Oracle Service Bus 11*g* Development Cookbook

Over 80 practical recipes to develop service and message-oriented solutions on the Oracle Service Bus

Guido Schmutz

Edwin Biemond

Eric Elzinga

Mischa Kölliker

Jan van Zoggel

BIRMINGHAM - MUMBAI

Oracle Service Bus 11*g* Development Cookbook

First published: January 2012

Production Reference: 1180112

Published by Packt Publishing Ltd.
32 Lincoln Road
Olton
Birmingham, B27 6PA, UK.

ISBN 978-1-84968-444-6

www.packtpub.com

Cover Image by David Gimenez (bilbaorocker@yahoo.co.uk)

Credits

Authors
Guido Schmutz
Edwin Biemond
Eric Elzinga
Mischa Kölliker
Jan van Zoggel

Reviewers
Jelle de Bruin
Matthias Furrer
Matt Wright
Peter van Nes

Acquisition Editor
Kerry George

Lead Technical Editor
Meeta Rajani

Technical Editors
Apoorva Bolar
Arun Nadar
Naheed Shaikh

Project Coordinator
Kushal Bhardwaj

Proofreaders
Matthew Humphries
Cecere Mario

Indexer
Rekha Nair

Graphics
Manu Joseph
Conidon Miranda

Production Coordinator
Aparna Bhagat

Cover Work
Aparna Bhagat

About the Authors

Guido Schmutz is an Oracle ACE director for Fusion Middleware and SOA and works for the Swiss Oracle Platinum Partner Trivadis—an independent consulting firm specializing in Oracle and Microsoft product stack. He has more than 25 years of technology experience, ranging from mainframes, integration, and SOA technologies in financial services, government, and logistics environments. At Trivadis he is responsible for SOA BPM and Application Integration solutions and leads the Trivadis Architecture Board. He has long-time experience as a developer, coach, trainer, and architect in the area of building complex Java EE and SOA-based solutions. Currently, he is focusing on SOA and application integration projects using the Oracle SOA Suite. Guido is a regular speaker at international conferences such as Oracle Open World, ODTUG, SOA Symposium, UKOUG conference, and DOAG. He is also co-author of the books *Service-Oriented Architecture: An Integration Blueprint*, *Spring 2.0 im Einsatz*, *Architecture Blueprints*, and *Integration Architecture Blueprints*. Guido runs his own blog at `http://guidoschmutz.wordpress.com`.

First of all I would like to thank all my co-authors for their hard work that lead to this book. I enjoyed working with you guys a lot!

Thanks a lot to the reviewers Matthias Furrer, Jelle de Bruin, Matt Wright and Peter van Nes for their work. Your feedback was very valuable and helpful!

A book like this one is not possible without a lot of work from the publisher. In the name of my fellow co-authors, I would like to thank the team at Packt Publishing for their help and support, especially Kerry George, Kushal Bhardwaj, Meeta Rajani, and Arun Nadar. It has been a long process with a lot of work, but we are very happy with the result we have achieved!

Thanks to my employer Trivadis for the support and for giving me the opportunity to write this book.

Last but not least I would like to thank my wonderful wife Renata and my family for their love and all the support. Without their help and understanding, this book would not have been possible.

Hope you like this book as much as I enjoyed writing it!

Edwin Biemond is an Oracle ACE and solution architect at Amis, specializing in messaging with Oracle SOA Suite and Oracle Service Bus. He is an expert in ADF development, WebLogic administration, high availability, and security. His Oracle career began in 1997 when he was developing an ERP CRM system with Oracle tools. Since 2001, Edwin changed his focus to integration, security, and Java development. Edwin was awarded with the Java Developer of the Year 2009 award by Oracle Magazine and in 2010 won the EMEA Oracle Partner community award, he contributed some content to the SOA Handbook of Lucas Jellema. He is also an international speaker at Oracle OpenWorld & ODTUG and has a popular blog called Java/Oracle SOA blog at—`http://biemond.blogspot.com`.

Eric Elzinga is an Oracle ACE for Fusion Middleware and SOA. He has over 10 years of experience in IT. His Oracle career started around 2001 as an Oracle database programmer and building enterprise portal applications. Lately, he is focusing on SOA and integration solutions based on the Oracle SOA Suite, Oracle Service Bus, and open source frameworks. He is also experienced in designing and maintaining middleware solutions, messaging, and creating business solutions using agile software development with Scrum. He is the owner of Xenta Consultancy. Eric is an active contributor to the Oracle Community/Forums and blogs on his website at `http://blog.xenta.nl`.

A thanks goes out to all the co-authors for their months of hard work. I really enjoyed the time!

I want to thank my mom for the never-ending support and believing in me. My dad, RIP, I hope you're proud of me.

Mischa Kölliker is a principal consultant at the Oracle consultancy company Trivadis. He has been working for more than 15 years in the area of integration solutions with technologies such as C++, Java EE, and Oracle Service Bus. At Trivadis he works as a solution architect, developer and trainer in SOA, integration, and Java EE projects. In his current assignments, he works on OSB-based integration solutions for Swiss railway and touristic organizations as well as on a Java EE project for a Swiss bank. His avocation is HTML5 and all related technologies. Mischa is a co-author of other books, including the Architecture Blueprints and the Business Communication Architecture Blueprint.

Jan van Zoggel is a principal Oracle Fusion Middleware consultant and works for the Dutch Oracle Gold Partner Rubix. He is experienced with process and system integration based upon the products Oracle Service Bus, Oracle Weblogic, and the Oracle SOA Suite. His IT career began in 2000 and in 2004, he changed his focus to message brokers, Enterprise Application Integration (EAI) and Business-to-Business (B2B) which later shifted towards Service Oriented Architecture (SOA) based upon the Oracle (BEA) and Tibco software suites. He has worked in different roles as a middleware operational support, process and service developer, solution architect, and as a trainer. His main area of interest is middleware architecture, high availability, reliable messaging, security, and cloud technology. Jan runs his own blog at `http://jvzoggel.wordpress.com`

I would like to thank all the other co-authors for their hard work, and especially Guido who went beyond the call of duty to finish this project successful. This was my first experience as a co-writer and I really enjoyed it. But especially I would like to thank my family and loved ones for their support, understanding, and in particular their ever-lasting patience.

About the Reviewers

Jelle de Bruin is a very experienced IT consultant. Having started his career on mainframe systems, he moved to the Java world at the end of the last century. In 2007, he joined the professional services department of BEA Systems Netherlands. During his time at BEA and later at Oracle, he worked extensively in customer facing assignments with the AquaLogic Service Bus or the Oracle Service Bus as it is now called. Although he has extensive knowledge and experience with other Oracle Fusion Middleware products, the Service Bus has become his specialty.

Now, he is working as an independent consultant on a variety of projects, ranging from enterprise architecture to working with Oracle Fusion Middleware products. In his role as an independent consultant, he is still asked by Oracle to help them out on occasions.

Matthias Furrer has been working in different roles for more than 20 years in IT. Throughout his career he worked as an application developer, consultant, and architect in many complex integration projects. Now, he is working as a senior consultant for Trivadis—a leading solution provider for infrastructure engineering, application development, and business intelligence operating in Switzerland, Germany, and Austria.

Peter van Nes is an Oracle Fusion Middleware consultant and works within a partnership of the Oracle SOA Specialized Gold Partner, The Future Group. In 1991, he started his career as a Systems Management consultant and changed his focus in 2005 to Oracle products and Java. In his current assignment, he mainly develops BPEL processes and OWSM security pipelines for an international financial services provider, and, as a senior developer, he is actively involved in the migration to 11g SOA Suite, using BPEL and OSB. In addition, Peter contributes to the Oracle community by blogging on his website, `http://www.petervannes.nl`.

www.PacktPub.com

Support files, eBooks, discount offers and more

You might want to visit www.PacktPub.com for support files and downloads related to your book.

Did you know that Packt offers eBook versions of every book published, with PDF and ePub files available? You can upgrade to the eBook version at www.PacktPub.com and as a print book customer, you are entitled to a discount on the eBook copy. Get in touch with us at service@packtpub.com for more details.

At www.PacktPub.com, you can also read a collection of free technical articles, sign up for a range of free newsletters, and receive exclusive discounts and offers on Packt books and eBooks.

http://PacktLib.PacktPub.com

Do you need instant solutions to your IT questions? PacktLib is Packt's online digital book library. Here, you can access, read, and search across Packt's entire library of books.

Why Subscribe?

- Fully searchable across every book published by Packt
- Copy and paste, print, and bookmark content
- On demand and accessible via web browser

Free Access for Packt account holders

If you have an account with Packt at www.PacktPub.com, you can use this to access PacktLib today and view nine entirely free books. Simply use your login credentials for immediate access.

Table of Contents

Preface

The **Oracle Service Bus 11***g* (**OSB**) is a scalable SOA integration platform that delivers an efficient, standards-based infrastructure for high-volume, mission critical SOA environments. It is designed to connect, mediate, and manage interactions between heterogeneous services, legacy applications, packaged applications, and multiple Enterprise Service Bus (ESB) implementations (such as other OSB instances, Microsoft BizTalk, IBM WebsSphere ESB, SAP-XI, ...and so on) across an enterprise-wide service network. Oracle Service Bus is a core component of the Oracle SOA Suite.

This practical cookbook shows you how to develop service- and message-oriented (integration) solutions on the Oracle Service Bus 11*g*.

The book contains more than **80 practical recipes**, showing how to efficiently develop on the Oracle Service Bus. In addition to its cookbook style, which ensures the solutions are presented in a clear step-by-step manner, the explanations go into great detail, which makes it good learning material for everyone who has experience with the OSB and wants to improve. Most of the recipes are designed in such a way that each one is presented as a separate, standalone entity and reading of prior recipes is not required. The finished solution of each recipe is also made available electronically.

What this book covers

Chapter 1, Creating a Basic OSB Service, teaches how to structure a project through the Eclipse OSB plugin, what conventions and best practices to apply, and how to use proxy and business service to create a simple message flow on the Oracle Service Bus. We will also learn how to test an OSB service through the Service Bus console and through soapUI.

Chapter 2, Working Efficiently with OSB Artifacts in Eclipse OEPE, presents some tips and tricks for simplifying working in Eclipse with the OSB Plugin. We will also learn how to use the visual debugger for step-by-step debugging of OSB services.

Chapter 3, Messaging with JMS Transport, shows how to use the JMS transport for sending and receiving message through JMS queues and topics. Additionally this chapter also shows how to use other tools such as soapUI and QBrowser to support the testing of JMS applications.

Chapter 4, Using EJB and JEJB Transport, teaches us how to use the EJB and JEJB transport for integrating and exposing EJB session beans.

Chapter 5, Using HTTP Transport, presents how to use the HTTP transport for implementing RESTful web services and how to implement a custom transport which uses WebSockets to implement server-side push messaging.

Chapter 6, Using File and Email Transports, shows how to use the File and FTP transport for reading and writing files and how to use the Email transport for receiving and sending emails from an OSB service.

Chapter 7, Communicating with the Database, shows with different recipes how the DB adapter can be used to integrate an OSB service with a relational database, and how the AQ adapter can be used to implement messaging between OSB and an Oracle database.

Chapter 8, Communicating with SOA Suite, teaches us how to use the SOA direct transport to natively communicate between SOA Suite service components and OSB services.

Chapter 9, Communication, Flow Control, and Message Processing, presents how to use different actions from the Communication, Flow Control, and Message Processing section of the OSB Design Palette.

Chapter 10, Reliable Communication with the OSB, contains recipes that will show how to use the various features of the OSB and WebLogic JMS to implement reliable message processing.

Chapter 11, Handling Message-level Security Requirements, shows different options for securing OSB services on the message-level to guarantee end-to-end security between an initial sender and an ultimate receiver.

Chapter 12, Handling Transport-level Security Requirements, contains recipes for securing OSB services on the transport protocol level.

What you need for this book

To develop and test the recipes in this book, an Oracle Service Bus 11g Patch Set 3 (11.1.1.4 or higher) and an Oracle Database11g (XE or Enterprise edition) needs to be installed on the system. For *Chapter 8*, a full installation of Oracle SOA Suite 11g (11.1.1.4 or higher) including Enterprise Manager needs to be installed as well.

An installation of JDeveloper with the SOA Suite extension (11.1.1.4 or higher) is necessary for *Chapter 2*, *Chapter 3*, *Chapter 7* and *Chapter 8*.

To use the web-based consoles, either Internet Explorer or Firefox is necessary.

We have developed all the recipes on the so-called *"developers"* installation of Oracle Service Bus 11*g* and Oracle SOA Suite 11*g*. This means that all the software is running on one single Admin Server and there are no additional Managed Servers needed, limiting the resources needed on the system. When we started writing the book, Oracle Service Bus Patch Set 3 (11.1.1.4) was the actual release and we have implemented all the recipes using this version. Keep that in mind when interpreting the screenshots, although most of the time this is transparent and not relevant. A place where it is certainly relevant is when entering the URI of the OSB server (that is, to open the Service Bus console). In our installation, having only an Admin Server, the port we use throughout the book is always 7001. Make sure to change that in case of a different installation.

For testing some of the recipes, the latest version of soapUI needs to be available. In *Chapter 3*, QBrowser and HermesJMS will be used to test JMS queues and topics.

For *Chapter 6*, an FTP server needs to be available. The corresponding recipe guides you through the installation of CoreFTP Server. Also in *Chapter 6*, an e-mail server and e-mail client is needed. The corresponding recipe describes the necessary steps for installing Apache James as the mail server and Mozilla Thunderbird as the e-mail client.

To guide you through the installation of the various components, we have written an extra document only available electronically. To download the installation guide, go to the Packt homepage for the OSB cookbook and download the ZIP file containing the code for the book. Included in the ZIP file is a PDF document named `OsbCookbookInstallationGuide.pdf`.

OSB Cookbook standard environment

The OSB Cookbook standard environment is a set of artifacts, representing the environment that most of the recipes make use of.

Part of the environment is a database schema to be installed in an Oracle database, containing a few tables and AQ objects. The database schema can be installed by running the script `setup\database\install.cmd`.

Another part of the environment is installed on the WebLogic server. This includes artifacts stored in the JNDI tree, such as DataSource or Connection Factories as well as the necessary JMS objects for *Chapter 3*. These artifacts are installed through a WLST script, which is called from an ANT script. Install it by running the script `setup\wlst\install.cmd`.

These two scripts are part of the ZIP file for this book, downloadable from the Packt website.

Who this book is for

If you are an intermediate SOA developer who is using Oracle Service Bus to develop service and message-orientated applications, then this book is for you. The book assumes that you have a working knowledge of fundamental SOA concepts and Oracle Service Bus.

Recipes

To keep the initial preparation of each recipe short, a lot of the recipes start from a base setup, which in most cases is an already existing OSB project including some initial artifacts and some base configuration. All the base setup artifacts are available in the `chapter-<N>\getting-ready\<recipe-name>` folder available in the ZIP file for this book. Each recipe refers to the corresponding folder in the *Getting Ready* section.

It will often be necessary to import an existing OSB project into Eclipse OEPE (for example, the OSB Plugin). The recipe *Importing an already existing project into Eclipse OEPE* in *Chapter 1, Creating a Basic OSB Service*, explains how to do that.

The solution of each recipe is available electronically in the folder `chapter-<N>\solution\<recipe-name>`, which is also part of the ZIP file for this book.

For most of the recipes we have created a simple, schematic diagram, representing the solution and the participating artifacts. The following image shows such a diagram taken from *Chapter 1, Creating a Basic OSB Service*.

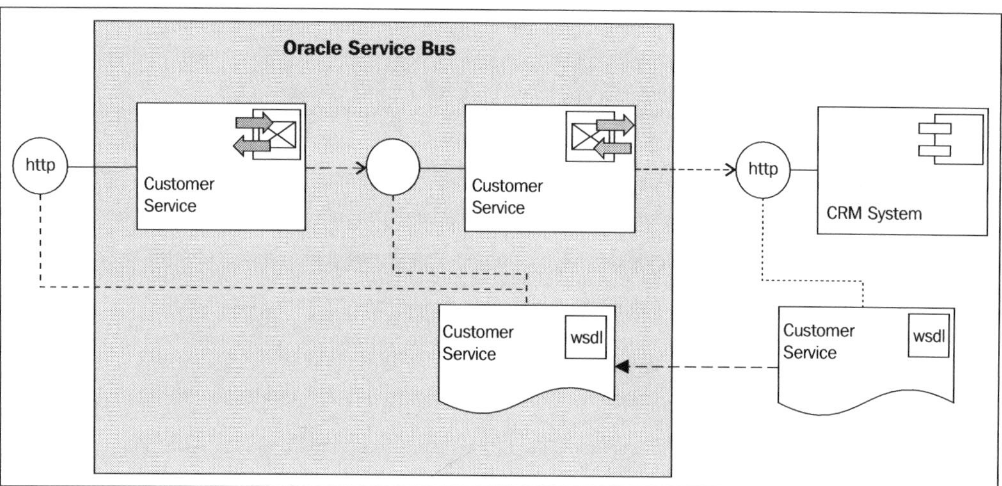

The following diagram shows a legend with the different symbols and their meanings used throughout this book.

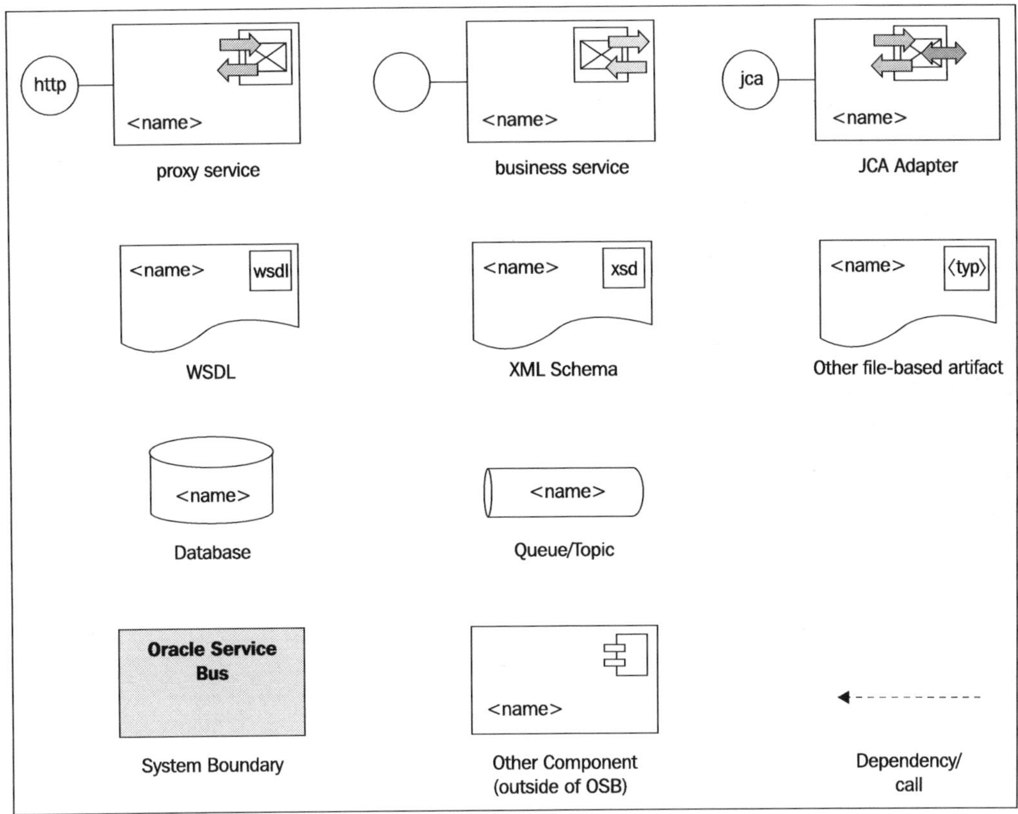

We strongly believe in the adage *"a picture is worth a thousand words"* and hope that these schematic diagrams will help the reader to quickly understand the setup of each recipe.

Conventions

In this book, you will find a number of styles of text that distinguish between different kinds of information. Here are some examples of these styles, and an explanation of their meaning.

Code words in text are shown as follows: "Open `<HERMES_HOME>\bin\hermes.bat` and add the following `JAVA_HOME` and `PATH` variable right at the beginning".

A block of code is set as follows:

```
<configuration>
  <location>
    <directory>c:\work\files\in</directory>
    <filename>OtherProperties.xml</filename>
  </location>
</configuration>
```

Any command-line input or output is written as follows:

```
keytool -exportcert -alias clientKey -storepass welcome -keystore c:\
client_2.jks -file c:\client_2.cer
```

New terms and **important words** are shown in bold. Words that you see on the screen, in menus or dialog boxes for example, appear in the text like this: "Navigate to the **Configuration tab**, and select the **Outbound Connection Pools** tab".

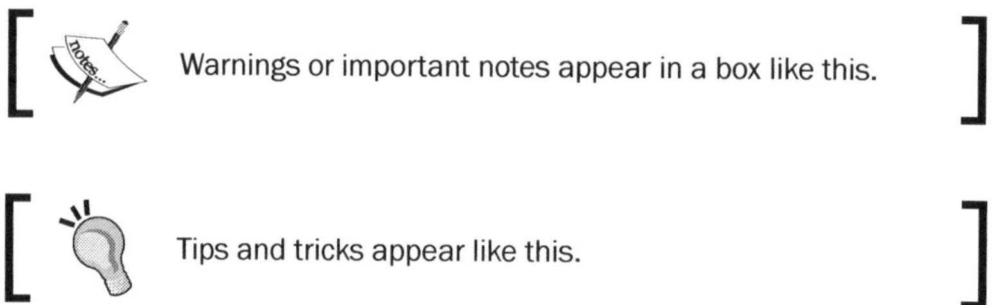

Warnings or important notes appear in a box like this.
Tips and tricks appear like this.

Reader feedback

Feedback from our readers is always welcome. Let us know what you think about this book—what you liked or may have disliked. Reader feedback is important for us to develop titles that you really get the most out of.

To send us general feedback, simply send an e-mail to `feedback@packtpub.com`, and mention the book title through the subject of your message.

If there is a topic that you have expertise in and you are interested in either writing or contributing to a book, see our author guide on `www.packtpub.com/authors`.

Customer support

Now that you are the proud owner of a Packt book, we have a number of things to help you to get the most from your purchase.

Downloading the example code

You can download the example code files for all Packt books you have purchased from your account at `http://www.packtpub.com`. If you purchased this book elsewhere, you can visit `http://www.packtpub.com/support` and register to have the files e-mailed directly to you.

Errata

Although we have taken every care to ensure the accuracy of our content, mistakes do happen. If you find a mistake in one of our books—maybe a mistake in the text or the code—we would be grateful if you would report this to us. By doing so, you can save other readers from frustration and help us improve subsequent versions of this book. If you find any errata, please report them by visiting `http://www.packtpub.com/support`, selecting your book, clicking on the **errata submission form** link, and entering the details of your errata. Once your errata are verified, your submission will be accepted and the errata will be uploaded to our website, or added to any list of existing errata, under the Errata section of that title.

Piracy

Piracy of copyright material on the Internet is an ongoing problem across all media. At Packt, we take the protection of our copyright and licenses very seriously. If you come across any illegal copies of our works, in any form, on the Internet, please provide us with the location address or website name immediately so that we can pursue a remedy.

Please contact us at `copyright@packtpub.com` with a link to the suspected pirated material.

We appreciate your help in protecting our authors, and our ability to bring you valuable content.

Questions

You can contact us at `questions@packtpub.com` if you are having a problem with any aspect of the book, and we will do our best to address it.

1
Creating a basic OSB service

In this chapter, we will cover the following topics:

- Creating a new OSB project
- Defining a folder structure for the OSB project
- Importing an already existing project into Eclipse OEPE
- Creating a business service to call an external SOAP-based web service
- Generating a pass-through proxy service
- Deploying the OSB configuration from Eclipse OEPE
- Testing the proxy service through the OSB console
- Testing the proxy service through soapUI
- Creating a proxy service with a WSDL-based interface
- Using a routing action to statically route to another service
- Using an operational branch to implement multiple WSDL operations in a proxy service
- Using an XQuery transformation to map between the different data models of the services

Introduction

In this chapter, we will cover some basic recipes to get the reader started working with the **Oracle Service Bus** (**OSB**). We will first develop the simplest possible service on the OSB with only one proxy service and then recipe by recipe add some more functionality to that service. In contrast to the other chapters, the recipes in this chapter are dependent on each other, and all the recipes of this chapter should therefore, be done in order. On the other hand, each single recipe can also be applied standalone by importing the 'getting-ready' project referenced in the *Getting Ready* section of each recipe.

In some of the recipes, we will also define the best practices and development conventions that we will use for this book, however, they are also applicable in any other project. We teach how to best structure a project using Eclipse OEPE (with the OSB plugin installed).

In this recipe, we will implement a mediation service in the OSB, which consumes a web service from an external CRM system.

Creating a new OSB project

In order to develop on the Oracle Service Bus, an OSB project needs to be available. This recipe will show how such an empty OSB project can be created. Such a project can either be created through the web-based OSB console or through the more developer-friendly Eclipse OEPE. **Eclipse OEPE** is an Eclipse IDE with **Oracle Enterprise Plugin for Eclipse** (**OEPE**) and the OSB plugin installed.

Getting ready

Make sure that you have access to a working Eclipse OEPE.

How to do it...

In Eclipse OEPE, perform the following steps:

1. From the **File** menu, pick **New** | **Other**.
2. Type `Oracle Service Bus` in the **Wizards** tree list:

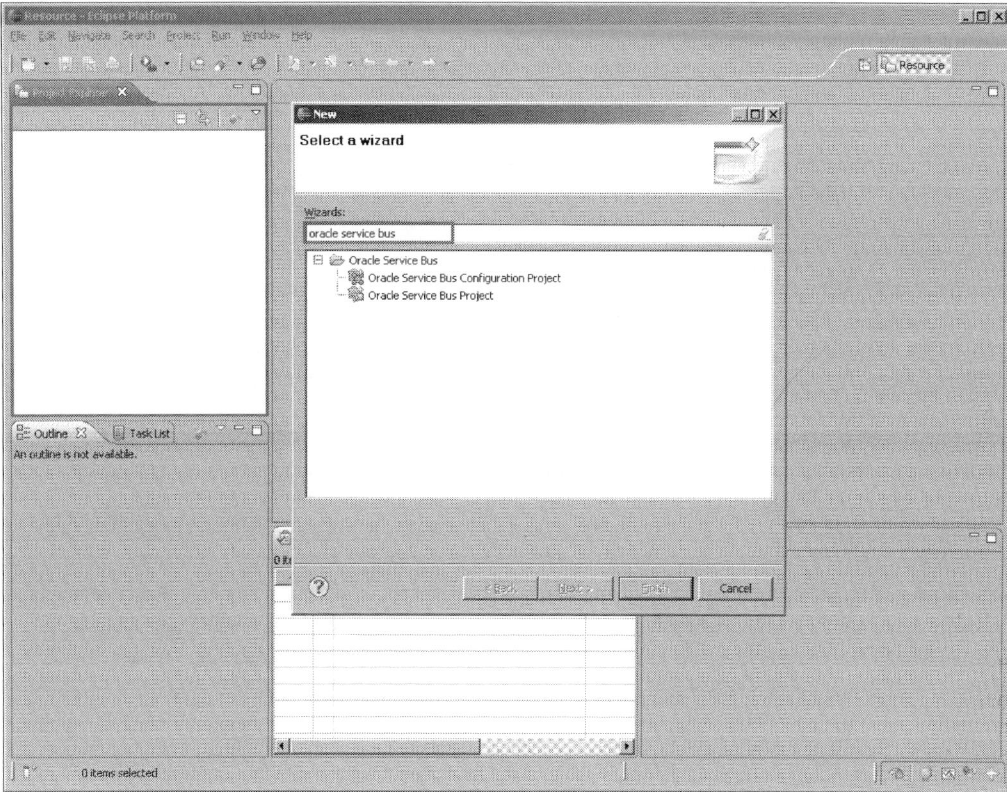

3. Choose **Oracle Service Bus Project** from the list and click on the **Next** button.
4. Enter `basic-osb-service` into the **Project name** field:

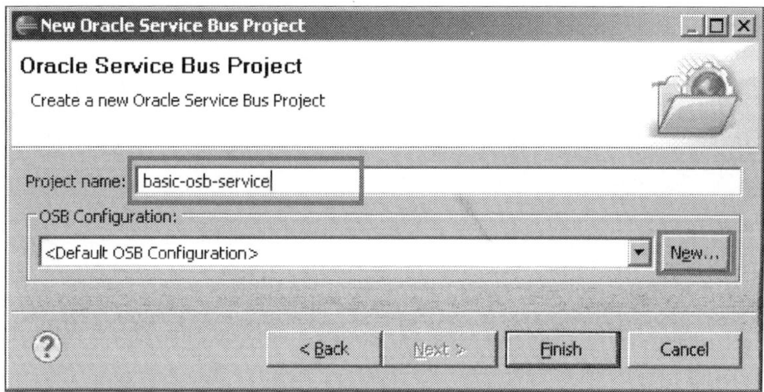

5. Click on the **New** button to create an OSB Configuration (if there is not yet one).

6. Enter `osb-cookbook-configuration` into the **Configuration name** field.
7. Click on the **Finish** button to create the empty `OSB project`.
8. Click on **Yes** to confirm that Eclipse OEPE will switch to the **Oracle Service Bus perspective**.

We have now created an empty OSB project inside our Eclipse workspace.

How it works...

An OSB project created through Eclipse OEPE is just a folder created below the location of the workspace. Visually, Eclipse OEPE shows it wrapped inside the **osb-cookbook-configuration** OSB configuration, but they are really both on the same level, just a subfolder of the workspace folder.

The project contains a `.project` file and a `.settings` folder like any Eclipse project. These files hold the necessary meta information about the project. An OSB project has the special **Oracle Service Bus** facet assigned.

This empty project can now be used to create the different OSB artifacts necessary for an OSB service. They can either be placed directly inside the project folder or a subfolder structure can be created in order to organize the `OSB project`. How to create a folder structure will be shown in the next recipe, *Defining a folder structure for the OSB project*.

There's more...

A new `OSB project` can also be created through the OSB console. The main difference to the approach shown before is that, through the OSB console we directly work on a running Oracle Service Bus instance. When using Eclipse OEPE, the project is stored in the Eclipse workspace and needs to be later deployed to an OSB instance. See the *next recipe*, to learn how to create a folder structure for holding the different OSB artifacts.

Defining a folder structure for the OSB project

After creating the empty OSB project, we will prepare a folder structure to be used to organize the project. OSB allows you to use folders to build-up a project structure which helps to better find the various artifacts inside the OSB project.

Getting ready

Make sure that the empty OSB project—`basic-osb-service` from the previous recipe is available in the Eclipse OEPE. Also make sure that the **Oracle Service Bus perspective** is active in Eclipse. The active perspective can be identified in the upper-right corner of the Eclipse window:

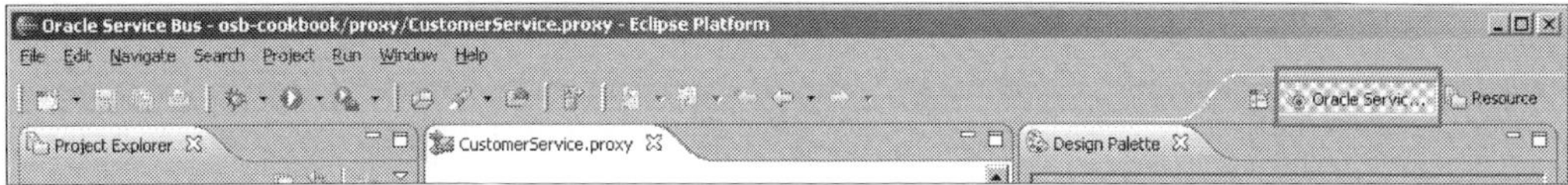

To switch to another perspective, click on the **Window** menu, select **Open Perspective** | **Other** and then select the **Oracle Service Bus** in the list of perspectives.

If after a while a certain perspective gets messed up and some windows or views are missing, then the perspective can always be reset to the factory settings by clicking on the menu **Window** | **Reset Perspective** and then confirming the dialog with the **OK** button.

How to do it...

In Eclipse OEPE, perform the following steps:

1. Right click on the **basic-osb-service** project and select **New** | **Folder**.
2. Enter `proxy` in the **Folder name** field:

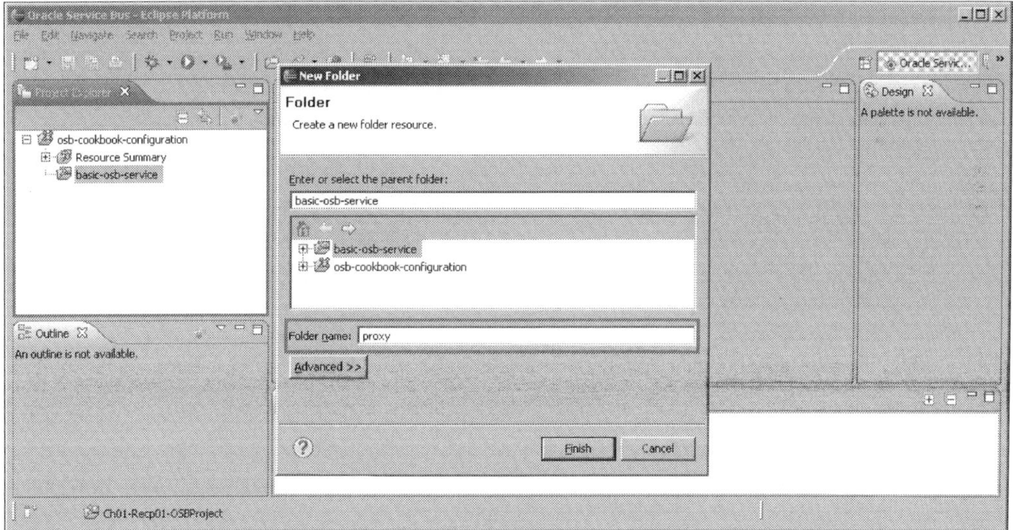

3. Repeat these two steps for the folders `business`, `wsdl`, `xsd`, and `transformation`. These are the most common folders and they altogether form the basic OSB project structure used in this book.

How it works...

Folders help to structure the projects and by that organize the different artifacts that we will create later. The folder structure will also be visible after the deployment of a project in the OSB console. So at runtime, if someone (that is, the administrator) needs to navigate to a certain artifact through the console, a clever folder structure can make life much easier.

The meaning of the folder structure that we will use in this book is listed in the following table:

Folder name	Used for organizing
`business`	business services artifacts
`proxy`	proxy services artifacts
`wsdl`	SOAP-based web service interfaces
`xsd`	the XML schema files
`transformation`	Artifacts for doing data model transformations, such as XQuery and XSLT scripts

In some specific recipes, we will add some additional folders. The ones shown in this recipe just represent the most commonly used ones.

Importing an already existing project into Eclipse OEPE

Working with Eclipse OEPE, there is often a need to open an already existing OSB project, which is (no longer) in your Eclipse workspace. This recipe will show how to import an existing project. It should be used in all future recipes, when the *Getting ready* section asks for importing an existing OSB project as the base for following the recipe.

Getting ready

Make sure that you have access to a working Eclipse OEPE.

How to do it...

In Eclipse OEPE, perform the following steps:

1. From the **File** menu select **Import**.
2. Type `Existing` in the **Select an import source** tree list.
3. Select **Existing Projects into Workspace** from the tree and click **Next**.
4. Click on the **Browse** button to specify the root directory from where to import the project.
5. Navigate to the `\chapter-1\getting-ready` folder and click on the **OK** button.
6. Select the **already-existing-osb-project** from the list of projects to import and select the Copy projects into workspace option:

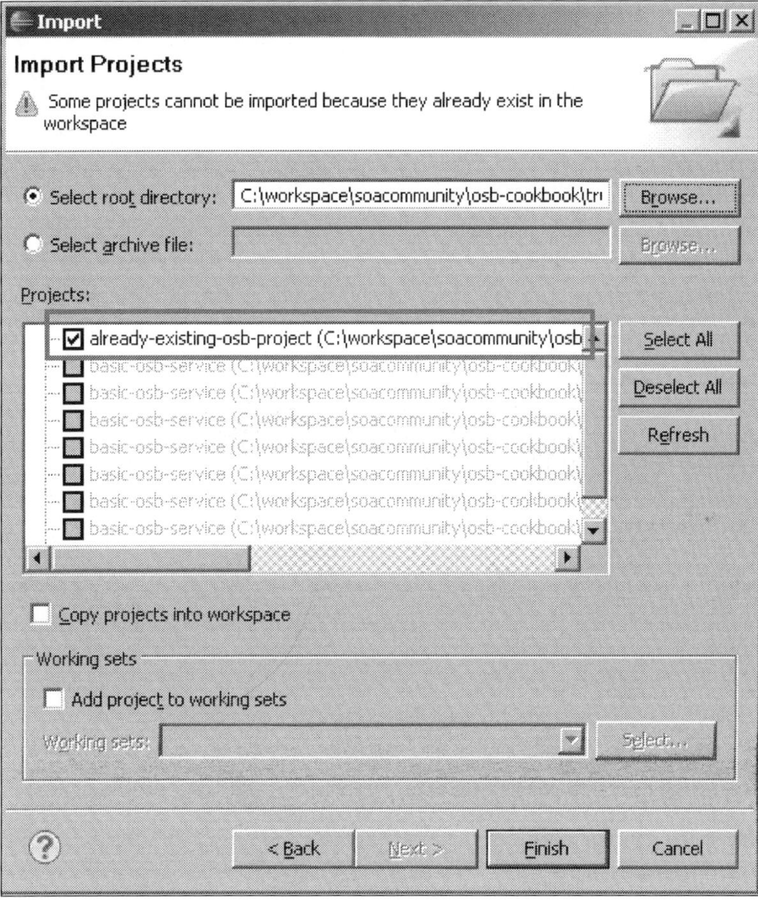

7. Click on the **Finish** button.

The project is now imported in Eclipse OEPE but will be placed outside of the OSB Configuration and therefore, will have an error marker.

To move it into the OSB Configuration, just drag the imported **already-existing-osb-project** in the **Project Explorer** into the `osb-cookbook-configuration project`. Now the project is ready to be used.

How it works...

To import the OSB project into Eclipse OEPE, we just used the standard import functionality of Eclipse. In order for that to work, the project needs to have the `.project`, which is automatically created when using Eclipse OEPE to create an OSB project.

The project has to be moved into the OSB configuration in order to be able to work with it, that is, deploy it to the OSB server. Dragging the project into the OSB configuration is only reflected inside Eclipse, it does not change the location of the files on the disk.

Creating a business service to call an external SOAP-based web service

With the basic folder structure of the OSB project in place, we are ready to create our first OSB service. We will start with the **business service** Customer Service which will act as a wrapper of the external service. Business services in OSB are required definitions to exchange messages with enterprise information systems—such as databases and queues or other web services. The external service is a web service offered by a fictive CRM system. The business service will allow the definition of all sorts of properties for controlling how the external service is invoked:

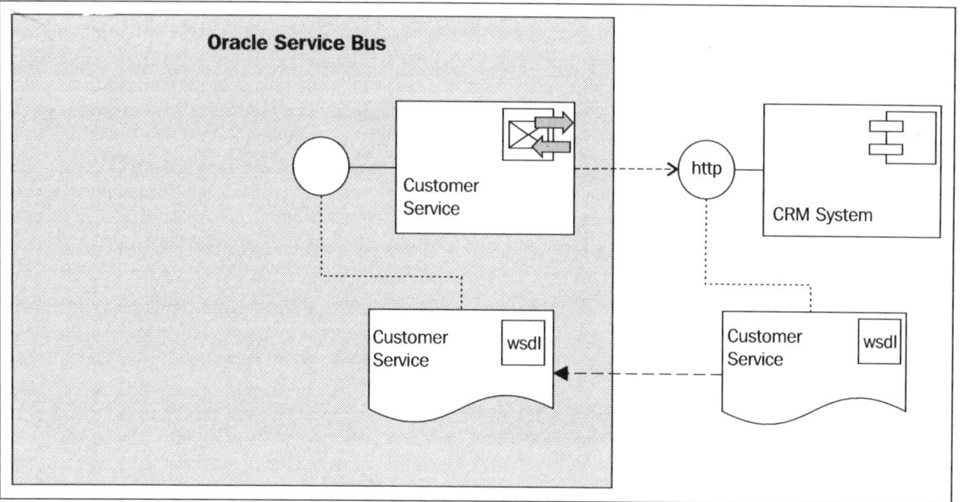

Getting ready

Make sure that the external web service we want to invoke is started by running the script `\chapter-1\getting-ready\misc\customer-external-webservice\start-service.cmd`. This service is implemented using soapUI's capabilities for creating mock services.

Verify that the service is running and available by asking it for its WSDL definition. Enter the following URI in a browser window: **http://localhost:8088/mockCustomerServiceSOAP?WSDL**:

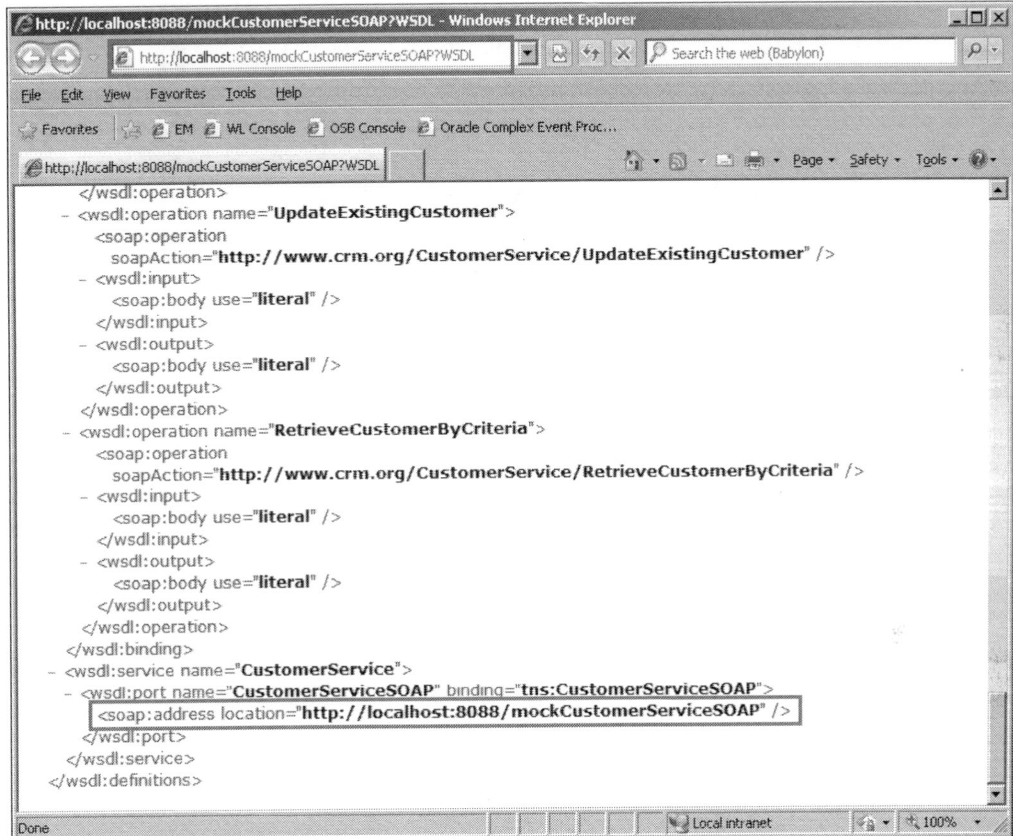

How to do it...

In Eclipse OEPE, perform the following steps:

1. In the project tree, right-click on the **business** folder and select **New | Business Service**.
2. Enter `CustomerService` into the **File name** field, check a second time that the **business** folder is selected, and click on the **Finish** button:

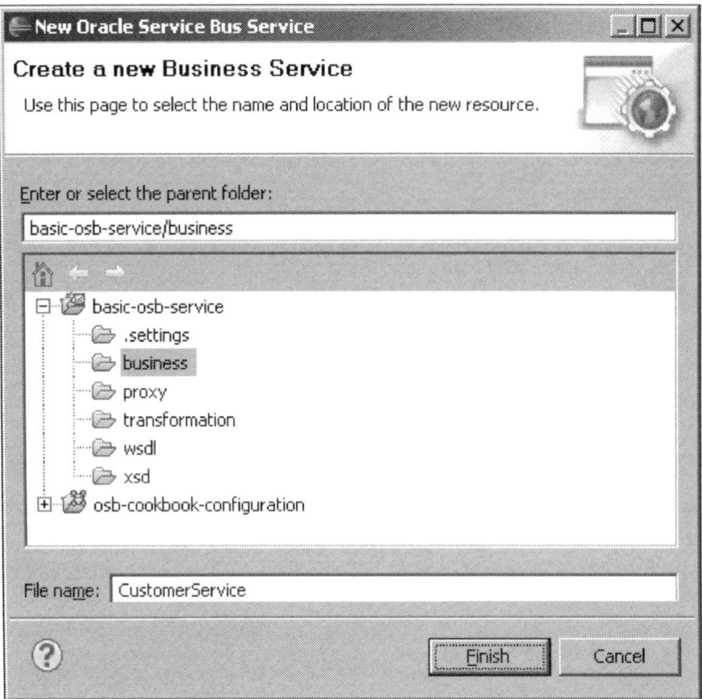

3. A new business service artifact is created in the `business` folder and the editor for the business service opens automatically.
4. Navigate to the **General** tab, if it does not already have the focus, and select the **WSDL Web Service** radio button.
5. Click on the **Browse** button and a pop up window will show up, where the WSDL resource of the external service to be wrapped, can be selected.
6. Click on the **Consume** button.

7. A second pop-up window will show up where the WSDL resource can be specified:

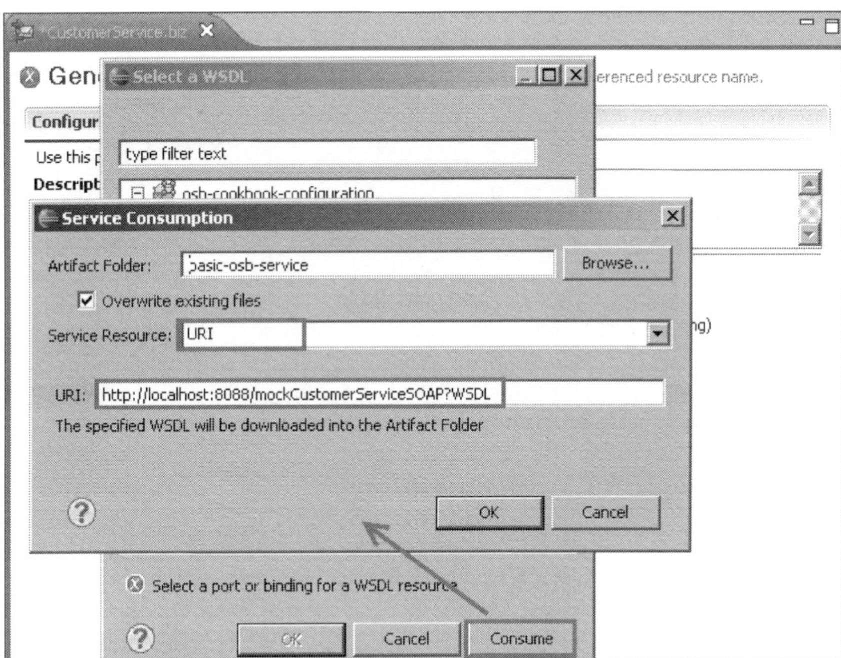

8. Select **URI** in the **Service Resource** drop-down listbox.
9. In the **URI** field, enter the URL of the WSDL resource to consume. The external service provides its WSDL through the following URL: **http://localhost:8088/mockCustomerServiceSOAP?WSDL**.
10. Click on the **OK** button and Eclipse will consume the WSDL from this URL.
11. Select the **CustomerServiceSOAP** port on the next window.
12. Click on the **OK** button.
13. Select **Yes** on the pop-up message window to confirm that the transport configuration settings will be overwritten by the information from the selected WSDL.
14. Save the OSB project by selecting File | Save.
15. In the **Project Explorer**, right-click on the imported WSDL file **mockCustomerServiceSOAP.wsdl** and select **Rename**. Enter `CustomerService.wsdl` into the **New name** field of the pop-up window and confirm.
16. In the **Project Explorer**, drag the **CustomerService.wsdl** file into the **wsdl** folder and drop it there. All the references to the WSDL file are automatically adapted by Eclipse OEPE.

17. Navigate to the **Transport** tab and check that the **Endpoint URI** has been replaced with the service endpoint setting from the WSDL that we consumed:

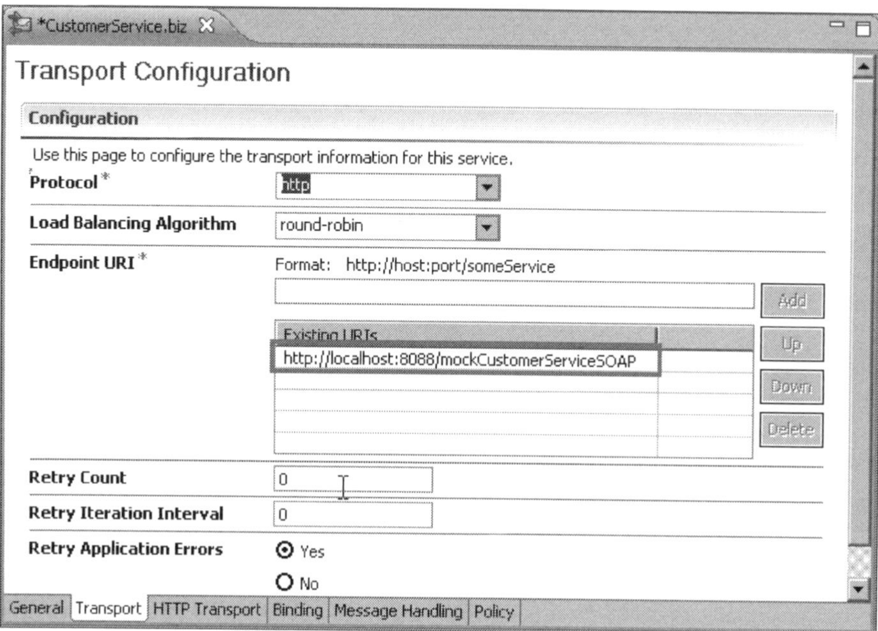

18. Save the artifact by selecting **File | Save** or by clicking on the **Save** toolbar button.

How it works...

The business service acts as a wrapper of our external service. Once created, we will no longer have to use the WSDL to refer to the external service, but can use the business service. This forms an additional abstraction layer, which will become handy later in some of the more advanced recipes to enable functionality in the OSB, which is applied before the real endpoint is invoked, such as SLA monitoring, service throttling, service pooling, and others. Sentence is too long, runs on too long. Would be better split into two sentences.

Generating a simple pass-through proxy service

After we have created the business service wrapping the external web service, we can now create the proxy service. The proxy service will allow a consumer to call our service on the OSB. If the OSB needs to support the same web service interface as the backend service does, then the quickest and easiest way is to create a pass-through service:

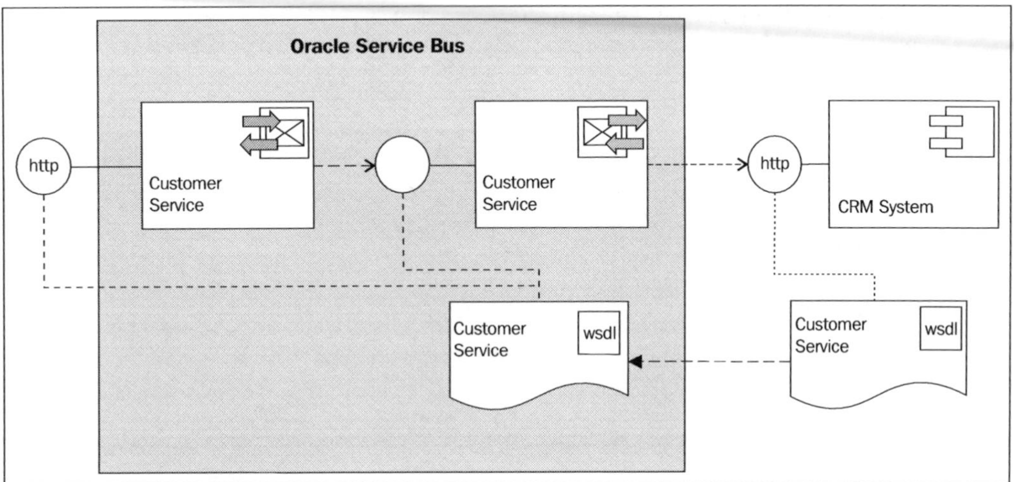

Getting ready

This recipe continues with the result of the previous recipe. If necessary, the `basic-osb-service project` at that stage can be imported from here: `\chapter-1\getting-ready\business-service-created`.

How to do it...

In Eclipse OEPE, perform the following steps:

1. In the project tree, right-click on the **CustomerService.biz** artifact and select **Oracle Service Bus | Generate Proxy Service**.
2. Enter `CustomerService` in the **File name** field and select the **proxy** folder for the location of the new proxy service.
3. Click on the **Finish** button.
4. Click on the **Transport** tab and check the value of the **Endpoint URI** field. It should be `/basic-osb-service/proxy/CustomerService`.

5. Navigate to the **Message Flow** tab and have a look at the message flow, which has been generated by Eclipse OEPE. A **Route** node with a nested **Routing** action has been created with its **Invoking** properties set to **Use inbound operation for outbound**:

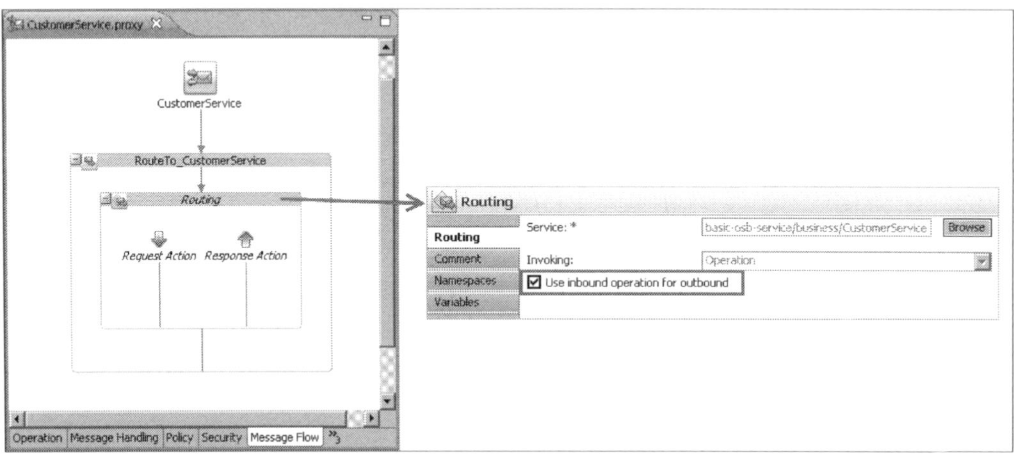

How it works...

Applying this recipe created the simplest possible proxy service. The proxy service offers the same SOAP-based web service interface as the business service/external service, so it's basically just doing a pass-through of the request and response message.

This can be handy if we want to use the OSB for adding an additional abstraction layer to apply service virtualization. If all the service consumers no longer access the external services directly, but only through the OSB proxy-service, a lot of the features of OSB can be used transparently by a service consumer, such as SLA monitoring and alerting, service pooling and throttling, or message validation. This directly supports the main goal of service virtualization—adding operational agility.

By setting the **Invoking** property to **Use inbound operation for outbound**, we make sure that the whole WSDL with all its operations is handled by one single **Routing** action. The inbound operation name on the proxy service is used as the outbound operation name invoked on the business service. Apart from the **Routing** action there are no other actions in this proxy service. By that, both the request and the response messages in the `$body` variable are not touched by the OSB. This guarantees that the overhead of adding OSB as a service virtualization layer has minimal impact on the performance.

See also

See recipe *Creating a proxy service with a WSDL-based interface*, if the proxy should offer a different web service interface than the external service provider.

For deploying and testing the service check the next two recipes in this chapter.

Deploying the OSB configuration from Eclipse OEPE

Before we can test an OSB service, we need to deploy it to a running OSB server. Such a server can either be locally on the same machine or it can be on another, remotely accessible server. In this recipe, we will only use the functionality provided by Eclipse OEPE to deploy our service, because it's the simplest of the possible options for deployment. Of course there exists other, more automatic and repeatable ways for deployment through WLST or Apache Ant, but in this book, the deployment through Eclipse OEPE as shown here is good enough.

Getting ready

Make sure that the OSB server is running locally on your machine. The easiest way to check that it's up and running is navigating to the OSB console in a browser window. Enter the URL `http://[OSBServer]:[Port]/sbconsole` (replacing `[OSBServer]` with the name of the server and `[Port]` with the port of your installation) and you should get the login window of the OSB console. Check if the OSB server is up and running, especially when running the OSB on a managed server.

Make sure that the **Oracle Service Bus perspective** is the active one in Eclipse OEPE. The perspective is visible in the top-right corner of the Eclipse window.

Make sure that the project with the result from the previous recipe is available in Eclipse OEPE. If not then it can be imported from here: `\chapter-1\getting-ready\pass-through-proxy-service-created`.

How to do it...

First we need to create the server reference inside Eclipse OEPE and after that we can deploy the OSB configuration with its projects to the server.

In Eclipse OEPE, perform the following steps to create a server:

1. Switch to the **Servers** tab and right-click in the empty window.
2. Select **New | Server**.

3. In the **Define a New Server** window, select the right WebLogic Server version (**Oracle WebLogic Server 11gR1 PatchSet 3** in our case, this might vary).
4. Click on the **Next** button twice.
5. Select the **Local** option and select the **Domain Directory** of the local OSB server installation. If the **Domain Directory** drop-down list is empty, then click on **Browse** button to navigate to the domain directory on your machine:

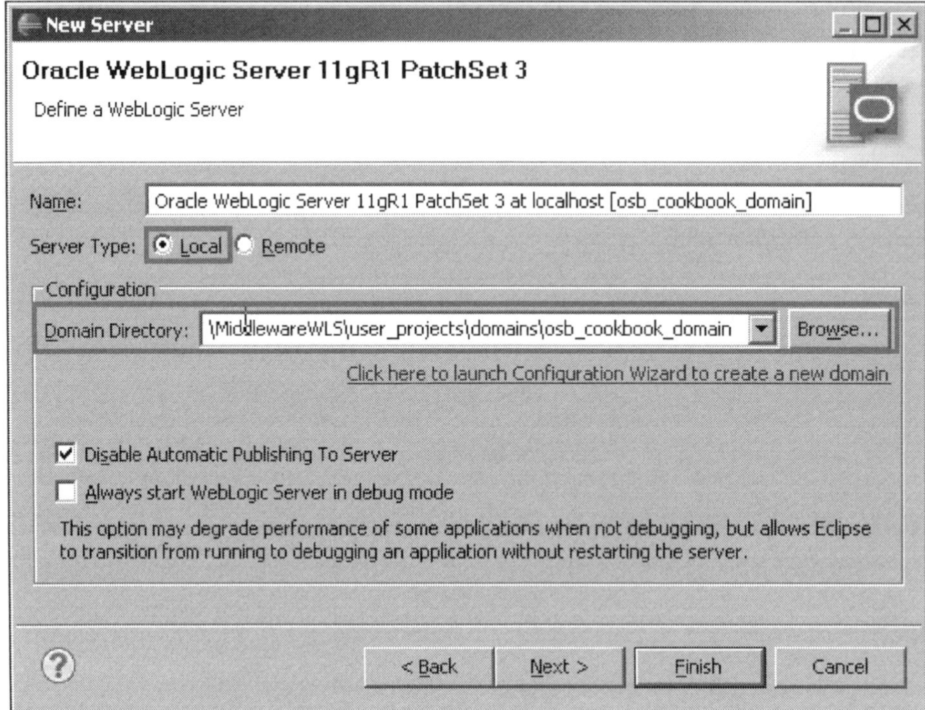

6. Click on the **Finish** button.

Now the local OSB server is configured in Eclipse OEPE. The next step is to deploy the OSB configuration to this sever. Still in Eclipse OEPE, perform the following steps:

7. On the **Servers** tab, right-click on the server item that you just created and select **Add and Remove**.
8. In the **Available** list on the left, click on the **osb-cookbook-configuration** OSB configuration.
9. Click on **Add** to move it to the **Configured** list on the right and click on the **Finish** button.

10. The OSB configuration is deployed to the running OSB server and after a while the status will change from **[Started]** to **[Started, Republish]**.
11. Right-click on the OSB server and select **Publish**.
12. After a while the status will change to **[Started, Synchronized]**, indicating that Eclipse OEPE and the OSB server are synchronized.
13. Expand the tree and the status of each single OSB project within the OSB configuration is shown:

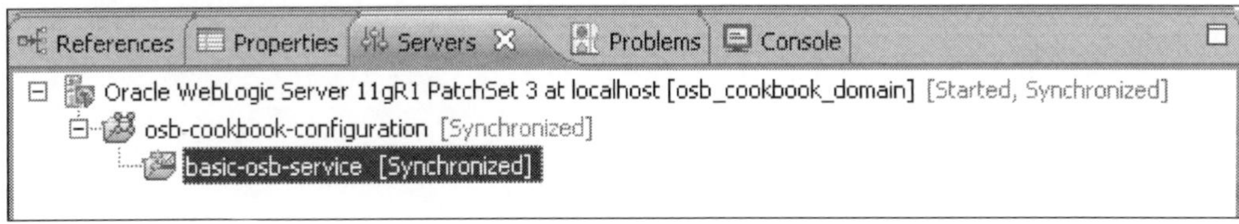

The OSB configuration is now successfully deployed and ready to be used.

How it works...

Behind the scenes, Eclipse OEPE is creating a JAR file (a Java Archive) with all the artifacts which belong to the OSB configuration and deploys that archive to the OSB server.

The mechanism to deploy directly from Eclipse should only be used during development. Later when deploying to integration, quality assurance, or a production system, of course, a more automatic and reproducible way is necessary. This can be achieved through Apache Ant and WLST.

There's more...

In this section, we will show the alternative ways for deploying a project to an OSB server.

Deploying to a remote server from Eclipse OEPE

Eclipse OEPE can also be used to deploy to a remote server. Just click on the **Remote** option when defining the WebLogic Server in the **New Server** wizard:

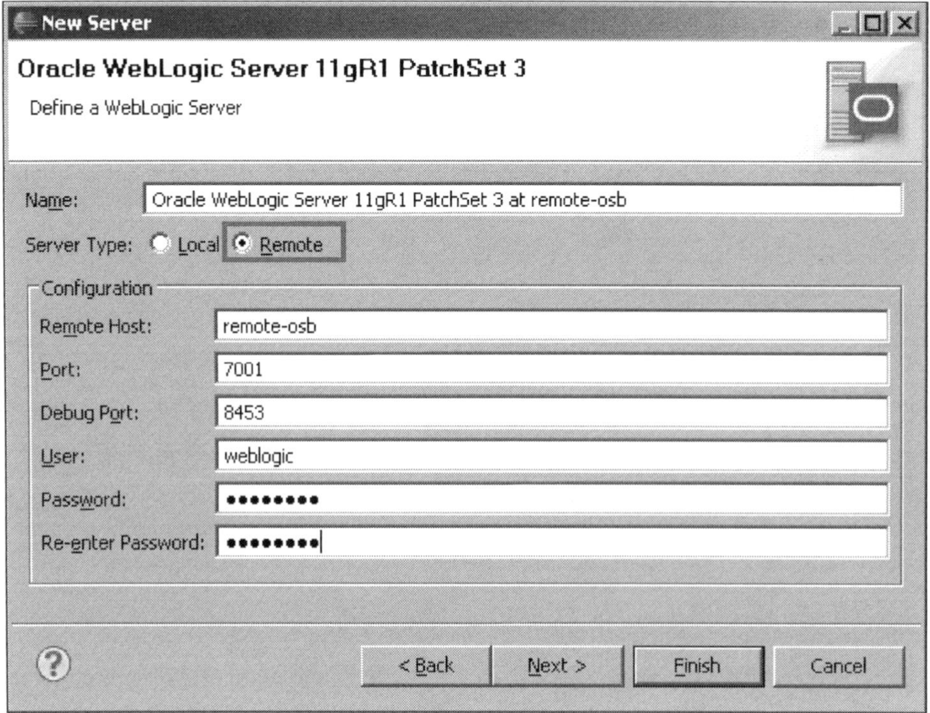

Creating an OSB Configuration Jar and use the OSB console to deploy it

An OSB configuration can also be deployed by using the **OSB console**. In Eclipse OEPE, perform the following steps:

1. In the **Project Explorer**, right-click on the **OSB Configuration** that you want to deploy to and select **Export | Oracle Service Bus - Configuration Jar**.
2. In the pop-up window, select the resources to export, enter the location of the configuration jar into the **Jar File** field and click on the **Finish** button.

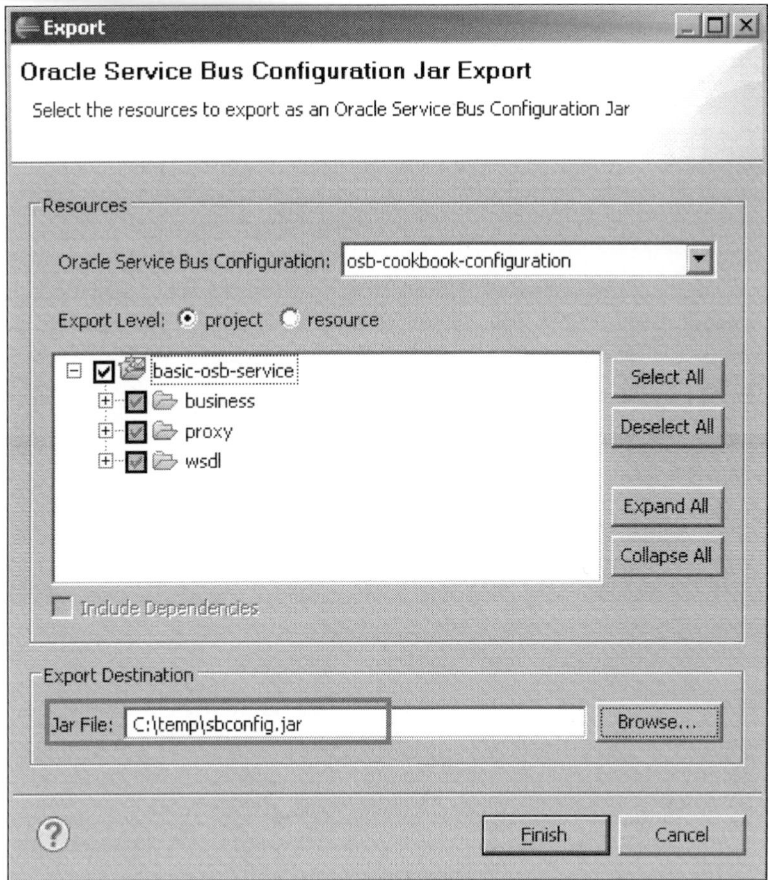

In the OSB console, perform the following steps to import the Configuration Jar that we just created:

3. Select the menu **System Administration** on the left-hand side. You might have to use the scroll bar in order to see all the menu items.
4. Click on **Create** in the **Change Center** to start a new change session.
5. Click on the **Import Resources** button and use **Browse** to select the file created in the export (`c:\temp\sbconfig.jar`).
6. Click on the **Next** button.

7. Check that the right sources will be imported:

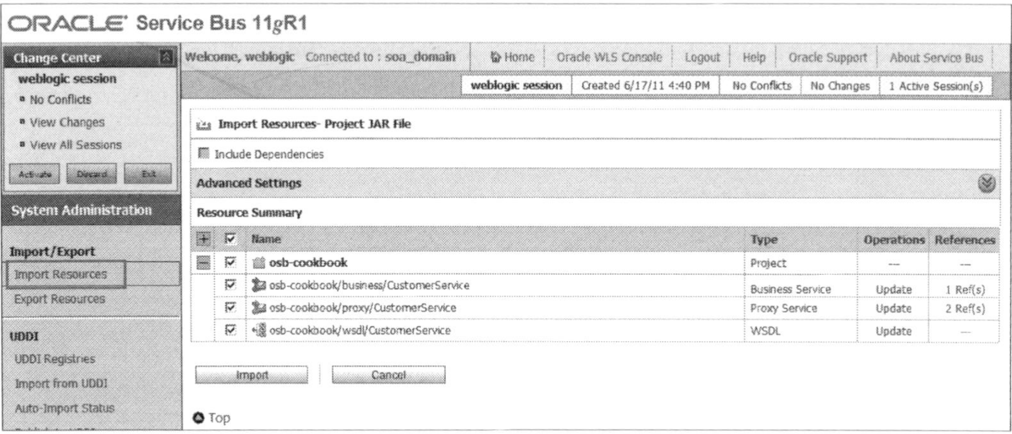

8. Click on the **Import** button to start the import.
9. The successful import is confirmed by the message **the import was completed successfully**.
10. Click on the **Activate** button in the **Change Center**.
11. Enter a text describing the changes into the **Description** field and click on the **Submit** button to activate the changes.

If we need to adapt some properties like endpoint URI to match the target environment, we can use a customization file and apply that when doing the deployment.

Testing the proxy service through the OSB console

With the OSB configuration deployed successfully to our OSB server, it's time to test it. This recipe will show the most basic way to test, using the OSB console. This is good enough for some initial test but in the long term something more repeatable is necessary. One alternative option is using soapUI, which will be covered in the next recipe.

Getting ready

Navigate to the OSB console and login as the Administrator (that is, weblogic).

How to do it...

In the OSB console, perform the following steps:

1. Click on the menu item **Project Explorer** on the left-hand side of the OSB console.
2. In the project tree, click on **basic-osb-service** and in the **details** section on the right, the project folder tree will be shown.
3. Click on the **proxy** link.
4. The proxy service Customer Service should be displayed in the **details** section (might have to scroll down to see it):

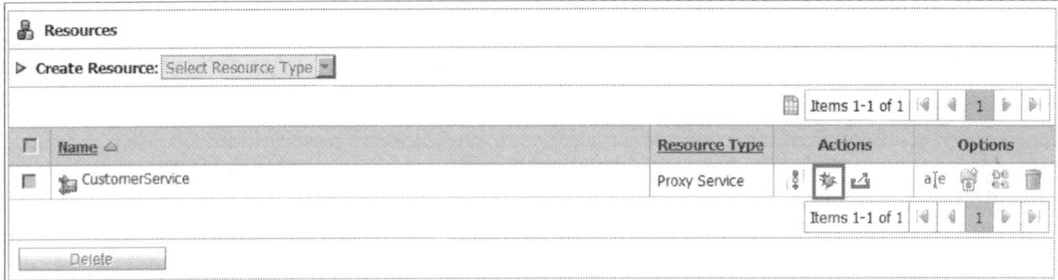

5. Click on the bug symbol in the **Actions** section (highlighted in red in the preceding screenshot) to open the test window for the Customer Service proxy service.
6. In the **Proxy Service Testing** window, make sure you select the right operation in the **Available Operations** drop-down list. We want to test the **RetrieveCustomerByCriteria** operation.

7. Change the **Payload** field as shown in the following screenshot:

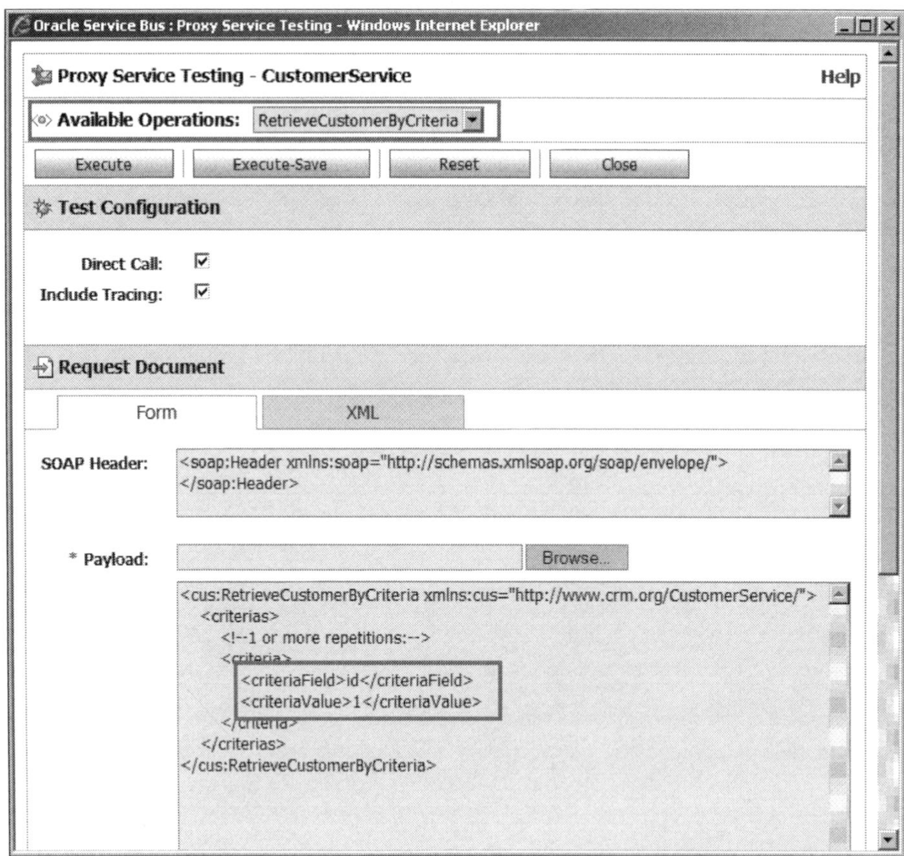

8. Click on the **Execute** button to run the test. The test results are returned after a while in the same window:

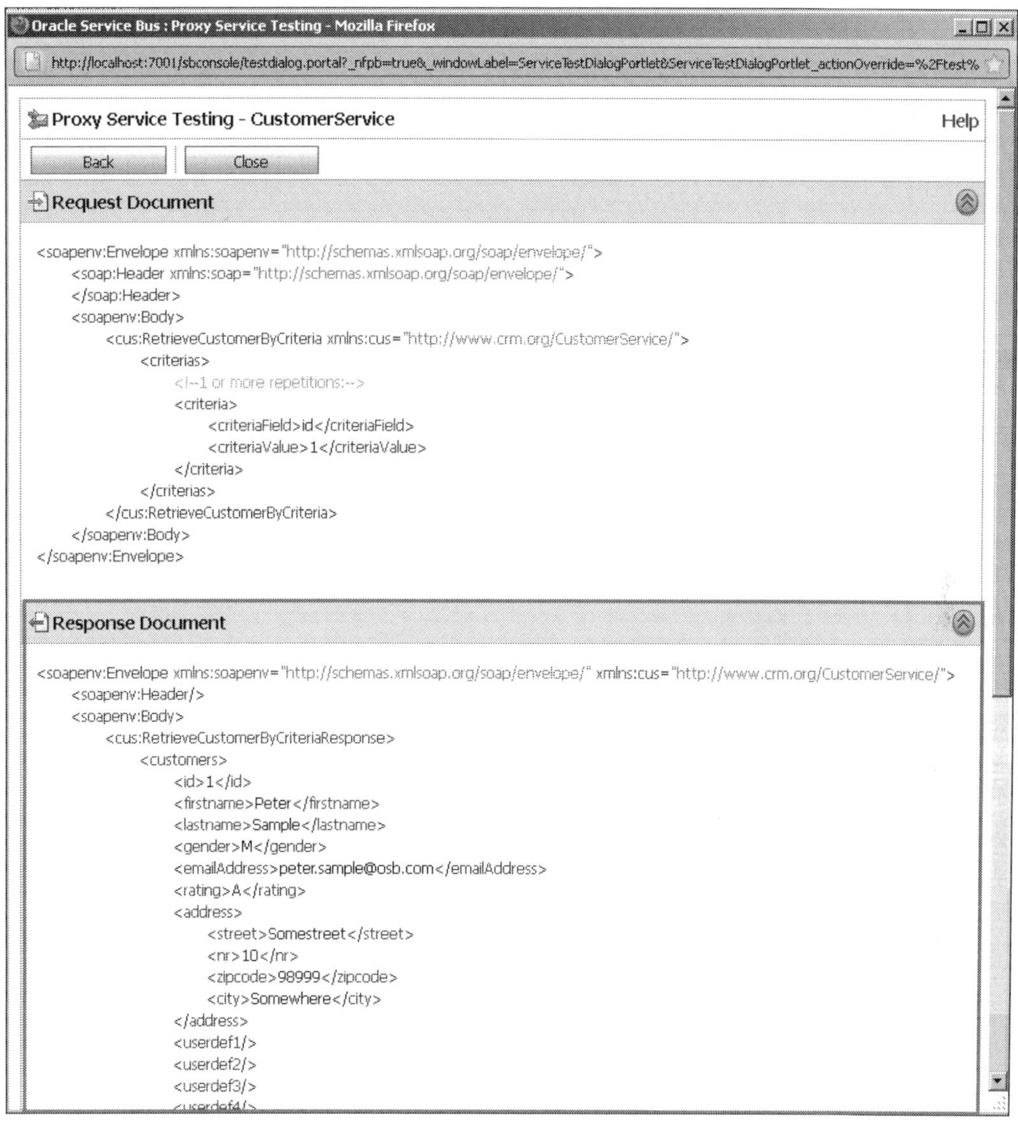
Oracle Service Bus : Proxy Service Testing - Mozilla Firefox
http://localhost:7001/sbconsole/testdialog.portal?_nfpb=true&_windowLabel=ServiceTestDialogPortlet&ServiceTestDialogPortlet_actionOverride=%2Ftest%
Proxy Service Testing - CustomerService
Help
Back
Close
Request Document
<soapenv:Envelope xmlns:soapenv="http://schemas.xmlsoap.org/soap/envelope/">
<soap:Header xmlns:soap="http://schemas.xmlsoap.org/soap/envelope/">
</soap:Header>
<soapenv:Body>
<cus:RetrieveCustomerByCriteria xmlns:cus="http://www.crm.org/CustomerService/">
<criterias>
<!--1 or more repetitions:-->
<criteria>
<criteriaField>id</criteriaField>
<criteriaValue>1</criteriaValue>
</criteria>
</criterias>
</cus:RetrieveCustomerByCriteria>
</soapenv:Body>
</soapenv:Envelope>
Response Document
<soapenv:Envelope xmlns:soapenv="http://schemas.xmlsoap.org/soap/envelope/" xmlns:cus="http://www.crm.org/CustomerService/">
<soapenv:Header/>
<soapenv:Body>
<cus:RetrieveCustomerByCriteriaResponse>
<customers>
<id>1</id>
<firstname>Peter</firstname>
<lastname>Sample</lastname>
<gender>M</gender>
<emailAddress>peter.sample@osb.com</emailAddress>
<rating>A</rating>
<address>
<street>Somestreet</street>
<nr>10</nr>
<zipcode>98999</zipcode>
<city>Somewhere</city>
</address>
<userdef1/>
<userdef2/>
<userdef3/>

9. Check that the right customer (with `ID = 1`) information is being returned by the OSB service.

10. Scroll down in the window to see the **Invocation Trace** section. This will show steps that the OSB proxy service has executed and values of the variables during execution:

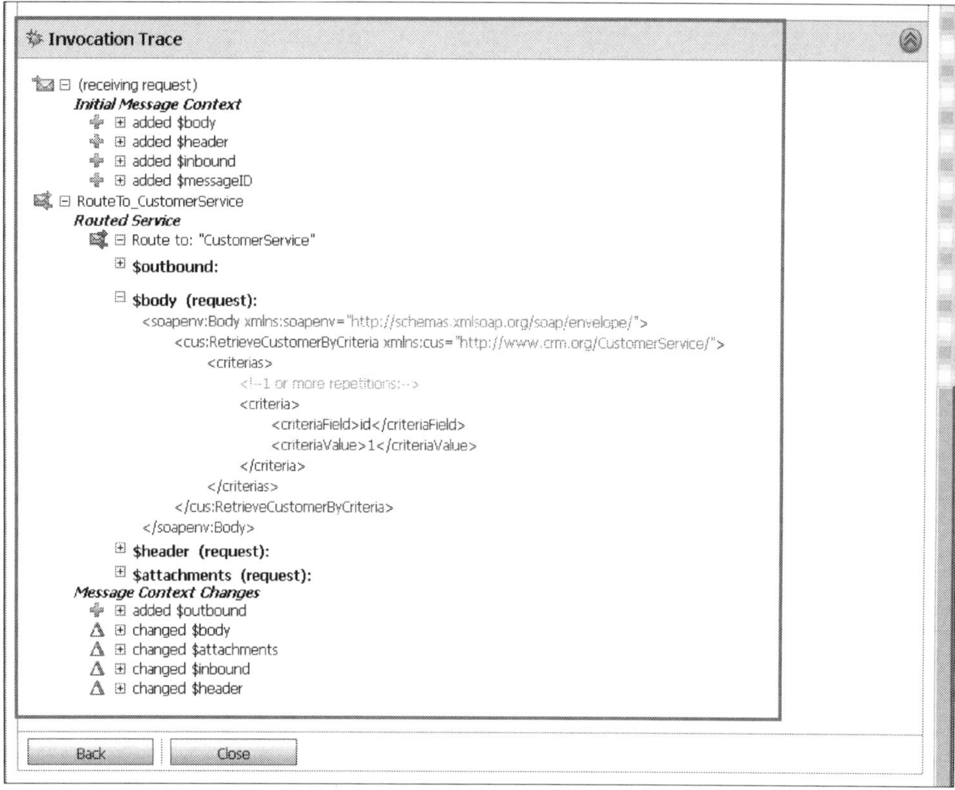

How it works...

Due to the fact that the interface of the proxy service is clearly defined through the WSDL, the OSB console is capable of showing us a sample test message in the **Payload** field. If we have a proxy service without a WSDL, then testing that service will still be possible through that window, but there will no longer be a sample message shown, as the OSB console does not know about the structure.

The testing capabilities offered by the OSB console are good for some initial tests or if the execution trace is of value, possibly for debugging if using the graphical debugger is not an option. The limitation of the OSB console for testing is clearly that there is no way to persist a test case to be able to run it again later. By that it's also not possible to automate and repeat testing, for example, to start tests inside a nightly build. For that, soapUI, which will be shown in the next recipe, is much better suited.

See also

An alternative way for testing proxy services can be found in the next recipe *Testing the proxy service through soapUI*.

Testing the proxy service through soapUI

In the previous recipe, we used the OSB console for testing the proxy service. This is ok to just quickly see, if the service is working. But for automatic and repeatable tests, the OSB console is not the right tool.

One advantage of using standards such as the web service standard and the SOAP-based web services is the fact that we can mix and match products from different vendors. The web service standards are vendor-neutral.

Especially for testing web services, there exists a lot of specialized products from different vendors. **soapUI** is such a specialized tool, which offers both a free as well as a pro version. The free version supports the testing web services with a lot of convenient functionalities. In this recipe, we will show how to test our simple proxy service through soapUI.

Getting ready

To perform this recipe, soapUI needs to be downloaded and installed. We can get it from here: `http://www.soapui.org`.

In order to test the service from soapUI, we need to know the WSDL URL of the deployed proxy service. The URL is constructed by the OSB at deployment time, based on the location of the OSB server (`http://[OSBServer]:[Port]`) and the endpoint URI specified in the proxy service (that is, `/basic-osb-service/proxy/CustomerService`). We need to concatenate the two and add the suffix `?wsdl` to get the WSDL URL of the OSB proxy service:

`http://localhost:7001/basic-osb-service/proxy/CustomerService?wsdl`.

How to do it...

In soapUI, perform the following steps:

1. In the **File** menu, select **New soapUI Project**.
2. Enter the URL of the WSDL, for the service to be tested (`http://localhost:7001/basic-osb-service/proxy/CustomerService?wsdl`) into the **Initial WSDL/WADL** field.

3. Enter `CustomerService` into the **Project Name** field.
4. Click on the **OK** button.

SoapUI will analyze the WSDL and creates a project with some initial requests for all operations defined by the WSDL. Still in soapUI, perform the following steps:

5. Expand the project in the **Navigator** on the left.
6. Double-click on the **Request 1** entry of the **RetrieveCustomerByCriteria** operation.

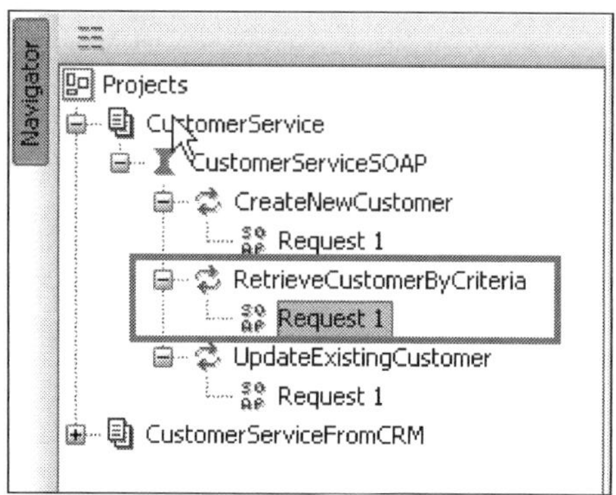

7. A new window for the **Request 1** will open in the **details** section.
8. Replace the **?** character in the request message on the left by the input parameter values for the test. The following screenshot shows the request with the ? characters replaced:

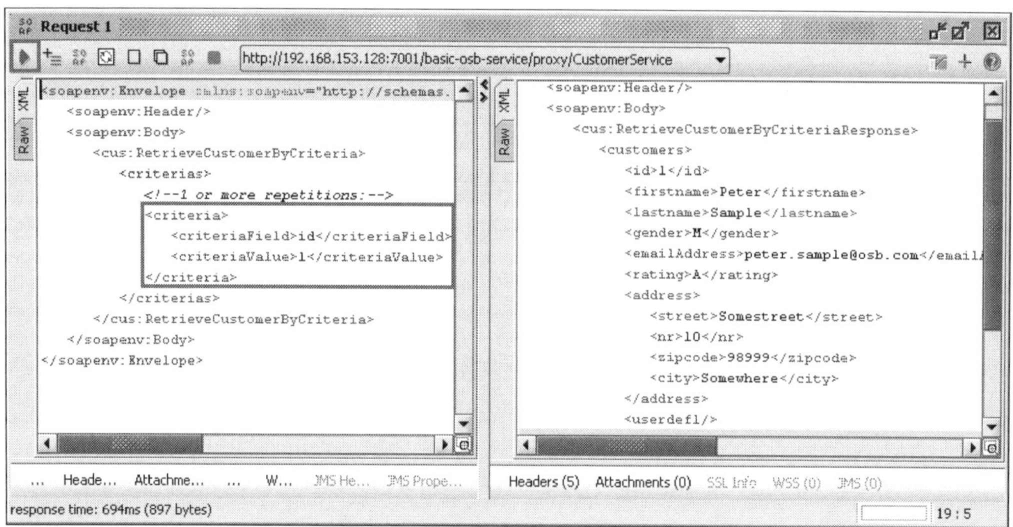

9. Click on the green arrow to start the test.

10. Check that a valid customer is returned in the response window on the right.
11. Save the soapUI project so that it is available to use later.

How it works...

Thanks to the standardization through web services, a tool such as soapUI can create the right requests for a service just by analyzing the provided WSDL of the service. SoapUI creates requests for each operation of the service. These requests are persisted in the soapUI project and they can be combined into a test suite. This allows them to be automatically executed, that is, they can be used together with continuous integration.

There's more...

SoapUI is very powerful and it's worth checking the online documentation available on their website (`http://www.soapui.org`). In any real-live project work, we suggest you to look at the pro version as well. It simplifies a lot of the service testing even further.

Validate that the response is correct

In soapUI, perform the following steps to validate the response from the proxy service against the XML schema in the WSDL:

1. Right-click on the response message window and select **Validate**.
2. Either a pop-up window will appear indicating that the XML message is valid or the validation errors will be displayed in a window below the response message, as shown in the following screenshot:

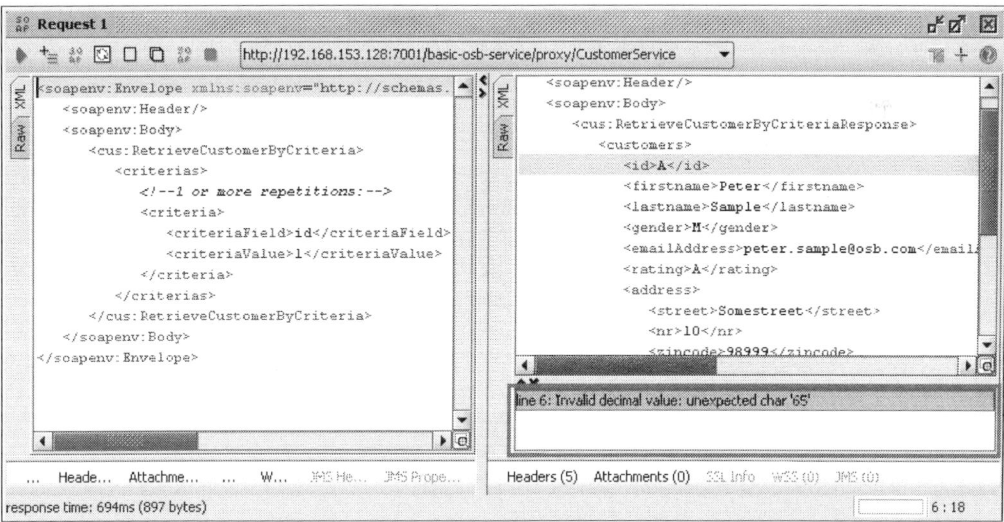

Creating another request for the same operation

SoapUI supports more than one request per operation, so that a request can be created for each test case to be executed. It's recommended to properly name the different requests in order to be able to identify them later and to clearly indicate the case tested by a given request.

To rename a request, just right-click on the request and select **Rename**.

An existing request can also be cloned. This reduces the amount of work necessary to correctly set up all the information in the request message. To create a copy of a request, right-click on the request and select **Clone Request**.

To create a new request from scratch, right-click on the operation and select **New request**.

See also

To learn more about soapUI check their website: `http://www.soapui.org/`. There is also a pro version available, which has a lot more interesting features, a lot of them simplifying the use of soapUI for web service testing.

Creating proxy service with a WSDL based interface

In the previous recipe, we have created an OSB service with a pass-through proxy service, which offered the same SOAP-based interface as the external service.

In this recipe, we will create a proxy service Customer Management which uses its own WSDL (CustomerManagement) to define a SOAP-based web service interface to its consumers:

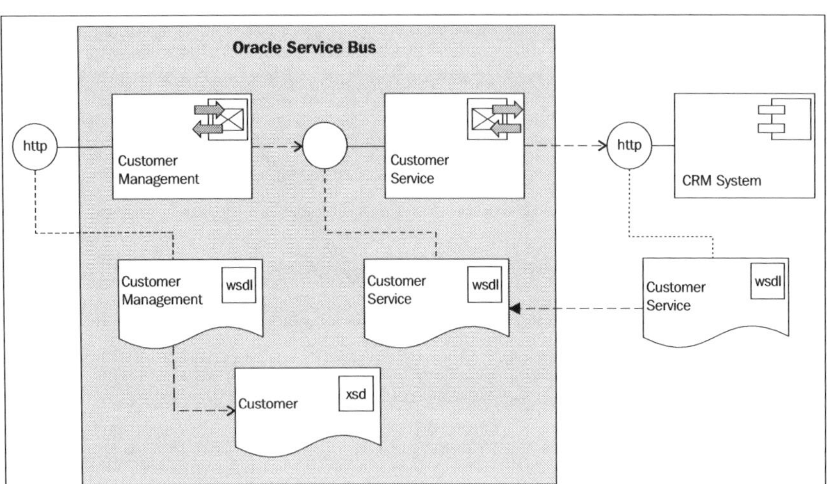

Getting ready

Make sure that you have the **basic-osb-service** project from the previous recipes available in Eclipse OEPE. We will start the recipe from there. If needed, it can be imported from here: `\chapter-1\getting-ready\pass-through-proxy-service-created`. Delete the pass-through proxy service by right-clicking on **CustomerService.proxy**, selecting **Delete**, and then confirm the deletion by clicking on the **OK** button.

How to do it...

In order to create the proxy service, we need to define the service interface (WSDL) for that new service. We won't create the WSDL in this recipe. The WSDL file and the corresponding XML schema files are available in the `\chapter-1\getting-ready\definition\xsd\` folder.

We start this recipe by first copying the WSDL and the corresponding XML schema files into the OSB project, and then create the new proxy service.

In Eclipse OEPE, perform the following steps:

1. Copy the **Customer.xsd** and **CreditCard.xsd** files from the `\chapter-1\getting-ready\definition\xsd` folder into the **xsd** folder of the project.
2. Copy the **CustomerManagement.wsdl** from the `\chapter-1\getting-started\definition\wsdl` folder into the **wsdl** folder in the OSB project.
3. Make sure that the project looks like the following screenshot (you might need to hit *F5* to refresh the project in Eclipse OEPE):

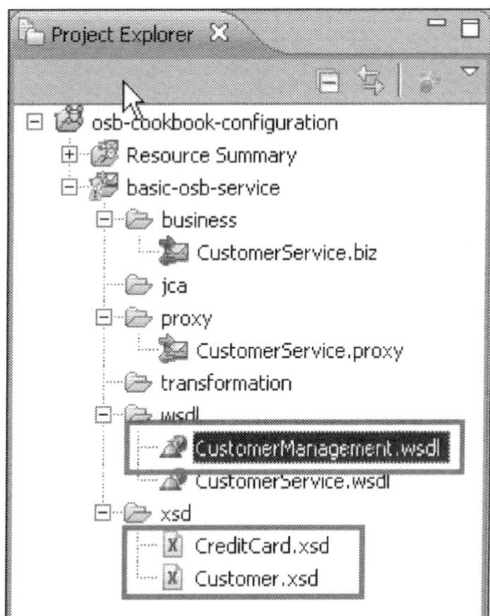

With the WSDL file in place, we can create the proxy service. Still in Eclipse OEPE, perform the following steps:

4. Right-click on the **proxy** folder and select **New | Proxy Service**.
5. Enter `CustomerManagement` for the name of the proxy service into the **File name** field and click on the **Finish** button.
6. The new proxy service artifact is created and the proxy service window is shown, with the **General** tab with the focus on.
7. We want to create a proxy service with a WSDL interface, so let's select the option **WSDL** web service and click on the **Browse** button.
8. In the pop-up window, expand the project tree and navigate to the **CustomerManagement.wsdl** file in the **wsdl** folder.
9. Click on the node to expand it and select the **CustomerManagementSOAP** port.
10. Click on the **OK** button:

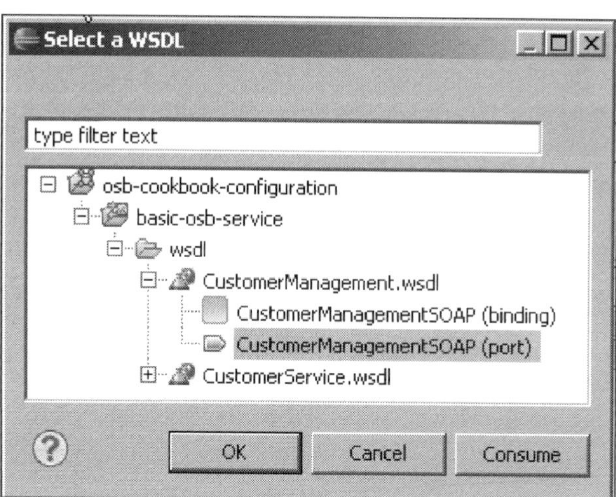

11. Click on **Yes**, on the confirmation dialog to overwrite the transport settings with the values from the WSDL.
12. Navigate to the **Transport** tab and check the **Endpoint URI** field. This value will be needed when invoking the service or when consuming the WSDL of the proxy service when deployed on the OSB server.

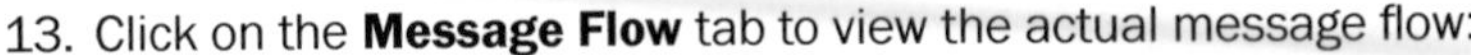

13. Click on the **Message Flow** tab to view the actual message flow:

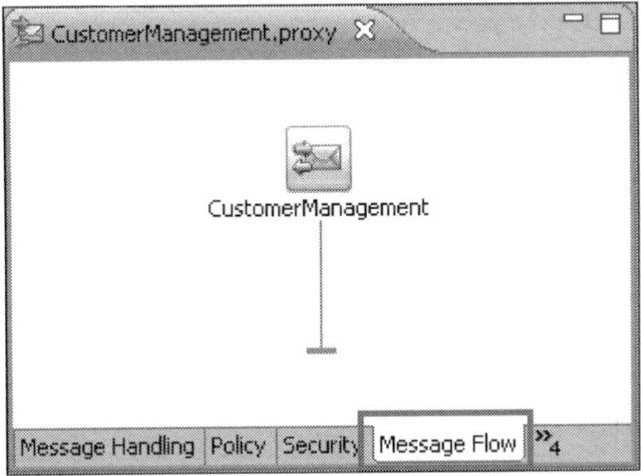

How it works...

So far the message flow only consists of the interface, which is based on the WSDL. The flow logic itself is empty. If no further actions are added to the message flow, the proxy service works in an 'echo mode'. All the request messages sent to the proxy service are returned unchanged.

Try it by deploying the project to the OSB server and test it through the console or soapUI. To use soapUI for that, create a new soapUI project and import the WSDL. It should be available from here: `http://[OSBServer]:[Port]/basic-osb-service/proxy/CustomerManagement?wsdl`.

The following screenshot shows the behavior of the 'echo proxy service', when invoked from soapUI:

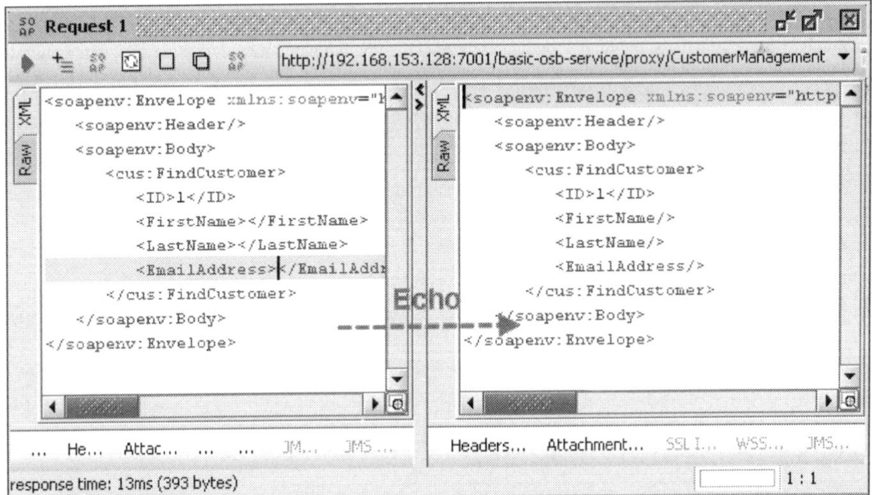

This is not the behavior that we want from our proxy service. In the next recipe, we will add a **Routing** action to the message flow, so that the business service the external service is called.

Use the echo behaviour to implement a simple mock service

The echo behaviour seems to be strange at the beginning and it's hard to find a use case in the way just shown. But it's good to see and know that the message flow just returns if there are no (more) actions to execute. Whatever the `$body` variable holds at that time is returned as the response message.

This behaviour can be used to implement a very simple mock service.

A **mock service** is a service which simulates the behaviour of the real service or part of it. If we have the WSDL but not yet an implementation, we can create a proxy service and due to the echo behaviour, all we need is an assignment to the `$body` variable (to set up the response), just before the request message is passed back. This can be achieved by a **Replace** or **Assign** Action inside a **Pipeline Pair Node/Stage** pair.

We can also use soapUI to implement mock services. SoapUI provides a lot of functionality to implement very flexible mock services.

Using a routing action to statically route to another service

To route the message to another service (to a business service or even to another proxy service) a routing action inside a **Route** node needs to be used.

Getting ready

Make sure you have the current state of the **basic-osb-service** project available in Eclipse OEPE. We will start this recipe from there. If necessary, it can be imported from here: `\chapter-1\getting-ready\echo-proxy-service-created`.

How to do it...

In Eclipse OEPE, perform the following steps:

1. Drag a **Route** node from the **Design Palette** and drop it on the message flow path below the interface. A green circle indicates that the item can be dropped here:

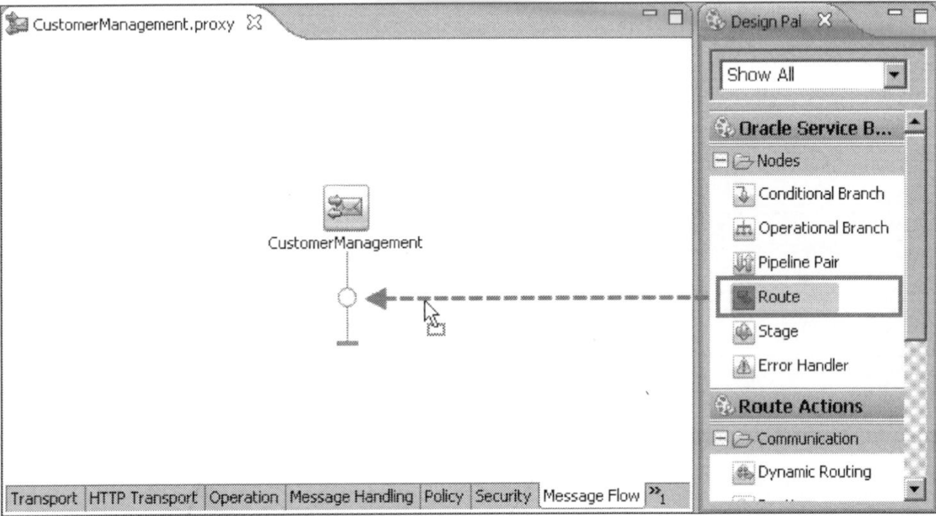

2. Rename the **Route** node to **RouteToCustomerService**.
3. Drag a **Routing** action from the **Communication** section of the **Design** Palette into the **Route** node:

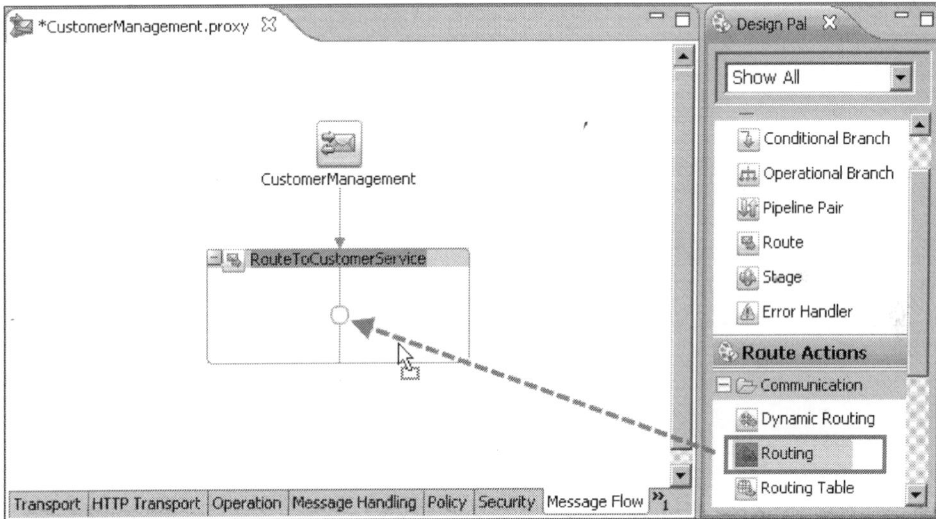

4. In the **Properties** of the **Routing** action click on the **Browse** button next to the **Service** field and select the business service **CustomerService.biz** (to be found in the `business` folder).

5. In the **Invoking** drop-down list, select **RetrieveCustomerByCriteria** as the operation to be called:

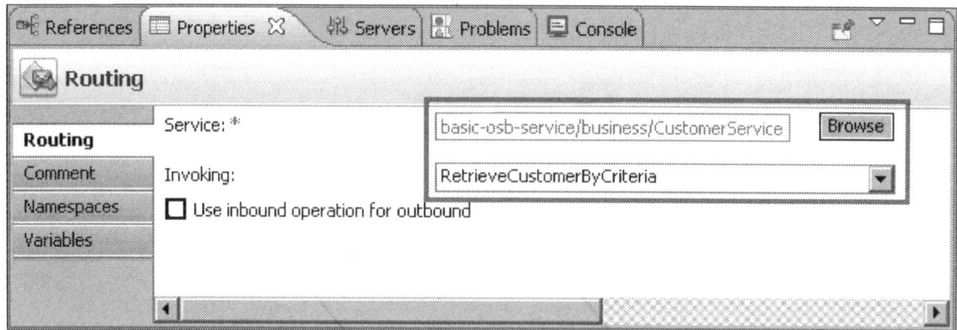

6. Click on the **Save** button.

How it works...

We have created a single route to the operation **RetrieveCustomerByCriteria** of the external web service. But we not only have one operation on the proxy service to implement, our WSDL contains two operations, which we need to route to different operations on the external service. Therefore, just a single **Routing** action is not enough. We need to use an **Operational Branch** with a branch containing a different **Routing** action. Using an **Operation Branch** node will be shown in the next recipe.

We cannot select the **Use inbound operation for outbound** option, because the WSDL on the proxy service is no longer the same as the one on the business service (external service), that is, the operation names do not match.

See also

Check the next recipe for how to add an Operational Branch to the proxy service.

Adding an operational branch to support the different WSDL operations of the proxy service

To support the different operations of the WSDL we need different branches, which will hold the necessary flow logic. This can be achieved with an **Operational Branch** node.

Getting ready

Make sure you have the current state of the **basic-osb-service** project available in Eclipse OEPE. We will start this recipe from there. Delete the existing routing node by right-clicking on it and then select **Delete**. We again have an empty message flow to start with. If needed, it can be imported from here: `\chapter-1\getting-ready\echo-proxy-service-created`.

How to do it...

1. Drag an **Operational Branch** node from the **Design Palette** on the right and drop on the **Message Flow** below the interface.
2. Change the name of the **Operational Branch** node to **HandleOperationBranch**, by editing the **Name field** in the property window.
3. The branch node contains two branches, one for the operation **FindCustomer** and the **Default** branch. We need one more branch for the **StoreCustomer** operation.
4. Click on the **+** symbol in the upper-right corner of the operation branch and a new branch is added and selected:

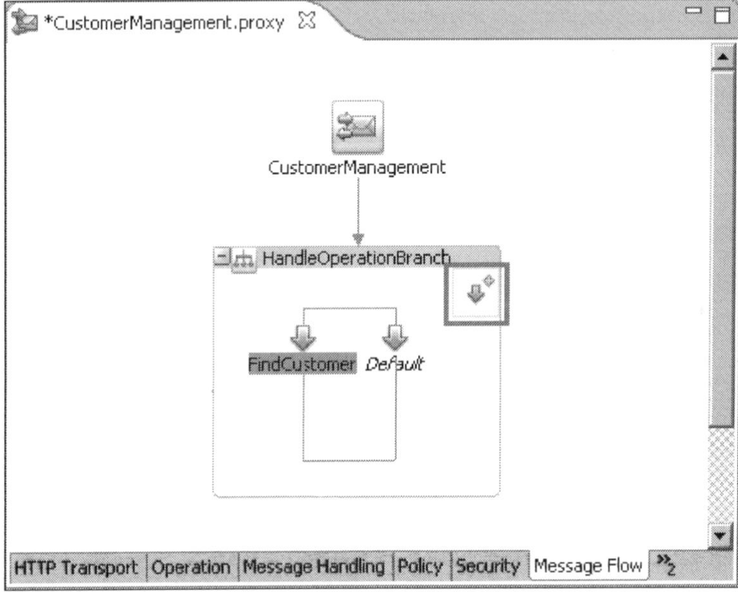

5. Navigate to the **Properties** tab of the new branch and change the **Operation** in the drop-down list to **StoreCustomer**.
6. Drag a **Route** node from the Design Palette and drop it on the **FindCustomer** branch.

7. Drag another **Route** node from the Design Palette and drop it on the **StoreCustomer** branch.
8. Rename the **Route** nodes to **FindCustomerRoute** and **StoreCustomerRoute**.
9. Drag a **Routing** Action from the **Communication** section of the **Design Palette** to both **Route** nodes:

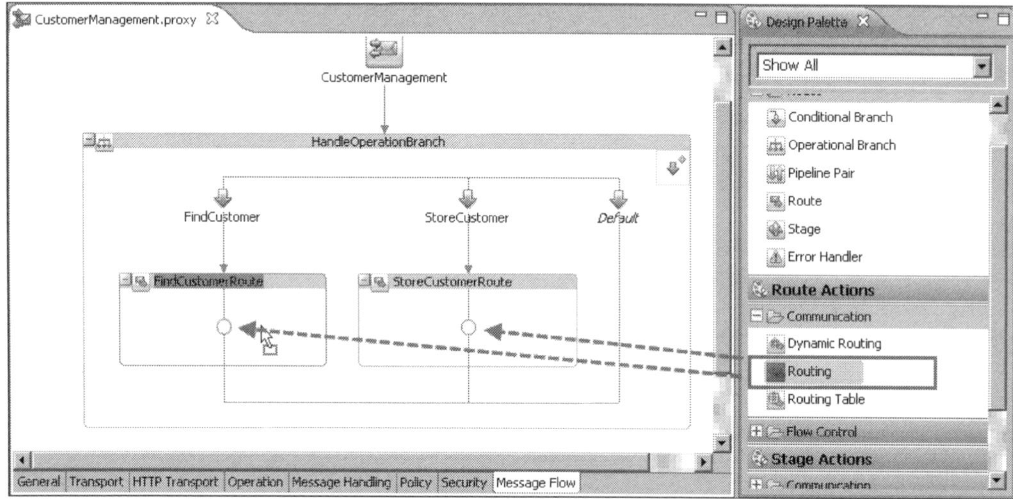

10. In the **Properties** of the **Routing** action, inside the **FindCustomerRoute**, click on **Browse** next to the **Service** field and select the business service **CustomerService.biz** (to be found in the `business` folder).
11. In the **Invoking** drop-down list, select **RetrieveCustomerByCriteria** as the operation to be called.
12. Repeat steps 8-10 for the **Routing** action of the **StoreCustomerRoute**, but this time select the **CreateNewCustomer** in the **Invoking** drop-down list.
13. Click on the **Save** button.

How it works...

The operational branch allows for implementing each operation of a multi-operational WSDL in a different way. In the **Message Flow** that we have implemented so far, the difference was just the routing to another operation on the external service. If the WSDL only contains one operation, then an operational branch is not really necessary. But we suggest to always use it from the beginning, in order to be prepared if an additional operation is added later. This also provides an option to handle invalid invocations or unsupported operations in the default branch.

With that in place, the service will now correctly route the calls on the different operations. What is not yet done is the adaption between the data models of the two services. This will be covered in the next recipe.

There's more...

In this section, we will discuss the default branch of an Operational Branch node and show how to handle an operation which is not (yet) supported.

Do I have to implement a branch for each operation?

Each single operation does not need to have its own branch. If an operation has no branch, then a call on that operation will end up in the default branch and all calls to an operation without a dedicated branch have to be handled there. If the default handler is left empty, then the behaviour will be an echo, similar to the empty proxy service that we have seen a few recipes back. So every message sent on an operation without a branch will be sent back untouched and unchanged.

The default branch can be used to either generically handle all other messages not handled by a specific branch or to return an error, that this operation is not (yet) supported (see next section).

How to handle operations which are not yet supported?

Use the default branch to raise an error by performing the following steps:

1. Drag a **Pipeline Pair** node from the palette and drop it on the **Default** branch flow.
2. Rename the pipeline pair to **HandleUnsupportedOpsPipelinePair**.
3. Drag a **Stage** node from the pallet and drop it on the **Request Pipeline** flow.
4. Drag a **Raise Error** action from the design palette and drop it into the stage flow.

5. Enter the error-code into the **Code** field and a meaningful error message into the **Message** field:

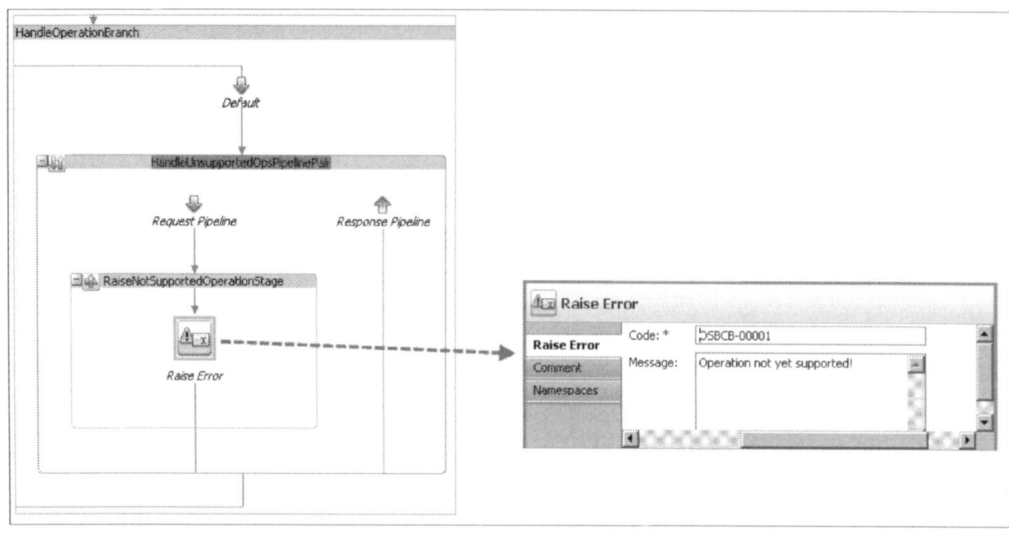

An operation branch should not be left empty just because it will only be implemented later and is not supported with the current release. If a branch is empty, then it will have the 'echo' behavior, resulting in a message sent to such an operation being returned just as is. It might be very difficult for a potential caller of such an operation to find out what happened. It's better to remove the branch completely and let the **Default** branch handle it or to add a **Raise Error** to the operational branch to signal an error:

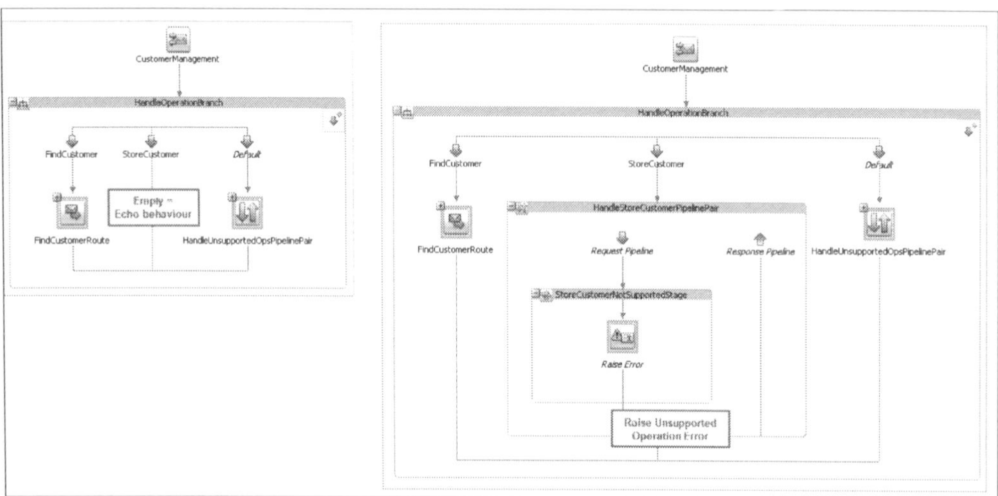

When using a branch specific for each operation, the name of the operation can be specified in the error message. If somebody is using the not yet supported **StoreCustomer** operation, the following SOAP fault will be returned:

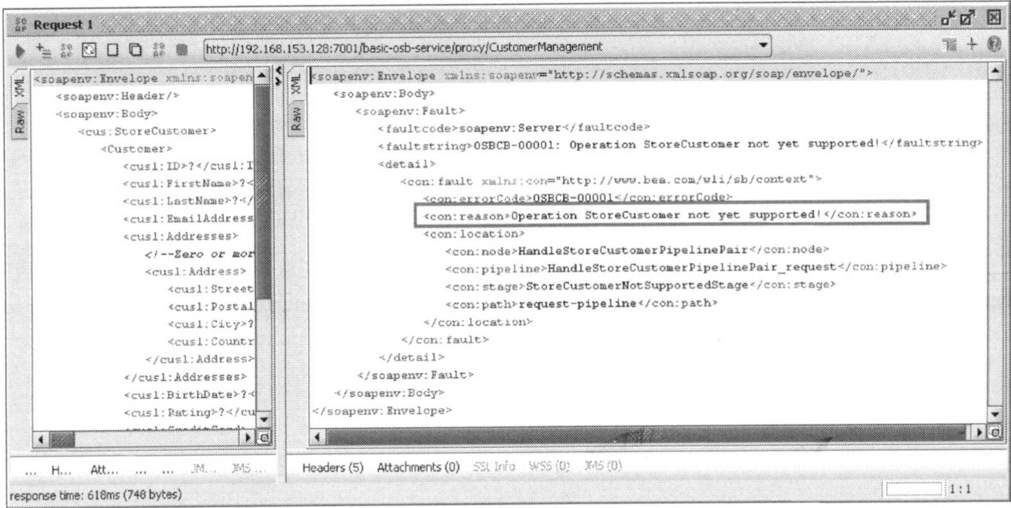

See also

See the next recipe for how to map between the different data models the two services use.

Using an XQuery transformation to map between the different data models of the services

Due to the fact that on the proxy service we use a different WSDL than the external service offered, we need to adapt the data models between these two interfaces when sending the request message as well as on the way back when returning the response message. There are different ways to achieve that, probably the most common one in OSB being the use of an XQuery script.

Getting ready

Make sure that you have the current state of the `basic-osb-service` project available in Eclipse OEPE. We will start this recipe from there. If necessary, it can be imported from here: `\chapter-1\getting-ready\operational-branch-proxy-service-created`.

How to do it...

First we will need to create the transformation for the request message to be passed to the external service, which has not many data elements to transform.

1. Create a new XQuery script by right-clicking on the `transformation` folder in the `Project` folder and then select **New | XQuery Transformation**.
2. Enter `TransformFindCustomerRequest` into the **File name** field and then click on **Next**.
3. In the **Available Source Types** tree, select the source type for the transformation: **FindCustomer from the CustomerManagement.wsdl**.
4. Click on the **Add** button to add it to the **Selected Source Types**, as shown in the following screenshot:

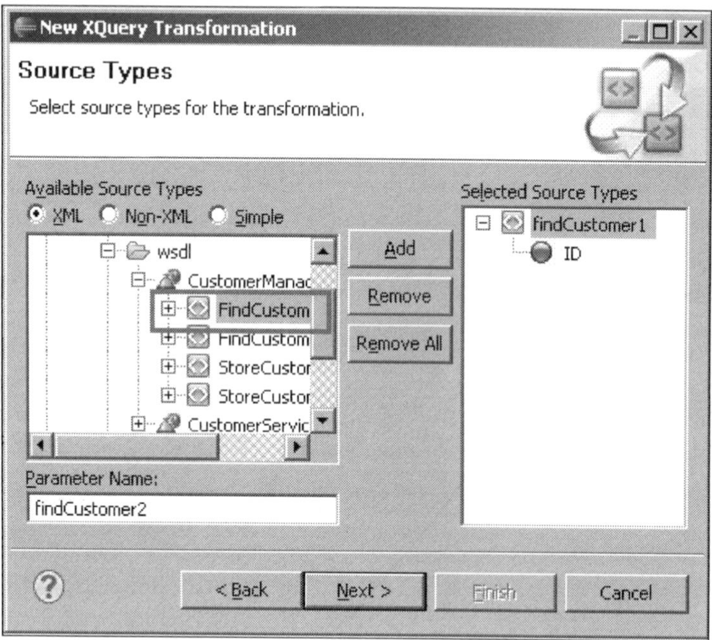

5. Click on the **Next** button.
6. In the **Available Target Types** tree, select the target type for the transformation: **RetrieveCustomerByCriteria from the CustomerService.wsdl**.
7. Click on the **Add** button to move it to the **Selected Target Types**.
8. Click on the **Finish** button.
9. Click on **Yes** to confirm switching to the XQuery Transformation perspective.

The graphical XQuery transformation editor opens, with the source on the left and the target structure on the right. We can now start mapping source to target values. In the case of the **FindCustomer** request, the target side is a generic query operation with a list of criteria elements. In this recipe, we will only map the ID, assuming that at the moment only the ID value needs to be supported. To map it, follow the ensuing steps:

10. Right-click on the **criteriaField** node on the right side (target) and select **Create Constant**.
11. Enter `id` into the **Constant Value** field of the pop-up window.
12. Click on the **OK** button.
13. The **criteriaField** is annotated with a little **c**, indicating that a constant is specified.
14. Select the **criteriaValue** on the right side and click on the **Target Expression** tab (make sure that the XQuery Transformation perspective is active, otherwise the **Target Expression** tab will not be available).
15. From the available **XQuery Functions** on the left, drag the string **Type Conversion Functions** to the expression editor. The expression will read **xs:string($item*-var)**.
16. Drag the **ID** element from the **Source** type and replace the **$item*-var** parameter value within the parentheses:

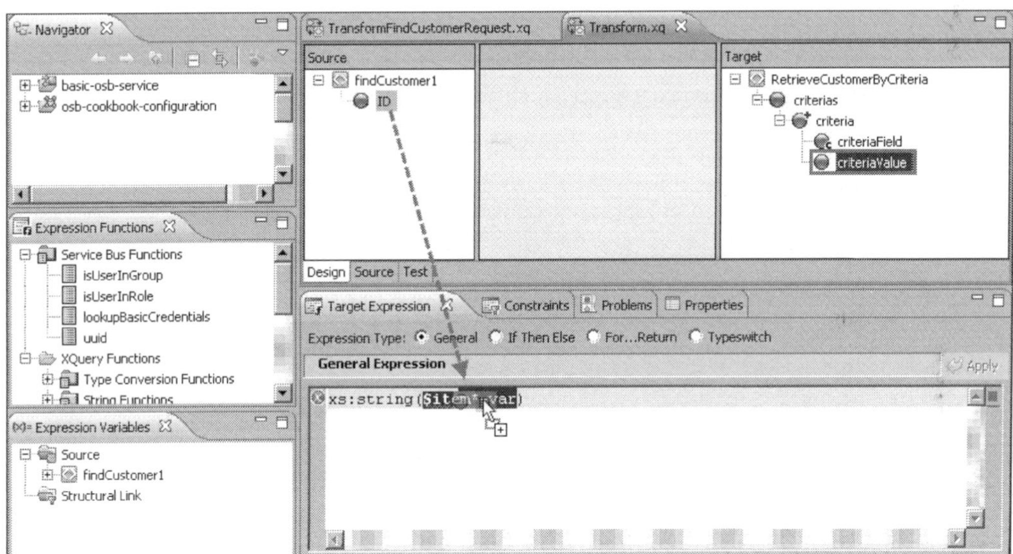

17. Click on **Apply** on the left of the **Target Expression** tab window to accept the expression and a line for the mapping should be displayed. The small **f** on the **criteriaValue** node indicates the usage of an XQuery function:

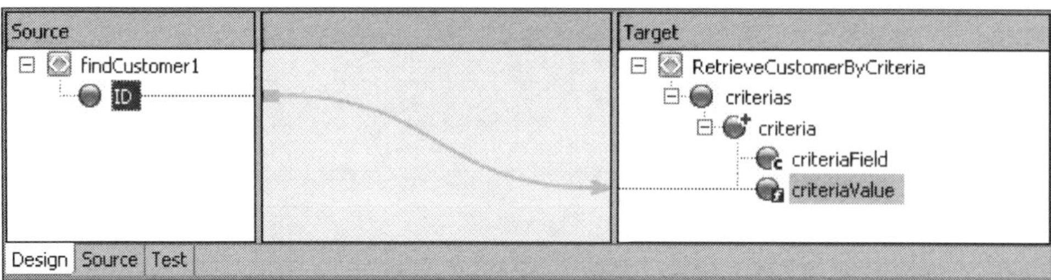

18. Save the XQuery script

The transformation for the request of the **findCustomer** operation is now ready to be used. Before we will apply it in the **Messagse Flow**, let's create the transformation for the response message. Perform the following steps:

19. Repeat steps 1-10 with the following differences:
    - Name the XQuery **TransformFindCustomerResponse**
    - Select the **RetrieveCustomerByCriteriaResponse** element of the **CustomerService** WSDL as the source type of the transformation
    - Select the **FindCustomerResponse** element of the **CustomerManagement** WSDL as the target type of the transformation
20. Map the source to the target values in the XQuery Transformation editor as shown in the following screenshot. The `ID` value cannot be directly mapped, a type conversion using the `xs:long` function is needed:

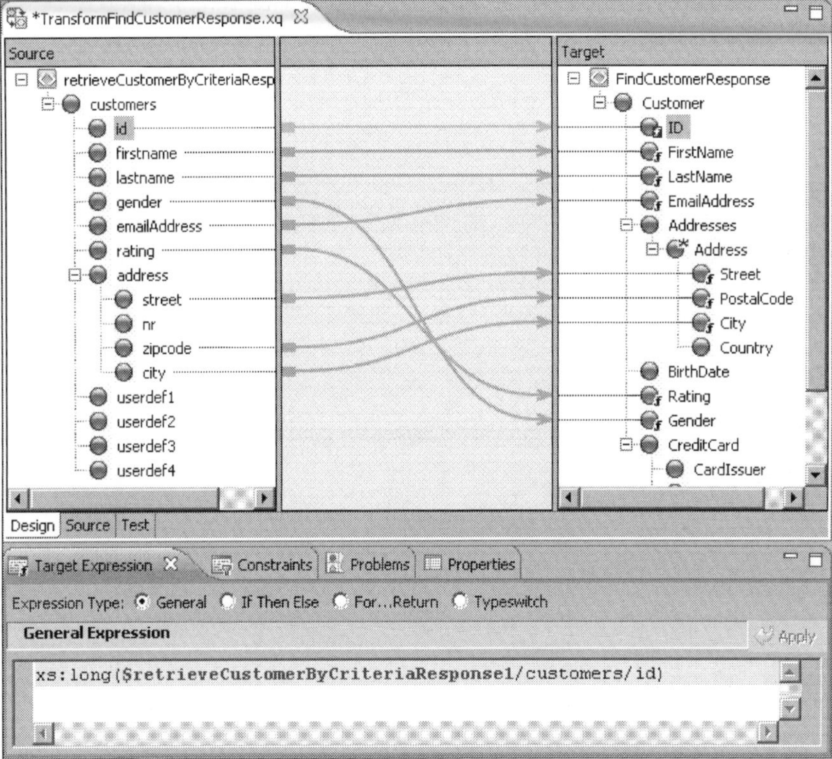

21. Now with the two XQuery transformations in place, let's use them in the message flow.
22. Switch to the **Oracle Service Bus** perspective.
23. Open the **CustomerManagement** proxy service and click on the **Message Flow** tab.

24. Drag a **Replace** action from the **Message Processing** section of the **Design** palette into the **Request Action** of the **Routing** for the **FindCustomer** operation:

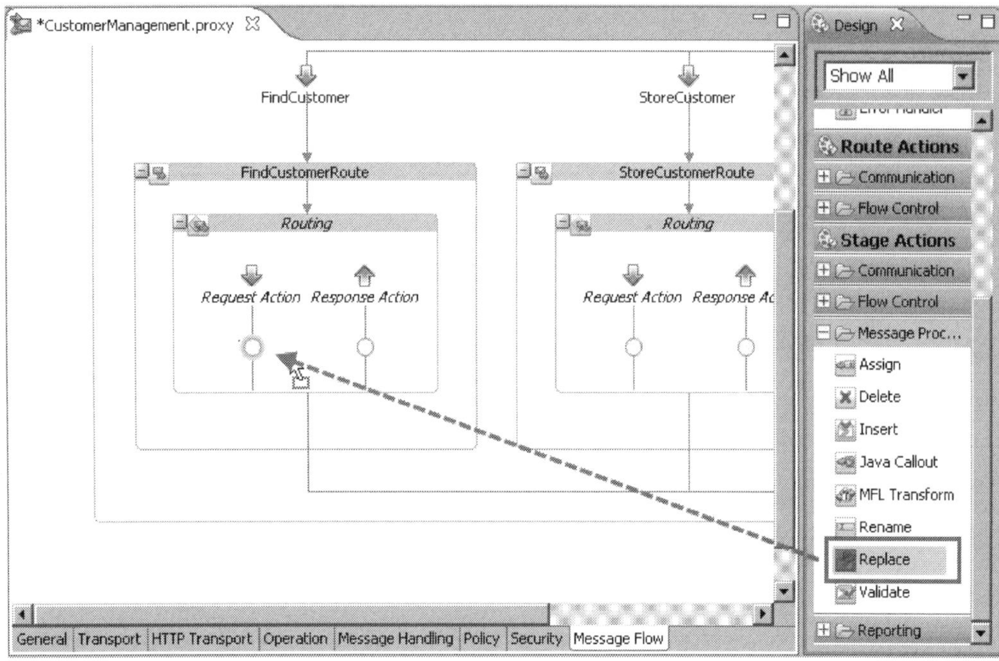

25. Select the **Replace** action and click on the **Properties** tab to show the properties of the **Replace**.
26. Enter `body` into the **In Variable** field.
27. Click on the **<Expression>** link.
28. In the **Expression Editor** pop-up, click on the **XQuery Resources** tab.
29. Click on **Browse** and select **TransformFindCustomerRequest.xq** from the `transformation` folder.
30. Click on the **OK** button.

31. Drag the **FindCustomer** node on the right side and drop it onto the **Binding Variables** field. The value of the binding should read `$body/cus:FindCustomer`.

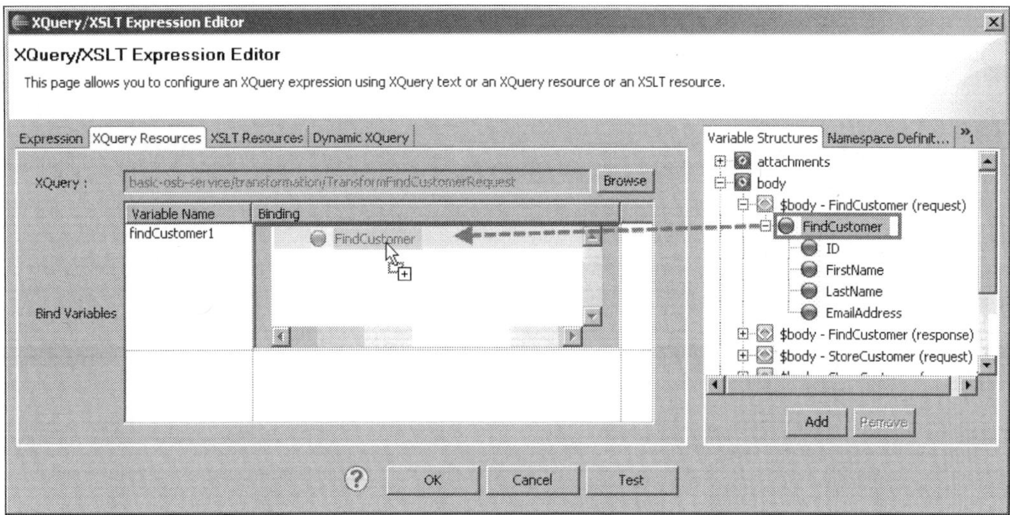

32. Click on the **OK** button.
33. Select the radio button **Replace node contents**.
34. Save the changes.

We have added the transformation of the request message. Let's repeat the same steps for the response message:

35. Drag a **Replace** action from the **Message Processing** section of the **Design Palette** into the **Response Action** of the Routing for the **FindCustomer** operation.
36. Select the **Replace** action and click on the **Properties** tab to show the properties of the **Replace**.
37. Enter `body` into the **In Variable** field.
38. Click on the **Expression** link.
39. In the **Expression Editor** pop-up click on the **XQuery Resources** tab.
40. Click on **Browse** and select **TransformFindCustomerResponse.xq** from the `transformation` folder.
41. Click on **OK**.
42. Enter `$body/ext:RetrieveCustomerByCriteriaResponse` into the **Binding Variables** field. An error is shown because the namespace alias `ext` is not defined. Click on **OK**.

43. Select the radio button **Replace node contents**.

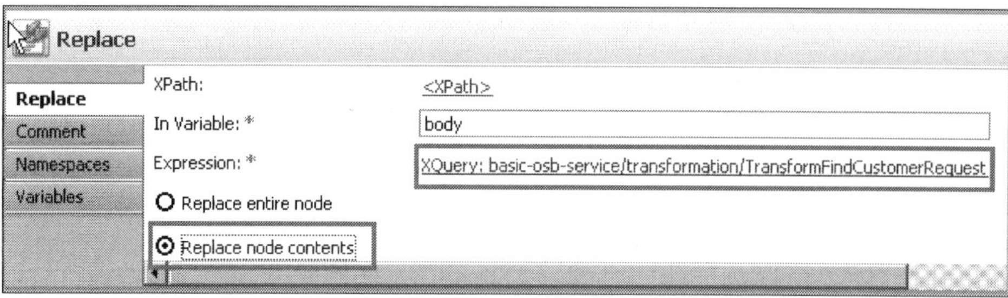

44. Click on the **Namespaces** tab on the left of the **Properties** window.
45. Click on **Add**.
46. Enter `ext` into the **Prefix** field and `http://www.crm.org/CustomerService/` into the **URI** field.
47. Click on **OK**.
48. Save the proxy service and close it.
49. Deploy the project to the OSB server by right-clicking on the server and select **Publish**.
50. Use soapUI to test the behavior of the service. The following screenshot shows the result of successfully executing a test containing the find result of the external service:

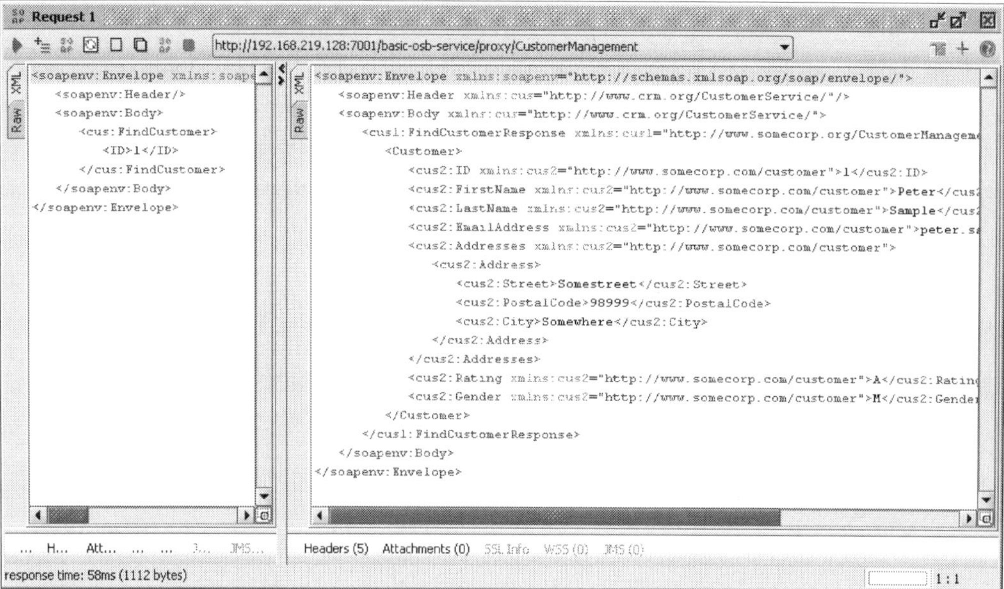

The request as well as the response message in the soapUI test window represents the format defined in the Customer Management WSDL.

How it works...

We have used two standalone XQuery scripts to define and execute the transformation of the request as well as the response message. XQuery is a very efficient way of executing such transformations.

We have used a **Replace** action to do each of the two transformations. This allows doing the transformation and assignment to the body variable in one single action. The setting **Replace node contents** is important because it takes care of the wrapping of the information returned by the transformation inside a `<soap-env:Body>` element.

The transformation could also be done with an **Assign** action. But in that case two **Assign** actions are necessary, the first one doing the transformation into a temporary variable and a second one to wrap the result of the transformation within the `<soap-env:Body>` element and assign it to the body variable.

Using the **Replace** action is not only the most efficient way of doing a transformation, it's also the easiest one to use. Therefore, we highly recommend using it if all you need is a transformation from one value to another.

2

Working Efficiently with OSB Artifacts in Eclipse OEPE

In this chapter, we will cover:

- Setting up an OSB project to work with JCA adapters
- Using context menu to add nodes and actions to message flow
- Moving nodes/actions in Eclipse OEPE by drag-and-drop
- Copying nodes/actions in Eclipse OEPE from one place to another
- Moving artifacts inside the same OSB project
- Copying artifacts from one project into another
- Debugging OSB services through Eclipse OEPE

Introduction

In this chapter, we present different recipes for making the daily work with the Oracle Service Bus (OSB) more efficient. The Eclipse OEPE has some good-to-know features, which supports the creation and changing/refactoring of the message flow of a proxy service as well as the refactoring of the project structure.

We will also show how to set up an OSB project so that the JCA adapters known from the Oracle SOA Suite can be efficiently used within the OSB.

Also in this chapter, we will cover how to debug a proxy service using the graphical debugger built into the Eclipse OEPE development environment and we will see how to reuse functionality through *private* proxy services.

Setting up an OSB project to work with JCA adapters

Since Oracle Service Bus 11g, the JCA adapter's framework is available at runtime, but the definition of the adapters through the wizards is only available in JDeveloper and not in Eclipse OEPE. To be able to use the adapters, JDeveloper with the SOA Suite extension installed needs to be available.

This recipe will show the basis for how to use the JCA adapters together with an OSB project. The idea is to avoid having to copy metadata from one place to the other by nesting the JDeveloper project inside the OSB project. This approach will be used by all other recipes working with the JCA adapters, such as the File, DB and AQ adapter recipes.

Getting ready

In order to use this recipe, both a working Eclipse and JDeveloper IDE needs to be available. In JDeveloper, you also need to install the SOA Suite extension.

How to do it...

First we create an empty OSB project with the correct folder structure. In Eclipse OEPE, perform the following steps:

1. Create a new OSB project and name it `working-with-jca-adapter`.
2. Create an `adapter` folder in the OSB project.
3. Right-click on the `adapter` folder and select **Properties** from the context window.
4. Copy the path of the `adapter` folder under **Location** into the clipboard. We will need it for the location of the SOA project in JDeveloper.

Now we switch to JDeveloper and create a SOA project, located inside the `adapter` folder just created previously. In JDeveloper, perform the following steps:

5. Click on **File** | **New...**.
6. Enter `soa` into the search field.
7. Select the **SOA Project** from the list of items as shown in the following screenshot:

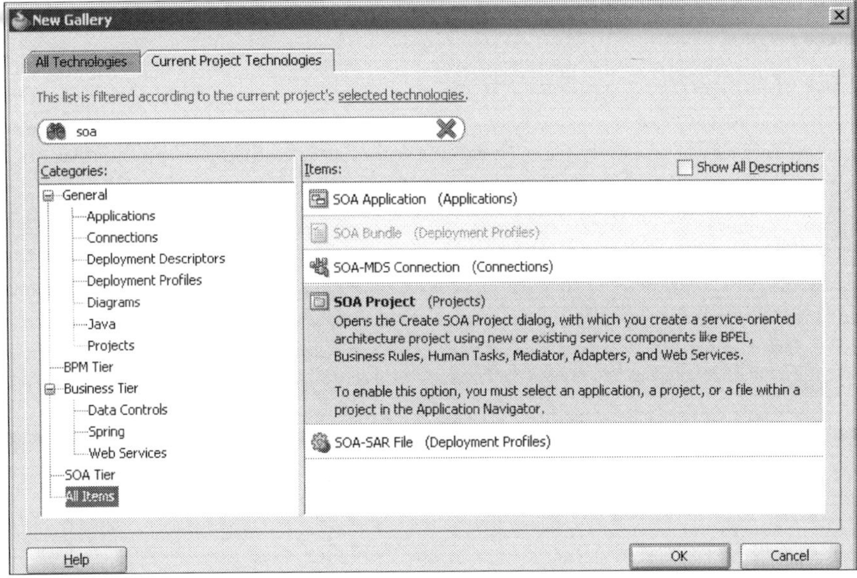

8. Click **OK**.
9. On the **Name your project** screen, enter `AdapterSOAProject` into the **Project Name** field.
10. Make sure that the project is placed within the **adapter** folder of the OSB project. Copy the path from the clipboard (the one copied from the **Properties** in Eclipse OEPE before) into the **Directory** field and add **AdapterSOAProject** to the path.

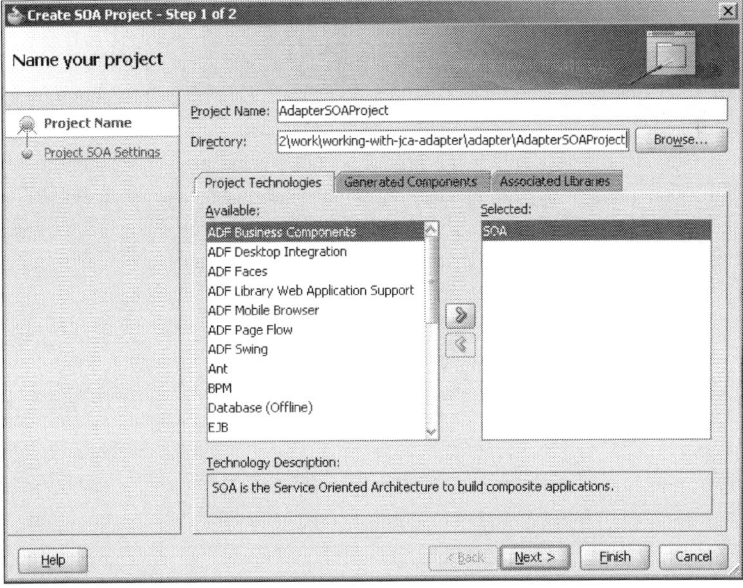

11. Click **Next** and then choose **Empty Composite**.
12. Click **Finish**.
13. The SOA project is created and the empty SOA composite window is shown. The composite can now be used to create the adapters. This is not part of this recipe and will be shown in most of the recipes in *Chapter 7, Communicating with the Database*.
14. Go back to Eclipse OEPE and do a refresh (*F5*) on the **adapter** folder of the OSB project.

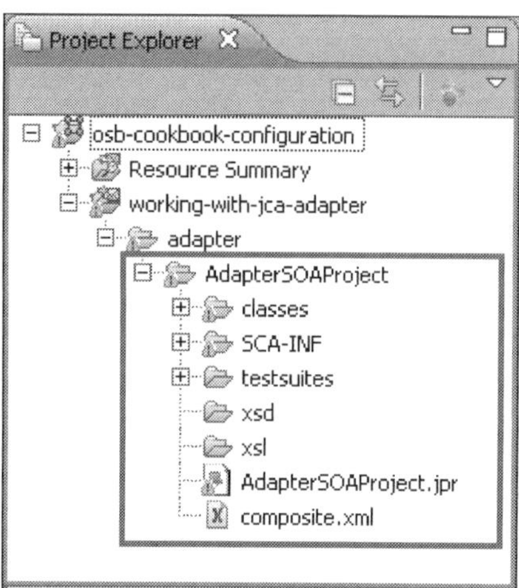

This finishes the basic set up of the **AdapterSOAProject** nested inside the OSB project. We have not yet created an adapter. This will be shown in many other recipes throughout the book.

How it works...

We have created a SOA project, which is located inside the `adapter` folder of the OSB project. Whenever something is changed on the adapters in JDeveloper, or a new adapter is added to the composite, all we have to do is refresh the adapter to have all necessary artifacts available in the OSB project and in Eclipse OEPE.

An empty SCA composite has been created as the base, which can now be used to define the adapters. Every composite has three swim lanes or sections, the **Exposed Services** located on the left, the **External References** on the right, and the **Components** section located in the middle of the composite window.

Think of the **Components** section as the place where the OSB proxy and business services are located. Using that mnemonic trick we can place the adapters in the same way as we are used to from working with SOA Suite 11*g*. Inbound adapters (file polling, database polling, and de-queuing) should be placed on the **Exposed Services** swim lane and outbound adapters (file write, database read/write, and enqueuing) should be placed on the **External References** swim lane.

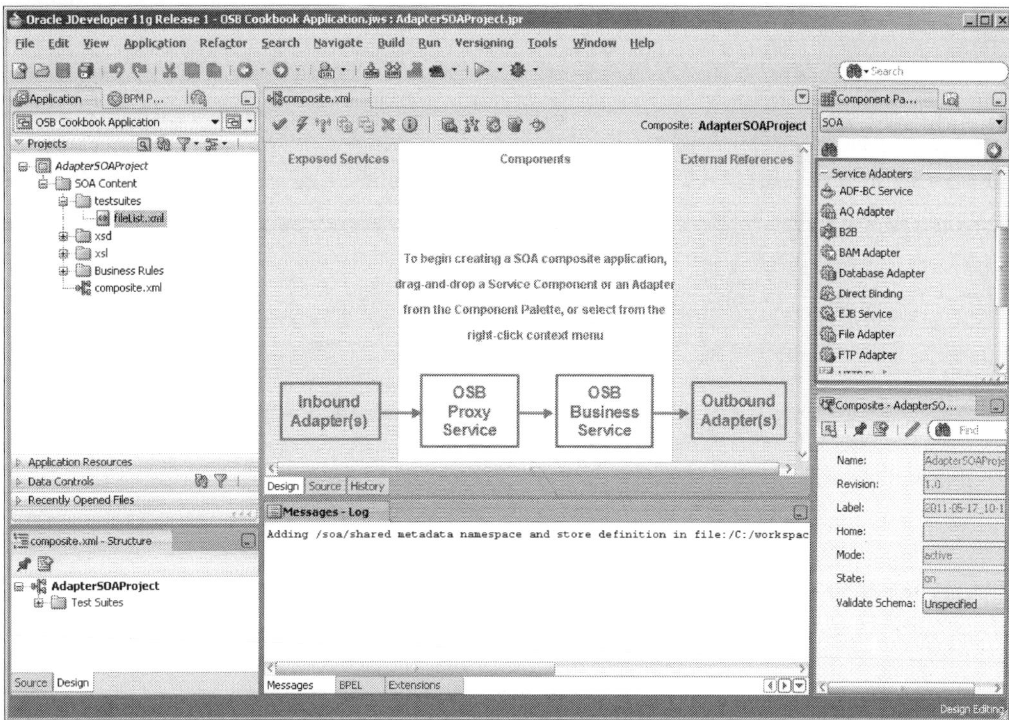

See also

Now with the basic project structure in place, we can start using the JCA adapter for either inbound or outbound communication. Check the recipes in the *Chapter 6, Using File and Email Transport* for the usage of the File adapter, and in *Chapter 7, Communicating with the Database* for the usage of the DB and AQ adapters. All of these recipes will reuse the basic setup of this recipe.

Using context menu to add nodes and actions to message flow

So far we have used the drag-and-drop feature for adding nodes and actions to the message flow of a proxy service. However, there is also a more developer-friendly approach, where we don't have to know where in the palette a given item is and especially which items are allowed in a given context.

Getting ready

You can import the OSB project containing the base setup for this recipe into Eclipse OEPE from `\chapter2\getting-ready\using-context-menu-to-add-nodes-actions`.

How to do it...

Navigate to the **Message Flow** tab and perform the following steps:

1. In the message flow, right-click on any element, for example, on the **Default** branch of the operational branch node.
2. In the given context, **Insert Into** and **Insert After** are possible.
3. Select **Insert Into** and then the element to be added. In the given context, the Default handler, only a **Conditional Branch**, an **Operational Branch**, a **Pipeline Pair**, or a **Route** are valid and therefore the context menu only holds these items.

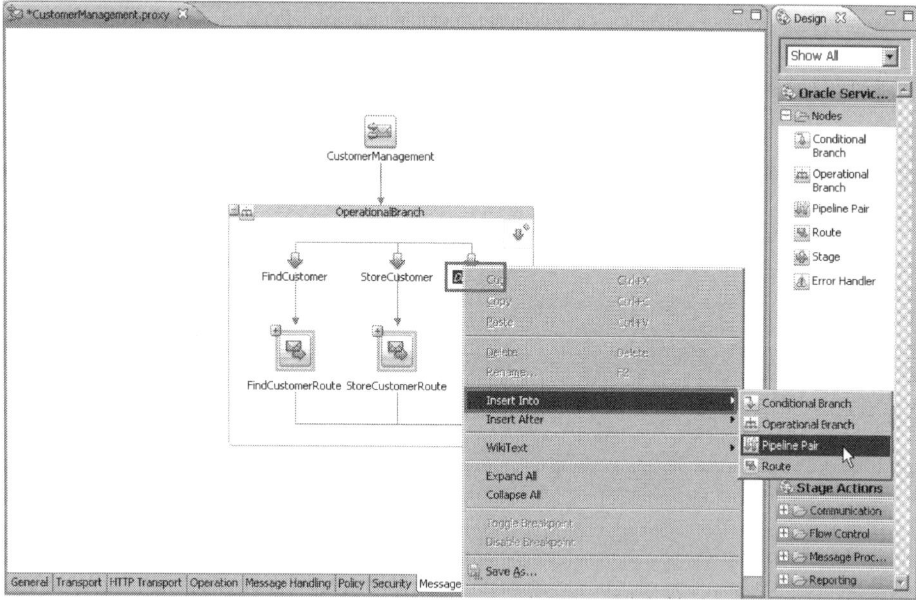

4. Select **Pipeline Pair** to add the unsupported error-handling code as shown in the previous screenshot.
5. Right-click on the **Request Pipeline** of the pipeline pair just added earlier and check the context menu.
6. Only **Insert Into** | **Stage** is available in this context.

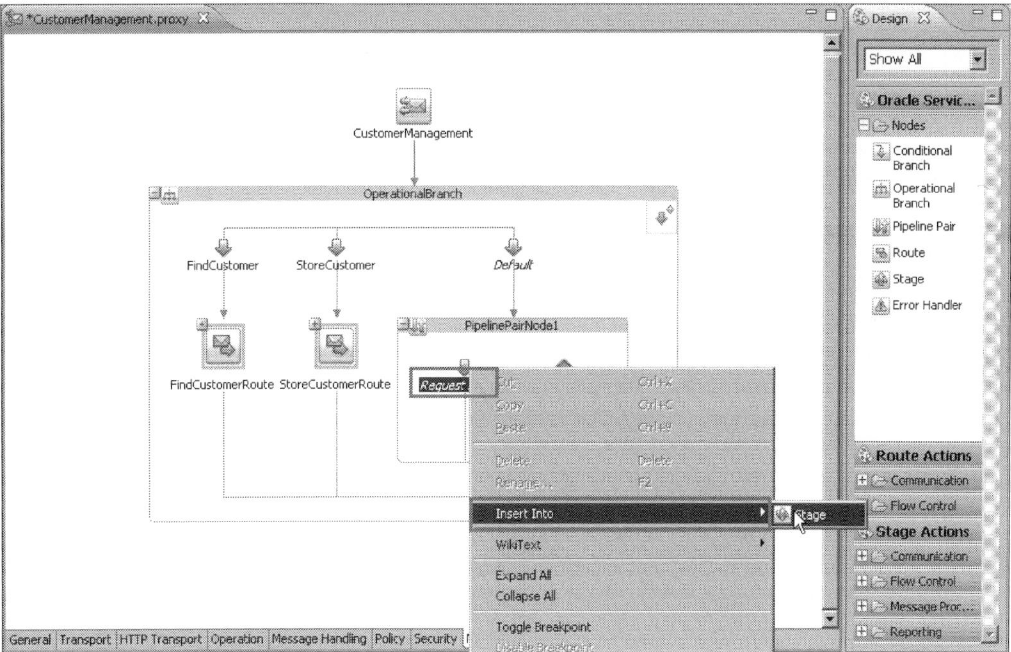

How it works...

The context-sensitive menu helps in choosing the right element at a given place in the message flow. There is an **Insert Into** and an **Insert After** menu, the first inserting the element *into* the element that holds the focus and the second one adding it *after* the one holding the focus.

This is very helpful, especially for a beginner, because this way we no longer have to exactly know which elements are allowed at a given place in the message flow. If using the drag-and-drop feature, the drop will not be possible for a certain action or node, if it's not allowed in the given context. Only those elements that are valid at the given context can be chosen.

Moving nodes/actions in Eclipse OEPE by drag-and-drop

This recipe will just present a simple approach for doing refactoring of nodes and actions within a single message flow. It uses the drag-and-drop functionality of the Eclipse OEPE to move around the items on the graphical representation of the message flow.

Getting ready

You can import the OSB project containing the base setup for this recipe into Eclipse OEPE from `\chapter2\getting-ready\moving-nodes\actions-by-drag-and-drop`.

How to do it...

If an existing message flow needs to be refactored and some nodes or actions need to be moved around, the Eclipse OEPE provides us with the drag-and-drop functionality, and a simple way to achieve this. For example to move a Pipeline Pair node from one place to another, perform the following actions in Eclipse OEPE:

1. Open the **CustomerManagement** proxy service and navigate to the **Message Flow** tab.
2. Select the node to move, for example, the **PipelinePair** node in the **FindCustomer** branch.
3. Drag the selected node and immediately Eclipse OEPE will show all the valid contexts, where the node could be dropped by a green circle. In our case, as the next screenshot shows, these are three places:

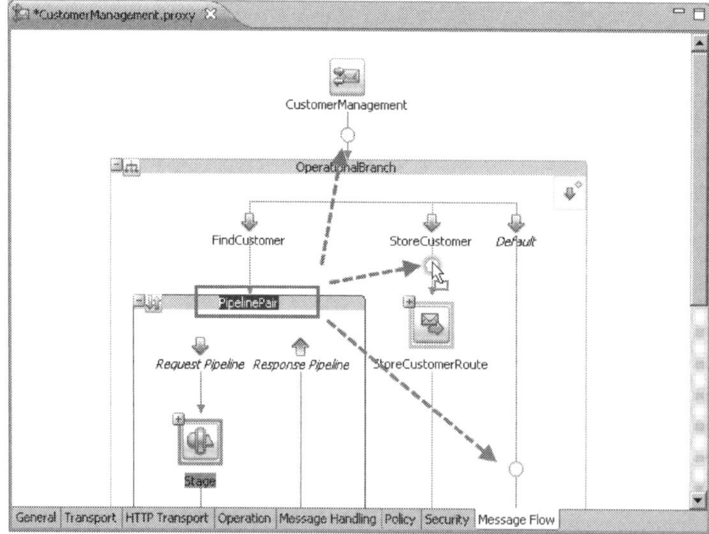

4. Drop it in the **StoreCustomer** branch, just above the **StoreCustomerRoute** route node. The circle will change to yellow before the selected node can be dropped.
5. The whole **PipelinePair** including all other items it might contain, **Stage** in our case, will be moved as well.

We have moved a whole node with all subitems from one place to another. The same can be done on a single-action level as well. To move an action to another place, similarly perform the following steps in Eclipse OEPE:

6. Select the **Log** action inside the Stage nested in the **PipelinePair** node.
7. Drag the **Log** action to the **Routing** action of the **StoreCustomerRoute** and drop it on the **Request Action** flow. Again the green circles show the places where a drop of the selected item is valid.

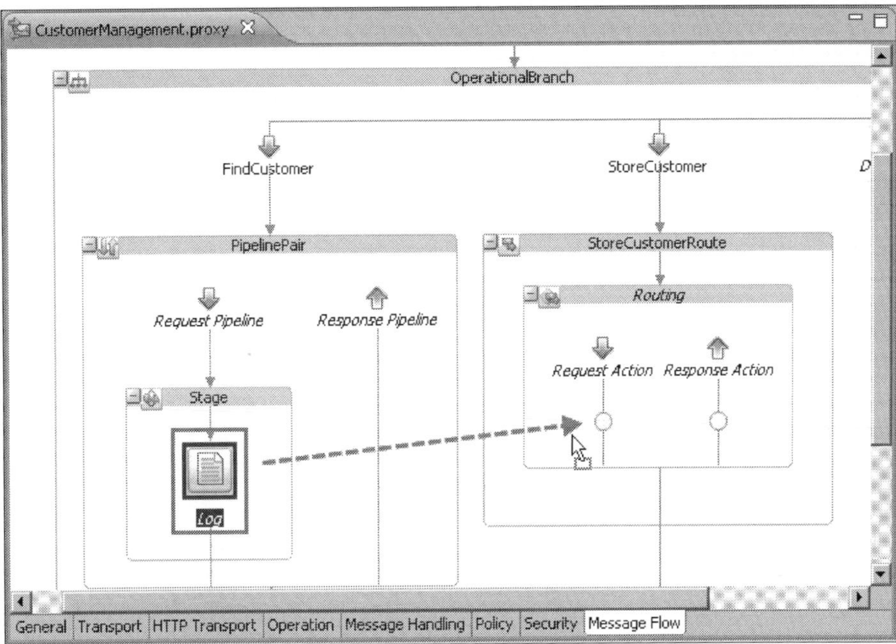

How it works...

This functionality is only available within the same message flow and does not work from one proxy service to another. In that case, you need to copy the nodes as shown by the next recipe *Copying nodes/actions from one place to another*.

Copying nodes/actions from one place to another

This recipe will just present a simple approach for doing refactoring of nodes and actions. It uses the copy/paste functionality of the Eclipse OEPE to copy a node/action from one place to another.

Getting ready

You can import the OSB project containing the base set up for this recipe into Eclipse OEPE from `\chapter2\getting-ready\copying-nodes-actions`.

How to do it...

Often when creating a new message flow, some node/actions are very similar. Instead of creating all of them from scratch, there is a way to copy them in Eclipse OEPE. To duplicate a **PipelinePair** node, perform the following steps:

1. Open the **CustomerManagement** proxy service and navigate to the **Message Flow** tab.
2. Right-click on the node/action to copy, for example, the **PipelinePair** node in the **FindCustomer** branch and select **Copy**.
3. Right-click on the **PipelinePair** node and select **Paste**.
4. The **PipelinePair** has been duplicated under the new name **PipelinePair1**.

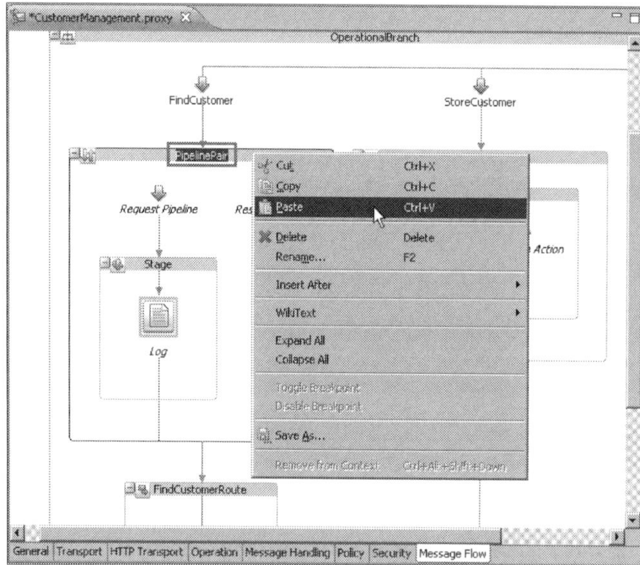

5. The whole **PipelinePair** node including all nested nodes and actions is duplicated.
6. The new node can now be moved to another place, if necessary, by applying the previous recipe *Moving nodes/actions in Eclipse OEPE by drag-and-drop*.

How it works...

The copy functionality in Eclipse OEPE provides a simple and efficient way to duplicate functionality in another place. This is handy because often the same kind of functionality is needed and there is no way to reuse code within a single message flow other than by copying it.

Sometimes it might not be possible to *paste* at the right place because the menu item is not available in both the context-sensitive menu as well as the main menu. In that case, duplicate the given node/action where it is allowed and then move it by applying the *Moving nodes/ actions in Eclipse OEPE by drag-and-drop* recipe.

The copy/paste functionality also works across proxy services. Just open both artifacts and copy from one to the other. This is similar to copying text from one editor to another.

Moving artifacts inside the same OSB project

This recipe will show how to refactor the structure of an OSB project inside Eclipse OEPE. Simply use the drag-and-drop functionality to move an artifact from one place to another and Eclipse OEPE will make sure that all internal links are updated accordingly.

We will use a simple OSB project with one proxy service calling another proxy service:

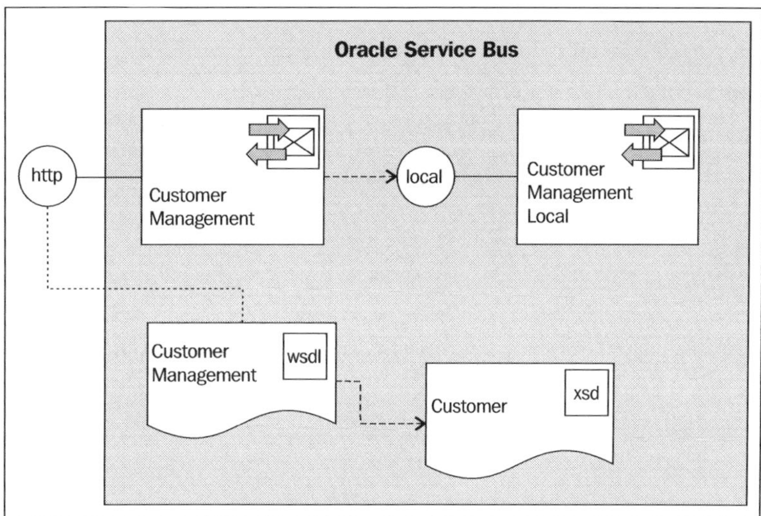

Both proxy services implement the same WSDL interface. We will show how the proxy services can be refactored so that the *private* proxy service is located in its own folder. In the second step, we will also move the WSDL file into another folder.

Getting ready

Import the base OSB project for this recipe from here: `\chapter-2\getting-ready\moving-artifacts-inside-osb-project`.

How to do it...

First let's move the proxy service **CustomerManagementLocal** into a **local** folder located inside the **proxy** folder. In Eclipse OEPE, perform the following steps:

1. Create a new folder inside the **proxy** folder by right-clicking on the **proxy** folder and select **New** | **Folder** and name it **local**.
2. Drag the proxy service **CustomerManagementLocal.proxy** and drop it on the **local** folder.

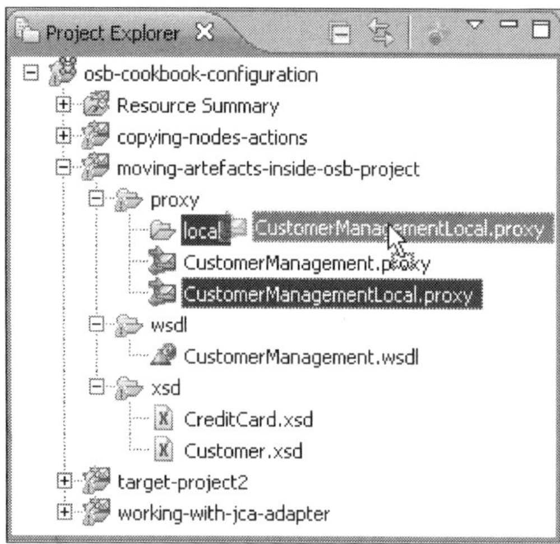

3. The **CustomerManagementLocal** proxy service is now located inside the **local** folder.

The moving of the artifact this way through Eclipse OEPE will make sure that all the invocation of the proxy service will be changed as well. If we check the **Routing** action inside the message flow of the **CustomerManagement** proxy service, we can see that the **Service** field reflects the new location of the **CustomerManagementLocal** proxy service being invoked.

Now let's see what happens if a WSDL file is moved to another folder. In Eclipse OEPE, perform the following steps:

4. Create a new folder inside the **wsdl** folder and name it `customer-mgmt`.
5. Drag the **CustomerManagement.wsdl** file and drop it on the `customer-mgmt` folder.

The moving of the WSDL into another folder is also reflected in the General section of the two proxy services. The location of the WSDL Web Service now points to the location of the WSDL.

How it works...

When it comes to refactoring operation inside an OSB project, the Eclipse OEPE behaves as expected. Drag-and-drop functionality on artifacts (files) is supported. It's important that these operations are done inside Eclipse OEPE and not directly on the filesystem. Only then is the refactoring applied on all other artifacts depending on the artifact being moved.

Copying artifacts from one project into another

This recipe will show how to copy artifacts from one OSB project into another OSB project. This is useful for duplicating artifacts in order to reuse them.

We will use the same project as in the previous recipe, with one proxy service calling another proxy service.

Getting ready

Import the base OSB project for this recipe from here: `\chapter-2\getting-ready\copying-artifacts-from-project-to-other`.

How to do it...

Let's see how we can copy the proxy, `wsdl` and `xsd` artifacts into another OSB project. For that we first create a new OSB project in the same OSB configuration and then copy the artifacts. In Eclipse OEPE, perform the following steps:

1. Create a new OSB project and name it **copy-of-artifacts**.
2. Select the **proxy**, **wsdl**, and **xsd** folder with a multiselect in the **copying-artifacts-from-project-to-other** project, right-click and select **Copy**.
3. Right-click on the **copy-of-artifacts** project and select **Paste**.

4. The artifacts are copied into the new OSB project and the project gets flagged with the error marker.

5. If we navigate into the **proxy** folder, which also has an error marker, we can see that the two proxy services are invalid.

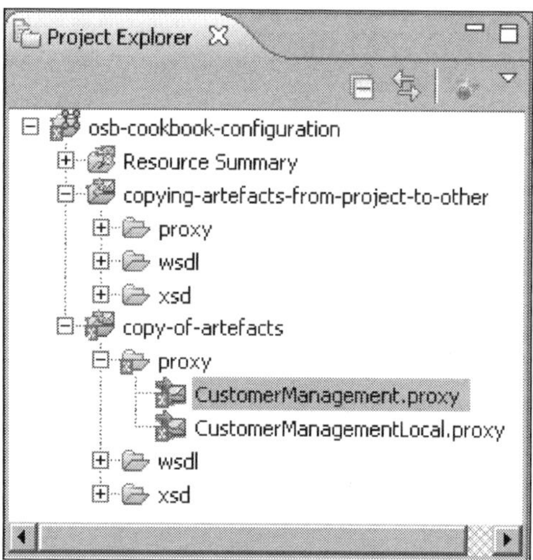

6. Open the **CustomerManagement** proxy service to see the reason for the error. The location of the **CustomerManagement** WSDL is still holding the name of the origin project.

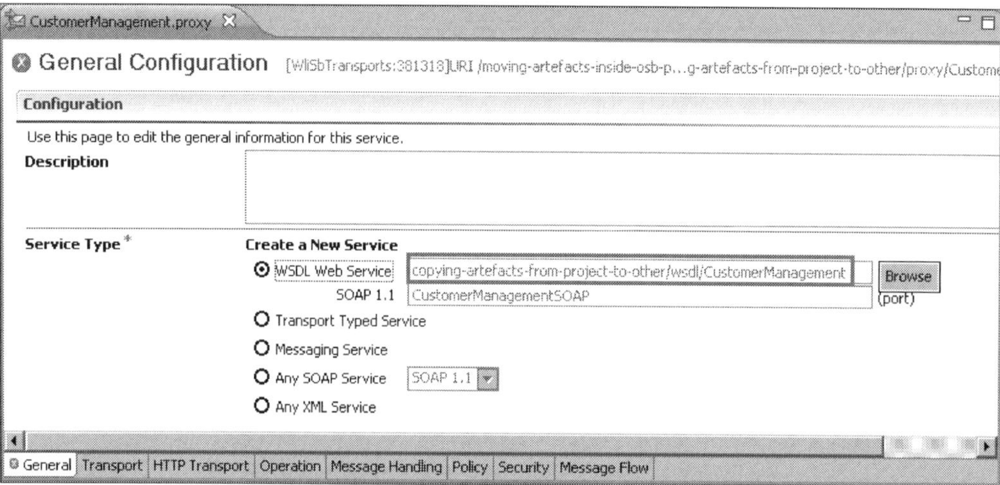

7. Click **Browse** and navigate to the WSDL file local to the new **copy-of-artifacts** project.
8. Select **No** on the **Transport Configuration Change** pop-up window, to confirm the overwriting of the transport configuration.
9. Navigate to the **Transport** tab to manually change the value of **Endpoint URI** so that it no longer contains the name of the origin project.
10. Repeat step 6 to 9 for the **CustomerManagementLocal** proxy service.

Save all the artifacts and the error marker should disappear. There is one last thing to adapt. The **CustomerManagement** proxy service is invoking the **CustomerManagementLocal** proxy service and the **Routing** action is also including the project name in the **Service** configuration. This has to be change too:

11. Open the **CustomerManagement** proxy service.
12. Navigate to the **Message Flow** tab.
13. Select the **Routing** action inside the **StoreCustomerRoute** node.
14. On the **Properties** of the **Routing** action, click **Browse** and select the correct proxy service to call. This overwrites the other settings of the **Routing** action.
15. Change the value of the **Invoking** drop-down list box back to **StoreCustomer**.

This finishes the necessary refactorings for this simple case. Depending on the complexity of the artifacts and their interrelationships, many more actions might be necessary.

How it works...

If we copy artifacts from one OSB project to another within Eclipse OEPE, then all the links referring to other artifacts are not changed as well. This may be correct, if the link is pointing to an artifact residing outside of the originating project. If the link is referring to a local artifact, then this is probably wrong and has to stay local, that is, it needs to be changed manually after copying the resources.

The same steps will be necessary if artifacts are copied from outside, that is, from a file explorer into Eclipse OEPE.

We have also seen that not all the wrong links will be marked as an error. A **Routing** action will still be fine as long as the artifact its invoking is still there, even if it's in another project.

There's more...

Instead of changing the errors caused by the copy of the artifacts manually through the different Eclipse OEPE editors, it can also be done directly on the source (XML representation) of the proxy service.

To open the source representation of the **CustomerManagement** proxy service, perform the following steps in Eclipse OEPE:

1. Close the **CustomerManagement** proxy service editor window if it's still open.
2. Right-click on the **CustomerManagement** proxy service and select **Open With | Text Editor**.
3. Change all occurrences of the origin project name **copying-artifacts-from-project-to-other** to the new name with a `find/replace` operation, which can be found in the menu **File | Find Replace**.

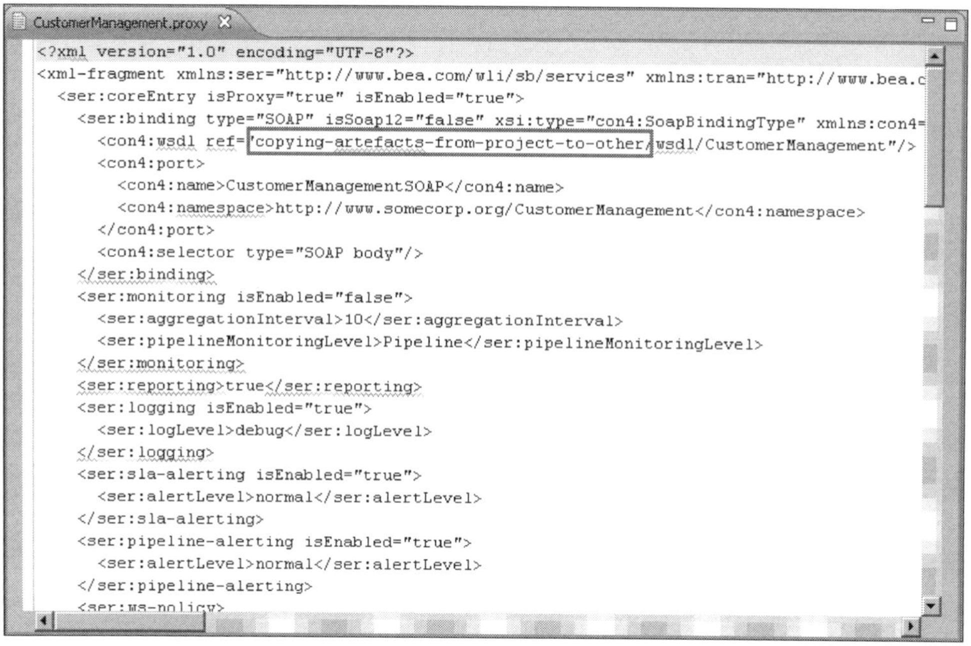

CustomerManagement.proxy

```
<?xml version="1.0" encoding="UTF-8"?>
<xml-fragment xmlns:ser="http://www.bea.com/wli/sb/services" xmlns:tran="http://www.bea.c
  <ser:coreEntry isProxy="true" isEnabled="true">
    <ser:binding type="SOAP" isSoap12="false" xsi:type="con4:SoapBindingType" xmlns:con4=
      <con4:wsdl ref="copying-artefacts-from-project-to-other/wsdl/CustomerManagement"/>
      <con4:port>
        <con4:name>CustomerManagementSOAP</con4:name>
        <con4:namespace>http://www.somecorp.org/CustomerManagement</con4:namespace>
      </con4:port>
      <con4:selector type="SOAP body"/>
    </ser:binding>
    <ser:monitoring isEnabled="false">
      <ser:aggregationInterval>10</ser:aggregationInterval>
      <ser:pipelineMonitoringLevel>Pipeline</ser:pipelineMonitoringLevel>
    </ser:monitoring>
    <ser:reporting>true</ser:reporting>
    <ser:logging isEnabled="true">
      <ser:logLevel>debug</ser:logLevel>
    </ser:logging>
    <ser:sla-alerting isEnabled="true">
      <ser:alertLevel>normal</ser:alertLevel>
    </ser:sla-alerting>
    <ser:pipeline-alerting isEnabled="true">
      <ser:alertLevel>normal</ser:alertLevel>
    </ser:pipeline-alerting>
    <ser:ws-policy>
```

Of course, we have to be very careful to not invalidate the structure of the XML when doing changes directly on the XML source code of the proxy service. Otherwise the editor view will no longer work.

If the same changes have to be applied on multiple file, then a global search and replace on the whole project can be done. A global search and replace is available through the **Search** menu:

4. In the **Project Explorer**, select the project **copy-of-artifacts**.
5. Click on the menu **Search | Search**.
6. Enter the text to search **copying-artifacts-from-project-to-other** into the **Containing text** field.

7. In the **Scope** section, select the **Enclosing projects** option and click on **Replace**.
8. On the **Replace Text Matches** pop-up window, enter the replacement text **copy-of-artifacts** into the **With** field.
9. Click **Preview** to review the changes that will be applied and then select **OK**.

Again be careful to really change the right occurrences only.

When directly manipulating the XML source code of the OSB artifacts, it's always a good idea to keep a copy of the previous version, that is, in a version control system such as Subversion or GIT.

Debugging services through Eclipse OEPE

We have already seen in the *Testing the proxy service through the OSB console* recipe that the OSB provides an Invocation Trace when executing an OSB service through the test console. The Invocation Trace is one possible solution for debugging if something is not working as expected. But its use is limited to the test console.

This recipe will show a more developer-friendly way for debugging. We will show how to use the visual debugger available with the Eclipse OEPE.

Getting ready

Make sure to have the current state of the **basic-osb-service** project from *Chapter 1, Creating a Basic OSB Service* available in Eclipse OEPE. We will use it for this recipe. If necessary, it can be imported from here: `\chapter-1\solution\with-transformation-proxy-service-created`.

For this recipe, we also have to make sure that the OSB server runs in debug mode. The status of a server in the **Servers** tab in the Eclipse OEPE indicates in which mode the server is started. A value of **[Debugging, ...]** means in debug mode, whereas the value **[Started, ...]** indicates the normal mode.

In order to switch to debug mode, right-click on the server and select **Restart in Debug**. After a while the status will switch to **[Debugging, ...]** and Eclipse OEPE will automatically switch into the debug perspective.

How to do it...

In order to debug a proxy service, some breakpoints are needed to tell the debugger where to halt the request processing. This is important as we cannot start the message flow from within Eclipse, the trigger is always something external such as the test console or soapUI and the message flow will run until the first breakpoint is reached. In Eclipse OEPE, perform the following steps to add a breakpoint:

1. Open the **CustomerManagement** proxy service and click on the **Message Flow** tab.
2. Navigate to the **Replace** action in the **Request Action**, right-click on it and select **Toggle Breakpoint**.
3. Select the **Routing** node, right-click on it and again select **Toggle Breakpoint**.

We have created two breakpoints in the message flow indicated by the blue dots in front of the **Replace** action and the **Routing** node, as shown in the following screenshot:

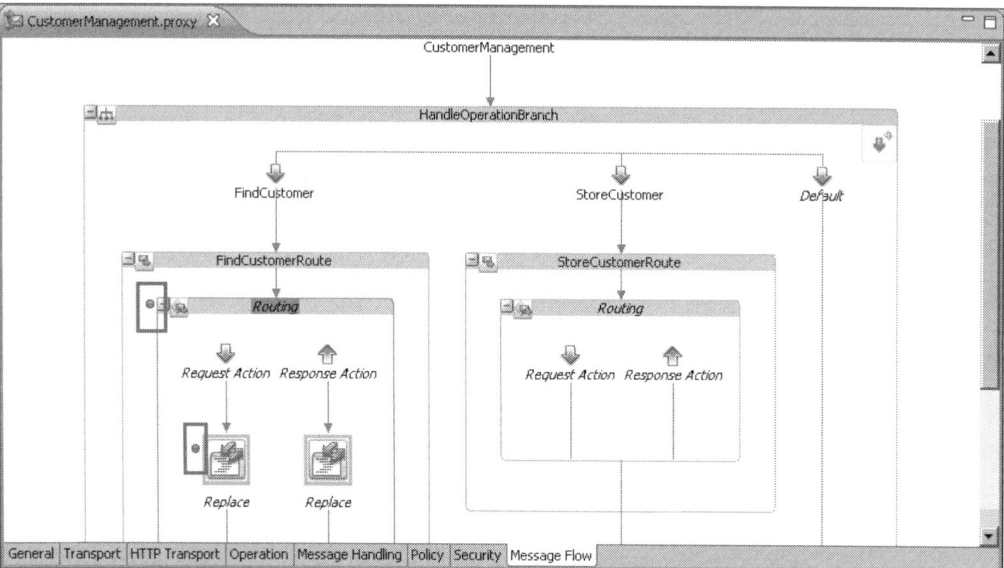

Let's see how the debugger works by executing a test. We can either use the OSB console or any other SOAP consumer (that is, soapUI) to send a request to the proxy service. The debugger will step in and halt execution at the first breakpoint.

The place where the execution is halted is indicated by the green arrow, shown in the next screenshot. We can also see the content of the variables in the upper-right window (**Variables** tab).

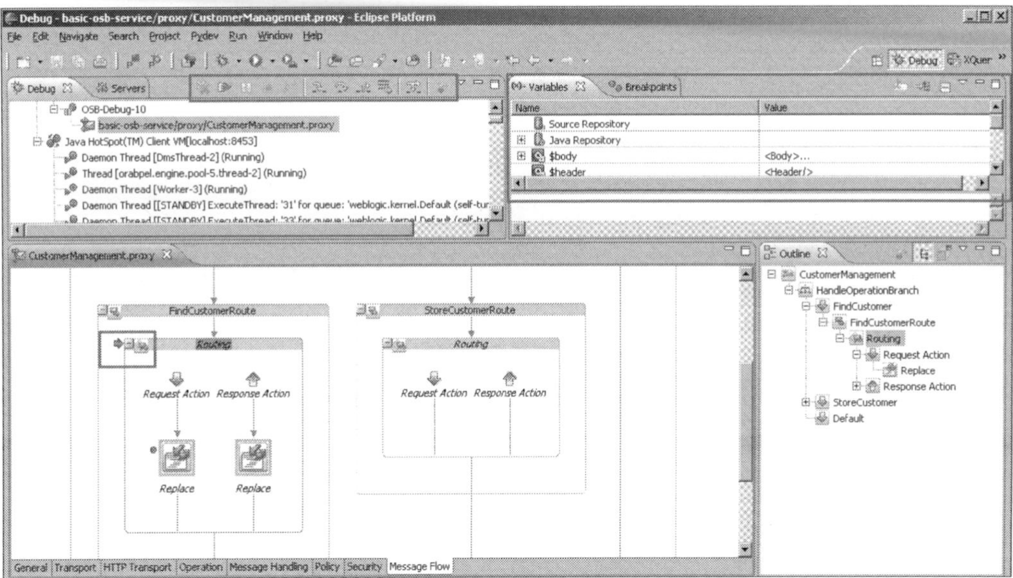

If we are interested in the content of the body variable at the given breakpoint (**Routing** action) we have to select the **$body** variable in the **Variables** window and the content is shown below the variable tree.

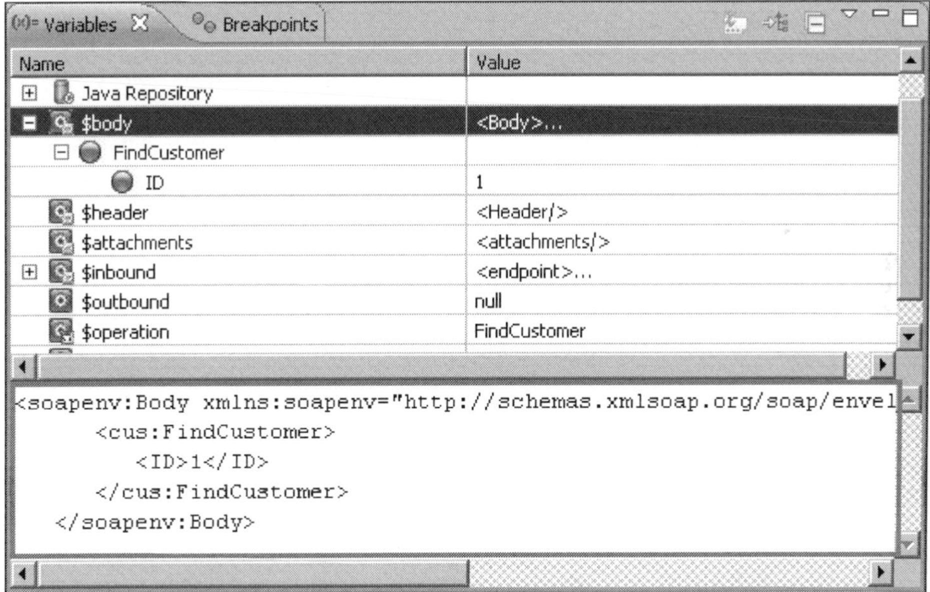

The content of the variables can also be changed.

We can continue either step-by-step by using the **Step-Into**, **Step-Over**, **Step-Return** actions or go forward to the next breakpoint by using the **Resume** action. These commands are available in the toolbar next to the **Servers** tab.

How it works...

The debugger is only available when working with Eclipse OEPE but not in the OSB console. The look and feel is very similar to the debugging of Java code in Eclipse. So if we know how to debug Java, it's very easy to also work with the OSB debugger.

In order for the debugger to work, the OSB server needs to be in debug mode. The mode can either be changed, as shown earlier, directly from Eclipse OEPE (if a local server is used) or the OSB server can simply be started in debug mode.

If we are working and testing on a remote OSB server, then it might not always be possible to switch on debug mode. In that case, it can be handy to also know how to use and interpret the Invocation Trace of the OSB test console.

3

Messaging with JMS Transport

In this chapter, we will cover:

- Sending a message to a JMS queue/topic
- Changing JMS Transport message headers and properties at runtime
- Consuming messages from a JMS queue
- Consuming messages from a topic with nondurable or durable subscription
- Consuming messages from a JMS queue/topic selectively
- Accessing JMS Transport message headers and properties in message flow
- Using request-response messaging with JMS
- Using QBrowser Admin GUI for accessing JMS queues/topics
- Testing JMS with soapUI

Introduction

The Java Message Service (JMS) specification defines a standard API for accessing messaging systems. It allows applications to consume and send messages to any JMS-compliant messaging server. JMS supports two distinct message models:

- **point-to-point** – The message producer (sender) creates a message and sends it to destination known as a **queue**. Message consumers (receivers) process messages placed in a queue. Each message can only be processed by one receiver and they are by default delivered in first-in-first-out (FIFO) order. This is also known as **point-to-point messaging model**.

- **publish-subscribe** – The message producer (sender) creates a message and sends it to a destination known as a **topic**. Messages sent or published to a topic are delivered to active consumers, known as **subscribers**. Subscribers have indicated their interest by subscribing to a topic. Subscriptions can either be **durable** or **nondurable**. A nondurable subscription only last as long as the subscriber is connected to JMS. A durable subscriber can disconnect and will get all messages published while disconnected as soon as he reconnects. This is also known as **publish-subscribe messaging model**.

WebLogic Server provides an enterprise-class messaging system called WebLogic JMS that completely supports the JMS API and makes it easy to use JMS from any applications.

Oracle Service Bus integrates very well with JMS. Using WebLogic JMS from an OSB project is very easy. The recipes in this chapter show the basic working with JMS from OSB and how to browse for the messages which are in a queue or topic. This is helpful in case of testing. In *Chapter 10, Reliable communication with OSB*, we cover how to use JMS to implement reliable messaging.

First let's check which queues exist in the OSB Cookbook standard environment. In the WebLogic console perform the following steps:

1. Expand the **Services** node in the **Domain Structure** tree.
2. Click the **Messaging** node and in the details view click on **JMS Modules**.
3. Click on **OsbCookbookResources**.

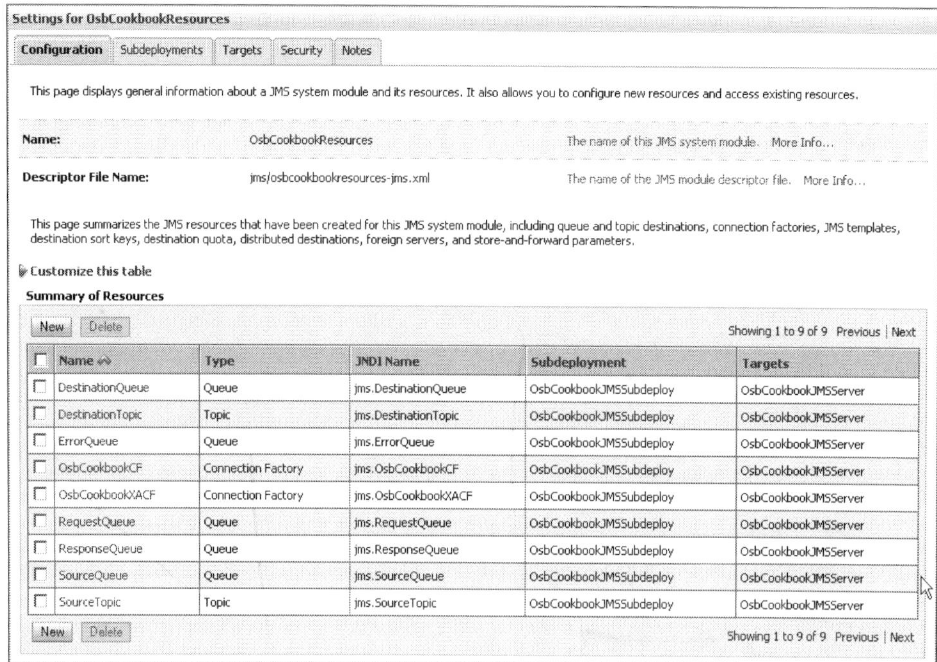

We can see the different queues, topics, and the connection factories available in the OSB Cookbook standard environment of our cookbook, created in the *Preface* chapter.

Sending a message to a JMS queue/topic

In this recipe, we will create a Business Service which sends a message to either a JMS queue or to a JMS topic. Since writing to a queue and topic is very similar from the business service perspective, we decided to combine it into one single recipe. We will use and configure the **JMS Transport** provided by the Oracle Service Bus.

Getting ready

For this recipe, we will use the **DestinationQueue** or the **DestinationTopic** from the OSB Cookbook standard environment and implement a business service to send messages to the queue/topic. We will not implement the proxy service in this recipe and instead test the business service directly on the OSB console.

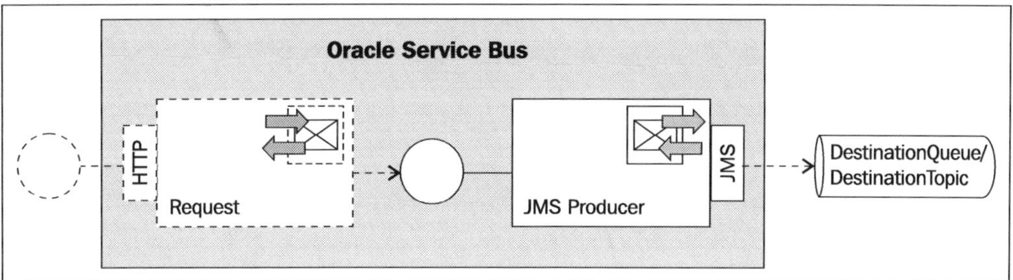

How to do it...

First let's create the **JMSProducer** business service which sends the messages to the **DestinationQueue**. In the *There's more* section we will show the necessary changes to send a message to the JMS topic. In Eclipse OEPE, perform the following steps:

1. Create a new OSB project `writing-to-a-jms-queue` and create a `business` folder within it.
2. Create a new business service and name it `JMSProducer`.
3. Navigate to the **General** tab.
4. Set the **Service Type** option to **Messaging Service**.
5. Navigate to the **Messaging** tab.
6. Set the **Request Message Type** option to **Text**.

7. Set the **Response Message Type** to **None**.
8. Navigate to the **Transport** tab.
9. Select **jms** for the value of the **Protocol** drop-down listbox.
10. Enter `jms://localhost:7001/weblogic.jms.XAConnectionFactory/jms.DestinationQueue` into the **EndpointURI** field and click **Add.**
11. Navigate to the **JMS Transport** tab.
12. Set the **Destination Type** option to **Queue**.
13. Set the **Message Type** option to **Text**.
14. Set **Response queues** option to **None**.

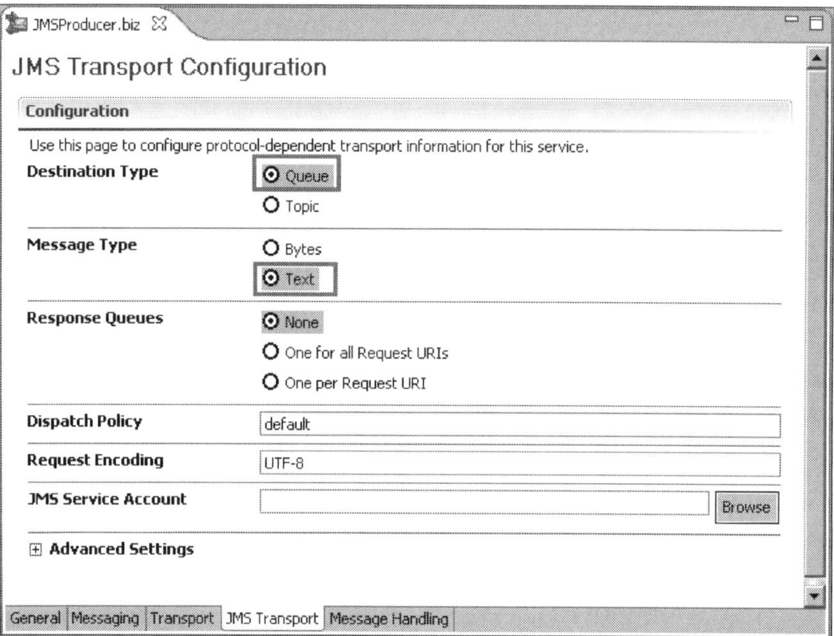

15. Deploy the project to the OSB server.

This is all what is needed to send a message to a queue.

Let's test the business service. In the OSB console, perform the following steps:

16. Navigate to the **JMSProducer** business service by clicking on **Projects** | **writing-to-jms-queue** | **business** in the **Project Explorer** tree on the left.
17. Click on the **Launch Test Console** icon (bug icon) in the **Actions** cell.

18. Enter the message to send as text into the **Payload** field.

19. Click **Execute**.
20. The business service is invoked and a **There was no response** message is shown in the *response document*. This is because we have configured a one-way message exchange pattern by selecting **Messaging Service** with the **Response Message Type** set to **None**. If we invoke the business service from a proxy service, we would also get no response.

Let's check if the message is in the **DestinationQueue** by performing the following steps in the WebLogic console:

21. In the Domain Structure tree on the left, navigate to **Services** | **Messaging** | **JMS Modules**.
22. Click on **OsbCookbookResources**.
23. Click on **DestinationQueue**.
24. Navigate to the **Monitoring** tab.
25. Enable the checkbox in front of **OsbCookbookResources!DestinationQueue**:

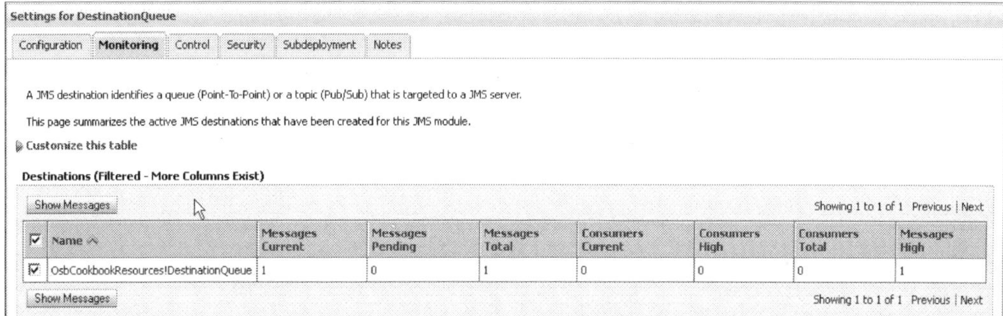
Settings for DestinationQueue

Configuration | Monitoring | Control | Security | Subdeployment | Notes

A JMS destination identifies a queue (Point-To-Point) or a topic (Pub/Sub) that is targeted to a JMS server.

This page summarizes the active JMS destinations that have been created for this JMS module.

Customize this table

Destinations (Filtered - More Columns Exist)

Show Messages — Showing 1 to 1 of 1 Previous | Next

☑	Name	Messages Current	Messages Pending	Messages Total	Consumers Current	Consumers High	Consumers Total	Messages High
☑	OsbCookbookResources!DestinationQueue	1	0	1	0	0	0	1

Show Messages — Showing 1 to 1 of 1 Previous | Next

26. Click on **Show Messages**.
27. Click on the ID of the message **ID: <nnnnn.nnnnnnnn.n>**:

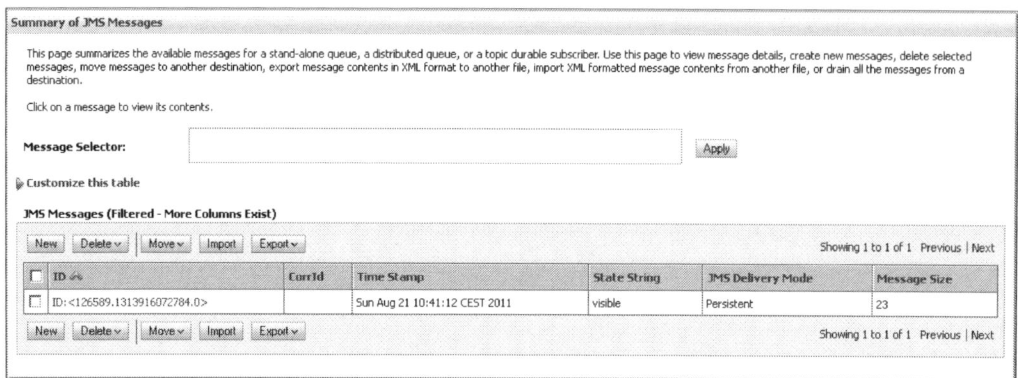

28. The details of the message with the payload and the JMS properties are shown:

How it works...

Configuring a business service with the JMS Transport is enough to send a message from OSB to a JMS queue or topic. The queue or topic can reside on:

- the same WebLogic instance as the OSB server
- a remote WebLogic instance
- any JMS-compliant JMS server

We have only configured the business service and tested it through the OSB console. In real life the business service would be called from a proxy service either by a *routing* or *publish* action. If there is no need to transform the message, a simple pass-through proxy service is enough, as shown in the *Generating a "pass through" proxy service* recipe.

There's more...

This section will first discuss some of the advanced settings on the JMS Transport tab and then discuss the necessary changes to the recipe in order to send to a JMS topic instead of a JMS queue.

Advanced settings on JMS Transport

There are some advanced settings which can be set on the **JMS Transport** tab on the business service configuration as shown on the following screenshot:

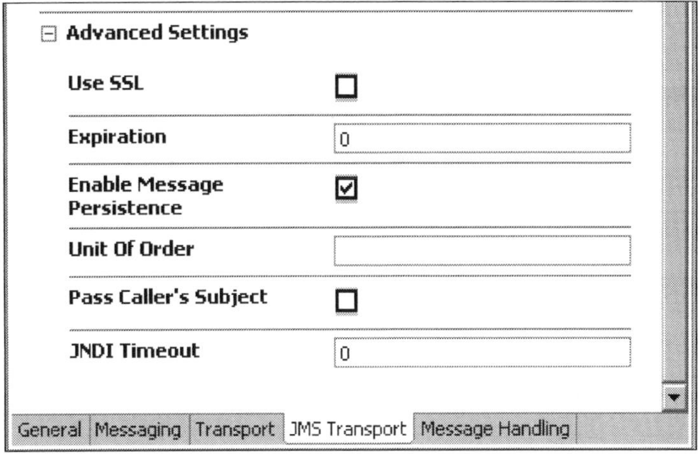

The option **Enable Message Persistence** is by default enabled, which guarantees message delivery because the messages persist and will survive server shutdowns and failures. To improve throughput, deselect this option if the occasional loss of a message is tolerable. There is a separate recipe covering this option in the *Chapter 10, Reliable Communication with OSB*.

Set a time interval in milliseconds in the **Expiration** field to specify the message time-to-live. After the time-to-live is passed, the message will automatically be treated according to the **Expiration Policy** defined on the JMS destination (that is, the queue) and either discarded, logged, or redirected to another JMS destination.

The default value of `0` for **Expiration** means that a message never expires and therefore waits to be consumed forever or until the server is shutdown, if the message is not persistent.

Any JMS destination can override the **Expiration** set on the business service by setting the **Time-to-Live Override** setting through the WebLogic console when configuring the JMS destination.

Sending to a JMS topic

The same steps as shown in the *How to do it...* section apply for sending to a JMS topic too. To change from the queue to the JMS topic **DestinationTopic**, make sure to enter `jms://localhost:7001/weblogic.jms.XAConnectionFactory/jms.DestinationTopic` into the **EndpointURI** in step 10 and to set the **Destination Type** option to **Topic** in step 12. Redeploy the project to the OSB server.

With that the business service will now write to the JMS topic. This can be tested through the OSB console by performing the following steps:

1. Navigate to the **JMSProducer** business service by clicking on **Projects** | **writing-to-jms-topic** | **business** in the **Project Explorer** tree on the left.
2. Click on the **Launch Test Console** icon (bug icon) in the **Actions** cell.
3. Enter `This is a text message!` into the **Payload** field.
4. Click on **Execute**.
5. The business service is executed and a **There was no response** message is shown in the *response document*. This is because we have configured a one-way message exchange pattern by selecting **Messaging Service** and only a **Request Message Type**.

Let's check if the message is in the **DestinationTopic** by performing the following steps in the WebLogic console:

6. In the Domain Structure tree on the left, navigate to **Services** | **Messaging** | **JMS Modules**.
7. Click on **OsbCookbookResources**.
8. Click on **DestinationTopic**.
9. Navigate to the **Monitoring** tab.

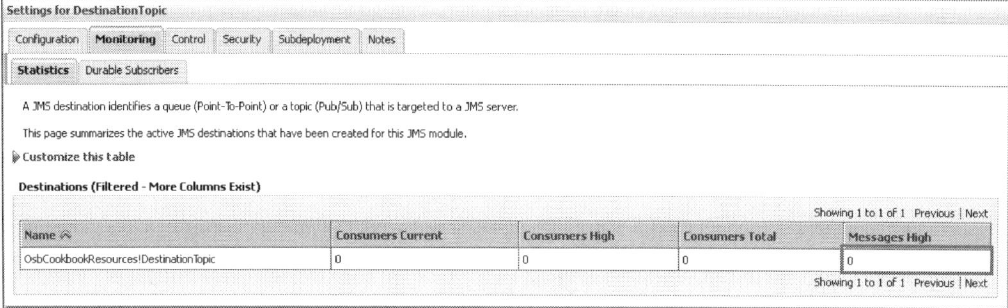

Because we don't have any subscribers on the topic, the message is not persisted. So let's add a subscriber to the topic:

10. Navigate to the **Durable Subscribers** tab.
11. Click on **New**.
12. Enter `TopicSubscriber` into the **Subscription Name** field.
13. Enter `TopicSubscriber` **into the Client ID field.**
14. Click **OK.**

Retest the business service, and refresh the **Durable Subscribers** tab.

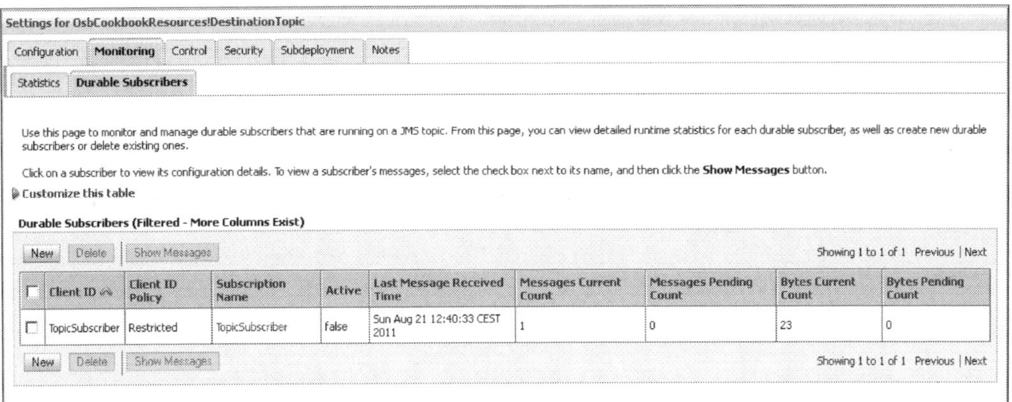

Client ID	Client ID Policy	Subscription Name	Active	Last Message Received Time	Messages Current Count	Messages Pending Count	Bytes Current Count	Bytes Pending Count
TopicSubscriber	Restricted	TopicSubscriber	false	Sun Aug 21 12:40:33 CEST 2011	1	0	23	0

15. Select the checkbox in front of **TopicSubscriber**.
16. Click **Show Messages**.
17. Click on the ID of the message **ID: <nnnnn.nnnnnnnn.n>**.
18. The details of the message with the payload and the JMS properties are shown here:

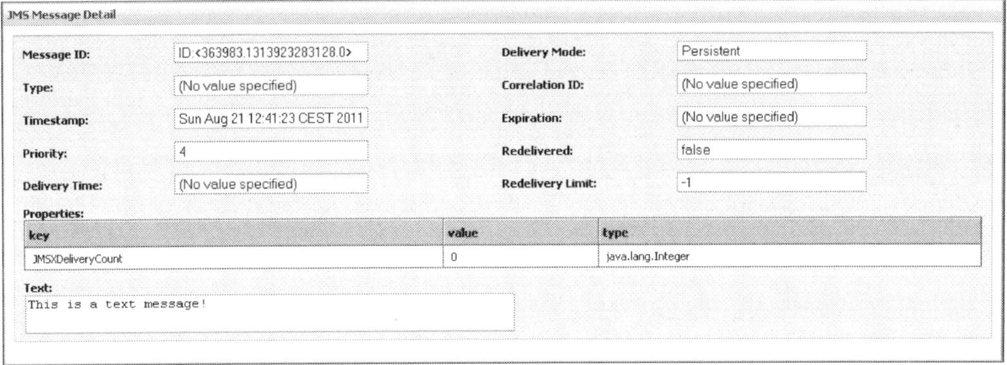

See also

See the *Enabling JMS Message Persistence* recipe in *Chapter 10, Reliable Communication with the OSB* for details of how to enable and use message persistence.

Changing JMS Transport message headers and properties at runtime

When sending a message to JMS queue or topic through a business service, default values for several JMS Transport message headers are used. The message headers as well as the message properties can be overwritten by using a **Transport Header** action in a proxy service when routing to the business service.

We will use it to both define the priority of the message by setting the **JMSPriority** header and to pass a user-defined property `myProperty` with the value `red`.

Getting ready

For this recipe, we will use the solution of the recipe *Sending a message to a JMS queue* and extend it with a simple pass-through proxy service and then add a **Transport Header** action.

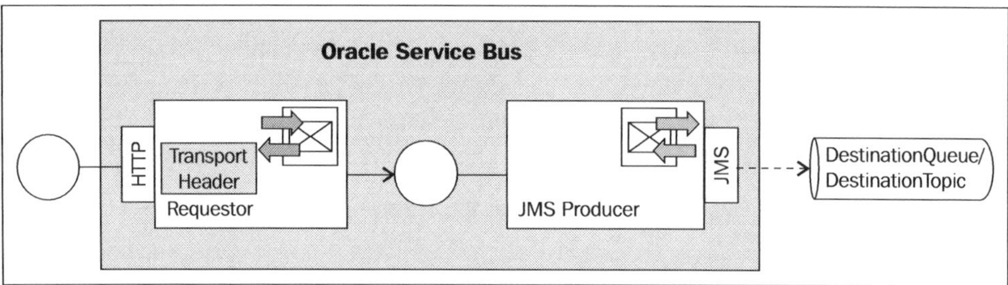

You can import the base OSB project containing the solution from this previous recipe into Eclipse from `\getting-ready\chapter-3\changing-jms-transport-headers-properties`.

How to do it...

First we will add the pass-through proxy service which routes the message to the JMSProducer business service. In Eclipse OEPE, perform the following steps:

1. Create a `proxy` folder in the **changing-jms-transport-headers-properties** OSB project.
2. Right-click on the **JMSProducer.biz** business service and select **Oracle Service Bus | Generate Proxy Service**.
3. Select the **proxy** folder in the tree and enter **Requestor** into the **File name** field.
4. Click **Finish**.

Now we can add the **Transport Header** to the message flow of the proxy service. We will use it to set the priority of the message to the highest possible value **9** and to pass a user-defined property "my-property" to the value of `test`.

In Eclipse OEPE, perform the following steps:

5. Open the **Requestor** proxy service and navigate to the **Message Flow** tab.
6. Right-click on the **Request Action** flow of the **Routing** action and select **Insert Into | Communication | Transport Header**.
7. Select the **Transport Header** action and navigate to the **Properties** tab.
8. Select **Outbound Request** in the **Direction** drop-down listbox.
9. Click on **Add Header**.
10. Select the **Defined** option and select **JMSPriority** in the drop-down listbox.
11. Select the **Set Header to** option and click on the **<Expression>** link.
12. Enter **9** into the **Expression** field and click **OK**.
13. Click **Add Header** to add an additional row for the user-defined property.
14. Select the **Other** option and enter `myProperty` into the field next to the **Other** radio button.
15. Select the **Set Header to** option and click on the **<Expression>** link.

16. Enter **"red"** into the **Expression** field and click **OK**.

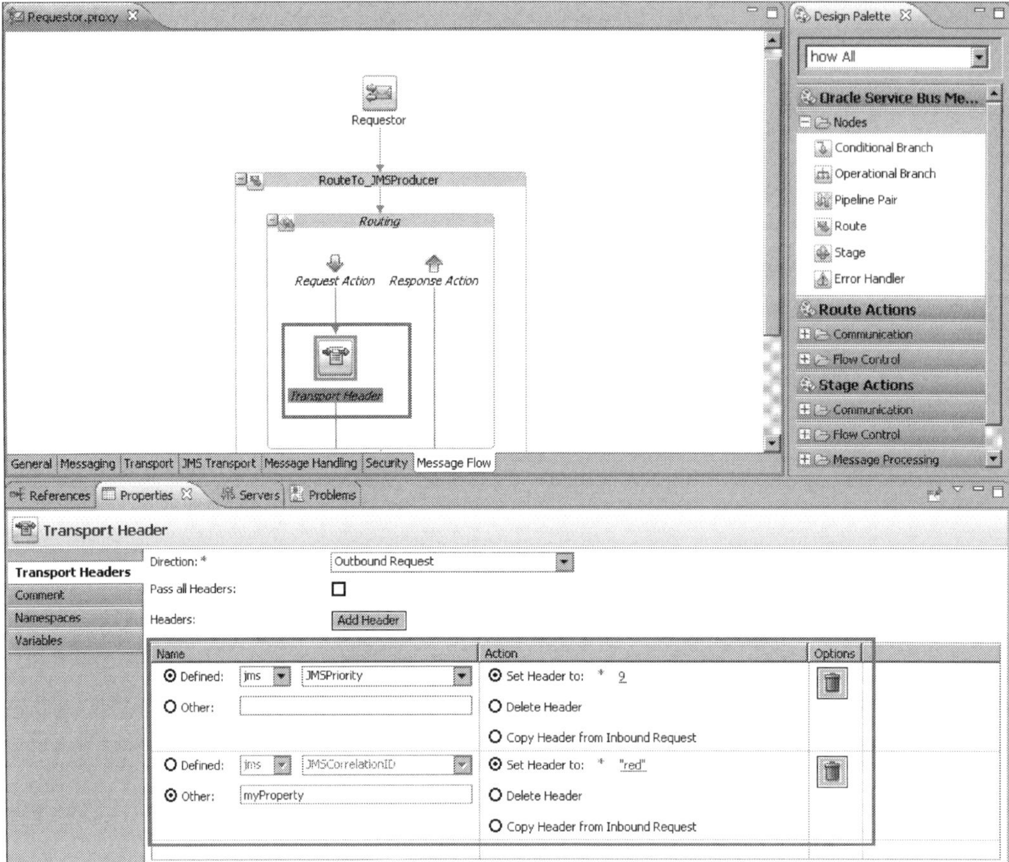

17. Save the project and deploy it to the OSB server.

Invoke the proxy service to see whether the **JMSPriority** header has been overwritten and the user-defined property has been added by the **Transport Header** action.

In the OSB console, perform the following steps.

18. In **Project Explorer** click **Projects** | **changing-jms-transport-headers-properties** | **proxy**.
19. Click on the **Launch Test Console** icon of the **Requestor** proxy service.
20. Enter `This is a text message!` into the **Payload** field and click **Execute**.
21. The proxy service is executed and a **There was no response** message is shown in the Response Document.

Let's check the details of the message through the WebLogic console by performing the following steps:

22. In the Domain Structure tree on the left, navigate to **Services | Messaging | JMS Modules**.
23. Click **OsbCookbookResources** and then click on **DestinationQueue**.
24. Navigate to the **Monitoring** tab.
25. Enable the checkbox in front of **OSBBookJMSModule!DestinationQueue.**
26. Click **Show Messages**.
27. Click on the ID of the message **ID: <nnnnn.nnnnnnnn.n>**.
28. The details of the message with the payload and the JMS properties are shown:

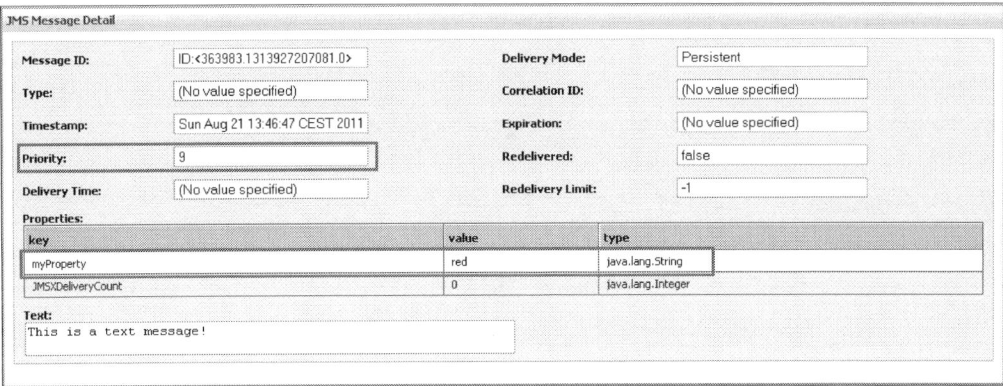

We can see that both the header and the user-defined property have been set.

How it works...

A business service using the **JMS Transport** defines the default values of the JMS message headers and properties. Some of these values, such as the **JMSExpiration** can be specified on the **JMS Transport** tab when configuring the business service. We have demonstrated that in the *Sending a message to a JMS queue* recipe. At runtime, these values can be overwritten before routing to the business service by using a **Transport Header** action. The **Transport Header** action can be placed into the **Request Action** of the **Routing** action or **Publish** action.

Consuming messages from a JMS queue

A message in a queue can only be consumed by a single consumer. To consume a message on the OSB, a proxy service with the **JMS Transport** needs to be setup.

In this recipe, we will show how to implement a proxy service as a message consumer for the queue. The proxy service will act as a listener on the JMS queue and will get active as soon as a message can be consumed from the queue.

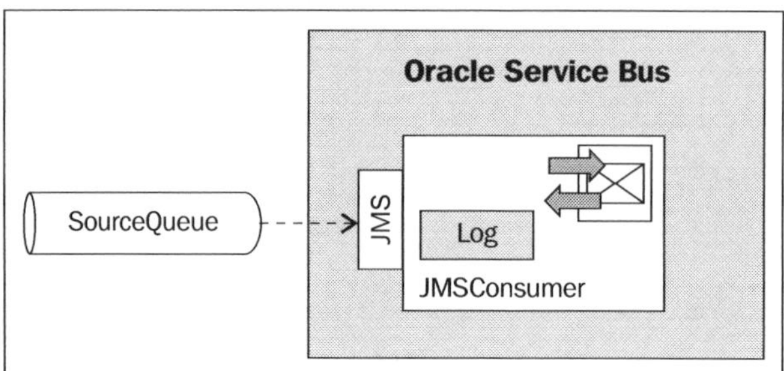

Getting ready

For this recipe, we need one queue from the OSB Cookbook standard environment and will then implement the proxy service to dequeue the messages from the queue.

How to do it...

Let's create the proxy service to consume messages from the **SourceQueue**. In Eclipse OEPE, perform the following steps:

1. Create a new OSB project `consuming-from-jms-queue` and create a `proxy` folder within it.
2. Create a new proxy service and name it `JMSConsumer`.
3. Navigate to the **General** tab.
4. Set the **Service Type** option to **Messaging Service**.
5. Navigate to the **Messaging** tab
6. Set the **Request Message Type** option to **Text**.
7. Set the **Response Message Type** option to **None**.
8. Navigate to the **Transport** tab.
9. Select **jms** for the value of the **Protocol** drop-down listbox.

10. Enter `jms://localhost:7001/weblogic.jms.XAConnectionFactory/jms.SourceQueue` into the **EndpointURI** field.

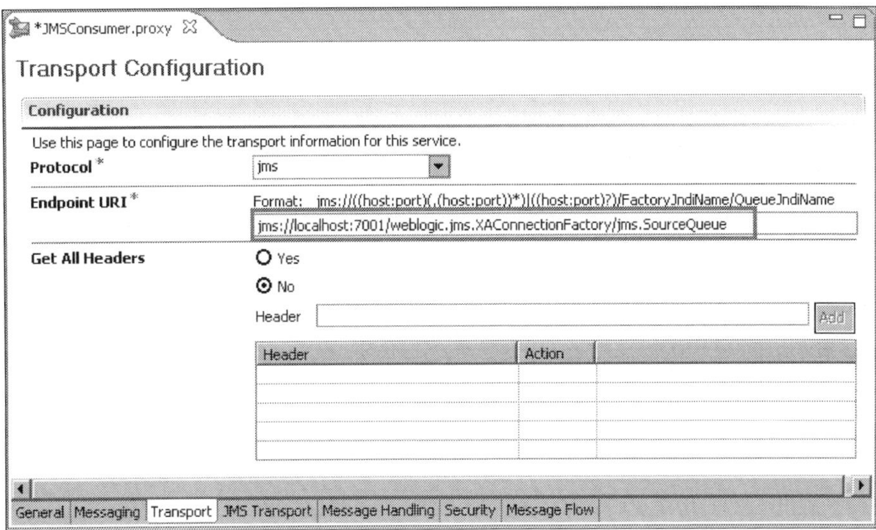

11. Navigate to the **JMS Transport** tab
12. Set the **Destination Type** option to **Queue.**

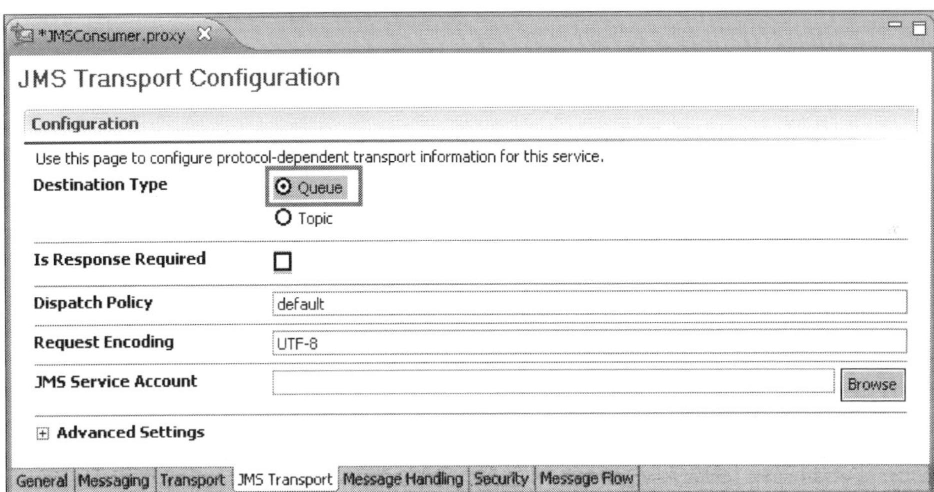

13. Navigate to the **Message Flow** tab.
14. Insert a **Pipeline Pair** node and add a **Stage** node to the **Request Pipeline.**

15. Place a **Log** action into the stage.

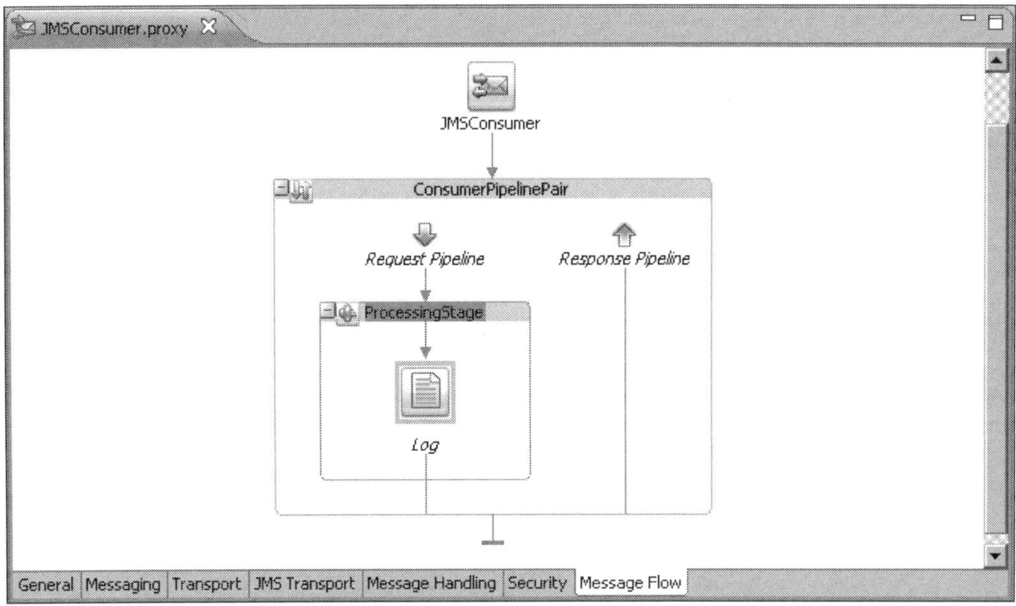

16. Enter `$body` for the **<Expression>**, Content of `$body` in Request into the **Annotation** field and select **Warning** as the value of the **Severity** drop-down listbox.
17. Save the project but **do not yet deploy it** to the OSB server.

Now it's time to test the behavior of the OSB service. In WebLogic console, perform the following steps to put a message into the queue:

18. Expand the **Services** node in the **Domain Structure** tree.
19. Click on the **Messaging** node.
20. Click on **JMS Modules** and in the list of modules click on **OsbCookbookResources.**
21. Click on the queue **SourceQueue.**
22. Click on the **Monitoring** tab.
23. Enable the checkbox in front of **OsbCookbookResources!SourceQueue** and click **Show Messages.**
24. Click on **New** to create a message.
25. Enter `This is a text message!` into the **Body** field and click **OK.**

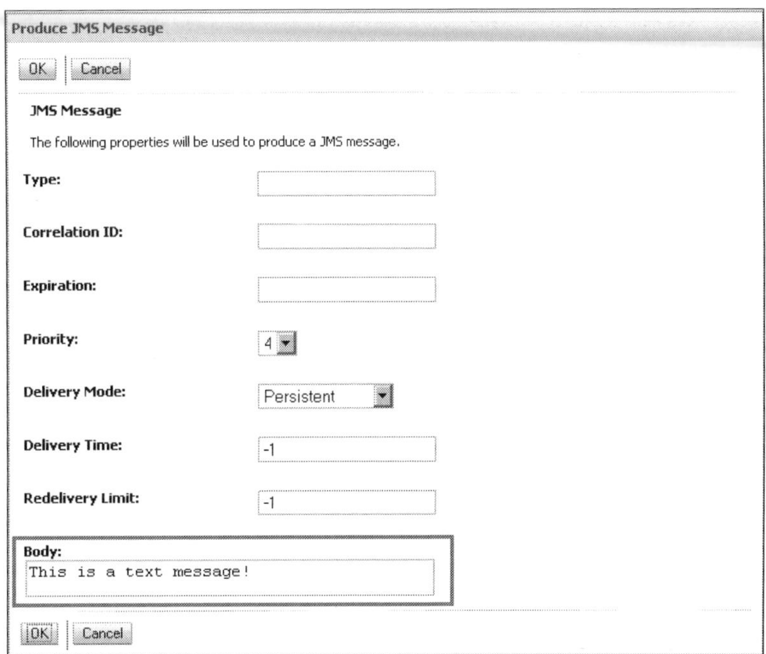

26. The message appears in the queue as shown in the following screenshot:

27. Click on the **ID: <nnnnn.nnnnnnn>** link to get the details of the message.

Now go back to Eclipse OEPE and deploy the project to the OSB server. The message should get consumed immediately and the OSB console output window should show the content of message (that is, the body variable).

Even though we have only sent a plain text string `This is a text message!`, on the OSB server the content is wrapped inside a **<soapenv:Body>** element. This is important to know if you require access to the value of the message.

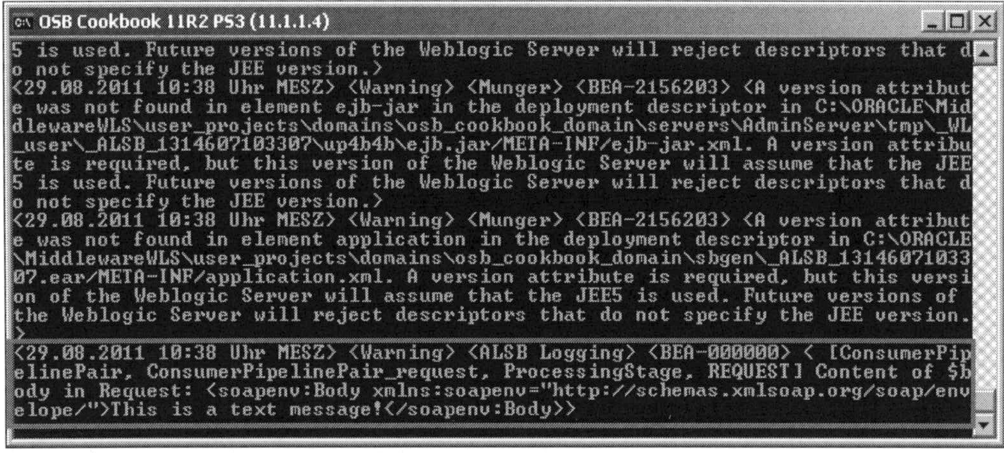

In WebLogic console refresh the **Summary of JMS Messages** view for the **SourceQueue** and check whether the message has really been consumed.

How it works...

Setting the **Service Type** of a proxy service to **Messaging Service** allows us to set the **Protocol** to **jms**. On a proxy service, the JMS protocol always works inbound, that is, the proxy service is consuming messages from a queue. On a business service in contrast, the JMS protocol always works outbound, that is, the business service is putting the message to a queue.

The queue which should be used by the proxy service is specified by the **Endpoint URI**, together with the hostname and port of the JMS server and the connection factory to use.

After deploying the proxy service, it listens to the queue for messages and will consume it immediately and passes it to the message flow of the proxy service for execution.

Consuming messages from a topic with non-durable/durable subscription

Subscribing to and consuming messages from a JMS topic is similar to consuming messages from a JMS queue. The main difference between a topic and a queue is that the topic can have multiple subscribers and that a subscription can either be durable or non-durable. With a durable topic, a message that cannot be delivered due to the subscriber being unavailable will be kept by the JMS server and delivered later when the subscriber is back online.

In this recipe, we will show you how to implement a proxy service as a subscriber for the topic. The proxy service will act as a listener on the JMS topic and will get active as soon as a message arrives in the topic. First we implement the non-durable subscription and show the durable subscription in the *There's more...* section later.

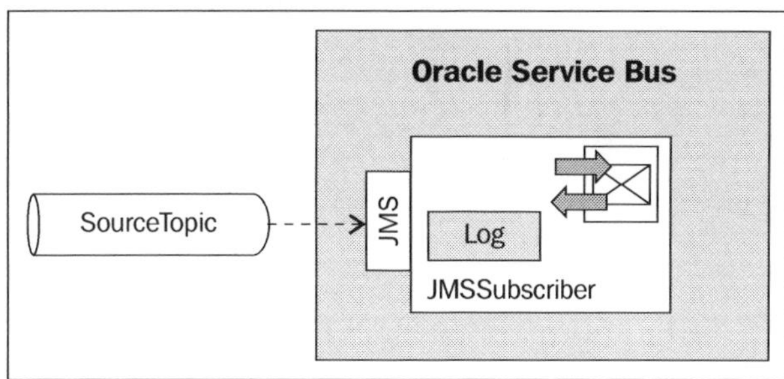

Getting ready

For this recipe, we need the JMS topic **SourceTopic** from the OSB Cookbook standard environment.

How to do it...

Let's implement the proxy service subscribing and accepting the messages from the topic.

In Eclipse OEPE, perform the following steps:

1. Create a new OSB project `consuming-from-jms-topic` and create a `proxy` folder within it.
2. Create a new proxy service and name it `JMSSubscriber`.
3. Navigate to the **General** tab.
4. Set the **Service Type** option to **Messaging Service**.

5. Navigate to the **Messaging** tab
6. Set the **Request Message Type** option to **Text**.
7. Set the **Response Message Type** option to **None**.
8. Navigate to the **Transport** tab.
9. Select **jms** for the value of the **Protocol** drop-down listbox.
10. Enter `jms://localhost:7001/weblogic.jms.XAConnectionFactory/jms.SourceTopic` into the **EndpointURI** field.
11. Navigate to the **JMS Transport** tab
12. Set the **Destination Type** option to **Topic.**

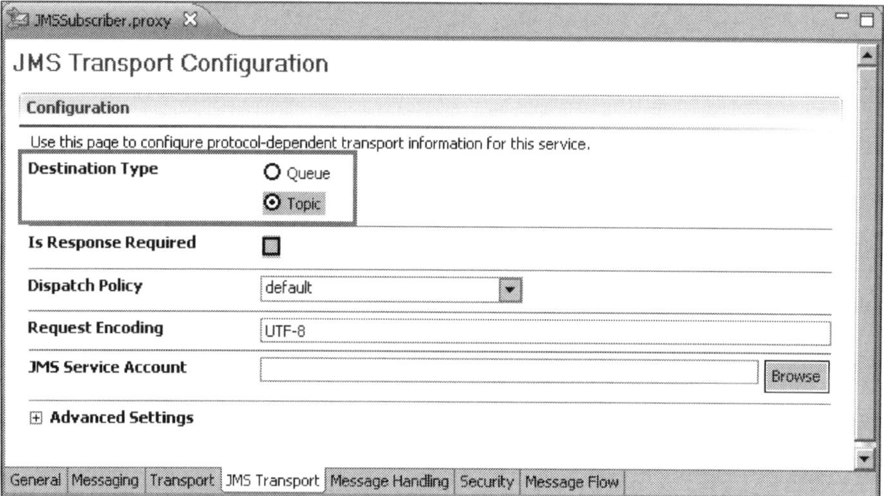

13. Navigate to the **Message Flow** tab.
14. Insert a **Pipeline Pair** node, add a **Stage** node, and place a **Log** action into the stage.

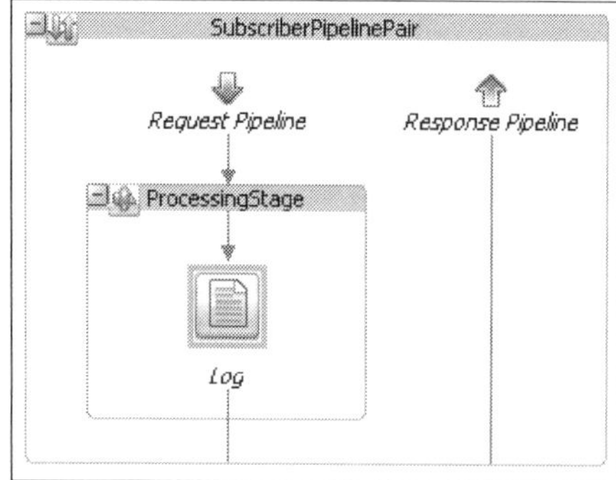

15. Enter `$body` for the **<Expression>**, Content of `$body` in Request into the **Annotation** field and select **Warning** as the value of the **Severity** drop-down listbox.
16. Save the project and deploy it to the OSB server.

Now we can test the subscription of the proxy service to the **SourceTopic** by putting a message into the topic.

Sending a message to a JMS topic is not supported by the WebLogic console. So we cannot use the same approach as shown in the previous recipe when consuming from a queue.

We can either use a business service to send a message to the topic (reusing the *Sending a message to a topic* recipe and reconfiguring it to use the **SourceTopic**, or use a tool such as JMS Browser or Hermes JMS for doing that. The recipe *Sending a message to a queue/topic with JMS Browser* recipe shows how to do that.

After putting a message into the JMS topic, check whether the following log statement shows up in the WebLogic console log window:

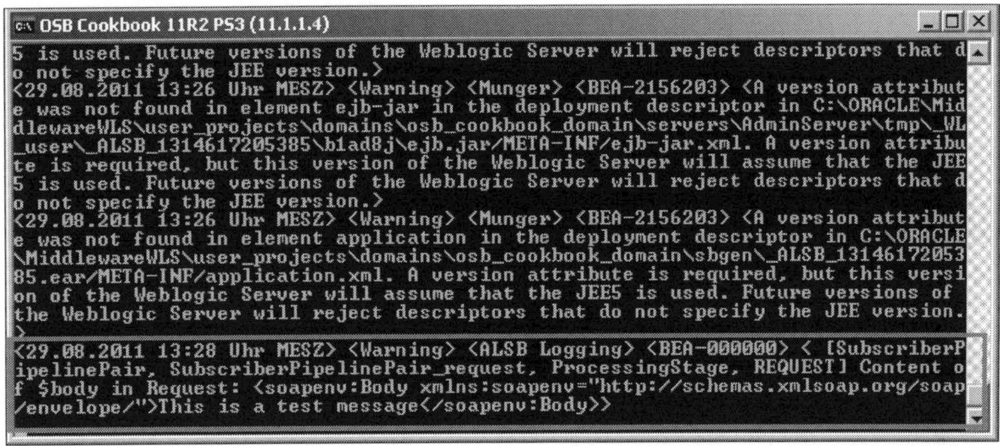

Now let's see what happens if the proxy service is not active, that is, it is in the disabled state. In the Service Bus console, perform the following steps to disable the **JMSSubscriber** proxy service:

17. Click on **Project Explorer** and in the **Projects** tree, expand the **consuming-from-jms-topic** node and click on the **proxy** node.
18. Click on the **JMSSubscriber** link.
19. Navigate to the **Operational Settings** tab by clicking on the link.
20. Click **Create** to start a new change session.
21. Deselect the **Enabled** checkbox in the **State** row.

22. Click **Update**.
23. Click **Activate**.
24. Enter **Disabled JMSSubscriber proxy service** into the **Description** field and click **Submit**.

Send a new message to the topic and check the Service Bus console log window.

There should be no new log message. Since the proxy service is no longer active, there is no longer an active subscription on the **SourceTopic** for the proxy service and therefore the message is not consumed from the topic.

Re-enable the proxy service by following the same steps (17-24) shown previously, but this time by selecting the **Enabled** checkbox. After activating the change session, the proxy service is back online and will again subscribe on the topic. Because the subscription was not durable, the topic does not keep the message and the message is lost. Check the OSB console where no new log message will be shown, indicating that the proxy service has not consumed any message after coming online again.

A message is lost if the proxy service is not active and the subscription is **not durable**.

How it works...

The proxy service acts as a subscription to the JMS topic. That means any message published to the topic will be consumed by the proxy service and sent through the message flow configured on the proxy service. A subscription can either be **durable** or **non-durable**. A durable subscription will be active, even if the proxy service itself is disabled and therefore in an inactive state. So far in this recipe we have shown the behavior of a proxy service creating a non-durable subscription. In the next section, we will demonstrate how to make the subscription durable.

A topic can have multiple subscribers at the same time differentiated by a unique client ID specified when subscribing to the topic. If a proxy service is used to subscribe on a topic, then the client ID is generated by the OSB. It has a value similar to the following: `RequestEJB-8542223846829071810-6ec035ed.13223f36c8d.-7fcf.`

If a message is sent/published to a topic, then all of subscribers, will get the message if they are alive.

There's more...

To make sure that the subscriber always gets a message published on a topic, even if he is unreachable or unavailable, the proxy service needs to create a **durable subscription**. In Eclipse OEPE, perform the following steps:

1. Open the **JMSSubscriber** proxy service.
2. Navigate to the **JMS Transport** tab.

3. Expand **Advanced Settings**.
4. Enable the **Durable Subscription** option.

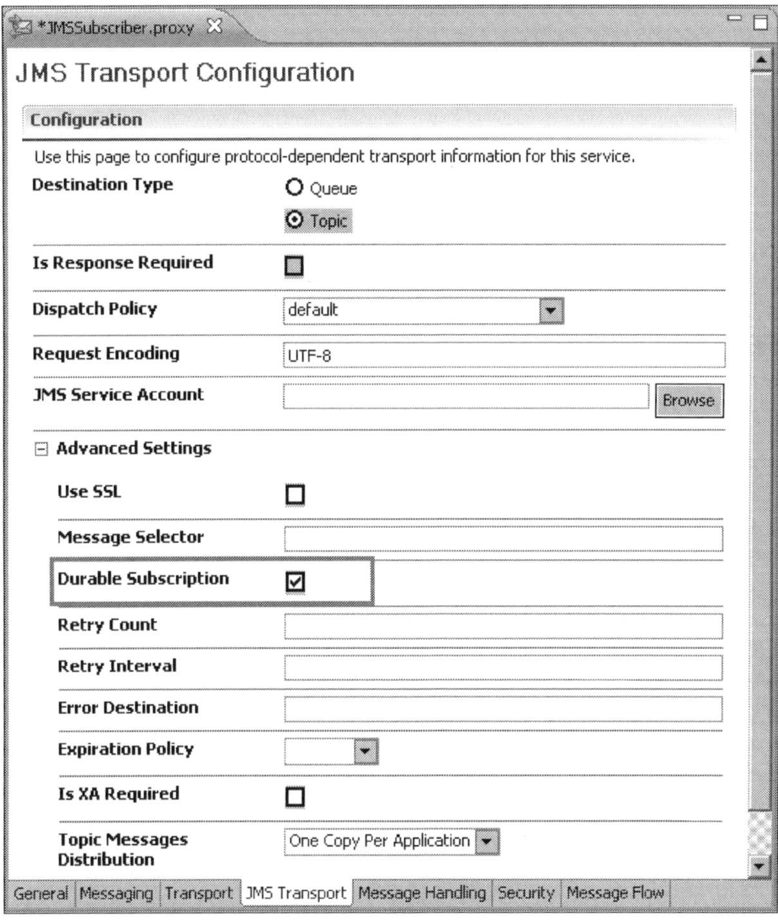

5. Save the proxy service and deploy it to the OSB server.

To view all durable subscribers registered on a topic, perform the following steps on the Service Bus console:

6. In the **Domain Structure** tree, expand **Services** | **Messaging** and select **JMS Modules**.
7. Click on **OsbCookbookResources**.
8. Click on **SourceTopic**.

4. Navigate to the **Monitoring** tab and inside that go to the **Durable Subscribers** tab and the subscribers will be displayed.

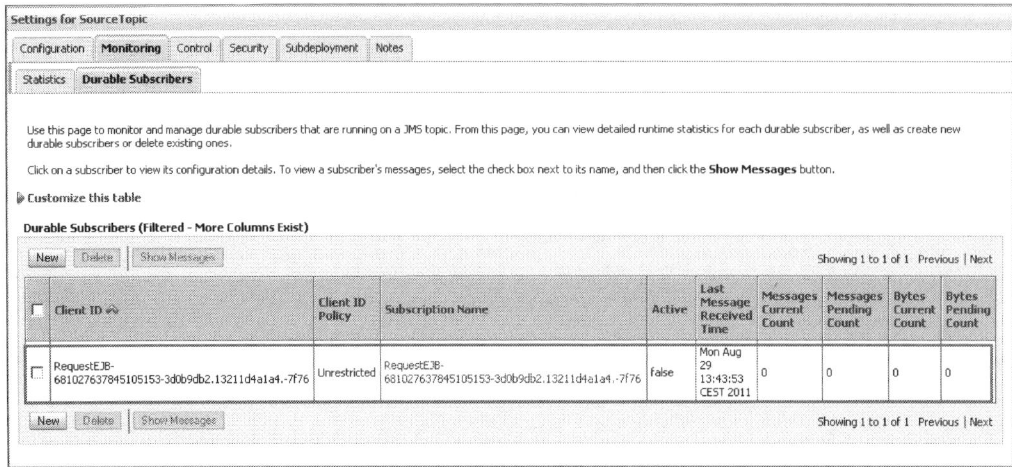

WebLogic JMS will keep track of which subscribers (again using the unique **Client id**) got a certain message delivered.

If we disable our proxy service now and send a message to the topic, the message will be kept by WebLogic JMS until the now durable subscriber receives it.

Consuming messages from a JMS queue/topic selectively

A proxy service can be configured to only consume messages that match a given criteria. This is done through the **Message Selector** in the **JMS Transport Advanced Settings**. A message selector is a logical statement similar to an SQL `WHERE` clause that the JMS provider evaluates against each message header or properties to determine whether the consumer should receive the message.

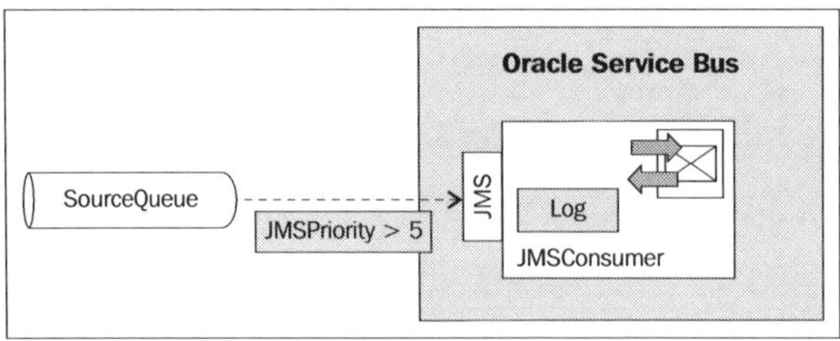

In this recipe, we will change the proxy service from the previous recipe *Consuming messages from a JMS queue* to only consume message with a priority higher than `5`.

Getting ready

For this recipe, we will use the queue **SourceQueue** from the OSB Cookbook standard environment.

You can import the base OSB project containing the solution from the previous recipe into Eclipse from `\chapter-3\getting-ready\consuming-messages-from-queue-topic-selectively`.

How to do it...

To add a message selector, which only consumes messages with a priority greater than `5`, perform the following steps in Eclipse OEPE:

1. Open the proxy service and navigate to the **JMS Transport** tab.
2. Expand the **Advanced Settings**.
3. Enter the `JMSPriority > 5` into the **Message Selector** field.

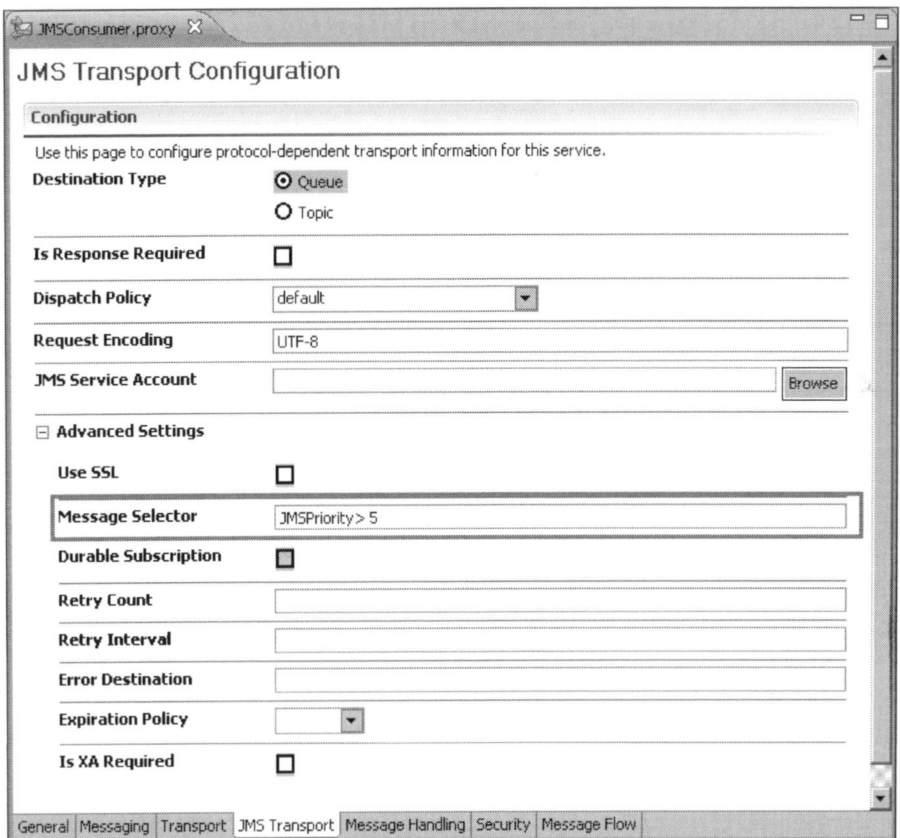

How it works...

A message selector is similar to the `WHERE` clause in SQL. A message selector is a logical statement which the JMS provider evaluates against each message's header or properties to determine whether the consumer, that is, the proxy service, should receive the message.

In WebLogic JMS, all selector evaluation and filtering takes place on the JMS server. A message selector can be specified for queues as well as topics.

For topics, WebLogic JMS evaluates each subscriber's message selector against every message published to the topic to determine whether to deliver the message to the subscriber.

For queues, WebLogic JMS will evaluate the message against each active consumer's message selector until it finds a match. If no active consumer's message selector matches the message, the message will remain in the queue.

Message selectors can get slow, especially when a consumer is activated later on a queue that already has a large backlog. In that case, the message selector has to be evaluated against each message in the queue. In such a case, it might be better to use multiple destinations and by that eliminate the need for message selectors.

This has nothing to do with OSB itself and is purely related to the implementation of WebLogic JMS. When using JMS with OSB, it's good to know about JMS and especially about the features and properties of the JMS provider, which in this case is WebLogic JMS.

There's more...

In this section, we will show how to use user-defined properties and compound expressions for the message selector.

Using user-defined properties in a message selector

A message selector also works on a user-defined JMS property. For example, to set a message selector on a user-defined property **myProperty** and test for the value **'red'**, the message selector should be as shown in the following screenshot:

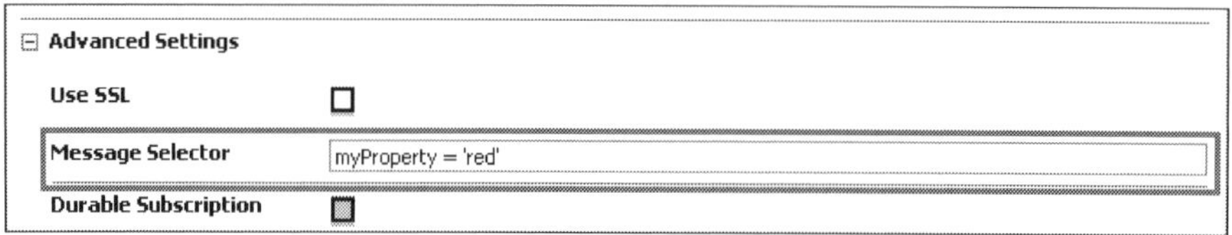

Using compound expressions in a message selector

Message selectors should be as simple as possible in order to not risk a performance penalty. The more complex a selector is, the slower its evaluation would be. A message selector can contain compound expressions with operators such as OR and AND. The next screenshot shows how to select all messages where both the priority is greater than **5** and the **myProperty** has a value of **'red'**.

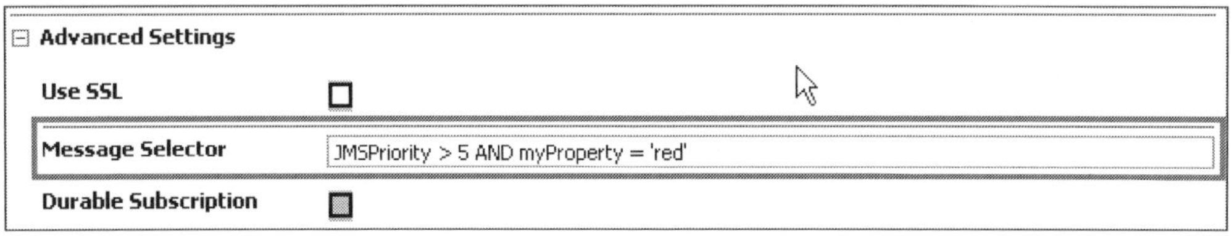

Advanced Settings
Use SSL
Message Selector JMSPriority > 5 AND myProperty = 'red'
Durable Subscription

When using compound selectors, the order matters. The evaluation is done from left-to-right. WebLogic JMS will short-circuit a message selector's evaluation once it determines the message does not match. So in our example, if a lot of messages have a priority of `5` or less, then these messages will not match the first evaluation criteria **JMSProperty > 5** of the compound expression.

See also

See *Accessing user-defined JMS properties in the message flow* recipe for how to implement a routing based on a user-defined property.

Accessing JMS Transport headers and properties in message flow

In this recipe, we will show how to access the JMS Transport headers and properties in the message flow. This can be useful, for example, to decide for which different business services the message should be routed to.

We will implement a decision based on the JMS header **JMSPriority** and another decision based on the user-defined property **myProperty**.

Getting ready

For this recipe, we will use the queue **SourceQueue** from the OSB Cookbook standard environment.

Import the base OSB project containing the solution from the previous recipe into Eclipse from `\chapter-3\getting-ready\accessing-jms-transport-headers-in-message-flow`.

How to do it...

In Eclipse OEPE, perform the following steps to add the two decisions to the message flow of the proxy service:

1. Open the proxy service **JMSConsumer** of the **accessing-jms-transport-headers-in-message-flow**.
2. Navigate to the **Message Flow** tab.
3. Right-click on the **Log** action and select **Insert After** | **Flow Control** | **If Then** to add an **If Then** action after the **Log** action.
4. Select the **If: <Condition>** and navigate to the **Properties** tab.
5. Click on **<Condition>**.
6. In the **Variable Structures** tree on the right, expand the **inbound** node until you get to the **JMSPriority** of the **transport** | **request - jms** node.
7. Drag the **JMSPriority** into the **Expression** field on the left. Add a `> 5` to the right of the generated expression so that it reads: `$inbound/ctx:transport/ctx:request/tp:headers/jms:JMSPriority > 5`.
8. Click **OK**.

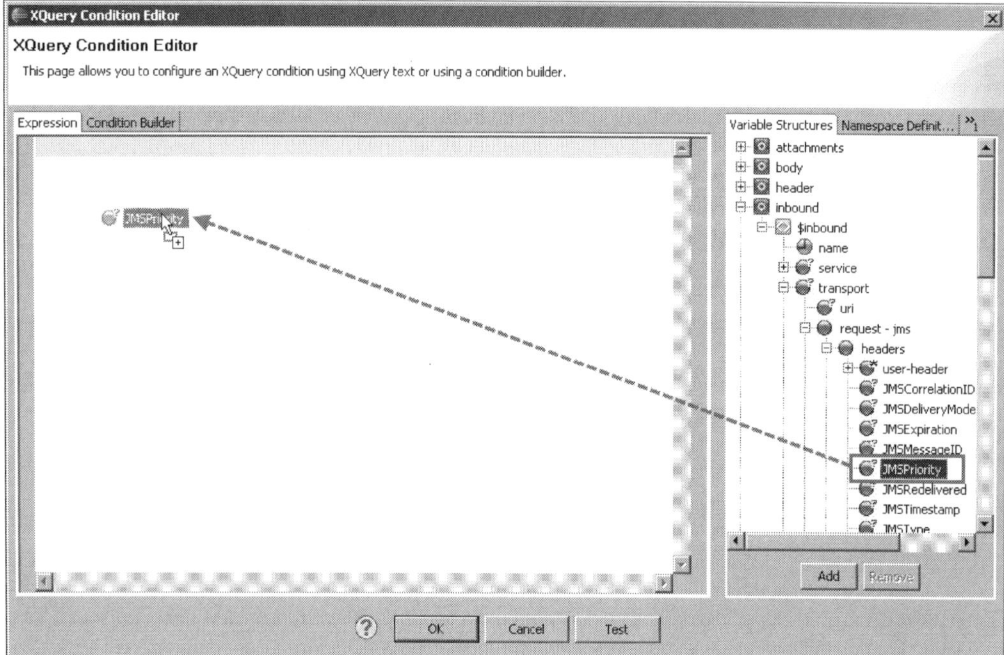

9. Right-click on **If: $inbou...** and select **Insert Into** | **Reporting** | **Log** to add a **Log** action into the branch.
10. Navigate to the **Properties** of the **Log** action, click **<Expression>** and set the expression to **'HIGH PRIORITY'**. Click **OK**.
11. Set the **Severity** drop-down listbox to **Warning**.
12. Right-click on the **Log** action just created and select **Copy**.
13. Right-click on the **Else** branch and select **Paste** to paste the **Log** action into the else branch.
14. Change the expression **'HIGH PRIORITY'** to **'LOW PRIORITY'**.

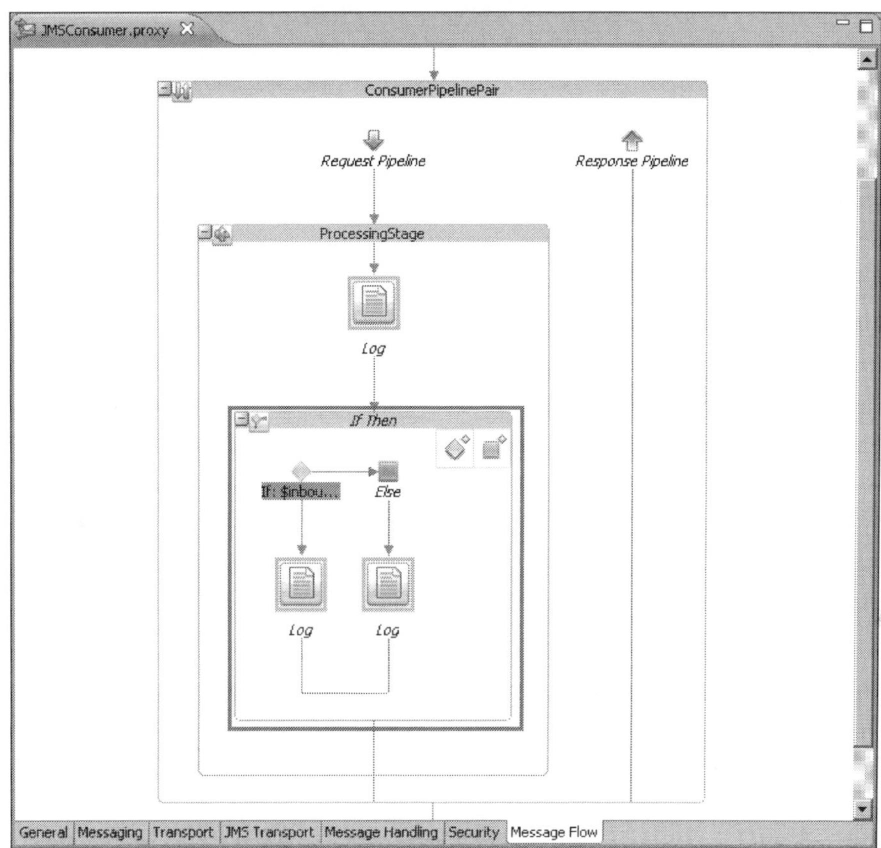

15. Deploy the proxy service to the OSB server.

Now it's time to test the changes to the proxy service.

16. Send a message with **JMSPriority** set to **6** and a **HIGH PRIORTY** log message should show up on the console window.
17. Send a message with **JMSPriority** set to **3** and a **LOW PRIORITY** log message should show up on the console window.

How it works...

In the incoming message in the proxy service, the transport-specific header and property values are available through the **inbound** context variable. Depending on the transport configured on the proxy service, the inbound variable holds different values in the **request** and **response** inside the **transport** node. In the case of JMS, we can find the different JMS headers, such as **JMSPriority** in the request node under the **transport** node (in the inbound variable).

By using XPath, these values can be accessed and used for the expressions of the OSB actions, such as **If Then** or **Routing Table**, for example, to implement a routing based on JMS header values.

There's more...

Here, we will learn how we can access user-defined JMS properties:

Accessing user-defined JMS properties

The user-defined JMS properties are only available if the headers are passed into the proxy service. This feature is disabled by default on a proxy service. To enable it, perform the following steps in OEPE:

1. Navigate to the **Transport** tab of the **JMSConsumer** proxy service.
2. Change the **Get All Headers** option to **Yes**.

Now the user-defined JMS properties are passed into the proxy service and can be accessed through the inbound context variable. Let's add a **Log** action to print out the value of the **myProperty** JMS property:

3. Navigate to the **Message Flow** tab.
4. Add a **Log** action after the **If Then** action.
5. On the **Properties** tab of the **Log** action, click on **<Expression>**.
6. On the **Variable Structures** tab on the right, navigate to the **user-header** node below **request - jms | headers**.

7. Drag the **name** element to the **Expression** field as shown in the following screenshot:

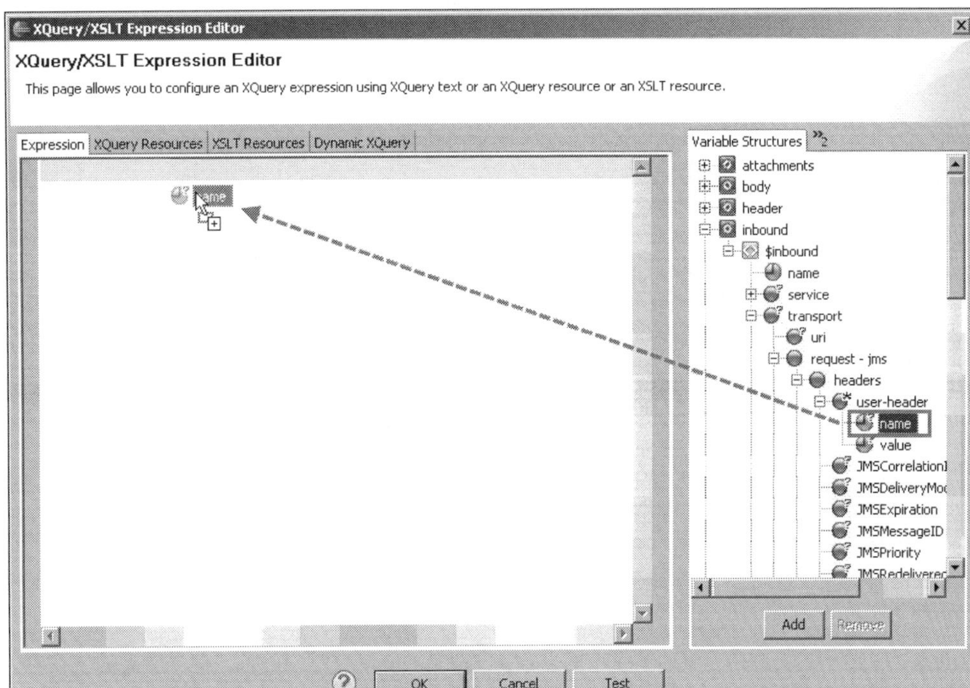

8. Extend the expression so that it accesses value attribute of the **myProperty** user-defined property: `$inbound/ctx:transport/ctx:request/tp:headers/tp:user-header[@name = 'myProperty']/@value`.
9. Click **OK**.
10. Change the **Severity** to **Warning**.
11. Deploy the project to the OSB server.

Now, retest the project by sending a message to the **SourceQueue** with a user-defined property **myProperty**. The value passed should be shown on the console window.

Using request-response messaging with JMS

This recipe shows you how to implement the request/reply design patterns over JMS. For this we need two queues, the **RequestQueue** where the request is sent to and consumed by the replier, and the **ResponseQueue** where the answer/reply is sent to by the replier and then consumed by the initial requester.

This is shown in the following diagram where on the left the requestor is implemented by a business service on OSB, and on the right the replier is implemented as a proxy service on OSB.

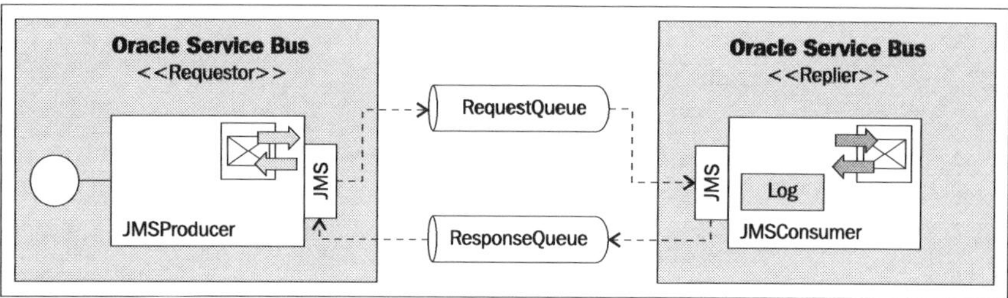

In a real case, the OSB normally only plays one role of either the requestor or the replier, and hence it is only on one side. On the other side, we would usually find legacy systems only capable of communicating through queues, such as a mainframe system.

Getting ready

For this recipe, we will use the two queues **RequestQueue** and **ResponseQueue** from the OSB Cookbook standard environment.

In order to start, we will use the setup from the recipe *Consuming messages from a JMS queue*. Import the base OSB project into Eclipse from `\chapter-3\getting-ready\sync-request-response-over-jms-queue`.

How to do it...

With the setup from the *Consuming messages from a JMS queue* recipe, we already have the replier side partially implemented with the **JMSConsumer** proxy service consuming from the **RequestQueue**. Let's change the behavior of the proxy service to send a response on the **ResponseQueue**. Perform the following steps in OEPE:

1. Open the **JMSConsumer** proxy service and navigate to the **Transport** tab.
2. Change the **EndpointURI** to consume from the **RequestQueue** instead of the **SourceQueue**.
3. Navigate to the **Messaging** tab.
4. Set the **Response Message Type** to **Text** to define that the proxy service will return an answer.
5. Navigate to the **JMS Transport** tab.
6. Enable the **Is Response Required** checkbox.
7. Set the **Response Pattern** to **JMSCorrelationID**.

8. Set the **Response Message Type** option to **Text**.
9. Enter `jms://localhost:7001/weblogic.jms.XAConnectionFactory/jms.ResponseQueue` into the **Response URI** field.

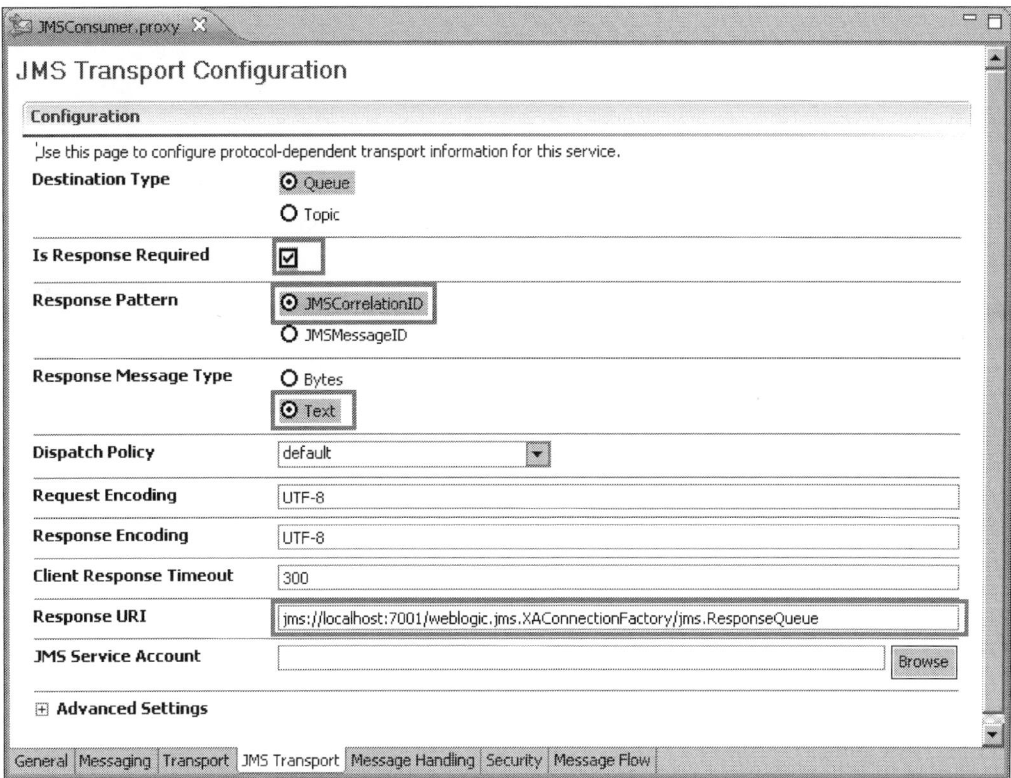

10. Navigate to the **Message Flow** tab.
11. Insert a **Stage** node into the **Response Pipeline**.
12. Insert an **Assign** action into the stage.
13. On the **Properties** tab for the **Assign** enter `body` into the **Variable** field.
14. Click **<Expression>** and enter the following expression into the **Expression** field:

```
<soap-env:Body>This is the response for this request: {$body/text()}
</soap-env:Body>
```

15. Click **OK**.

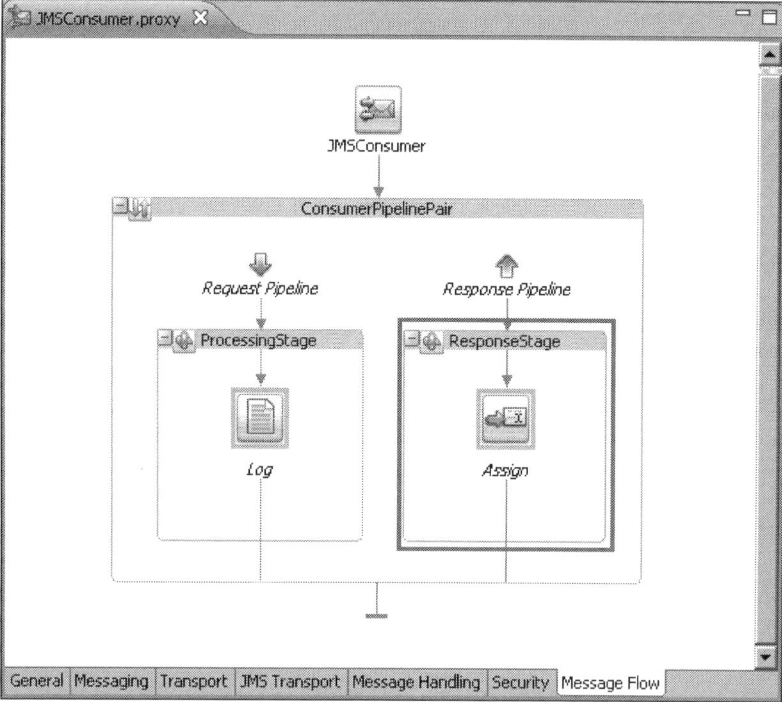

16. Deploy the project to the OSB server.

We have the replier side ready and working. So let's test this by putting a message into the **RequestQueue** and then check the **ResponseQueue** for the answer message. We will use QBrowser here, as it makes testing of multiple queues much easier. Check the *Using QBrowser Admin GUI for accessing JMS queues/topics* recipe for how to install and use QBrowser.

In QBrowser, perform the following steps:

17. Right-click on the **RequestQueue** and select **Send message to**.
18. Enter `This is the request message` into the **Message body** field.
19. Add **JMSCorrelationID** to **JMS Header** and set it to the value **123456789**.
20. Click **Send**.
21. Confirm the next two pop-up windows by clicking **Send** and then **OK**.
22. Click on the **ResponseQueue** and check whether a new message arrived.

23. Double-click on the message and you will see the reply from the proxy service. The value of the **JMSCorrelationID** matches what we passed in the request message and the content of the **Message Body** shows the manipulation done by the **Assign** action.

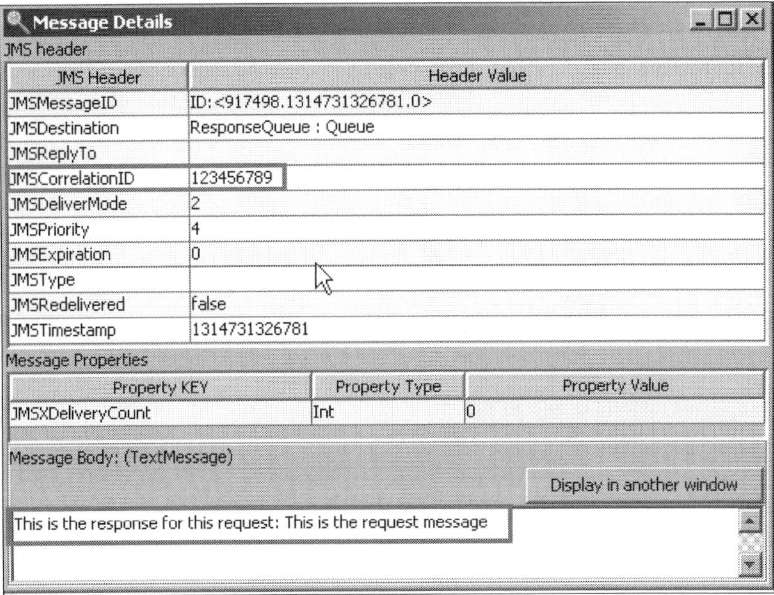

So the replier side works perfectly. Let's now implement the requestor side with the business service sending the request to the **RequestQueue** and waiting for the response on the **ResponseQueue**. In OEPE, perform the following steps to implement the business service:

24. Add a `business` folder to the **sync-request-response-over-jms-queue** project and create the `JMSProducer` business service.
25. On the **General** tab select **Messaging Service** for the **Service Type**.
26. Navigate to the **Messaging** tab and select **Text** for both the **Request Message Type** and the **Response Message Type**.
27. Navigate to the **Transport** tab and select **jms** for the **Protocol**.
28. Change the **EndpointURI** field to `jms://localhost:7001/weblogic.jms.XAConnectionFactory/jms.RequestQueue` and click **Add**.
29. Navigate to the **JMS Transport** tab and select **Text** for the **Message Type**.
30. Select **One for all Request URIs** for the **Response Queues** option.
31. Set the **Response Pattern** to **JMSCorrelationID** matching the settings on the proxy service.

32. Enter `jms://localhost:7001/weblogic.jms.XAConnectionFactory/jms.ResponseQueue` into the **ResponseURI** field.

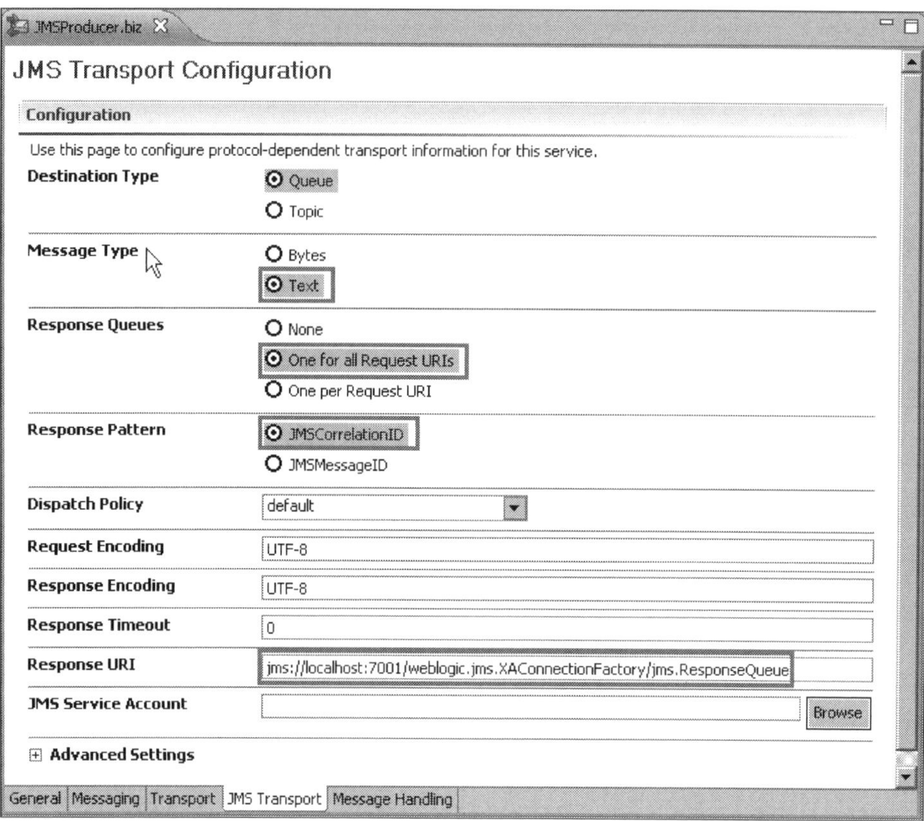

33. Deploy the project to the OSB server.

Now we have both the requestor and replier role implemented in OSB, once as a business service and once as a proxy service. Let's test the business service to see that the request-response pattern works. In OSB console, perform the following steps:

34. In the **Project Explorer** tree click on **sync-request-response-over-jms-queue | business**.
35. Click on the **Launch Test Console** icon (little bug icon) to open the test console.
36. Enter **This is a request message** into the **Payload** field and click **Execute**.

37. The business service will wait for the reply message on the **ResponseQueue** and shows it as the **Response Document**. It reflects the action of the **Assign** in the proxy service.

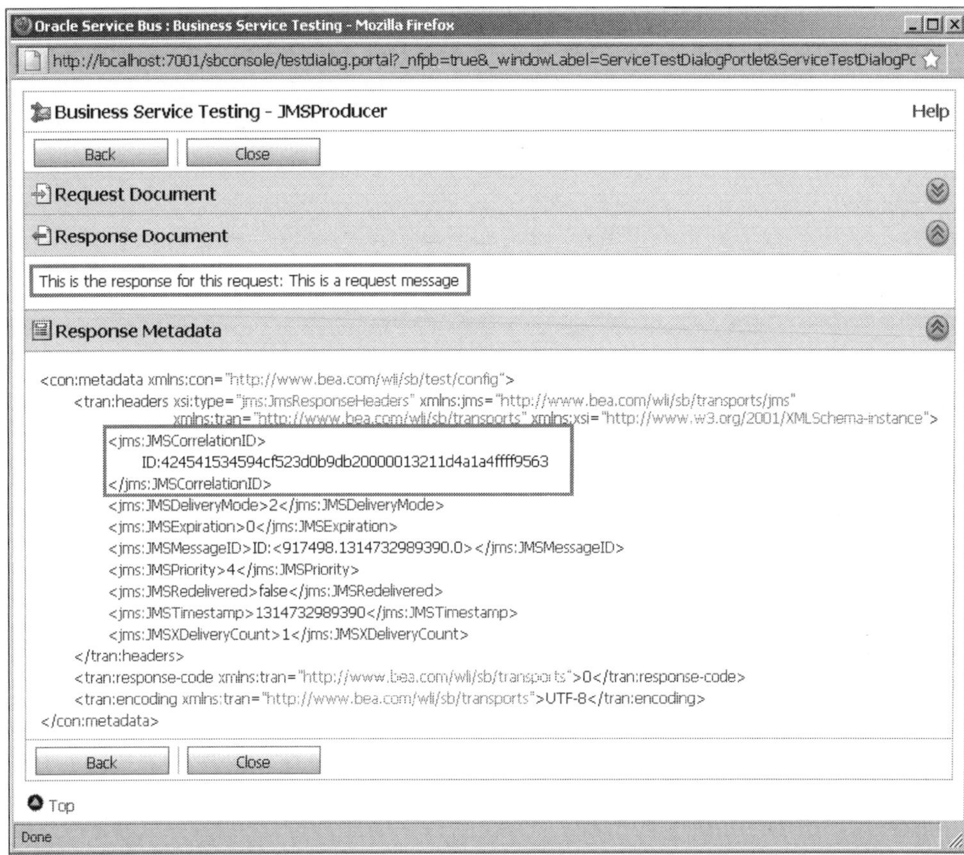

In the **Response Metadata** section, the JMS headers are shown. We can see the value of the **JMSCorrelationID** used for correlating the request and response on the business-service side.

How it works...

This recipe implements a sync-to-async bridging, where on the business service (the requestor side) the request-response processing is done in a synchronous manner. The business service will wait until the reply message from the replier arrives. The communication between the requestor and replier is done in an asynchronous manner using two queues. To make sure that the requestor can correlate the original request to the correct reply message, some correlation information is passed between the requestor and the replier by using the JMS Header **JMSCorrelationID**.

When the requestor creates a request message, it has to assign a unique identifier to the request that is different from those for all other currently outstanding requests (for example, requests that do not yet have replies). When the receiver processes the request, it saves the identifier and adds the request's identifier to the reply.

JMS request/response messaging does not provide reliable responses because the mapping of the correlation ID is stored in memory. If there is a failure/restart in between sending the request message and receiving the reply message, the response will be discarded.

If this is a problem, then JMS request/response should not be used. It can be replaced by two JMS one-way proxies. The first one-way JMS proxy delivers the message and a second one-way JMS proxy in the reverse direction delivers the reply message. This scenario is shown in the *There's more* section.

There's more...

The request-reply pattern over queues can also be implemented asynchronously, without using the correlation feature of the OSB as shown in the recipe so far.

In that scenario, we still use two queues, the **RequestQueue** holding the request message and the **ResponseQueue** holding the reply message. Instead of configuring the proxy service on the replier side to send a response message, an additional business service **JMSReplyProducer** is called that writes to the queue. To consume the reply message on the requestor side, an additional proxy service **JMSReplyConsumer** is needed. This is represented in the following diagram:

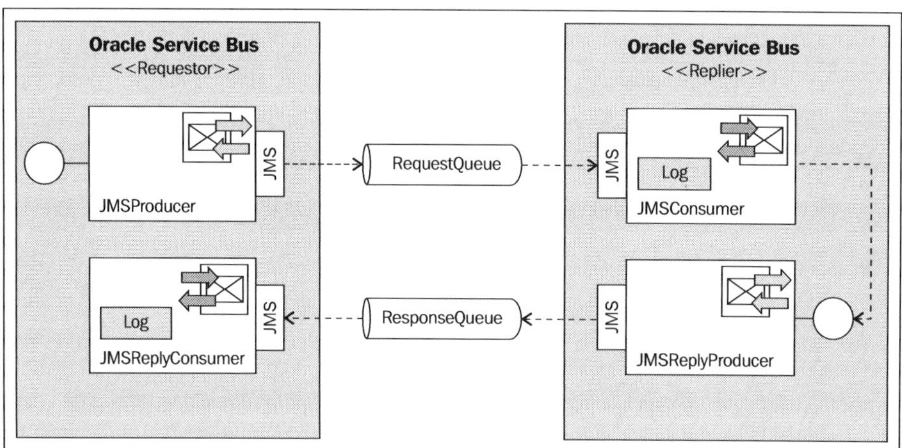

Compared to the synchronous version shown in the previous diagram, the asynchronous version won't support any correlation on the requestor side. So the request and the response processing are completely separate on the requestor side.

We won't show the implementation of the recipe here. Based on the recipes *Sending a message to a JMSqueue* and *Consuming messages from a JMS queue* of this chapter, the reader should be able to implement this recipe without a problem.

Using QBrowser Admin GUI for accessing JMS queues/topics

In the recipes in this chapter, we have seen how to use the WebLogic console to send messages to queues and to browse for messages in a queue/topic. This can be good enough for some simple quick tests.

In this recipe, we will show you how the testing and browsing can be supported by using an external tool called QBrowser.

Getting ready

Download the latest version (**QBrowser_light_V2.5.2.2** at the time of writing) of QBrowser from here: `http://sourceforge.net/projects/qbrowserv2/files/`. Unzip the download to a local folder.

Before the tool can be started, open the file `run_wls_mq_for_default_install_location.bat` and change the settings of the `BEA_HOME` and `WL_HOME` variables according to your environment. After that, double-click on the file to start QBrowser.

How to do it...

First we have to connect to the JMS server. In QBrowser, perform the following steps:

1. Select the **File** menu and click **New Connection**.
2. Change the URL provider according to your installation, especially hostname and port number.
3. Enter `weblogic` into the User field and `welcome1` into the Password field.
4. Click **OK**.

5. A tree on the left shows the available queues and topics on the JMS server.

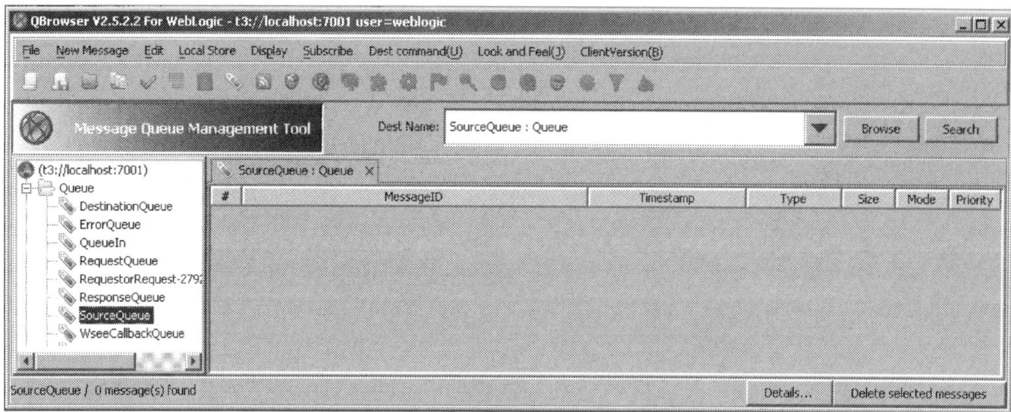

To put a message into the **SourceQueue**, perform the following steps:

6. Right-click on **SourceQueue** and select **Send message to**.
7. Enter the message to send into the **Message body** field.
8. Select **TextMessage** from the **Input Type** drop-down listbox.
9. Optionally add a JMS Header by clicking on the **+** button to the right of **JMS Header**. Select the **JMS Header** from the drop-down, for example, **JMSPriority** and set the value in the **Header Value** cell.
10. Optionally add a user-defined JMS message property by clicking on the + button to the right of **Message Properties**. Specify **myProperty** for the **Property KEY** set the **Property Type** drop-down listbox to **String** and enter **red** into the **Property Value** cell.

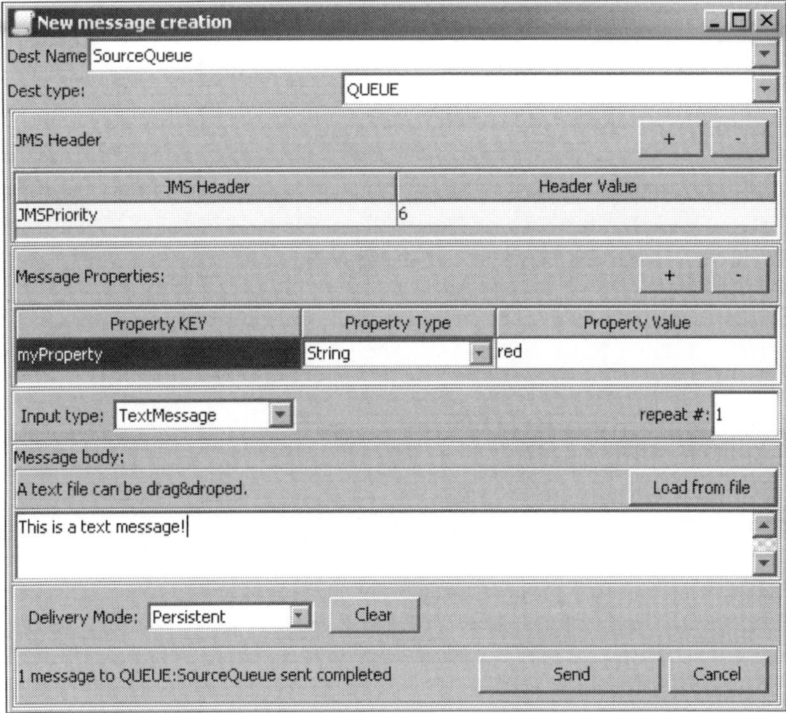

11. Click on **Send**.
12. Confirm the message sending by clicking on **Send** on the pop-up window.
13. A pop-up window showing the progress info will be shown. Confirm it by clicking on **OK**.

The message is placed on the **SourceQueue** and if one of the OSB recipes consuming from the queue is deployed, the message will immediately get consumed by the proxy service.

Messages in a given queue can also be browsed in QBrowser. Perform the following steps to check for the messages in the **DestinationQueue**:

14. In the tree on the left, click on **DestinationQueue**.
15. The detail window on the right will display all the messages that are currently in the **DestinationQueue**.

3. Double-click on the first message to show the details of the message.

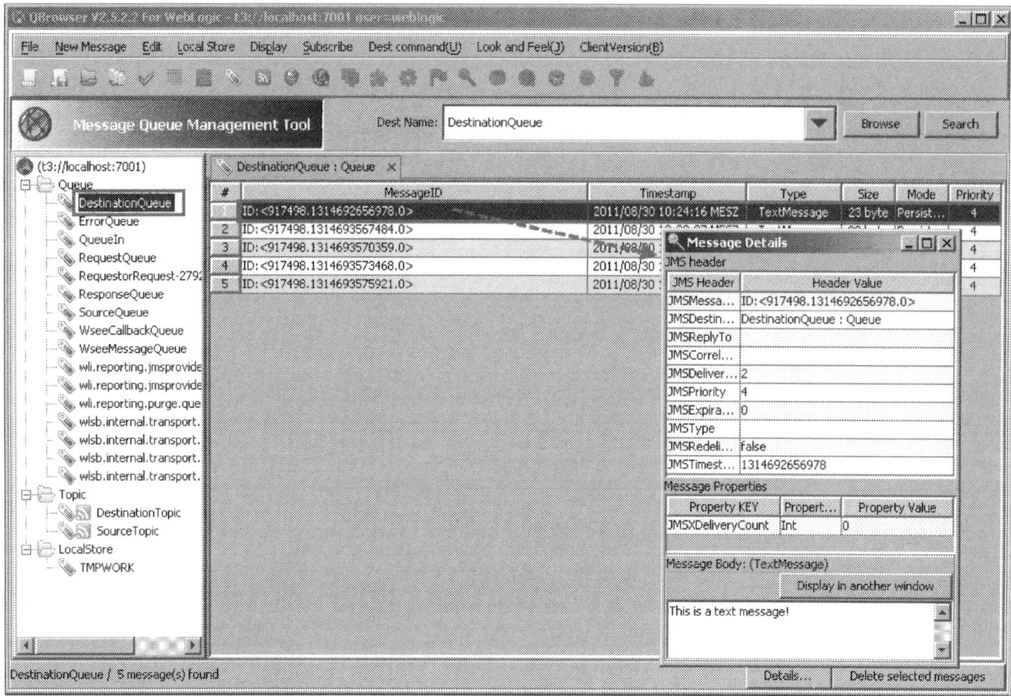

How it works...

Since the JMS defines a standard way of how to access queues, there are other third-party tools available for accessing JMS queues and topics. This can simplify working with JMS with the downside of having to install an additional program.

See also

There are other tools that support similar functionality such as QBrowser, they are:

- JMSBrowser: `http://jmsbrowser.com/`
- HermesJMS: `http://www.hermesjms.com/confluence/display/HJMS/Home`

We will see HermesJMS used and configured in the next recipe *Testing JMS with soapUI*.

Testing JMS with soapUI

We have already seen soapUI being used for Web Services testing. In this recipe, we will demonstrate how soapUI can also be used for testing JMS-based interfaces.

We will use the solution from the recipe *Accessing JMS Transport message headers and properties in message flow*, which implemented a proxy service consuming from the **SourceQueue** of the OSB Cookbook standard environment. In that recipe, we have used the WebLogic console and replace it now in this recipe by soapUI.

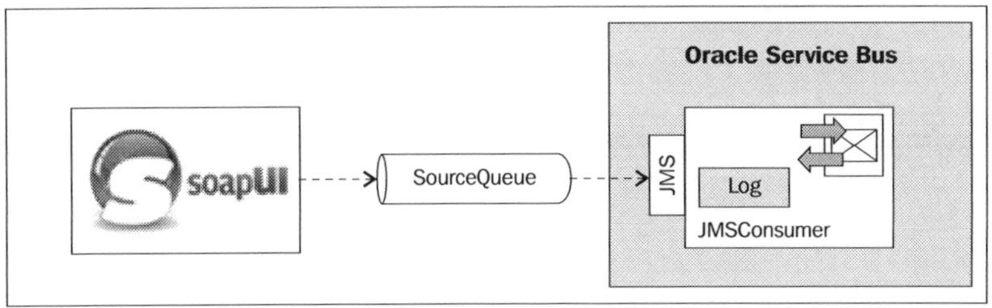

The advantage of using soapUI for testing is the persistence of the different test cases and by that the possibility to automate tests. This is not achievable through the console, and also QBrowser shown in the previous recipe cannot be used for automating tests.

Getting ready

Download and install the latest version of soapUI (**soapUI 4.0** at the time of writing) from here: `http://www.soapui.org`. Make sure that you also select and install HermesJMS when asked by the soapUI installer.

Import the **finished solution** from the previous recipe into Eclipse from `\chapter-3\solution\accessing-jms-transport-headers-in-message-flow`.

How to do it...

Before we can use soapUI for testing JMS, we need to configure JMS. This is done in HermesJMS, another external tool for working with JMS, which is used behind the scenes by soapUI. Perform the following steps to configure HermesJMS:

1. Navigate to the installation folder of HermesJMS nested in the soapUI installation.
2. Make sure that HermesJMS is using the same JVM as the WLS we want to connect to. Open `<HERMES_HOME>\bin\hermes.bat` and add the following `JAVA_HOME` and `PATH` variable right at the beginning:

```
SET JAVA_HOME=[FMW_HOME]\jrockit_160_22_D1.1.1-3
SET PATH=%JAVA_HOME%\bin
```

3. Start soapUI.
4. Click the **Tools** menu and select **HermesJMS**.
5. In the **Sessions** tree on the left side, right-click on the sessions node and select **New | New session**.
6. Navigate to the **Providers** tab.
7. Right-click and select **Add Group**.
8. Enter `Weblogic` into the **Classpath group name** field and click **OK**.
9. Right-click on **Library** and select **Add JAR(s)**.
10. Navigate to the **weblogic.jar** in: `<WEBLOGIC_HOME>\server\lib\weblogic.jar` and click **Open**.
11. Click **Don't scan** when asked and click **Apply**.

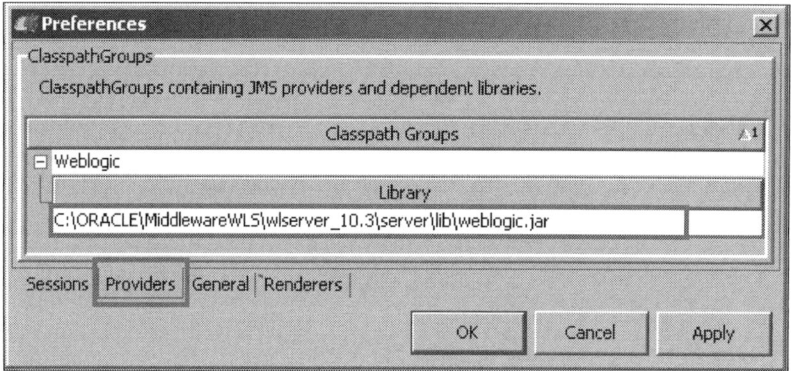

12. Navigate to the **Sessions** tab.
13. Enter `OsbCookbook` into the **Session** field.
14. Select **Weblogic** for the **Loader** drop-down listbox.
15. Select **BEA WebLogic** for the **Plugin** in drop-down listbox.
16. Select **hermes.JNDIConnectionFactory** for the **Class** drop-down listbox.
17. For the **Connection Factory**, add the following properties through **Add property**.

Property	**Value**
`binding`	`javax/jms/QueueConnectionFactory`
`initialContextFactory`	`weblogic.jndi.WLInitialConetxtFactory`
`providerURL`	`t3://<managedServer>:<port-number>`
`securityCredentials`	`weblogic`
`securityPrincipal`	`<password-of-weblogic>`

18. Click **Apply** and then click **OK**.

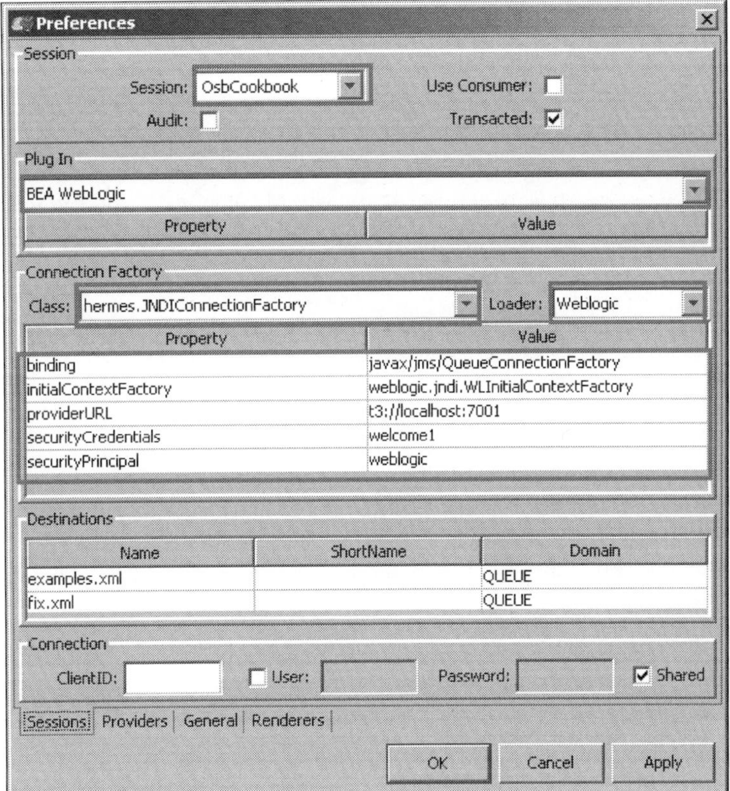

19. Right-click on the newly created session **OsbCookbook** and select **Discover...**.
20. After a while a pop-up window will show up stating **Discovered # destinations**.
21. Click **Yes** to confirm.

HermesJMS is now ready and can be used to administer the JMS server. The configuration is stored in the `.hermes/hermes-config.xml` file.

Now we can go back to soapUI and use the HermesJMS configuration to send a message to a queue through a soapUI request. In soapUI perform the following steps:

22. Right-click on the **Projects** tree node and select **New soapUI Project**.
23. Enter `SendToSourceQueue` into the **Project Name** field and enable the **Add REST Service** option and click **OK**.
24. Enter `SendToSourceQueueService` into the **Service Name**, enable the **Create Resource** option and click **OK**.

25. Enter `SourceQueue` into the **Resource Name** field and click **OK**.
26. Enter **send** into the **Method Name** and select **POST** for the **HTTP Method** drop-down listbox.
27. Click **OK**.

We have added a RESTful interface with one method `SendMessage`. To be able to use JMS, we have to add a JMS endpoint:

28. Right-click on **SendToSourceQueueService** and select **Add JMS endpoint**.
29. Click on **Browse** and navigate to the folder where the `hermes-config.xml` created previously can be found (`c:\.hermes` on my machine).
30. Select **OsbCookbook** for the **Session**.
31. Select **jms/SourceQueue** for the **Send/Publish destination**.
32. Click **OK**.

Now the interface to the queue is defined in soapUI and we can finally execute a test and send a message to the **SourceQueue**. In soapUI, perform the following steps:

33. Open **Request 1** of the **send** method if not yet opened.
34. Select the created endpoint **jms://OsbCookbook::queue_jms/SourceQueue** form the drop-down listbox.
35. Enter **This is a text message!** into the field below the **Media Type** drop-down listbox.
36. Navigate to the **JMS Header settings and properties** tab and enter **6** into the **JMSPriority** field.

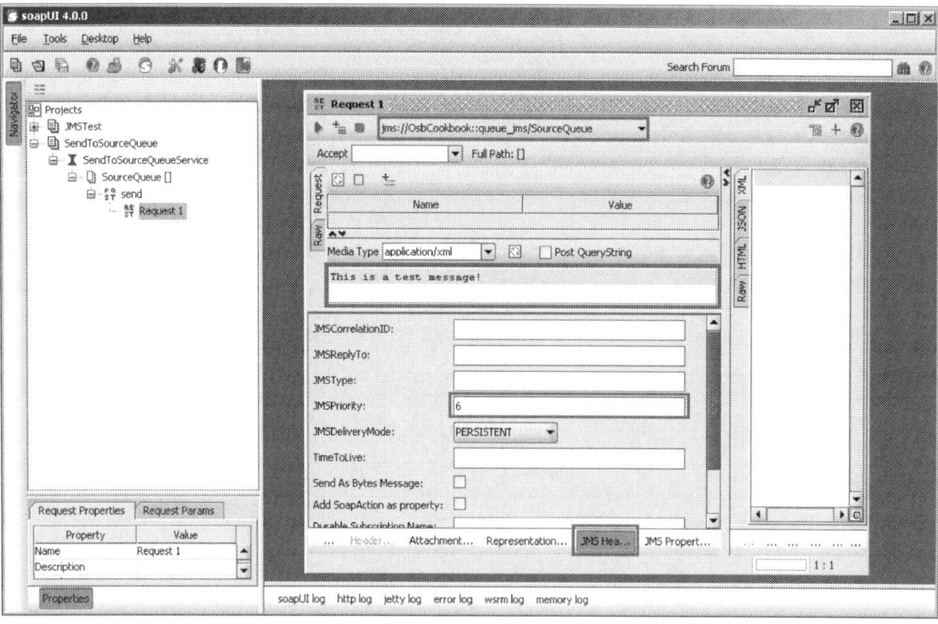

37. Navigate to the **JMS Property** tab and click on the **+** button to add a new user-defined JMS property.
38. Enter `myProperty` into the **Specify name of JMS Property to add** field of the pop-up window. Click **OK**.
39. Enter `red` into the **Value** cell for the value of **myProperty**.

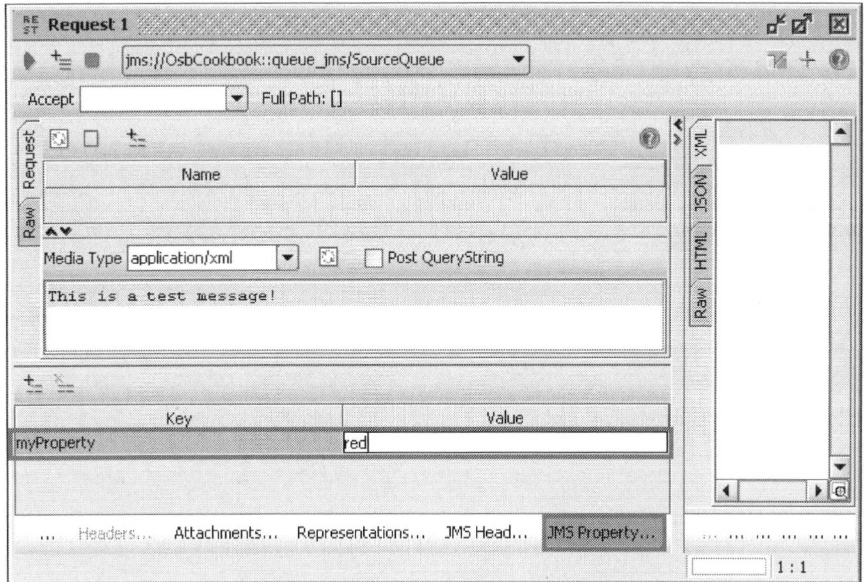

40. Click on the green arrow on the upper-left corner to execute the test.
41. An empty response **<xml/>** will be shown in the response window indicating that the message has been sent.
42. The OSB console should show some new log messages indicating that the proxy service has consumed and processed the message successfully.

```
OSB Cookbook 11R2 PS3 (11.1.1.4)
<30.08.2011 13:05 Uhr MESZ> <Warning> <ALSB Logging> <BEA-000000> < [ConsumerPip
elinePair, ConsumerPipelinePair_request, ProcessingStage, REQUEST] Content of $b
ody in Request: <soapenv:Body xmlns:soapenv="http://schemas.xmlsoap.org/soap/env
elope/">This is a test message!</soapenv:Body>>
<30.08.2011 13:05 Uhr MESZ> <Warning> <ALSB Logging> <BEA-000000> < [ConsumerPip
elinePair, ConsumerPipelinePair_request, ProcessingStage, REQUEST] HIGH PRIORITY
>
<30.08.2011 13:05 Uhr MESZ> <Warning> <ALSB Logging> <BEA-000000> < [ConsumerPip
elinePair, ConsumerPipelinePair_request, ProcessingStage, REQUEST] red>
```

A *high priority* message has been consumed because we have set the **JMSPriority** to a value greater than `6` and the **myProperty** had the value **red** in the proxy service (remember the behavior of the previous recipe). This shows that the soapUI test was successful.

How it works...

SoapUI supports SOAP-based as well as RESTful requests. Because we don't want to send a SOAP message to our queue, we have used the REST features and configured a RESTful request. By adding a JMS endpoint we made sure that the request is not sent through HTTP, which is the default protocol soapUI uses, but through JMS. Adding a JMS endpoint is only possible if the JMS server has been previously setup in HermesJMS. SoapUI uses the HermesJMS configuration to communicate with the JMS server. In this recipe, we have configured HermesJMS to work with WebLogic JMS, but any other JMS-compliant server would work as well.

There's more...

SoapUI can also be used to do request/reply messaging through JMS, where the request queue and response queue are different. Just specify the second queue in the **Receive/ Subscribe destination**.

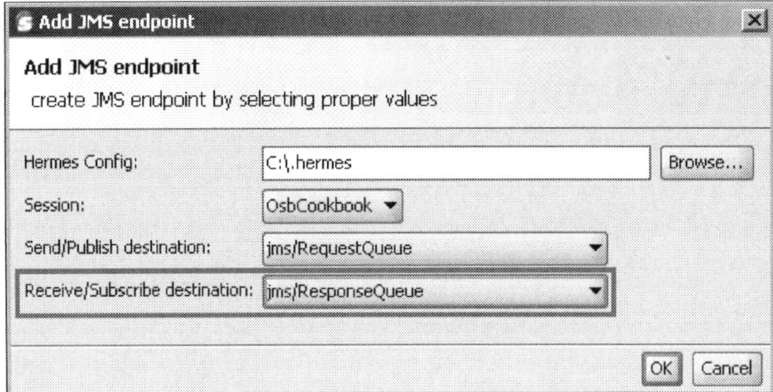

SoapUI can also be used to test SOAP over JMS. The usage of SOAP over JMS will be shown in *Chapter 10*, Sending SOAP over JMS.

4
Using EJB and JEJB transport

In this chapter, we will cover:

- Exposing an EJB session bean as a service on the OSB using the EJB transport
- Using JNDI Provider to invoke an EJB session bean on a remote WebLogic domain
- Using the `Converter` class with EJB transport to help converting data types
- Exposing an EJB session bean as an EJB on the OSB using the JEJB transport
- Manipulating the response of the JEJB transport by a Java Callout action

Introduction

With the release 11g of the Oracle Service Bus there are two transports for directly communicating to an EJB session bean layer, the EJB, and the JEJB transport. The first was already available in previous versions of OSB whereas the latter, the JEBJ transport, has been introduced with 11g.

The EJB transport is only available for business services whereas the JEJB transport can be used both on a proxy service as well as for business services.

- The EJB transport uses the **Java Web Services** (**JWS**) framework to invoke remote EJBs
- The JEJB transport uses an RMI serialization/deserialization cycle and passes **Plain Old Java Objects** (**POJOs**) directly through the OSB to the remote EJBs.

The EJB and JEJB business services both call the session beans, but there is an important difference between these two transports. With the JEJB transport the request and response remain Java object (POJO) and will not be transformed to XML. This is great for performance but it means you cannot change the request or response with the default OSB activities. To manipulate the request or response you should use a java callout in the proxy service. To a J2EE client, a JEJB proxy service pipeline looks like a stateless session bean.

The EJB transport behaves the same as a HTTP or a JCA DB adapter business service.

In order to perform the recipes in this chapter, we need an EJB session bean available on a server. To simplify life, we can deploy it directly to the OSB server, although in real life the EJB is often to be found on a separate machine.

The EJB session bean we are using here for the tests, implements the following interface:

```
@Remote
public interface CustomerManagement {

    public Customer findCustomer(Long id);
    public List findAllCustomers();
}
```

We have already created a JAR file with the EJB session bean, which can be deployed through the WebLogic console by performing the following steps:

1. Click on **Deployments** in the **Domain Structure** tree on the left.
2. Click on **Install** on the detail page.
3. Navigate to the `\chapter-4\getting-ready\ejb-jdev-workspace\ejb\deploy` folder.
4. Select **customerManagementEJB.jar** and click on the **Next** button.

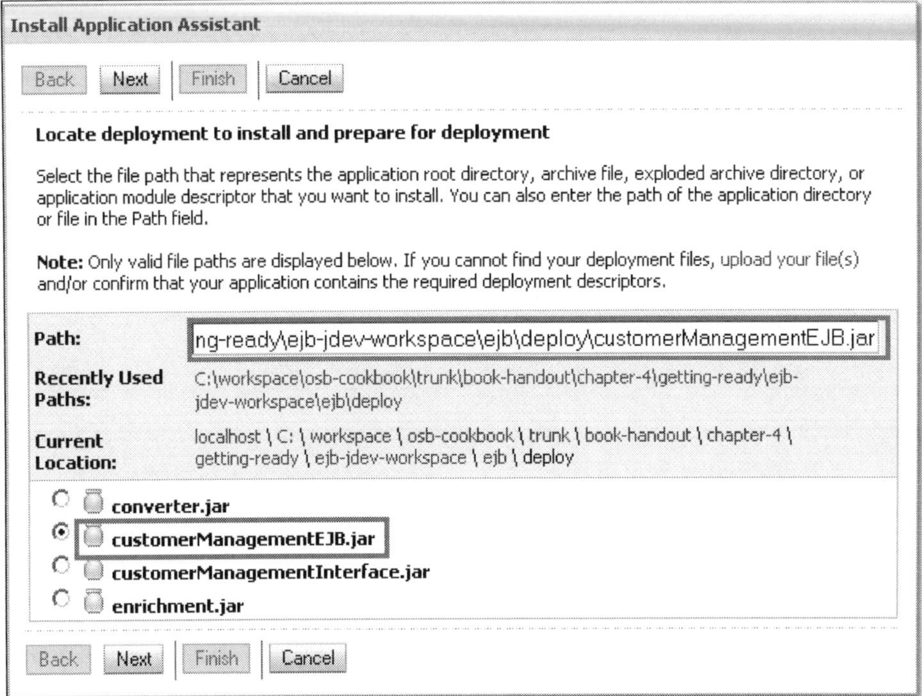

5. Select the **Install this deployment as an application** option and click on **Next**.
6. Click on the **Finish** button.

Now with the EJB session bean in place, let's test it through the test class provided in the JDeveloper workspace. In JDeveloper, perform the following steps:

1. Open the `osbbook_jejb.jws` workspace.
2. Expand the `client` project until you reach the `CustomerManagementClient.java` class.
3. Open the class and check that the password in the `getInitialContext()` is correct for the environment.

4. Right-click on the `CustomerManagementClient.java` file and select **Run**:

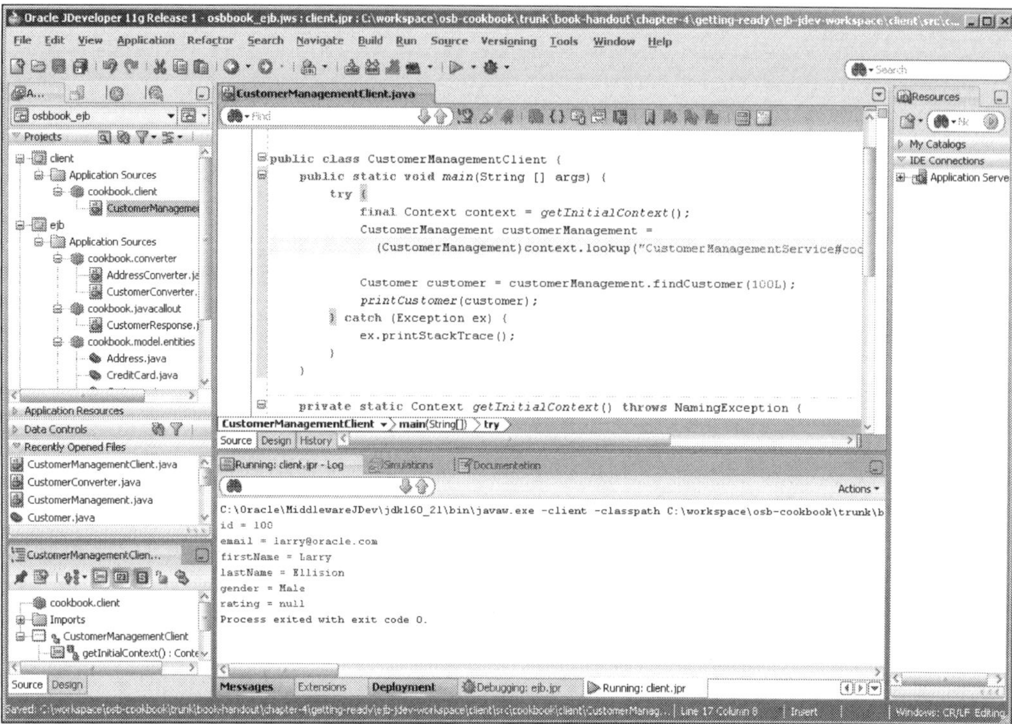

We can see that the data about the customer with the `id = 100` is returned. That tells us the environment is ready for the coming recipes.

Exposing an EJB session bean as a service on the OSB using the EJB transport

As the version of OSB is 11gR1 we can use an EJB version 3.0 session bean in an OSB business service. Before 11gR1, only EJB version 2.1 was supported.

In this recipe, we will create and test a business service—JB and JEJB transport. The business service calls a session bean that returns the Java object in XML or as a Java object with the JEJB transport.

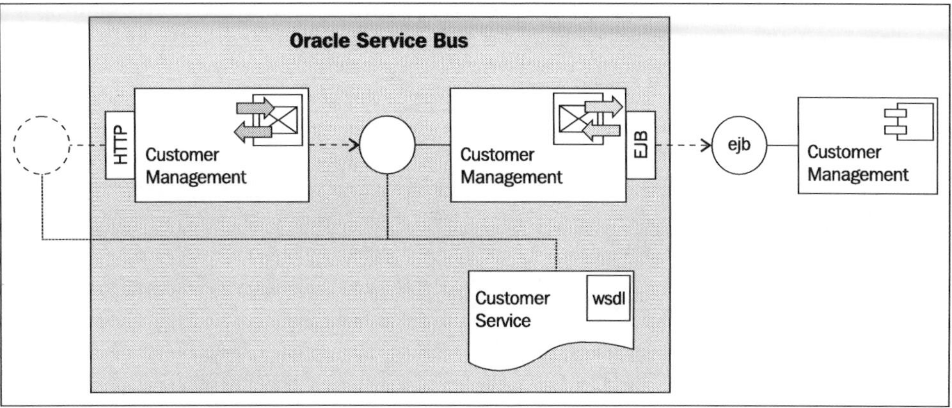

Getting ready

Make sure that the EJB session bean is deployed to the OSB server as shown in the *Introduction* section of this chapter.

How to do it...

First we will have to register an **EJB client JAR** as a resource in Oracle Service Bus. The EJB client JAR contains the necessary interfaces and classes needed by the business service to access the EJB session bean.

In Eclipse OEPE, perform the following steps:

1. Create a new OSB project and name it `exposing-session-bean-as-webservice` and create a `jar`, `business`, and `proxy` folder within it.
2. Open a file explorer window and navigate to the `ejb-jdev-workspace\ejb\deploy` folder.

3. Drag the **customerManagementInterface.jar** file to the Eclipse OEPE and drop it on the **jar** folder of the project, as shown in the following screenshot:

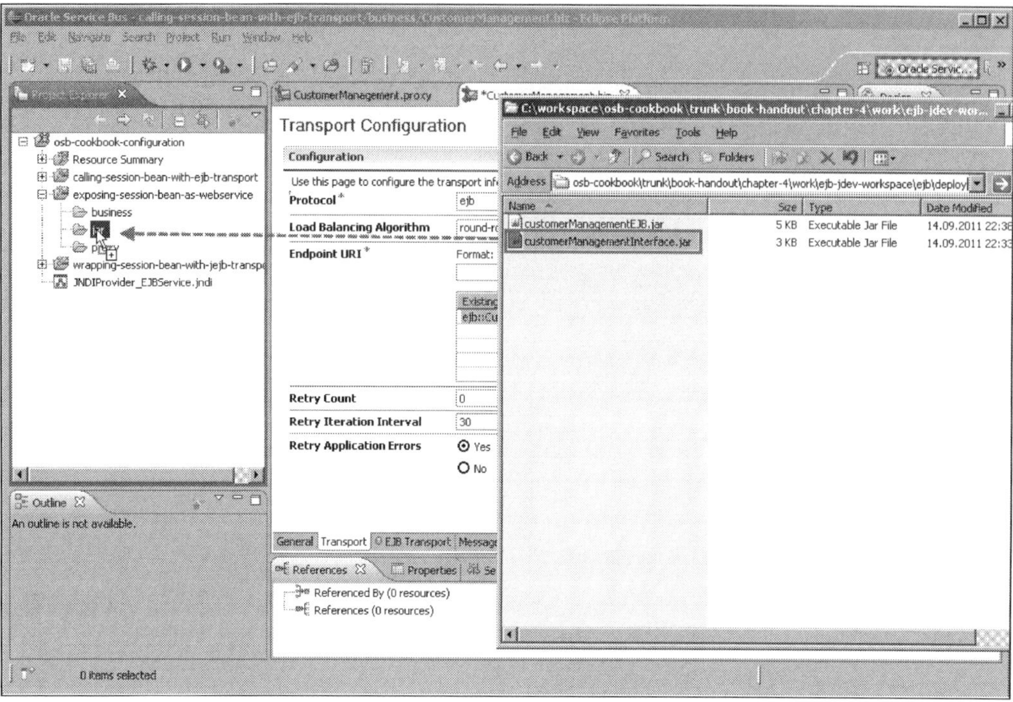

4. On the **File Operation** pop-up window, select the **Copy files** option, and click on **OK**.

Next we create the business service and register the EJB client JAR within the EJB transport configuration. In Eclipse OEPE, perform the following steps:

5. In the `business` folder, create a new business service and name it `CustomerManagement`.
6. On the **General** tab, select the **Transport Typed Service** option for **Service Type**.
7. Navigate to the **Transport** tab.
8. Select **ejb** for the **Protocol**.
9. In the **Endpoint URI** field enter `ejb::CustomerManagementService#cookbook.model.services.CustomerManagement`
10. Click on **Add** to add the URL to the **Existings URIs**.

11. Navigate to the **EJB Transport** tab.
12. Enable the **EJB 3.0** checkbox.
13. Click on **Browse** on the **Client Jar** field, select the **customerManagementInterface.jar** and click **OK**.
14. Based on the information in the EJB client JAR, Eclipse OEPE shows the available methods with the signatures.
15. Rename the **Return** name of the **findAllCustomers** operation to `customers`.
16. Rename the first parameter in the **Parameters** section of the **findCustomer** operation to `id`.
17. Rename the **Return** name of the **findCustomer** operation to `customer`:

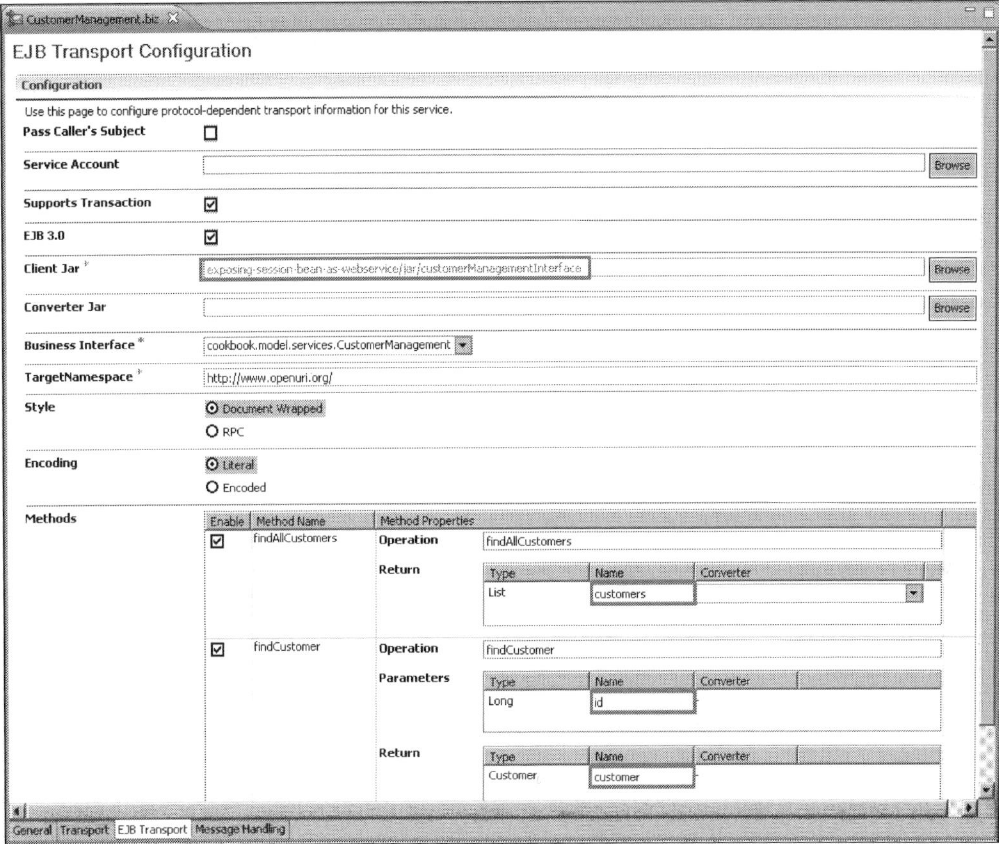

18. Deploy the project to the OSB server.

Now we can already test the business service directly through the OSB console. Perform the following steps:

19. In the **Project Explorer** tree on the left, select the **business** folder of the **exposing-session-bean-as-webservice** project.
20. Click on the **Launch Test Console** icon of the **CustomerManagement** business service.
21. Select the **findCustomer** item from the **Available Operations** drop-down listbox.
22. Change the `id` of the request payload to `100` and click on **Execute**.
23. The **Response Document** section shows the response of the EJB automatically transformed to XML:

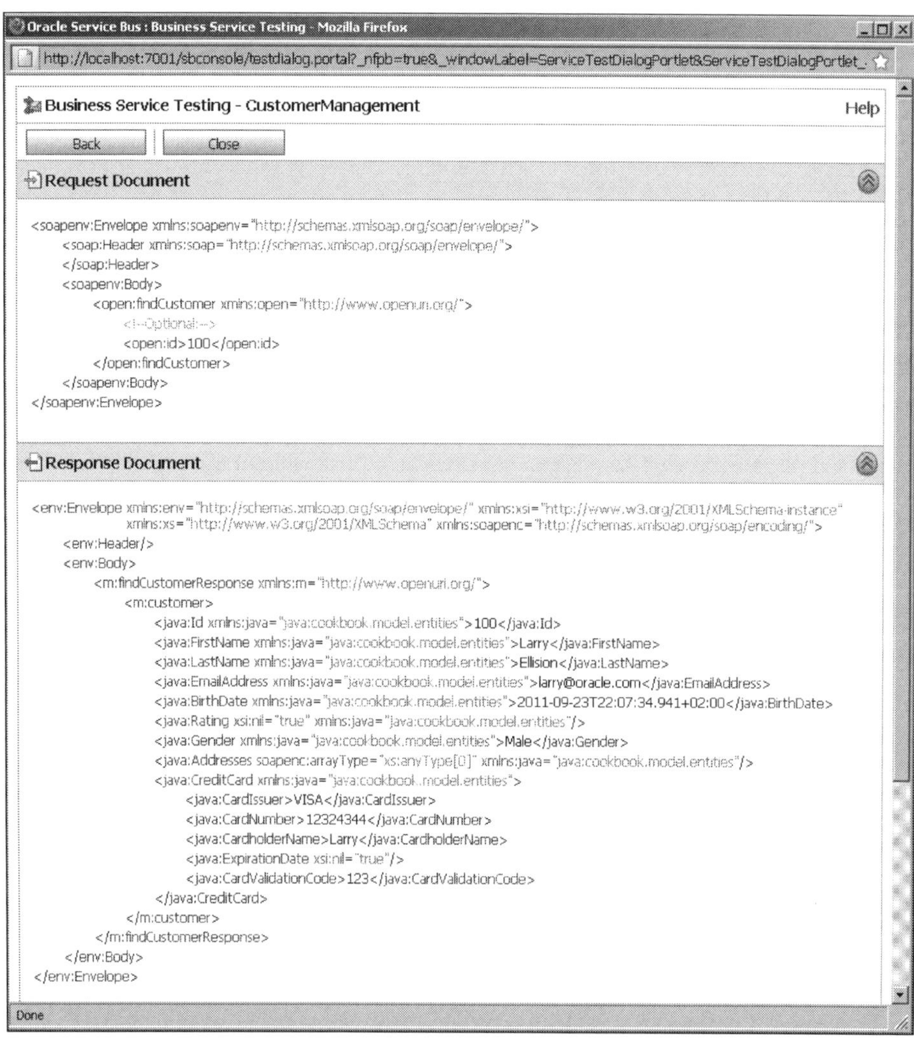

This business service, similar to any other business service, cannot be invoked from outside of OSB. To make it available, we can expose it as a web service.

In order to expose the business service as a web service, we need to know the WSDL of the business service. To retrieve the WSDL of the business service, perform the following steps in the Service Bus console:

24. In the **Project Explorer** tree on the left, select the **business** folder of the **exposing-session-bean-as-webservice** project.
25. Click on the **Export WSLD** icon of the **CustomerManagement** business service.
26. On the pop-up window click on **Save File**.
27. Open the exported file **CustomerManagment_wsdl.jar** with an unzip program such as WinRAR.

In Eclipse OEPE, perform the following steps:

28. Create a **wsdl** folder in the OSB project.
29. Drag the **CustomerManagement.wsdl** file from WinRAR and drop it on the **wsdl** folder.

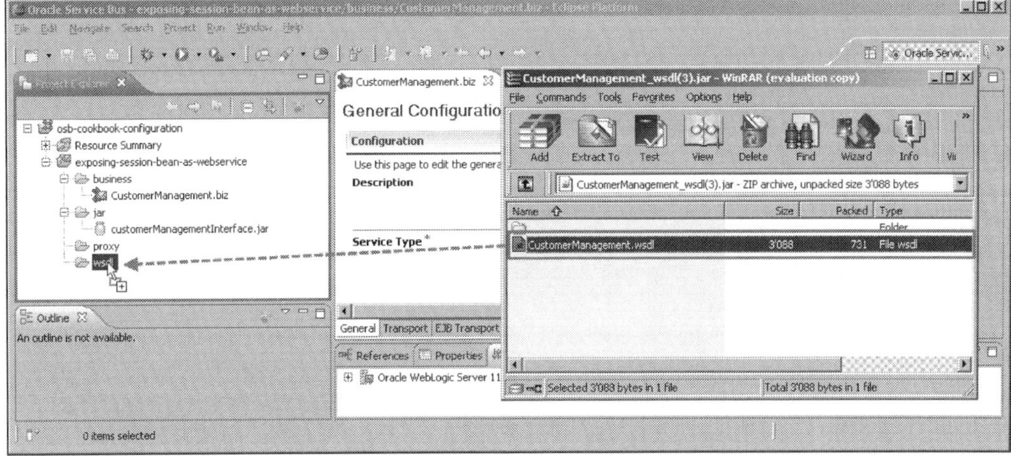

30. On the **File Operation** pop-up window, select **Copy Files**, and click on **OK**.
31. Create a new proxy service and name it **CustomerManagement**.
32. Select **WSDL Web Service** as the **Service Type**.
32. Click on **Browse**, navigate to the **CustomerManagement.wsdl** and select the **JwsServiceSoapBinding (binding)** node.

33. Click on **OK**.
34. Navigate to the **MessageFlow** tab.
35. Drag a **Route** node to the message flow, name it **InvokeEJBRoute**, and add a **Routing** action.
36. On the **Properties** tab of the **Routing** action, click on **Browse** and select the **CustomerManagement.biz** business service.
37. Select the **Use inbound operation for outbound** option.
38. Deploy the project to the OSB server.

Test the web service by either using Service Bus console or soapUI as shown in *Chapter 1, Testing the proxy service through soapUI*. Make sure that you test the `findCustomer` operation and pass 100 for the `id`.

How it works...

We have configured a business service to use the EJB transport so that we can invoke it from the message flow. The EJB transport uses the JAX-RPC stack to perform the Java to XML bindings and vice versa. That's why we have seen the response returned from the business service formatted as XML. The EJB transport natively supports all primitive types, XmlObject, schema-generated XML Beans, and JavaBean classes. If an EJB method uses parameters/return types that are not supported by the JAX-RPC engine or do not map directly to XML, an error will occur. This happens if Java Collections like List, Set, or Map objects are used. In order to support such cases, a custom converter needs to be written and registered to the EJB transport.

This business service can be used like any other business service. It provides a WSDL, holding the definition of the service interface. Such a business service can be used in **Publish**, **Service Callout**, and **Routing** actions.

We have shown the latter in this recipe and implemented a proxy service that exposes the functionality of the EJB session bean on the OSB as a SOAP-based web service. We have directly reused the WSDL the business service provides for simplicity. This should be used with care, as it tightly couples the consumer with the EJB session bean. It's usually far better to let the proxy service implement its own service interface based on a canonical data model, and then use a transformation action to convert between the different XML formats as demonstrated in *Chapter 1, Using an XQuery transformation to map between different data models of the services*.

There's more...

Locate an EJB in the JNDI tree

If we do not know the JNDI name for an EJB, we can browse the EJB Server JNDI tree. In the WebLogic console, perform the following steps:

1. Click on **Environment** of the **Domain Structure** tree.
2. Click on **Servers** on the detail window.
3. Click on the OSB server, that is, **AdminServer (admin)** if it is an admin-only installation.
5. Click on **View JNDI Tree**:

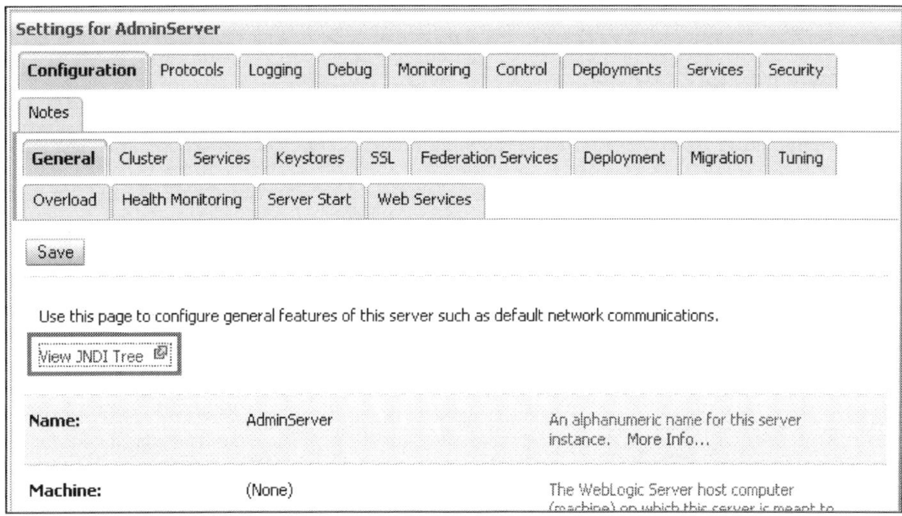

6. A new window with the **JNDI Tree** will show up.

7. In the **JNDI Tree Structure**, navigate to the **CustomerManagementService** EJB session bean:

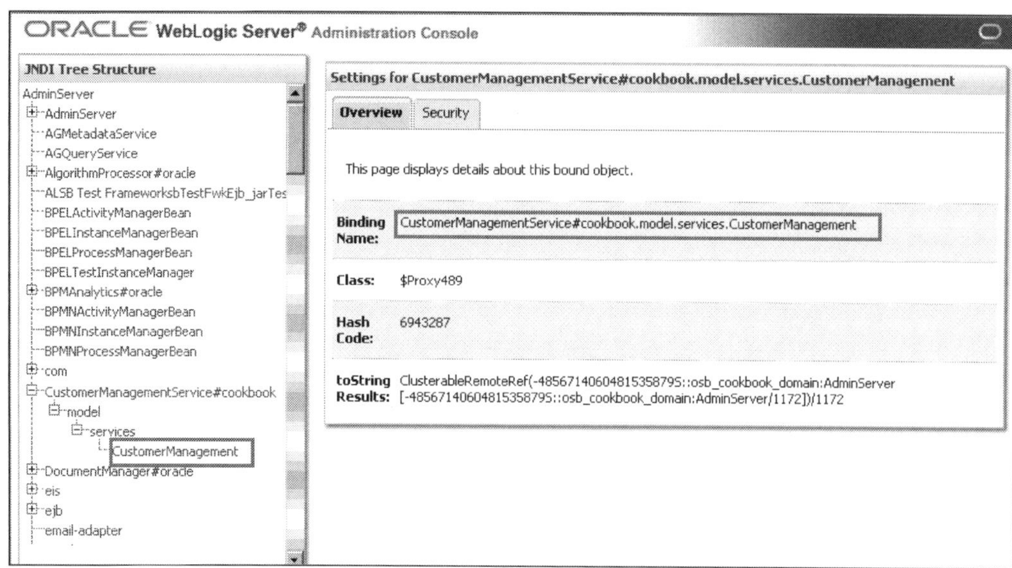

Navigate to the **model** | **services** | **CustomerManagement** interface and the **Binding Names** on the detail view on the right side shows the JNDI name of the session bean.

What if the EJB method returns a list of objects?

If we invoke the `findAllCustomers` method, which returns a list of `Customer` instances, then the list is returned as a soap array in the result and the items of the collection are untyped. This can be seen in the following screenshot:

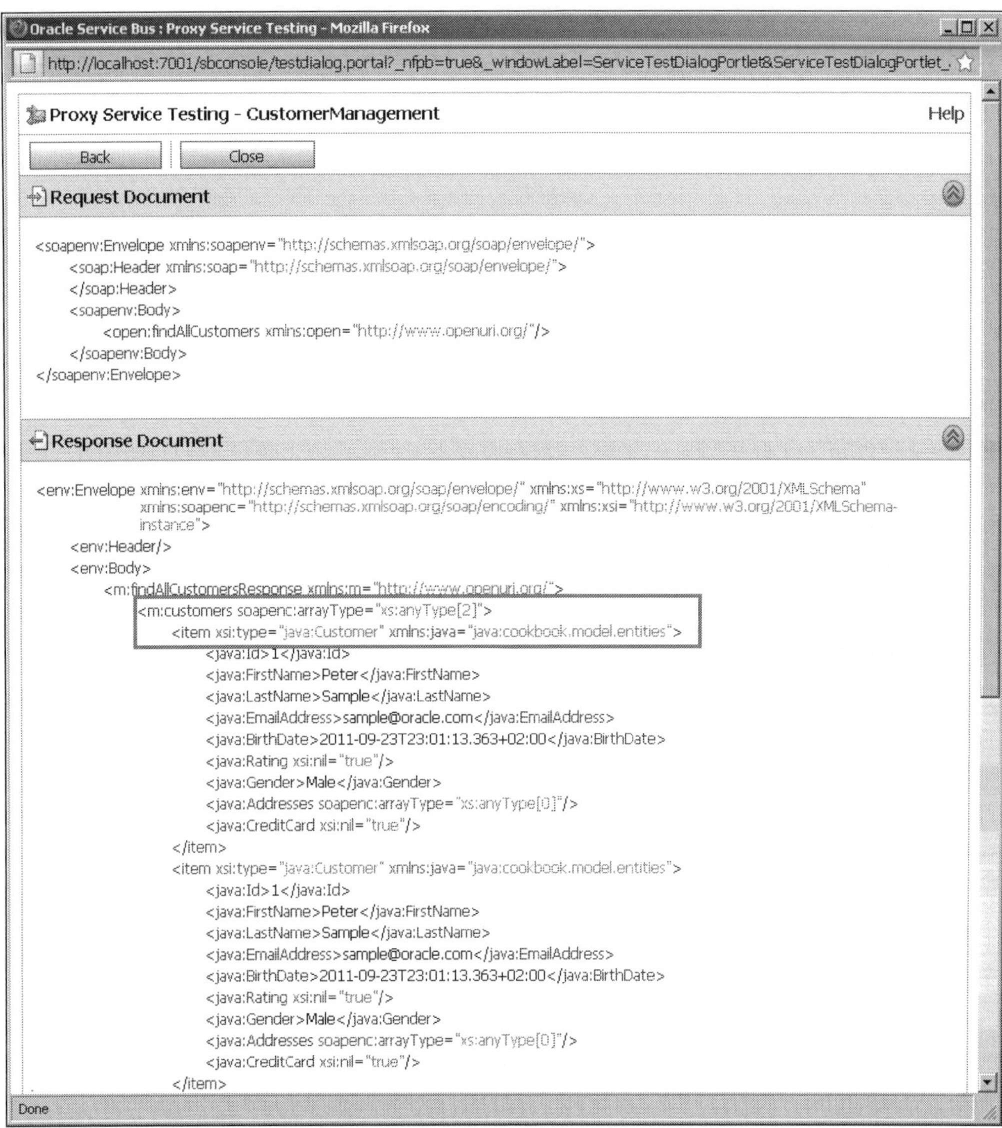

The reason for this is that the JAX RPC engine can't infer the type in the collection. Returning such a soap array can cause some serious interoperability issues, so we should try to avoid that.

The recipe, *Using converter class with EJB transport to help converting data types*, will show how this can be fixed by implementing a `Converter` class.

Using JNDI Provider to invoke an EJB session bean on a remote WebLogic domain

In the recipe, *Exposing an EJB session bean as a service on the OSB using the EJB transport*, we have assumed that the EJB session bean is deployed on the OSB server and by that in the same WebLogic domain.

If the EJB session bean to invoke is deployed on another WebLogic domain, which in the real world is the more typical scenario, then a JNDI Provider resource needs to be created on the OSB configuration.

Getting ready

Make sure that the EJB session bean is deployed to the OSB server as shown in the *Introduction* section of this chapter.

Import the OSB project containing the solution from the recipe, *Exposing an EJB session bean as a service on the OSB using the EJB transport*, into Eclipse from `\chapter-4\getting-ready\using-jndi-provider-to-invoke-remote-ejb`.

How to do it...

In Eclipse OEPE, perform the following steps to register a JNDI Provider resource:

1. Right-click on the **obs-cookbook-configuration** configuration project and select **New | JNDIProvider**.
2. Enter `JNDIProviderEJB` into the **File name** field and click on **Next**.
3. Enter the URL of the JNDI Provider, in our case `t3://localhost:7001` into the **Provider URL** field.
4. If access to the target JNDI Provider requires a username and password, enter it into the **User Name**, **Password**, and **Confirm Password** fields:

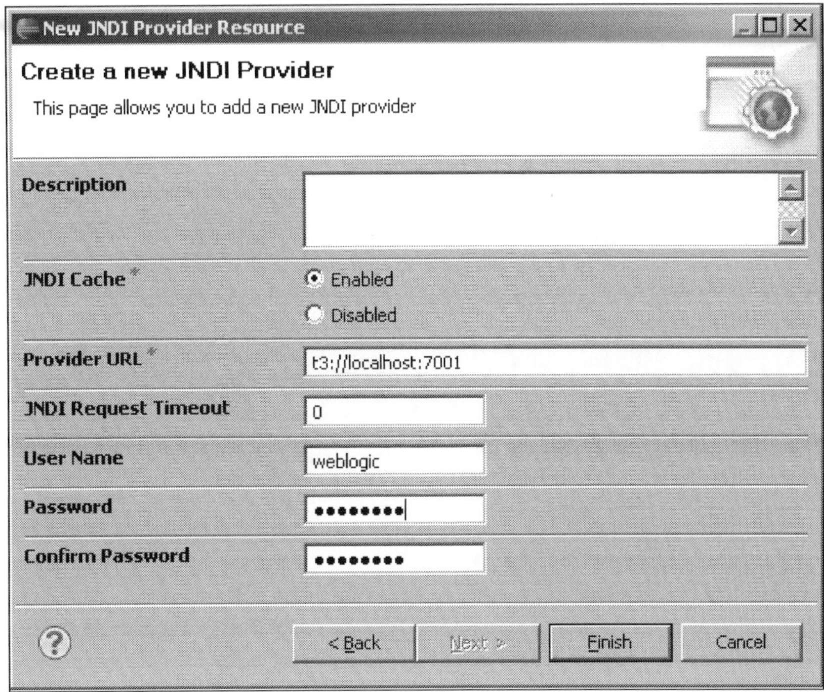

5. Click on the **Finish** button.
6. In order for the business service to use the JNDI Provider, the Endpoint URI needs to be changed:
7. Navigate to the **Transport** tab of the **CustomerManagement.biz** business service.
8. Delete the existing URI by clicking on **Delete** on the right side of the list.
9. Enter the following value into the **Endpoint URI** field and click on **Add**: `ejb:JNDIProviderEJB:CustomerManagementService#cookbook.model.services.CustomerManagement`. The only difference to the old URI is the JNDI Provider specified after the `ejb:` prefix.
10. Deploy the project to the OSB server.

The business service is now using the configured JNDI Provider to get and cache the EJB stubs.

The preferred communication mechanism from an OSB to a WebLogic server domain is either **t3** or **t3s**, as used here.

How it works...

A JNDI Provider allows us to specify the communication protocols and security credentials used to retrieve the EJB subs bound in a JNDI tree located on a remove WebLogic server domain.

The JNDI Provider also implements an efficient caching mechanism for the remote connections as well as the EJB stubs.

If the EJBs are located in the same domain, a JNDI Provider can also be used to specify credentials and take advantage of the caching mechanism, but it's optional.

Using converter class with EJB transport to help converting data types

Usually, data conversion between an EJB and OSB is done for you in OSB. However, when dealing with EJBs, there are times when automatic conversion is simply not possible. For example, if the EJB returns any of the following, the JAX RPC engine will not be able to infer the true type being returned:

- `java.lang.Object`
- `java.lang.Object[]`
- Java Collections that are not strongly typed
- Java classes that do not follow JavaBean conventions (like the Map class)

In such cases, we can help the JAX RPC engine, by providing `converter` classes that convert from these types to the supported types.

In this recipe, we will change the mapping of the `findAllCustomers` method by using a `converter` class from the EJB transport on the business service, so that the method returns a typed result.

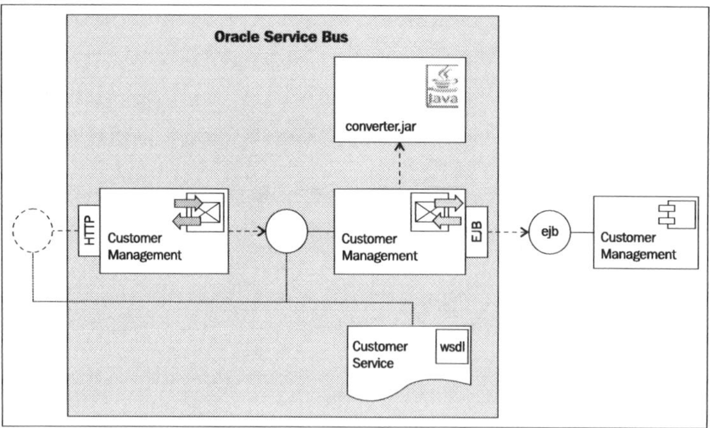

We have already created a `converter` class that converts the list of customers to a customer array. The following screenshot shows the implementation of the converter, which is available in the `converter.jar` archive file in the `ejb-jdev-workspace\ejb\deploy` folder:

```
package cookbook.converter;

import ...;

public class CustomerConverter implements ITypeConverter {
    public static Customer[] convert(List customerList) {
        int listSize = customerList.size();
        Customer[] custArray =  new Customer[listSize];
        custArray = (Customer[])customerList.toArray(custArray);
        return custArray;
    }

}
```

The important things to know when implementing a `converter` class are:

- You must implement the `com.bea.wli.sb.transports.ejb.ITypeConverter` interface, available in the `sb-kernel-api.jar` file that is found in the `osb_10.3\lib` directory of the OSB installation.
- You must have a public static method named `convert`. The return value of this method may be any type at all, but the arguments to the method must be an `Object`, `Object []`, Collection, List, Map, etc. Otherwise the OSB will not show the class as an available converter.

Getting ready

Make sure that the EJB session bean is deployed to the OSB server as shown in the *Introduction* section of this chapter.

Import the OSB project containing the solution from the recipe, *Exposing an EJB session bean as a service on the OSB using the EJB transport*, into Eclipse from `\chapter-4\getting-ready\using-converter-with-ejb-transport`.

How to do it...

In Eclipse OEPE, perform the following steps:

1. Copy the `converter.jar` from the `ejb-jdev-workspace\ejb\deploy` folder into the `jar` folder of the project.

2. Open the **CustomerManagement** business service and navigate to the **EJB Transport** tab.
3. Click on the **Browse** button, to the right of the **Converter Jar** field.
4. Select the `converter.jar` file inside the `jar` folder:

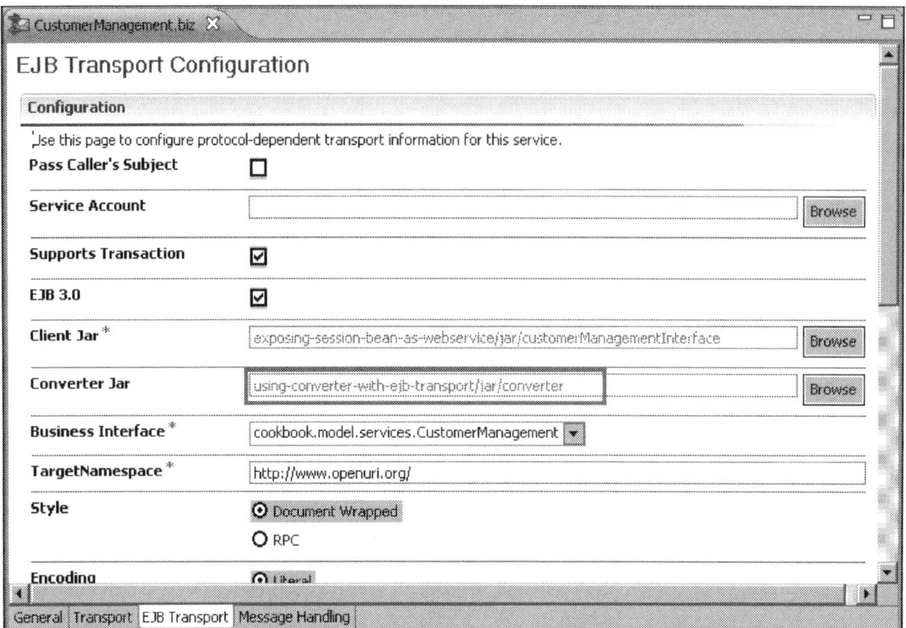

5. Scroll down to the **Methods** section. Select the **cookbook.converter. CustomerConverter** class for the **Return** value of the **findAllCustomers** method:

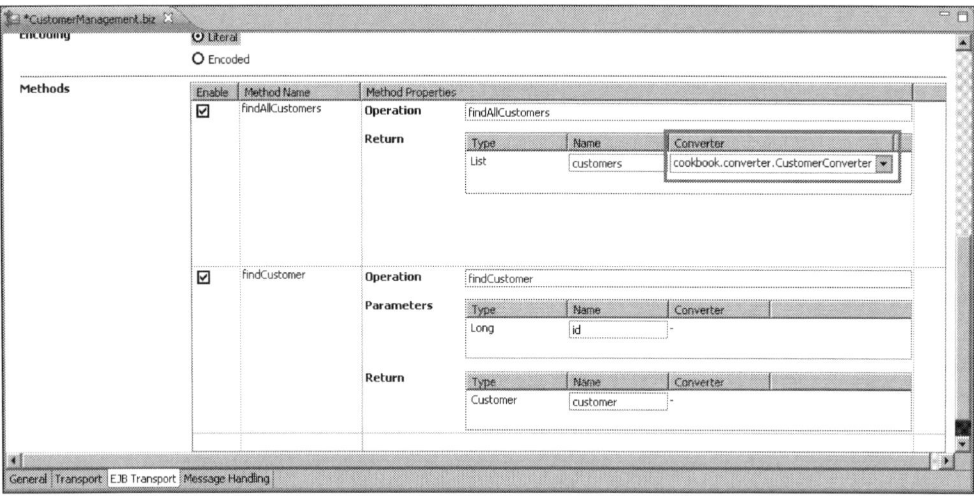

6. Deploy the project to the OSB server.

Now, retest the proxy service from the Service Bus console. Invoke the **findAllCustomers** operation from the Test console and the following result should be shown:

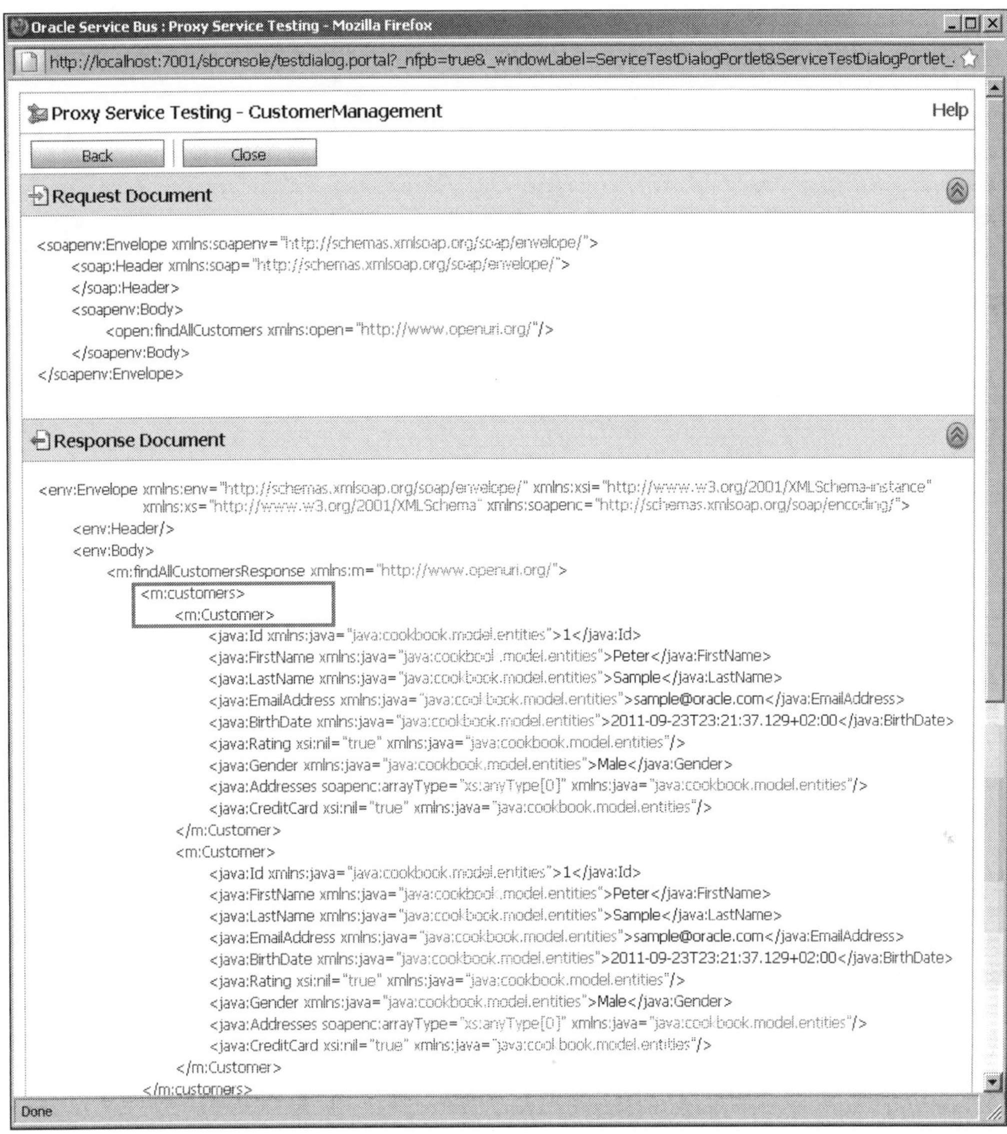

If you compare that to the result we have seen in the previous recipe, we can see that there is no longer a soap array being returned.

How it works...

By implementing a `converter` class and registering it on the EJB transport configuration of the business service, we were able to change the mapping of the list of customers being returned by the `findAllCustomers` method. Instead of the untyped soap array, which can cause a lot of interoperability issues, we now return a collection of `customer` objects, that more closely matches the signature of the EJB session bean method.

The `converter` class translated the list of customers to a customer array, which the JAX RPC engine understands.

Exposing an EJB session bean as an EJB on the OSB using the JEJB transport

The JEJB transport allows passing POJOs through the OSB. We can use the JEJB transport on proxy service and expose the proxy service as a remote EJB. For the consumer/client, the proxy service looks like a normal stateless session bean. This will add an additional layer between the client and some existing EJB session beans, which provides additional functionality and agility, such as:

- Replacing the original EJB by something else, that still provides the same interface to the existing clients
- Doing some transformations between the EJB client and the EJB session bean implementation
- Implementing logging
- Using the capabilities of OSB to monitor SLA's

In this recipe, we will implement the same EJB session bean interface on the OSB and just pass-through the messages:

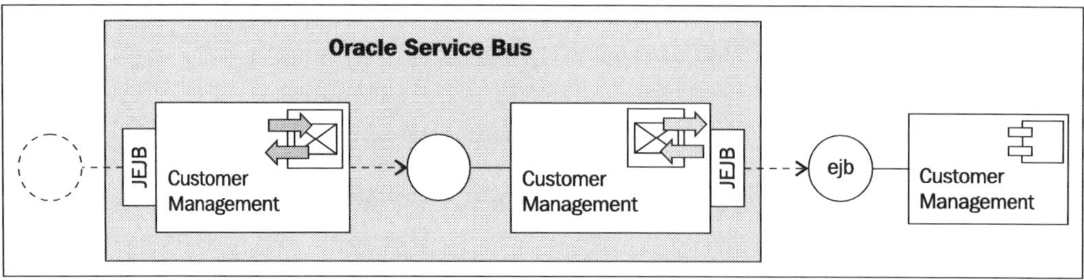

Getting ready

Make sure that the EJB session bean is deployed to the OSB server as shown in the *Introduction* section of this chapter.

How to do it...

First we have to create a new OSB project and then register the customer management service interface JAR. To make the JAR available, we will use the `Import` functionality of Eclipse OEPE. This is an alternative way to the copy-paste approach we have used in the previous recipe. In Eclipse OEPE, perform the following steps:

1. Create a new OSB project `exposing-session-bean-as-ejb` and create a `jar`, `business`, and `proxy` folder in this new project.
2. Select the `jar` folder and from the **File** menu select **Import**.
3. Expand the `General` folder, select **File System**, and click on **Next**.
4. Click on **Browse** next to the **From directory** field and navigate to the `deploy` folder in the `Model` project folder.
5. Only select the **customerManagementInterface.jar** and click on **Finish**:

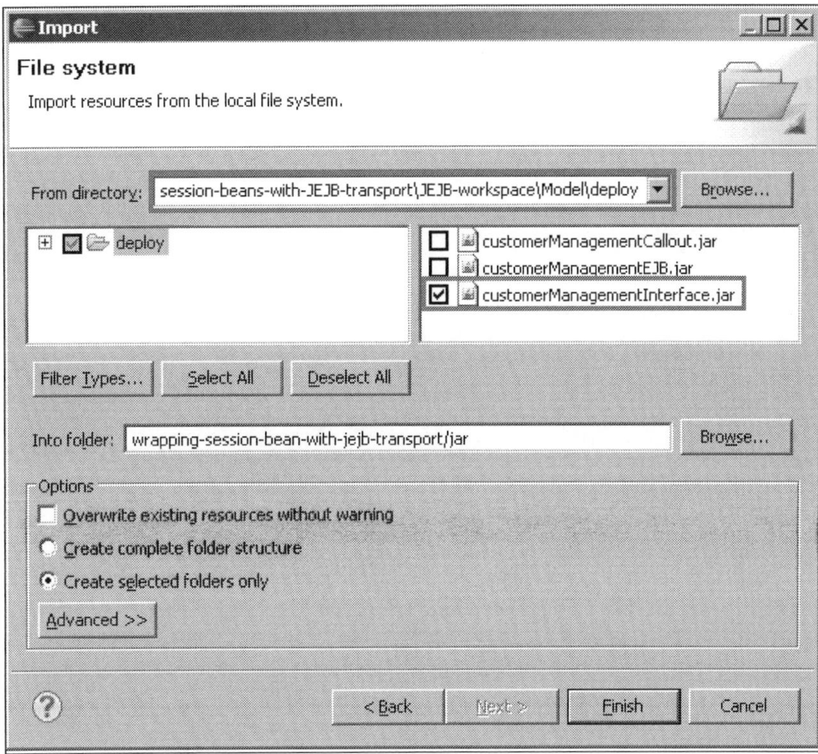

Next, we will create a new business service that will call the customer management EJB session bean:

1. Within the `business` folder, create a new business service and name it `CustomerManagement`.
2. On the **General** tab select **Transport Typed Service** as the **Service Type**.
3. Navigate to the **Transport** tab.
4. Select **jejb** for the **Protocol** drop-down listbox.
5. Enter `jejb::CustomerManagementService#cookbook.model.services.CustomerManagement` into the **Endpoint URI** field and click on **Add**.
6. Navigate to the **JEJB Transport** tab.
7. Choose **3.0** for the **EJB Spec Version**.
8. Click on the **Browse** button next to the **Client Jar** field.
9. In the **Select a Java Archive Resource** window, expand the **wrapping-session-bean-with-jejb-transport** project.
10. Select the **customerManagementInterface.jar** and click on **OK**.
11. Rename the **Return** name of the **findAllCustomers** operation to `customers`.
12. Change the **Parameters name** field of the **findCustomer** method to `id`.
13. Rename the **Return** name of the **findCustomer** operation to `customer`:

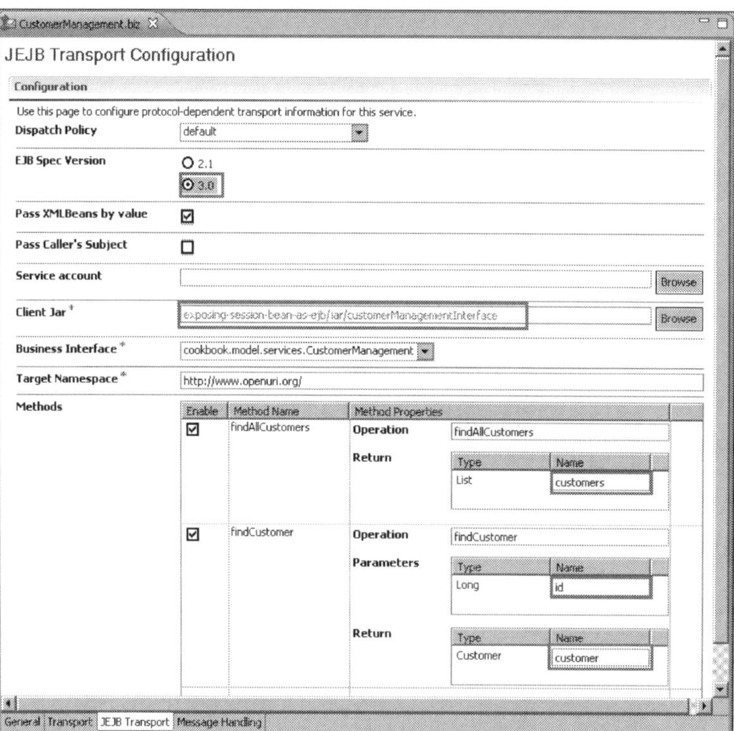

Create a proxy service with a JEJB transport, which calls this business service. In Eclipse OEPE, perform the following steps:

14. Right-click on the **CustomerManagement.biz** business service and select **Oracle Service Bus | Generate Proxy Service**.
15. Select the **proxy** folder in the tree and enter `CustomerManagement` into the **File name** field.
16. Navigate to the **JEJB Transport** tab.
17. Choose **3.0** for the **EJB Spec Version** option and make sure that the **Pass XMLBeans by value** checkbox is enabled.
18. Click on the **Browse** button next to the **Client Jar** field.
19. In the **Select a Java Archive Resource** window, expand the **wrapping-session-bean-with-jejb-transport** project, select the **customerManagementInterface.jar**, and click on **OK**.
20. Rename the **Return** name of the **findAllCustomers** operation to `customers`.
21. Change the **Parameters name** field of the **findCustomer** method to `id`.
22. Rename the **Return** name of the **findCustomer** operation to `customer`:

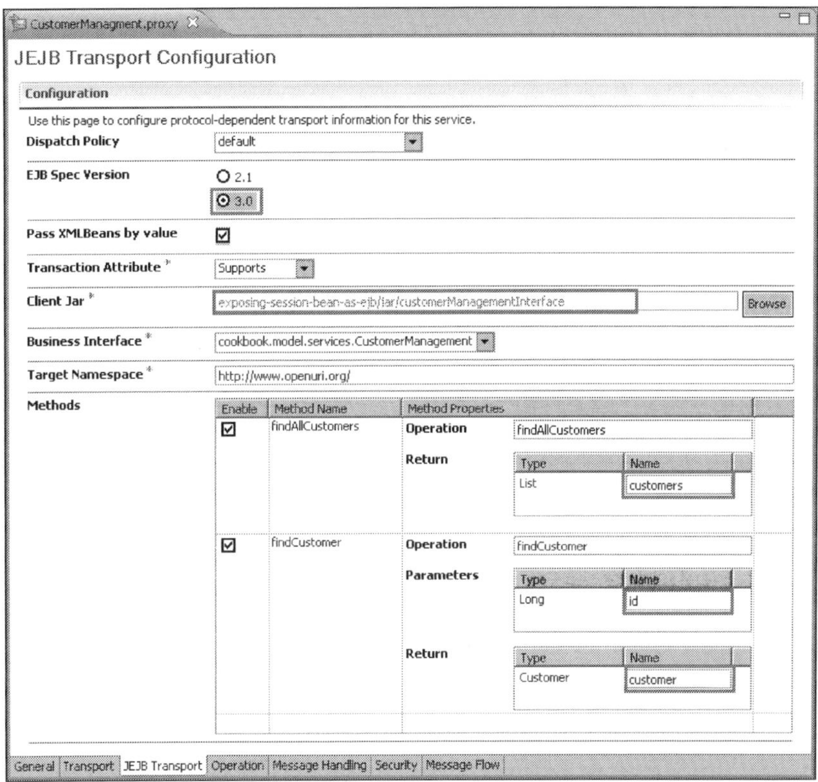

23. Navigate to the **Message Flow** tab.
24. Navigate to the **Properties** tab of the **Routing** action, which has been generated and enable the **Use inbound operation for outbound** option.
25. To see the information passed into the proxy service we log the value of the `$body` variable. Right-click on the **Request** action and select **Insert Into | Reporting | Log** to add a **Log** action.
26. Click on **Expression**, enter `$body` as the expression, and click on the **OK** button.
27. Enter `$body in Request` into the **Annotation** field and select **Warning** for the **Severity** drop-down listbox.
28. To see the information returned by the EJB session bean, we log the value of the `$body` variable. Copy the **Log** action from the **Request Action** and paste it into the **Response Action**.
29. Enter `$body in Response` into the **Annotation** field:

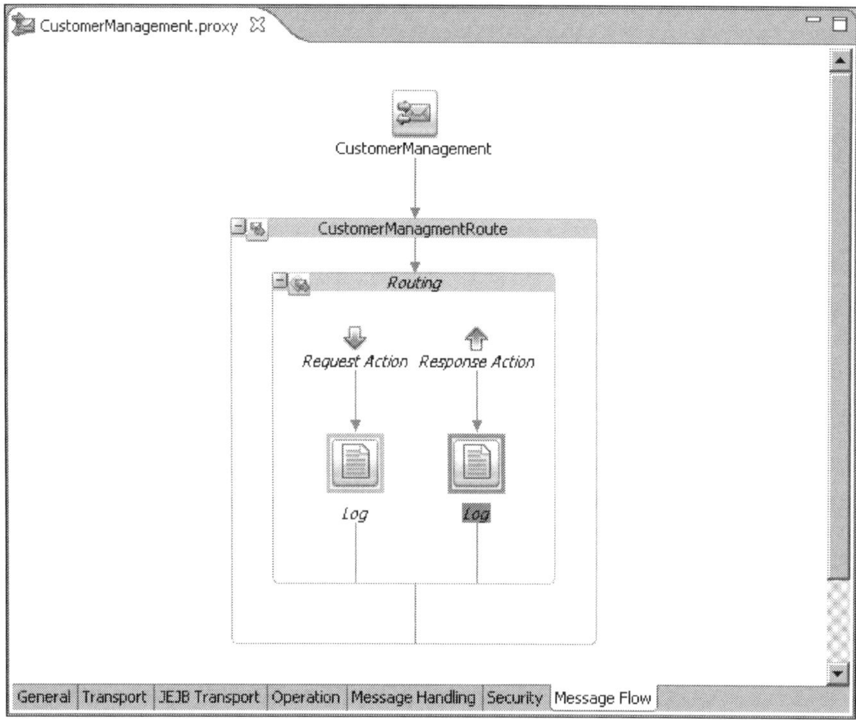

30. Save the project and deploy it to the OSB server.

Now it's time to test the OSB service. In JDeveloper, again open the `osbbook_jejb.ws` workspace and perform the following steps to change the already used Java test class to no longer invoke the EJB session bean, but invoke the proxy service with the JEJB transport:

31. Open the **osbbook_jejb.jws** workspace and expand the **client** project until reaching the **CustomerManagementClient.java** class.
32. Change the JNDI name of the `context.lookup` code:

```
CustomerManagement customerManagement = (CustomerManagement)
context.lookup("CustomerManagement#cookbook.model.services.
CustomerManagement");
```

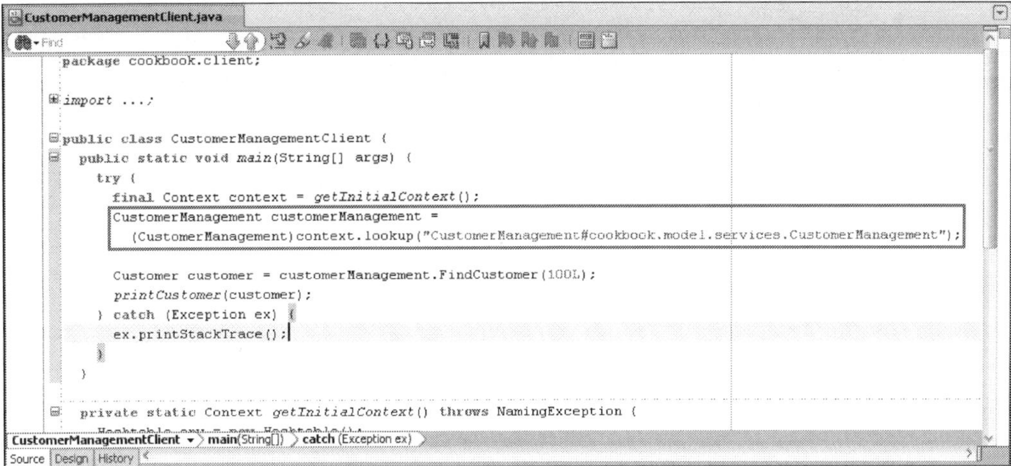

33. Right-click on the `CustomerManagementClient.java` file and select **Run**.
34. Check that the output in the JDeveloper **Log** window is the same as before, when testing the EJB session bean directly.

35. We can check that the proxy service really was executed by checking the output of the two **Log** actions:

```
OSB Cookbook 11R2 PS3 (11.1.1.4)
ot enabled for the EJB 'exposing_session_bean_as_ejb_busine4371EJB'. The server
will have better performance if it is enabled. To enable call-by-reference, set
the enable-call-by-reference element to True in the weblogic-ejb-jar.xml deploym
ent descriptor or corresponding annotation for this EJB.>
<18.09.2011 13:05 Uhr MESZ> <Warning> <ALSB Logging> <BEA-000000> < [RouteTo_Cus
tomerManagement, null, null, REQUEST] $body in Request: <soap:Body xmlns:soap="h
ttp://schemas.xmlsoap.org/soap/envelope/">
  <ns:findCustomer xmlns:ns="http://www.openuri.org/">
    <ns:id>100</ns:id>
  </ns:findCustomer>
</soap:Body>>
<18.09.2011 13:05 Uhr MESZ> <Warning> <ALSB Logging> <BEA-000000> < [RouteTo_Cus
tomerManagement, null, null, RESPONSE] $body in Response: <soap:Body xmlns:soap=
"http://schemas.xmlsoap.org/soap/envelope/">
  <ns:findCustomerResponse xmlns:ns="http://www.openuri.org/">
    <ns:customers>
      <con:java-content ref="jcid:-7e89d5a5:1327b339122:-7f9b" xmlns:con="http:/
/www.bea.com/wli/sb/context"/>
    </ns:customers>
  </ns:findCustomerResponse>
</soap:Body>>
```

The value of the request, which on the transport level is a Java bean, is translated into an XML representation with all the properties (`id` in our case) as elements. We have triggered this behavior by enabling the **Pass XMLBeans by value** on the JEJB transport configuration of the proxy service. This is of course helpful if we need to trigger some action based on the value of the request message or we need to simply log the request message.

This is not the case with the response. In the response, we only get a reference to the Java object. If we need access to the values, then we have to use a Java Callout action that we will cover in the next recipe, *Manipulating the response of the JEJB transport by a Java Callout action*.

How it works...

The JEJB transport lets us pass POJOs through the OSB. We created a proxy service which implements the same EJB interface as the business service wrapping the EJB session bean on the EJB server. To switch to the EJB implementation on the OSB in the consuming Java class, we only had to change the JNDI alias of the context lookup to point to the EJB interface implemented by the proxy service.

To the Java EE client, the JEJB proxy service looks like an EJB stateless session bean.

The JEBJ transport is always synchronous and the message exchange pattern is always request-response.

Manipulating the response of the JEJB transport by a Java Callout action

In this recipe, we show how to change the response and enrich the message by a value for the rating attribute. For that, we have to create a Java class that we will call from the message flow of the proxy service through a Java Callout action:

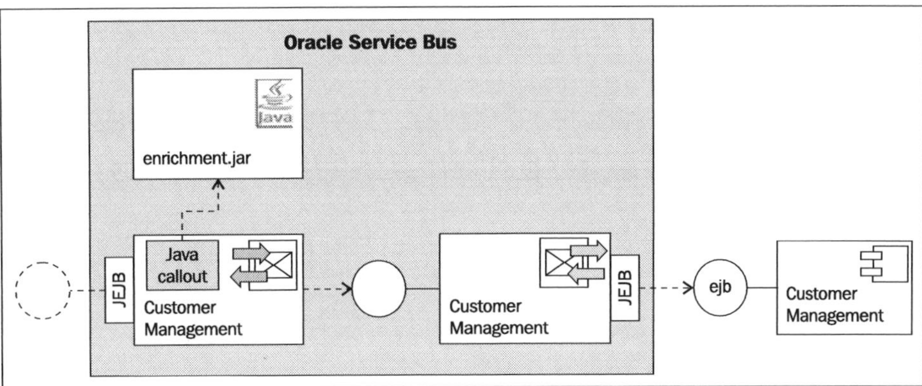

We have created a simple Java class as shown in the following screenshot:

CustomerResponse.java

```
package cookbook.javacallout;

import ...;

public class CustomerResponse {
    public CustomerResponse() {
    }

    public static Object enrichCustomerResponse(Object cust ){
      Customer customer = (Customer)cust;

      // assign the rating ....
      if (customer.getFirstName().equals("Larry")) {
        customer.setRating("AAA");
      } else {
        customer.setRating("AA");
      }

      return customer;
    }
}
```

CustomerResponse ▾ › enrichCustomerResponse(Object)

Source | Design | History

As we can see, this Java class has one method, which enriches the value of the rating attribute of a customer object based on the value of the first name attribute. The method accepts a parameter of type `Object` and cast this to a `Customer` type.

To make it available to OSB, we have to package the Java classes into a JAR. This JAR is available as `enrichment.jar` in the `ejb-jdev-workspace\ejb\deploy` folder.

Getting ready

Make sure that the EJB session bean is deployed to the OSB server as shown in the *Introduction* section of this chapter.

Import the base OSB project containing the necessary schemas and the right folder structure into Eclipse from `\chapter-4\getting-ready\change-response-of-jejb-transport`.

How to do it...

Let's make the Java class available in the OSB project. In Eclipse OEPE, perform the following steps:

1. Copy the JAR file `enrichment.jar` from the `ejb-jdev-workspace\ejb\deploy` folder and paste it into the `jar` folder.
2. To add the **Java Callout** action, open the **CustomerManagement** proxy service and navigate to the **Message Flow** tab
3. In the **Response Action**, insert a **Java Callout** action after the **Log** action. Right-click on the **Log action** inside the **Response** Action and select **Insert After | Message Processing | Java Callout**.
4. On the **Properties** tab of the **Java Callout** action, click on **Browse**.
5. Expand the tree and navigate to the `enrichmentByCallout.jar` file.
6. Click on **OK**.
7. Expand the **CustomerResponse** node and select the static `enrichCustomerResponseByRating` method:

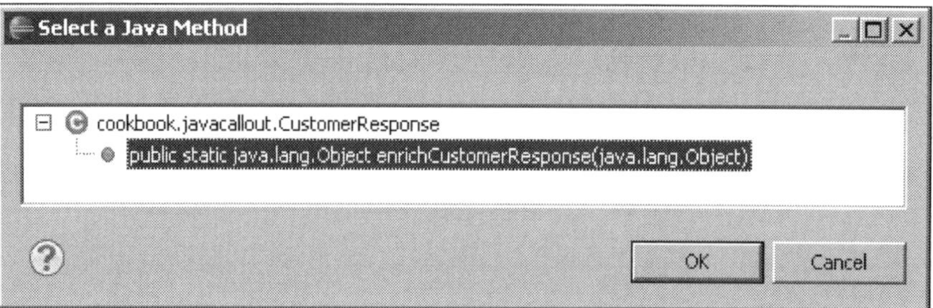

8. Click on **OK**.
9. On the **Properties** tab of the **Java Callout** action, click on **Expression** in the **Action** cell.
10. Enter `$body/open:findCustomerResponse/open:customer/ctx:java-content` into the **Expression** field.
11. Click on **OK**.
12. Back on the **Properties** tab of the **Java Callout** action enter `changedResponse` into the **Result Value** field:

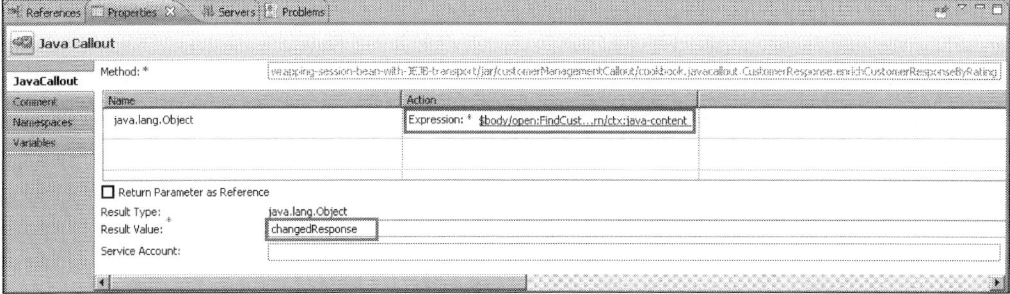

13. Right-click on the **Java Callout** action and select **Insert After | Message Processing | Replace**.
14. On the **Properties** tab of the **Replace** action enter `body` into the **In Variable** field.
15. Click on **XPath** and enter `/open:findCustomerResponse/open:customer/ctx:java-content`.
16. Click on **Expression** and enter `$changedResponse`, which holds the reference to the POJO returned from the **Java Callout** action.
17. Enable the **Replace entire node** option:

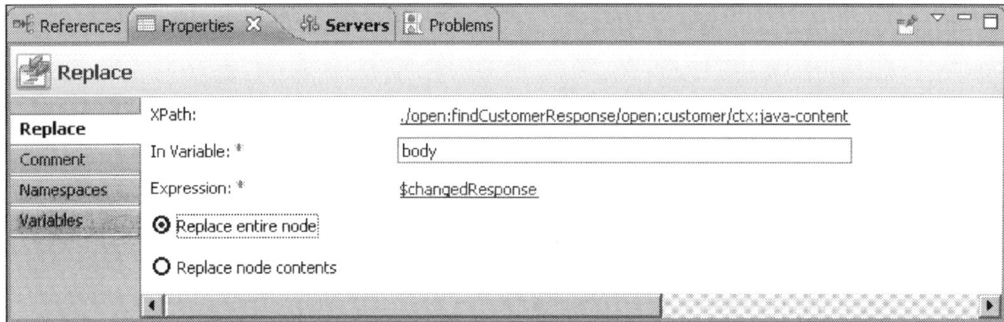

18. The message flow should now look as shown in the following screenshot:

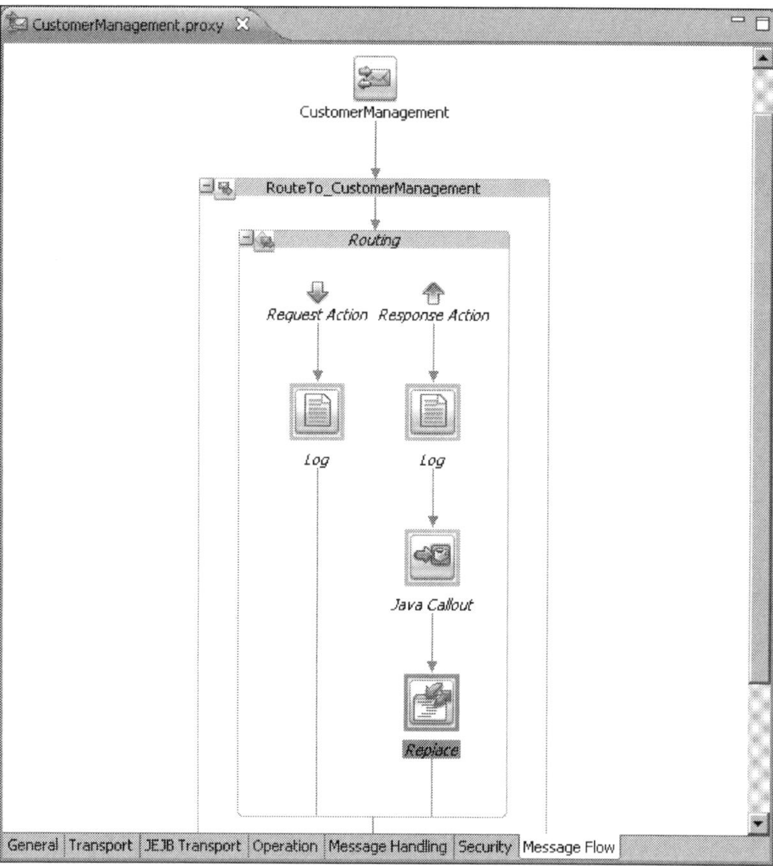

19. Save the project and deploy it to the OSB server.

Retest the implementation by using the same Java test class. The rating should no longer be null:

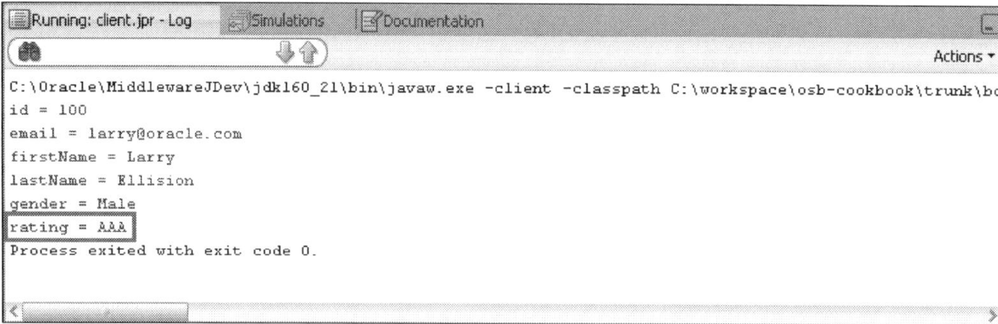

How it works...

When we examine the log output, we can see that the response from the EJB session bean contained in the body has the following content:

```
<soap:Body xmlns:soap="...">
  <ns:findCustomerResponse xmlns:ns="http://www.openuri.org/">
    <ns:customer>
      <con:java-content
         ref="jcid:-6bfa91a1:132950119a5:-7f3a"
         xmlns:con="http://www.bea.com/wli/sb/context"/>
    </ns:customer>
  </ns:findCustomerResponse>
</soap:Body>
```

The value of the `con:java-content` element, holds the reference to the POJO being passed back by the EJB session bean method. By passing that value of `con:java-content` to the **Java Callout**, we can then access the POJO in our enricher Java class.

The object returned from the enricher Java Callout is also in the form of `con:java-content`, which is used in the **Replace** action to overwrite the `con:java-content` part of the `body` variable.

There's more...

Be careful when using the **Variable Structures** tree to specify an expression into the `java-content` part (step 10 in the recipe).

If the argument names of the methods have been renamed, that is, from return to customer in our case, then the drag-and-drop feature implemented in Eclipse OEPE will not be aware of it.

If we drag the **java-content** element as shown in the following screenshot into the **Expression** field, then we manually have to replace **return** by **customer**, to get the correct expression `$body/open:findCustomerResponse/open:customer/ctx:java-content`:

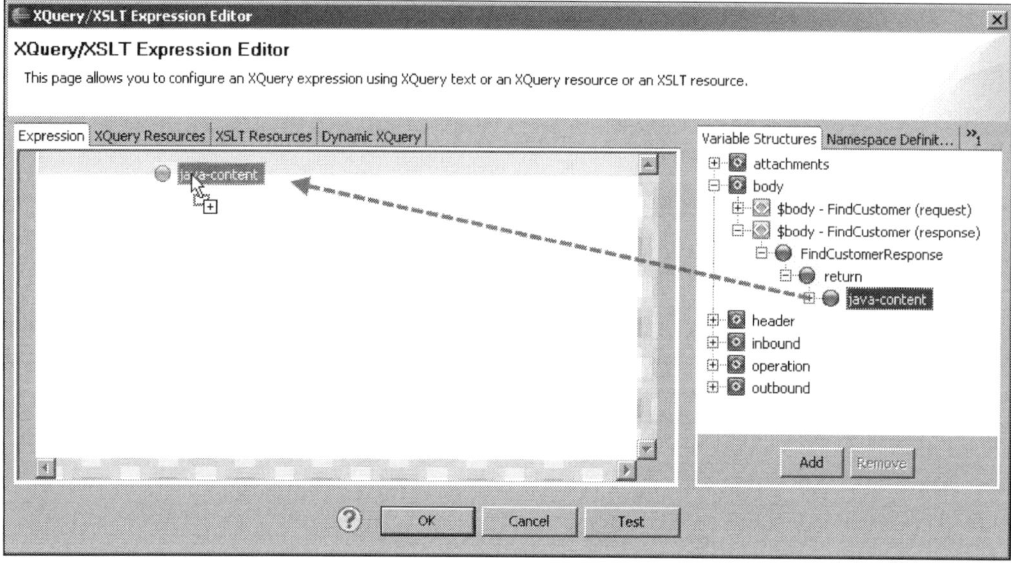

5

Using HTTP Transport

In this chapter, we will cover:

- Using HTTP transport to implement messaging over HTTP
- Exposing a RESTful service on the OSB
- Consuming a RESTful service from the OSB
- Creating a generic RESTful gateway on the OSB
- Implementing a WebSocket transport for server-side push

Introduction

In this chapter, we will cover the HTTP transport.

The HTTP transport allows sending messages between clients and service providers through Oracle Service Bus using the http(s) protocol. The HTTP transport also provides support for working with RESTful (**REST** = **Representational State Transfer**) services.

The HTTP transport can be used on the proxy service to accept inbound messages over the HTTP protocol as well as on the business service to implement outbound communication over HTTP.

We have already used the HTTP transport when implementing the SOAP-based service in *Chapter 1, Creating a basic OSB service*. In this chapter, we will present how to work with the HTTP transport without using SOAP.

Using HTTP transport to implement messaging over HTTP

Instead of sending SOAP over HTTP, the HTTP transport can be used for doing simple messaging over HTTP. In this recipe, we will show how easy it is to implement a proxy service on the OSB accepting text/XML messages:

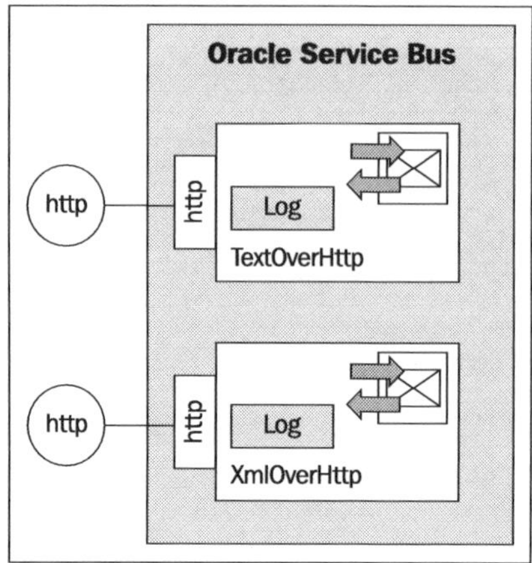

How to do it...

We will first create a proxy service that accepts any text-based messages over HTTP. In Eclipse OEPE, perform the following steps:

1. Create a new project and name it `using-http-for-msg-over-http`.
2. Create a `proxy` folder.
3. In the `proxy` folder, create a new proxy service and name it `TextOverHttp`.
4. On the **General** tab select **Messaging Service** for the **Service Type**.
5. Navigate to the **Messaging** tab and select **Text** for the **Request Message Type**.
6. Leave the **Response Message Type** to **None**.
7. Navigate to the **Message Flow** tab and insert a **Pipeline Pair** node named **HandleMessagePipeline**.
8. Insert a **Stage** node into the **Pipeline Pair** and name it `LogStage`.
9. Insert a **Log** action into the **LogStage**.
10. On the **Properties** tab of the **Log** action, click **<Expression>** and enter `$body` into the **Expression** field. Click **OK**.
11. Change the **Severity** level of the **Log** action to **Warning**.

Next let's implement a similar proxy, but this time accepting only XML. In Eclipse OEPE, perform the following steps:

12. In the `proxy` folder, create a new proxy service and name it `XmlOverHttp`.
13. On the **General** tab select **Messaging Service** for the **Service Type**.
14. Navigate to the **Messaging** tab and select **Xml** for the **Request Message Type**.
15. Leave the **Response Message Type** to **None**.
16. Navigate to the **Message Flow** tab, copy **HandleMessagePipeline** from the **TextOverHttp** proxy service and paste it here.
17. Deploy the project to the OSB server.

We now have two proxy services in place, one accepting Text and the other XML. Let's test the behavior through the console. In the Service Bus console, perform the following steps:

18. In the **Project Explorer**, navigate to the **TextOverHttp** proxy service and click on the **Launch Test Console** icon.
19. Enter `Hello from OSB!` into the **Payload** field and click **Execute**.
20. The Service Bus console log window will show the message from the Log action.

```
<06.10.2011 08:06 Uhr MESZ> <Warning> <ALSB Logging> <BEA-000000>
< [HandleMessagePipeline, HandleMessagePipeline_request, LogStage,
REQUEST]
<soapenv:Body
  xmlns:soapenv="http://schemas.xmlsoap.org/soap/envelope/">
  Hello from OSB!
</soapenv:Body>>
```

21. Now test again by clicking **Back**, entering the XML fragment `<message>Hello from OSB!</message>` into the **Payload** field and then clicking **OK**.

```
<06.10.2011 08:08 Uhr MESZ> <Warning> <ALSB Logging> <BEA-000000>
< [HandleMessagePipeline, HandleMessagePipeline_request, LogStage,
REQUEST]
<soapenv:Body
  xmlns:soapenv="http://schemas.xmlsoap.org/soap/envelope/">&lt;
  message>Hello from OSB!&lt;/message>
</soapenv:Body>>
```

We can see that a proxy service using **Text** for the **Message Type** handles everything as plain text.

Now let's test the second service, the **XmlOverHttp** proxy service.

22. Click on the **Launch Test Console** icon of the **XmlOverHttp** proxy service.
23. Enter the XML fragment `<message>Hello from OSB!</message>` into the **Payload** field and then click **OK**.

```
<06.10.2011 08:11 Uhr MESZ> <Warning> <ALSB Logging> <BEA-000000>
< [HandleMessagePipeline, HandleMessagePipeline_request, LogStage,
REQUEST]
<soapenv:Body
  xmlns:soapenv="http://schemas.xmlsoap.org/soap/envelope/">
  <message>Hello from OSB!</message>
</soapenv:Body>>
```

We can see that a proxy service using **Xml** for the **Message Type** now really handles the message as XML and embeds it inside the `<soapenv:Body>` element.

How it works...

This recipe showed how easy it is to send messages over HTTP. We have used **Text** as well as **Xml** for the **Message Type** of the **Messaging Service Type** of proxy service.

In the case of the Text type, the message is handled as text and any text will be accepted. If we send a text message with XML in it, then it is still handled as simple text. If we need to process the XML inside the proxy service, then the `fn-bea:inlinedXML($body)` method can be used to transform from text to an XML node.

In all cases, the message available in the `$body` variable is wrapped inside a `<soapenv:Body>` element, even though we are not using SOAP over HTTP.

Here we only used the **Log** action to write the content of the `$body` variable to the console. In real life, we would probably call another service through a business service, for example, to write the content to a file.

There's more...

A Messaging Service typed proxy service together with the HTTP transport can be handy to start some processing without requiring the passing of parameters. In that case, a simple invoke on the **Endpoint URI** of the proxy service is enough to invoke the proxy service. This can be done with any HTTP method, such as **GET**.

To invoke the **TextOverHttp** proxy service, the following URI can be used directly from a browser: `http://localhost:7001/using-http-for-xml-over-http/proxy/TextOverHttp`:

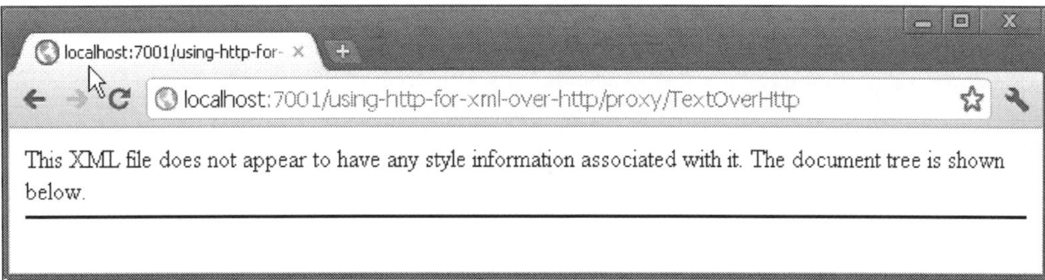

The message appears because the interface on the proxy service is defined as one-way, so no answer is returned and therefore the browser cannot display anything.

If a status message should be shown, then the proxy service can also be changed to return a message:

1. Navigate to the **Messaging** tab of the **TextOverHttp** proxy service and select **Text** for the **Response Message Type.**
2. Navigate to the **Message Flow** tab and insert a **Stage** node into the **Response Pipeline**.
3. Insert a **Replace** action into the **Stage**.
4. On the **Properties** tab of the **Replace** action, enter **body** into the **In Variable** field.
5. Click on **<Expression>** and enter `TextOverHttp started successfully`**!** into the **Expression** field.
6. Select the **Replace node contents** option.
7. Deploy the project to the OSB server.
8. Re-execute the test in the browser:

Exposing a RESTful service on the OSB

In this recipe, we will show how to REST-enable an existing service. We will reuse the CRM mock service used in *Chapter 1, Creating a Basic OSB Service*, but instead of exposing it as a SOAP-based web service as shown in *Chapter 1, Creating a Basic OSB Service*; we will expose it as a RESTful web service.

For that we first implement a business service that wraps the SOAP-based web service of the CRM system (a soapUI mock service). Then we create a proxy service using the HTTP transport and conditionally executing an action based on the HTTP method passed by the consumer:

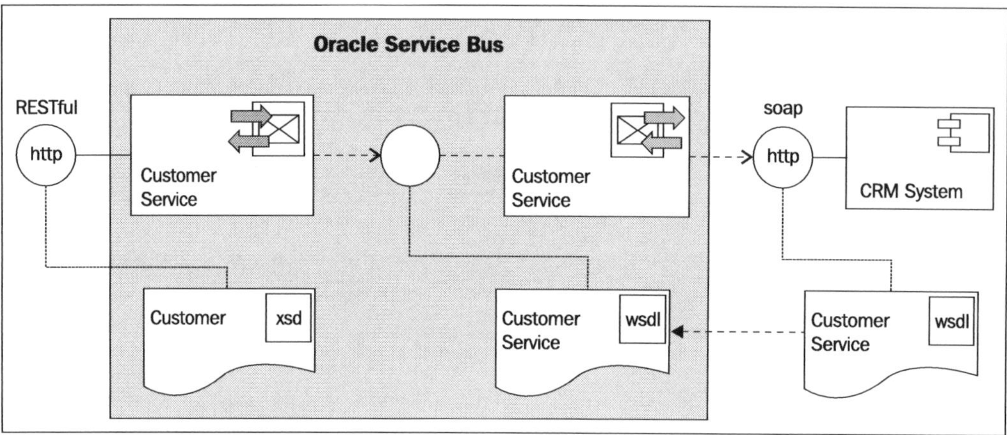

Getting ready

Import the SoapUI project `CustomerServiceCRM-soapui-project.xml` from the location `\chapter-5\getting-ready\exposing-restful-service\soapui` into your SoapUI. Start the mock service `CustomerServiceSOAP MockService`.

Import the base OSB project containing the right folder structure and the necessary XQuery transformations into Eclipse from `\chapter-5\getting-ready\exposing-restful-service`.

How to do it...

We will start with the business service, which will wrap the SOAP-based web service of the CRM system (the soapUI mock service).

In Eclipse OEPE, perform the following steps:

1. In the `business` folder of the `exposing-restful-service` project, create a new business service and name it `CustomerServiceCRM`.
2. On the **General** tab select **WSDL Web Service** for the **Service Type** and click **Browse**.
3. Navigate to `CustomerServiceCRM.wsdl` from the `wsdl` folder and select the **CustomerManagementSOAP (port)**.
4. Click **OK** and confirm the pop-up window with **Yes**.
5. Navigate to the **Transport** tab and change the **Endpoint URI** to `http://localhost:8088/mockCustomerServiceSOAP`.

Now, we can create the proxy service that will expose the RESTful interface. In Eclipse OEPE, perform the following steps:

6. In the `proxy` folder create a new proxy service and name it `CustomerService`.
7. On the **General** tab select **Messaging Service** for the **Service Type** option.
8. Navigate to the **Messaging** tab and select **XML** for both **Request Message Type** and **Response Message Type**.
9. Navigate to the **Transport** tab and select **http** for the **Protocol**.
10. Change the **Endpoint URI** to `/exposing-restful-service/CustomerService`.
11. Navigate to the **Message Flow** tab.
12. Drag a **Conditional Branch** node from the Design palette and drop it below **CustomerService**.
13. On the **Properties** of the **Conditional Branch** node, navigate to the **Flow** tab and enter `MethodBranch` into the **Name** Field
14. Navigate to the **Conditional Branch** tab and click on `<XPath>` link.
15. Enter `./ctx:transport/ctx:request/http:http-method/text()` into the **Expression** field and click **OK**.
16. Enter **inbound** into the **In Variable** field.

17. On the **Conditional Branch** node, add three new branches by clicking the **Add Branch** three times:

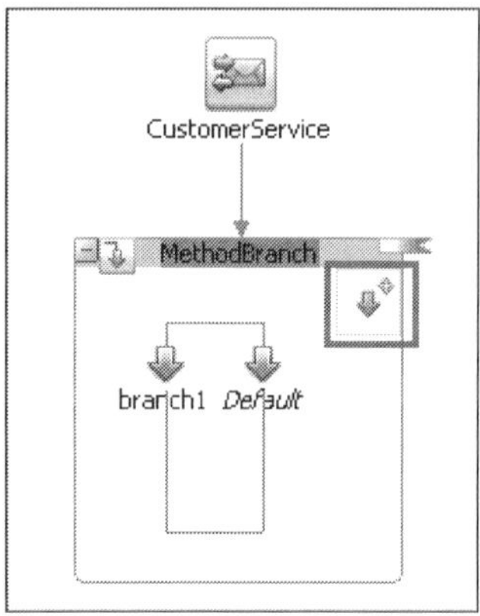

18. Click on the first branch, **branch1** and navigate to the **Properties** tab.
19. Enter `GET` into the **Label** field.
20. Leave = selected for the **Operator** drop-down listbox.
21. Enter `'GET'` (don't forget the quotes) into the **Value** field
22. Repeat the last three steps for the other three branches and use **PUT**, **DELETE**, and **POST** for the **Label** and the **Value** fields:

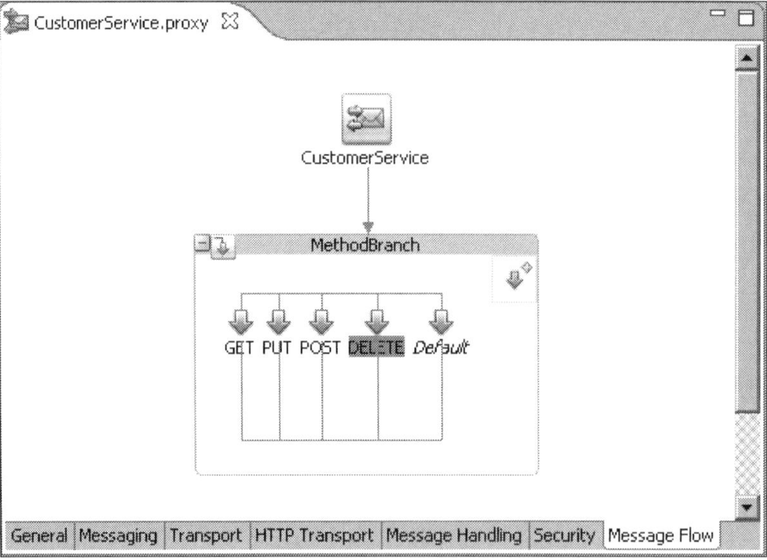

We have now created the basic structure of our RESTful service with the four HTTP methods representing the CRUD operations. Let's now implement each of the four operations. We start with the `GET` method, which will invoke the **RetrieveCustomerByCriteria** operation on the business service.

23. Drag a **Route** node and drop it on the **GET** branch and change the name to **RetrieveCustomerRoute**.
24. Right-click on the **Route** node and select **Insert Into | Communication | Routing**.
25. On the **Properties** of the **Routing** node, click on **Browse** and select the business service **CustomerServiceCRM**.
26. Select **RetrieveCustomerByCriteria** for the **Invoking** drop-down listbox.
27. Right-click on the **Request Action** and select **Insert Into | Message Processing | Replace**.
28. Enter `body` into the **In Variable** and click on **<Expression>**.
29. Navigate to the **XQuery Resources** tab, click on **Browse**, select the `HttpGetToSoap.xq` resource from the `transformation` folder and click **OK**.
30. Enter `$inbound/ctx:transport/ctx:request/http:query-string/text()` into the **Binding** field of the `queryString` variable and click **OK**.
31. Select the **Replace node contents** option.
32. Copy the **Replace** action and paste it into the **Response Action** of the same **Routing** action.
33. On the **Properties**, click on the **Expression** link to replace it by the correct XQuery.
34. On the **XQuery Resources**, click on **Browse**, select the `SoapToHttpGet.xq` resource from the `transformation` folder and click **OK**.
35. Enter `$body/cus:RetrieveCustomerByCriteriaResponse` into the **Binding** field of the `retrieveCustomerByCriteriaResponse1` variable.
36. Add a new namespace and enter `cus` into the **prefix** and `http://www.crm.org/CustomerService/` into the **URI** field.
37. Click **OK** twice.
38. Add a **Transport Header** action after the **Replace** action in the **Response Action**.
39. Select **Inbound Response** for the **Direction** drop-down listbox.
40. Click **Add Header**.
41. Select **Defined | http | Content-type** for the **Name** part.
42. Enter `'text/xml; charset=utf-8'` into the **Set Header to** field of the **Action** part.
43. Click **Add Header**.

44. Select **Other** in the **Name** part and enter `Content-Length` into the field to the right of it.
45. Enter `string-length($body)` into the **Set Header to field** of the **Action** part.
46. Click **Add Header**.
47. Select **Defined** | **http** | **Date** for the **Name** part.
48. Enter `fn-bea:dateTime-to-string-with-format("E, dd MMM yyyy hh:mm:ss",fn:current-dateTime())` into the **Set Header to** field of the **Action** part.
49. Click **Add Header**.
50. Select **Other** in the **Name** part and enter **Content-Encoding** into the field to the right of it.
51. Enter `'UTF-8'` into the **Set Header to** field of the **Action** part.
52. Click **Add Header**.
53. Select **Other** in the **Name** part and enter `Allow` into the field to the right of it.
54. Enter `'GET, POST, PUT, DELETE'` into the **Set Header to** field of the **Action** part:

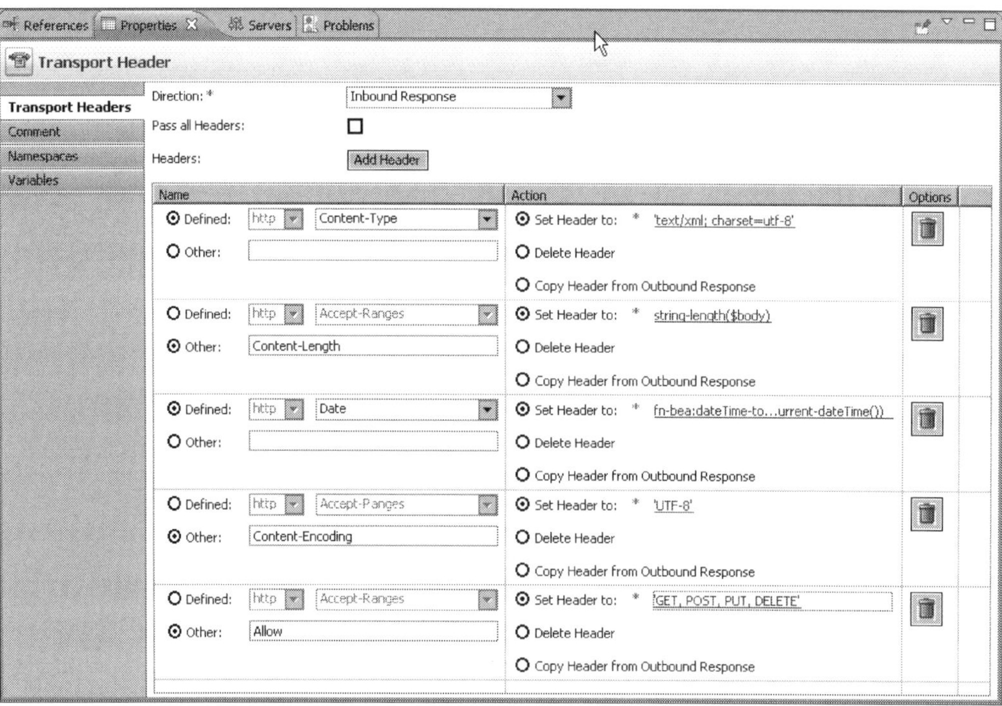

We have completed the implementation of the `GET` operation and the flow should look as shown in the following screenshot:

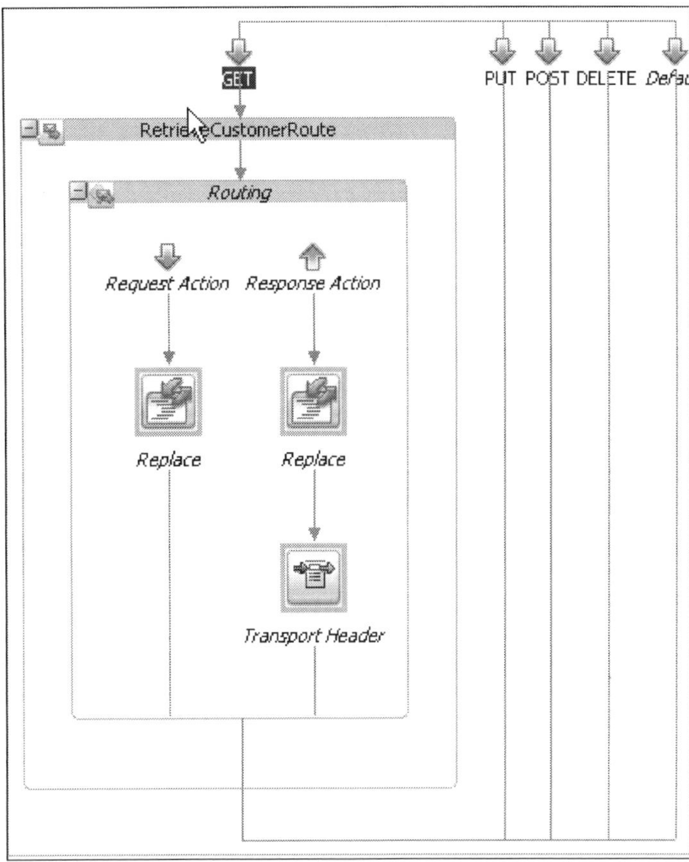

Next let's implement the **PUT** method, which will invoke the **UpdateExistingCustomer** operation on the business service.

55. Copy the **RetrieveCustomerRoute** node and paste it into the **PUT** flow.
56. Change the name to `UpdateExistingCustomerRoute`.
57. On the **Properties** tab of the **Routing** action, select the **UpdateExistingCustomer** operation for the **Invoking** drop-down listbox.
58. On the **Properties** tab of the **Replace** action in the **Request Action** of the **UpdateExistingCustomerRoute**, click on the **Expression** link.
59. On the **XQuery Resources**, click on **Browse**, select the `HttpPutToSoap.xq` resource from the `transformation` folder and click **OK**.

60. Enter `$body/cus1:Customer` into the **Binding** field of the `customer1` variable.
61. Add a new namespace and enter `cus1` into the **prefix** and `http://www.somecorp.com/customer` into the **URI** field.
62. Click **OK**.
63. On the **Properties** of the **Replace** action in the **Response Action** flow of **UpdateExistingCustomerRoute**, click on the **Expression** link.
64. Enter the following XML fragment into the **Expression** field:

```
<status>
    <code>OK</code>
    <message>record updated</message>
</status>
```

Next, let's implement the `POST` method, which will invoke the **CreateNewCustomer** operation on the business service.

65. Copy the **RetrieveCustomerRoute** node and paste it into the **POST** flow.
66. Change the name to `CreateNewCustomerRoute`.
67. On the **Properties** tab of the **Routing** action, select the **CreateNewCustomer** operation for the **Invoking** drop-down listbox.
68. Insert an **Assign** action into the **Request Action** flow, right before the **Replace** action.

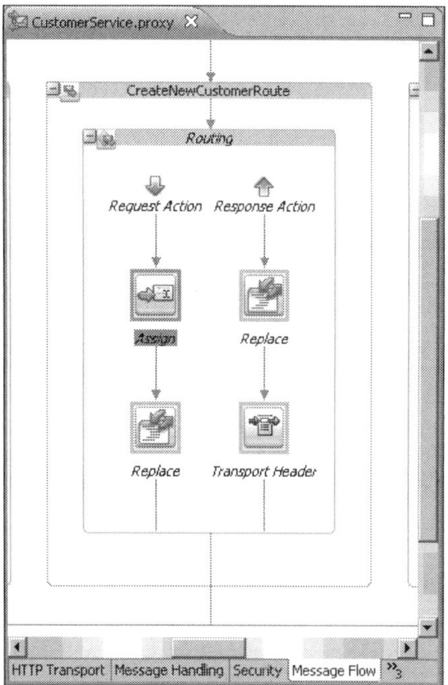

69. On the **Properties** tab of the **Assign** action, click on **<Expression>** and enter `$body` into the **Expression** field.
70. Enter `origRequest` into the **Variable** field.
71. On the **Properties** tab of the **Replace** action in the **Request Action** of the **CreateNewCustomerRoute**, click on the **Expression** link.
72. On the **XQuery Resources**, click on **Browse**, select the `HttpPostToSoap.xq` resource from the `transformation` folder and click **OK**.
73. Enter `$body/cus1:Customer` into the **Binding** field of the `customer1` variable.
74. Add a new namespace and enter `cus1` into the **prefix** and `http://www.somecorp.com/customer` into the **URI** field.
75. Click **OK**.
76. On the **Properties** of the **Replace** action in the **Response Action** flow of **CreateNewCustomerRoute**, click on the **Expression** link.
77. On the **XQuery Resources**, click on **Browse**, select the `SoapToHttpPost.xq` resource from the `transformation` folder and click **OK**.
78. Enter `$body/cus:CreateNewCustomerResponse` into the **Binding** field of the `createNewCustomerResponse1` variable.
79. Enter `$origRequest/cus1:Customer` into the **Binding** field of the `customer1` variable and click **OK**.

Last but not least, let's implement the `DELETE` method, which will invoke the **DeleteExistingCustomer** operation on the business service.

80. Copy the **UpdateExistingCustomerRoute** node and paste it into the **DELETE** flow.
81. Change the name to `DeleteExistingCustomerRoute`.
82. On the **Properties** tab of the **Routing** action, select the **DeleteExistingCustomer** operation for the **Invoking** drop-down listbox.
83. On the **Properties** tab of the **Replace** action in the **Request Action** of **DeleteExistingCustomerRoute**, click on the **Expression** link.
84. On the **XQuery Resources**, click on **Browse**, select the `HttpDeleteToSoap.xq` resource from the `transformation` folder and click **OK**.
85. Enter `$inbound/ctx:transport/ctx:request/http:query-parameters/http:parameter/@value[$inbound/ctx:transport/ctx:request/http:query-parameters/http:parameter/@name='id']` into the **Binding** field of the `id` variable and click **OK**.
86. On the **Properties** of the **Replace** action in the **Response Action** of **DeleteExistingCustomerRoute**, click on the **Expression** link.
87. Change message element content to `record deleted` and click **OK**.

Now we have implemented all required HTTP methods for the CRUD operations. But there are two other HTTP methods (`OPTIONS` and `HEADER`), which we won't need and which will trigger the default branch. Therefore, we will raise an error to communicate that these methods are not supported.

88. Add a **Pipeline Pair** node to the default branch and name it `NotSupportedMethodPipeline`.
89. Add a **Stage** to the **Pipeline Pair** node and name it `RaiseErrorStage`.
90. Insert a **Raise Error** action into the **Stage**.
91. On the **Properties** of the **Raise Error** action, enter `NOT_SUPPORT_HTTP_METHOD` into the **Code** field and `Unsupported HTTP Method` into the **Message** field.
92. Deploy the project to the OSB server.

The completed message flow definition is shown in the following screenshot:

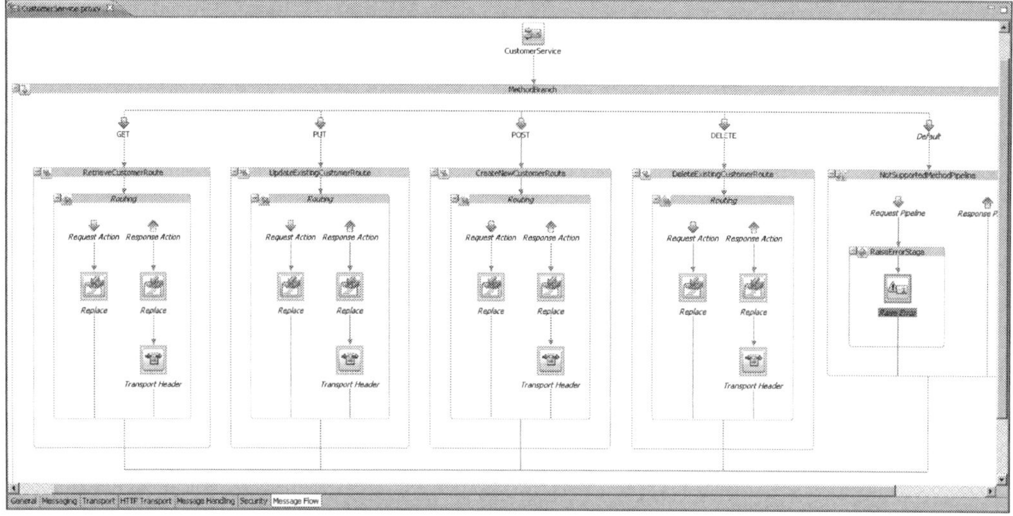

Now let's test our RESTful service. There are multiple ways for testing a RESTful service.

For testing the `GET` method, we can use a Web browser and enter the following URL: `http://localhost:7001/exposing-restful-service/CustomerService?id=100`:

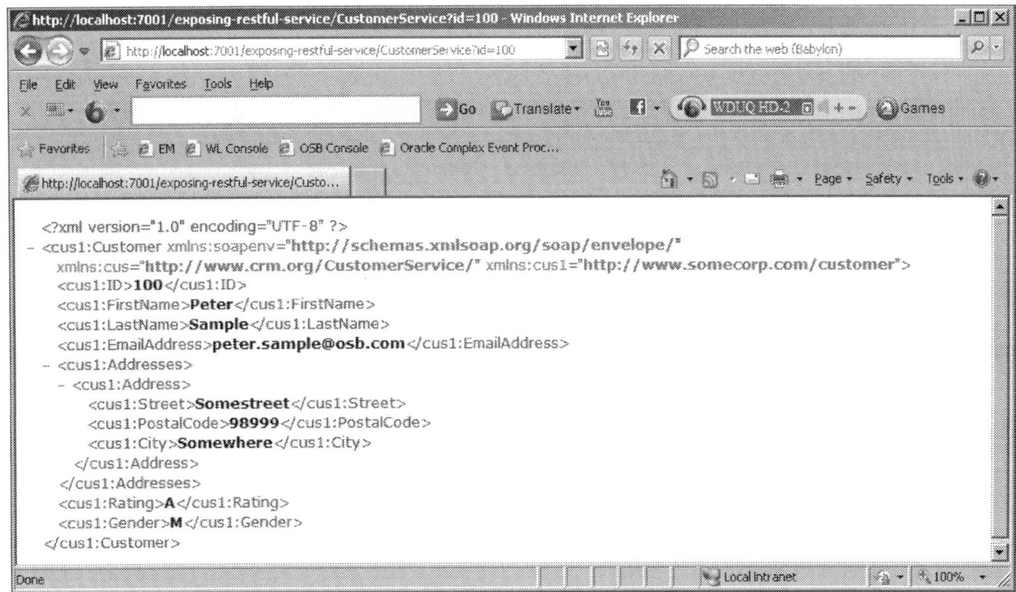

For testing the other implemented HTTP methods, we can use the Service Bus console.

To test the `PUT` method, perform the following steps in Service Bus console:

93. In the **Project Explorer**, navigate to **exposing-restful-service | proxy** and click on the **Launch Test Console** icon for the **CustomerService** proxy service.
94. Expand the **Transport** section.
95. Enter `PUT` into the `http-method` field.
96. Enter the following XML fragment into the **Payload** field.

```
<cus1:Customer xmlns:soapenv="http://schemas.xmlsoap.org/soap/
envelope/" xmlns:cus="http://www.crm.org/CustomerService/"
xmlns:cus1="http://www.somecorp.com/customer">
    <cus1:ID>1</cus1:ID>
    <cus1:FirstName>Peter</cus1:FirstName>
    <cus1:LastName>Sample</cus1:LastName>
    <cus1:EmailAddress>peter.sample@osb.com</cus1:EmailAddress>
    <cus1:Addresses>
        <cus1:Address>
            <cus1:Street>Somestreet</cus1:Street>
            <cus1:PostalCode>98999</cus1:PostalCode>
            <cus1:City>Somewhere</cus1:City>
```

```
            </cus1:Address>
        </cus1:Addresses>
        <cus1:Rating>A</cus1:Rating>
        <cus1:Gender>M</cus1:Gender>
    </cus1:Customer>
```

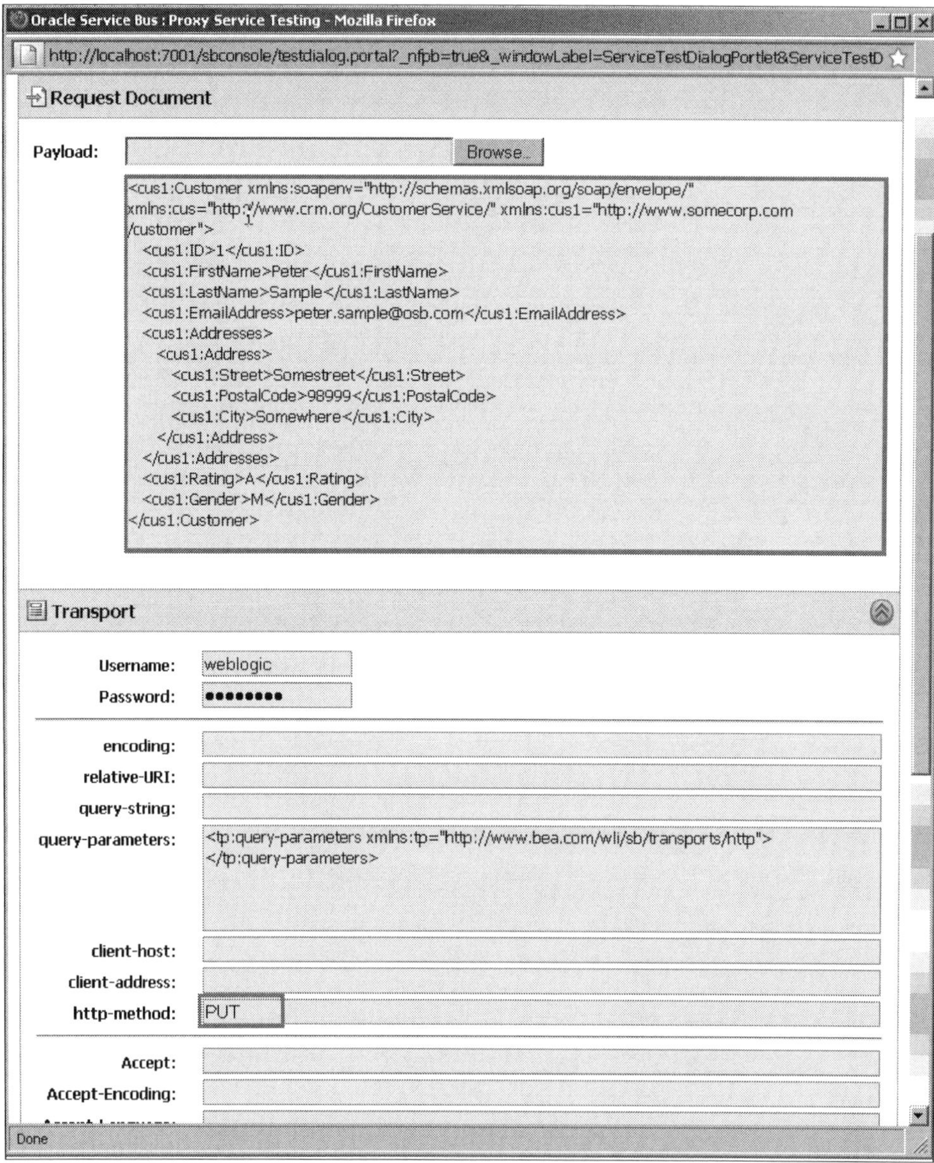

97. Click **Execute**.
98. The **Response Document** shows the **record updated** message and in soapUI a new request has been logged on the mock service.

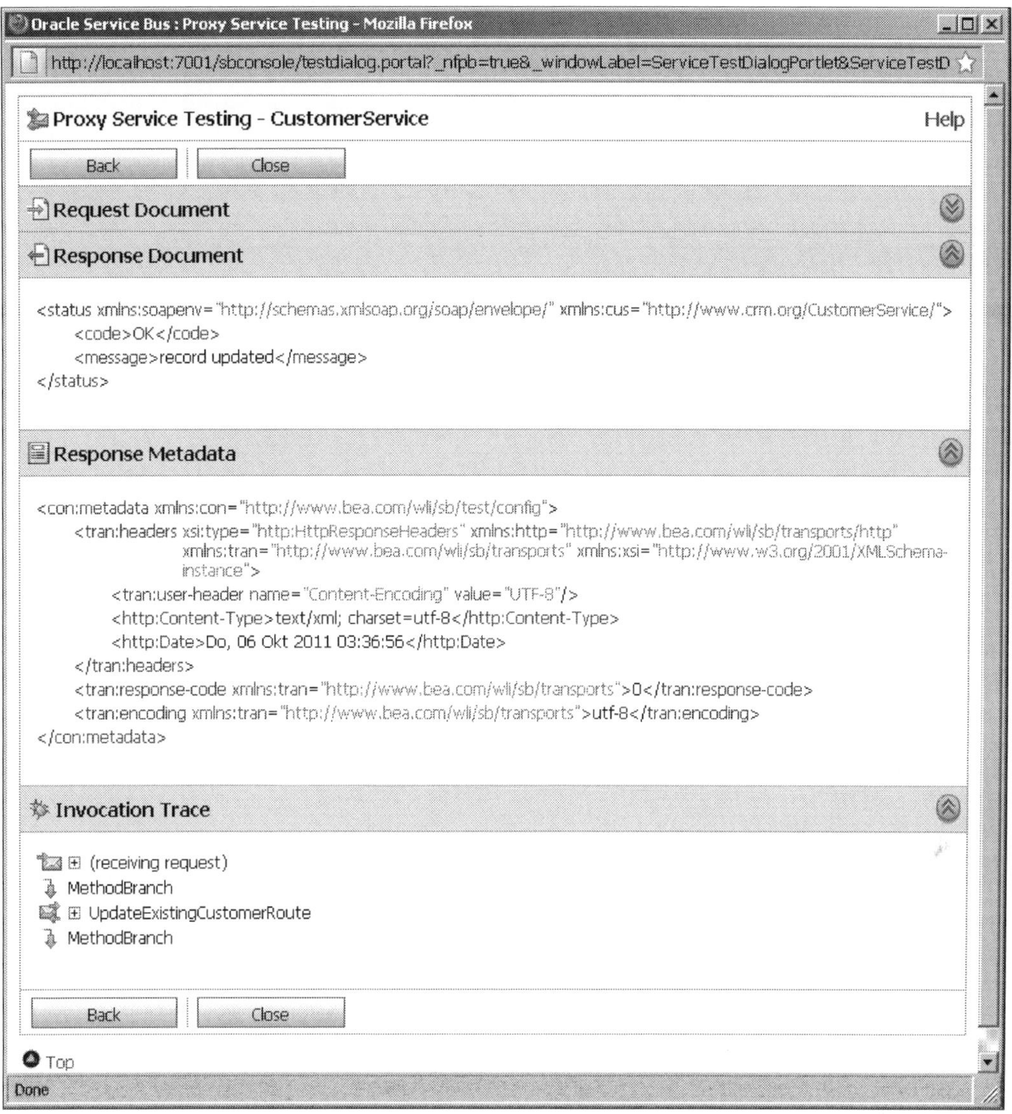

Testing the other HTTP methods is similar to the `PUT`, just replace the HTTP method and pass another message. To test the `DELETE` and `GET`, enter the value of the query string (that is, `id=100`) into the `query-string` field.

How it works...

In this recipe, we created a REST interface for an existing SOAP service. We have mapped each of the available HTTP methods to one of the CRUD operations of the customer service.

The HTTP methods we implemented are `PUT`, `POST`, `DELETE`, and `GET`.

Working with the HTTP methods is similar to working with a WSDL with multiple operations. But we can't use an operational branch for handling the different methods; we have to use a conditional branch. The conditional branch decides which HTTP method has been passed and triggers the right behavior.

For each method we have to transform the message we get through the RESTful interface to the message the backend SOAP-based web service expects. For that, we have used the **Replace** action together with XQuery scripts.

For the `GET` and `DELETE` method, all the necessary values are passed in the query string, that is, in the URL of the request. For example, to read the customer with `id=100`, we have defined and used the following URL:

`http://localhost:7001/exposing-restful-service/CustomerService?id=100`

The request URL will end up in the `$inbound` variable, the part with the information about the request is shown here:

```
<con:transport>
    <con:uri>/exposing-restful-service/CustomerService</con:uri>
    <con:request>
    <tran:headers>
        <http:Content-Type>text/plain;
            charset=utf-8</http:Content-Type>
    </tran:headers>
    <tran:encoding>utf-8</tran:encoding>
    <http:query-string>id=100</http:query-string>
    <http:query-parameters>
        <http:parameter name="id" value="100"/>
    </http:query-parameters>
    <http:http-method>GET</http:http-method>
    </con:request>
</con:transport>
```

We can see that the there is a separate element `http:query-string` only holding the value of the query string. Additionally there is a `http:query-parameters` collection with one element for each parameter.

In the implementation of the `GET` method, we have used the `http:query-string` element to pass the value of the query-string to the XQuery script by using the following XPath expression:

```
$inbound/ctx:transport/ctx:request/http:query-string/text()
```

The XQuery then uses the following FLOWER expression to create the criteria structure to be passed to the SOAP web service of the CRM system.

```
<criterias>
    {
    for $nameValue in fn:tokenize($queryString,"&amp;")
    return
        <criteria>
            <criteriaField>
                { fn:substring-before($nameValue,'=') }
            </criteriaField>
            <criteriaValue>
                { fn:substring-after($nameValue,'=') }
            </criteriaValue>
        </criteria>
    }
</criterias>
```

The implementation of the `DELETE` method is using the `http:query-parameters` collection to retrieve the value of the `id` parameter using the following expression:

```
$inbound/ctx:transport/ctx:request/http:query-parameters/
http:parameter/@value[$inbound/ctx:transport/ctx:request/http:query-
parameters/http:parameter/@name='id']
```

For the `PUT` and `POST` method, the message is passed as an XML fragment, which will end up in the `$body` variable in the message flow. The following screenshot shows the content of the `$body` for the `PUT` request when logged through a **Log** action.

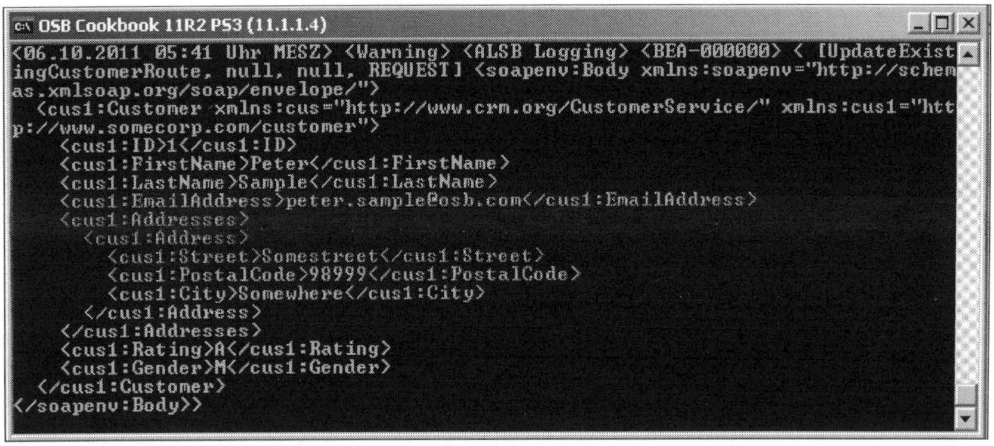

OSB Cookbook 11R2 PS3 (11.1.1.4)


```
<06.10.2011 05:41 Uhr MESZ> <Warning> <ALSB Logging> <BEA-000000> < [UpdateExistingCustomerRoute, null, null, REQUEST] <soapenv:Body xmlns:soapenv="http://schemas.xmlsoap.org/soap/envelope/">
  <cus1:Customer xmlns:cus="http://www.crm.org/CustomerService/" xmlns:cus1="http://www.somecorp.com/customer">
    <cus1:ID>1</cus1:ID>
    <cus1:FirstName>Peter</cus1:FirstName>
    <cus1:LastName>Sample</cus1:LastName>
    <cus1:EmailAddress>peter.sample@osb.com</cus1:EmailAddress>
    <cus1:Addresses>
      <cus1:Address>
        <cus1:Street>Somestreet</cus1:Street>
        <cus1:PostalCode>98999</cus1:PostalCode>
        <cus1:City>Somewhere</cus1:City>
      </cus1:Address>
    </cus1:Addresses>
    <cus1:Rating>A</cus1:Rating>
    <cus1:Gender>M</cus1:Gender>
  </cus1:Customer>
</soapenv:Body>>
```

There's more...

In the previous recipe, we used the query string part of the URL to pass the values to the `GET` and `DELETE` method. Another way of passing these values is as so-called **clean URLs**, which are purely structural URLs that do not contain a query string but instead define the path of the resource through the URL. So instead of using the following URL for the `GET`:

```
http://localhost:7001/exposing-restful-service/CustomerService?id=100
```

we could use a clean URL, such as this one:

```
http://localhost:7001/exposing-restful-service/CustomerService/id/100
```

Even if the request URL is longer, the existing proxy listening on Endpoint-URI `/exposing-restful-service/CustomerService` will still be triggered. The interesting part of the `$inbound` variable in this case would hold the following values:

```
<con:transport>
    <con:uri>/exposing-restful-service/CustomerService</con:uri>
    <con:request>
        <tran:headers>
            <http:Content-Type>text/plain;
                charset=utf-8</http:Content-Type>
        </tran:headers>
        <tran:encoding>utf-8</tran:encoding>
        <http:relative-URI>id/100</relative-UR>
        <http:http-method>GET</http:http-method>
    </con:request>
</con:transport>
```

We can see that the part of the path after the Endpoint-URI of the proxy can be found in the `http:relative-URI` element. Using a tokenize function, it's easy to access the different values, for example, for the value of the `id` we could use:

```
fn:tokenize($inbound/ctx:transport/ctx:request/http:relative-URI/
text(),'/')[2]
```

Consuming a RESTful service from the OSB

In this recipe, we will show you how to consume an existing RESTful service from the OSB. We will reuse the service we have provided in the previous recipe and implement a proxy service/business service pair to expose it as a SOAP-based web service.

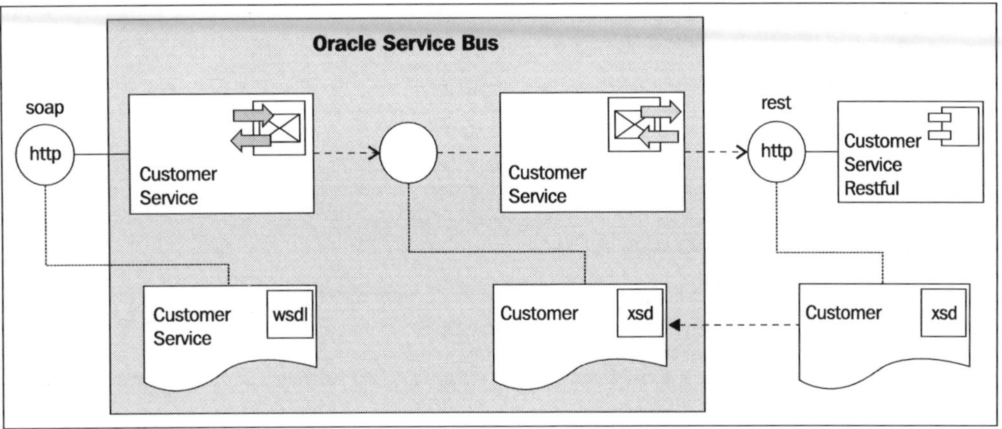

The business service is using the HTTP transport to invoke the RESTful service and a proxy service is exposing this as a SOAP-based web service, also using the HTTP transport.

In this recipe, we will only implement the **RetrieveCustomerByCriteria** operation.

Getting ready

Import the SoapUI project `CustomerServiceCRM-soapui-project.xml` from the location `\chapter-5\getting-ready\exposing-restful-service\soapui` into your SoapUI. Start the mock service `CustomerServiceSOAP MockService`.

Import the OSB project containing the implementation of the RESTful service into Eclipse OEPE from `\chapter-5\solution\exposing-restful-service`.

Import the base OSB project containing the right folder structure and the necessary XQuery transformations into Eclipse from `\chapter-5\getting-ready\consuming-restful-service`.

How to do it...

We will start with the business service, which will wrap the RESTful service. In Eclipse OEPE, perform the following steps:

1. In the `business` folder of the **consuming-restful-service** project, create a new business service and name it `CustomerService`.
2. On the **General** tab select **Messaging Service** for the **Service Type**.

3. Navigate to the **Messaging** tab and select **XML** for both the **Request Message Type** and the **Response Message Type**.
4. Navigate to the **Transport** tab, enter `http://localhost:7001/exposing-restful-service/CustomerService` into the **Endpoint URI** field and click **Add**.

The business service wrapping the RESTful service is in place. Let's now create the proxy service that will expose the SOAP-based interface. In Eclipse OEPE, perform the following steps:

5. In the `proxy` folder create a new proxy service and name it `CustomerService`.
6. On the **General** tab select **WSDL Web Service** for the **Service Type** and click **Browse**.
7. Navigate to the `CustomerServiceCRM.wsdl` from the `wsdl` folder and select the **CustomerServiceSOAP (port)**.
8. Click **OK** and confirm the pop-up window with **Yes**.
9. Navigate to the **Message Flow** tab, insert an **Operational Branch** node and name it `OperationalBranch`.
10. Click on the first branch and select **RetrieveCustomerByCriteria** in the **Operation** drop-down listbox.
11. Insert a **Route** node into the **RetrieveCustomerByCriteria** branch and name it `InvokeGetRoute`.
12. Insert a **Routing** action into the **Route** node.
13. On the **Properties** tab of the **Routing** action, click **Browse**, select the **CustomerService** business service in the `business` folder and click **OK**.
14. Insert a **Transport Header** action into the **Request Action** flow of the **Routing** action.
15. On the **Properties** tab of the **Transport Header** action, enable the **Pass all Headers** option.
16. Insert an **Insert** action after the **Transport Header** action.
17. On the **Properties** tab of the **Insert**, click **<Expression>** and enter `<http:http-method>GET</http:http-method>` into the **Expression** field. Click **OK**.
18. Click on **<XPath>**, enter `./ctx:transport/ctx:request` into the **Expression** field and click **OK**.

19. Enter `outbound` into the **In Variable** field.

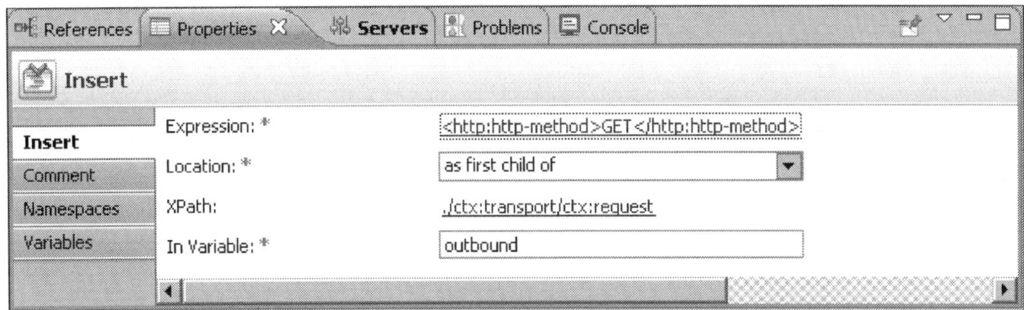

20. Add another **Insert** action right after the one created above in step 16.
21. On the **Properties** tab of the **Insert**, click **<Expression>** and navigate to the **XQuery Resources** tab.
22. Click **Browse**, select the `SoapToHttpGet.xq` resource in the `transformation` folder and click **OK**.
23. In the **Variable Structures** on the right, expand **body | $body – RetrieveCustomerByCriteria (request)** and drag the node **RetrieveCustomerByCriteria** to the **Binding** of the **retrieveCustomerByCriteria1** variable.

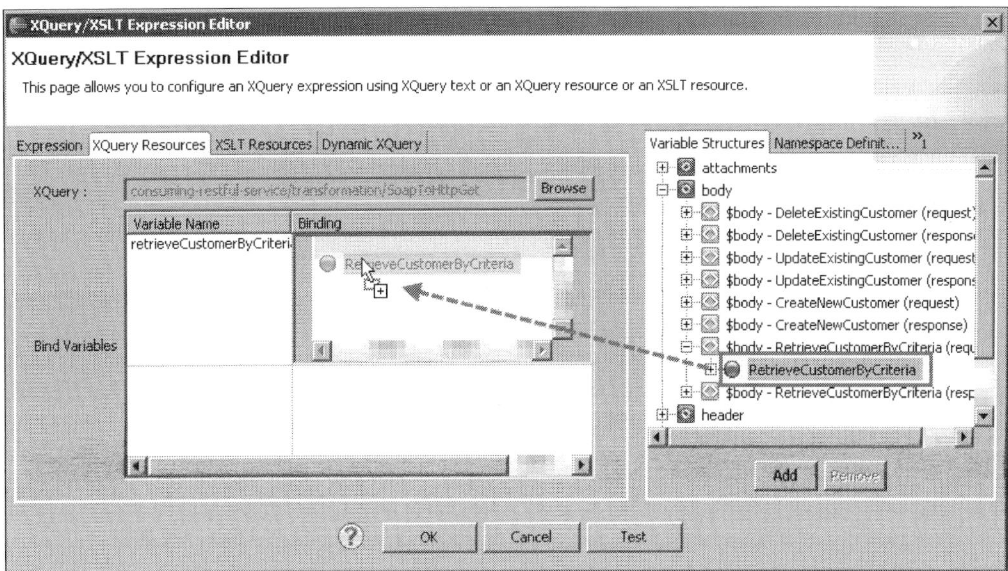

24. Click on **<XPath>**, enter `./ctx:transport/ctx:request` into the **Expression** field and click **OK**.
25. Enter `outbound` into the **In Variable** field.

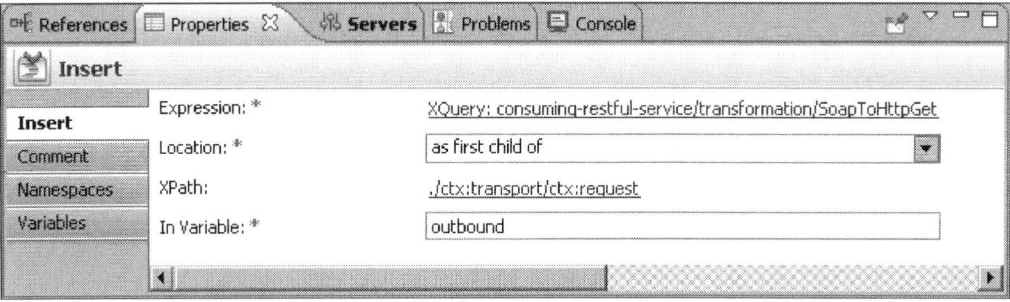

26. Insert a **Replace** action into the **Response Action** flow.
27. On the **Properties** tab of the **Replace** action, enter `body` into the **In Variable** field.
28. Click **<Expression>**, navigate to the **XQuery Resources** tab and click **Browse**.
29. Select the `HttpGetToSoap.xq` resource in the `transformation` folder and click **OK**.
30. Enter `$body/cus1:Customer` into the **Binding** field of the **customer1** variable.
31. Add a new namespace and enter `cus1` into the **prefix**, `http://www.somecorp.com/customer` into the **URI** field and click **OK**.
32. Select the **Replace node contents** option.

By doing that the processing for the **RetrieveCustomerByCriteria** operation is complete. We won't implement the other operations of the **Operational Branch** in this recipe. It's a good practice to raise an error if a *not-yet-supported* operation is called. We can do this by adding a **Raise Error** action in the default branch:

33. Insert a **Pipeline Pair** node into the **Default** branch and name it `UnsupportedOpPipeline`.
34. Insert a **Stage** node into the **Pipeline Pair** and name it `RaiseErrorStage`.
35. Insert a **Raise Error** action into the **RaiseErrorStage**.

36. On the **Properties** tab of the **Raise Error** action, enter `OPERATION_NOT_SUPPORTED` into the **Code** field and `The operation is not yet supported!` into the **Message** field.

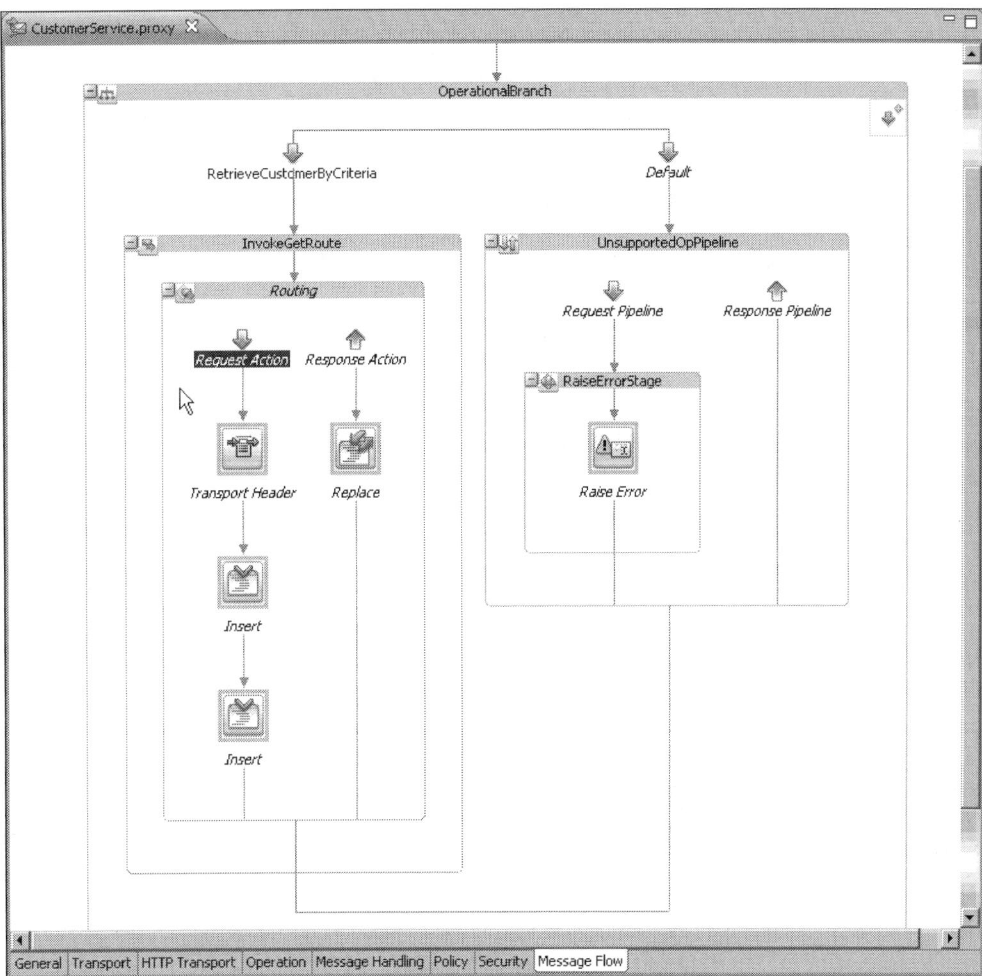

37. Deploy the project to the OSB server.

Our SOAP-based web service is now ready and can be tested. In the Service Bus console, perform the following steps:

38. In the **Project Explorer** navigate to the **CustomerService** proxy service inside the **proxy** folder and click on the **Launch Test Console** icon.
39. In the **Available Operations** drop-down listbox make sure to select the **RetrieveCustomerByCriteria** operation.
40. In the **Payload** field, enter `id` into the `criteriaField` and `100` into the `criteriaValue` element and click **Execute**.

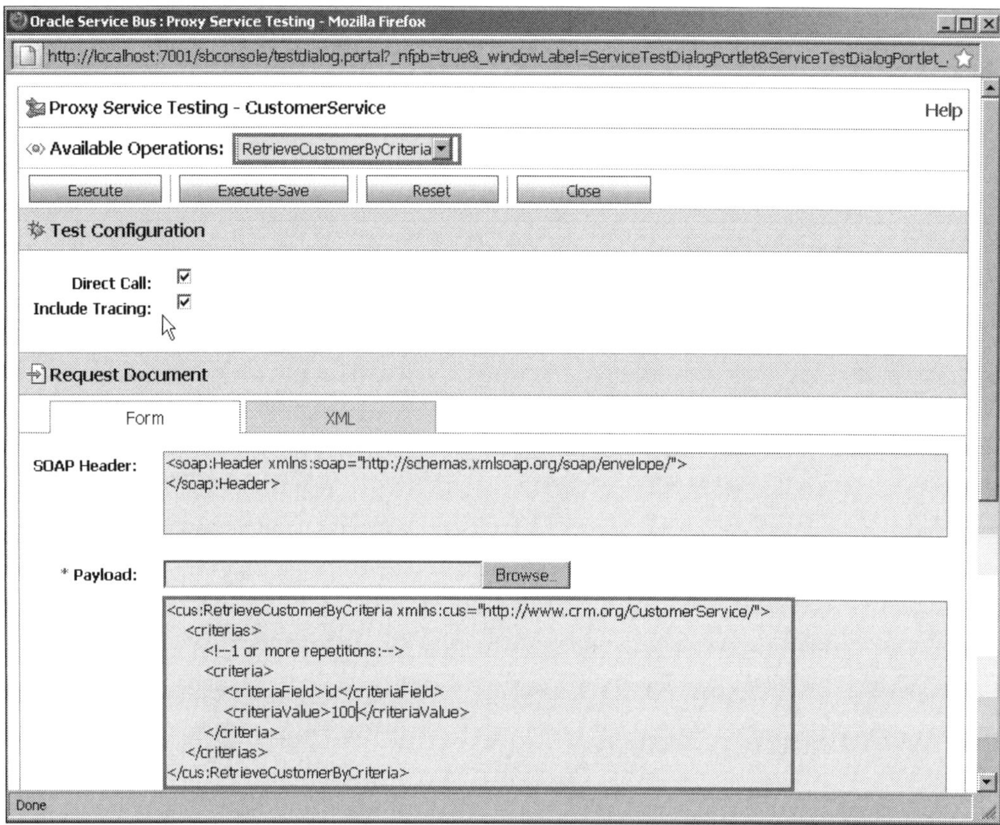

41. The **Response Document** in the next window will show the result of our SOAP-based web service.

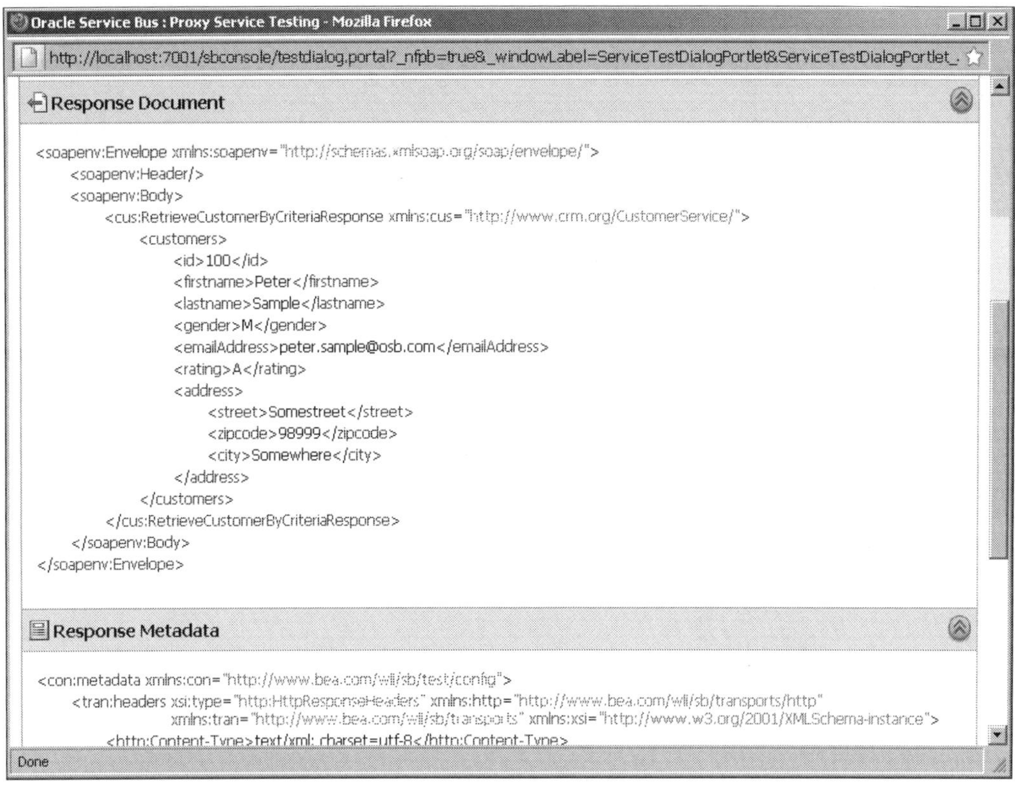

How it works...

In this recipe, we created a SOAP-based web service for an existing RESTful service. We have mapped the SOAP request into the corresponding RESTful message and vice versa.

On the business service, wrapping the RESTful service, the HTTP method is defined at development time (`POST` by default). However, through the use of the **Transport Header** action together with the two **Insert** actions, we are able to overwrite/define the HTTP method being used in a given call. In our case, where we only implemented the **RetrieveCustomerByCriteria**, it's the HTTP `GET` method we want to use.

The next screenshot shows the value of the metadata in the `$outbound` variable in the **Routing** action.

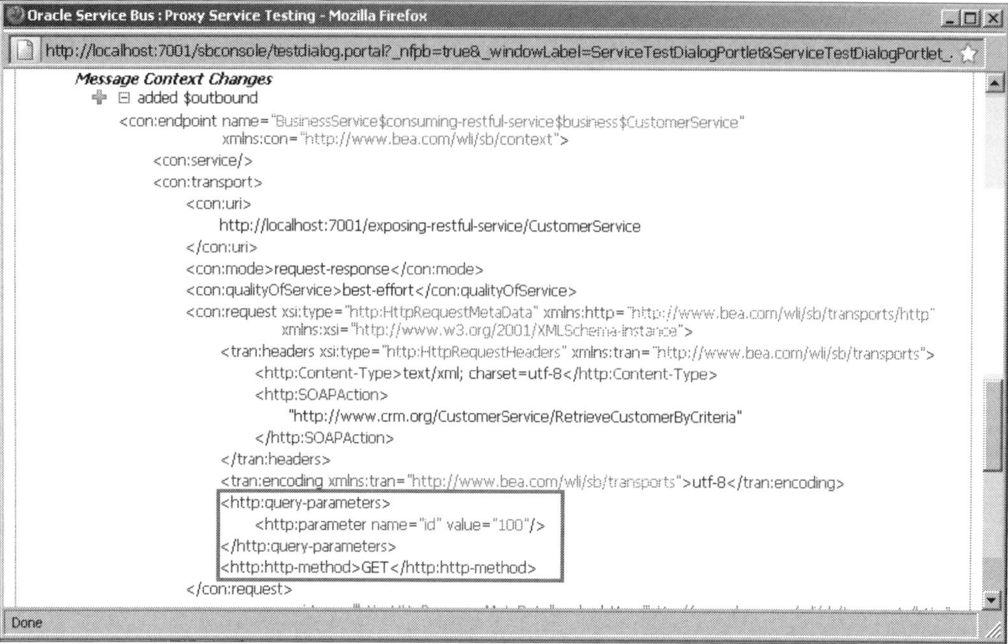

We can see that the value of the `http-method` and the `query-parameters` elements that have been added by the two **Insert** actions.

For the creation of the `query-parameters` in the XQuery script, we have reused the standard OSB XML Schema `HttpTransport.xsd`. In there the `query-parameters` structure is defined as a complex type.

Creating a generic RESTful gateway on the OSB

In this recipe, we will show you how to implement a RESTful gateway on the OSB, which will accept RESTful requests and then routes these requests to the real implementation of the service that can also be a RESTful service. This adds an additional layer of processing logic, which can be used for things such as auditing, security, and SLA monitoring.

We will use an external public service called **Brewery DB**, which offers a RESTful API (`http://www.brewerydb.com/api/documentation`) to execute queries for breweries, beers, styles, and other information about beer.

The gateway we implement will be generic in such a way that it accepts all the different requests through one single proxy service and then routes the request directly to the business service, wrapping the external RESTful API of the Brewery DB service.

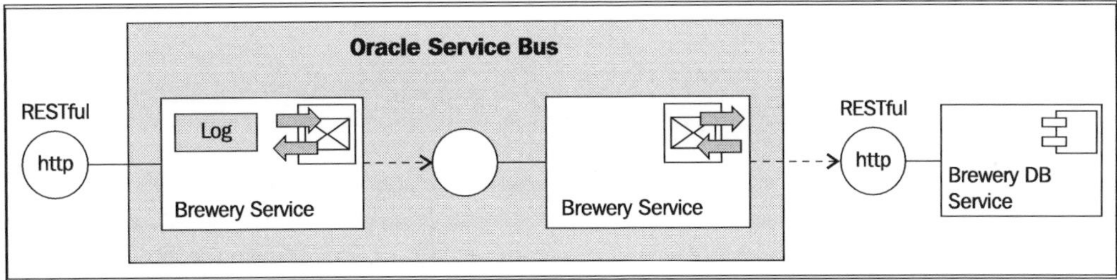

Getting ready

To use the Brewery DB service API, an API key is needed. Just register for such an API key here: `http://www.brewerydb.com/api/register`.

Make sure to have access to the Internet and check that the Brewery DB API is accessible, by executing the following request from a browser: `http://www.brewerydb.com/api/styles?apikey=<api-key>`. Make sure that you replace the `<api-key>` with your own key. The service should respond with an XML document holding the different styles of beers.

How to do it...

We will start with the business service, which will wrap the Brewery DB service API. In Eclipse OEPE, perform the following steps:

1. Create a new OSB project, name it `creating-generic-restful-gateway` and add a `business` and `proxy` folder to the project.
2. In the `business` folder of the project, create a new business service and name it `BreweryService`.
3. On the **General** tab select **Messaging Service** for the **Service Type**.
4. Navigate to the **Messaging** tab and select **XML** for both the **Request Message Type** and the **Response Message Type**.
5. Navigate to the **Transport** tab, enter `http://www.brewerydb.com/api` into the **Endpoint URI** field and click **Add**.

By doing that the business service wrapping the Brewery DB service API is in place.

Next, let's create the proxy service that will offer the same RESTful API and just passes request messages through to the Brewery DB service using the business service created previously. In Eclipse OEPE, perform the following steps:

6. Right-click on the business service `BreweryService.biz` and select **Oracle Service Bus | Generate Proxy Service**.
7. Enter `BreweryService` into the **File name** field and select the `proxy` folder for the location of the proxy service from the tree.
8. Click **Finish**.
9. Navigate to the **Transport** tab and enter `/BreweryService` into the **EndpointURI** field.
10. Navigate to the **Message Flow** tab and check that a **Route** node with a **Routing** action, which invokes the business service, has been generated.
11. Insert an **Insert** action into the **Request Action** flow of the **Routing** action.
12. On the **Properties** of the **Insert** action, enter `outbound` into the **In Variable** field.
13. Click **<Expression>**, enter `<http:http-method>{$inbound/ctx:transport/ctx:request/http:http-method}</http:http-method>` into the **Expression** field and click **OK**.
14. Click **<XPath>**, enter `./ctx:transport/ctx:request` into the **Expression** field and click **OK**.
15. Leave the **Location** on **as first child of**.
16. Duplicate the **Insert** action by copying and pasting it into the **Request Action**.
17. On the **Properties** of the second **Insert** action, click on the link to the right of **Expression**, enter `<http:query-string>{$inbound/ctx:transport/ctx:request/http:query-string}</http:query-string>` into the **Expression** field and click **OK**.
18. Duplicate the **Insert** action by copying and pasting it into the **Request Action**.
19. On the **Properties** of the third **Insert** action, click on the link to the right of **Expression**, enter `<http:relative-URI>{$inbound/ctx:transport/ctx:request/http:relative-URI}</http:relative-URI>` into the **Expression** field and click **OK**.
20. Insert a **Log** action into the **Response Action** flow of the **Routing** action.
21. On the **Properties** tab of the **Log** action, click **<Expresssion>**, enter `$body` and click **OK**.
22. Select **Warning** for the **Severity** drop-down listbox.

23. The message flow of the proxy service should look as shown in the following screenshot:

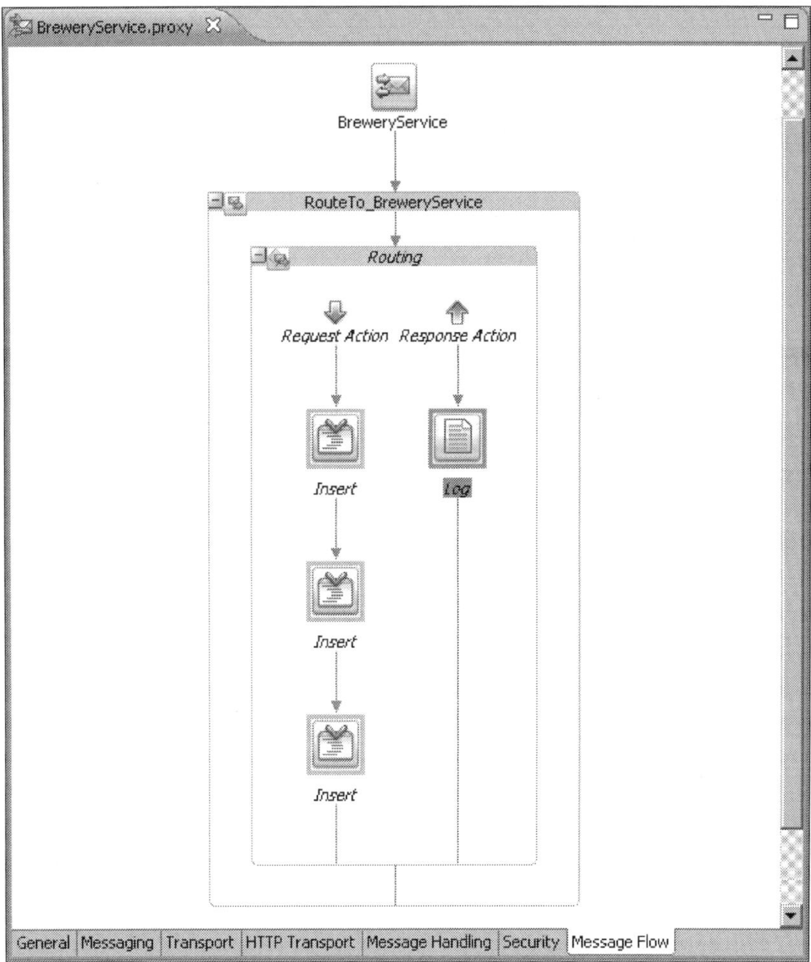

24. Deploy the project to the OSB server.

Our generic RESTful service gateway is now ready and can be tested. Open a browser window and perform the following steps:

25. Send a request using the following URL (replace the <api-key> with your key): http://localhost:7001/BreweryService/beers?apikey=<api-key>&format=xml.
26. The response should be shown in the browser window and holds a XML document with a list of beers as shown in the following screenshot:

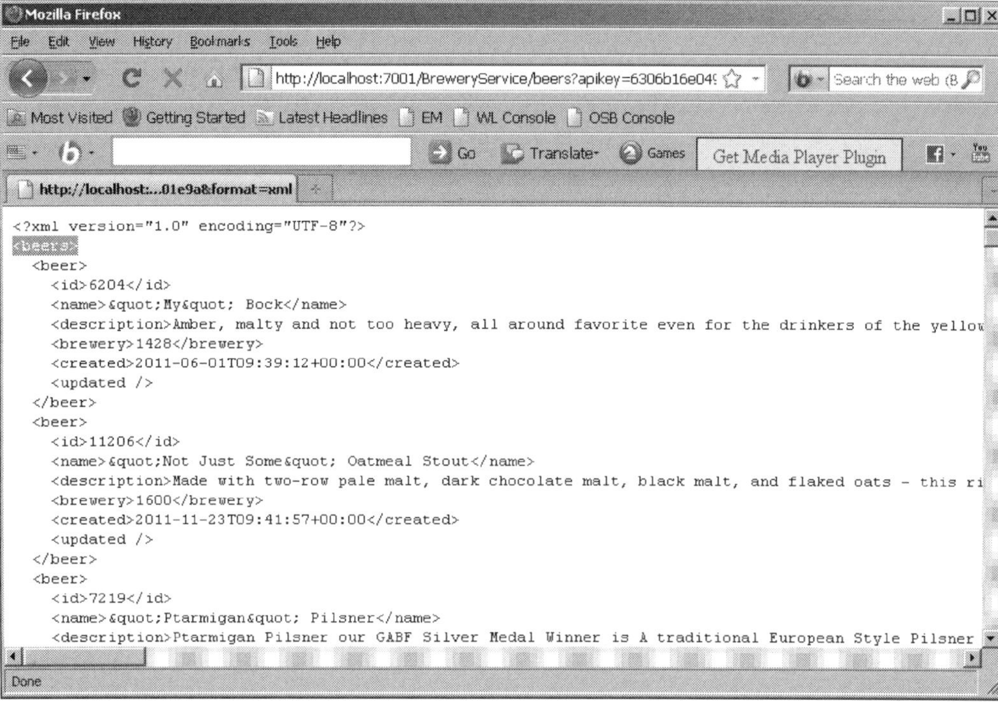

27. The response should also be shown in the OSB console log window.
28. Send a request using the following URL (replace the <api-key> with your key): http://localhost:7001/BreweryService/beers?apikey=<api-key>&format=json.
29. The response in the browser window will now contain a list of beers in JSON format.
30. Send a request using the following URL (replace the <api-key> with your key): http://localhost:7001/BreweryService/breweries?apikey=<api-key>.
31. The response in the browser window will contain a list of breweries formatted as XML.

How it works...

In this recipe, we created a generic RESTful service gateway that accepts RESTful requests and passes it through to the Brewery DB RESTful service API.

We have created one single proxy service, accepting requests on the (base) Endpoint URI: `http:\\<osbserver>:<osb-port>\BreweryService`. By doing that, the message flow of the proxy service will be triggered for all requests using this base URI, such as:

- `http://localhost:7001/BreweryService/beers?apikey=<api-key>&format=xml`
- `http://localhost:7001/BreweryService/breweries?apikey=<api-key>`

By adding the three **Insert** actions into the message flow of the proxy service we make sure that the HTTP method, the relative part of the URI (such as `/beers` and `/breweries`), as well as the query parameters (such as `apikey` and `format`) are copied from the `inbound` into the `outbound` variable. This is important, as the generic business service also only holds the base part of the Endpoint URI: `http://www.brewerydb.com/api`. When sending a request to the Brewery DB service, the values of the `<http:relative-URI>` and `<http:query-string>` elements in the `outbound` variable are combined with the Endpoint URI.

So far only the response of the Brewery DB service is logged. But this centralized, additional layer of processing logic can be useful for many other things, such as:

- monitoring the response time of the different services centrally and alerting an administrator if an SLA is violated
- routing to other external services, depending on the request sent to the proxy service
- mapping other security credentials to the API keys used by the external service

Implementing a WebSockets transport for server-side push

In this recipe, we will install and use a custom transport. We do not actually write a custom transport because it would take way too many pages to describe the implementation from scratch. But we have implemented a fully functional WebSocket transport and provide it with this book.

Our WebSocket transport implementation is derived from the socket transport example that comes with the OSB installation. It is located in `MW_HOME\Oracle_OSB1\samples\servicebus`.

If you are keen on implementing your own custom transport, you may want to look at the source code as a starting place and adapt it according to your own requirements.

How does our custom WebSockets transport basically work? The transport communicates with a local WebSocket servlet, which in turn is accessed by a WebSocket-capable browser. Since the WebLogic server does not support WebSocket servlets yet, the transport starts an embedded Jetty server which runs the WebSocket servlet and handles WebSocket requests. The WebSocket servlet communicates with the transport interface classes, which in turn interact with business and proxy services through the WebLogic Integration transport manager framework.

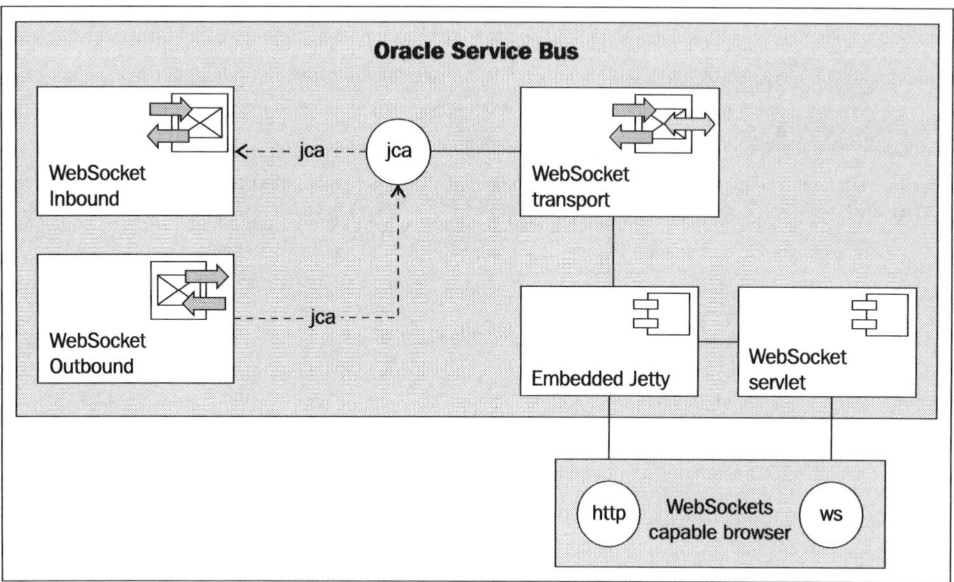

The WebSocket transport implementation is divided into two projects and deployment units:

- A transport EAR containing the OSB transport SDK
- A JAR containing the embedded Jetty server with an example WebSocket servlet

Getting ready

The Jetty part of the WebSocket transport is built and deployed with Apache Maven. Even though Maven can be executed through the command line, it is sometimes easier to have Maven support built in to the IDE. This is especially true when modifying dependencies in `pom.xml`, which require build path-updates in Eclipse OEPE.

We can easily add Maven support to Eclipse, by performing the following steps in Eclipse OEPE:

1. Navigate to **Help** | **Install New Software**.
2. Click **Add** to create a new update site and enter `M2Eclipse` into the **Name** field and `http://download.eclipse.org/technology/m2e/releases` into the **Location** field.
3. Click **OK**.
4. Select the complete **Maven Integration for Eclipse** package and click **Next** twice.
5. Accept the license agreement and click **Finish**.
6. Confirm the warning dialog by clicking **OK**.
7. Restart Eclipse OEPE by clicking **Restart Now**.

We build the WebSocket transport from the sources provided with this book. Copy the folders `static-files`, `websocket-server`, and `websocket-transport` from `\chapter-5\getting-ready\implementing-websockets-transport\` to a working folder. In the following instructions, we use `C:\work`. The file structure of the `work` folder should look as shown in the following screenshot:

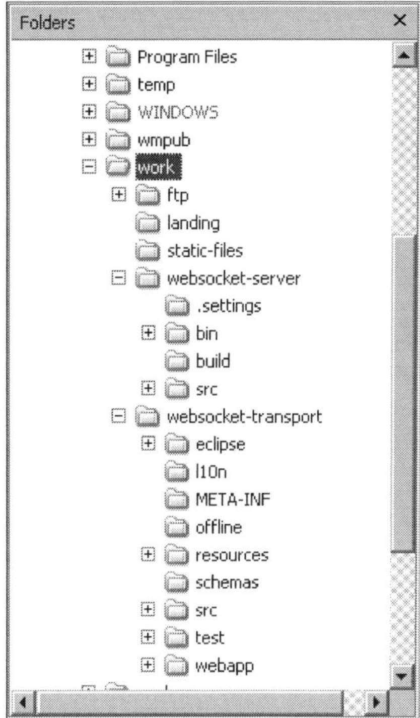

Import the two projects **websocket-server** and **websocket-transport** into Eclipse OEPE:

8. From the **File** menu select **Import | Existing Projects into Workspace**.
9. Select the option **Select root directory** and enter `c:\work` into the field and hit **Enter**.
10. Make sure that the option **Copy projects into workspace** is not selected.
11. Select the two projects **websocket-transport** and **websocket-server** and click **Finish**.

Now, we need to configure the run configuration, which allows the execution of the build scripts from the IDE. In Eclipse OEPE, perform the following steps:

12. Right-click on the file `pom.xml` in the **websocket-server** project and select **Run As | 2 Maven build...**.
13. Enter `websocket-server install` into the **Name** field.
14. Enter `clean install` into the **Goals** field.
15. Navigate to the **Common** tab.
16. Select **Run** in **Display in favorites menu**.
17. Click **Apply** and then click **Close**.

Now, some configuration files must be adjusted. In Eclipse OEPE, perform the following steps:

18. Open the `pom.xml` file in the **websocket-server** project and modify the property `mw.home` to reflect the path of the OSB installation.
19. Open the `build.properties` file in the **websocket-transport** project and modify the properties `wls.username` and `wls.password` to reflect your environment.

The Ant build script of the WebSocket transport heavily relies on environment variables specific to the WebLogic server. Thus it is easier to execute this script in a command shell than configure it in the IDE.

20. Open a command shell (for example, `cmd.exe` on Windows).
21. Execute the script `MW_HOME\user_projects\domains\osb_cookbook_domain\bin\setDomainEnv.cmd`.
23. Switch to the folder where the **websocket-transport** sources are. In our case, this is `C:\work\websocket-transport`.
24. Keep the window open as we will use it shortly.

The **WebSocket Transport** project references a variable `MW_HOME`, which must be set in Eclipse OEPE, if not already done.

25. Navigate to **Window | Preferences**.
26. In the **Preferences** window navigate to **Java | Build Path | Classpath Variables**.

27. Click **New**.
28. Enter `MW_HOME` into the **Name** field.
29. Enter the path to your Middleware installation into the **Path** field.
30. Click **OK** twice and confirm the full rebuild by clicking **Yes**.

Now, everything is ready to build and deploy the custom transport. There might still be some errors in Eclipse OEPE. They will disappear after the projects are built using Ant and Maven.

How to do it...

First we will build the **websocket-server** project. This component contains the embedded Jetty server and an example WebSocket servlet. The JAR containing everything will be copied to the `<domain_dir>\lib` folder. All the JAR files in this folder will automatically be added to the system classpath when the WebLogic server is starting up.

In Eclipse OEPE, perform the following steps:

1. From the **Run** button drop-down list, select **websocket-server install**. If everything worked fine, you should see a **BUILD SUCCESS** message in the **Console** view.
2. In the next step, we build and deploy the WebSocket transport.

In the prepared command shell window, perform the following task (OSB server must be started):

3. Execute the following command: `ant clean build stage deploy`.
4. If you see a deployment completed message in the command window, everything went fine.
5. Now restart both the OSB server and Eclipse OEPE.

If the deploy step was successfully completed once, it must not be repeated on later executions of the build. So, if we modify the transport and want to deploy it again, we can just execute `ant clean build stage` and restart both the OSB server and Eclipse OEPE.

The WebSocket transport and the embedded Jetty server are now installed and ready to be used both on the OSB server and from within Eclipse OEPE.

In the next step, we create the proxy and business service implementing the communication with the servlet that was installed with the WebSocket-server component. First, we create the proxy service which just logs the incoming messages from the WebSocket-servlet.

In Eclipse OEPE, perform the following steps:

6. Create a new OSB project and name it `using-websocket-transport`.
7. Create a `proxy` and `business` folder.

8. In the `proxy` folder, create a new proxy service and name it `WebSocketInbound`.
9. On the **General** tab, select **Any XML Service**.
10. Navigate to the **Transport** tab.
11. From the **Protocol** drop-down list, select **websocket**. If this protocol does not appear, something in the previous steps went wrong or Eclipse OEPE has not been restarted after installing the transport.
12. Enter `/pass` into the **Endpoint URI** field.
13. Navigate to the **WebSocket Transport** tab.
14. Enter `8085` into the **port** field.
15. Enter the path to the static files folder, `C:\work\static-files` in our case, into the **WebApp Static Files Directory** field. Leave everything else on default.

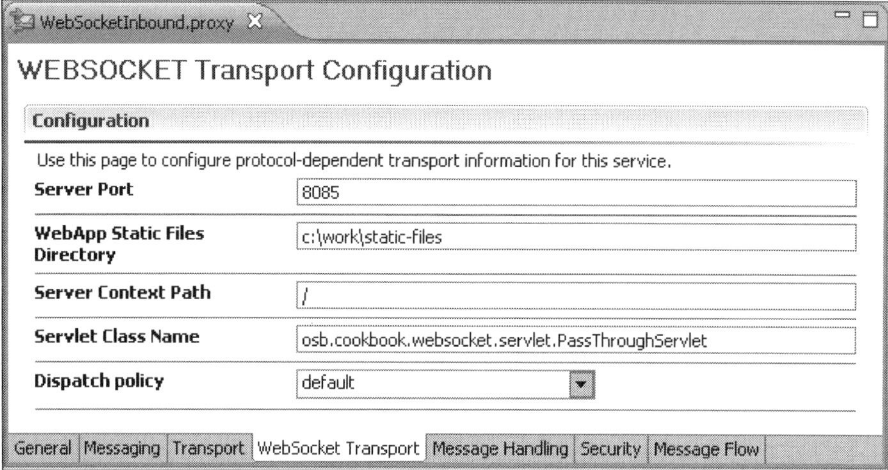

16. Navigate to the **Message Flow** tab, insert a **Pipeline Pair** and name it `RequestPipelinePair`.
17. Add a **Stage** to the **Request Pipeline** and name it `LogStage`.
18. Add a **Log** to the stage.
19. On the **Properties** of the **Log** action, click on **<Expression>** and enter `$body` into the **Expression** field.
20. Set the **Severity** level to **Warning**.
21. Deploy the project to the OSB server.

In the Service Bus console log window some messages will appear indicating that the Jetty server has been started:

```
OsbCookbookServletContext.createServer().run() start of method
2011-08-05 18:01:18.703:INFO::jetty-7.x.y-SNAPSHOT
2011-08-05 18:01:18.796:INFO::started o.e.j.s.ServletContextHandle
r{/,null}
OsbCookbookServletContext.addServlet(): called with osb.cookbook.
websocket.servlet.PassThroughServlet and path /pass
2011-08-05 18:01:18.828:INFO::Started
SelectChannelConnector@0.0.0.0:8085 STARTING
OsbCookbookServletContext.run start requested
```

In a WebSocket-capable browser, such as Google Chrome, perform the following steps:

22. Navigate to the following URL: `http://localhost:8085/`.
23. A simple chat application appears.

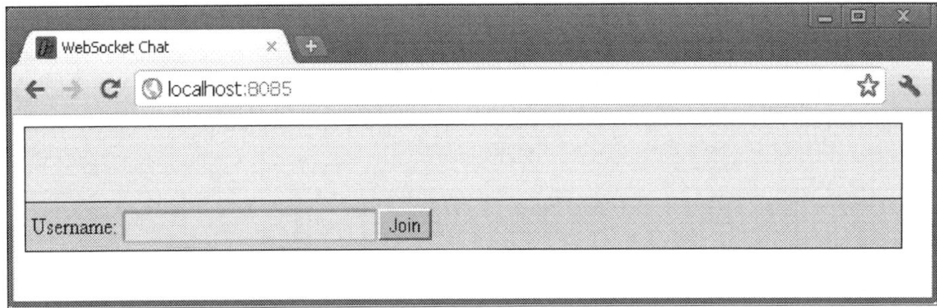

24. Enter a value into the **Username** field and click **Join**.
25. In the Service Bus console Log window, a log message indicating that the connection has been established will appear. Additionally the logged message from the chat application is shown:

```
PassThroughServlet$PassThroughSocket.onOpen()
PassThroughServlet$PassThroughSocket.onMessage(): John:has joined!
<Aug 5, 2011 6:24:35 PM CEST> <Warning> <ALSB Logging> <BEA-
000000> < [PipelinePairNode1, PipelinePairNode1_request, stage1,
REQUEST] <soapenv:Body xmlns:soapenv="http://schemas.xmlsoap.org/
soap/envelope/">
  <msg>John:has joined!</msg>
</soapenv:Body>>
```

The inbound communication is now finished. We can start sending messages via the chat application. The proxy service will be invoked and executed for every single message.

Keep the browser window open as we will use it again in a few minutes.

To communicate back to the user connected via the WebSocket servlet we need to implement a business service using our new WebSocket transport. In Eclipse OEPE, perform the following steps:

26. In the `business` folder, create a new business service and name it `WebSocketOutbound`.
27. On the **General** tab, select **Any XML Service**.
28. Switch to the **Transport** tab.
29. From the **Protocol** drop-down list, select **websocket**.
30. Enter `/pass` into the **Endpoint URI** field and click **Add**.
31. Navigate to the **WebSocket Transport** tab.
32. Enter the path to the static files folder, `C:\work\static-files` in our case, into the **WebApp Static Files Directory** field. .
33. Enter `8085` into the **port** field.
34. Deploy the project to the OSB server.

Now, we can invoke the business service to send a message back to the browser. Make sure that there was no timeout in the chat browser window. If so, join again.

In the Service Bus console perform the following steps:

35. In the **Project Explorer** navigate to the **WebSocketOutbound** business service.
36. Click on the **Launch Test Console** icon.
37. Enter `<x>Hello from OSB</x>` into the **Payload** field and click **Execute**.
38. The message will appear in the chat window a little bit later:

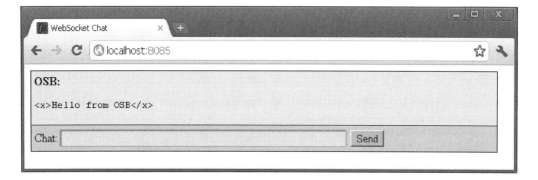

How it works...

The example WebSocket transport implementation starts one single Jetty instance that is shared among all services using the WebSocket transport. This instance deploys one single JEE web-application, which is also shared. Thus, all services must define the same values for **Server Port**, **WebApp Static Files Directory** and **Server Context Path**. This is not very user friendly, but it simplifies the example transport implementation.

Every service defines a WebSocket servlet by providing the **Servlet Class Name** on the **WebSocket Transport** tab and the **Endpoint URI** on the **Transport** tab. The **Endpoint URI** is used as the instance identifier of the servlet. There is one servlet instance for every URI.

More than one business service may register for the same Endpoint URI, but it is only possible to register one proxy service for a certain Endpoint URI. This is not a limitation of the OSB transport framework, but a design choice. Every incoming message starts the proxy service in its own thread. If it would be possible to register more than one proxy service on the same servlet, there would be multiple threads processing the same message, which would not be very efficient.

There is no request-response pattern available with our WebSocket transport. This would not make a lot of sense because normally both ends of the connection, server and client, will send messages individually in any order and at any time.

One characteristic of the WebSocket protocol, similar to the HTTP protocol, is that the client initiates a connection. However, both ends may end a connection. The example transport never ends the connection. Timeouts occur after 30 seconds, which is the default HTTP timeout in Jetty.

There's more...

There are a few main classes which implement the larger part of the WebSocket transport. On the web server side, there is the WebSocket servlet class `osb.cookbook.websocket.servlet.PassThroughServlet`, which—as its name suggests—passes messages from the WebSocket client to the WebSocket transport and vice versa. Messages are converted back and forth by this servlet, from `String` on the web server side to `org.apache.xmlbeans.XmlObject` on the transport side.

The other important class on the web server side is `osb.cookbook.websocket.OsbCookbookServletContext`. It mainly creates and starts the embedded Jetty server, adds servlets configured in the WebSocket transport, and passes messages between the transport and the servlets. The latter is implemented in the methods `update()` and `notifyOSB()`.

On the transport side, there are lot of classes that implement all the tooling around Eclipse OEPE and Service Bus console. Two other classes are responsible for receiving and sending messages. The class which is handling the sending of messages from OSB is `com.bea.alsb.transports.websocket.WebSocketOutboundMessageContext`. Its method `send()` communicates via `OsbCookbookServletContext` with the web server. The class responsible for receiving messages is `com.bea.alsb.transports.websocket.WebSocketTransportReceiver`. Its `receive()` method is called by the `OsbCookbookServletContext`'s `notifyOSB()` method.

This call is performed by reflection to avoid cyclic dependencies of the involved classes (the web server side does not have to know the transport classes). The method `receive()` stores the message in a linked list and immediately returns. The `WebSocketTransportReceiver` class has started a thread which listens on the linked list and schedules a `WebSocketInboundMessageContext` for every incoming message. With this context, the proxy service is invoked.

6
Using File and Email Transports

In this chapter, we will cover:

- Using the **File** or **FTP Transport** to trigger a proxy service upon arrival of a new file
- Using the File JCA adapter to read a file within the message flow
- Using the **File** or **FTP Transport** to write a file
- Using **Email Transport** to receive e-mail
- Using **Email Transport** to send e-mail

Introduction

In this chapter, we will cover the so called Poll-based transports, the **File** or **FTP Transport**, the **Email Transport**, as well as the File JCA adapter.

As the name implies, the **File** or **FTP Transport** can be used to do operations on files. When using the **File Transport**, the file needs to be local to the OSB Server or reachable via a file share, whereas when using the **FTP Transport**, the file can be on any FTP server reachable from the OSB. When using these transports on a proxy service, then the given location will be constantly polled for new files, and each file will be processed by the message flow of the proxy service. When the two transports are used on a business service, then a file will be written to the configured location upon invoking the business service.

The File JCA adapter allows treating the operation on a file as a service, which also allows for the reading of a file through a service invocation in the message flow of a proxy service.

The **Email Transport** supports both, the receiving as well as the sending of e-mails, with or without attachments. Using the **Email Transport** with a proxy service will consume new e-mails from an e-mail server whereas using the **Email Transport** on a business service will send an e-mail through the given e-mail server.

Using the File or FTP transport to trigger a proxy service upon arrival of a new file

In this recipe, we will trigger a proxy service upon arrival of a file in a certain location. We will implement both, a proxy service listening on a folder in a local filesystem as well as one listening to a remote location via FTP.

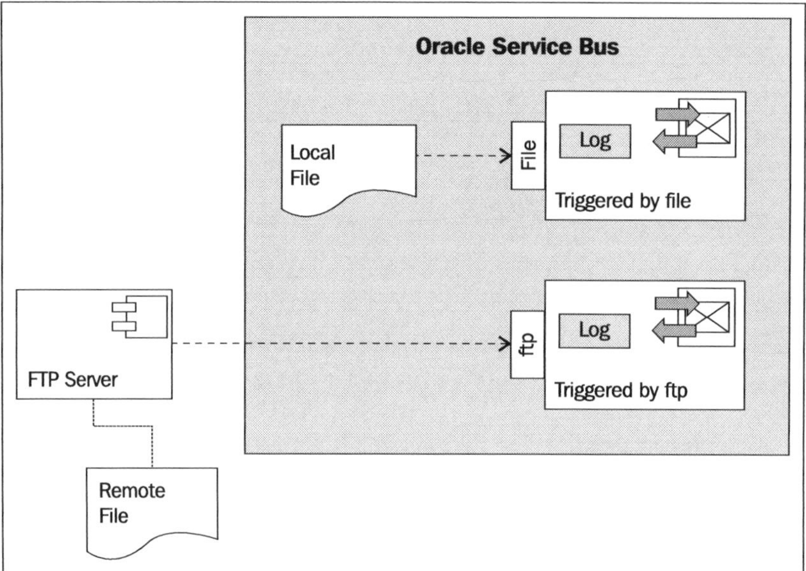

Getting ready

In order to make working with the FTP example as simple as possible, we first install a simple local FTP server:

1. From `http://coreftp.com/server/index.html`, download the **Core FTP Server**.
2. Start the installer and click through it (leave all options on default).
3. Create a folder `C:\work\ftp`.
4. Launch the Core FTP Server executable.

5. Click on **Setup**.
6. Click on **New**.
7. Enter `OSB` in the **Domain Name** field.
8. Enter `localhost` in the **Domain IP/Address** field.
9. Enter `C:\work\ftp` in the **Base directory** field.
10. Click on **OK**.

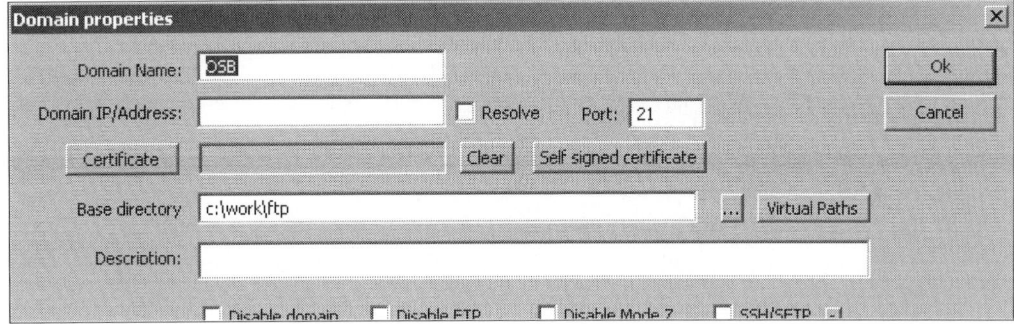

11. Back on the main setup window, select the newly created domain and click **New** on the lower half of the window, to create a user.
12. Enter `osb` in the **User name** field.
13. Enter `osb` in the **Password** field.

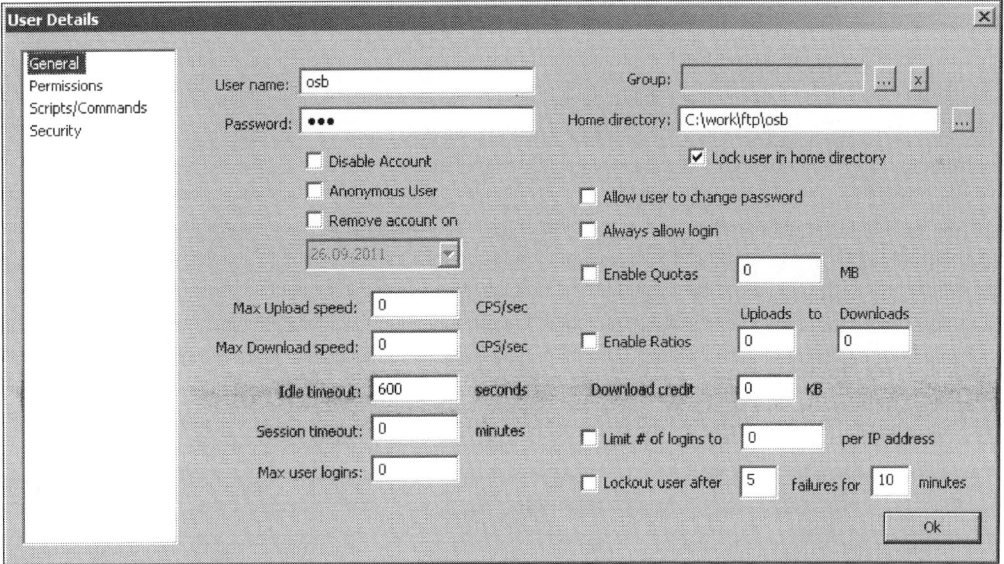

14. Click **OK** and then click **Yes** to confirm the creation of the home directory.
15. Click **OK** in the main setup window.
16. Click **Start** on the Core FTP Server main window.

The FTP server is started and ready to be used.

How to do it...

We begin with a proxy service listening on a local folder for new files. In Eclipse OEPE, perform the following steps:

1. Create a new OSB project, name it `using-file-transport-to-trigger-service` and add a `proxy` folder to that new project.
2. In the `proxy` folder, create a new proxy service named `TriggeredByFile`.
3. On the **General** tab select **Messaging Service** for the **Service Type** option.
4. Navigate to the **Messaging** tab and select **Text** as the **Request Message Type**.
5. Leave the **Response Message Type** on **None**.
6. Navigate to the **Transport** tab select **file** from the **Protocol** drop-down list.
7. Enter `file:///C:/work/landing` into the **Endpoint URI** field.
8. Navigate to the **File Transport** tab and enter `5` into the **Polling Interval** field.
9. Select **archive** from the **Post Read Action** drop-down list.
10. Enter `C:\work\stage` into the **Stage Directory** field, `C:\work\archive` into the **Archive Directory** field and `C:\work\error` into the **Error Directory** field.

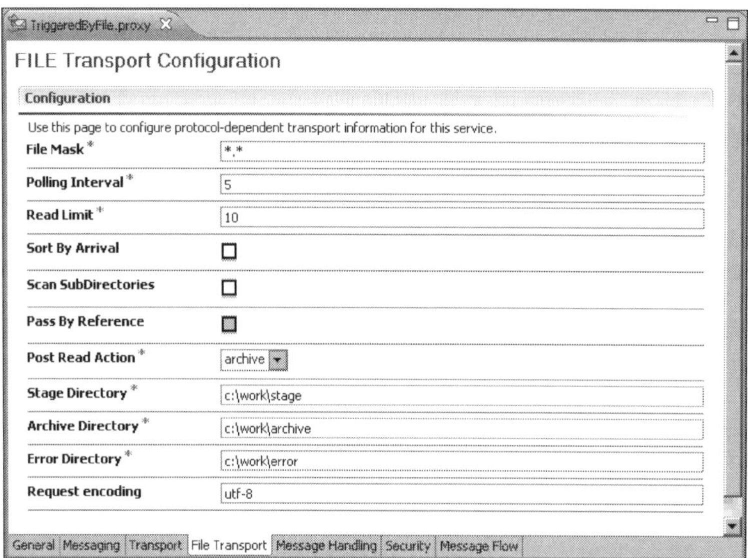

11. Navigate to the **Message Flow** tab, insert a **Pipeline Pair** and name it `FileProcessingPipelinePair`.
12. Insert a **Stage** node into the **Request Pipeline** and name it `LogStage`.
13. Insert a **Log** action into the stage.
14. Enter `$inbound` as the log **Expression** and set the **Severity** to **Warning**.
15. Insert a second **Log** action into the stage.
16. Enter `$body/text()` as the log **Expression** and set the **Severity** to **Warning**.

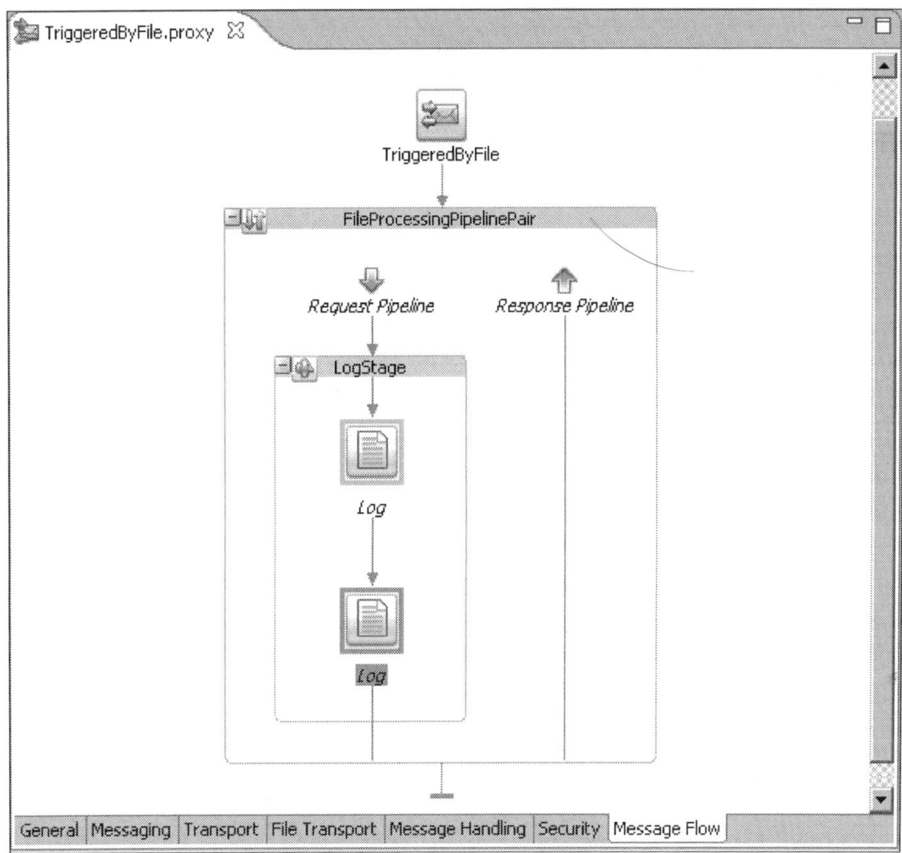

17. Deploy the project to the OSB server.

Now our simple file polling service, implemented by a proxy service using the **File Transport**, is ready and can be tested.

Copy a text file into the folder `C:\work\landing`. Within five seconds, the file will disappear from that folder and two log messages, one with metadata from `$inbound` and one with the content of the file, are shown on the Service Bus console log window.

```
OSB Cookbook 11R2 PS3 (11.1.1.4)
0 vorhanden ist. Der neuere Snapshot ersetzt den ölteren.>
<30.09.2011 16:38 Uhr MESZ> <Warning> <ALSB Logging> <BEA-000000> < [FileProcess
ingPipelinePair, FileProcessingPipelinePair_request, LogStage, REQUEST] <con:end
point name="ProxyService$file-transport-to-trigger-service$proxy$TriggeredByFile
" xmlns:con="http://www.bea.com/wli/sb/context">
  <con:service/>
  <con:transport>
    <con:uri>file:///C:/work/landing</con:uri>
    <con:mode>request</con:mode>
    <con:qualityOfService>exactly-once</con:qualityOfService>
    <con:request xsi:type="file:FileRequestMetaData" xmlns:file="http://www.bea.
com/wli/sb/transports/file" xmlns:xsi="http://www.w3.org/2001/XMLSchema-instance
">
      <tran:headers xsi:type="file:FileRequestHeaders" xmlns:tran="http://www.be
a.com/wli/sb/transports">
        <file:fileName>C:\work\landing\hello.txt</file:fileName>
      </tran:headers>
      <tran:encoding xmlns:tran="http://www.bea.com/wli/sb/transports">utf-8</tr
an:encoding>
      <file:isFilePath>false</file:isFilePath>
    </con:request>
  </con:transport>
  <con:security>
    <con:transportClient>
      <con:username>&lt;anonymous></con:username>
    </con:transportClient>
  </con:security>
</con:endpoint>>
<30.09.2011 16:38 Uhr MESZ> <Warning> <ALSB Logging> <BEA-000000> < [FileProcess
ingPipelinePair, FileProcessingPipelinePair_request, LogStage, REQUEST] Hello wo
rld!>
```

We have implemented a proxy service listening and process files arriving on a local folder. Now, let's implement a proxy service consuming files from a remote FTP location.

In Eclipse OEPE, perform the following steps:

18. In the `proxy` folder create a new proxy service named `TriggeredByFtp`.
19. On the **General** tab select **Messaging Service** as the **Service Type** option.
20. Navigate to the **Messaging** tab and select **Text** as the **Request Message Type**.
21. Leave the **Response Message Type** on **None**.
22. Navigate to the **Transport** tab and select **ftp** from the **Protocol** drop-down list.
23. Enter `ftp://localhost/` into the **Endpoint URI** field.
24. Navigate to the **FTP Transport** tab enter `5` into the **Polling Interval** field.
25. Select **archive** from the **Post Read Action** drop-down list.
26. Enter `C:\work\archive` into the **Archive Directory** field, `C:\work\stage` into the **Download Directory** field and C:\work\error into the **Error Directory** field.

In order to access the FTP server, the proxy service needs to authenticate itself. To provide the credentials, we first need a Service Account, which can then be used on the proxy service.

27. Within the **file-transport-to-trigger-service** project create a new folder and name it `security`.
28. Right-click on the folder `security` and choose **New | Service Account**.
29. Enter `FTPUser` into the **File name** field and click **Finish**.
30. Select **Static** for the **Resource Type** option.
31. Enter `osb` into the **User Name** field and `osb` into the **Password** and **Confirm Password** fields.

The Service Account is now configured and ready to be used from our proxy service.

32. Reopen the **TriggeredByFtp** proxy service and navigate to the **FTP Transport** tab.
33. Select **external user** for the **User Authentication** option.
34. Right to the **Service Account** field, click **Browse** and select the service account created previously:

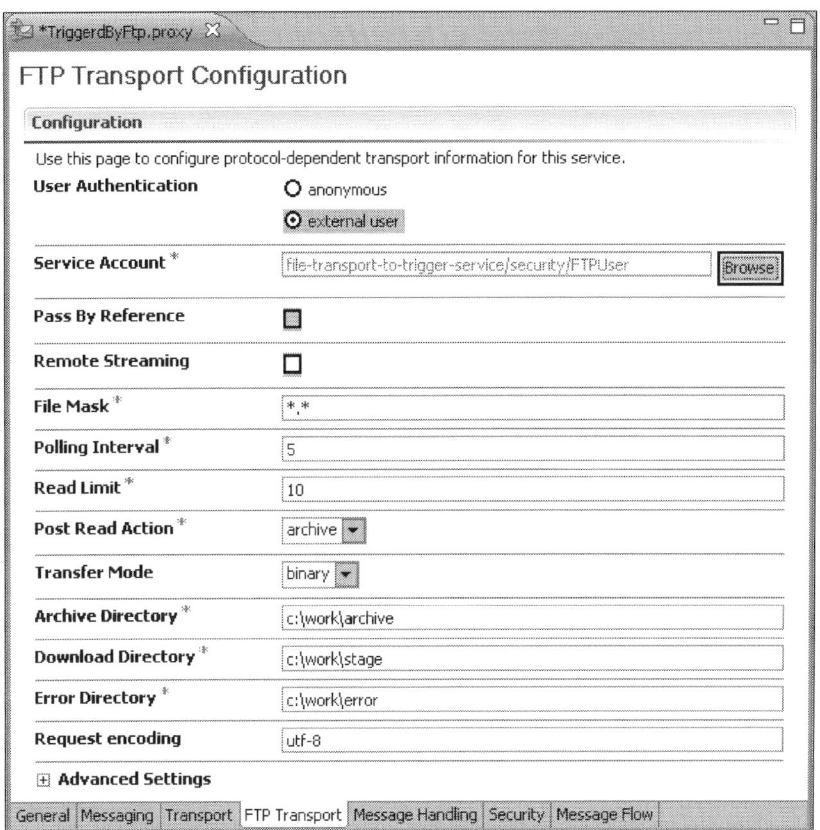

35. Navigate to the **Message Flow** tab, insert a **Pipeline Pair** and name it `FileProcessingPipelinePair`.
36. Insert a **Stage** to it and name it `LogStage`.
37. Add a first **Log** action to the stage with `$inbound` as the log **Expression** and set the **Severity** to **Warning**.
38. Add a second **Log** action to the stage with `$body/text()` as the log **Expression** and set the **Severity** to **Warning**.
39. Redeploy the project to the OSB server.

Now our file polling service, implemented by a proxy service using the **FTP Transport** is ready and can be tested.

Copy a text file to the directory `C:\work\ftp\osb`. Within five seconds the file will disappear from that folder and two log messages, one with the metadata of `$inbound` and one with the content of the file, are shown on the Service Bus console log window.

How it works...

Both transports, the File and the **FTP Transport** work similarly. The main difference is the file retrieval mechanism. Of course, polling through FTP is more costly than polling on the local filesystem using the **File Transport**. Take that into account when defining the polling frequency.

If the transport discovers a new file in polling location, then the file is copied into the staging directory. The file remains in there until the execution of the proxy service is finished. The absolute path of the processed file is available within the message flow through the `$inbound` variable.

If the proxy service finishes with an uncaught error, the file is moved to the `error` folder. If the proxy service terminates without an error, the file is moved to the `archive` folder—or deleted, depending on the option chosen for **Post Read Action**. Files in the `error` and `archive` folders are automatically prefixed with a UUID to make the filename unique.

Proxy service execution started through either the **File** or **FTP Transport** can be transactional. A new transaction is started upon execution. Both the **File** and **FTP Transport** are one-way only; it is not possible to return a response.

There's more...

In this section, we discuss the difference between the **File** or **FTP Transport** and the JCA adapters, show how to process files selectively and how to handle files with binary content.

File and FTP transports versus JCA adapters

The File and FTP transports are not as feature-rich as the corresponding File and FTP JCA adapters, known from the Oracle SOA Suite and also available for OSB.

For instance, with both the File and FTP transports, it is not possible to read a file within a message flow. A file can only be read inbound through polling, meaning that a new proxy service message flow is started. This is the behavior we have shown in this recipe.

To read a file from inside an already started and active message flow, use the File or FTP JCA adapter, as covered in the *Using the File JCA adapter to read a file within the message flow* recipe.

When using the **File** or **FTP transport** on a business service, then the behavior is always outbound, meaning that a file can only be written. This is covered in the recipe *Using the File or FTP transport to write a file*.

Furthermore, the JCA adapter also provides far richer metadata about the file being processed.

Selectively processing files

You can selectively process files inside the polling directory, by using the **File Mask** on the **FTP Transport** tab.

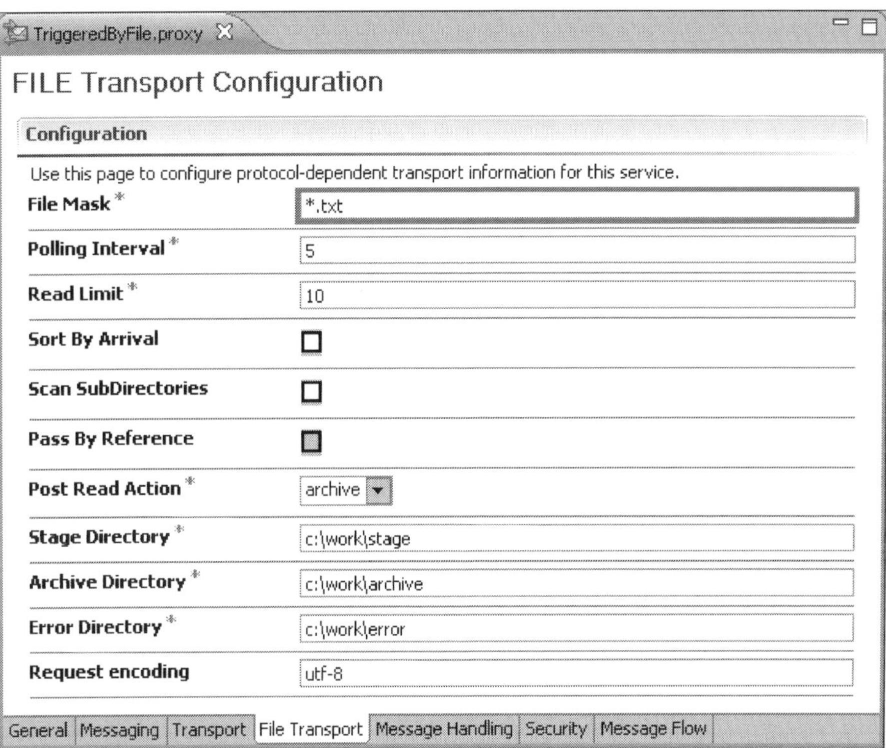

Processing binary files

When working with files, we often end up with the requirement that we have to be able to handle files with binary content, such as images, movies, or other digital content.

The OSB offers no direct support for manipulating binary data inside the message flow of a proxy service. Binary data will be represented as a reference. If we change the **Request Message Type** on the **Messaging** tab of the proxy service from **Text** to **Binary**, the body will have the following content when copying a binary file into the polling folder:

```
<soapenv:Body
    xmlns:soapenv="http://schemas.xmlsoap.org/soap/envelope/"
    xmlns:con="http://www.bea.com/wli/sb/context">
  <con:binary-content ref="cid:6af7caf5:132a6198e59:6a40" />
</soapenv:Body>
```

We can see that the content of the file is no longer present inside the <soapenv:Body> element, but only a reference is.

Such references to binary data can be passed as a byte array to an EJB message-driven bean or to an EJB session bean, where it can then be processed using Java.

Binary content can also be passed through the proxy service to a business service, which is using an outbound **File** or **FTP Transport**. In that case, we just pass the content of the `body` variable untouched to the business service.

Another option is to pass the binary content to a **Java Callout** action. A method accepting binary data can have the following signature.

```
public static void fileProcessing(byte[] inputData) {
  ...
}
```

When calling this method from a **Java Callout** action inside the message flow of a proxy service, the following XPath expression must be used to bind the `inputData` parameter:

```
$body/ctx:binary-content
```

Using this expression, the OSB automatically converts the reference contained in the <binary-content> element into a byte array, which can then be accessed in the Java code.

See also

Check the *Using the File JCA adapter to read a file within the message flow* recipe to see how to read the content of a file inside an active message flow.

Using the File JCA adapter to read a file within the message flow

If there is a need to read the contents of a file inside a message flow of an already active proxy service, then neither the **File Transport** nor the FTP transport can be of any help. Reading a file with the **File** or **FTP Transport** is always only available inbound, implemented as a polling operation and starting a new message flow/proxy service upon detecting a new file.

This recipe will show how we can use the File JCA adapter to read a file at runtime, for example, to enrich data at runtime or to retrieve some configuration information. The JCA adapters are available since OSB 11g and are the same ones we know from the SOA Suite.

We will create a business service wrapping the artifacts created by the JCA adapter wizard in JDeveloper. By that the business service is just as any other business service seen so far and can be invoked from a proxy service using a **Routing** or **Service Callout** action as shown in this recipe.

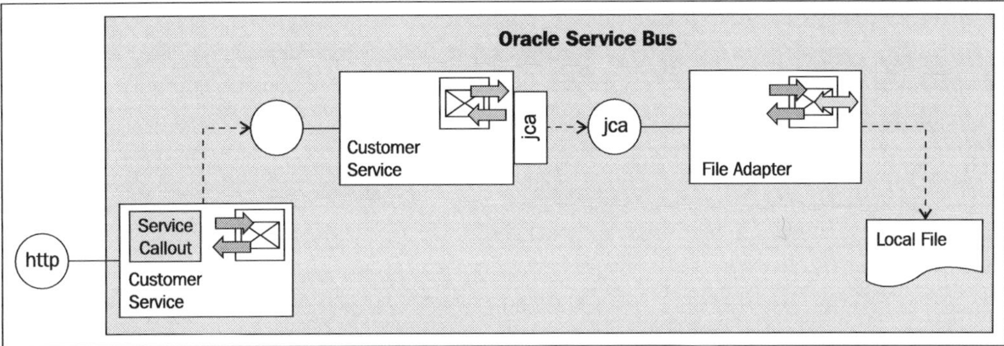

The scenario shown can be helpful if you need to retrieve some configuration data or you'll have to enrich the message, and the data is already available as a file.

Getting ready

Import the base OSB project containing the folder structure and the nested JDeveloper project as shown in recipe *Setting up OSB project to work with JCA adapters* into Eclipse from `\chapter-6\getting-ready\reading-a-file-within-a-message-flow`.

How to do it...

First, we will use JDeveloper to create the File adapter, using the nested SOA project inside the `adapter` folder of the Eclipse OEPE project. In JDeveloper, perform the following steps:

1. Open the `AdapterSOAProject.jpr` file inside the `adapter` folder of the OSB project, by selecting **File | Open**.
2. In the SOA project, double-click on the `composite.xml` file to open the SCA composite.
3. To be able to create the File adapter, we need a XML Schema defining the data we will read. Copy the prepared XML Schema file from `\chapter-6\getting-ready\reading-a-file-within-a-message-flow\Properties.xsd` and paste it into the `xsd` folder inside the SOA project:

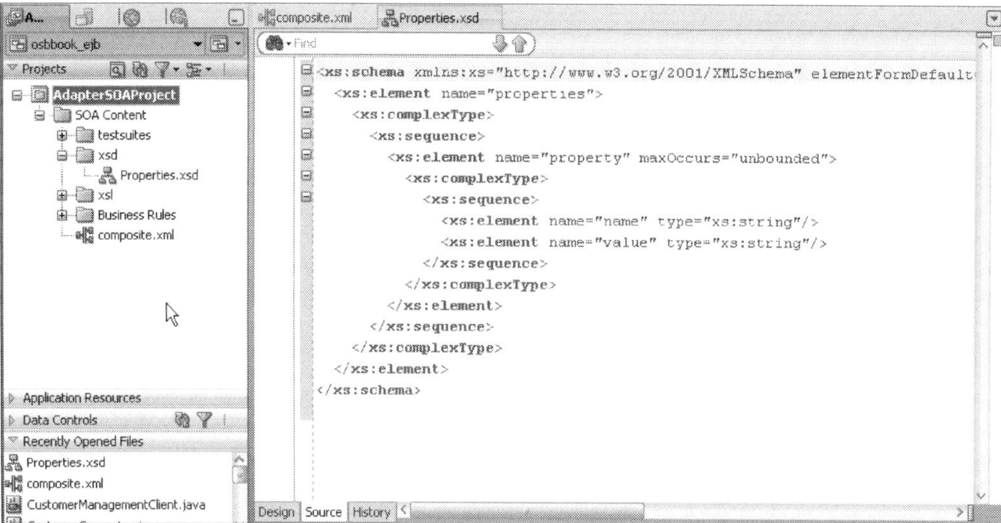

4. On the SOA Composite view, drag a new **File Adapter** from the **Component Palette** and drop it on the **External References** swim lane on the right-hand side.

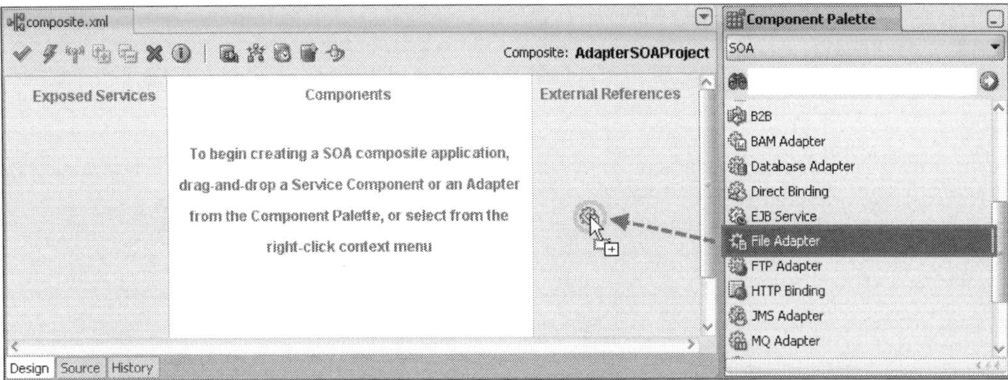

5. Click **Next**.
6. Enter `FileReadingService` into the **Service Name** field and click **Next**.
7. Select the **Define from operation and schema (specified later)** option and click **Next**.
8. Select **Synchronous Read File** for the **Operation Type** option.
9. Leave `SynchRead` in the **Operation Name** field and click **Next**.

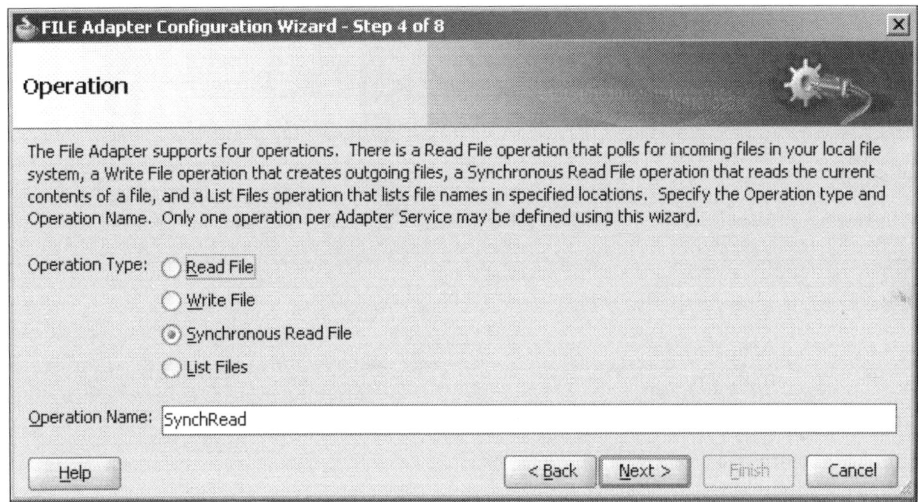

10. Select **Physical Path** for the **Directory names are specified as** option.
11. Enter `C:\work\files\in` into the **Directory for Incoming Files** field.

12. The option **Delete files after successful retrieval** is enabled but grayed out and cannot by changed (reason for that not known). This is probably not we want here, because we want the file to stay. We will later see the possibility to change the flag when creating/configuring the business service.
13. Click **Next**.

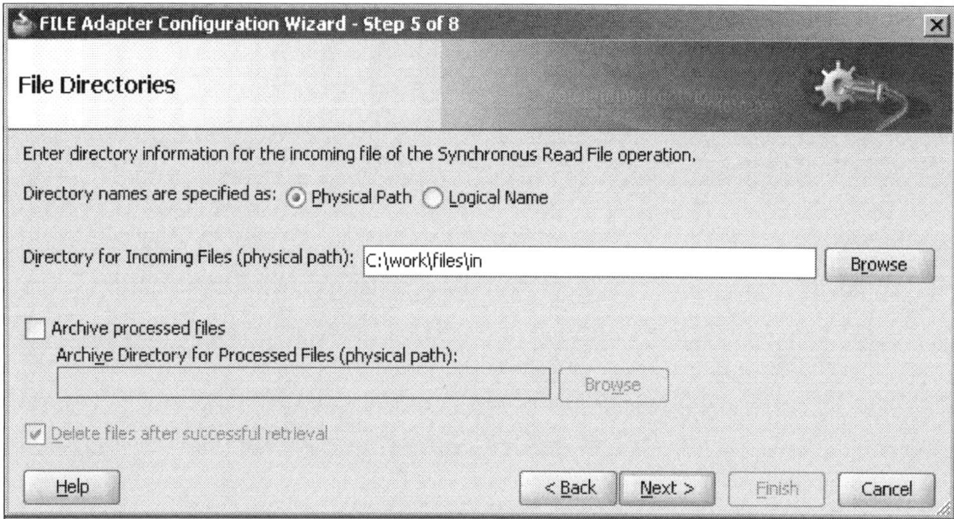

14. Enter `Properties.xml` into the **File Name** field and click **Next**.
15. Deselect the **Native format translation is not required** option.
16. Enter `xsd/Properties.xsd` into the **URL** field.
17. Select **properties** in the **Schema Element** drop-down listbox.
18. Click **Next** and then click **Finish**.
19. Save the SOA project in JDeveloper.

This is all we have to do in JDeveloper to get the necessary artifacts describing the File adapter service. We can now go back to Eclipse OEPE and generate a business service based on the JCA metadata.

In Eclipse OEPE, perform the following steps:

20. Refresh the `adapter` folder inside the OSB project.

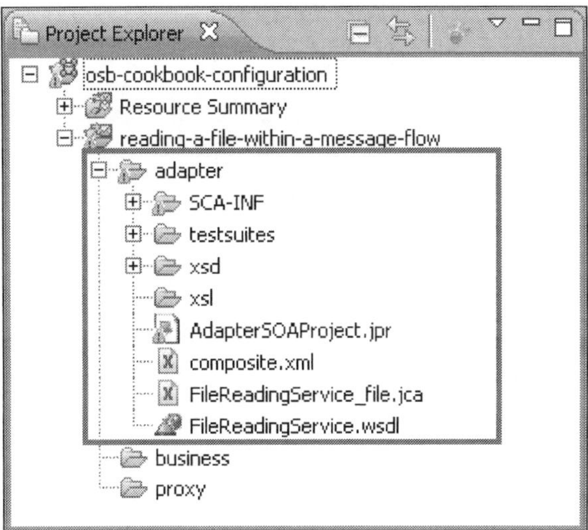

21. Right-click on the `FileReadingService_file.jca` file and select **Oracle Service Bus | Generate Service** to generate a business service based on the JCA adapter definition.
22. Select the `business` folder in the **Select the location for the WSDL and Service** tree.
23. Enter `FileReadingService` into the **Service name** and **WSDL name** field and click **OK**.

The business service is generated. We could already use it like that. But we have to configure the adapter to not remove the file after reading it. In Eclipse OEPE, perform the following steps to configure the business service:

24. Open the generated **FileReadingService** business service and navigate to the **JCA Transport** tab.
25. Expand the **Advanced Settings** at the bottom of the window.

26. Disable **Always use configuration from JCA file** and set the **Delete File** field value to `false`.

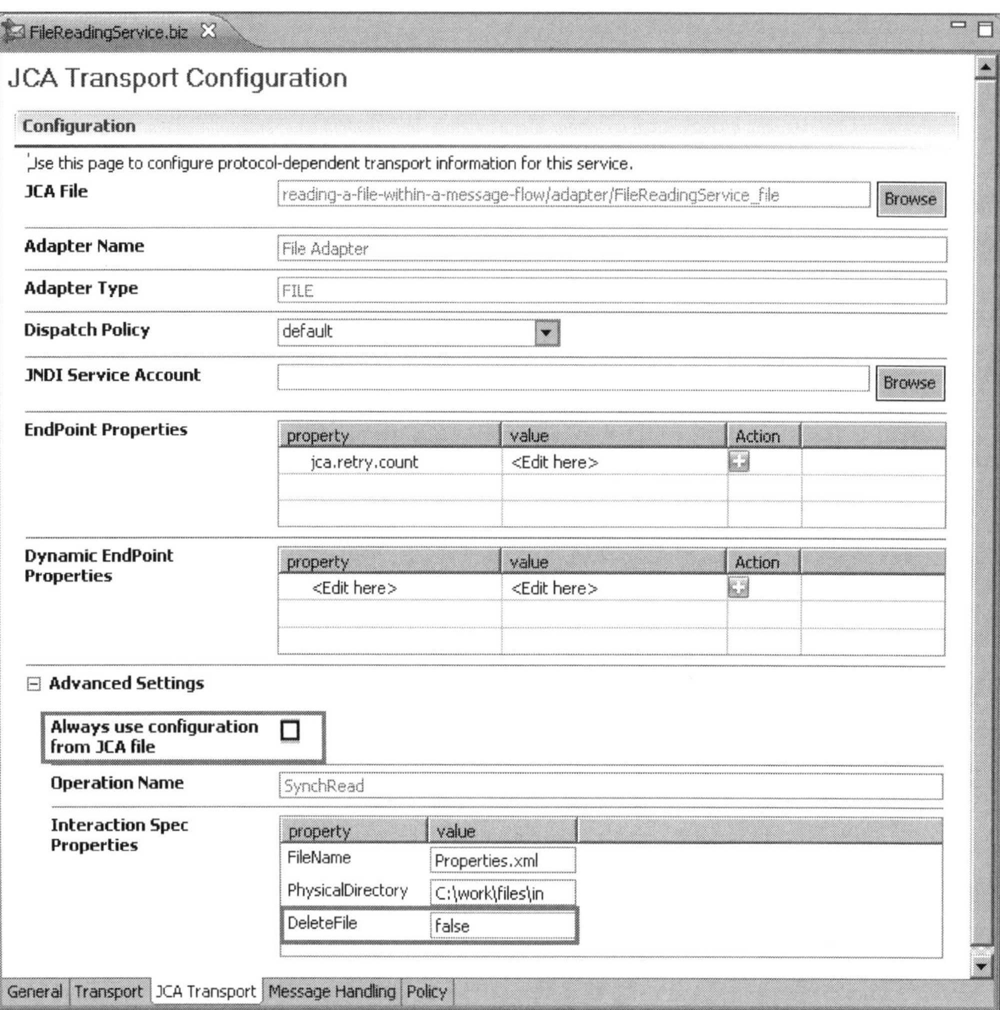

Next we will create the proxy service, which will invoke the business service generated previously, through a **Service Callout** action.

27. Inside the `proxy` folder, create a new proxy service and name it `FileReader`.
28. Select **Any XML Service** for the **Service Type** option.
29. Navigate to the **Transport** tab.
30. Select **http** for the **protocol** drop-down listbox.

31. Navigate to the **Message Flow** tab.
32. Insert a **Pipeline Pair** action and name it `ReadFilePipelinePair`.
33. Insert a **Stage** node into the **Request Pipeline**, and name it `FileReadStage`.
34. In the **FileReadStage** stage, insert a **Service Callout** action.

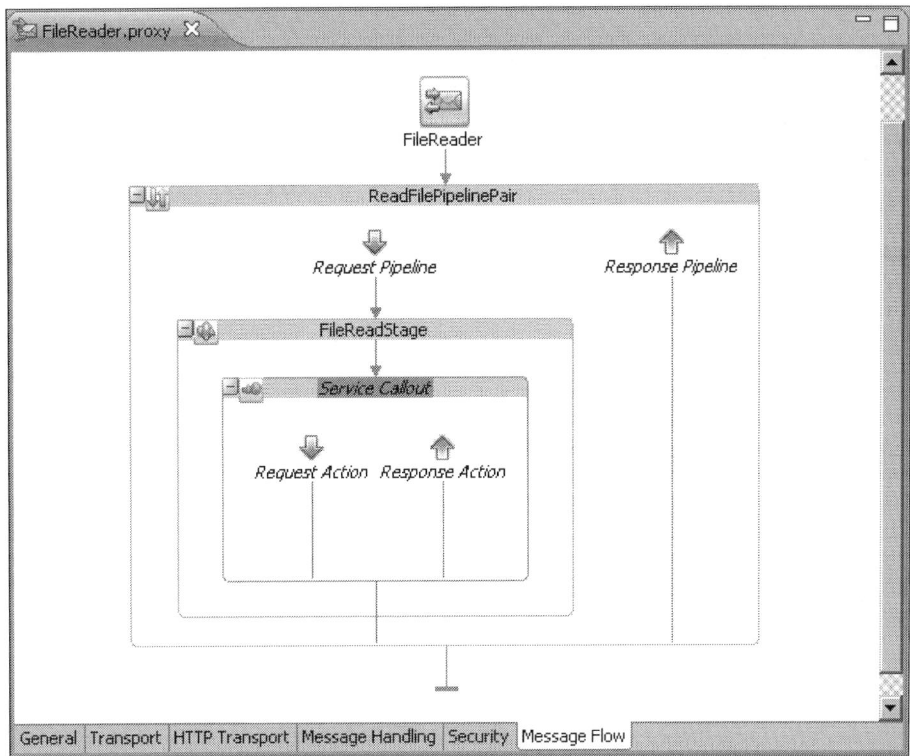

35. Navigate to the **Properties** tab of the **Service Callout** action, click **Browse** and select the **FileReadingService** business service.
36. Select the **SynchRead** operation for the **Invoking** drop-down listbox.
37. Select the **Configure Payload Document** option.

38. Enter `fileRequest` into the **Request Variable** field and `fileResponse` into the **Response Variable** field:

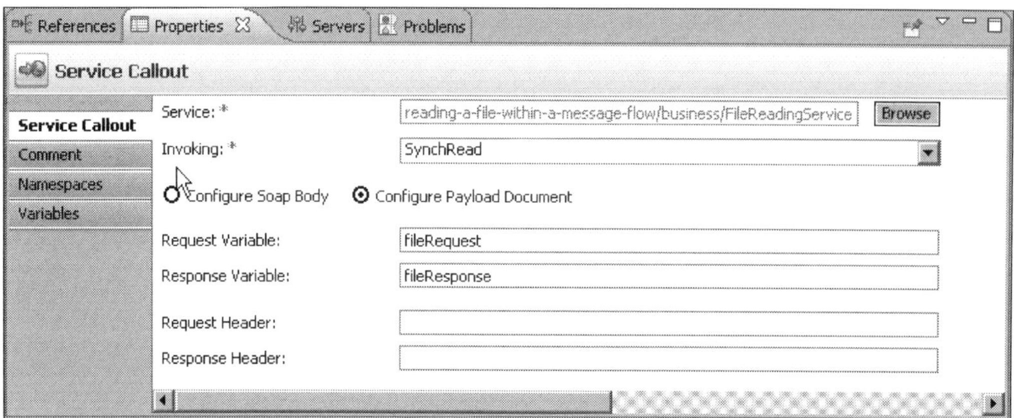

39. Deploy the project to the OSB server.
40. Copy the file `\chapter-6\getting-ready\reading-a-file-within-a-message-flow\misc\Properties.xml` into the `c:\temp\in\files` folder.

Now we're ready to test the service. On the Service Bus console perform the following steps:

41. In the **Project Explorer** navigate to the **FileReader** proxy service inside the `proxy` folder.
42. Click on the **Launch Test Console** icon and click **Execute**.
43. Check the **Invocation trace** to see that the content of the file is available in the `fileResponse` variable.

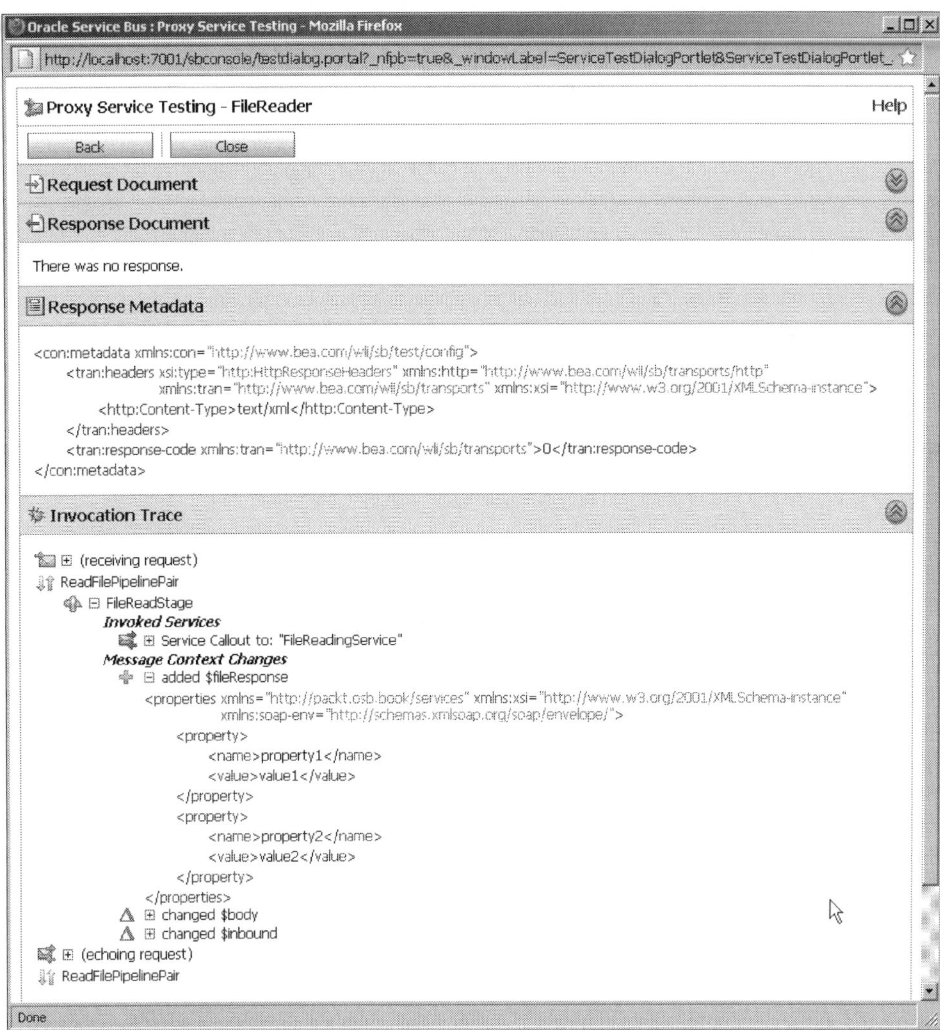

How it works...

In this recipe, we have used the File JCA adapter for reading files from the local filesystem (local to the OSB server) from within a message flow of a proxy service. With the **File Transport**, reading a file can only be used in a polling scenario, where a proxy service together with the **File Transport** constantly polls for new files to arrive and a new message flow is started for each file. So the file itself is the trigger when using the **File Transport**. When using the File JCA adapter, the operation on the file (write or read) is exposed as a service and being wrapped by an OSB business service it can be invoked as any other service. The JCA adapter actually creates a WSDL, which acts as the contract for the service, although behind the scenes, JCA is used as the protocol and not SOAP or HTTP.

We have used the **Service Callout** action to invoke the File adapter service, but we could have used a **Routing** action as well. Reading a file is typically only one of the (preparing) steps in a proxy flow and a **Service Callout** action needs to be used, as no further (request) actions can follow a **Routing** action in a message flow.

There's more...

In this section, we show how to set file/folder names dynamically at runtime and how to read a file through an XQuery script, as an alternative to the File JCA adapter.

Setting the filename and folder name dynamically at runtime

When going through the File adapter in JDeveloper, we have specified the file and directory name to be used for reading the file. These settings are used at runtime, if not overwritten by the invoker. To overwrite them, we can use the **Transport Header** action inside the **Service Callout** and specify some JCA-specific transport header properties.

In Eclipse OEPE, open the **FileReader** proxy service and perform the following steps:

1. In the **Request Pipeline** of the **Service Callout** action, insert a **Transport Header** activity.

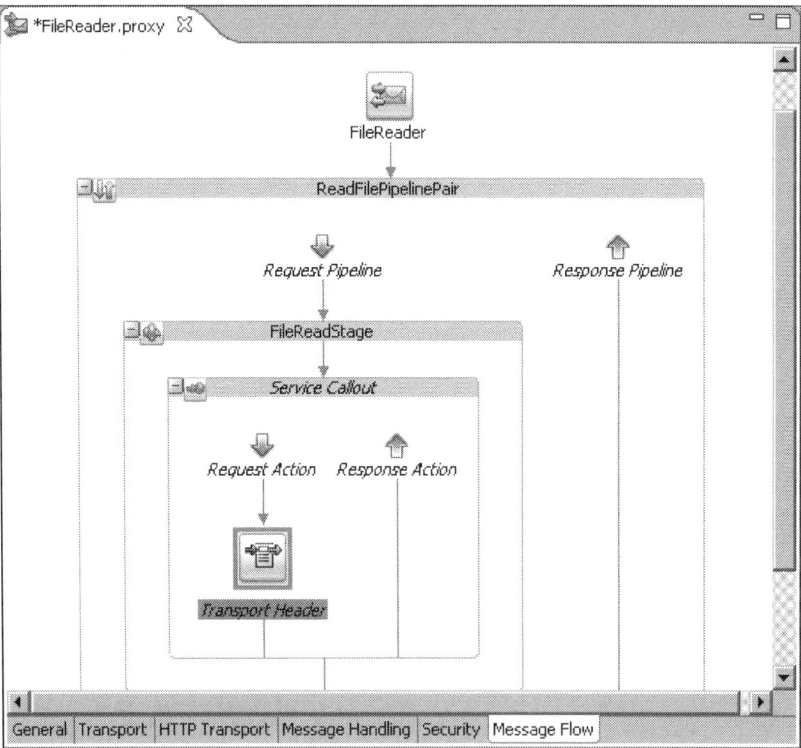

2. On the **Properties** tab of the **Transport Header** action, click **Add Header** twice.
3. Set the **Defined** drop-down list to **jca** and select the **jca.file.FileName** property with the following **Set Header to** expression: `data($body/configuration/location[1]/filename)`.
4. Set the **Defined** drop-down list for the second header again to **jca** and select the **jca.file.Directory** property with the following **Set Header to** expression: `data($body/configuration/location[1]/directory)`.

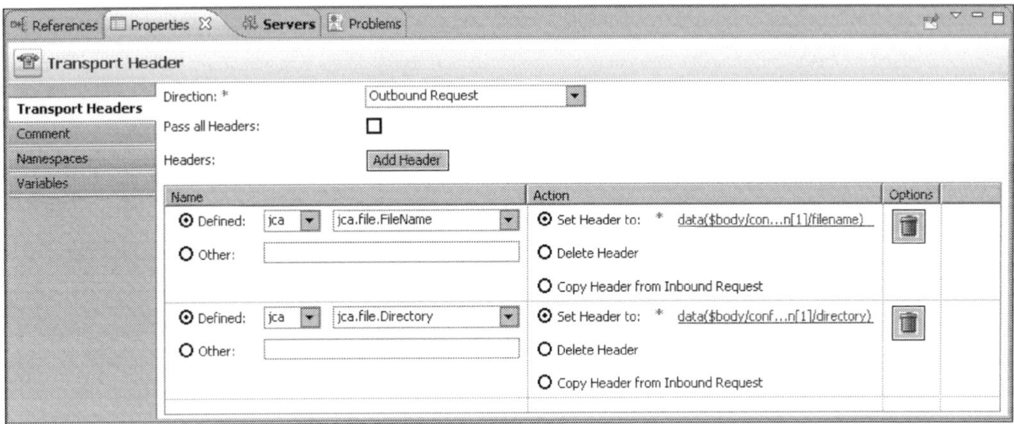

5. Deploy the project to the OSB server.
6. Copy the file `\chapter-6\getting-ready\reading-a-file-within-a-message-flow\misc\OtherProperties.xml` into the `c:\temp\in\files` folder.

Now, let's test the change. In Service Bus console, perform the following steps:

7. In the **Project Explorer** navigate to the **FileReader** proxy service inside the `proxy` folder.
8. Click on the **Launch Test Console** icon.
9. Set the **Payload** field to the following value:

```
<configuration>
  <location>
    <directory>c:\work\files\in</directory>
    <filename>OtherProperties.xml</filename>
  </location>
</configuration>
```

10. Check the **Invocation trace** to see that the content of the file is available in the `fileResponse` variable.

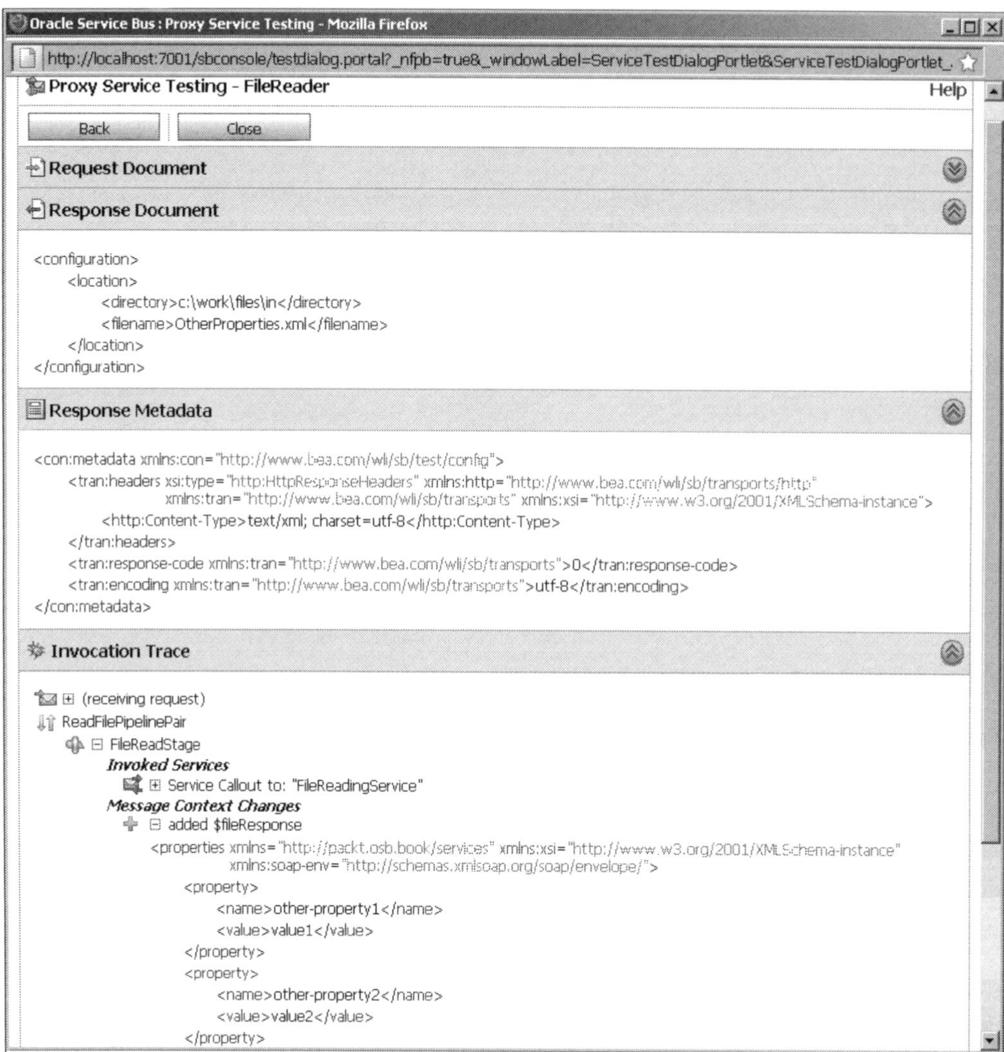

Reading file resources through a XQuery script

Another possibility for reading a file from the local filesystem from a proxy service is by using the XQuery doc function.

To read a file through XQuery, perform the following steps in Eclipse OEPE:

1. Create a `xquery` folder and copy the file `\chapter-6\getting-ready\reading-a-file-within-a-message-flow\misc\ReadFile.xq` into that folder.

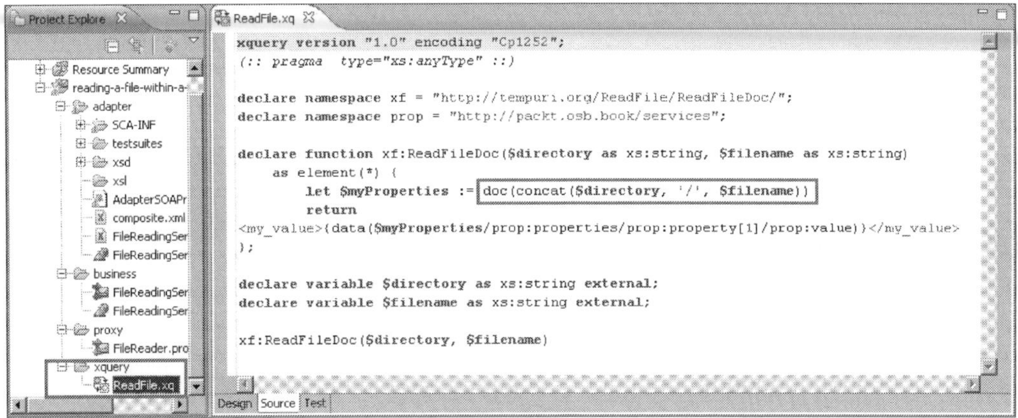

2. Insert an **Assign** action into the **FileReadStage**.
3. On the **Properties** tab of the **Assign**, type `xqueryFileResponse` into the **Variable** field.
4. Click on the **<Expression>**.
5. Select the **XQuery Resources** tab and click **Browse**.
6. Select the **ReadFile.xq** resource from the `xquery` folder.
7. Enter `data($body/configuration/location[1]/directory)` into the **directory** field.
8. Enter `data($body/configuration/location[1]/directory)` into the **filename** field.

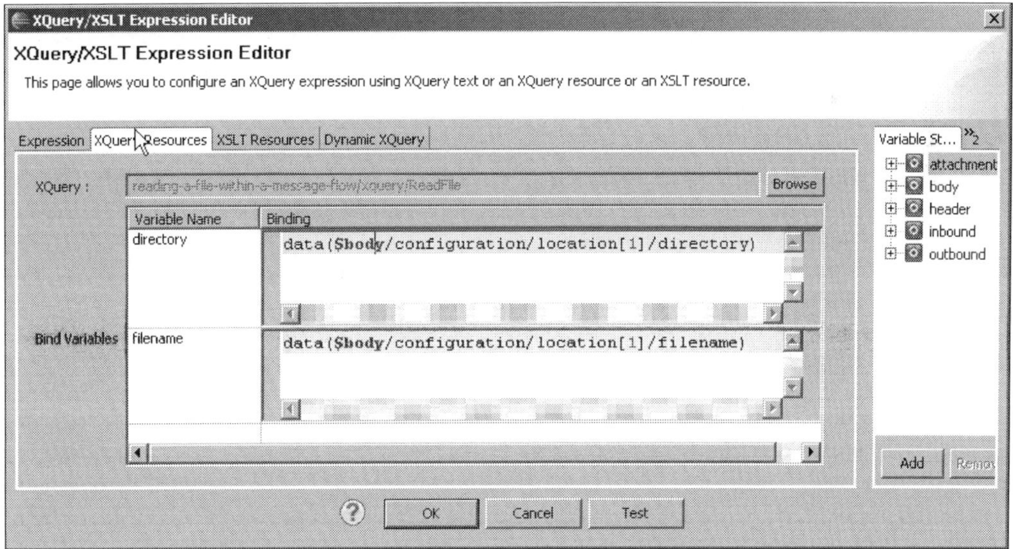

Now, let's test the change. In Service Bus console, perform the following steps:

9. In the **Project Explorer** navigate to the **FileReader** proxy service inside the `proxy` folder.
10. Click on the **Launch Test Console** icon.
11. Set the **Payload** field to the following value:

```
<configuration>
  <location>
    <directory>c:\work\files\in</directory>
    <filename>OtherProperties.xml</filename>
  </location>
</configuration>
```

12. Check the **Invocation trace** to see that the content of the file is available in the `xqueryFileResponse` variable.

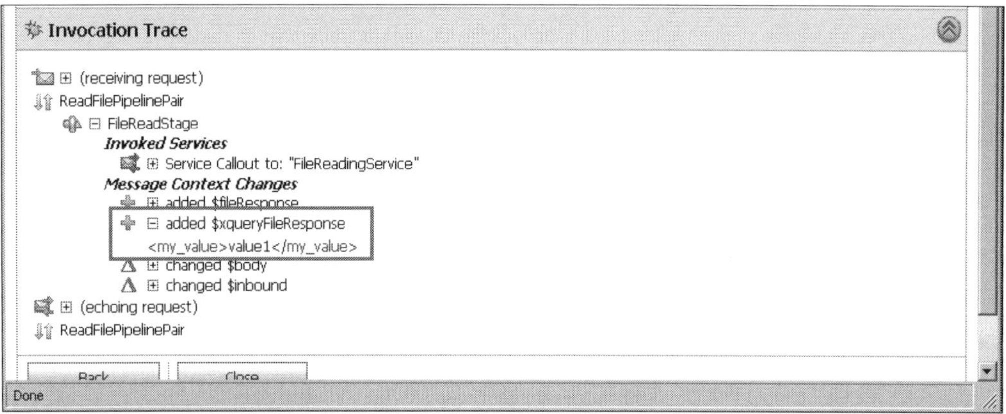

See also

If you want to read the file over and over again, then you can use the Result Cache functionality on the business service. Check the *Caching result information in the OSB* recipe to see how easily this can be enabled.

Using the File Transport to write to a file

In this recipe, we will write a file to the local filesystem (local to the OSB server). We will implement a business service which uses the **File Transport** to do that. Additionally, we will create a proxy service and control the filename of the file being written by using a **Transport Header** action.

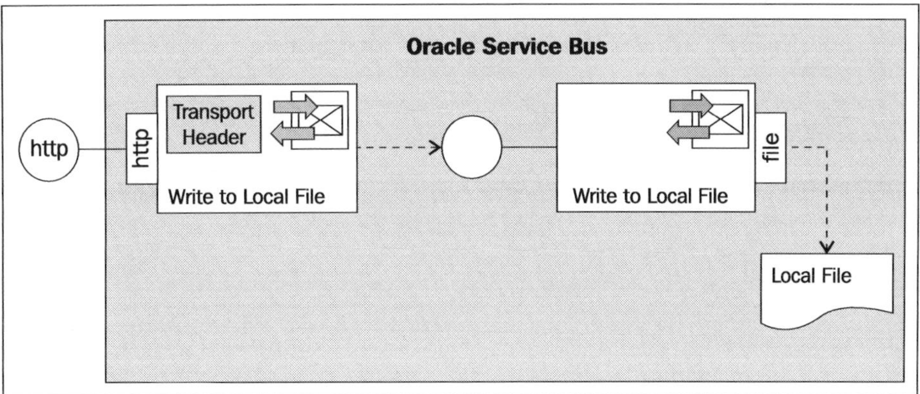

Getting ready

No special actions necessary.

How to do it...

We begin with a business service writing a file to a local folder. In Eclipse OEPE, perform the following steps:

1. Create a new OSB project and name it `using-file-transport-to-write-to-file`.
2. Create a `business` folder in that new project.
3. In the `business` folder create a new business service named `WriteToLocalFile`.
4. On the **General** tab select **Messaging Service** as the **Service Type** option.
5. Navigate to the **Messaging** tab and select **Text** as the **Request Message Type**.
6. Leave the **Response Message Type** on **None**.
7. Navigate to the **Transport** tab and select **file** from the **Protocol** drop-down list.

8. Enter `file:///C:/work/destination` into the **Endpoint URI** field and click **Add**.
9. Navigate to the **File Transport** tab.
10. Enter `Hello` into the **Prefix** field and `.txt` into the **Suffix** field.

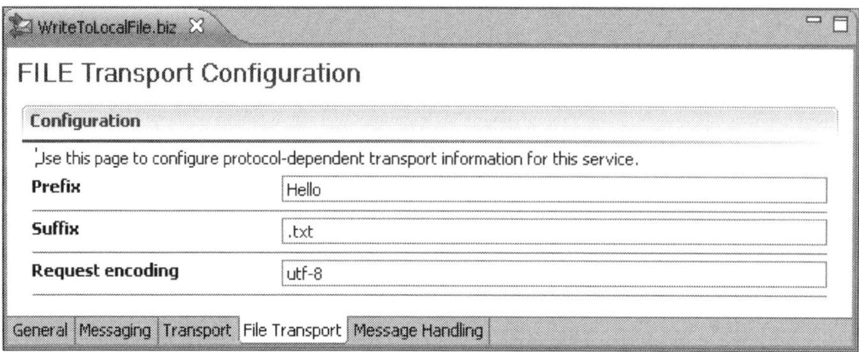

11. Deploy the project to the OSB server.

The business service to write a file is now configured and we can test it through the test console. In the Service Bus console, perform the following steps:

12. Click on **Project Explorer** in the menu on the left and navigate to the **WriteToLocalFile** business service.
13. Click on the **Launch Test Console** icon.
14. Enter `Hello world!` For the content to write to the local file into the **Payload** field.
15. Click **Execute**.
16. The result of the test is presented as shown in the following screenshot. There is now response, as writing a file is always a one-way operation. But the content of the metadata returns the file path, that is, a generated name with the prefix **Hello** and the suffix **.txt**.

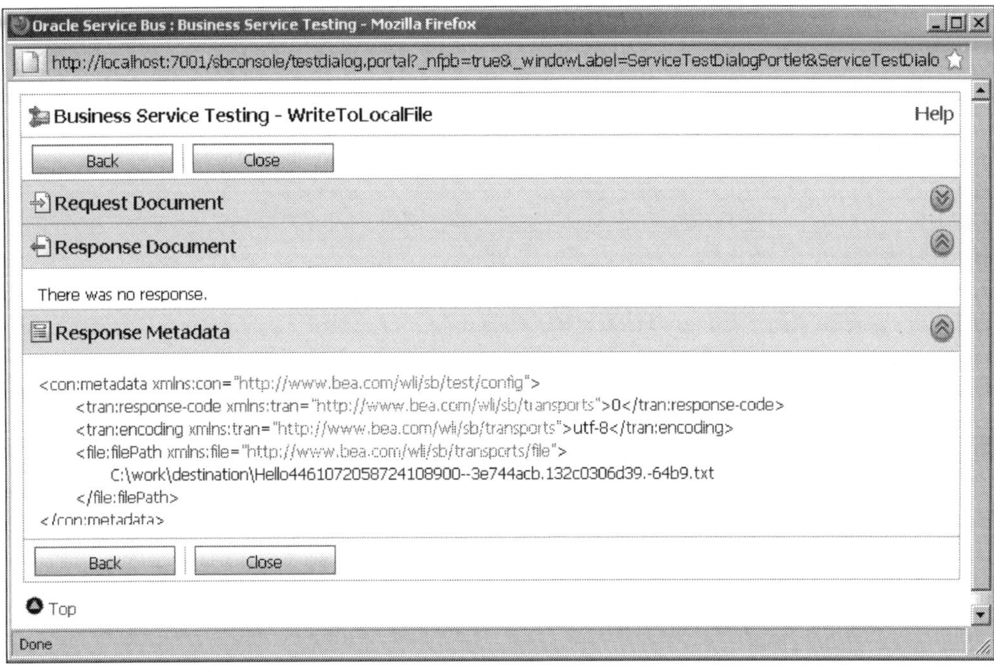


```
<con:metadata xmlns:con="http://www.bea.com/wli/sb/test/config">
    <tran:response-code xmlns:tran="http://www.bea.com/wli/sb/transports">0</tran:response-code>
    <tran:encoding xmlns:tran="http://www.bea.com/wli/sb/transports">utf-8</tran:encoding>
    <file:filePath xmlns:file="http://www.bea.com/wli/sb/transports/file">
        C:\work\destination\Hello4461072058724108900--3e744acb.132c0306d39.-64b9.txt
    </file:filePath>
</con:metadata>
```


6. Check that a file has been created at the given location.

We have a business service through which we can write to a local file. The filename is generated. We can only control the prefix and suffix being used through the configuration of the **File Transport**.

To specify the complete filename, a **Transport Header** action can be used in the **Routing** action of the proxy service which is invoking the business service.

How it works...

Simply using a business service configured with the **File Transport** is enough to be able to write a file to a local folder. The Endpoint URI configured on the **File Transport** defines where that target local folder resides. If the folder does not yet exist, then it is created by the **File Transport** upon writing the first file.

The **File Transport** allows some control over the filename by the prefix and suffix option. However, the middle part of the filename is by default generated based on a UUID-like string. By that it's guaranteed that the filenames are always unique. If this is not the behavior we want, then we can overwrite the filename by using a **Transport Header** action, as shown in the next recipe *Specifying a filename at runtime*.

If a file already exists, a `_N` will be appended, where `N` is a number starting from `0`. The string will be added before the suffix, so an original filename `targetFile.txt` would be extended to `targetFile_0.txt`, if `targetFile.xml` already exists in the destination folder.

There's more...

In this section, we discuss how to specify the filename dynamically at runtime and how to use the **FTP Transport** to write a file to a remote folder through FTP.

Specifying a filename at runtime

If we want to overwrite the filename generated by the **File Transport**, then we have set some transport headers using a **Transport Header** action when invoking the business service from a proxy service.

So let's create a proxy service which invokes the business service created previously. To simplify things, we just use the Generate Service functionality to create a proxy service based on the existing business service and change the protocol to HTTP transport. In Eclipse OEPE, perform the following steps:

1. Create a `proxy` folder.
2. Right-click on the business service **WriteToLocalFile** and select **Oracle Service Bus** | **Generate Proxy Service**.
3. Select the `proxy` folder in the **Enter or select the parent folder** tree, enter `WriteToLocalFile` into the **File name** field and click **Finish**.
4. Navigate to the **Transport** tab and change the **Protocol** to **http**.
5. Navigate to the **Message Flow** tab.
6. Insert a **Transport Header** action into the generated **Request Action** of the **Routing** node.
7. On the **Properties** tab of the **Transport Header** action, click on **Add Header**.
8. Select the **Defined** option and select **file** and **fileName** in the corresponding drop-downs.
9. Select the **Set Header to** option and click on **<Expression>**.

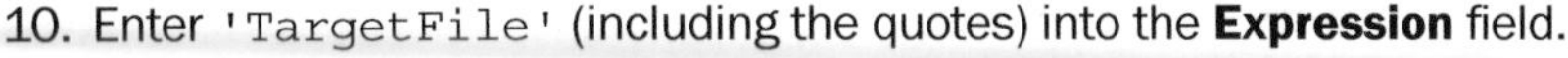

10. Enter `'TargetFile'` (including the quotes) into the **Expression** field.

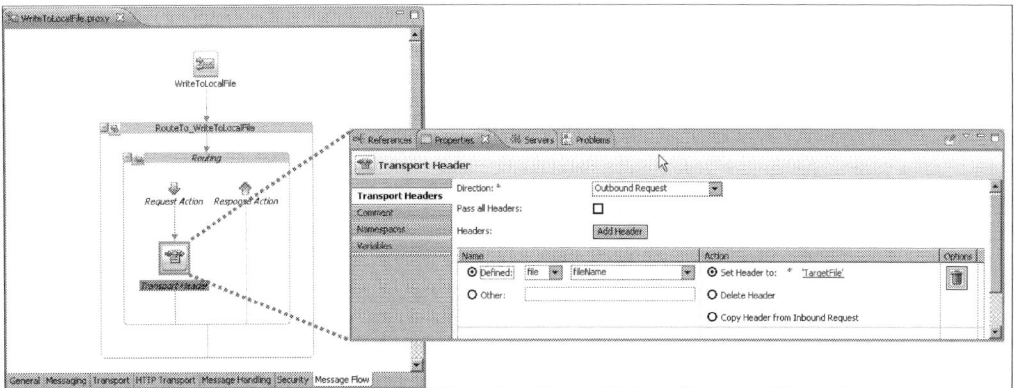

11. Deploy the project to the OSB server.

We can now test the proxy service through the test console. In the Service Bus console, perform the following steps:

12. Click on **Project Explorer** in the menu on the left and navigate to the **WriteToLocalFile** proxy service inside the `proxy` folder.
13. Click on the **Launch Test Console** icon.
14. Enter `Hello world!` For the content to write to the local file into the **Payload** field.
15. Click **Execute**.

5. The result of the test should be similar to that shown in the following screenshot. The outbound variable will show the value of the complete **filePath** used to write the file. The filename is created with the prefix **Hello** and the suffix **.txt** from the **File Transport** configuration and the name **TargetFile** from the **Transport Header** action.

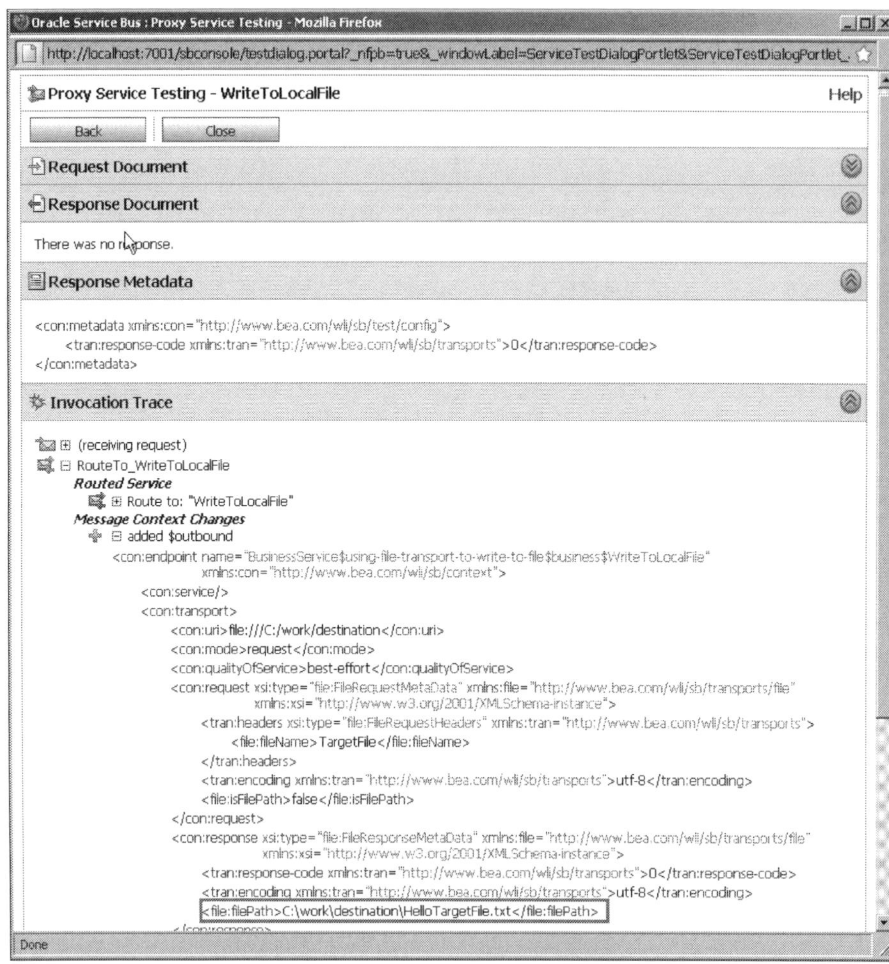

6. Check that a file has been created at the given location.

Writing a file to a remote folder through FTP

Similar to shown in the *Using the File or FTP Transport to trigger a proxy service upon arrival of a new file* recipe, we can replace the **File Transport** by a **FTP Transport** to write to a remote filesystem through FTP.

To write the file to an FTP server, perform the following steps in Eclipse OEPE:

1. Create a Service Account artifact called `FTPUser.sa` in the same way as shown in the *Using the File or FTP Transport to trigger a proxy service upon arrival of a new file* recipe.
2. Create a new business service `WriteToFtpFile` in the `business` folder.
3. On the **General** tab select **Messaging Service** as the **Service Type** option.
4. Navigate to the **Messaging** tab and select **Text** as the **Request Message Type**.
5. Leave the **Response Message Type** on **None**.
6. Navigate to the **Transport** tab ad select **ftp** from the **Protocol** drop-down list.
7. Enter `ftp://localhost/` into the **Endpoint URI** field and click **Add**.

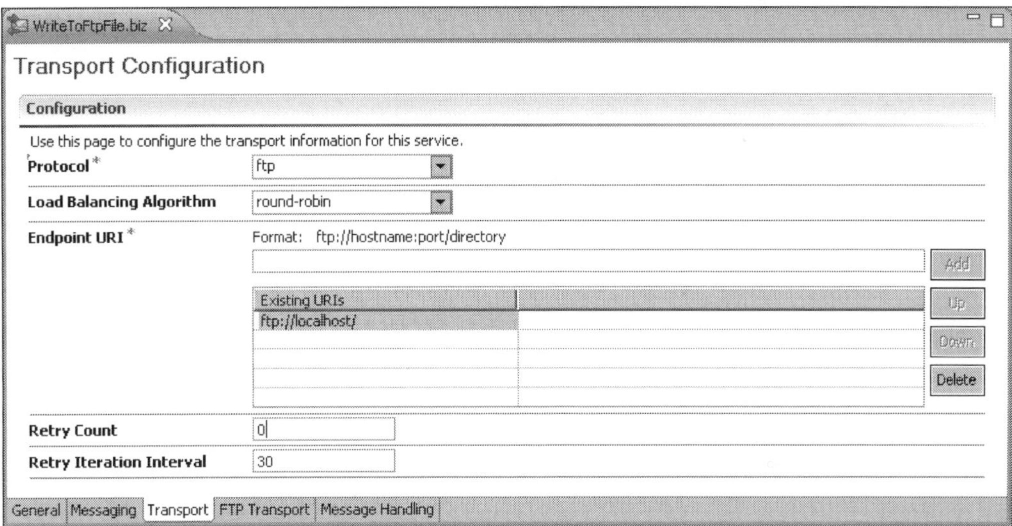

8. Navigate to the **FTP Transport** tab.
9. Select **external user** for the **User Authentication** option, click **Browse** and select the **FTPUser** Service Account artifact.
10. Enter `Hello` into the **Prefix for destination File Name** and `.txt` into the **Suffix for destination File Name** field.

11. Select **ascii** for the **Transfer Mode** option.

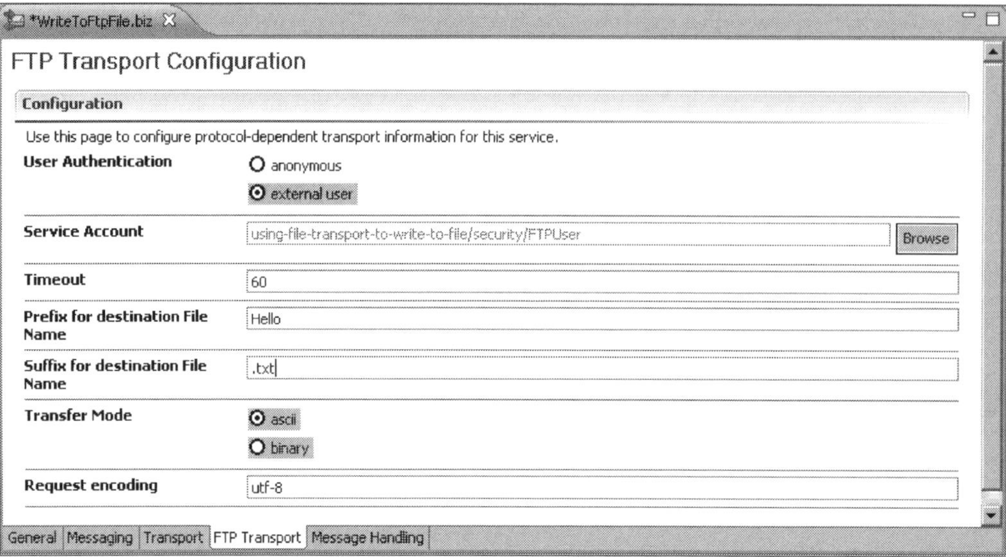

This business service can now be invoked from the proxy service instead and the file is written to the FTP server.

Using Email Transport to receive e-mail

Oracle Service Bus offers the **Email Transport** for both receiving and sending e-mails.

In this recipe, we will show how we can set up a proxy service to listen on a mailbox for new e-mail messages. For each new e-mail message, the message processing as defined in the message flow of the proxy service is executed.

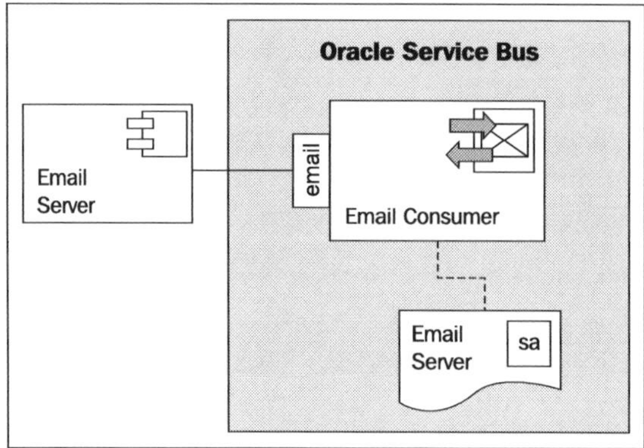

Getting ready

In order to be able to receive e-mails on the OSB, we need a running mailserver. We could connect to an already existing e-mail server, but for this recipe to be standalone, we will use the Apache James mailserver. Perform the following steps for the installation of Apache James on the local machine:

1. Download the latest version of Apache James binary from: `http://james.apache.org/download.cgi#Apache_James_2.3.2_is_the_stable_version`.
2. Unzip the file into a local folder.
3. Navigate to the `bin` folder within the Apache James binaries.
4. Locate and execute the `run.bat`.

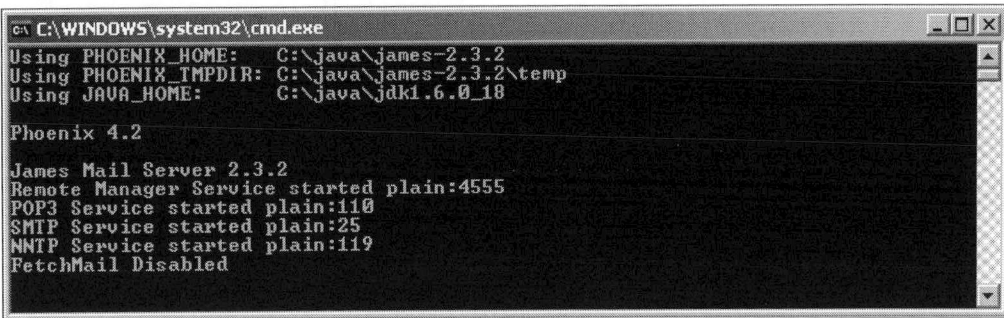

5. Open a command window and open a telnet session by entering `telnet localhost 4555`.
6. Enter `root` on the **Login id** prompt.
7. Enter `root` on the **Password** prompt.
8. Create a new user by entering the command `adduser <user> <password>`.
9. Create the `osbuser` and `osbadmin` user.

```
Telnet localhost
JAMES Remote Administration Tool 2.3.2
Please enter your login and password
Login id:
root
Password:
root
Welcome root. HELP for a list of commands
adduser osbuser osbuser
User osbuser added
adduser osbadmin osbadmin
User osbadmin added
listusers
Existing accounts 2
user: osbadmin
user: osbuser
```

10. List the users by entering the `listusers` command.
11. Enter `quit` to exit the telnet session and close the command window.

Now, let's install an e-mail client in order to send and receive e-mails. We will use Mozilla Thunderbird here, but it can be replaced by any other e-mail client. Perform the following steps to set up Thunderbird:

12. Download and install Mozilla Thunderbird from: `http://www.mozilla.org/en-US/thunderbird/`.
13. Start Thunderbird by double-clicking on the icon installed on the desktop.
14. On the main window click **Create a new account**.
15. Enter `OSB User` into the **Your name** field.
16. Enter `osbuser@localhost` into the **Email address** field. Ignore the warning message.
17. Enter `osbuser` into the **Password** field.
18. Click **Continue**.
19. The configuration should be found and the account can be created by clicking on **Create Account**.
20. Repeat step 14-19 for the `OSB Admin` user.

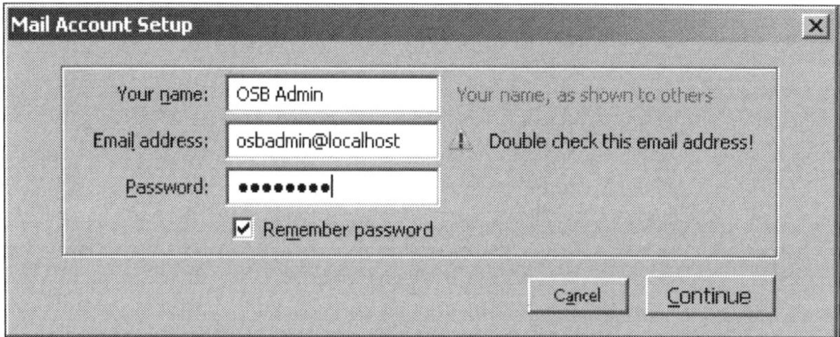

21. Test the two e-mail accounts by sending an e-mail message from the `OSB User` account to the `OSB Admin` account (E-mail address: `osbadmin@localhost`).

We have now configured the e-mail server and an e-mail client. Let's now implement the proxy service which consumes e-mail messages from the `osbadmin@localhost` mailbox.

How to do it...

First, we will create a service account object, which we will use in the proxy service to authenticate against the e-mail server. In Eclipse OEPE, perform the following steps:

1. Create a new OSB project and name it `consuming-emails`.
2. Create the folder structure with a `proxy` and `security` folder.
3. Right-click on the `security` folder and select **New | Service Account** to create a new Service Account object.
4. Enter `EmailServer` into the **File Name** field and click **Finish**.
5. Select **Static** for the **Resource Type** option.
6. Enter `osbadmin` into the **User Name** field and `osbadmin` into the **Password** and **Confirm Password** fields.

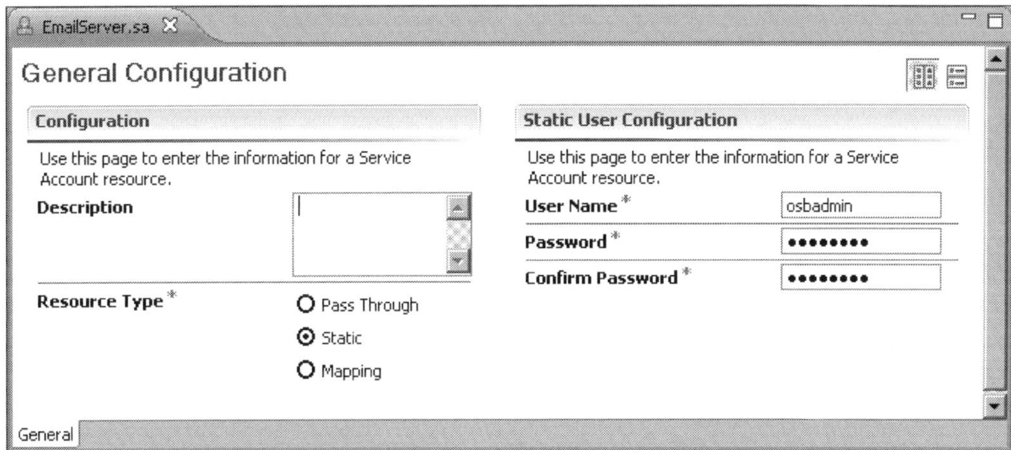

Now, we create the proxy service, which will use the service account to retrieve the e-mails from the e-mail server:

7. Create a new proxy service in the `proxy` folder and name it `EmailConsumer`.
8. Select **Messaging Service** for the **Service Type** option.
9. On the **Messaging** tab, select the **Text** option for **Request Message Type**.
10. Leave the **Response Message Type** option to **None**.
11. Navigate to the **Transport** tab and select **email** for **Protocol**.
12. Enter `mailfrom:localhost:110` into the **Endpoint URI** field.
13. Navigate to the **Email Transport** tab.

14. Click **Browser** and select the **EmailServer** for the **Service Account**.
15. Enter `10` into the **Polling Interval** to configure polling every 10 seconds.
16. Enter `c:\temp\emails-download` into the **Download Directory** field.
17. Enter `c:\temp\error` into the **Error Directory** field.
18. Navigate to the **Message Flow** tab.
19. Insert a **Pipeline Pair** node and name it **MailConsumerPipelinePair**.
20. Insert a **Stage** node into the **Request Pipeline** and name it **LogStage**.
21. Insert a **Log** action into the **LogStage**.
22. On the **Properties** of the **Log** action, enter `$body` into the **Expression** field and select **Warning** for the **Severity**.
23. Deploy the project to the OSB server.

Now it's time to test the proxy service. In Mozilla Thunderbird (or any other email client), perform the following steps in order to send a message to the `osbadmin@localhost` e-mail address.

24. Click **Write a new message**.
25. Enter `osbadmin@localhost` into the **To** field.
26. Enter `Email to OSB Server` into the **Subject** field.
27. Enter `This is a message for the OSB Server!` for the body of the e-mail message.

28. Click on **Send**.

After a while (around 10 seconds), the log message should appear on the Service Bus console window with the content of the e-mail body:

```
<16.10.2011 20:48 Uhr MESZ> <Warning> <ALSB Logging> <BEA-000000> <
[MailConsume
rPipelinePair, MailConsumerPipelinePair_request, LogStage, REQUEST]
Body of Emai
l: <soapenv:Body xmlns:soapenv="http://schemas.xmlsoap.org/soap/
envelope/">This
is a message for the OSB Server!</soapenv:Body>>
```

How it works...

Receiving e-mails by the OSB server is as simple as using a proxy service with the **Email Transport**. In order to be able to select the **Email Transport** protocol on the **Transport** tab, either a **Messaging Type** or **Any XML Service** type of proxy service needs to be configured.

A proxy service using the **Email Transport** must always be one-way, that is, the **Response Message Type** needs to be set to **None**.

The **Email Transport** is a polling transport, which means that it polls the E-mail server repeatedly for new e-mails. The **Polling Interval** property on the **Email Transport** tab defines the time in seconds the transport should wait in between.

Both POP3 and IMAP can be used for the e-mail protocol. POP3 is the default.

If there are multiple new e-mails waiting on the mail server for consumption, then each e-mail will cause a new proxy service to be started, that is, the message flow will handle always only exactly one e-mail message. The **Read Limit** property on the **Email Transport** tab controls the number of e-mails to consume in each poll.

The `body` variable in the message flow holds the content of the e-mail body, as we have seen in the log output previously. The other information of the e-mail, such as the to-email-address or the subject, can be found in the `transport` element of the `inbound` variable. Here is the content of the `transport` element for the test we did previously:

```
<con:transport xmlns:con="http://www.bea.com/wli/sb/context">
  <con:uri>mailfrom:localhost:110</con:uri>
  <con:mode>request</con:mode>
  <con:qualityOfService>exactly-once</con:qualityOfService>
  <con:request xsi:type="ema:EmailRequestMetaData"
    xmlns:ema="http://www.bea.com/wli/sb/transports/email"
      xmlns:xsi="http://www.w3.org/2001/XMLSchema-instance">
    <tran:headers xsi:type="ema:EmailRequestHeaders"
      xmlns:tran="http://www.bea.com/wli/sb/transports">
      <tran:user-header name="Delivered-To"
        value="osbadmin@localhost" />
      <tran:user-header name="MIME-Version" value="1.0" />
```

```
        <tran:user-header name="Message-ID"
          value="&lt;4E9B28D3.6070802@localhost>" />
        <tran:user-header name="Return-Path"
          value="&lt;osbuser@localhost>" />
        <tran:user-header name="Content-Transfer-Encoding"
          value="7bit" />
        <tran:user-header name="Received"
          value="from 127.0.0.1 ([127.0.0.1]) by soavm11
          (JAMES SMTP Server 2.3.2) with SMTP ID 98 for
          &lt;osbadmin@localhost>;
          Sun, 16 Oct 2011 20:56:19 +0200 (CEST)" />
        <tran:user-header name="User-Agent"
          value="Mozilla/5.0 (Windows NT 5.2; rv:7.0.1) Gecko/20110929
          Thunderbird/7.0.1" />
        <ema:To>osbadmin@localhost</ema:To>
        <ema:From>OSB User &lt;osbuser@localhost></ema:From>
        <ema:Date>Sun Oct 16 20:56:19 CEST 2011</ema:Date>
        <ema:Subject>Email to OSB Server</ema:Subject>
        <ema:Content-Type>text/plain; charset=ISO-8859-1; format=flowed
        </ema:Content-Type>
      </tran:headers>
      <tran:encoding xmlns:tran=
        "http://www.bea.com/wli/sb/transports">
        ISO-8859-1</tran:encoding>
    </con:request>
  </con:transport>
```

There's more...

E-mails with attachments are also supported by the **Email Transport**. Let's change the test case from before and add two additional attachments.

The first attachment is a text file and the second one is a BMP image, with binary content.

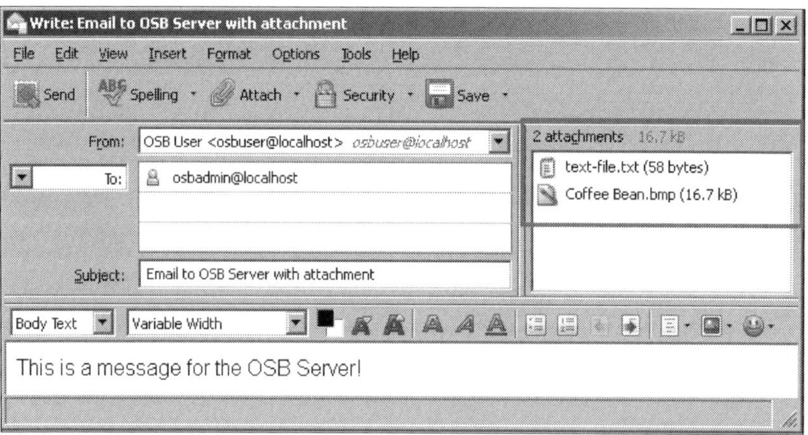

Information about the e-mail attachments is available through one of the standard OSB variables called `attachments`. The following screenshot shows the contents of the **attachments** variable during execution of the proxy service after consumption of the e-mail sent previously (content of the variables from the OSB debugger). **Attachments** hold a collection with an **attachment** element for each file attached to the e-mail.

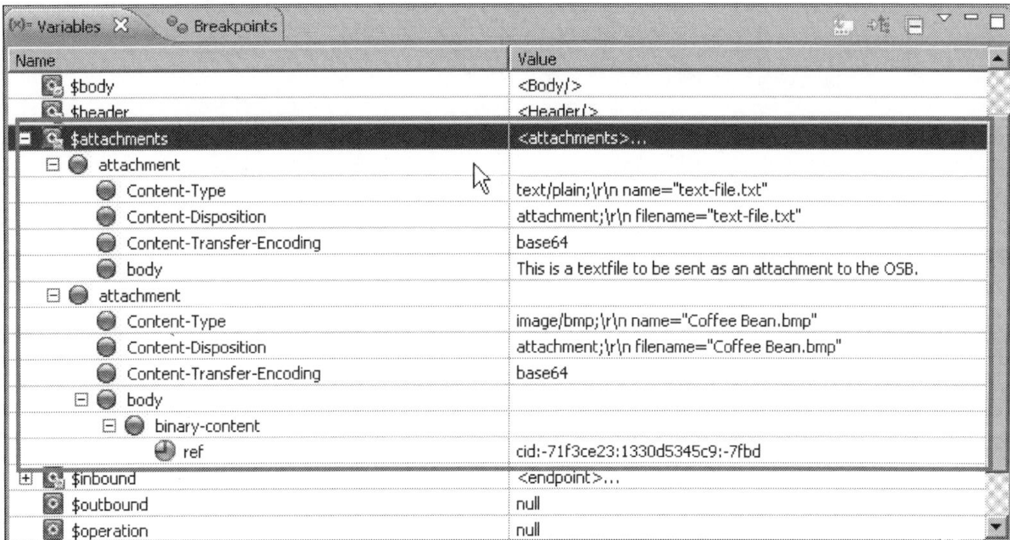

If an attachment is text-based (text/plain), then the content of the file is directly available through the body element. This is the case for the first attachment.

If an attachment is binary (image/bmp), then the body element only holds a reference to the binary content.

Using Email Transport to send e-mail

In this recipe, we will show how the **Email Transport** can be used to send e-mails. We will first implement a business service, which sends a message to a given e-mail address. The e-mail address is hardcoded in the endpoint of the business service.

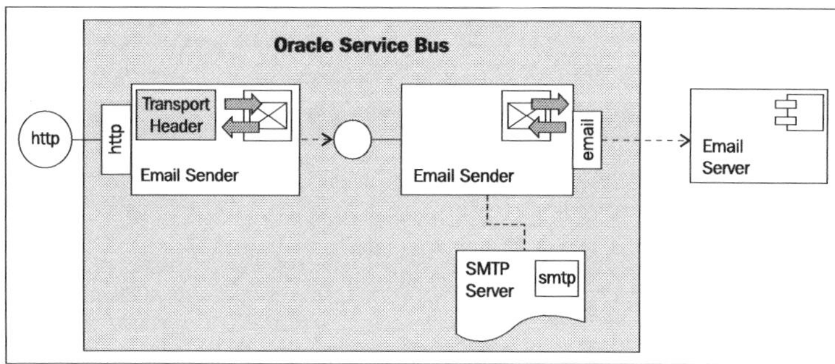

In order to make the sending more flexible, we will also show how to use the **Transport Headers** action to dynamically set the e-mail address, the subject, and the mail body in a proxy service, before invoking the business service.

Getting ready

Make sure that the mail server is installed and configured as shown in the *Using Email Transport to consume e-mails* recipe.

How to do it...

First we will create the SMTP Server object, holding the reference to the SMTP server. In Eclipse OEPE, perform the following steps:

1. Add a new **SMTP Server** to the configuration project and name it `SMTPServer`.
2. Enter `localhost` in the **Server URL** field.
3. Enter `osbuser` into the **User Name** field.
4. Enter `osbuser` into the **Password** and **Confirm Password** fields.

Now with the SMTP Server in place, we can create the OSB project with a business service. In Eclipse OEPE, perform the following steps:

5. Create new OSB project `sending-emails` and create a `business` folder within it.
6. Create a new business service and name it `EmailSender`.
7. On the **General** tab, set the **Service Type** option to **Messaging Service**.

8. Navigate to the **Messaging** tab.
9. Set the **Request Message Type** option to **Text**.
10. Leave the **Response Message Type** option to **None**.
11. Navigate to the **Transport** tab.
12. Select **email** for the value of the **Protocol** drop-down listbox.
13. Enter `mailto:osbuser@localhost` in the **Endpoint URI** field and click **Add**.
14. Navigate to the **Email Transport** tab.
15. Select **SMTPServer** for the value of the **SMTP Server** drop-down listbox.
16. Enter `OSB Admin` into the **From Name** field.
17. Enter `no_reply@localhost` into the **From Address**.

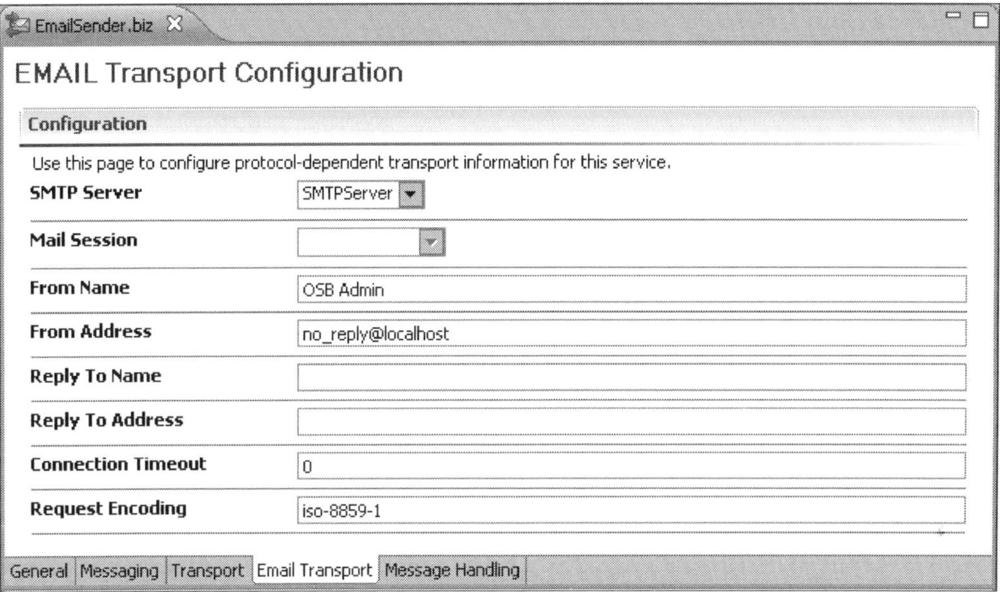

Let's now deploy the OSB project. By performing the following steps, we can make sure that we also deploy the SMTP Server resource:

18. Right-click on the OSB configuration project **osb-cookbook-configuration** and select **Export | Oracle Service Bus | Resources to Server**.
19. Select **resource** for the **Export Level** option.
20. Select the checkboxes for **sending-emails** and **osb-cookbook-configuration**.
21. Click **Next**.
22. Click **Finish**.

Now it's time for testing the business service. In Service Bus console, perform the following steps:

23. In the **Project Explorer**, navigate to the **EmailSender** business service located in the `business` folder of the **sending-emails** project.
24. Click on the **Launch Test Console** icon.
25. Enter the text to use for the mail into the **Payload** field, as shown in the following screenshot:

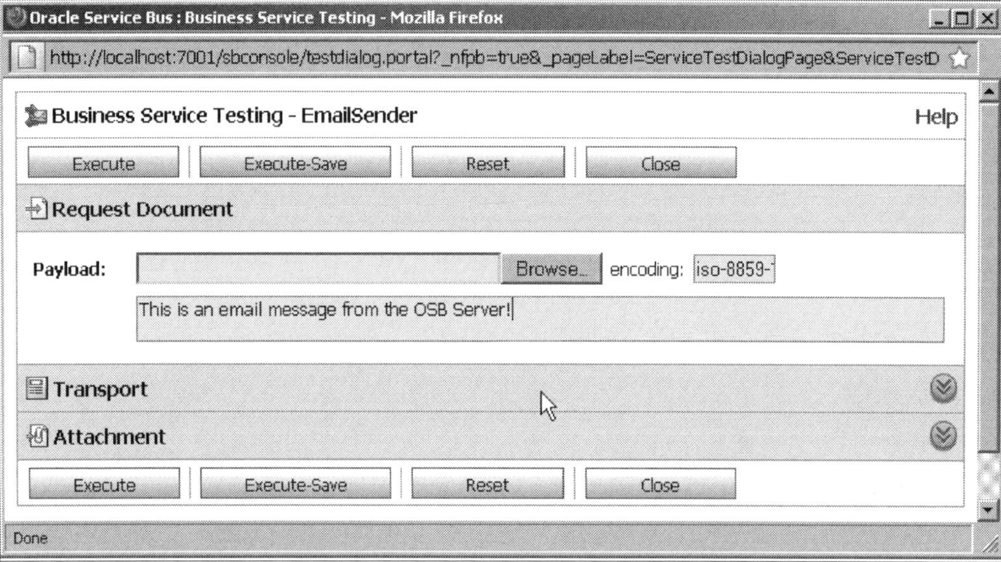

26. Click **Execute**.
27. The test window should show a **There was no response** message in the **Response Document** section.

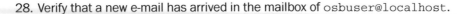

28. Verify that a new e-mail has arrived in the mailbox of `osbuser@localhost`.

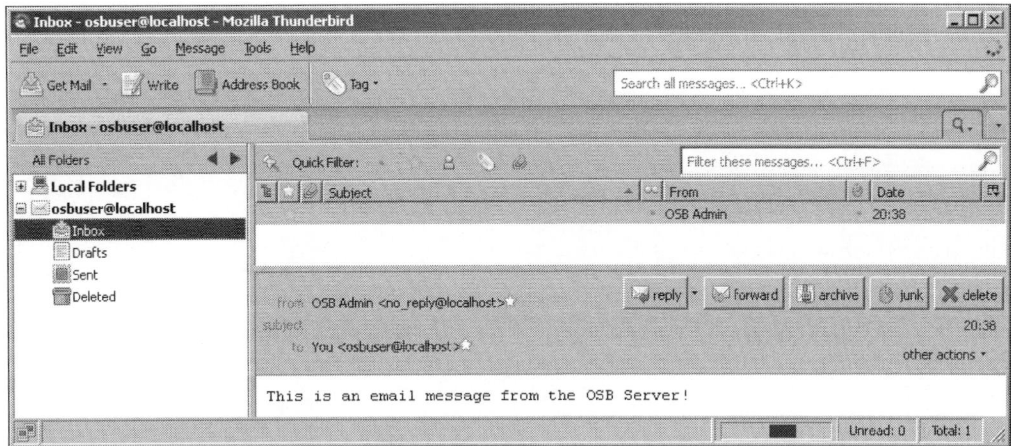

How it works...

Configuring a business service with the **Email Transport** creates a service which supports sending an e-mail to a given e-mail address. The e-mail address is hardcoded in the endpoint of the business service.

In order to reach to the e-mail server, we have created an OSB SMTP Server resource holding the configuration properties of our local e-mail server we want to talk to. This is a global resource and therefore it has to be created on an OSB configuration level and not on a single OSB project.

The content of the `body` variable upon invoking the business service determines the content of the e-mail message. If we look at the e-mail received in the previous screenshot, we can see that the subject is empty.

All the e-mail properties are available as transport-specific header properties. If we click on the **Transport** section on the test console, then we can specify a value for the subject, as shown in the following screenshot:

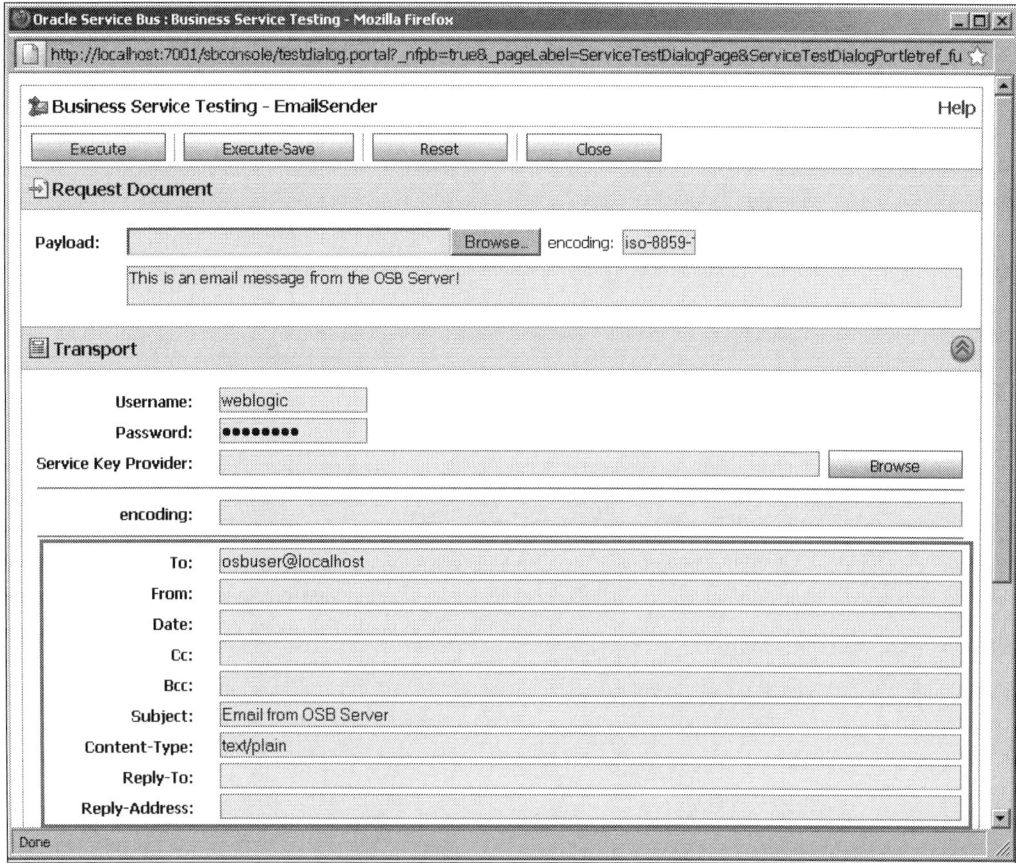

These properties can also be specified trough a **Transport Header** action, when invoking the business service from a proxy service.

There's more...

We often need to control the sending of an e-mail based on incoming information, that is, we want to be able to change the To-address dynamically.

In order to be able to override the default settings configured on the **Email Transport** tab of the business service (From name/Address, Reply to, ...), we have to use a **Transport Header** action in the proxy service upon invoking the business service. This also allows us to set a value for the subject of the e-mail.

In Eclipse OEPE, perform the following steps:

1. Create a new folder and name it `proxy`.
2. Right-click on the **EmailSender** business service and select **Oracle Service Bus** | **Generate Proxy Service**.
3. Enter `EmailSender` into the **File name** field, select the `proxy` folder for the location and click **Finish**.
4. Navigate to the **Transport** tab and select **http** for the **Protocol** drop-down listbox.
5. Navigate to the **Message Flow** tab.
6. Insert a **Transport Header activity** inside the **Request Action** of the **Routing** action.
7. Click **Add Header**.
8. Select **email** and **To** for the **Defined** drop-down listboxes, and click on **<Expression>**.
9. Enter `'osbuser@localhost'` into the **Expression** field and click **OK**.
10. Click **Add Header**.
11. Select **email** and **Subject** for the **Defined** drop-down listboxes, and click on **<Expression>**.
12. Enter `'Hello from OSB'` into the **Expression** field and click **OK**.

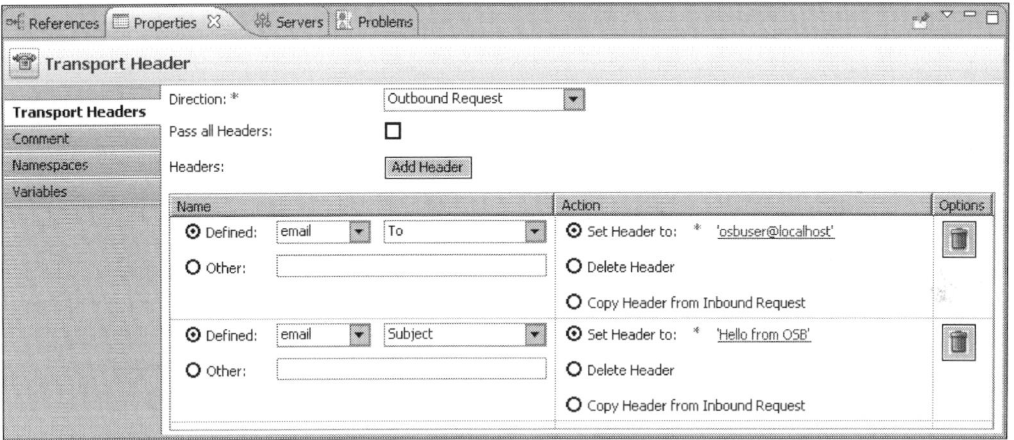

13. Deploy the project and test the new proxy service through the OSB test console.

7
Communicating with the Database

In this chapter, we will cover:

- Using DB adapter to read from a database table
- Using DB adapter to execute a custom SQL statement against the database
- Using DB adapter to update a database table
- Using DB adapter to poll for changes on a database the table
- Using the AQ adapter to consume messages from database
- Using the AQ adapter to send messages to the database

Introduction

In this chapter, we will show two different mechanisms to talk to the database:

1. **Using the DB adapter**: It enables the OSB to communicate with database endpoints, such as Oracle database servers and any relational databases that provide JDBC drivers. Allows the execution of SQL statements, such as select, insert, updating, deleting as well as calling stored procedures or functions. Can also be used inbound, by polling for changes on a database table.
2. **Using the AQ adapter**: It enables the OSB to talk to the Oracle **Advanced Queuing** (**AQ**) feature of an Oracle database. Oracle AQ offers queuing inside the database and is often used to implement asynchronous communication between applications in the database.

Both the DB adapter and the AQ adapter are JCA adapters and are well-known from the Oracle SOA Suite. As OSB 11g, they are also integrated with the OSB through the JCA transport.

The configuration of the JCA adapters is not available in Eclipse OEPE. For that, we have to use JDeveloper. The recipe, *Setting up OSB project to work with JCA adapters*, shows how to set up the project so that it's easy to share the different artifacts between JDeveloper and Eclipse OEPE.

Before we start with the recipes, we have to create the necessary connection factories on the DB and AQ adapter, which will be used by all the recipes.

To configure the DB adapter, perform the following steps in WebLogic Console:

1. In the domain structure tree on the left, navigate to **osb_cookbook_domain | Deployments**.
2. In the deployments list, locate the **DbAdapter** component and click on it.
3. Navigate to the **Configuration tab**, and select the **Outbound Connection Pools** tab.
4. Click on **New**:

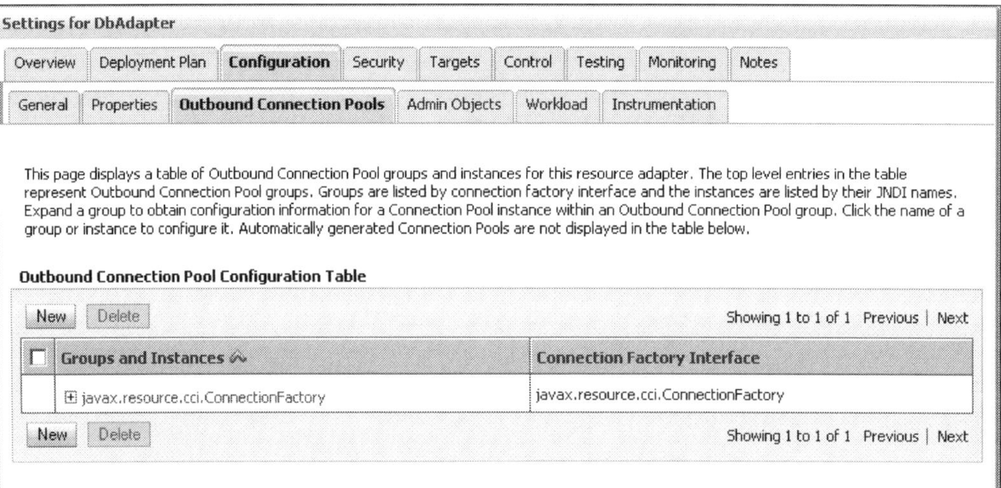

5. Select the **javax.resource.cci.ConnectionFactory** radio button (which is the only option).
6. Click on **Next**.
7. Enter `eis/DB/OsbCookbookConnection` into the **JNDI Name** field.
8. Click on **Finish**.
9. On the **Save Deployment Plan** screen, click on **OK**.

Now, we have to configure the connection factory that we just created:

10. Select the **Configuration** tab on the **Settings for DbAdapter** window.
11. On the **Outbound Connection Pools** tab, expand the **javax.resource.cci.ConnectionFactory** node.
12. Click on the **eis/DB/OsbCookbookConnection** link to open the connection properties.
13. Click on the **Property Value** column in the row **xADataSourceName**. The field changes to editable.
14. Enter `jdbc.OsbCookbookDS` for the **JNDI Name** field of the data source, which is part of the OSB Cookbook standard environment. Press *Enter* (this is important, otherwise the new value will not be saved).
15. Click on **Save**:

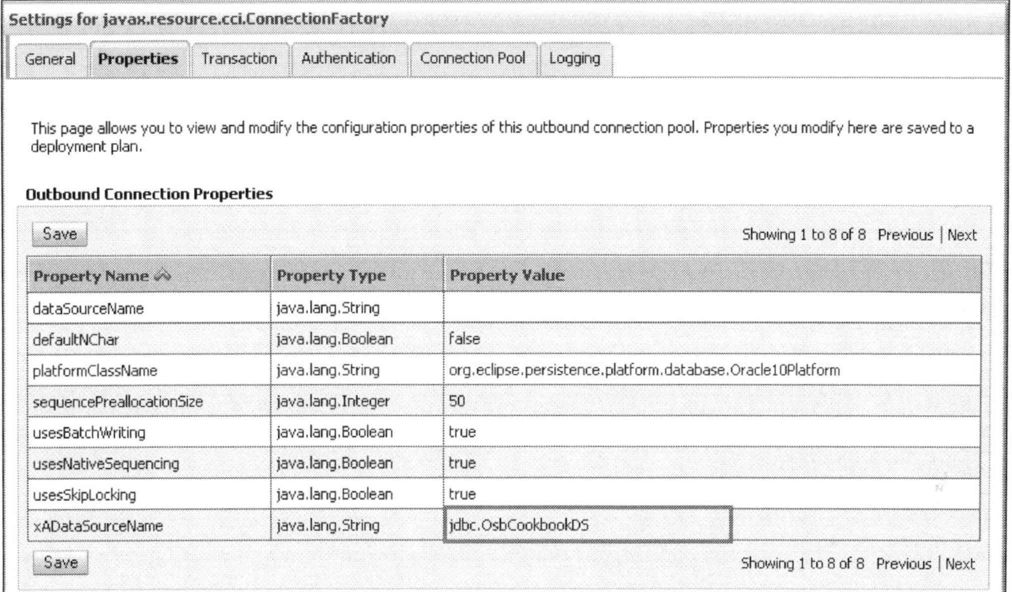

16. We have successfully configured the new connection factory. In order to make it active, we have to reload the DB adapter. In WebLogic Console, perform the following steps:
17. In the **Domain Structure** tree on the left, navigate again to **osb_cookbook_domain** | **Deployments**.
18. In the deployments list, locate the **DbAdapter** and select the checkbox in front.
19. Click on **Update**.
20. Click on **Finish**. This finishes the work for the DB adapter.

Now let's configure the connection factory for the AQ adapter. In WebLogic Console perform the following steps:

21. In the Domain Structure tree on the left, navigate to **osb_cookbook_domain | Deployments**.
22. In the deployments list, locate the **AqAdapter** component and click on it.
23. Navigate to the **Configuration** tab, and select the **Outbound Connection Pools** tab.
24. Click on **New**.
25. Select the **javax.resource.cci.ConnectionFactory** radio button (which is the only option).
26. Click on **Next**.
27. Enter `eis/aq/OsbCookbookConnection` into the **JNDI Name** field.
28. Click on **Finish**.

Now let's configure the connection factory that we just created:

29. Select the **Configuration** tab on the **Settings for AqAdapter** window.
30. On the **Outbound Connection Pools** tab, expand the **javax.resource.cci.ConnectionFactory** node.
31. Click on the **eis/aq/OsbCookbookConnection** link to open the connection properties.
32. Click on the **Property Value** column in the row **DataSourceName**. The field changes to editable.
33. Enter `jdbc.OsbCookbookDS` for **JNDI Name** field of the data source, which is part of the OSB Cookbook standard environment. Press *Enter* (this is important, otherwise the new value will not be saved).
34. Click on **Save**.

We have successfully configured the new connection factory. In order to make it active, we have to reload the Aq adapter. In WebLogic Console, perform the following steps:

35. In the **Domain Structure** tree on the left, navigate again to **osb_cookbook_domain | Deployments**.
36. In the deployments list, locate the **AqAdapter** and select the checkbox in front.
37. Click on **Update**.
38. Click on **Finish**.

The two adapters are now fully configured and we can use them.

Using DB adapter to read from a database table

In this recipe, we will configure an outbound DB adapter, in order to read data from multiple database tables. The adapter will be invoked from a business service, which can be generated using Eclipse OEPE.

The business service implements a WSDL-based interface. In a real life scenario, the business service would be exposed using a proxy service. We won't show that here, check the recipes in Chapter, *Creating a basic OSB service*, to learn how to do that:

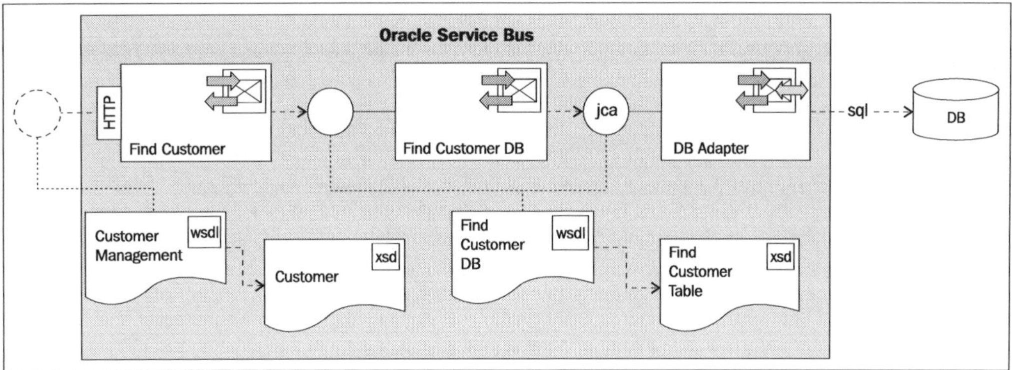

For the configuration of DB adapter, we will use JDeveloper and then switch to Eclipse to implement the proxy service wrapping the inbound DB adapter.

Getting ready

For this recipe, we will use the database tables created with the OSB Cookbook standard environment. Make sure that the connection factory is set up in the database adapter configuration as shown in the *Introduction* of this chapter.

You can import the OSB project containing the base setup for this recipe into Eclipse from `\chapter-7\getting-ready\using-db-adapter-to-read-from-table`.

How to do it...

First we create the DB adapter, which will implement the query from the database. In JDeveloper, perform the following steps:

1. Open the file `composite.xml` of the project `ReadFromDB`.
2. From the **Component Palette**, select the **SOA** components if not already done.

3. Drag the **Database Adapter** to the **External References** lane:

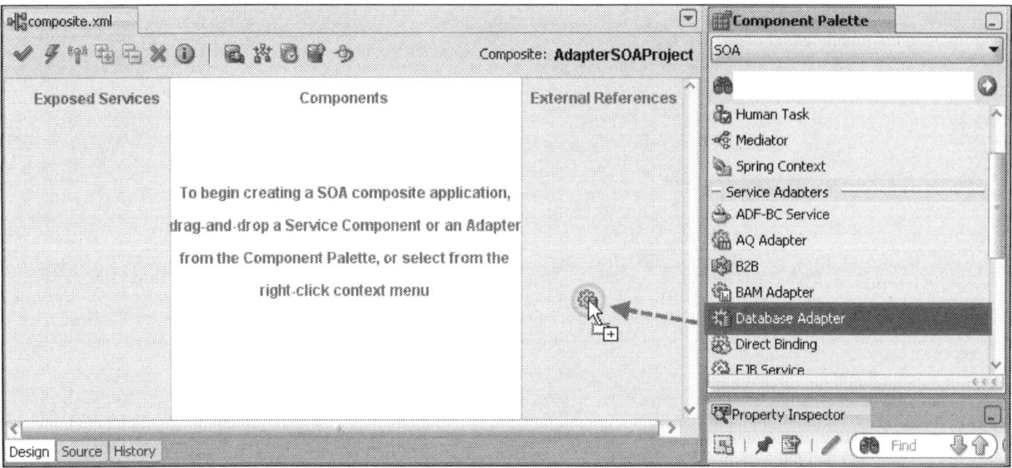

4. Click on **Next** and enter `FindCustomer` into the **Service Name** field.
5. Click on **Next**.
6. On the screen **Service Connection**, create a connection (if not already done). Click on the plus sign to the right of the drop-down list.
7. Enter `osbCookbookConnection` into the **Connection Name** field.
8. Enter `osb_cookbook` into the **Username** and **Password** field.
9. Change the Host Name, SID, and JDBC port according to the database instance the **osb_cookbook** schema is installed on.
10. Click on **Test Connection** to test the connection and a **Success!** message shows up.
11. Click on **OK**.
12. Check that the **JNDI Name** field is prefilled with `eis/DB/OsbCookbookConnection`. A DB connection factory with this JNDI alias has been created as shown in the *Introduction* section of this chapter.
13. Click on **Next**.
14. On the screen **Operation Type**, select **Perform an Operation on a Table**.
15. Check the **Select** checkbox, uncheck all others, and click on **Next**.
16. On the screen **Select Table**, click on **Import Tables**.
17. Make sure that the schema **OSB_COOKBOOK** is selected and click on **Query**.
18. Select the table **CUSTOMER_T**, **PERSON_T**, and **ADDRESS_T** and move them to the selected pane.

19. Click on **OK**.
20. Wait a few seconds until the selected table appears on the pane. Select the **CUSTOMER_T** as the root table for the query and click on **Next**.
21. Click on the **PERSON_T has a 1:M relationship with CUSTOMER_T** and click on **Remove**. Confirm the pop-up window by clicking on **Yes**.
22. Click on the **ADDRESS_T has a 1:1 relationship with PERSON_T** and click on **Remove**. Confirm the pop-up window by clicking on **Yes**.
23. Click on **Next**.
24. On the screen **Attribute Filtering** we can uncheck the attributes we don't want the adapter to return. In our case we return all the information.
25. Click on **Next**:

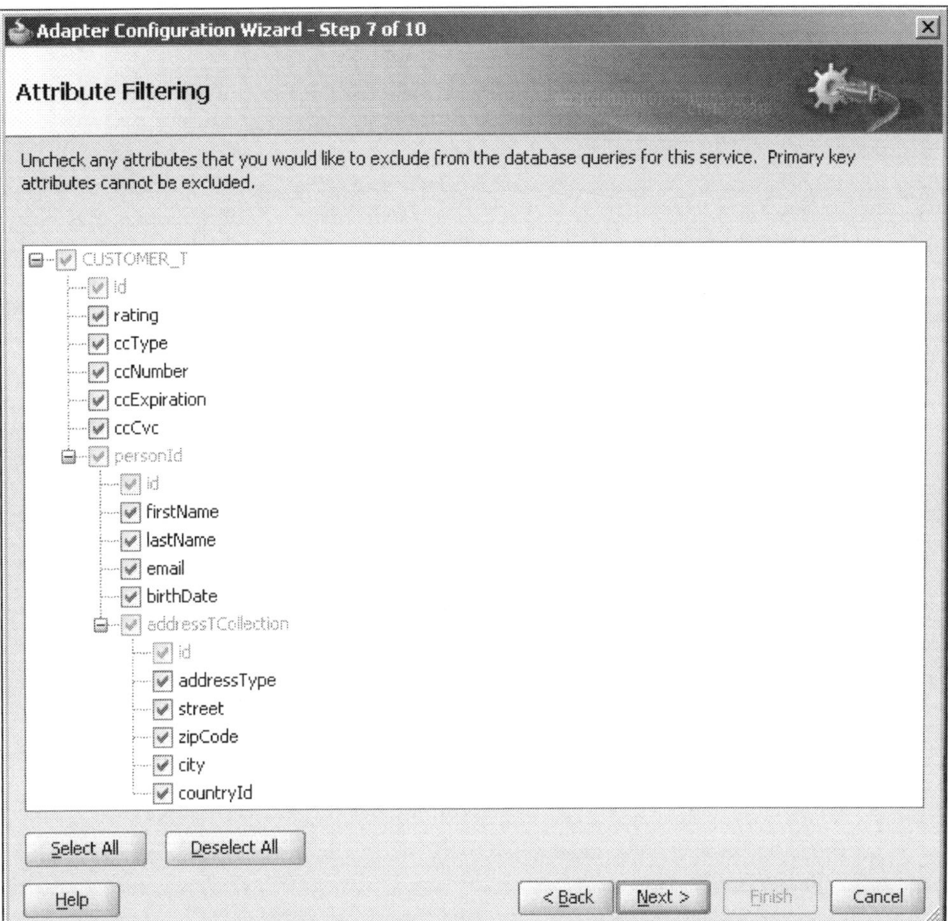

26. On the screen **Define Selection Criteria**, click on **Add.** Enter `customerId` into the **Parameter Name** field and click on **OK**.
27. Click on **Edit**, next to the **SQL** field.
28. Click on **Add**.
29. Select **id** as **Query Key**, **EQUAL** as **Operator**, and in the **Second Argument** section, select **Parameter** and **customerId** from the drop-down listbox.
30. Click on **Ok**.

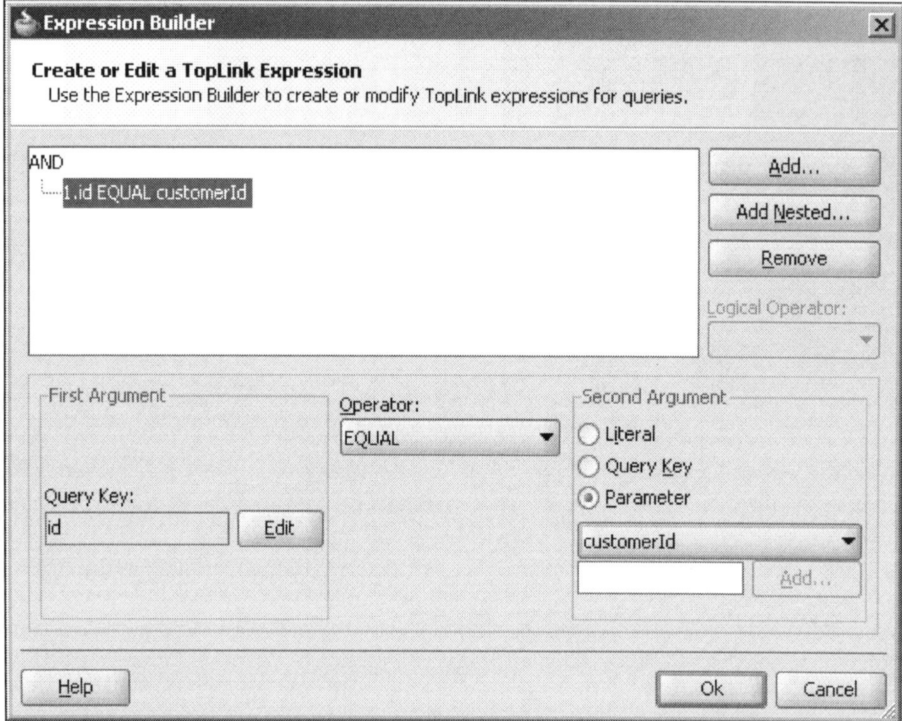

31. Click on **Next** two times.
32. Click on the **Finish** button and save the project.

We have created the DB adapter used to query a customer and its person and address data. This is all we need to do in JDeveloper. Let's go back to Eclipse OEPE and perform the following steps to make the DB adapter usable in the OSB:

1. On the OSB project hit **Refresh** (*F5*). The artifacts generated by JDeveloper in the previous steps will show up.
2. Right-click on the `FindCustomer_db.jca` file and select **Oracle Service Bus | Generate Service** from the context menu.

3. Select the `business` folder for the location of the business service.
4. Leave the **Service Name** and **WSDL name** as suggested by the wizard.
5. Click on **OK**.
6. A business service of type **WSDL Web Service** and a corresponding WSDL file is generated in the `business` folder.
7. Deploy the project to the OSB server.

Let's test the business service through the Service Bus console. Perform the following steps:

8. In the **Project Explorer**, navigate to the business service **FindCustomer_db**.
9. Click on the **Launch Test Console** icon under **Actions**.
10. Specify the value of the **Payload** field as shown in the following screenshot.
11. Click on **Execute**:

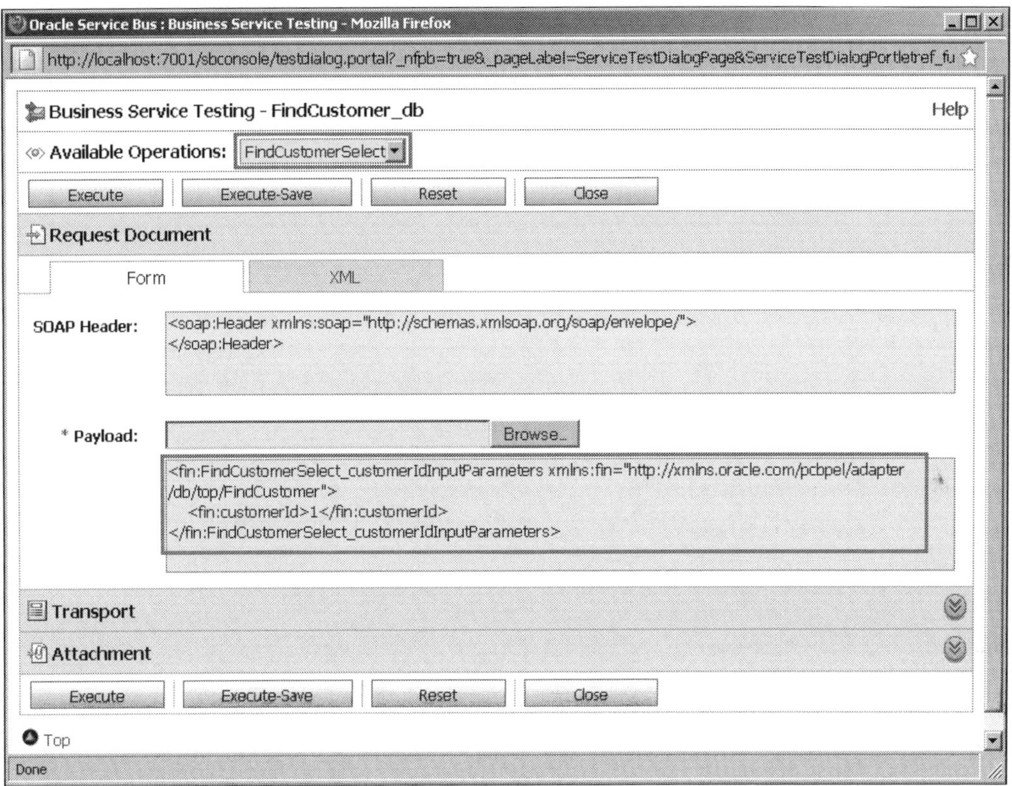

12. The **Response Document** on the next window, shows the result of the business service:

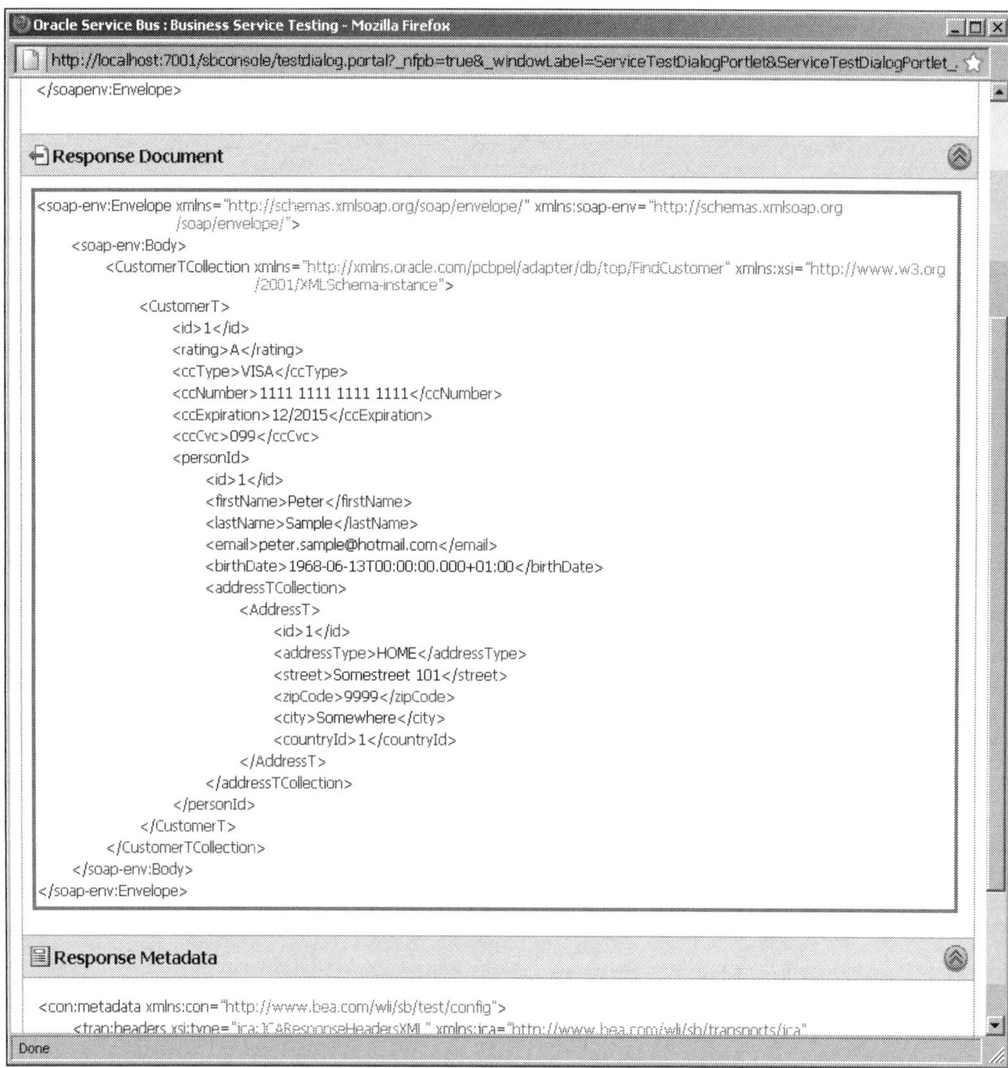

How it works...

We have used the DB adapter wizard to create an adapter configuration for retrieving data from the database. The DB adapter supports reading information from multiple tables and will create a hierarchical XML document, based on the relationships defined between the tables. Therefore, we had to specify the possible relations when configuring the DB adapter. The XML schema generated by the adapter reflects that hierarchy:

The DB adapter also generates a WSDL with one operation `FindCustomerSelect`, implementing the read from the tables. The business service generated from Eclipse OEPE will implement that WSDL. This means that the contract of the business service is created in a contract-last fashion, because it's generated based on the definition of the database. When testing the business service through the test console, we could see in the response the generated names, such as `CustomerTCollection` and `AddressT`. This is ok, as long as we don't expose these element names to the outside of the OSB, which is always assured on a business service, as it is not directly callable from outside. It's important that the proxy service we would use to expose the service implements its own WSDL and does not just use the one generated by the adapter. The *Chapter 1, Creating a basic OSB service*, has multiple recipes showing how to achieve that.

Using DB adapter to execute a custom SQL statement against the database

In this recipe, we will use an outbound DB adapter to execute a custom SQL statement against the database to reuse some database functionalities.

With that it's easy to call a function of the database to perform a certain value. We will use the `ORA_HASH` function to create a hash value for a given string, which we pass as a parameter to the DB adapter.

Getting ready

Make sure that the connection factory is set up in the database adapter configuration as shown in the *Introduction* section of this chapter.

You can import the OSB project containing the base setup for this recipe into Eclipse from `\chapter-7\getting-ready\using-db-adapter-to-execute-custom-sql`.

How to do it...

First we create the DB adapter, which will implement the query from the database. In JDeveloper, perform the following steps:

Open the file `composite.xml` of the project `ExecuteCustomSQL`.

1. From the **Component Palette**, select the **SOA** components if not already done.
2. Drag the **Database Adapter** to the **External References** lane.
3. Click on **Next** and enter `ExecuteCustomSql` into the **Service Name** field.
4. Click on **Next**.
5. Select the **OsbCookbookConnection** from the **Connection** drop-down listbox.

6. Make sure that the **JND Name** field has the value of **eis/DB/OsbCookbookConnection**, which matches the connection factory created in the *Introduction* of this chapter.
7. Click on **Next**.
8. On the screen **Operation Type**, select **Execute Pure SQL** and click on **Next**.
9. Enter `SELECT ORA_HASH(#value) as hashValue FROM dual` into the **SQL** field.
10. Upon typing the SQL statement into the **SQL** field, the corresponding XML schema representation for the input and output message is shown in the **XSD** field.
11. Add `xs:string` for the type of the value element and change the type of the `hashValue` element to `xs:string` as shown in the following screenshot.
12. Click on **Next**:

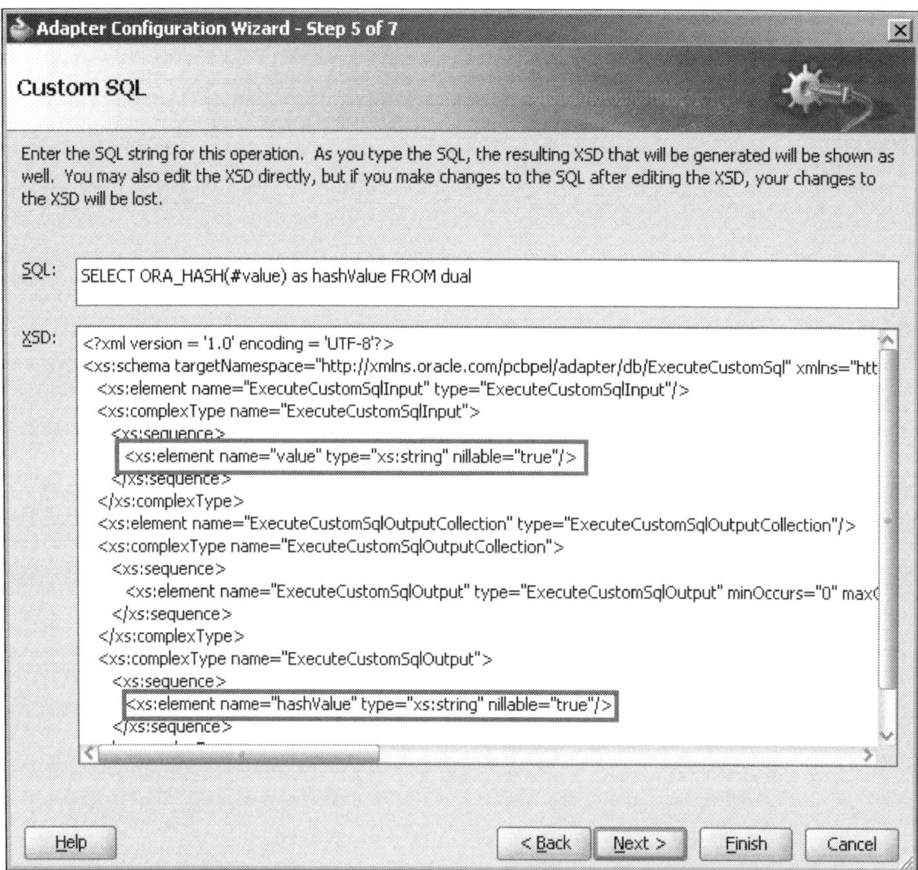

13. Click on the **Finish button**.
14. Click on **Save All** on the JDeveloper project.

We have created the DB adapter definition for the custom SQL. This is all we need to do in JDeveloper. Let's go back to Eclipse OEPE and perform the following steps to make the DB adapter usable in the OSB:

15. On the OSB project hit **Refresh** (*F5*) on the `adapter` folder. The artifacts generated by JDeveloper in the previous steps will show up.
16. Right-click on the `ExecuteCustomSql_db.jca` file and select **Oracle Service Bus | Generate Service** from the context menu.
17. Select the `business` folder for the location of the business service.
18. Leave the **Service Name** and **WSDL name** as suggested by the wizard and click on **OK**.
19. A business service of type **WSDL Web Service** and a corresponding WSDL file is generated in the `business` folder.
20. Deploy the project to the OSB server.

Let's test the business service through the Service Bus console. Perform the following steps:

21. In the **Project Explorer**, navigate to the business service **ExecuteCustomSql_db**.
22. Click on the **Launch Test Console** icon under **Actions**.
23. Enter a value into the value element in the **Payload** field and click on **Execute**:

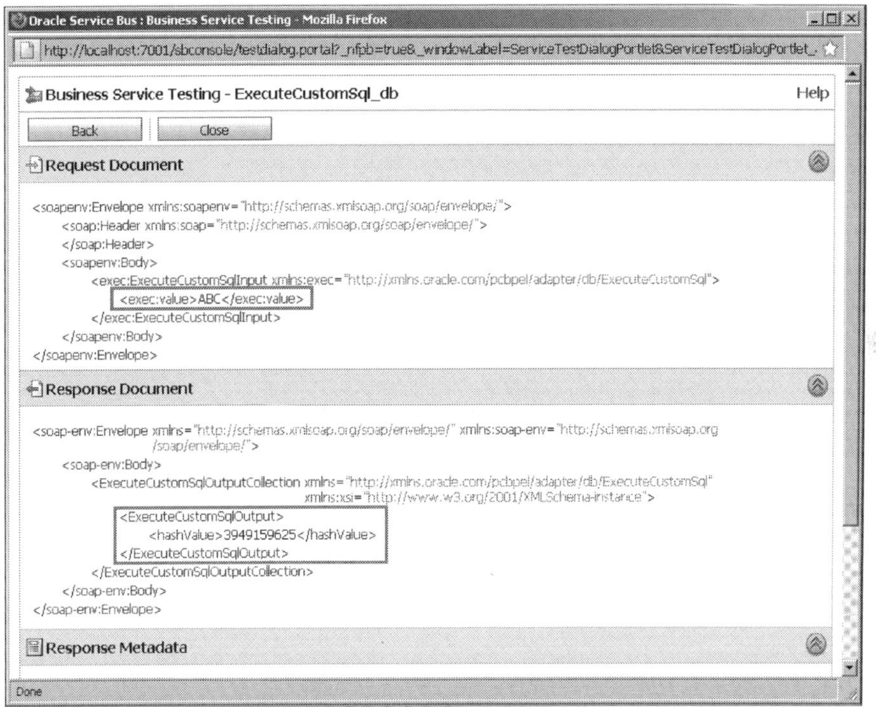

24. The **Response Document** section shows the response message with the `hashValue` for the string `ABC`.

How it works...

When selecting the **Execute Pure SQL** option in the DB adapter wizard, the SQL statement executed against the database can be custom defined. Based on the SQL statement entered, the wizard will try its best to generate the matching data structure for both the input and the output message. This will not always be possible, that is, for the parameter to the `ORA_HASH` function, the wizard was unable to know the data type and therefore, we had to manually change the XSD in the wizard and set the type to `xs:string` for the value parameter.

Often it might be possible and even easier to wrap the SQL statement to be executed in a view. In that case the normal **Perform an Operation on a Table** option can be used to select the data from the view. This might even be easier than using the **Execute Pure SQL**. In our case, where we have to pass a value to the database function, the wrapping in a view is not possible, so Execute Pure SQL is a good option.

Of course another valid alternative would be to use the **Call a Stored Procedure or Function** option on the DB adapter, especially if the procedure or function is more complicated than the simple `ORA_HASH` function used here.

There's more...

Instead of using the DB adapter to execute a SQL statement, the XQuery function `fn-bea:execute-sql`, already available before OSB 11g, can be used.

The function has the following signature:

```
fn-bea:execute-sql( $datasource as xs:string, $rowElemName as
xs:QName, $sql as xs:string, $param1, ..., $paramk) as element()*
```

The following screenshot shows the usage of the function to call the `ORA_HASH` database function. The expression is from an **Assign** action in a proxy service.

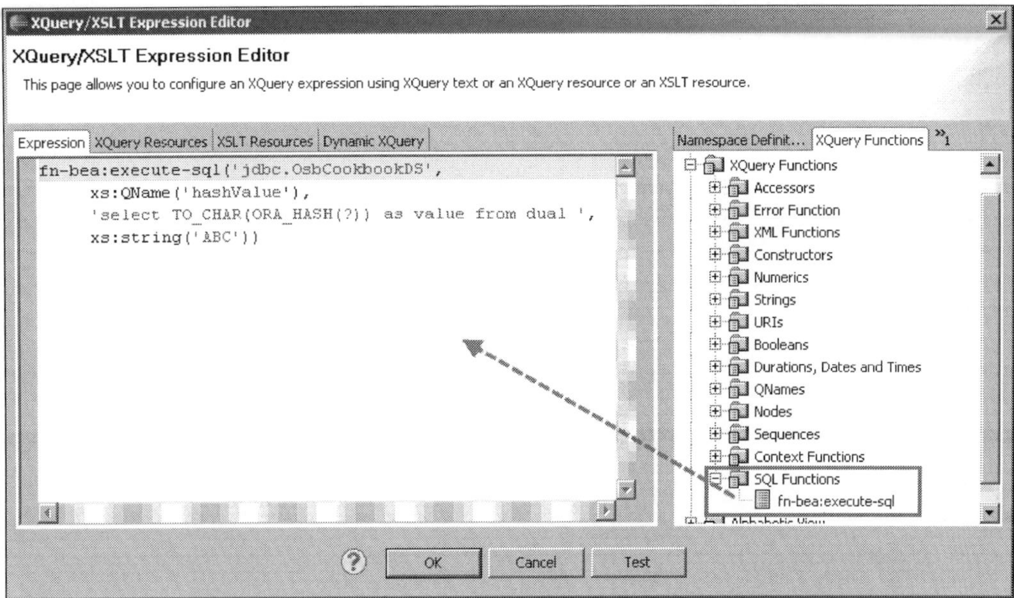

For the $datasource the JNDI name of a datasource configured on WebLogic has to be passed.

The XQuery function `execute-sql` has its value. It was actually the only way to access the database directly from Oracle Service Bus prior to version 11g. The big advantage of using the DB adapter compared to the `execute-sql` function is that the interface to the database is clearly defined by the WSDL, which is generated by the adapter wizard. By that it can be invoked from the message flow of a proxy service like any other service. But be careful, the WSDL generated does not follow a contract-first approach and therefore, should never be exposed to external consumers directly.

Additionally the DB adapter can also be used inbound, which we will see in the recipe, *Using the DB adapter to poll for changes on a database table*.

Using the DB adapter to update a database table

In this recipe, we will configure an outbound DB adapter, so that it can be used to update data in one or more tables. The adapter will be invoked from a business service, which can be generated using Eclipse OE:

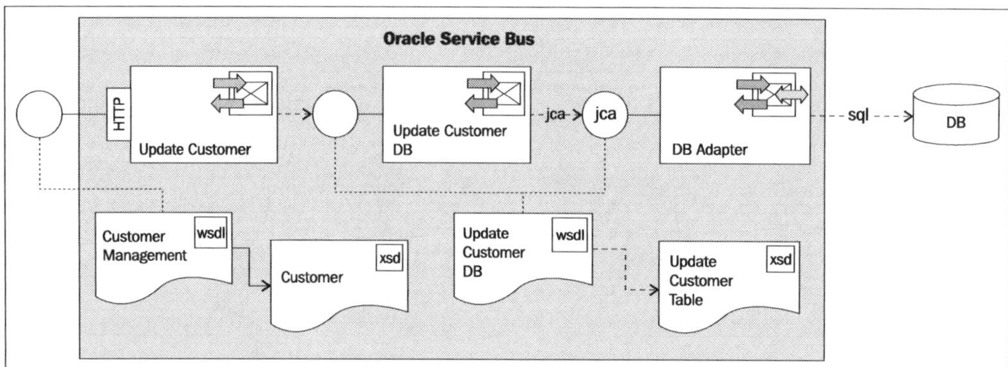

The business service implements a WSDL-based interface. The WSDL and XSD being used for that interface are generated by the DB adapter and are dependent on the database tables and their columns.

In this recipe, we will show how to wrap that business service with a proxy service using its own WSDL and XSD. By that we use a contract-first approach and have full control over the interface we offer to our consumers.

For the configuration of the DB adapter, we will use JDeveloper and then switch to Eclipse to implement the proxy service wrapping the inbound DB adapter.

Getting ready

For this recipe, we will use the database tables created with the OSB Cookbook standard environment. Make sure that the connection factory is set up in the database adapter configuration, as shown in the *Introduction* of this chapter.

You can import the OSB project containing the base setup for this recipe into Eclipse from `\chapter-7\getting-ready\using-db-adapter-to-update-to-table`.

How to do it...

First we create the DB adapter, which will implement the update to the database. In JDeveloper, perform the following steps:

1. Open the file `composite.xml` of the project `UpdateToDB`.
2. From the **Component Palette**, select the **SOA** components if not already done.
3. Drag the **Database Adapter** to the **External References** lane.
4. Enter `UpdateCustomer` in the **Service Name** field and click on **Next**.
5. Select the **OsbCookbookConnection** from the **Connection** listbox.
6. Check that **eis/DB/OsbCookbookConnection** is the value of **JNDI Name** field and click on **Next**.
7. On the **Operation Type** screen, select **Perform an Operation on a Table**.
8. Check the **Insert or Update (Merge)** checkbox, uncheck all others, and click on **Next**.
9. Click on **Import Tables**, click on **Query** and move the table `CUSTOMER_T` to the selected list and click on **OK**.
10. Back on the main wizard screen, click on **Next** three times.
11. On the **Advanced Options** screen, click on **Search** located below the **Sequence** listbox.
12. Select **CUSTOMER_SEQ** from the **Sequence** listbox.
13. Click on **Next**, and then on **Finish**.

    Due to a bug in the current version of the DB adapter generator, one of the generated files must be tweaked. Otherwise we will get an error in the OSB project in Eclipse OEPE.

14. Open the file `UpdateCustomer-or-mappings.xml`.
15. Locate the line `<sequence-field table="CUSTOMER_T" name="ID"/>`.
16. Modify the line to `<sequence-field name="ID"/>`.
17. Save the project.

The DB adapter used to create or update a customer is now ready to be used.

The work in JDeveloper is now done, let's switch to Eclipse OEPE and perform the following steps:

18. On the OSB project, hit **Refresh** (*F5*). The artifacts generated by JDeveloper in the previous steps will show up.
19. Right-click on the `UpdateCustomer_db.jca` file and select **Oracle Service Bus | Generate Service** from the context menu.

20. Select the `business` folder for the location of the business service.
21. Leave the **Service Name** and **WSDL name** as suggested by the wizard and click on **OK**.

Next we will create the proxy service, which implements the `StoreCustomer` operation defined in the `CustomerManagement.wsdl`. In Eclipse OEPE, perform the following steps:

22. In the `proxy` folder, create a proxy service and name it `CustomerManagement`.
23. On the **General** tab, select **WSDL Web Service** and click on **Browse**.
24. Select **wsdl** | **CustomerManagement.wsdl** | **CustomerManagementSOAP (binding)** and click on **OK**.
25. Confirm the pop-up window by clicking on **Yes**.
26. Navigate to the **Message Handling** tab and select the **Transaction Required** checkbox.
27. Navigate to the **Message Flow** tab, insert a **Route** node and name it `InvokeDBRoute`.
28. Insert a **Routing** action into the **Route** node.
29. On the **Properties** tab of the **Routing** action, click on **Browse** and select the **UpdateCustomer_db.biz** business service, and click on **OK**.
30. Select **merge** for the **Invoking** drop-down listbox.

We have created the proxy service that invokes the business service using the DB adapter. What we have not yet done is formatting the message according to the interface of the **UpdateCustomer_jca** business service. Next we will create an XQuery mapping file, which transforms the request message from the proxy service interface to the message the business service/DB adapter expects. In Eclipse OEPE, perform the following steps:

31. On the `transformation` folder, right-click and select **New** | **XQuery Transformation**.
32. Enter `createUpdateCustomerMsg` into the **File name** field and click on **Next**.
33. For the input parameter, select **wsdl** | **CustomerManagement.wsdl** | **StoreCustomer** and click on **Add**.
34. Enter `storeCustomer` into the **Parameter Name** field and click on **Next**.
35. For the second input parameter, select the **adapter** | **UpdateToDB** | **xsd** | **UpdateCustomer_table.xsd** | **CustomerTCollection** and click on **Add**.
36. Click on **Finish** and confirm the pop-up window with **Yes**.

37. Create the mapping by dragging elements from the left onto elements on the right. The last element **ccCvc** is mapped using the following expression: `xs:string($storeCustomer1/Customer/ns2:CreditCard/ns1:CardValidationCode)`. Select the target element, that is, **ccCvc**, navigate to the **Target Expression** tab to specify the expression, and click on **Apply**. You have to be in the **XQuery Transformation** perspective. The end result should look similar to the one shown in the following screenshot:

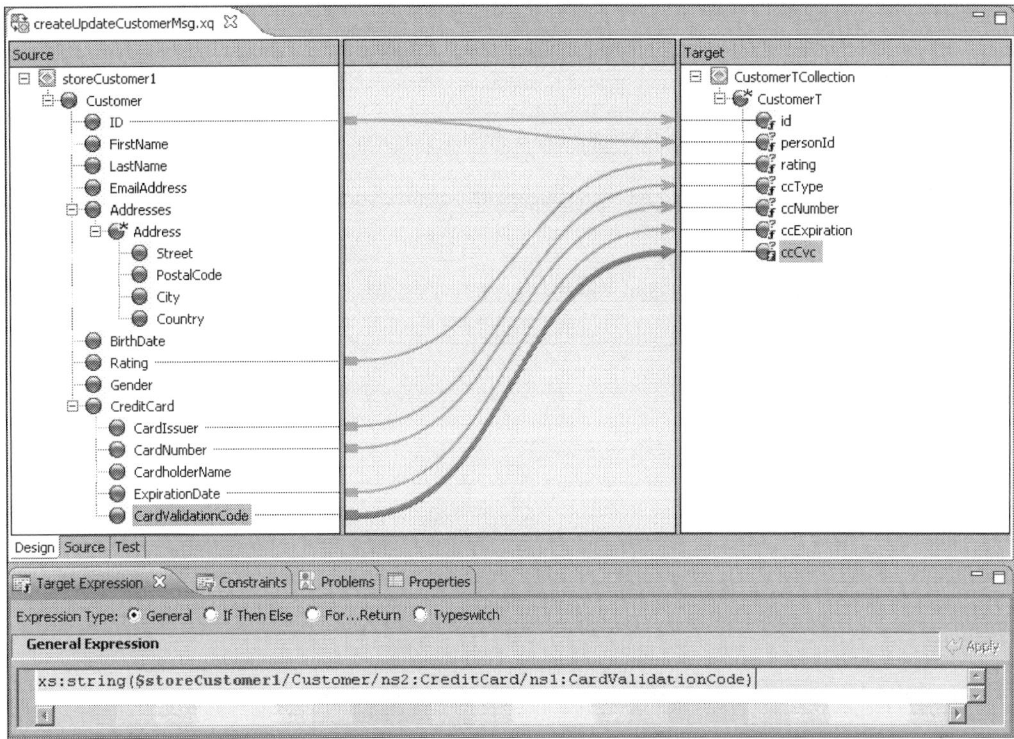

38. Switch back to the **Oracle Service Bus** perspective and reopen the **CustomerManagement** proxy service.

39. In the message flow, insert a **Replace** action into the **Request Action** flow of the **Routing** action.

40. On the **Properties** tab of the **Replace**, enter `body` into the **In Variable** field.

41. Click on **Expression**, navigate to the **XQuery Resources** tab, and click on **Browse**.

42. Select the **transformation** | **createUpdateCustomerMsg.xq** and click on **OK**.

43. Enter `$body/cus:StoreCustomer` into the **Binding** field for the **storeCustomer1** parameter and click on **OK**.

44. Back on the **Properties** of the **Replace** action; select the **Replace node contents** option.

So we have made sure that the message sent to the DB adapter is properly formatted. Next, we also have to treat the response that we get from the business service/DB adapter and format it appropriately. In Eclipse OEPE, perform the following steps:

45. In the message flow, insert an **Assign** action into the **Response Action** flow of the **Routing** action.
46. On the **Properties** tab of the **Assign**, enter `body` into the **Variable** field.
47. Click on the **Expression** link and enter the following XML fragment into the **Expression** field:

```
<soap-env:Body>
  <cus:StoreCustomerResponse>
    <cus:ID>{$body/upd:CustomerTCollection/upd:CustomerT/
upd:id}</cus:ID>
  </cus:StoreCustomerResponse>
</soap-env:Body>
```

48. Navigate to the **Namespace Definitions** tab on the right and click on **Add**.
49. Enter `upd` into the **Prefix** field and `http://xmlns.oracle.com/pcbpel/adapter/db/top/UpdateCustomer` into the **URI** field.
50. Click on **OK** twice.
51. Deploy the project to the OSB server.

Before we can test the proxy service, the connection factory used by the DB adapter must be modified, so that the **sequencePreallocationSize** property matches the database sequence increment, which is set to `1` for the `CUSTOMER_SEQ` sequence, as shown in the following screenshot:

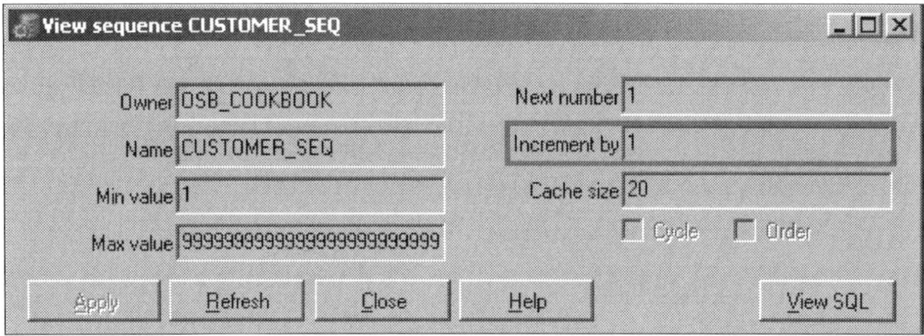

In the WebLogic Console, perform the following steps:

52. On the left side in the **Domain Structure** view, navigate to **osb_cookbook_domain | Deployments**.
53. In the list of deployments, click on the **DbAdapter** and select the tab **Configuration**, then select the tab **Outbound Connection Pools**.

54. Expand the **javax.resource.cci.ConnectionFactory** node and click on **eis/DB/OsbCookbookConnection**.
55. On the **Properties** tab, click on the **Property Value** field of the row **sequencePreallocationSize**. The field gets editable.
56. Enter `1` into the **Property Value** field and press *Enter* (this is important because otherwise the entered value will not be saved).
57. Click on **Save**.
58. Navigate back to the list of deployments and check the **DbAdapter** checkbox.
59. Click on **Update** (on top of the list).
60. Click on **Finish**.

The service can now be tested. In the Service Bus console, navigate to the test console and execute:

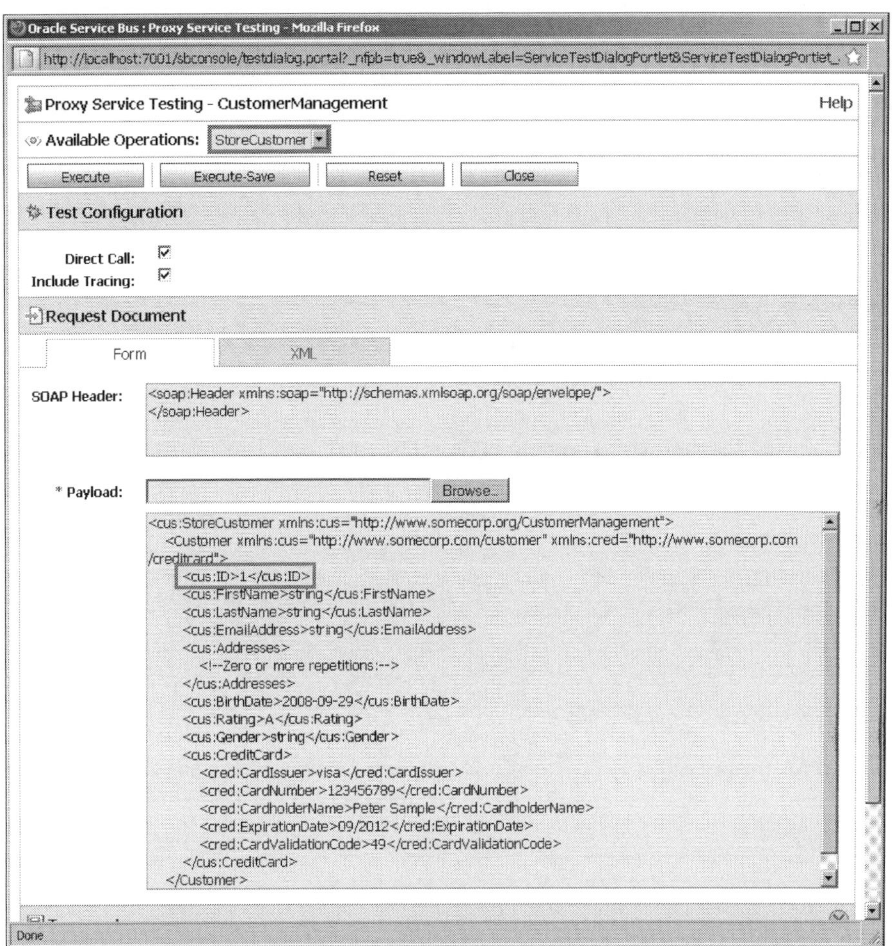

This modifies an existing customer with PK 1. When the row <cus1:ID>1</cus1:ID> is removed, a new customer will be inserted in the table.

How it works...

The merge operation of the DB adapter detects itself whether a record is already available in the table or not. Depending on that, either a SQL `UPDATE` or `INSERT` is applied. If there is no customer ID provided or the provided one could not be found, a new record is created.

If an ID is provided but no record can be found, the provided value will be used as the primary key of the new record. If no ID is provided, the value for the primary key will be retrieved from the database sequence before inserting the new record.

Note that, we have set the **Transaction Required** flag of the **CustomerManagement** proxy service. Setting this flag starts an XA transaction, even though the inbound protocol (HTTP) is not transactional.

Technically, the DB adapter is executed by the DbAdapter component, which is deployed on WebLogic server as a resource adapter. The adapter we created uses resources of the DbAdapter component. Therefore, we had to configure the connection factory there, which in turn uses the data source resource configured on WebLogic server as a standard data source.

The `CUSOMER_SEQ` database sequence is used by the DB adapter in case of an `INSERT` to generate a unique identifier for the primary key.

There's more...

Instead of using the `Merge` operation of the DB adapter, we could have chosen an `update-only` or an `insert-only` operation or even execute a pure SQL statement, which allows a completely self-written, self-tuned SQL statement, and permits bind parameters.

Two flags of the DB adapter deserve special mentioning, as their consequences and side effects are not always obvious:

A Note on the Detect Omissions Flag

The `Detect Omissions` flag can be set on the last page (**Advanced Options** screen) of the DB adapter wizard. The behaviour of this flag is sometimes mysterious to the beginner. It takes two values , which are as follows:

1. **Detect Omissions = true**: The DB adapter interprets missing elements in the target XML as *leave as default or do not touch*. For a `MERGE`, this will prevent valid but unspecified values from being overwritten with `NULL`. For `INSERT` operations, they will be omitted from the `INSERT` statement, allowing default values to take effect.
2. **Detect Omissions = false**: The DB adapter interprets a missing element as *set all left out values in the table explicitly to NULL*.

The latter behaviour (DetectOmissions = false) is often useful, as in an XQuery transformation, it is mostly easier to express a NULL value by the absence of an element rather than adding the attribute `xsi:nil="true"` to the element. This behaviour however, often steps in unexpectedly at first sight. Imagine the following situation: The `CVC` field of a credit card is often entered in a separate step in an application. If we design a service which allows updating only the `CVC` column in the `CUSTOMER_T` table, then a call to the DB adapter with only the CVC element set in the XML would clear out all other fields of the record. So, be cautious when setting `Detect Omissions` to `false` and prefer adding an `xsi:nil="true"` attribute, even though it looks like more work in the first place!

The side effect of the Get Active UnitOfWork flag

One more flag to be set on the **Advanced Options** screen is the `Get Active UnitOfWork`. It is intended to pin a JDBC connection to the global XA transaction. One side effect of setting this flag however, is that it delays all writes to the database until the commit of the global transaction.

By that, errors on inserts or updates due to constraints or trigger failures occur only when these operations are no longer under control of a proxy service. Such errors cannot be cached by an error handler in a proxy service. In cases where it is essential to be able to handle such errors, the `Get Active UnitOfWork` flag should not be enabled.

Using DB adapter to poll for changes on a database table

In this recipe, we will use the setup of the previous recipe and implement an inbound DB adapter. The DB adapter allows triggering execution of a proxy service upon changes on a table by using polling. The adapter is capable of marking or deleting read and processed rows in several ways. We will implement a proxy service which consumes from a DB adapter, as shown in the following screenshot:

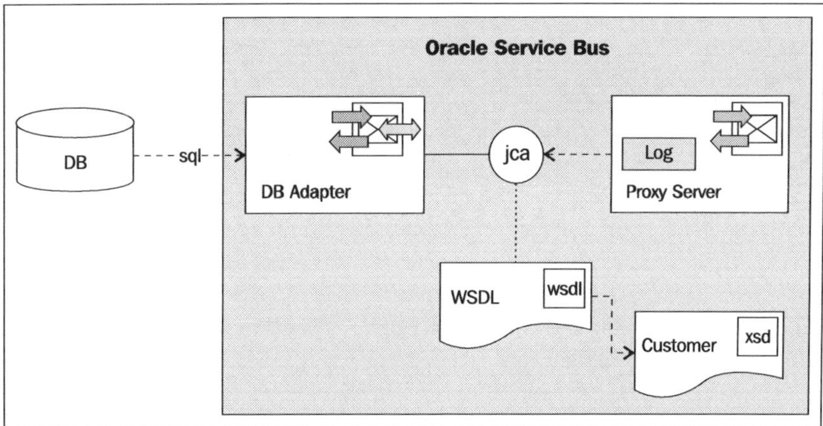

For the configuration of the DB Adapter we will use JDeveloper and then switch to Eclipse to implement the proxy service wrapping the inbound DB adapter.

Getting ready

For this recipe, we will use the database tables created with the OSB Cookbook standard environment. Make sure that the connection factory is set up in the database adapter configuration, as shown in the *Introduction* of this chapter.

You can import the OSB project containing the base setup for this recipe into Eclipse from `\chapter-7\getting-ready\using-db-adapter-to-poll-for-changes-on-db`.

How to do it...

First create the DB adapter used to poll the database. In JDeveloper perform the following steps:

1. Open the file `composite.xml` of the project `CustomerChangeDB`.
2. From the **Component Palette**, select the **SOA** components if not already done.
3. Drag a **Database Adapter** to the **Exposed Services** lane.
4. Click on **Next** and enter `CustomerAdded` in the **Service Name** field.
5. Click on **Next**.
6. On the screen **Service Connection**, create a connection (if not already done so): Click the plus sign to the right of the drop-down list.
7. Enter `OsbCookbookConnection` into the **Connection Name** field.
8. Enter `osb_cookbook` into the **Username** and **Password** field.
9. Change the Host Name, SID, and JDBC Port according to the database instance the **osb_cookbook** schema is installed on.
10. Click on **Test Connection** to test the connection and a **Success!** Message shows up.
11. Click on **OK**.
12. Check that the **JNDI Name** field is prefilled with the `eis/DB/OsbCookbookConnection`. We will configure the DB connection factory using that JNDI alias later through the WebLogic Console. Click on **Next**.

13. On the **Operation Type** screen, select **Poll for New or Changed Records in a Table** and click on **Next**.

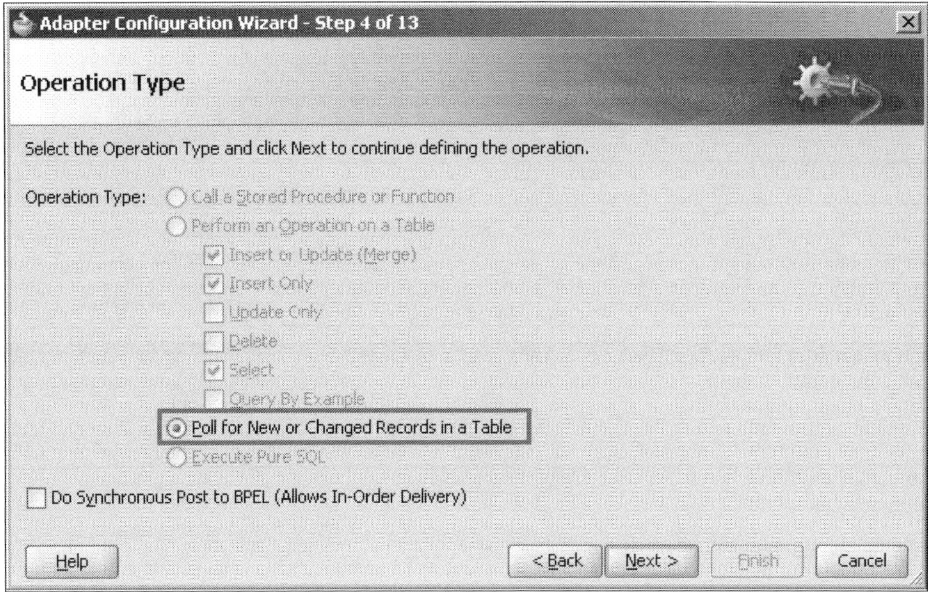

14. On the **Select Table** screen, click on **Import Tables**.
15. Make sure the schema **OSB_COOKBOOK** is selected. Click on **Query**.
16. Select the table `CUSTOMER_T`, move it to the selected pane and click on **OK**.
17. Wait a few seconds until the selected table appears on the pane, and then click on **Next** three times.
18. On the **After Read** screen, select **Update a Sequencing File** and click on **Next**:

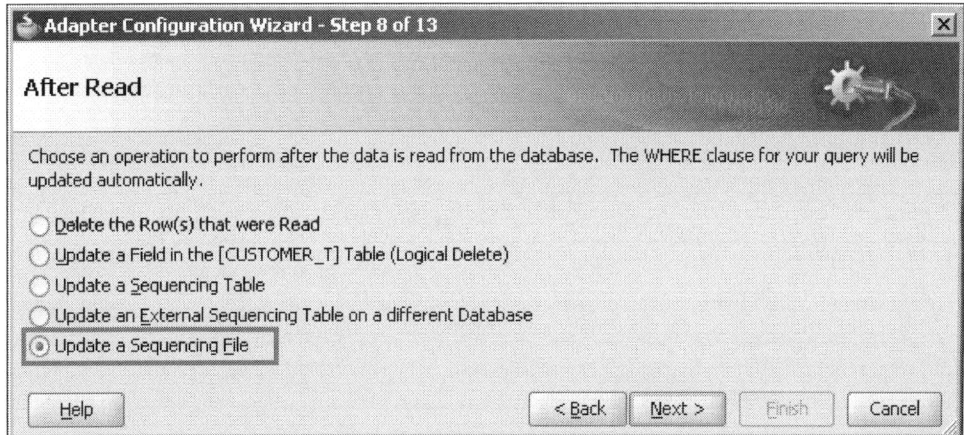

19. On the screen **Sequencing File** enter a location of a file, which the DB adapter will use to store the last read ID of the table CUSTOMER_T. This file location must be accessible at runtime by the OSB.
20. Select **ID** for **Sequenced ID Field**:

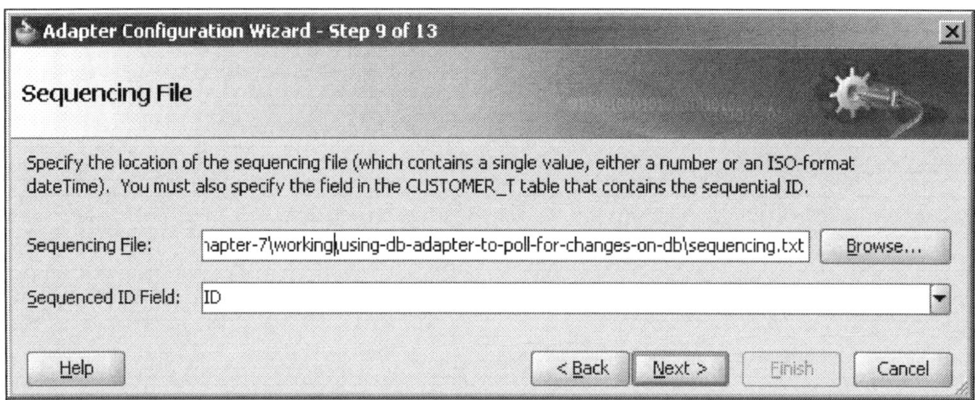

21. Click on **Next** four times to step over some more configuration options.
22. Click on **Finish**. JDeveloper now creates all the artifacts that define the adapter.

    You should now have a SCA composite with one exposed service, as shown in the following screenshot:

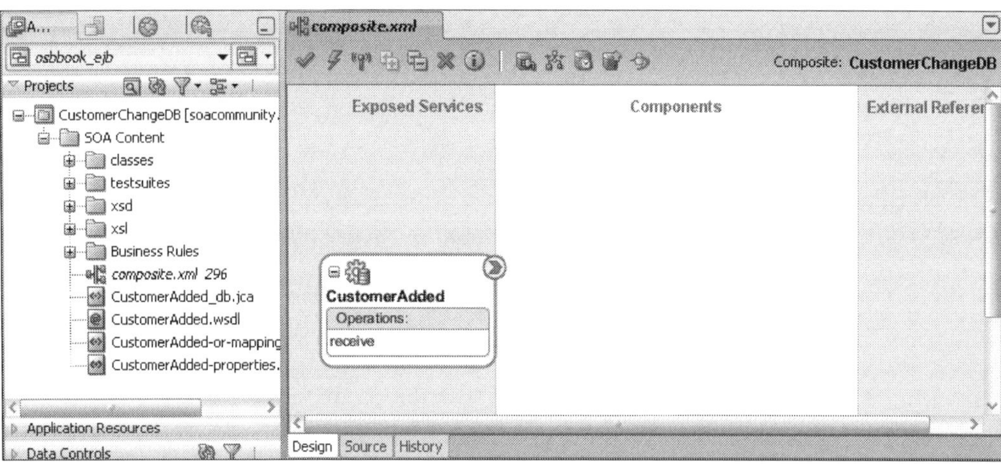

23. Click on **Save All**.

This is all we need to do in JDeveloper. Let's switch back to Eclipse OEPE and perform the following steps:

24. On the OSB project hit **Refresh** (*F5*). The artifacts generated by JDeveloper in the previous steps will show up.
25. Right-click on the `CustomerAdded_db.jca` file and select **Oracle Service Bus** | **Generate Service** from the context menu.
26. Select the `proxy` folder for the location of the proxy service.
27. Leave the **Service Name** and **WSDL name** field as suggested by the wizard.
28. Click on **OK**.
29. A proxy service and a WSDL file are generated in the `proxy` folder.
30. Open the generated proxy service **CustomerAdded_db.proxy**.
31. It's a **WSDL Web Service** using the WSDL just generated. Check that by navigating to the **General** tab.
32. Navigate to the **Message Flow** tab.
33. Drag a **Pipeline Pair** node to the message flow and change the name to **HandleCustomerAddedPipelinePair**.
34. Right-click on the **Request Pipeline** and select **Insert Into** | **Stage** to add a stage.
35. Change the name of the stage to `LoggingStage`.
36. Right-click on the **LoggingStage** and select **Insert Into** | **Reporting** | **Log**.
37. Click on the **Log** action, navigate to the **Properties** tab and click on the **Expression** link.
38. Enter `$body` into the **Expression** field and click **OK**.
39. Enter `Customer Added:` into the **Annotation** field.

40. Select **Warning** from the **Severity** drop-down list

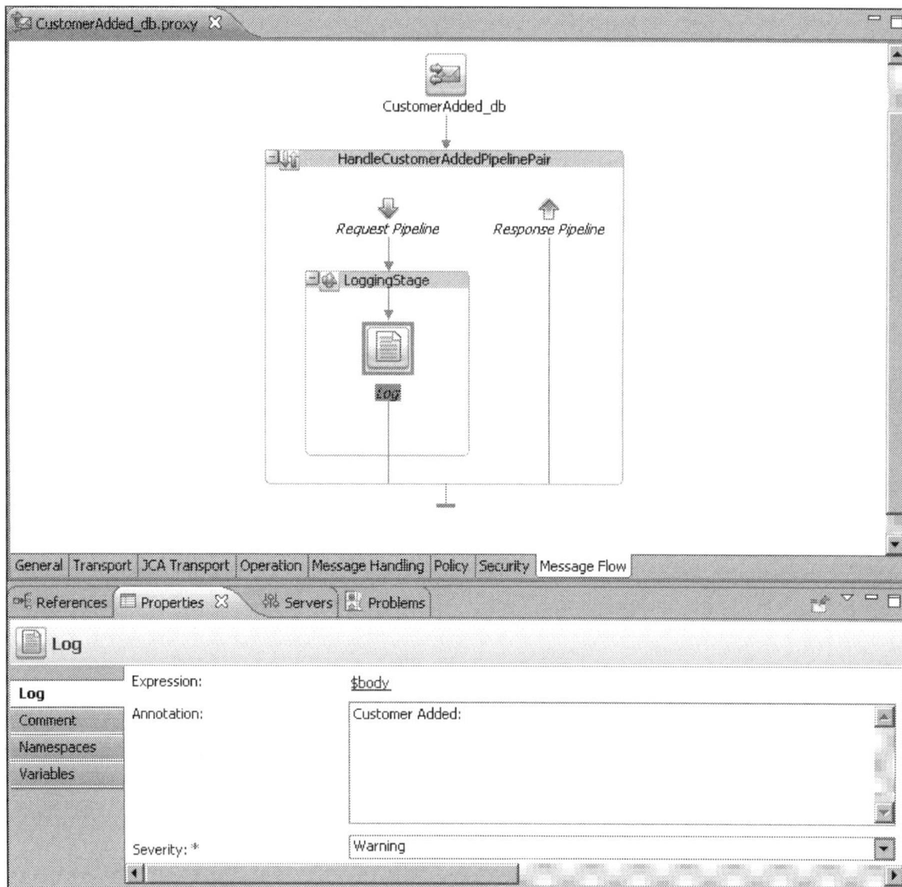

41. Deploy the project on OSB server.
42. To test it, run the script `\chapter-2\getting-ready\using-db-adapter-to-poll-for-changes-on-db\sql\insert_customer.sql`. It creates a new customer on the database.
43. A log message should appear in the Service Bus Console output window for every new row inserted into the `CUSTOMER_T table`.

How it works...

In JDeveloper, we created and configured a DB adapter, which periodically (default is every five seconds) polls a database table for added records. To know which was the last primary key processed, the value of the `ID` column of the polled table is stored in a sequencing file.

Technically, the DB adapter is executed by the DbAdapter component, which is deployed on WebLogic server as a resource adapter. The adapter we created references resources of this DbAdapter component. Therefore, we had to configure the connection factory there, which in turn uses datasource resources configured on WebLogic server as a standard datasource.

When the DB adapter detects a new row in `CUSTOMER_T` table, it invokes the proxy service providing an XML representation of data for the new row. Our proxy service then simply logs the XML using a **Log** action.

There's more...

The DB adapter provides a lot more options on how changes should be detected and how processed rows are marked. It allows modifying the query used to poll the database, to use bind parameters and to join tables to query a whole graph of data.

What kind of database changes may be detected

In our example, we have seen how to poll for new records. It is also possible to poll for changed records, but in this case it is not sufficient to store the ID of a processed record in the sequencing file. A possible solution would be to store a *last changed* timestamp in the sequencing file. However, this requires that this timestamp is updated with every change or insert operation on the table.

It is not possible to poll for deleted records. If this is a requirement, a good solution is to set up a trigger which writes every change into a queue (for example, AQ) or into a change-tracking table. However, such a solution is only feasible if you change the database you are polling on.

A third way to query changes is to execute a custom select or query by example. Both are also possible with the DB adapter. However, this select operation must be executed through a business service. So it is no longer the DB adapter, which periodically triggers the select action, but some other external timer. The timer triggers a proxy service, which in turn executes the business service. In that case, the DB adapter is used in an outbound operation.

What are the possibilities of marking processed rows

In our example, we just stored the ID of the last processed row in a sequencing file. This is a non-invasive solution, which only works if inserted rows get ascending keys. The **After Read** screen of the DB adapter wizard shows some more options to mark processed rows in a table:

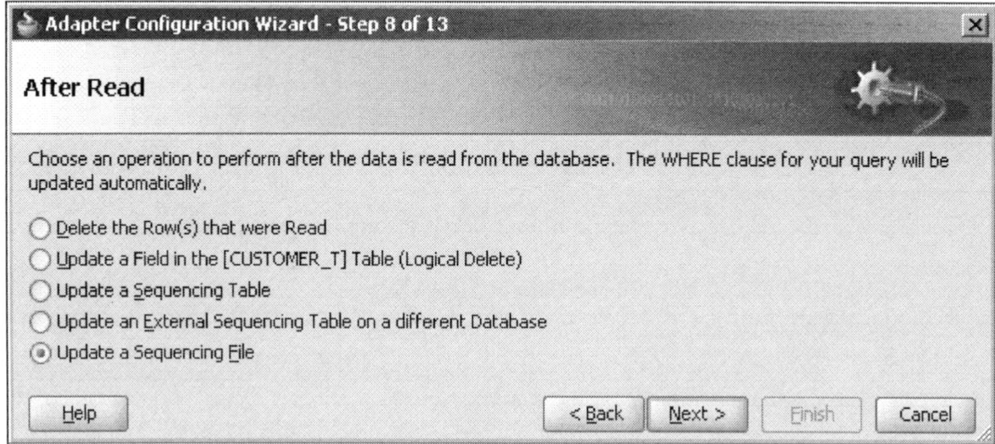

In fact, there are three ways to register whether a row was processed:

1. Delete the row read. This is suitable when change notifications are written into separate table by a trigger.
2. Update some field in the polled table, marking every row processed. This is the most common scenario when you have the option to add an extra flag column to an existing table.
3. Store the ID of the last processed record either in a file (as in our example) or in another table on the same or a different database.

How to modify the query when polling the database

When polling a table for changes, it is possible to add filters to the query, for example, to only match records which are released for processing. For instance, if we are only interested in customers with rating = '1', we could add the following filter on the **Define Selection Criteria** screen:

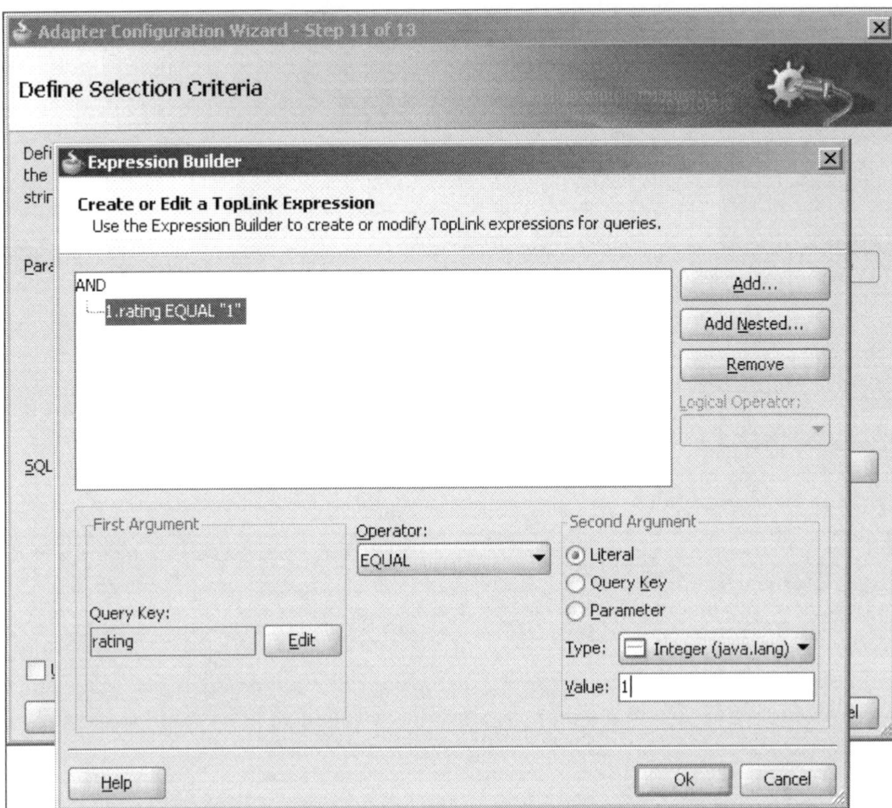

This results in the following query:

SQL:

```
SELECT ID, PERSON_ID, RATING, CC_TYPE, CC_NUMBER, CC_EXPIRATION,
CC_CVC FROM CUSTOMER_T WHERE ((RATING = '1') AND (ID > #LAST_READ_ID))
ORDER BY ID ASC
```

Edit...

Unfortunately, it is only possible to provide filters with constant values when polling. These filter values cannot be changed at runtime. If filter values need to be more dynamic and changeable at runtime, then a database view, implementing the dynamic filter, might be a solution, depending on the database product being used. This view can then be used instead of the table for the polling.

When using a select operation instead of polling, parameters can be sent to the query. As the select operation must be explicitly called through a business service, we have the opportunity to provide parameters in the request body.

Options regarding runtime behavior

There are some more options to be configured on the DB adapter within the JDeveloper wizard, namely, query timeout and retry-behavior in case of failures.

Other options, such as the dispatch policy or transaction usage, are configured on the **JCA Transport** and **Message Handling** tab of the proxy service within Eclipse OEPE.

It is recommended to use a dispatch policy, (which is in fact a Work Manager in WebLogic terms) which has its `Ignore Stuck Threads` flag enabled. Failure to do so results sooner or later in the infamous 'stuck thread' exceptions in the log file. This is because the DB adapter holds a thread used to poll the database which is never released after. WebLogic treats this as an error in its default configuration.

Using the AQ adapter to consume messages from the database

In this recipe, we will configure an inbound AQ adapter, so that it can be used to consume messages from a queue implemented in the database by Oracle AQ. The adapter will be used from a proxy service as shown in the following screenshot:

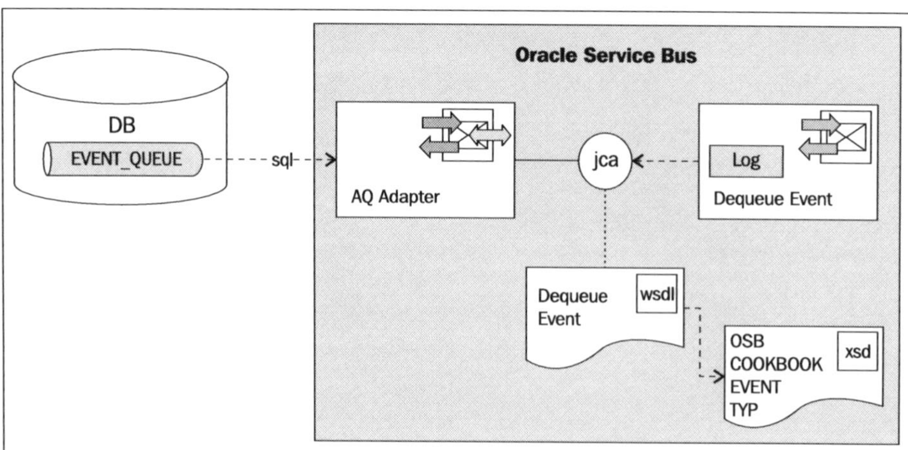

The queue EVENT_QUEUE that we will use has been set up with the OSB Cookbook standard environment using the following SQL and PL/SQL code:

```
--creating the object type, which defines payload
CREATE OR REPLACE TYPE event_typ as OBJECT
(
   id NUMBER(19)
   , event_type VARCHAR2(30)
   , event_time TIMESTAMP
)

-- creating queue table
BEGIN
  sys.dbms_aqadm.create_queue_table(
           queue_table => 'EVENT_QUEUE_T',
           queue_payload_type => 'OSB_COOKBOOK.EVENT_TYP',
           sort_list => 'ENQ_TIME',
           compatible => '10.0.0',
           primary_instance => 0,
           secondary_instance => 0,
           storage_clause => 'tablespace USERS pctfree 10
              initrans 1 maxtrans 255 storage ( initial 64K
              minextents 1 maxextents unlimited )');
END;
/

-- creating queue
BEGIN
  sys.dbms_aqadm.create_queue(
                queue_name => 'EVENT_QUEUE',
                queue_table => 'EVENT_QUEUE_T',
                queue_type => sys.dbms_aqadm.normal_queue,
                max_retries => 5,
                retry_delay => 0,
                retention_time => 0);

  sys.dbms_aqadm.start_queue( queue_name => 'EVENT_QUEUE',
                              enqueue => TRUE,
                              dequeue => TRUE);
END;
```

Getting ready

For this recipe, we will use the database queue `EVENT_QUEUE` available with the OSB Cookbook standard environment. Make sure that a connection factory is set up for the AQ adapter configuration, as shown in the *Introduction* of this chapter.

You can import the OSB project containing the base setup for this recipe into Eclipse from `\chapter-7\getting-ready\using-aq-adapter-to-dequeue-from-db`.

How to do it...

First we create the AQ adapter, which will implement the dequeue functionality from the database. In JDeveloper perform, the following steps:

1. Open the file `composite.xml` of the project `DequeueFromDB`.
2. From the **Component Palette**, select the **SOA** components if not already done.
3. Drag the **AQ Adapter** to the **Exposed Services** lane and click on **Next**.
4. Enter `DequeueEvent` in the **Service Name** field and click on **Next**.
5. Select the **OsbCookbookConnection** from the **Connection** listbox.
6. Check that **eis/aq/OsbCookbookConnection** is the value of the **JNDI Name** field.
7. Click on **Next**.
8. On the **Adapter Interface** screen, select the **Define from operation and schema (specified later)** option and click on **Next**.
9. On the **Operation** screen, select the **Dequeue** option and leave the value `Dequeue` for the **Operation Name** field.
10. Click on **Next**.
11. On the **Queue Name** screen, click on **Browse**.
12. On the **Select Queue** screen, select **EVENT_QUEUE** and click on **OK**.

13. Click on **Next**.

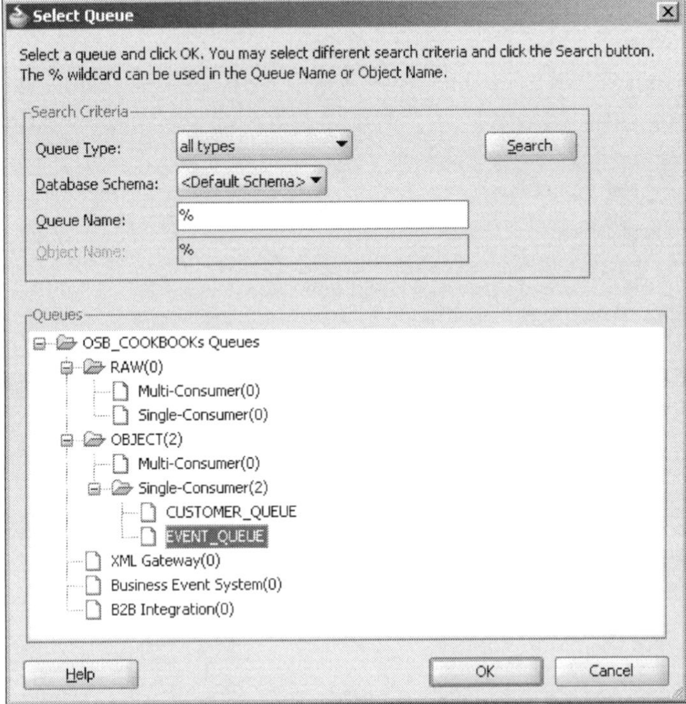

14. Leave the **Queue Parameters** screen as is and click on **Next**.
15. On the **Object Payload** screen, select the **Whole Object EVENT_TYP** option and click on **Next**.

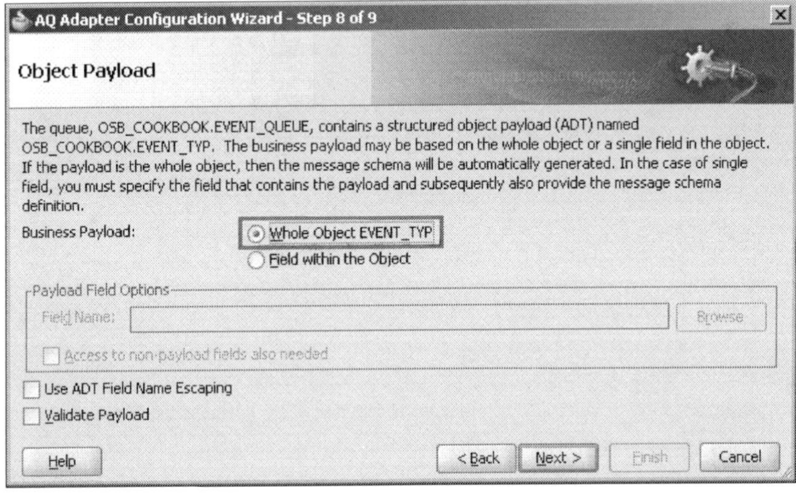

16. Click on **Finish**.
17. Click the **Save All** button to save the SOA project.

The definition of the AQ adapter for consuming messages from the `EVENT_QUEUE` is now ready. The work in JDeveloper is done by that and we can switch to Eclipse OEPE and perform the following steps to create a proxy service using the AQ adapter:

18. On the OSB project hit **Refresh** (*F5*). The artifacts generated by JDeveloper in the previous steps will show up.
19. Right-click on the `DequeueEvent_aq.jca` file and select **Oracle Service Bus | Generate Service** from the context menu.
20. Select the `proxy` folder for the location of the proxy service.
21. Leave the **Service Name** and **WSDL name** as suggested by the wizard.
22. Click on **OK**.

We now have a proxy service in place that uses the AQ adapter through the JCA transport. The interface of the proxy is defined by the **DequeueEvent** WSDL, which has been generated by the AQ adapter. Perform the following steps in Eclipse OEPE for implementing the message flow of the proxy:

23. Navigate to the **Message Flow** tab of the **DequeueEvent_aq** proxy service.
24. Insert a **Pipeline Pair** node and name it `HandleEventPipelinePair`.
25. In the **Request Pipeline** insert a **Stage** node and name it `HandleEventStage`.
26. Insert a **Log** action into the stage just created.
27. On the **Properties** tab of the **Log** action, click on **Expression** and enter `$body, $inbound` into the **Expression** field, to log both the content of the body as well as the content of the inbound metadata.
28. Click on **OK**.
29. Select **Warning** for the **Severity** drop-down listbox.
30. Deploy the project to the OSB server.
31. The service can now be tested. In a SQL window (that is, within SQL Plus), execute the following PL/SQL code block:

```
DECLARE
   enqueue_options dbms_aq.enqueue_options_t;
   message_properties dbms_aq.message_properties_t;
   msgid RAW(100);
   event event_typ;
BEGIN
   event := event_typ(1, 'NEW_CUSTOMER', CURRENT_TIMESTAMP);
```

```
    dbms_aq.enqueue(queue_name => 'EVENT_QUEUE'
                   , enqueue_options => enqueue_options
                   , message_properties => message_properties
                   , payload => event
                   , msgid => msgid);
END;
/
COMMIT;
```

The log statement showing the payload of the received message should be shown in the Service Bus Console window.

OSB Cookbook 11R2 PS3 (11.1.1.4)


```
<24.10.2011 15:14 Uhr MESZ> <Warning> <ALSB Logging> <BEA-000000> < [HandleEvent
PipelinePair, HandleEventPipelinePair_request, HandleEventStage, REQUEST] <soap-
env:Body xmlns:soap-env="http://schemas.xmlsoap.org/soap/envelope/">
  <osb:EVENT_TYP xmlns:osb="http://xmlns.oracle.com/xdb/OSB_COOKBOOK">
    <ID>1</ID>
    <EVENT_TYPE>NEW_CUSTOMER</EVENT_TYPE>
    <EVENT_TIME>2011-10-24T15:14:42.541Z</EVENT_TIME>
  </osb:EVENT_TYP>
</soap-env:Body><con:endpoint name="ProxyService$using-aq-adapter-to-dequeue-fro
m-db$proxy$DequeueEvent_aq" xmlns:con="http://www.bea.com/wli/sb/context">
  <con:service>
    <con:operation>Dequeue</con:operation>
  </con:service>
  <con:transport>
    <con:uri>jca://eis/aq/OsbCookbookConnection</con:uri>
    <con:mode>request</con:mode>
    <con:qualityOfService>exactly-once</con:qualityOfService>
    <con:request xsi:type="jca:JCARequestMetaDataXML" xmlns:jca="http://www.bea.
com/wli/sb/transports/jca" xmlns:xsi="http://www.w3.org/2001/XMLSchema-instance"
>
      <tran:headers xsi:type="jca:JCARequestHeadersXML" xmlns:tran="http://www.b
ea.com/wli/sb/transports">
        <jca:SOAPAction>Dequeue</jca:SOAPAction>
        <jca:jca.aq.Priority>1</jca:jca.aq.Priority>
        <jca:jca.aq.Correlation/>
        <jca:jca.aq.MessageId>AB0BDA27B0504F019BF8A7454DA6D7C2</jca:jca.aq.Messa
geId>
        <jca:jca.aq.Attempts>0</jca:jca.aq.Attempts>
        <jca:jca.aq.EnqueueTime>2011-10-24T15:14:42.000+02:00</jca:jca.aq.Enqueu
eTime>
        <jca:jca.aq.OrigMessageId/>
      </tran:headers>
      <tran:encoding xmlns:tran="http://www.bea.com/wli/sb/transports">UTF-8</tr
an:encoding>
    </con:request>
    <con:response xsi:type="jca:JCAResponseMetaDataXML" xmlns:jca="http://www.be
a.com/wli/sb/transports/jca" xmlns:xsi="http://www.w3.org/2001/XMLSchema-instanc
e">
      <tran:headers xsi:type="jca:JCAResponseHeadersXML" xmlns:tran="http://www.
bea.com/wli/sb/transports"/>
      <tran:response-code xmlns:tran="http://www.bea.com/wli/sb/transports">0</t
ran:response-code>
    </con:response>
  </con:transport>
  <con:security>
```

How it works...

Using the AQ adapter allows us to implement a proxy service, which is automatically invoked when a message arrives in the queue on the database, implemented by using Oracle AQ.

Based on the object type payload defined on the database when creating the AQ queue, the AQ adapter is generating the corresponding XML schema. This schema is then used to define the WSDL for the `DequeueEvent` proxy service. When using the AQ adapter configuration to generate a proxy service, the proxy service will automatically get a WSDL-based interface, based on the generated WSDL of the JCA adapter. Therefore, the body variable will contain a message according to the XML schema generated by the AQ adapter.

Using the AQ adapter , we can offer an alternative way of processing events from the database. In the recipe, *Using DB adapter to poll for changes on a database table*, we have seen that the DB adapter can be used to poll for changes in a table.

Using this recipe and the AQ adapter, the same can be achieved in a more event-driven fashion, where a database trigger would be used on a table to enqueue a message into the `EVENT_QUEUE` whenever a change is applied to a database table.

Dequeuing of the message works in a transaction and can be combined with another modification on another transactional resource (such as a database table or JMS queue) by using an XA transaction.

There's more...

If we only want to consume messages which meet a specific condition, then the **Dequeue Condition** on the **Queue Adapter** screen of the AQ adapter wizard can be used.

The **Dequeue Condition** is a Boolean expression using a syntax similar to the `WHERE` clause of a SQL query, but without using the `WHERE` keyword. The expression can include conditions on message properties, user object payload data, and PL/SQL or SQL functions. Message properties include the columns of the queue table, such as `priority` and `corrid`.

If the **Dequeue Condition** is specified and no messages meet the condition, then no dequeue will happen.

To specify a **Dequeue Condition** on a message payload (object payload), use attributes of the object type in the clause. Each attribute must be prefixed with `tab.user_data` as a qualifier to indicate the specific column of the queue table that stores the payload.

The following screenshot shows a possible restriction on the recipe, so that only messages with `event_type` equals to `UPD_CUSTOMER` are consumed:

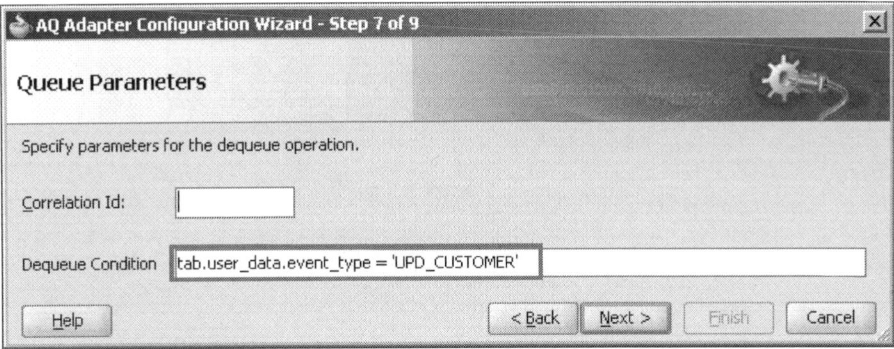

See also

See the Chapter, *Messaging with JMS transport*, for how to use the WebLogic JMS server for implementing JMS messaging in the Oracle Service Bus.

Using the AQ adapter to send messages to the database

In this recipe, we will configure an outbound AQ adapter, so that it can be used to publish messages from the Oracle Service Bus to an Oracle AQ queue on the database:

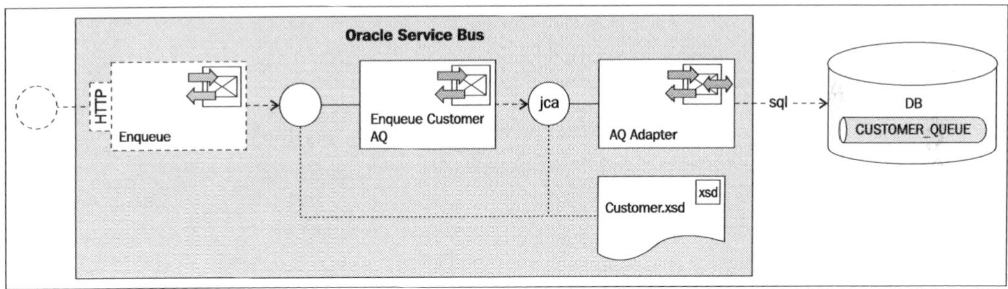

The AQ database queue `CUSTOMER_QUEUE`, which we will use has been set up with the OSB Cookbook standard environment using the following SQL and PL/SQL code:

```
BEGIN
  sys.dbms_aqadm.create_queue_table(
                queue_table => 'CUSTOMER_QUEUE_T',
```

```
                queue_payload_type => 'SYS.XMLTYPE',
                storage_clause => 'PCTFREE 10 PCTUSED 40 INITRANS 1
MAXTRANS 255',
                sort_list => 'ENQ_TIME',
                compatible => '8.1.3');
END;
/

BEGIN
  sys.dbms_aqadm.create_queue(
                queue_name => 'CUSTOMER_QUEUE',
                queue_table => 'CUSTOMER_QUEUE_T',
                queue_type => sys.dbms_aqadm.normal_queue,
                max_retries => 5,
                retry_delay => 0);
  sys.dbms_aqadm.start_queue( queue_name => 'CUSTOMER_QUEUE', enqueue
=> TRUE, dequeue => TRUE);

END;
```

Getting ready

For this recipe, we will use the database queue `CUSTOMER_QUEUE` available with the OSB Cookbook standard environment. Make sure that the connection factory is set up in the database adapter configuration, as shown in the *Introduction* of this chapter.

You can import the OSB project containing the base setup for this recipe into Eclipse from `\chapter-7\getting-ready\using-aq-adapter-to-enqueue-to-db`.

How to do it...

First we create the AQ adapter, which will implement the enqueue functionality to the database. In JDeveloper perform the following steps:

1. Open the file `composite.xml` of the project `EnqueueToDB`.
2. From the **Component Palette**, select the **SOA** components if not already done.
3. Drag the **AQ Adapter** to the **External References** lane and click on **Next**.
4. Enter `EnqueueCustomer` in the **Service Name** field and click on **Next**.
5. Select the **OsbCookbookConnection** from the **Connection** listbox.
6. Check that **eis/aq/OsbCookbookConnection** is the value of the **JNDI Name** field and click on **Next**.

7. On the **Adapter Interface** screen, select the **Define from operation and schema (specified later)** option and click on **Next**.
8. On the **Operation** screen, select the **Enqueue** option and leave the value `Enqueue` for the **Operation Name** field.
9. Click on **Next**.
10. On the **Queue Name** screen, click on **Browse**.
11. On the **Select Queue** screen, select **CUSTOMER_QUEUE** and click on **OK**.
12. Click on **Next**.
13. Leave the **Correlation Id** empty and click on **Next**.
14. On the **Messages** screen, select the **Browse for schema file** option.
15. Choose the **Customer** type from the **Customer.xsd** and click on **OK**.
16. Click on **Next**.

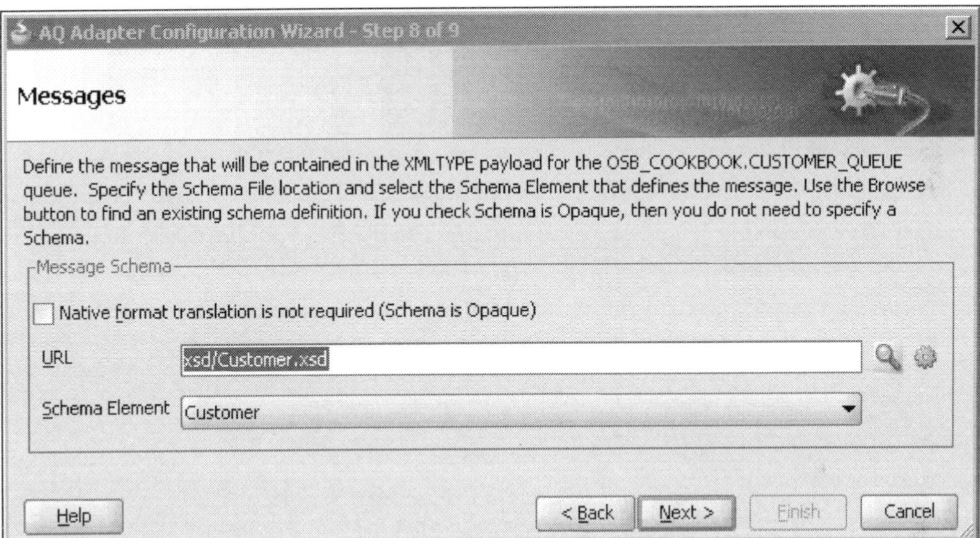

17. Click on **Finish**.

18. Click on the **Save All** to save the SOA project. The composite should look similar to the one shown in the following screenshot:

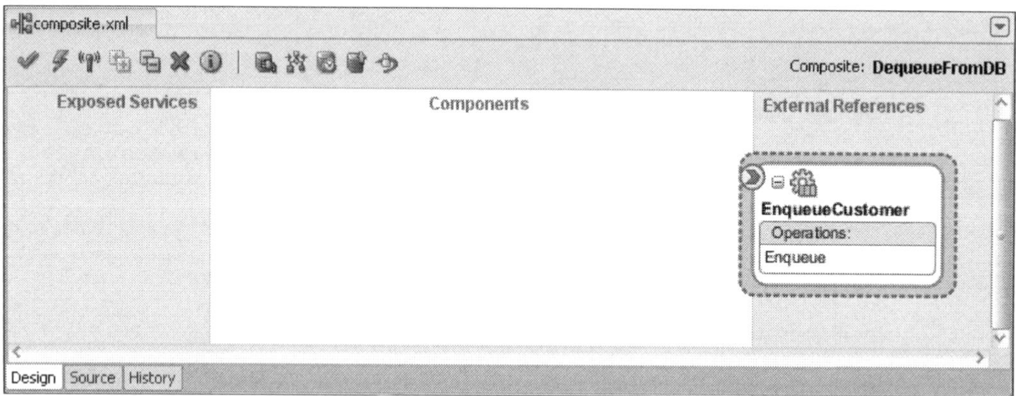

The definition of the AQ adapter for publishing messages to the `CUSTOMER_QUEUE` database queue is now ready. The work in JDeveloper is done and we can switch to Eclipse OEPE and perform the following steps to create a business service using the AQ adapter:

19. On the OSB project hit **Refresh** (*F5*) on the **adapter** folder. The artifacts generated by JDeveloper in the previous steps will show up.
20. Right-click on the `adapter/EnqueueCustomer_ac.jca` file and select **Oracle Service Bus** | **Generate Service** from the context menu.
21. Select the `business` folder for the location of the business service.
22. Leave the **Service Name** and **WSDL name** as suggested by the wizard.
23. Click on **OK**.
24. Deploy the project to the OSB server.

We now have a business service that allows the Oracle Service Bus to use the AQ adapter through the JCA transport. The interface of the business service is defined by the `EnqueueCustomer_aq` WSDL, which imports and uses the `EnqueueCustomer` WSDL generated by the AQ adapter. We could now create a proxy service, which allows us to send a Customer message over a common protocol, such as SOAP/HTTP. However, in this recipe we will just focus on testing the OSB to AQ communication.

In the Service Bus Console perform the following steps:

25. In the **Project Explorer**, navigate to the business service **EnqueueCustomer_aq**.
26. Click on the **Launch Test Console** icon under **Actions**.
27. Enter a valid customer message into the **Payload** field and click on **Execute**.

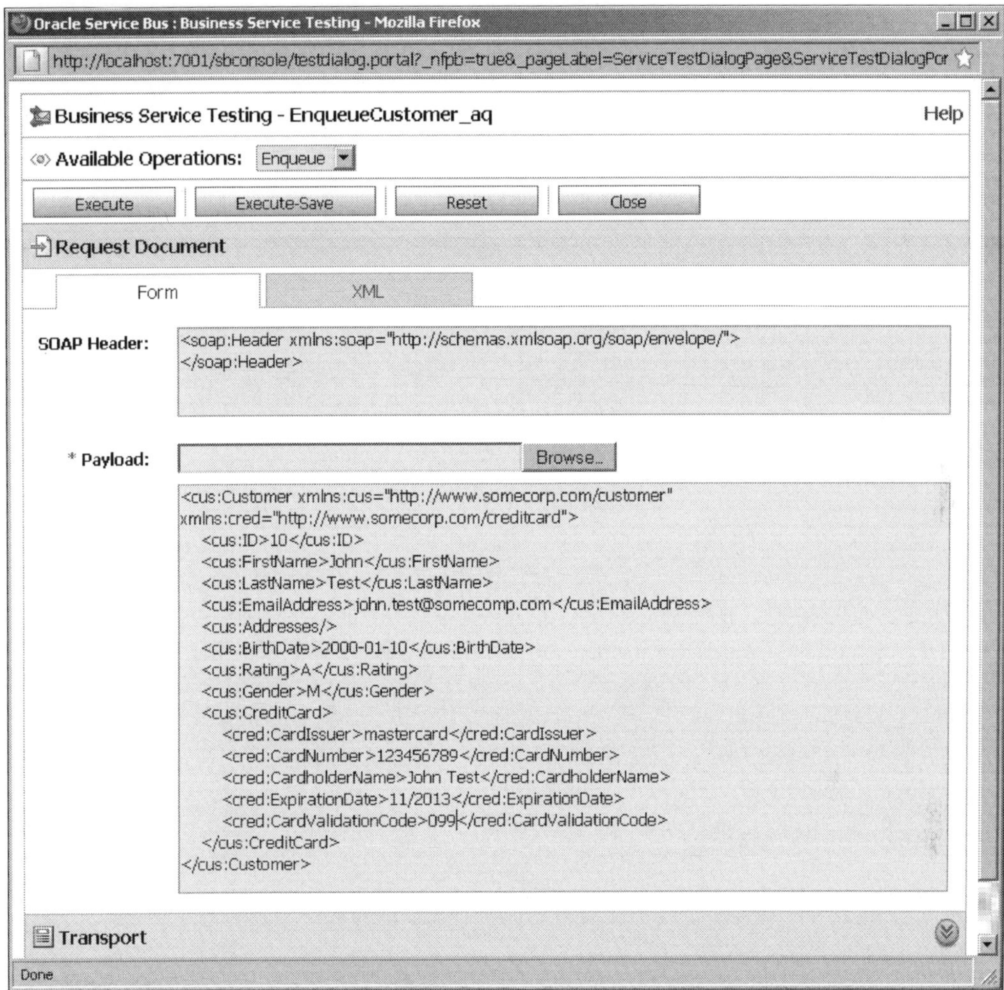

The business service publishes the message through the AQ Adapter to our queue. We can check the database if the message is located there.

29. Connect to the **OsbCookbookConnection** within JDeveloper.
30. Expand the tables and double-click on the **CUSTOMER_QUEUE_T** queue table.

31. Click on the **Data** tab.
32. Navigate to the `USER_DATA` column and click on the **Edit Value** button to see the complete text of the message.

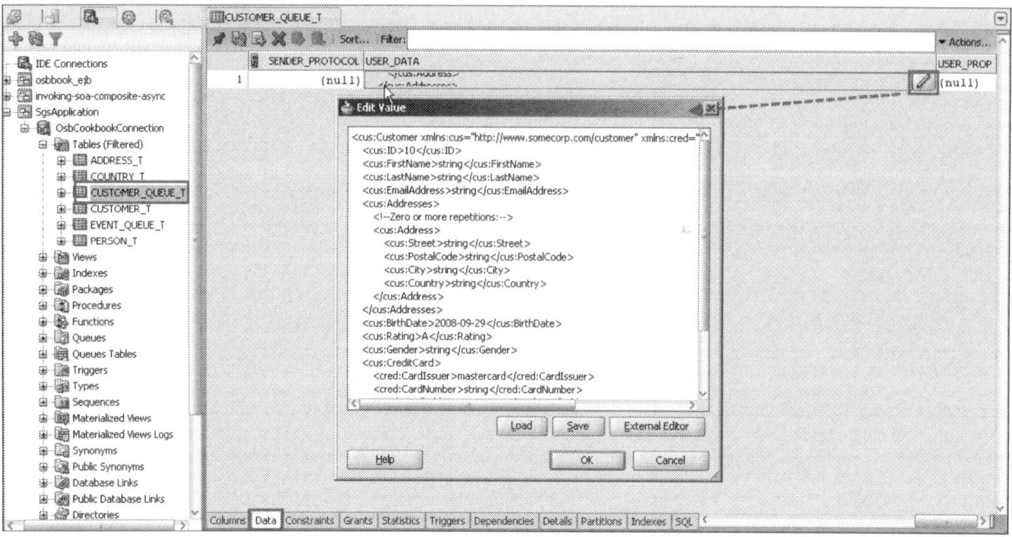

How it works...

Using the AQ adapter allows us to expose Oracle AQ queues to the Oracle Service Bus.

In practice, we would invoke the business service from within a proxy service, either in a **Routing** or **Publish** action. The proxy service would then expose any other transport, for example, a WSDL Web Service, to offer the publishing a message to an AQ queue through a SOAP-based Web Service.

There's more...

The queue table message has a column called `CORRID` that can store a correlation identifier. This is very helpful if you need to provide message tracking over multiple transactions.

The value can either be hard coded when configuring the adapter or passed dynamically when invoking the business service. When testing the business service through the test console, the value can be specified through the property in the **Transport** section.

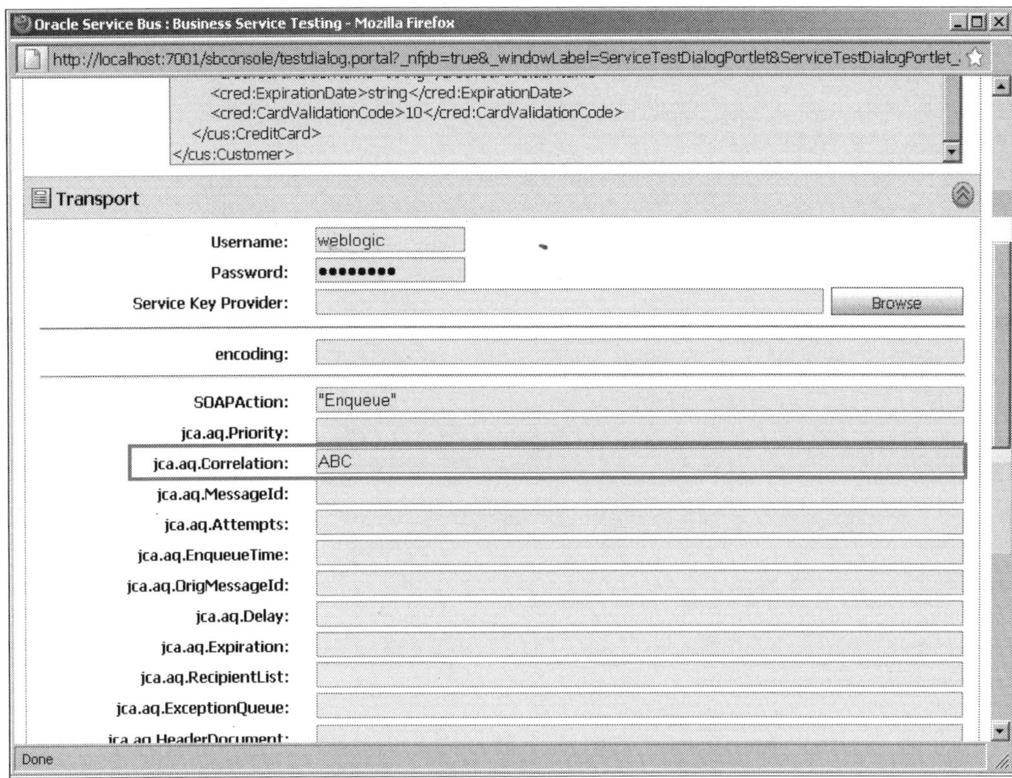

To pass a correlation identifier from a proxy service, the **Transport Header** action should be used within a **Routing** or **Publish** action, as shown in the following screenshot:

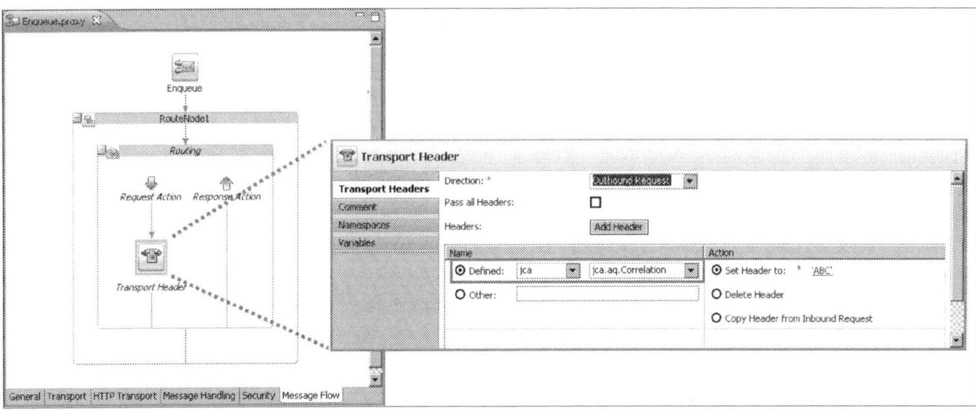

8
Communicating with SOA Suite

In this chapter, we will cover:

- Invoking a SCA composite synchronously from an OSB service
- Invoking a SCA composite asynchronously from an OSB service
- Invoking an OSB service from SCA composite synchronously
- Invoking an OSB service from SCA composite asynchronously

Introduction

The OSB provides a **SOA-DIRECT** transport that can be used to invoke Oracle SOA Suite service components, such as BPEL processes, human tasks, rules, and Oracle Mediator components.

The SOA-DIRECT transport provides native connectivity between OSB services and Oracle SOA Suite service components. Oracle SOA Suite provides a direct binding framework that can be used to expose Oracle SOA Suite service components of an SCA composite. The OSB SOA-DIRECT transport can be used to interact with those exposed services through the SOA Direct Binding framework, letting those service components interact in the service bus layer and leverage the capabilities and features of OSB.

The SOA-DIRECT transport supports the following features:

- Invocation of any SOA binding component services through Java **Remote Method Invocation** (**RMI**)
- WS-Addressing
- Identity propagation

- Transaction propagation
- Attachments
- Optimized RMI transport for invoking SOA services
- High availability and clustering support
- Failover and load balancing (not available for services in the service callback role)
- Connection and application retries on errors

The SOA-DIRECT transport uses WS-Addressing for message correlation in synchronous and asynchronous communications. We will see the WS-Addressing applied in the recipe, *Invoking an OSB proxy service from SCA composite asynchronously*.

Invoking a SCA composite synchronously from an OSB service

In this recipe, we will create a SOA Suite composite application, which has a BPEL service component with a synchronous Direct Binding service interface. The direct binding interface will be invoked from an OSB business service through the SOA-DIRECT transport:

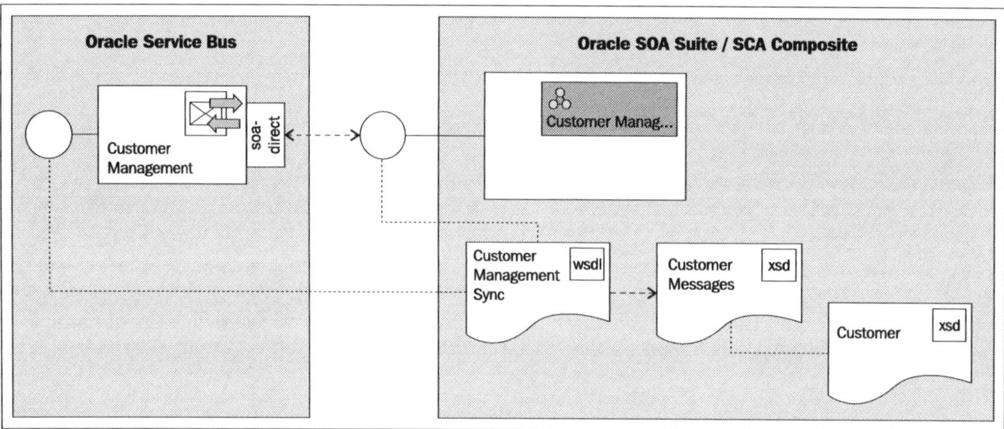

The SOA-DIRECT transport supports transactions and identity propagation across JVMs and uses the T3 RMI protocol to communicate with the SOA Suite server. It's important that the SOA Suite and the OSB server are on the same patch set level, otherwise we can get java class version errors.

Getting ready

Copy the `soa-suite-invoking-soa-composite-sync` holding the JDeveloper project from `\chapter-8\getting-ready\invoking-soa-composite-sync\` into a local workspace folder.

Import the base OSB project containing the necessary schemas and the right folder structure into Eclipse from `\chapter-8\getting-ready\invoking-soa-composite-sync`.

How to do it...

First we need a SOA Suite composite which exposes a synchronous Direct Binding interface. In JDeveloper perform the following steps to create it:

1. Open the SOA workspace in JDeveloper by selecting **File** | **Open** and navigating to the `invoking-soa-composite-sync.jws` file.
2. Click on the **composite.xml** located in the **CustomerManagement** project to open up the SCA composite view.
3. Drag a **BPEL Process** from the **Service Components** section of the **Component Palette** to the SCA composite and drop it on the **Components** area:

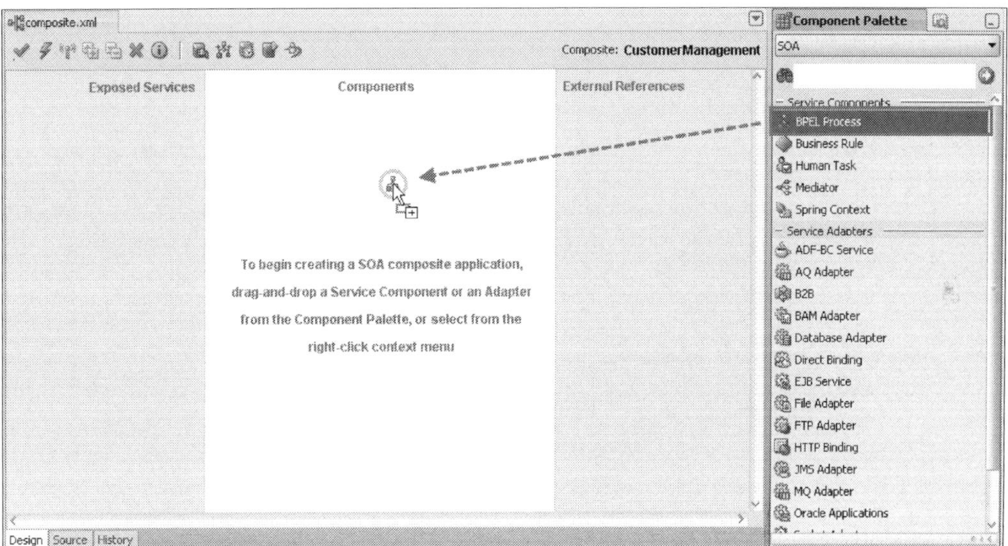

4. In the **Create BPEL Process** window, enter `CustomerManagentSync` into the **Name** field.
5. Choose **Synchronous BPEL Process** for the **Template** drop-down listbox.

6. Click on the magnifying glass button right to the **Input** field.
7. In the **Type Chooser** window expand the **CustomerMessages.xsd** inside the **Project Schema Files** folder:

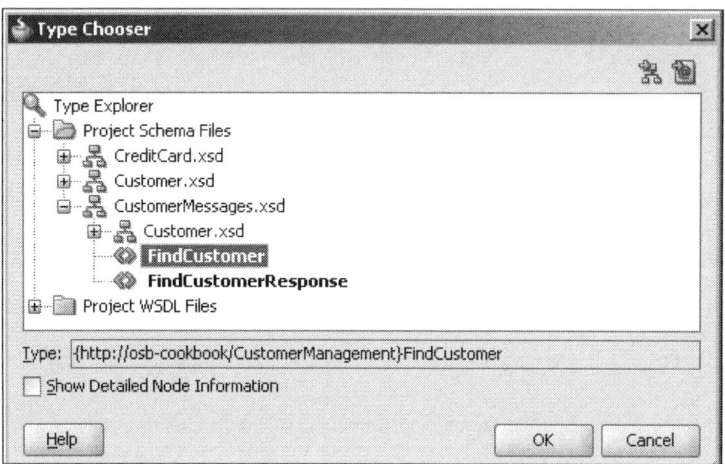

8. Select the **FindCustomer** element and click on **OK**.
9. Click on the magnifying glass button right to the **Output** field.
10. In the **Type Chooser** window expand the **CustomerMessages.xsd** inside the **Project Schema Files** folder.
11. Select the **FindCustomerResponse** element and click on **OK**:

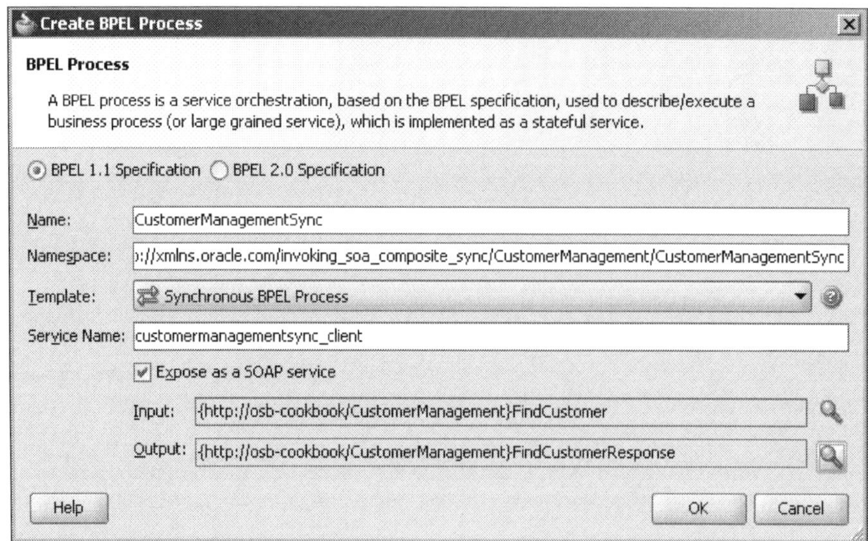

12. Click on **OK**.

This will create a BPEL component with an exposed SOAP binding as shown in the following screenshot:

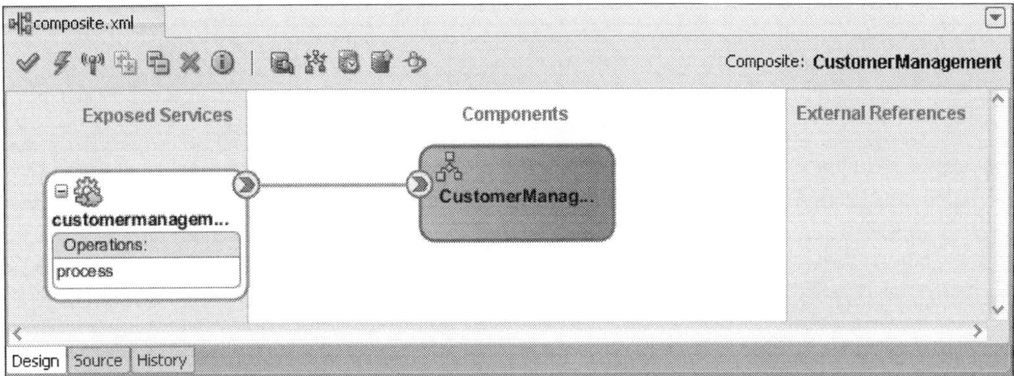

Now let's add a Direct Binding to the SCA composite. In JDeveloper perform the following steps:

13. From the **Component Palette** drag the **Direct Binding** from the **Service Adapter** section and drop it on the **Exposed Services** section of the SCA composite.
14. Enter `CustomerManagementSyncDirect` into the **Name** field.
15. Make sure that **Service** is pre-selected for **Type** drop-down listbox, if you have not probably dropped the **Direct Binding** component on the wrong lane.
16. Click on the icon with the green arrow next to the **WSDL URL** field to browse for the `WSDL` file created earlier. Select the `CustomerManagementSync.wsdl` file and click on **OK**.

17. Click on **OK** to finish the **Create Direct Binding** dialog:

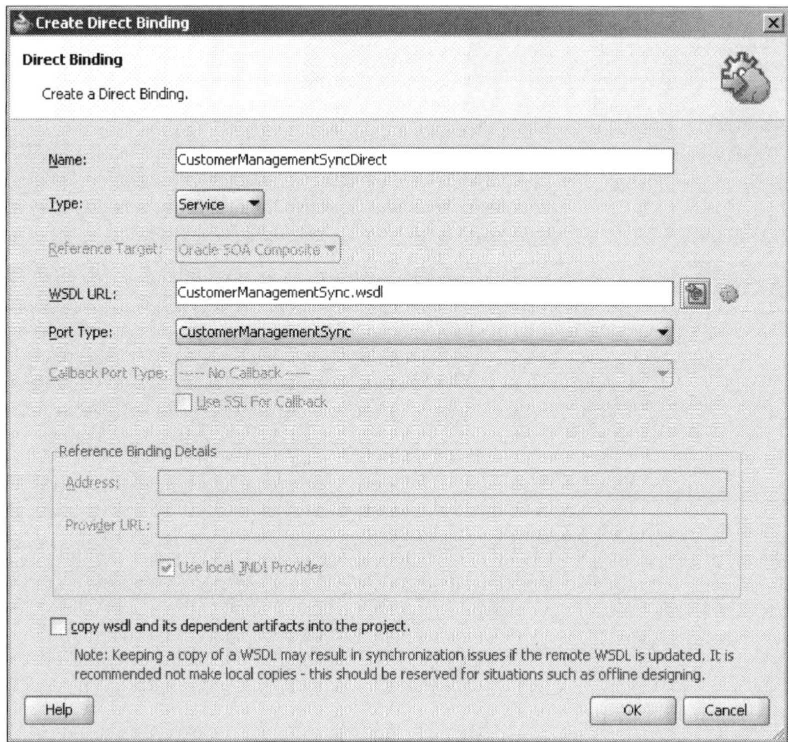

18. Drag a wire from the **CustomerManagementSyncDirect** exposed service to the **CustomerManagement** BPEL component:

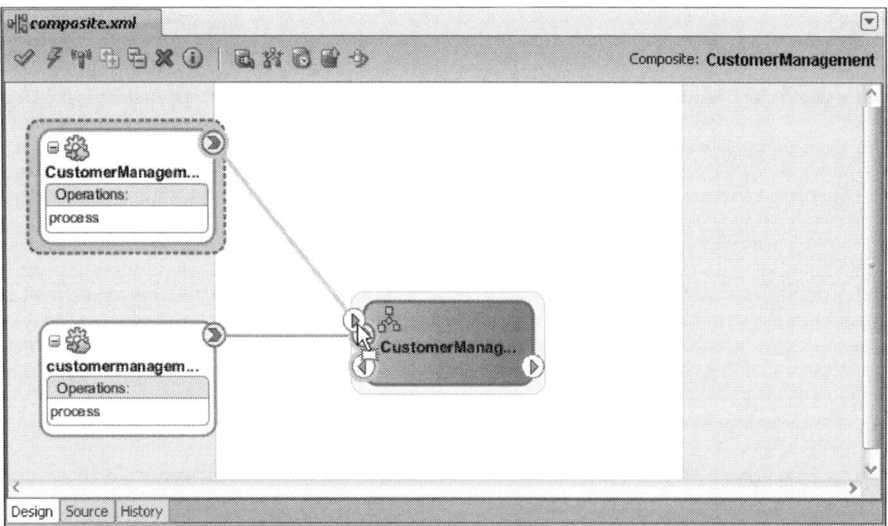

Next, we will change the BPEL component so that it will return the customer test data:

19. Double-click on the BPEL component symbol on the SCA composite.
20. Drag an **Assign** activity from the **Component Palette** and drop it inbetween the **receiveInput** and **replyOuput** activity.

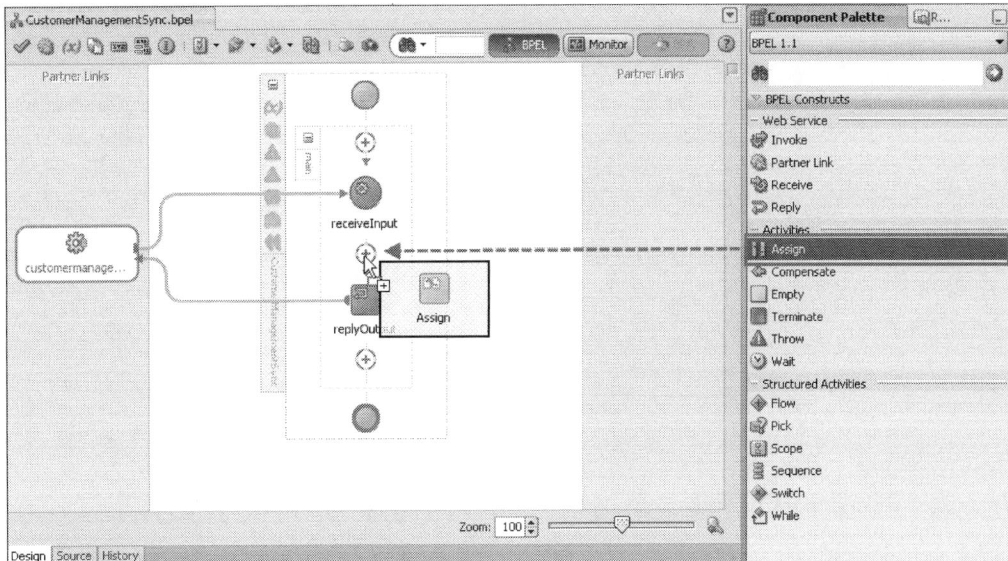

21. Double-click on the **Assign** activity.
22. Navigate to the **General** tab and overwrite the **name** field with **AssignOutput**.
23. Navigate to the **Copy Rules** tab.
24. In the tree on the right (the target section) right-click on **outputVariable** and select **Expand All Child Nodes**.

25. Drag XML fragment to the **Customer : CustomerTyp** element:

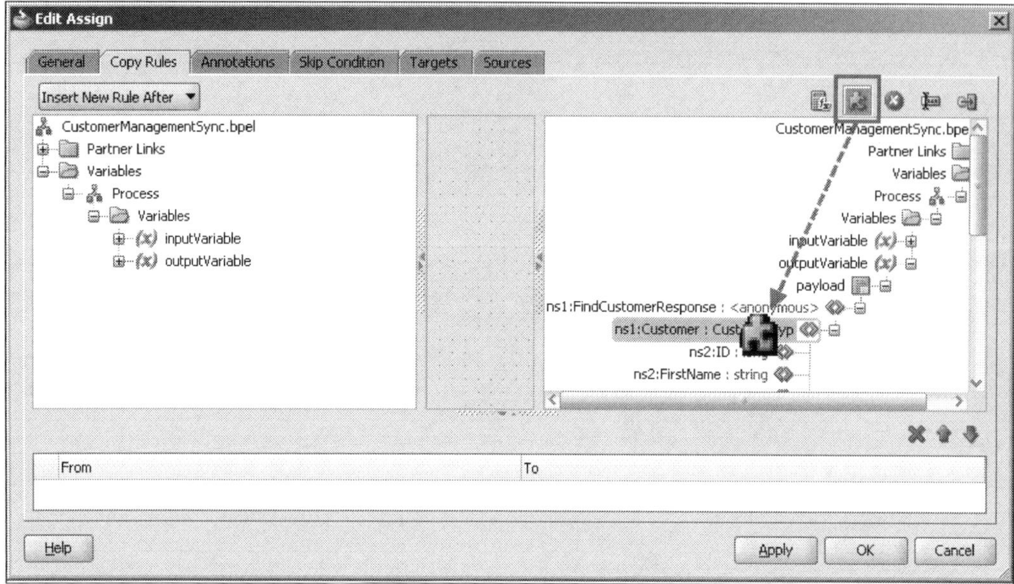

26. Enter the following xml fragment into **XML Fragment** field of the pop-up window:

```
<Customer xmlns="http://osb-cookbook/CustomerManagement"
xmlns:cus1="http://osb-cookbook/customer" xmlns:cred="http://osb-
cookbook/creditcard">
        <cus1:ID>100</cus1:ID>
        <cus1:FirstName>Larry</cus1:FirstName>
        <cus1:LastName>Ellison</cus1:LastName>
        <cus1:EmailAddress>larry.ellison@oracle.com</
cus1:EmailAddress>
        <cus1:Addresses/>
        <cus1:BirthDate>1967-08-13</cus1:BirthDate>
        <cus1:Rating>A</cus1:Rating>
        <cus1:Gender>Male</cus1:Gender>
        <cus1:CreditCard>
                <cred:CardIssuer>visa</cred:CardIssuer>
                <cred:CardNumber>123</cred:CardNumber>
                <cred:CardholderName>Larry</cred:CardholderName>
                <cred:ExpirationDate>2020-01-01</
cred:ExpirationDate>
               <cred:CardValidationCode>1233</
cred:CardValidationCode>
        </cus1:CreditCard>
</Customer>
```

27. Click on **OK** to close the pop-up window.
28. Click on **OK** to close the detail window of the **Assign** activity.
29. Click on **Save All** and close the `CustomerMangementSync.bpel` and `composite.xml`.

Now we can deploy the SCA composite to the SOA Suite server. In JDeveloper perform the following steps:

30. Right-click on the **CustomerManagement** project and select **Deploy | CustomerManagement**.
31. Select **Deploy to Application Server** from the list of deployment actions and click on **Next**.
32. Enable the **Overwrite any existing composites with the same revision ID** check box and click on **Next**.
33. Select the **ApplicationServerConnection** from the list of application servers and click on **Finish**.
34. Check the **SOA-Log** and **Deployment** status window for errors. The deployment is successful, if a **deployment finished** message is shown.

Next let's test **CustomerManagement** composite. In Enterprise Manager, perform the following steps:

35. Expand the `SOA` folder in the tree on the left.
36. Expand `soa-infra` folder and click on the **default** node.
37. Click on **CustomerManagement [1.0]** in the list of composites and the details of the composite are displayed:

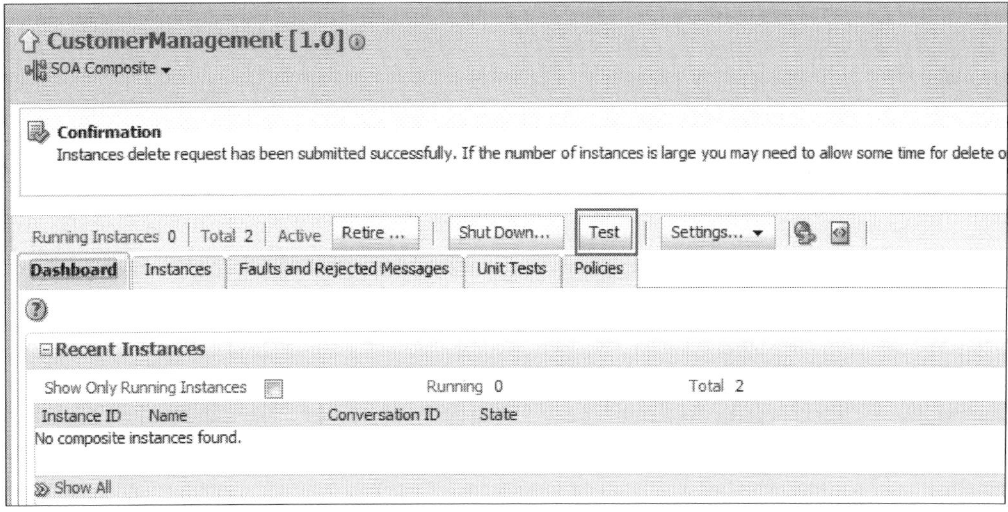

38. Click on the **Test** tab.
39. The **Test Web Service** screen is shown, which allows us to test the SOAP Binding of the composite.
40. On the **Request** tab, in the **Input Arguments** section enter `100` into the **ID** field and click on **Test Web Service** in the top-right corner.
41. The result of the test is shown in the **Response** tab:

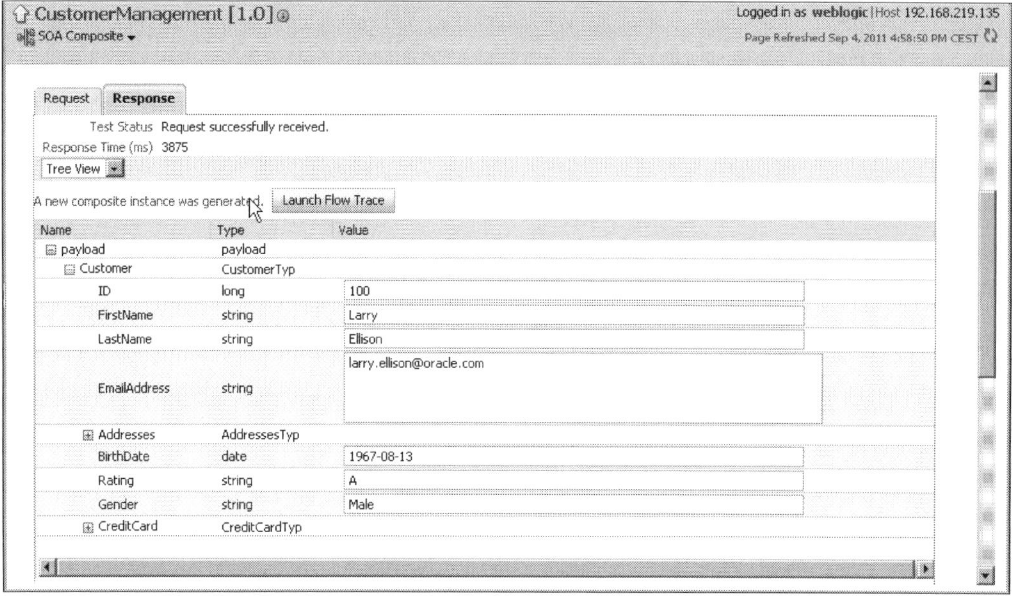

So far we have successfully created and tested the service provider side in SOA Suite. Now, let's implement the service consumer side on the OSB. First we need to get the WSDL of the SOA Direct Binding interface. We will retrieve the URL of the WSDL in JDeveloper and then use that URL to consume it in Eclipse OEPE.

In JDeveloper perform the following steps to retrieve the URL of the WSDL:

42. Navigate to the **Resource Palette** tab on the right side of JDeveloper and expand the **Application Server** node.
43. Expand the **ApplicationServerConnection | SOA | [SOAManagedServerName] | default | CustomerManagement [Default 1.0]**, right-click on **CustomerManagementSyncDirect (direct)** and select **Copy Path**:

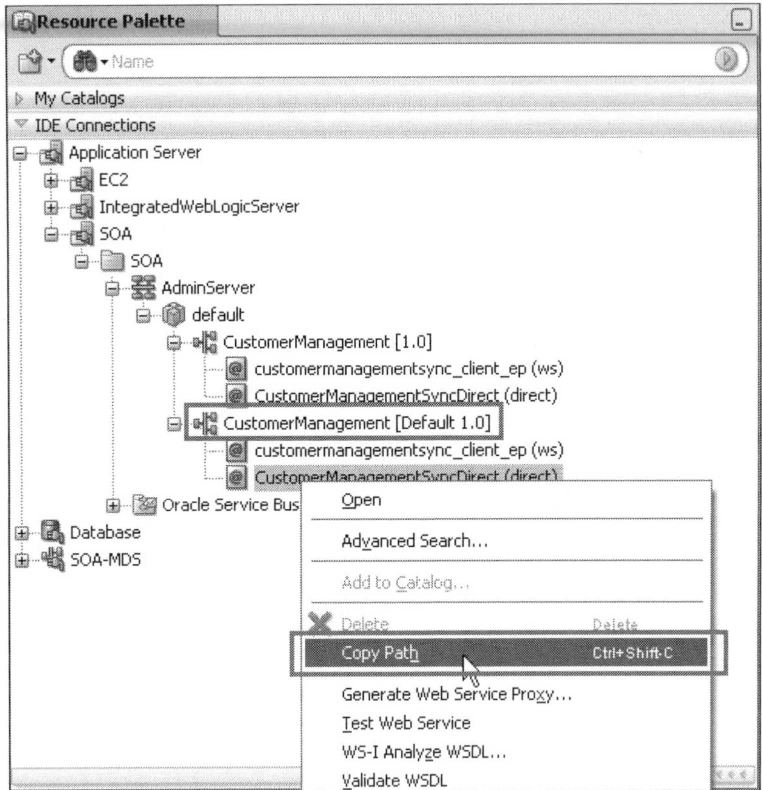

With the URL of the WSDL in the clipboard, let's create the business service by consuming the WSDL from the URL. In Eclipse OEPE, perform the following steps:

44. In the `business` folder, create a new business service and name it `CustomerManagement`.
45. On the **General** tab select **WSDL Web Service**.
46. Click on **Browse** to define the WSDL.
47. We want to consume the WSDL through the URL in the clipboard, so click on **Consume**.
48. Select **URI** for the **Service Resource**, paste the URL into the **URI** field and click on **OK**.
49. Select **CustomerManagementSyncDirectDirectBindingPort12 (port)** and click on **OK**.
50. Confirm the **Transport Configuration Change** dialog with **Yes**.

51. The WSDL is stored in the project folder itself. We can easily refactor by dragging it to the `wsdl` folder. The reference in the business service is automatically updated.
52. The necessary XML schemas are also consumed and stored in the project. However, they have generated names, so let's replace them by the ones we have used in the SOA Suite project. They are already available in the `xsd` folder of the OSB project.
53. Double-click on the **CustomerMangementSyncDirect.wsdl** and replace the value of **schemaLocation** for the import by `../xsd/CustomerMessages.xsd`:

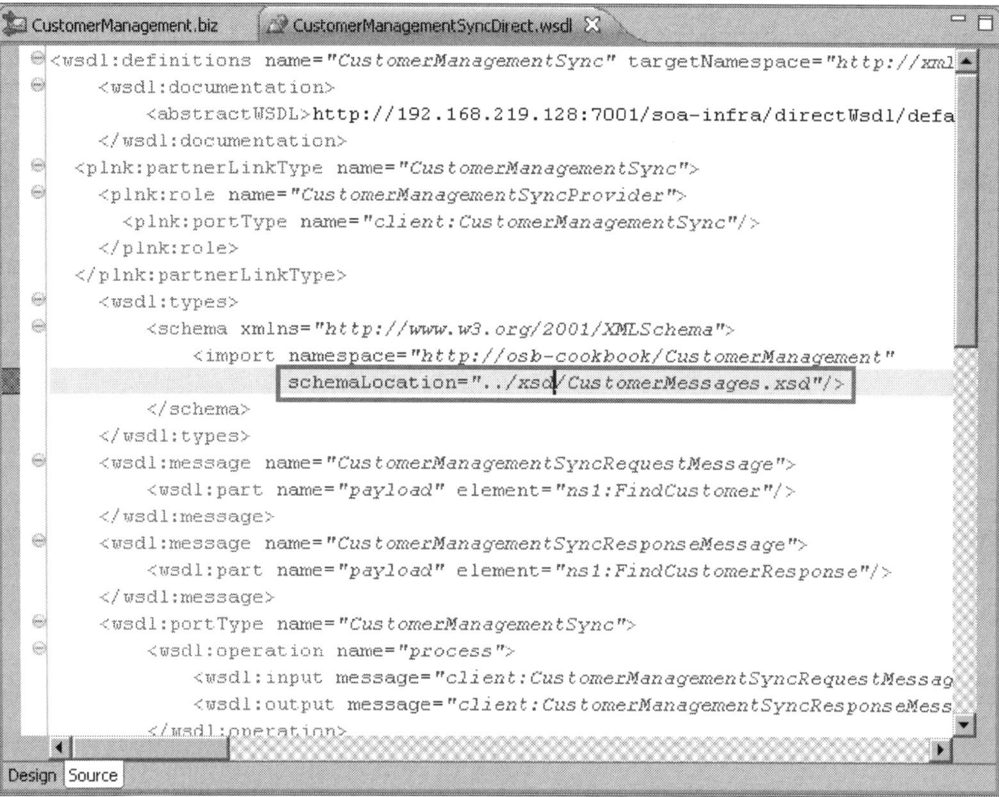

54. Save and close the `wsdl` file.
55. Now delete the three generated XML schema files.
56. Back on the `CustomerMangagement.biz` business service, navigate to the **Transport** tab.
57. Check the **Endpoint URI**.
58. Navigate to the **SOA-DIRECT Transport** tab.
59. **Synchronous client** should be selected for the **Role** radio-button.
60. Save the project and deploy it to the OSB server.

Now let's test the service. In the Service Bus Console, perform the following steps:

61. In the **Project Explorer** expand the **invoking-soa-composite-sync** node and click on the **business** node.
62. Click on the **Launch Test Console** icon (icon with the bug) for the **CustomerManagement** business service.
63. Change the **ID** to `100` and click on **Execute**.
64. The response message from the BPEL component is shown in the **Response Document** section:

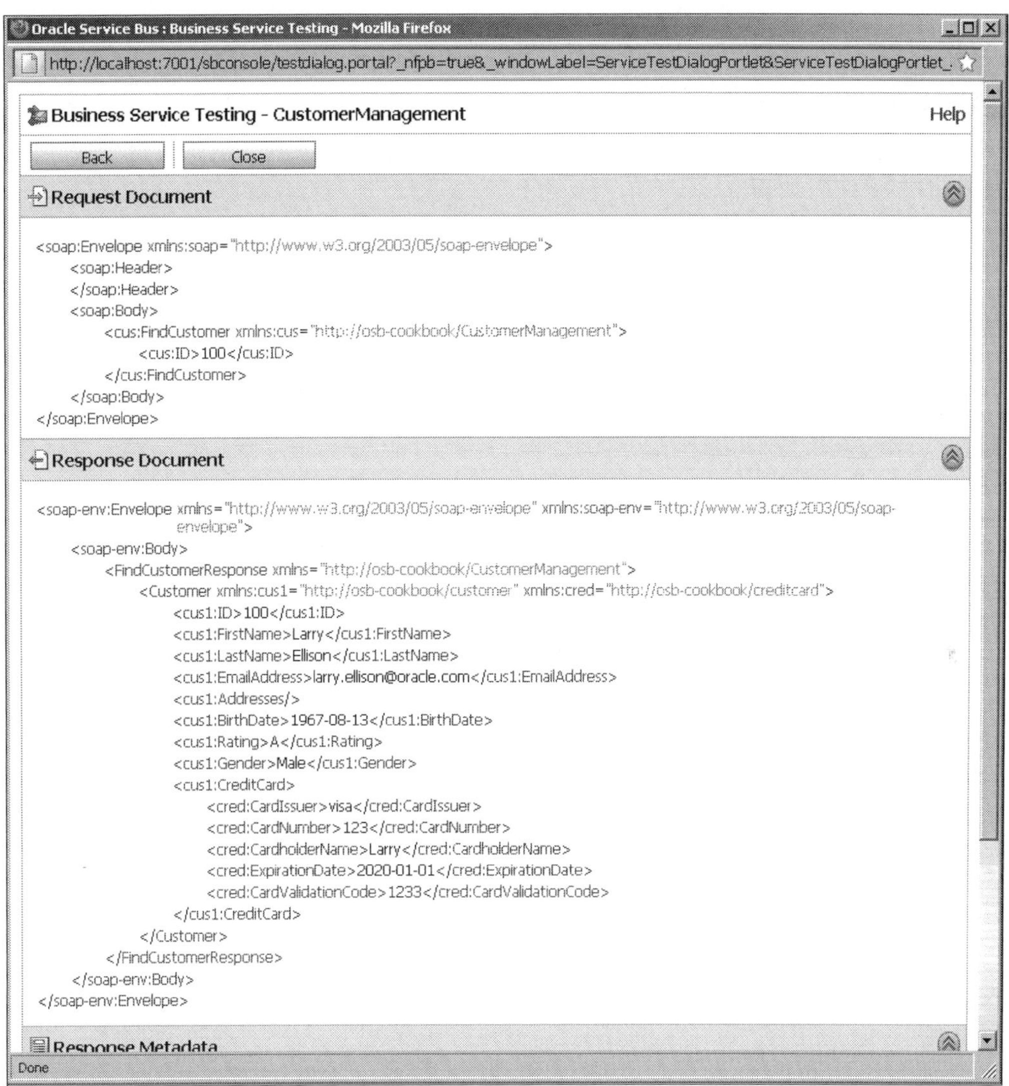

How it works...

A business service can call a SOA Suite Direct Binding service wired to a SCA component by using the SOA-DIRECT transport.

In this recipe, we have used a BPEL component, but it could have been any other SCA component, such as a Mediator or Rule component. OSB will use the T3 RMI protocol to communicate to the SOA Suite server but IIOP could be used as well. Because the WSDL of the SOA Direct Binding interface defines a synchronous request/response message exchange pattern, the business service will wait for the response.

There's more...

If the OSB and the SOA Suite are not in the same WebLogic domain, a service account needs to be created. The business service will use the service account to authenticate against the SOA Suite server.

1. Right-click on the **security** folder and select **New | Service Account**.
2. Enter `ServiceAccountSOA` into the **File name**.
3. Click on **Finish**.
4. Select **Static** at the **Resource Type** radio button.
5. Enter `weblogic` into the **User Name** field.
6. Enter the password of the SOA Server into the **Password** and **Confirm Password** field.
7. Save and close the service account.
8. Go back to the `CustomerManagement.biz` business service and open the **SOA-DIRECT Transport** tab.
9. Expand **Advanced Settings**.
10. Click on **Browse** on the **Invocation Service Account** field.
11. In the pop-up window navigate to the `security` folder in the `invoking-soa-composite-synchronously` project and select `ServiceAccountSOA.sa`.

12. Click on **OK**.

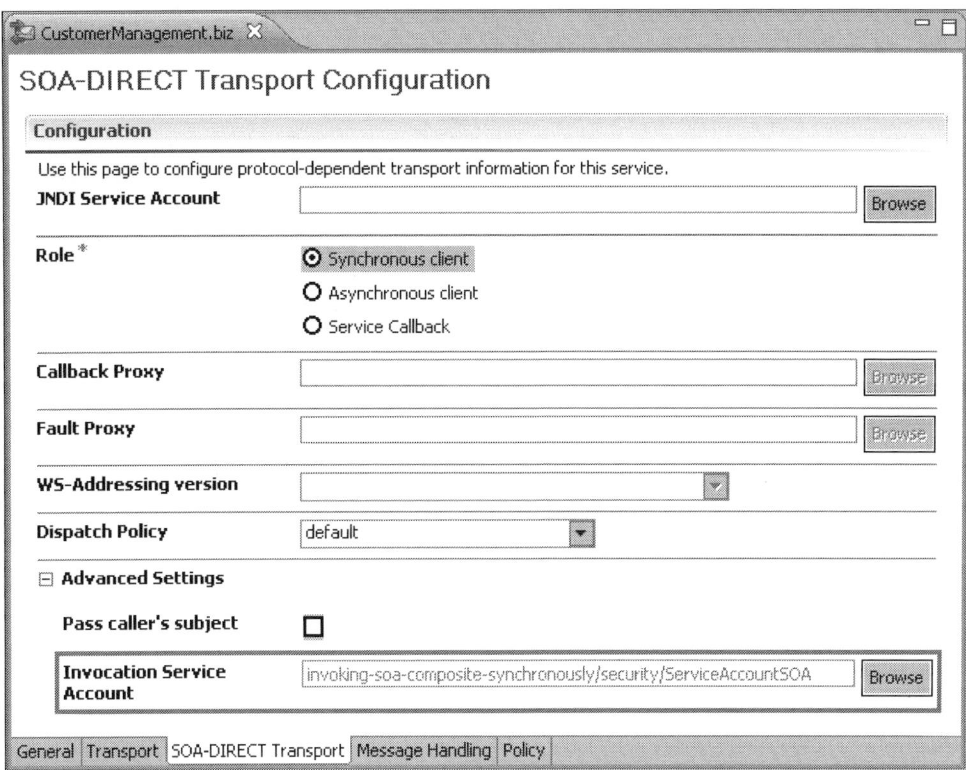

See also

For an asynchronous message exchange pattern, check the other recipe *Invoking a SCA composite asynchronously*.

Invoking a SCA composite asynchronously from an OSB service

In this recipe, we will create a SOA Suite composite application with a BPEL service component with an asynchronous direct binding service interface. The direct binding interface will be invoked from an OSB business service through the SOA-DIRECT transport. The callback message from the BPEL service will be handled by an OSB proxy service through the SB transport.

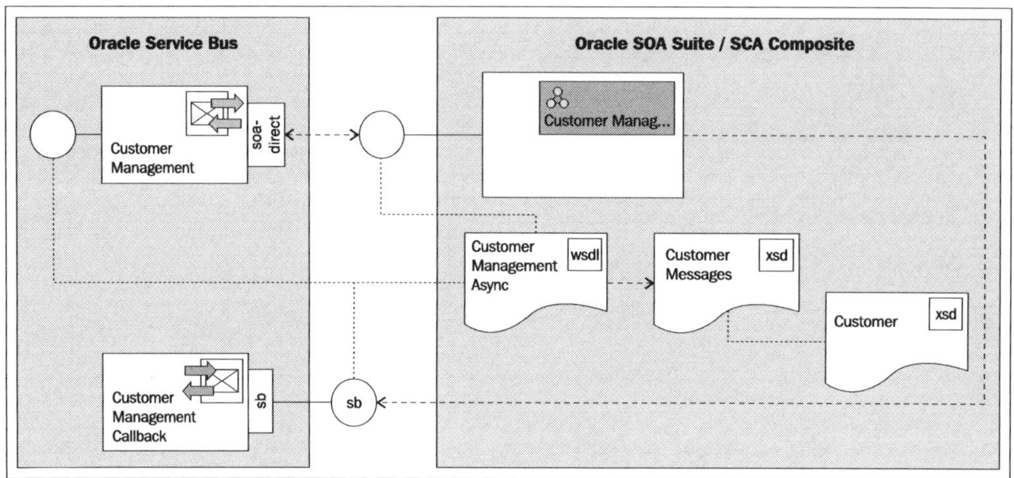

Getting ready

Copy the `soa-suite-invoking-soa-composite-async` holding the JDeveloper project from `\chapter-8\getting-ready\invoking-soa-composite-async\` into a local workspace folder.

Import the base OSB project containing the necessary schemas and the right folder structure into Eclipse from `\chapter-8\getting-ready\invoking-soa-composite-async`.

How to do it...

First we need a SOA Suite composite which exposes an asynchronous direct binding interface. In JDeveloper, perform the following steps to create it:

1. Open the workspace in JDeveloper by selecting **File** | **Open** and navigating to the `invoking-soa-composite-async.jws` file.
2. Click on the **composite.xml** located in the `CustomerManagement` project to open up the SCA composite view.

3. Drag a **BPEL Process** from the **Service Components** section of the **Component Palette** to the SCA composite and drop it on the **Components** area.
4. In the **Create BPEL Process** window, enter `CustomerManagentASync` into the **Name** field.
5. Choose **Asynchronous BPEL Process** for the **Template** drop-down listbox.
6. Click on the magnifying glass button, right to the **Input** field.
7. In the **Type Chooser** window expand the **CustomerMessages.xsd** inside the **Project Schema Files** folder.
8. Select the **FindCustomer** element and click on **OK**.
9. Click on the magnifying glass button right to the **Output** field.
10. In the **Type Chooser** window expand the **CustomerMessages.xsd** inside the **Project Schema Files** folder.
11. Select the **FindCustomerResponse** element and click on **OK**.
12. Click **OK** to create the BPEL component:

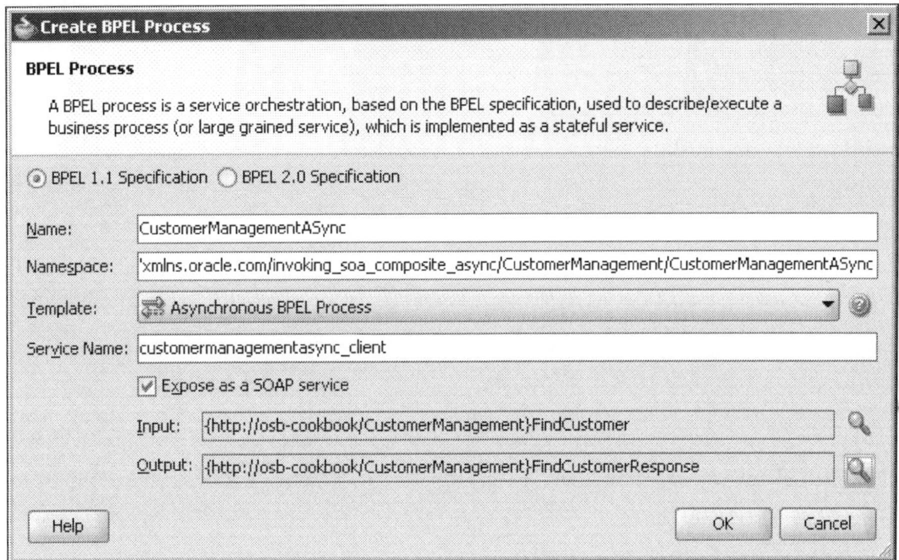

We have created a BPEL component with an exposed SOAP binding, defining an asynchronous interface. Similar to the synchronous recipe we will now add the direct binding to the SCA composite:

13. From the **Component Palette** drag the **Direct Binding** from the **Service Adapter** section and drop it on the **Exposed Services** section of the SCA composite.
14. Enter `CustomerManagementASyncDirect` into the **Name** field.
15. Make sure that **Service** is pre-selected for **Type** drop-down listbox. If not you have probably dropped the **Direct Binding** component on the wrong lane.
16. Click on the icon with the green arrow next to the **WSDL URL** field to browse for the WSDL file that we just created. Select the **CustomerManagementASync.wsdl** file.
17. Select **CustomerManagementAsync** for the value of **Port Type** drop-down listbox.
18. Select **CustomerManagementAsyncCallBack** for the value of **Callback Port Type** drop-down listbox and click on **OK**:

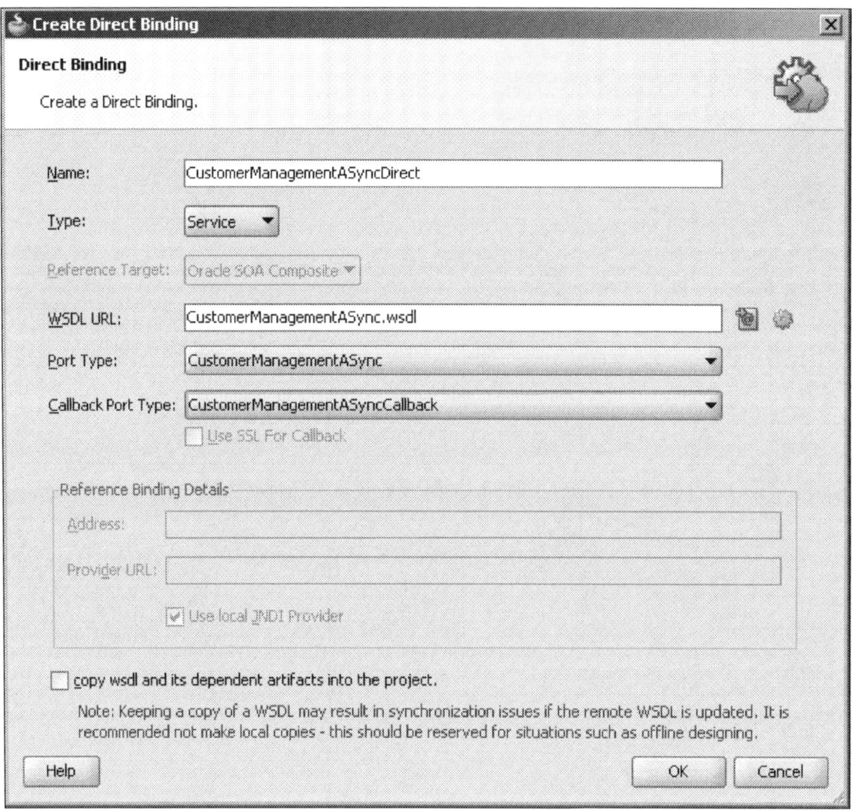

19. Drag a wire from the **CustomerManagementASyncDirect** exposed service to the **CustomerManagement** BPEL component.

    The SCA composite should look similar to the one shown in the following screenshot:

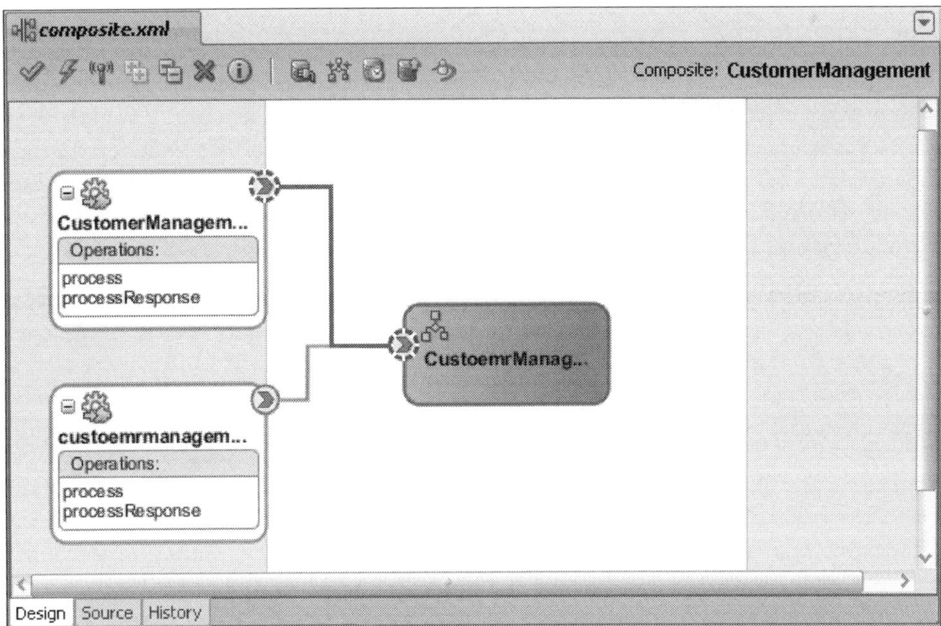

Perform the following steps to change the BPEL component, so that it will return the customer test data:

20. Double-click on the BPEL component icon in the SCA composite.
21. Drag an **Assign** activity from the **Component Palette** and drop it in between the **receiveInput** and **replyOuput** activity.
22. Double-click the **Assign1** activity.
23. Navigate to the **General** tab and overwrite the **name** field with `AssignOutput`.
24. Navigate to the **Copy Rules** tab.
25. In the tree on the right, (the target section) right-click on **outputVariable** and select **Expand All Child Nodes**.

26. Drag the XML fragment to the **Customer : CustomerTyp** element:

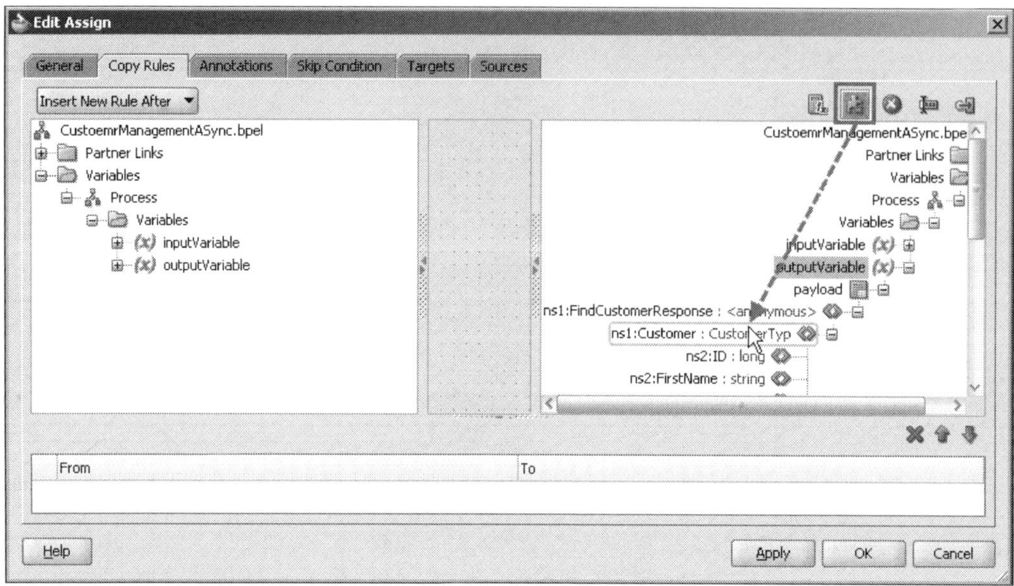

27. Enter the following XML fragment into **XML Fragment** field of the pop-up window:

```
<Customer xmlns="http://osb-cookbook/CustomerManagement"
xmlns:cus1="http://osb-cookbook/customer" xmlns:cred="http://osb-
cookbook/creditcard">
        <cus1:ID>100</cus1:ID>
        <cus1:FirstName>Larry</cus1:FirstName>
        <cus1:LastName>Ellison</cus1:LastName>
        <cus1:EmailAddress>larry.ellison@oracle.com</
cus1:EmailAddress>
        <cus1:Addresses/>
        <cus1:BirthDate>1967-08-13</cus1:BirthDate>
        <cus1:Rating>A</cus1:Rating>
        <cus1:Gender>Male</cus1:Gender>
        <cus1:CreditCard>
                <cred:CardIssuer>visa</cred:CardIssuer>
                <cred:CardNumber>123</cred:CardNumber>
                <cred:CardholderName>Larry</cred:CardholderName>
                <cred:ExpirationDate>2020-01-01</
cred:ExpirationDate>
               <cred:CardValidationCode>1233</
cred:CardValidationCode>
        </cus1:CreditCard>
</Customer>
```

28. Click on **OK** to save the XML fragment.
29. Click on **OK** to close the detail window of the **Assign1** activity.
30. Click on **Save All** and close the `CustomerMangementSync.bpel` and `composite.xml`.

Now we can deploy the SCA composite to the SOA Suite server. In JDeveloper, perform the following steps:

31. Right-click on the **CustomerManagement** project and select **Deploy | CustomerManagement**.
32. Select **Deploy to Application Server** from the list of deployment actions and click on **Next**.
33. Enable the **Overwrite any existing composites with the same revision ID** checkbox and click on **Next**.
34. Select the **ApplicationServerConnection** from the list of application servers and click on **Finish**.
35. Check the **SOA-Log** status window for errors. The deployment was successful, if a **BUILD SUCCESSFUL** message is shown.
36. By that the service provider side in SOA Suite is ready. Testing doesn't make sense, because of the asynchronous nature of the interface; we would not see any response in the Enterprise Manager.
37. The next step is to implement the service consumer side on the OSB. First, we need to get the WSDL of the SOA Direct Binding interface. We will retrieve the URL of the WSDL in JDeveloper and then use that URL to consume it in Eclipse OEPE.

In JDeveloper, perform the following steps to retrieve the URL of the WSDL:

38. Navigate to the **Resource Palette** tab on the right side of JDeveloper and expand the **Application Server** node.
39. Expand the **ApplicationServerConnection | SOA** | [SOAManagedServerName] | **default** | **CustomerManagement [Default 1.0]**, right-click on **CustomerManagementASyncDirect (direct)**, and select **Copy Path**.

    With the URL of the WSDL in the clipboard, let's create the business service by consuming the WSDL from the URL. In Eclipse OEPE, perform the following steps:

40. In the `business` folder, create a new business service and name it `CustomerManagement`.
41. On the **General** tab, select **WSDL Web Service**.
42. Click on **Browse** to define the WSDL.

43. We want to consume the WSDL with the URL in the clipboard, so click on **Consume**.
44. Select **URI** for the **Service Resource**, paste the `URL` into the **URI** field and click on **OK**.
45. Select **CustomerManagementASyncDirectDirectBindingPort12 (port)** and click on **OK**:

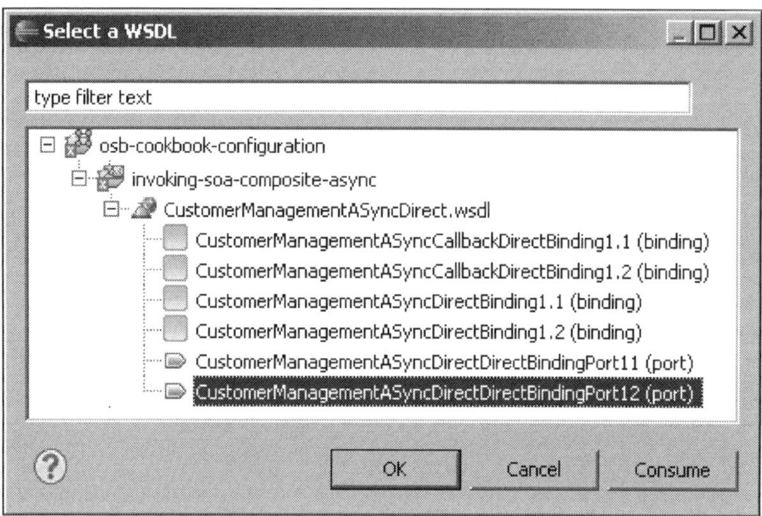

46. Confirm the **Transport Configuration Change** dialog with **Yes**.

    The `WSDL` file is stored in the `project` folder itself. We can easily refactor by dragging it to the `wsdl` folder. The reference in the business service is automatically updated.

    The necessary XML schemas are also consumed and stored in the project. However, they have generated names, so let's replace them by the ones we have used in the SOA Suite project. They are already available in the `xsd` folder of the OSB project.

47. Double-click on the **CustomerMangementASyncDirect.wsdl** and replace the value of **schemaLocation** for import by `../xsd/CustomerMessages.xsd`.
48. Save and close the `WSDL` file.
49. Now delete the three generated XML schema files.
50. Back on the `CustomerMangagement.biz` business service navigate to the **Transport** tab.
51. Check the **Endpoint URI**.
52. Navigate to the **SOA-DIRECT Transport** tab.
53. **Asynchronous client** should be selected for the **Role** radio button.

If the OSB and the SOA Suite are not in the same WebLogic domain, a service account needs to be created. Check the recipe, *Invoking a SOA composite synchronously from an OSB service*, for how to create a service account.

Next, we create the proxy service which handles the callback from the SOA Suite.

54. In the `proxy` folder, create a new proxy service and name it `CustomerManagementCallback`.
55. On the **General** tab select **WSDL Web Service**.
56. Click on **Browse** to define the WSDL.
57. The **Select a WSDL** pop-up window appears.
58. Expand **invoking-soa-composite-async | wsdl | CustomerManagementAsyncDirect.wsdl** and select **CustomerManagementAsyncCallbackDirectBinding1.2 (binding)** and click on **OK**:

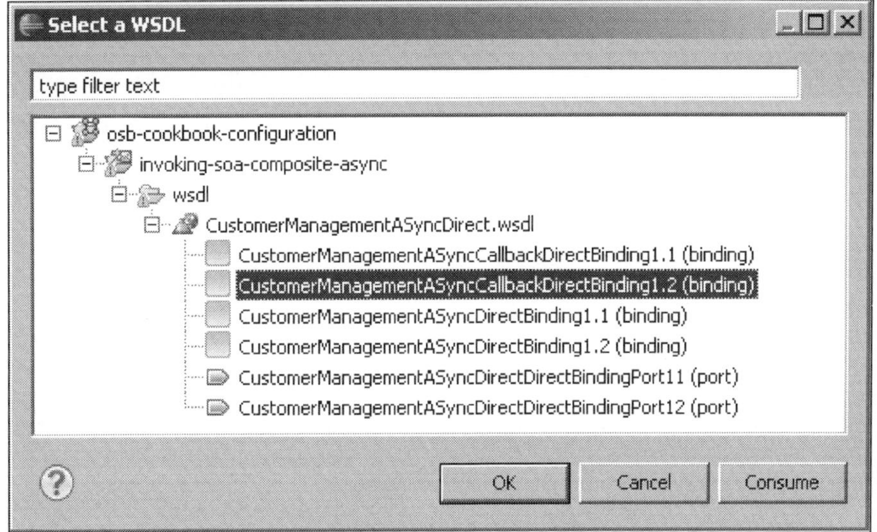

59. Confirm the **Transport Configuration Change** dialog with **Yes**.
60. Navigate to the **Transport** tab.
61. Change the value of the **Protocol** drop-down listbox to **sb**.
62. Navigate to the **Message Flow** tab.
63. Drag a **Pipeline Pair** node from the **Design Palette** and drop it below the interface. Name it **HandleCallbackPipelinePair**.

64. Right-click on the **Request Pipeline** and select **Insert Into | Stage**. Name it **LogStage**.
65. Right-click on the **LogStage** and select **Insert Into | Reporting | Log**.
66. On the **Properties** tab of the new **Log** action, click on the **<Expression>** link and enter `$body` into the **Expression** field.
67. Click on **OK**.
68. Enter `Customer Response` into the **Annotation** field.
69. Select **Warning** for the **Severity** drop-down listbox:

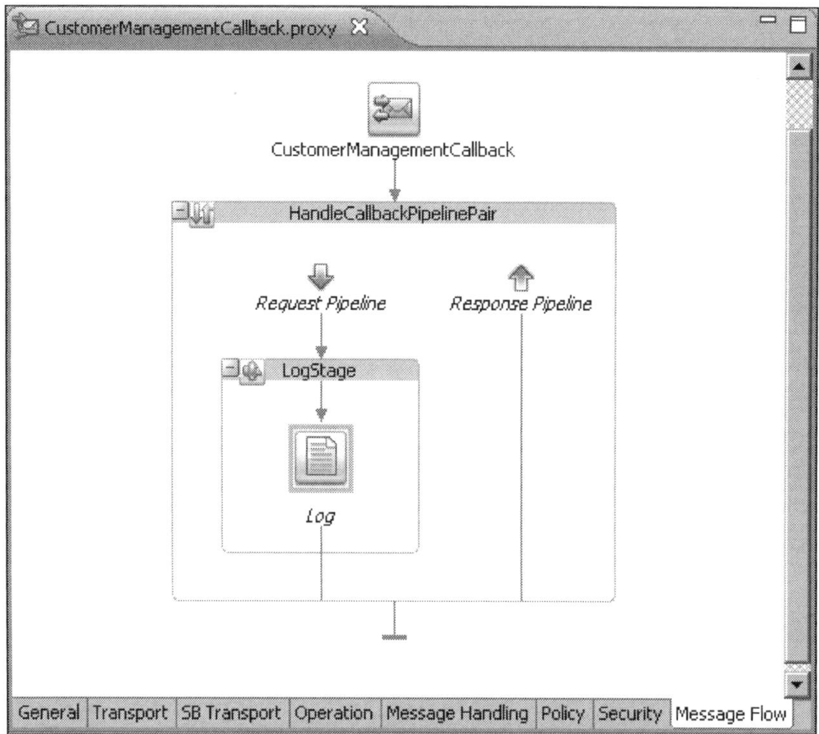

Now with the proxy service handling the callback in place, we have to configure it in the business service:

70. Open the `CustomerManagement.biz` business service.
71. Navigate to the **SOA-DIRECT Transport** tab.
72. On the **Callback Proxy** field, click on **Browse.**

73. On the **Select a Proxy Service Resource** pop-up window, expand the tree and select the **CustomerManagementCallback.proxy** proxy service.
74. Click on **OK**:

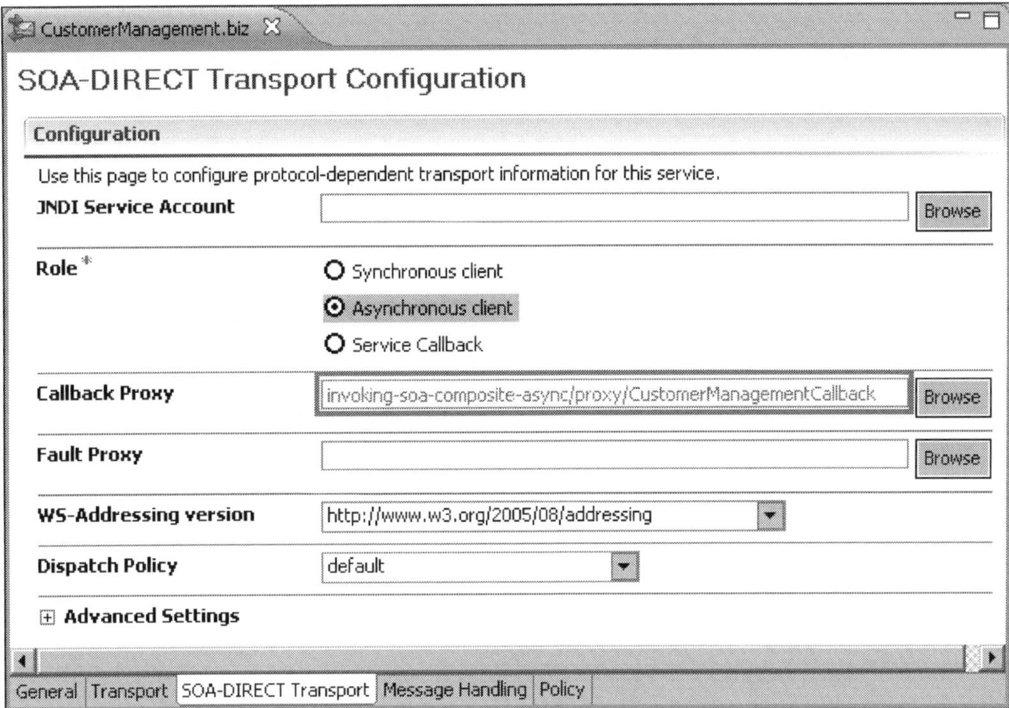

75. Deploy the project to the OSB server.

Now let's test the service. In the Service Bus Console, perform the following steps:

76. In the **Project Explorer** expand the **invoking-soa-composite-async** node and click on the **business** node.
77. Click the **Launch Test Console** icon (icon with the bug) for the **CustomerManagement** business service.
78. Change the **ID** to `100` and click on **Execute**.
79. The **Response Document** section should contain the message **There was no response**. This is correct, because the business service does not get an answer.

80. Check the Service Bus Console output window for the appearance of the log statement from the proxy service:

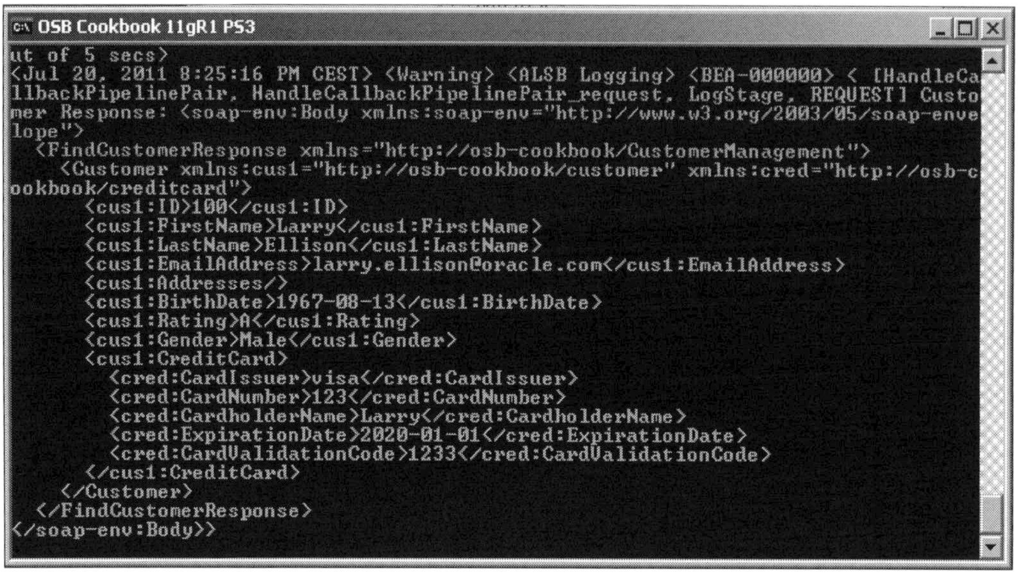

```
OSB Cookbook 11gR1 PS3
ut of 5 secs>
<Jul 20, 2011 8:25:16 PM CEST> <Warning> <ALSB Logging> <BEA-000000> < [HandleCa
llbackPipelinePair, HandleCallbackPipelinePair_request, LogStage, REQUEST] Custo
mer Response: <soap-env:Body xmlns:soap-env="http://www.w3.org/2003/05/soap-enve
lope">
  <FindCustomerResponse xmlns="http://osb-cookbook/CustomerManagement">
    <Customer xmlns:cus1="http://osb-cookbook/customer" xmlns:cred="http://osb-c
ookbook/creditcard">
      <cus1:ID>100</cus1:ID>
      <cus1:FirstName>Larry</cus1:FirstName>
      <cus1:LastName>Ellison</cus1:LastName>
      <cus1:EmailAddress>larry.ellison@oracle.com</cus1:EmailAddress>
      <cus1:Addresses/>
      <cus1:BirthDate>1967-08-13</cus1:BirthDate>
      <cus1:Rating>A</cus1:Rating>
      <cus1:Gender>Male</cus1:Gender>
      <cus1:CreditCard>
        <cred:CardIssuer>visa</cred:CardIssuer>
        <cred:CardNumber>123</cred:CardNumber>
        <cred:CardholderName>Larry</cred:CardholderName>
        <cred:ExpirationDate>2020-01-01</cred:ExpirationDate>
        <cred:CardValidationCode>1233</cred:CardValidationCode>
      </cus1:CreditCard>
    </Customer>
  </FindCustomerResponse>
</soap-env:Body>>
```

The proxy service is invoked when the callback message arrives from the BPEL component and the log statement shows the callback message handled by the proxy service.

How it works...

A business service can call an asynchronous SOA Suite Direct Binding service, wired to a SCA component by using the SOA-DIRECT transport.

OSB will use the T3 RMI protocol to communicate with the SOA Suite server. Because the WSDL of the SOA Direct Binding interface defines an asynchronous request/response message exchange pattern, the SOA Suite will callback on proxy server configured on the business service when the response message is ready. The callback URL of proxy service is passed by the business service to the SOA Suite as SOAP header information using WS-Addressing.

Invoking an OSB service from SCA composite synchronously

In this recipe, we will invoke an OSB proxy service from an SCA composite. This is the opposite of the recipe, *Invoking a SCA composite from an OSB service*.

The OSB service consists of a proxy service **CustomerManagement** accepting the call from a SOA Suite Mediator component through the SB transport. Because the **CustomerManagement** WSDL defines a synchronous request/reply message exchange pattern, the Mediator will wait for the proxy service to return its response message:

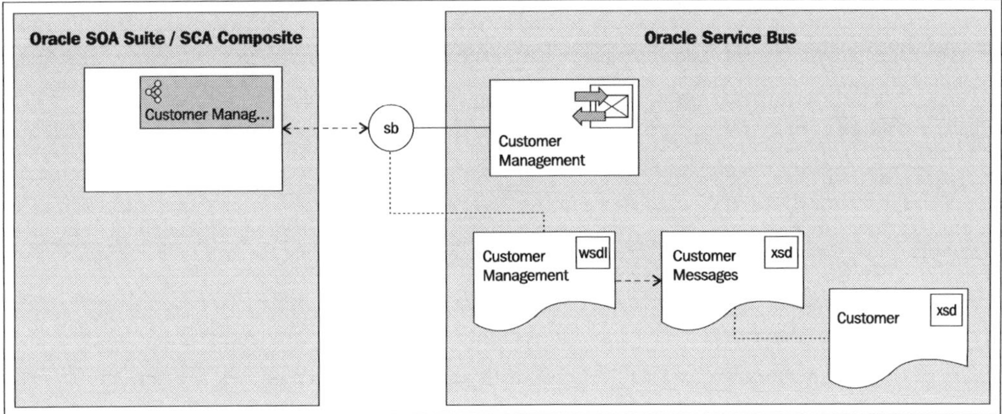

Getting ready

Copy the `soa-suite-invoking-osb-service-sync-from-sca-composite` holding the JDeveloper project from `\chapter-8\getting-ready\invoking-osb-service-sync-from-sca-composite\` into a local workspace folder.

Import the base OSB project containing the base implementation of the proxy service together with the WSDL and XML schemas into Eclipse from `\chapter-8\getting-ready\invoking-osb-service-sync-from-sca-composite`.

How to do it...

We start on the OSB side and change the `CustomerManagement` proxy service, available with the base OSB project imported from the `getting-ready` folder, so that it can be invoked by the SCA composite. The proxy service implements a synchronous interface and contains a pipeline pair, which always returns the same response.

In Eclipse OEPE, perform the following steps:

1. Open the `CustomerManagement` proxy service located in the `proxy` folder.
2. Go to the **Transport** tab where we need to change the protocol.
3. Choose **sb** as the **Protocol**.
4. Deploy the project to the OSB server.

Next, we will create a Mediator, which will call the proxy service synchronously through a direct binding reference. In JDeveloper, perform the following steps:

5. Open the `osb-cookbook` workspace in JDeveloper by selecting **File | Open** and navigating to the `osb-cookbook.jws` file.
6. Click on the `composite.xml` located in the `CustomerManagement` project to open up the SCA composite view.
7. Drag a **Mediator** component from the **Service Components** section of the **Component Palette** on the right and drop it on the **Components** area.
8. Enter `CustomerManagementSync` into the **Name** field.
9. Choose **Synchronous Interface** for the value of the **Template** drop-down listbox.
10. Click on the magnifying glass button right to the **Input** field.
11. In the **Type Chooser** window expand the **CustomerMessages.xsd** below the **Project Schema Files** node.
12. Select the **FindCustomer** node and click on **OK**:

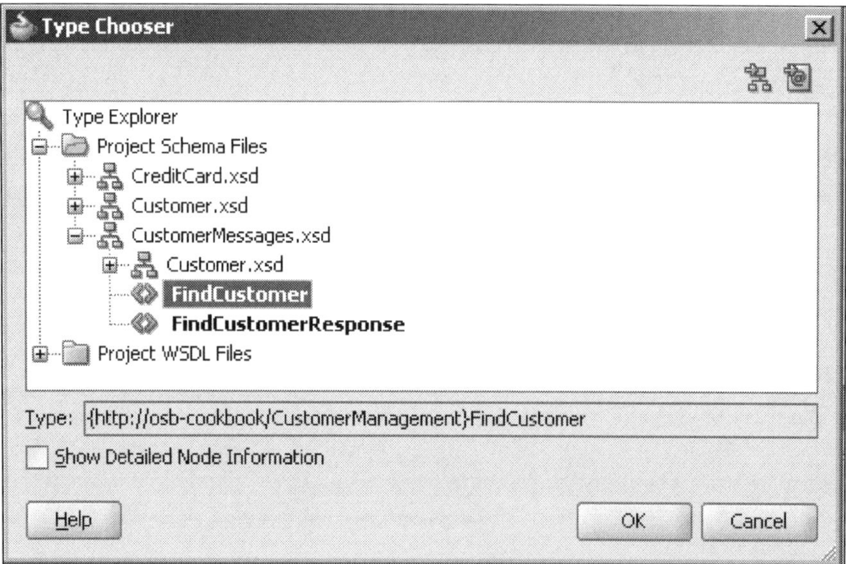

13. Click on the magnifying glass button right to the **Output** field.
14. In the **Type Chooser** window expand the **CustomerMessages.xsd** below the **Project Schema Files** node.
15. Select the **FindCustomerResponse** node and click on **OK**:

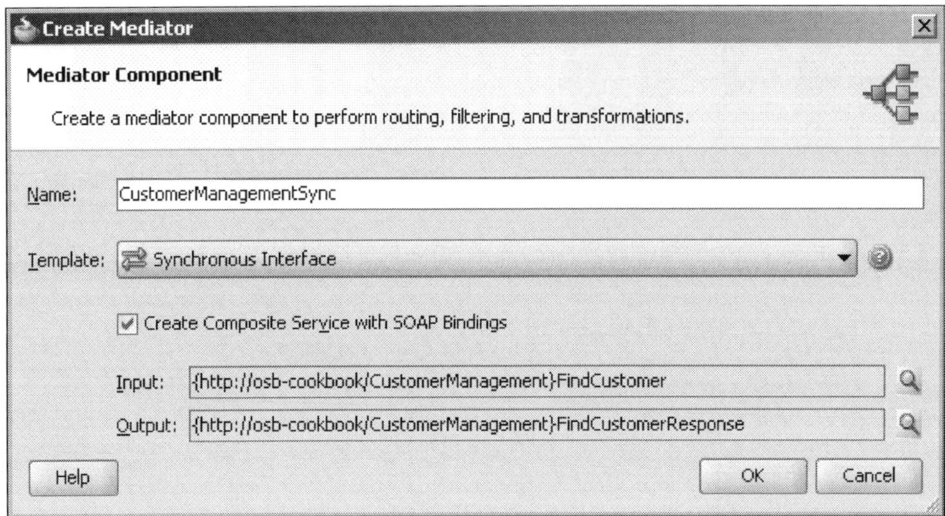

16. Click on **OK**. This will create a new Mediator component with an exposed SOAP binding as shown in the following screenshot:

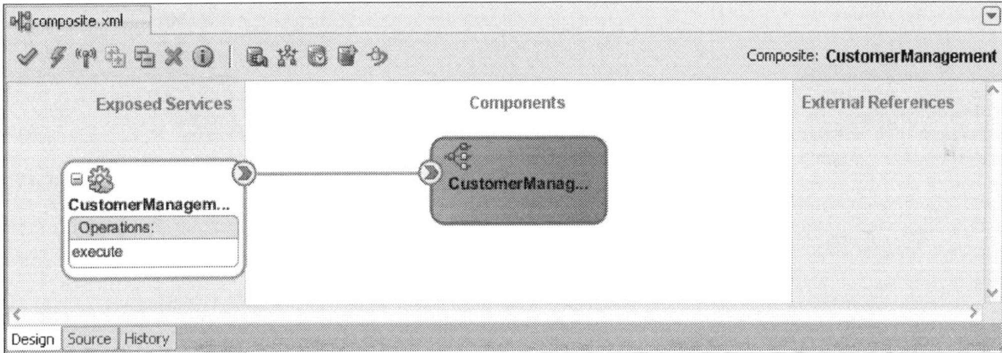

Now let's invoke the OSB proxy service from the Mediator. For that, we need to add a direct binding to the composite. In JDeveloper, perform the following steps:

17. On the **Component Palette**, drag the **Direct Binding** from the **Service Adapters** section and drop it on the **External References** section of the SCA composite.
18. Enter `CustomerManagementDirect` into the **Name** field.
19. Choose **Reference** for the **Type** drop-down listbox.
20. Choose **Oracle Service Bus** for the **Reference Target** drop-down listbox.
21. Click on the icon with the green arrow right to the **WSDL URL** field.
22. On the SOA Resource Browser pop-up window select **Resource Palette** and then expand the **ApplicationServerConnection** as shown in the following screenshot:

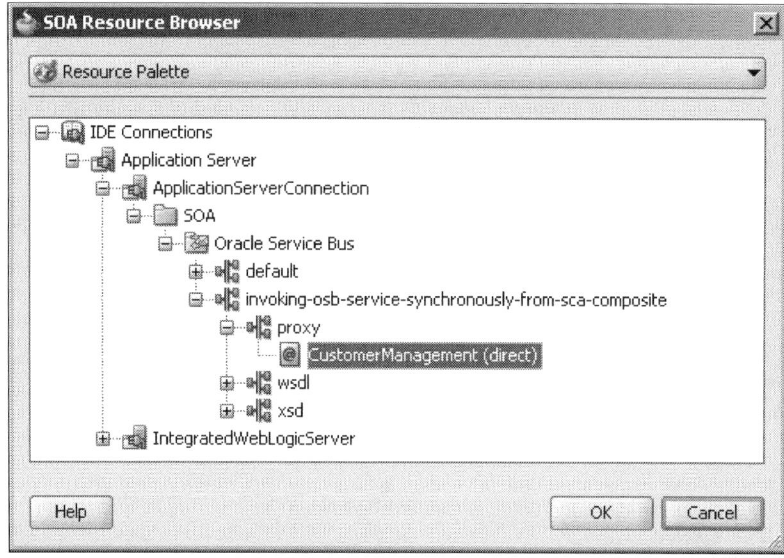

23. Navigate to the **CustomerManagment (direct)** proxy service and click on **OK**.

24. Enable **copy wsdl and its dependent artifacts into the project** option and click on **OK**:

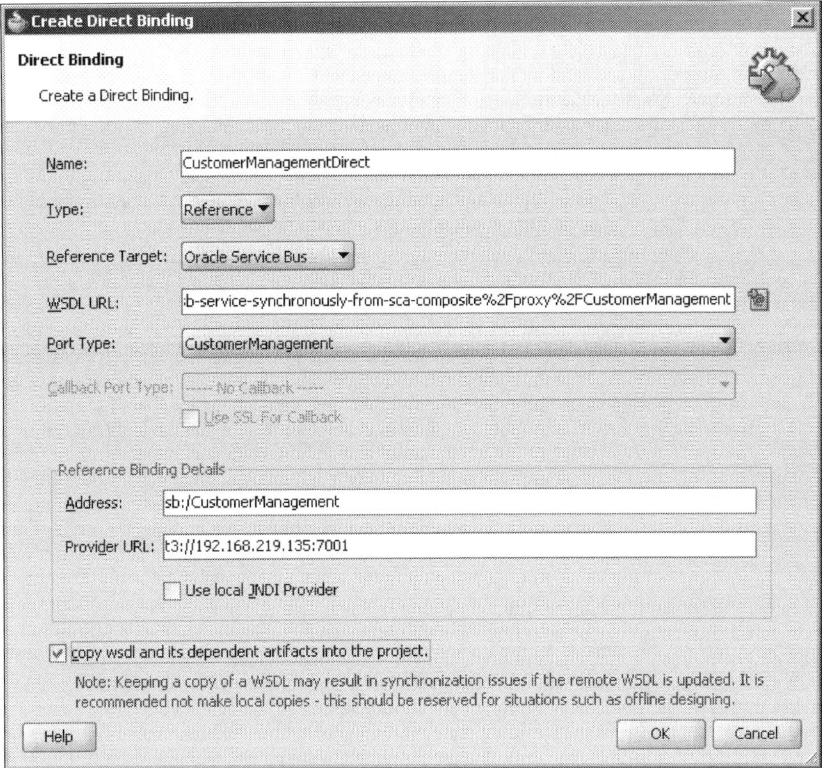

25. Confirm the popup window by clicking **OK**.

26. Drag a wire from the **CustomerManagementDirect** external reference to the **CustomerManagementSync** Mediator component:

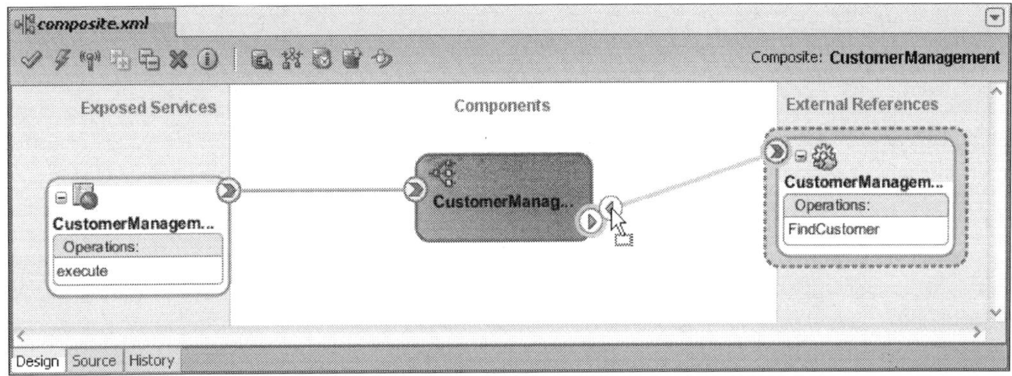

Next, we will change the Mediator component so that the request as well as the response message is passed through by the static routing rule:

27. Double-click on the **CustomerManagementSync** Mediator component.
28. Click on the icon right to the **Assign Value** of the request.
29. In the **Assign Value** pop-up window, click on the green plus icon.
30. In the **From** section, select **expression** for the **Type** drop-down listbox.
31. Enter `$in.request/inp1:FindCustomer` into the **Expression** field.
32. In the **To** section, select **expression** for the **Type** drop-down listbox.
33. Enter `$out.parameters/inp1:FindCustomer` into the **Expression** field and click on **OK** to close the **Assign Value** dialog:

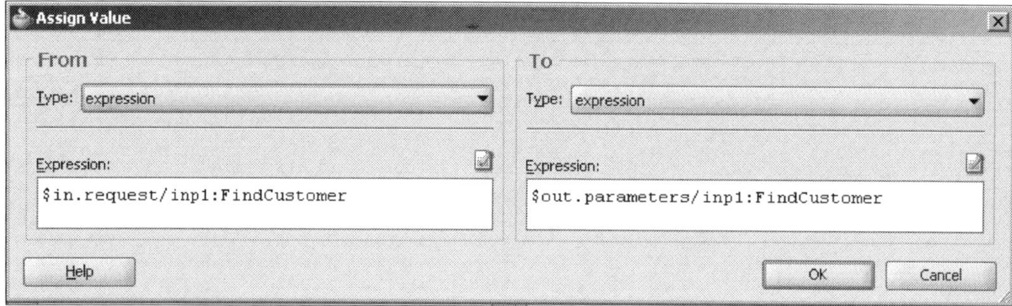

34. Click on **OK**.
35. Click on the icon right to the **Assign Value** of the synchronous reply.
36. In the **Assign Values** pop-up window click on the green plus icon.
37. In the **From** section, select **expression** for the **Type** drop-down listbox.
38. Enter `$in.parameters/tns:FindCustomerResponse` into the **Expression** field.
39. In the **To** section, select **expression** for the **Type** drop down listbox.
40. Enter `$out.reply/tns:FindCustomerResponse` into the **Expression** field and click on **OK** to close the **Assign Value** dialog.

41. Click on **OK**:

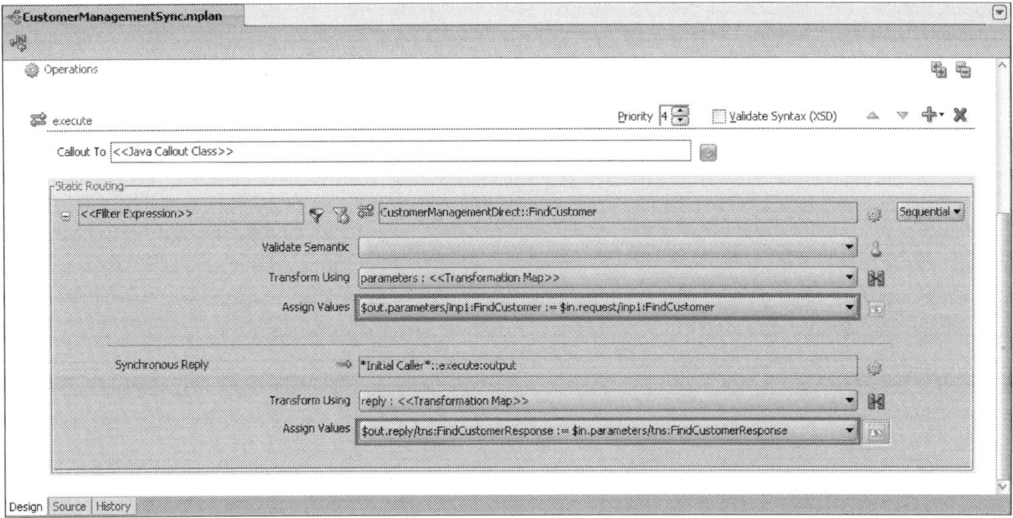

Now, we can deploy the SCA composite to the SOA Suite server. In JDeveloper, perform the following steps:

42. Right-click on the `CustomerManagement` project and select **Deploy | CustomerManagement**.
43. Select **Deploy to Application Server** from the list of deployment actions and click on **Next**.
44. Enable the **Overwrite any existing composites with the same revision ID** check box and click on **Next**.

Select the **ApplicationServerConnection** from the list of application servers and click on **Finish**.

45. Check the **SOA-Log** status window for errors. The deployment was successful, if a **BUILD SUCCESSFUL** message is shown.
46. Next, let's test the **CustomerManagement** composite. In Enterprise Manager, perform the following steps:
47. Expand the **SOA** node in the tree on the left.
49. Expand **soa-infra** node and click on the **default** node.
50. Click on **CustomerManagement [1.0]** in the list of composites. The details of the composite are displayed.

51. Click on the **Test** tab.
52. The **Test Web Service** screen is shown, which allows us to test the SOAP Binding of the composite.
53. On the **Request** tab, in the **Input Arguments** section enter `100` into the **ID** field.
54. Click on the **Test Web Service** button in the top-right corner.
55. The result of the test is shown in the **Response** tab:

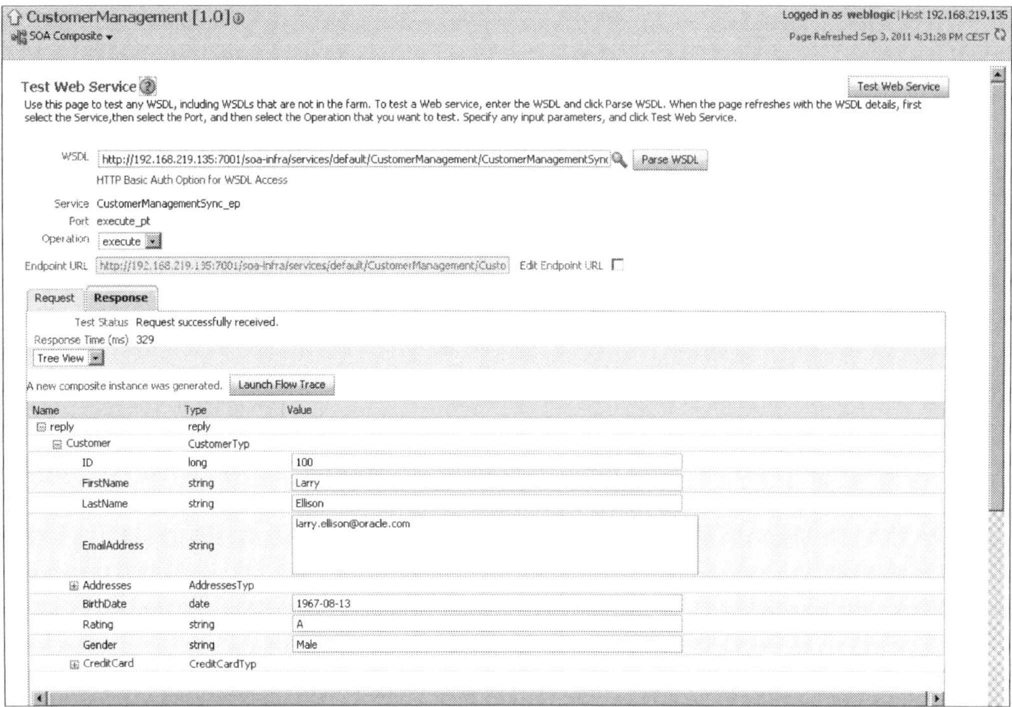

How it works...

This recipe demonstrated the use case, where a SCA composite invokes an OSB WSDL-based proxy service through the SB transport. To invoke an SB proxy service, the SCA service component needs to use a Direct Binding reference of target type Oracle Service Bus.

Invoking an OSB service from SCA composite asynchronously

In this recipe, we will call an OSB service from a SCA Suite composite. The OSB service consists of a proxy service **CustomerManagementAsync** with a one-way interface accepting the call and a business service **CustomerManagementCallback**, which implements the callback interface for sending the response back to the SOA Suite in an asynchronous manner:

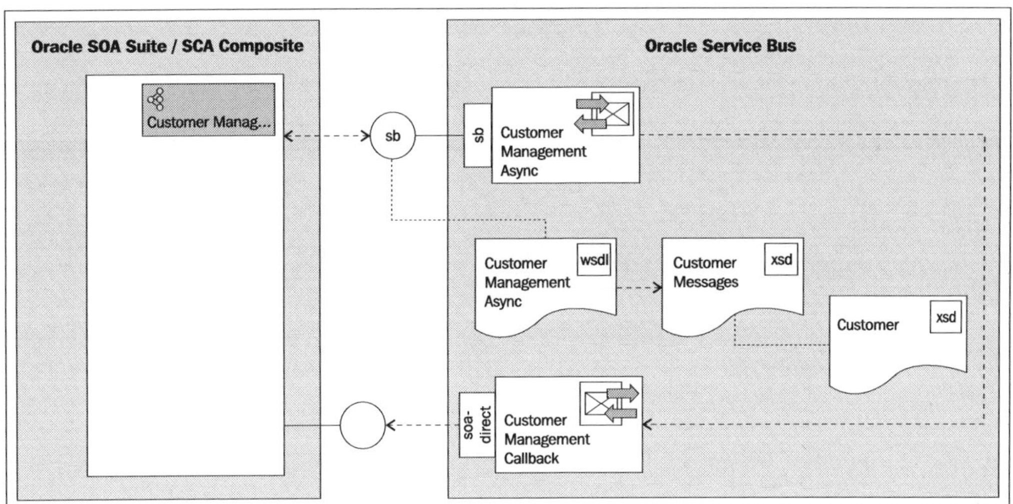

Getting ready

Copy the `soa-suite-invoking-osb-service-async-from-sca-composite` holding the JDeveloper project from `\chapter-8\getting-ready\invoking-osb-service-async-from-sca-composite\` into a local workspace folder.

Import the base OSB project containing the necessary schemas and the right folder structure into Eclipse from `\chapter-8\getting-ready\invoking-osb-service-async-from-sca-composite`.

How to do it...

We start with the OSB side where we will create a proxy service which has a one-way interface. In the proxy service we first only add a pipeline pair, which logs the SOAP header. By that we can examine the addressing part, which we need later to dynamically callback through a business service.

In Eclipse OEPE, perform the following steps:

1. Open the `CustomerManagementAsync.wsdl` in the `wsdl` folder.

   The WSDL defines two port types, one for the one-way request and one for the response as a callback:

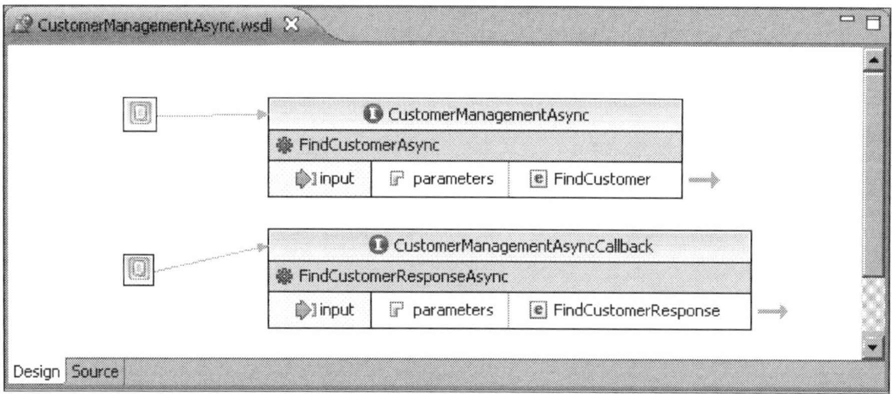

The **CustomerManagementAsync** port type will be implemented by the proxy service whereas the **CustomerManagementAsyncCallback** will be implemented by a business service. Let's start with the proxy service:

2. In the `proxy` folder, create a new proxy service and name it `CustomerManagementAsync`.
3. Navigate to the **General** tab and select **WSDL Web Service** as the **Service Type**.
4. Click on **Browse** and expand the `CustomerManagementAsync.wsdl` in the `wsdl` folder.
5. Select **CustomerManagementSOAPAsync (binding)** and click on **OK**:

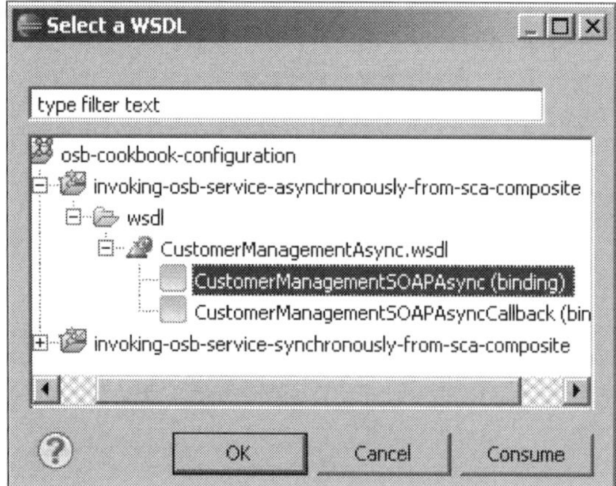

6. Confirm the **Transport Configuration Change** pop-up window by clicking on **Yes**.
7. Navigate to the **Transport** tab and check that **sb** is selected as **Protocol** value.
8. Navigate to the **Message Flow** tab and insert a **Pipeline Pair** node.
9. In the **Request Pipeline** insert a new stage.
10. Add a **Log** action to the stage.
11. Click on the **Expression** link in the **Properties** window for the **Log** action.
12. Drag **header** from the **Variable Structures** to the **Expression** field.
13. Select **Warning** for the **Severity** drop-down listbox:

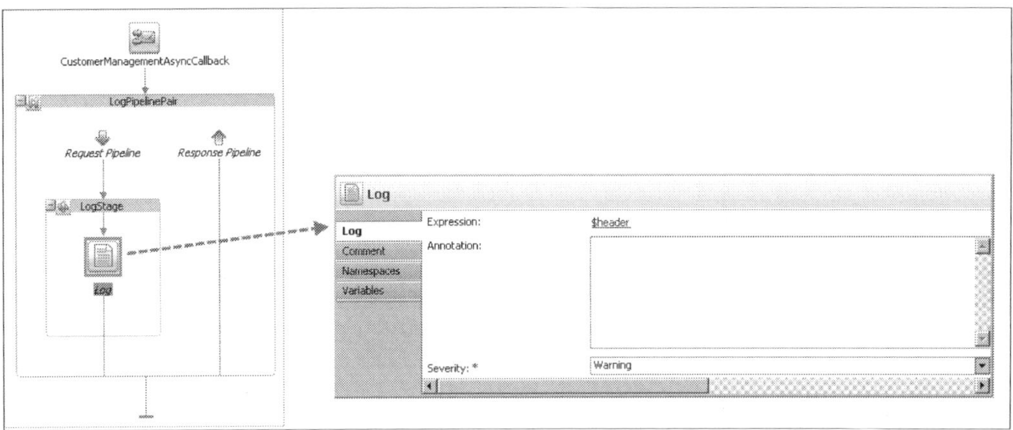

14. Deploy the project to the OSB server.

We have now created the proxy service, which logs the content of the header to the console. We will add the invocation of the callback business service later. Let's now create the Mediator on the SOA Suite side, which will call this proxy service through a direct binding. In JDeveloper perform the following steps:

15. Open the workspace in JDeveloper by selecting **File** | **Open** and navigating to the `invoking-async-from-sca-composite.jws` file.
16. Click on the **composite.xml** located in the **CustomerManagement** project to open up the SCA composite view.
17. Drag a **Mediator** component from the **Service Components** section of the **Component Palette** on the right and drop it on the **Components** area.
18. Enter `CustomerManagementASync` into the **Name** field.
19. Choose **One-Way Interface** for the **Template** drop-down listbox.
20. Click on the magnifying glass button right to the **Input** field.

21. In the **Type Chooser** window expand the **CustomerMessages.xsd** below the **Project Schema Files** node.
22. Select the **FindCustomer** node and click on **OK**.
23. Click on **OK** to create the Mediator component:

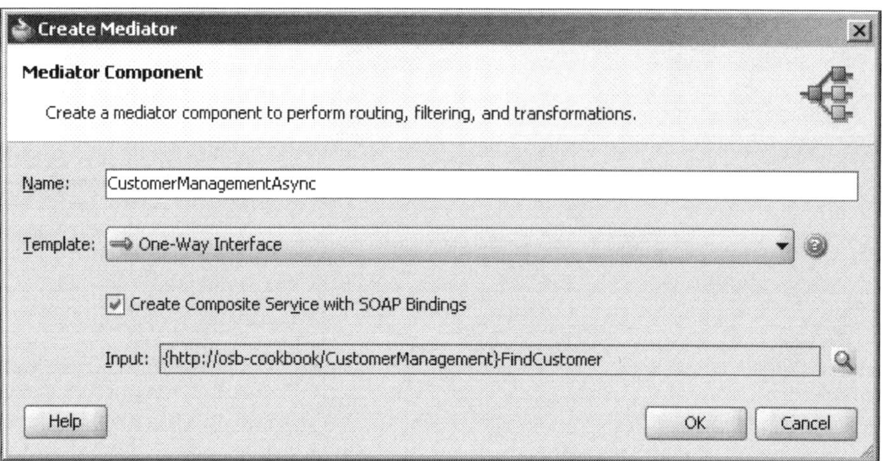

Now let's invoke the OSB proxy service from the Mediator. For that we need to add a direct binding to the composite. In JDeveloper, perform the following steps:

24. On the **Component Palette**, drag the **Direct Binding** from the **Service Adapters** section, and drop it on the **External References** section of the SCA composite.
25. Enter `CustomerManagementAsyncDirect` into the **Name** field.
26. Choose **Reference** for the **Type** drop-down listbox.
27. Choose **Oracle Service Bus** for the **Reference Target** drop-down listbox.
28. Click on the icon with the green arrow right to the **WSDL URL** field.

29. On the **SOA Resource Browser** pop-up window, select **Resource Palette** and then expand the **ApplicationServerConnection**:

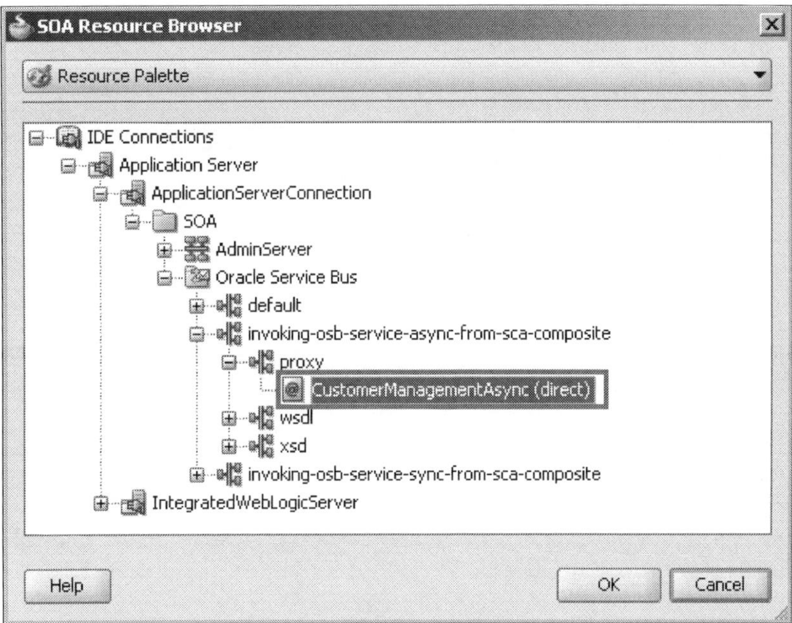

30. Navigate to the **CustomerManagmentAsync (direct)** proxy service and click on **OK**. If the WSDL file is not available, export it from Eclipse to the file system and import it into JDeveloper from there.

31. Back on the **Direct Binding** window, select **CustomerManagementAsync** for the **Port Type** and **CustomerManagemementAsyncCallback** for the **Callback Port Type**.

32. Enable **copy wsdl and its dependent artifacts into the project** option and click on **OK**:

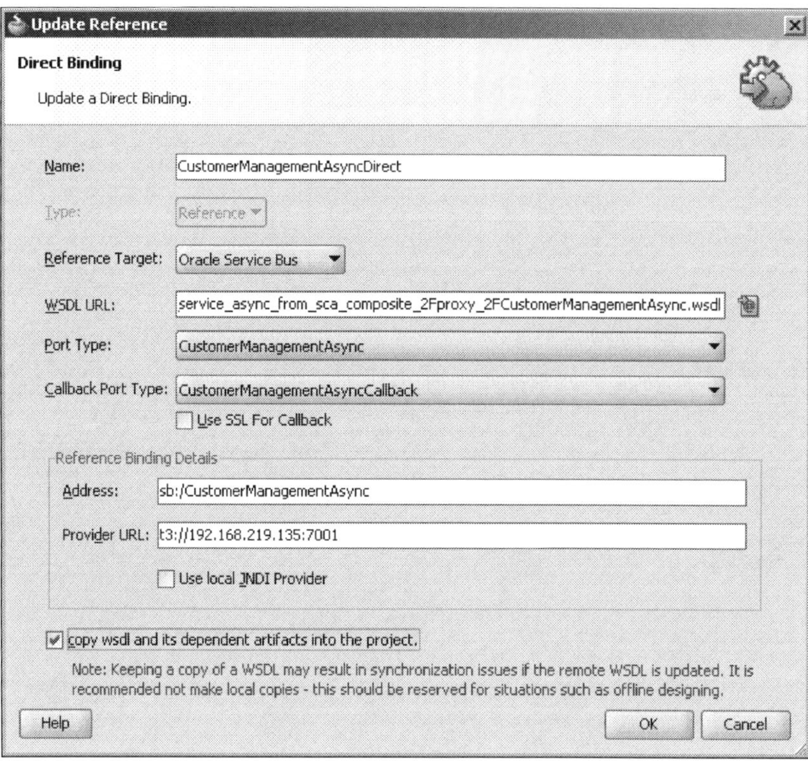

33. Confirm the pop-up window by clicking on **OK**.
34. Drag a wire from the **CustomerManagementDirect** external reference to the **CustomerManagementSync** Mediator component:

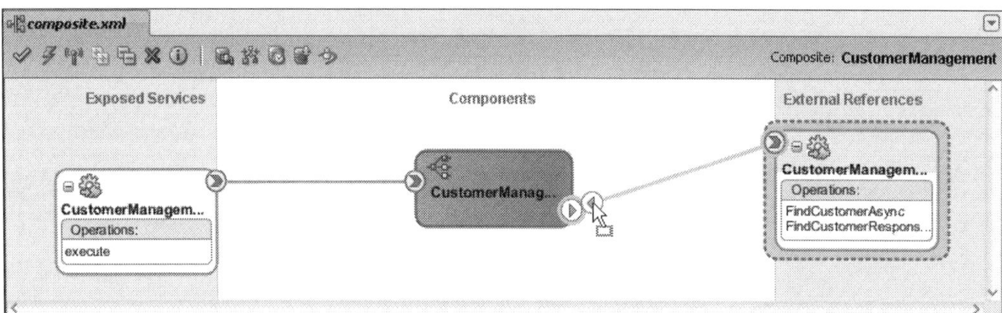

Next, we will change the Mediator component so that the request as well as the response message is passed through by the static routing rule. Perform the following steps to change the Mediator component:

35. Double-click on the **CustomerManagementAsync** Mediator component.
36. Click on the icon right to the **Assign Value** of the request.
37. In the **Assign Values** pop-up window, click on the green plus icon.
38. In the **From** section, select **expression** for the **Type** drop-down listbox.
39. Enter `$in.request/inp1:FindCustomer` into the **Expression** field.
40. In the **To** section, select **expression** for the **Type** drop-down listbox.
41. Enter `$out.parameters/ns2:FindCustomer` into the **Expression** field:

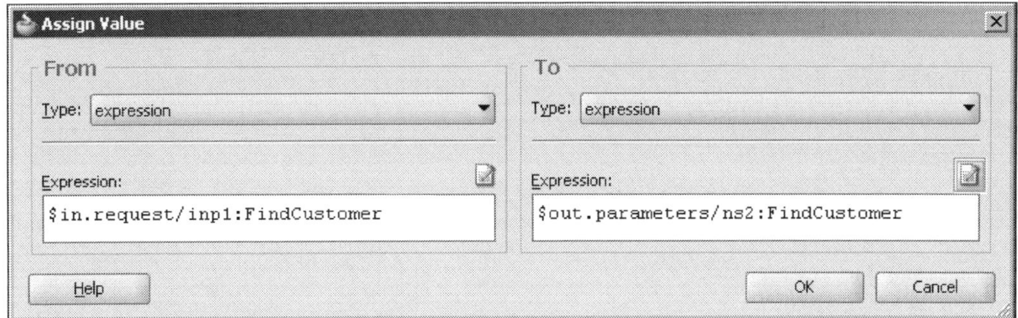

42. Click on **OK** twice.

Now let's deploy the SCA composite to the SOA Suite server to test the request. In JDeveloper, perform the following steps:

43. Right-click on the `CustomerManagement`, project and select **Deploy | CustomerManagement**.
44. Select **Deploy to Application Server** from the list of deployment actions and click on **Next**.
45. Enable the **Overwrite any existing composites with the same revision ID** check box and click on **Next**.
46. Select the **ApplicationServerConnection** from the list of application servers and click on **Finish**.
47. Check the **SOA-Log** and **Deployment** status window for errors. The deployment was successful, if a **deployment finished** message is shown.

Next, let's test the **CustomerManagement** composite. In Enterprise Manager, perform the following steps:

48. Expand the **SOA** node in the tree on the left, expand **soa-infra** node, and click on the **default** node.
49. Click on **CustomerManagement [1.0]** in the list of composites and details of the composite are displayed.
50. Click on the **Test** tab.
51. The **Test Web Service** screen is shown, which allows us to test the SOAP Binding of the composite.
52. On the **Request** tab, in the **Input Arguments** section enter `100` into the **ID** field and click on **Test Web Service** in the top-right corner.

We won't see a response because it is an asynchronous process and the SOA Suite instance will wait forever for this response because we didn't implement the callback in our proxy service.

The OSB console window will show the output of the **Log** action with the SOAP header of the SOA Suite request:

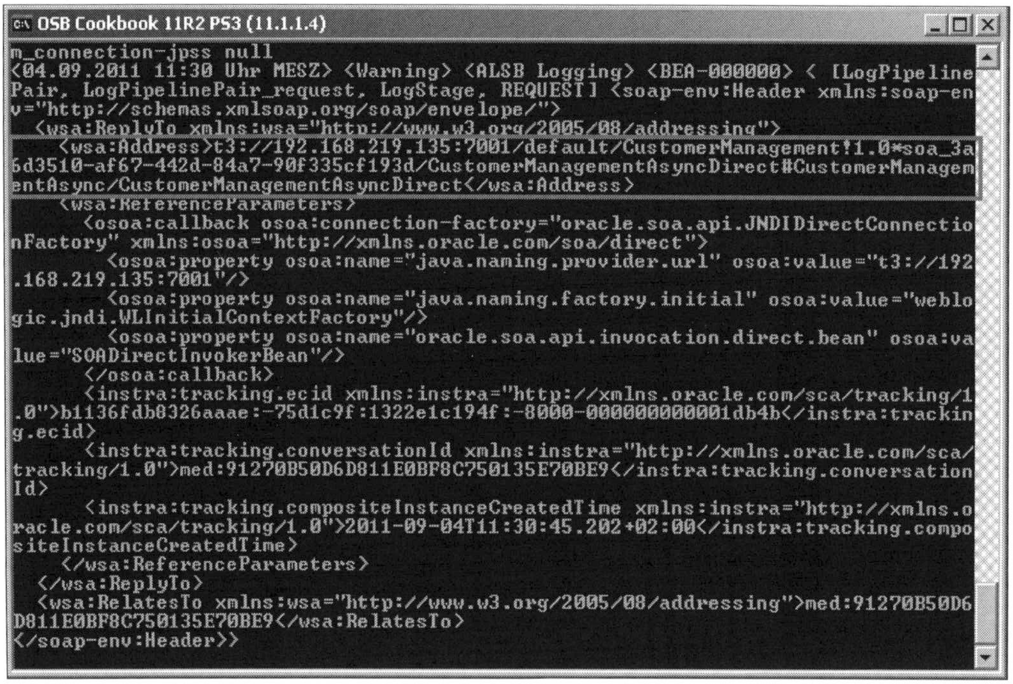

```
OSB Cookbook 11R2 PS3 (11.1.1.4)
m_connection-jpss null
<04.09.2011 11:30 Uhr MESZ> <Warning> <ALSB Logging> <BEA-000000> < [LogPipeline
Pair, LogPipelinePair_request, LogStage, REQUEST] <soap-env:Header xmlns:soap-en
v="http://schemas.xmlsoap.org/soap/envelope/">
  <wsa:ReplyTo xmlns:wsa="http://www.w3.org/2005/08/addressing">
    <wsa:Address>t3://192.168.219.135:7001/default/CustomerManagement!1.0*soa_3a
6d3510-af67-442d-84a7-90f335cf193d/CustomerManagementAsyncDirect#CustomerManagem
entAsync/CustomerManagementAsyncDirect</wsa:Address>
    <wsa:ReferenceParameters>
      <osoa:callback osoa:connection-factory="oracle.soa.api.JNDIDirectConnectio
nFactory" xmlns:osoa="http://xmlns.oracle.com/soa/direct">
        <osoa:property osoa:name="java.naming.provider.url" osoa:value="t3://192
.168.219.135:7001"/>
        <osoa:property osoa:name="java.naming.factory.initial" osoa:value="weblo
gic.jndi.WLInitialContextFactory"/>
        <osoa:property osoa:name="oracle.soa.api.invocation.direct.bean" osoa:va
lue="SOADirectInvokerBean"/>
      </osoa:callback>
      <instra:tracking.ecid xmlns:instra="http://xmlns.oracle.com/sca/tracking/1
.0">b1136fdb0326aaae:-75d1c9f:1322e1c194f:-8000-00000000001db4b</instra:trackin
g.ecid>
      <instra:tracking.conversationId xmlns:instra="http://xmlns.oracle.com/sca/
tracking/1.0">med:91270B50D6D811E0BF8C750135E70BE9</instra:tracking.conversation
Id>
      <instra:tracking.compositeInstanceCreatedTime xmlns:instra="http://xmlns.o
racle.com/sca/tracking/1.0">2011-09-04T11:30:45.202+02:00</instra:tracking.compo
siteInstanceCreatedTime>
    </wsa:ReferenceParameters>
  </wsa:ReplyTo>
  <wsa:RelatesTo xmlns:wsa="http://www.w3.org/2005/08/addressing">med:91270B50D6
D811E0BF8C750135E70BE9</wsa:RelatesTo>
</soap-env:Header>>
```

The SOAP Header contains an addressing element with the callback URL:

```
<wsa:Address>t3://<soaserver>:<port>/default/
CustomerManagement2!1.0*soa_fd4fbf3b-8708-4d19-acc7-ed375008370a/
CustomerManagementAsyncDirect#CustomerManagementAsyncMed/
CustomerManagementAsyncDirect</wsa:Address>.
```

For the callback URI in the business service we only need to use part of the URL: `/default/CustomerManagement2!1.0 /CustomerManagementAsyncDirect#CustomerManagementAsyncMed/CustomerManagementAsyncDirect`.

So we need to remove `*soa_fd4fbf3b-8708-4d19-acc7-ed375008370a` from the URL. This can be done using some XQuery functions in the expression of the **Routing Options** action.

Let's create the business service implementing the dynamic callback on the address provided by the SOAP header. In Eclipse OEPE, perform the following steps for that:

1. In the `business` folder, create a new business service and name it `CustomerManagementCallback`.
2. Navigate to the **General** tab and select **WSDL Web Service** as the **Service Type**.
3. Click on **Browse** and expand the **CustomerManagementAsync.wsdl** in the **wsdl** folder.
4. Select **CustomerManagementSOAPAsyncCallback (binding)** and click on **OK**:

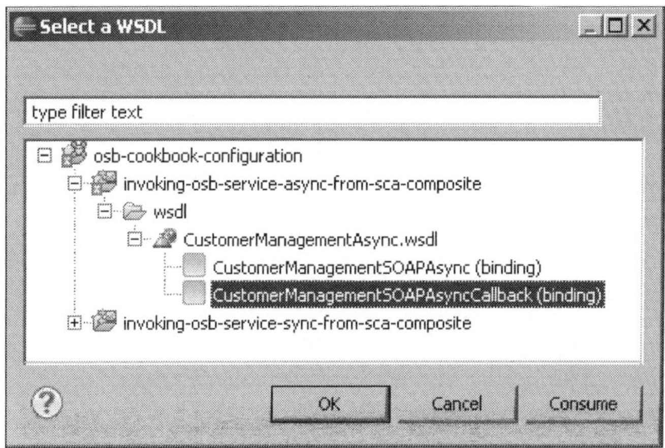

5. Confirm the **Transport Configuration Change** pop-up window by clicking on **Yes**.
6. Navigate to the **Transport** tab and check that **soa-direct** is selected as the **Protocol** value.

7. Enter `callback` in **Endpoint URI** field and click on **Add**:

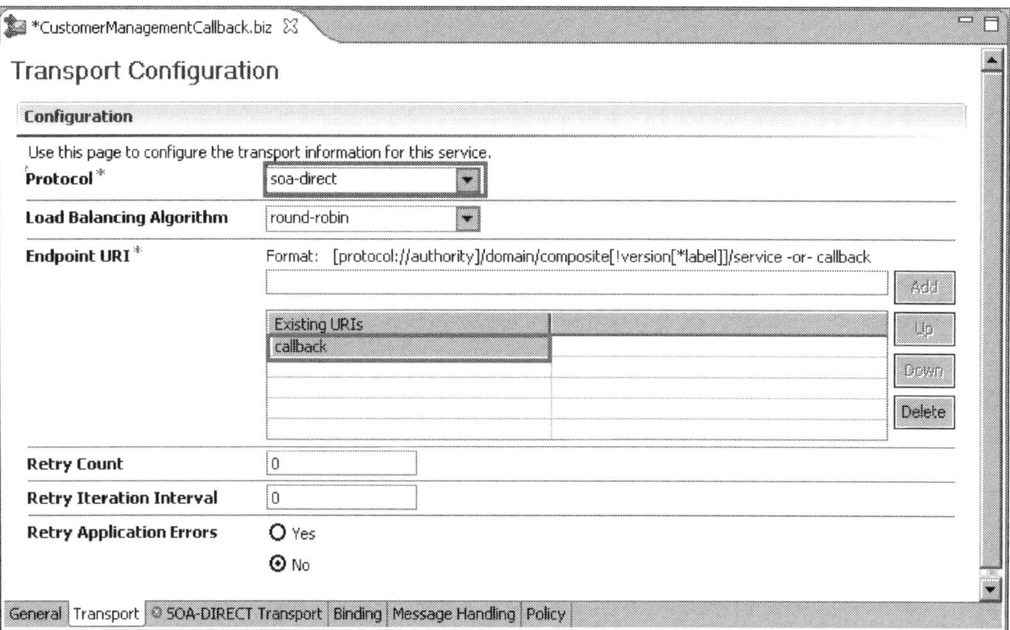

8. Navigate to the **SOA-DIRECT Transport** tab and select **Service Callback** for the **Role** option.

We have created the business service for the callback. Now let's add the necessary actions to dynamically specify the callback address, based on the WS-Addressing header values passed in the request. In Eclipse OEPE, perform the following steps:

9. Open the **CustomerManagementAsync** proxy service and navigate to the **Message Flow** tab.
10. Insert a **Route** node after the **Pipeline Pair** node and name it `CallbackRoute`.
11. Insert a **Routing** action into the **CallbackRoute**.
12. Navigate to the **Properties** tab of the **Routing** action and click on **Browse**.
13. In **Select a Service Resource** dialog, select **CustomerManagementCallback.biz** and click on **OK**.
14. Select **FindCustomerResponseAsync** as the value of the **Invoking** drop-down listbox.
15. Right-click on the **Request Action** of the **Routing** and select **Insert Into | Communication | Routing Options**.
16. On the **Properties** tab of the **Routing Options** action enable **URI**.

17. Click on the **Expression** link and add the following code in the **Expression** window to dynamically define and overwrite the callback URI:

```
fn:concat(
  fn:substring-before($header/wsa05:ReplyTo/wsa05:Address/
text(),'*')
  ,'/',
  fn:substring-after(
   fn:substring-after($header/wsa05:ReplyTo/wsa05:Address/
text(),'*')
    , '/'
  )
)
```

18. Click on **OK**:

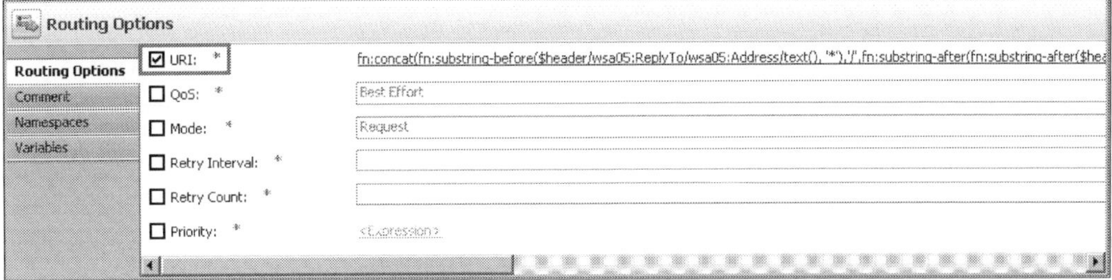

19. Insert a **Replace** action after the **Routing Options** action to provide a response.
20. On the **Properties** tab of the **Replace** action, click on the **Expression** link of the **Replace Properties** window.
21. Copy the following XML fragment into the **Expression** field:

```
<cus:FindCustomerResponse
  xmlns:cus="http://osb-cookbook/CustomerManagementAsync"
  xmlns:cus1="http://osb-cookbook/customer"
  xmlns:cred="http://osb-cookbook/creditcard">
        <Customer>
           <cus1:ID>100</cus1:ID>
           <cus1:FirstName>Larry</cus1:FirstName>
           <cus1:LastName>Ellison</cus1:LastName>
           <cus1:EmailAddress>larry.ellison@oracle.com</
cus1:EmailAddress>
           <cus1:Addresses/>
           <cus1:BirthDate>1967-08-13</cus1:BirthDate>
           <cus1:Rating>A</cus1:Rating>
           <cus1:Gender>Male</cus1:Gender>
           <cus1:CreditCard>
```

```
                    <cred:CardIssuer>visa</cred:CardIssuer>
                    <cred:CardNumber>123</cred:CardNumber>
                    <cred:CardholderName>Larry</cred:CardholderName>
                    <cred:ExpirationDate>2020-01-01</
cred:ExpirationDate>
                    <cred:CardValidationCode>1233</
cred:CardValidationCode>
                </cus1:CreditCard>
            </Customer>
</cus:FindCustomerResponse>
```

22. Click on **OK**.
23. Enter `body` into the **In Variable** field and select the **Replace node contents** option:

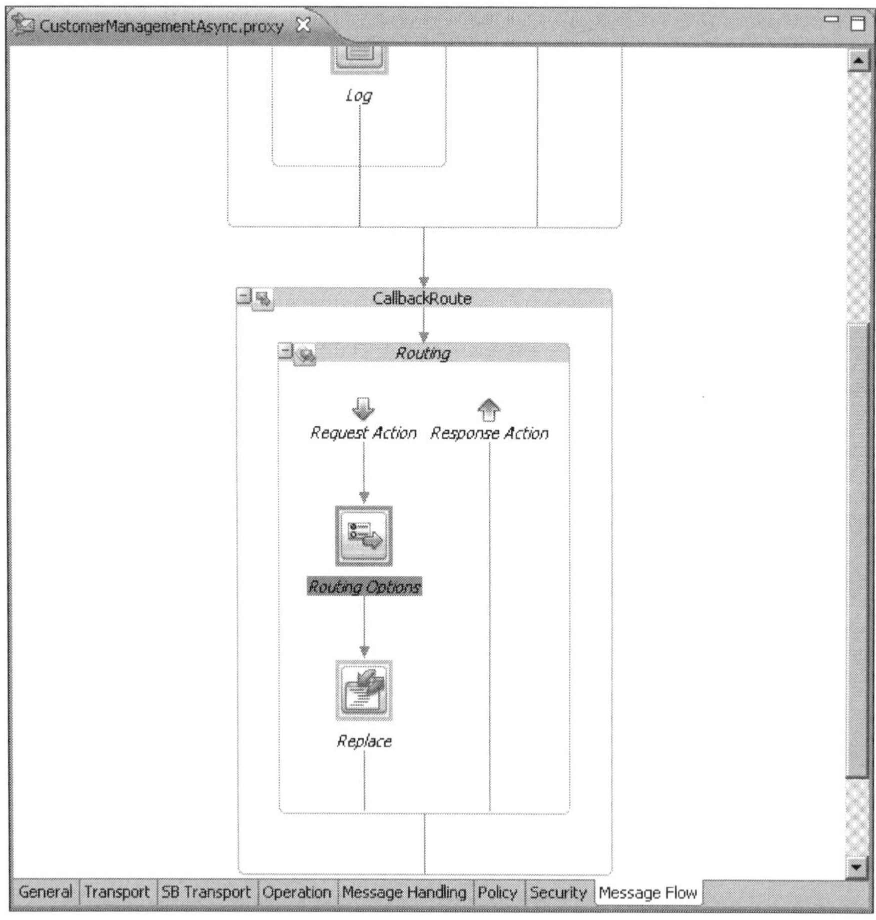

24. Deploy the project to the OSB server.

In order to see that the callback worked and the Mediator got the callback message, let's add a file adapter and write the callback message to a file. In JDeveloper, perform the following steps:

25. On the **Component Palette**, drag the **File Adapter** from the **Service Adapters** section and drop it on the **External References** section of the SCA composite.
26. Click on **Next**.
27. Enter `AsyncResponseToFile` into the **Service Name** field and click on **Next** twice.
28. Choose **Write File** for the **Operation Type** option and click on **Next**.
29. Enter `c:\temp` into the **Directory for Outgoing Files (physical path)** field.
30. Enter `async_response_%SEQ%.xml` into the **File Naming Convention** field and click on **Next**.
31. Click on the magnifying glass button right to the **URL** field.
32. In the **Type Chooser** window expand the **CustomerMessages.xsd** inside the **Project Schema Files** folder, select the **FindCustomerResponse** element, and click on **OK**.
33. Click on **Next** and **Finish**.
34. Double-click on the Mediator to open the `CustomerManagementAsync.mplan` and click on the **Browse for target service operations** icon next to **Callback**:

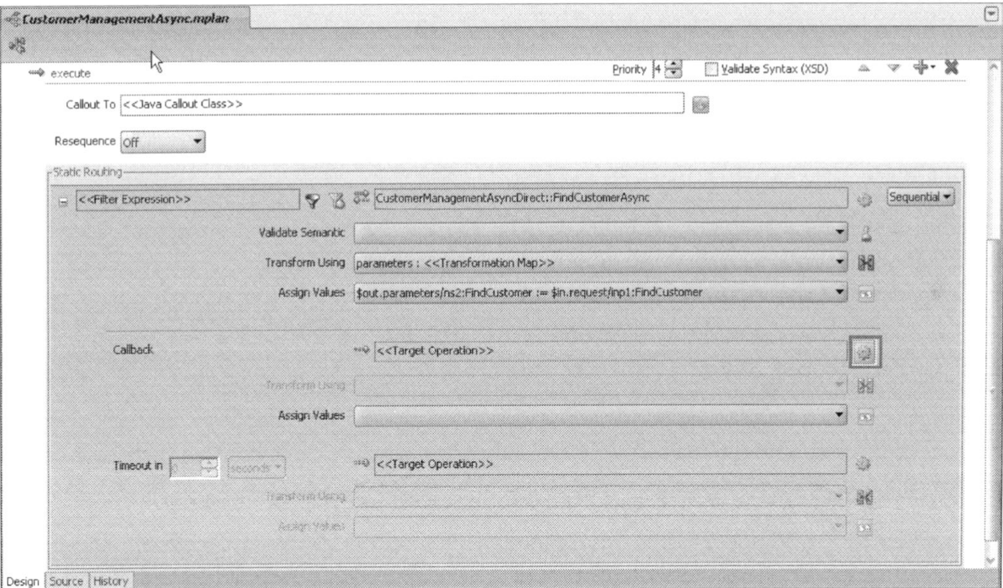

35. Click on **Service** on the **Target Type** pop-up window:

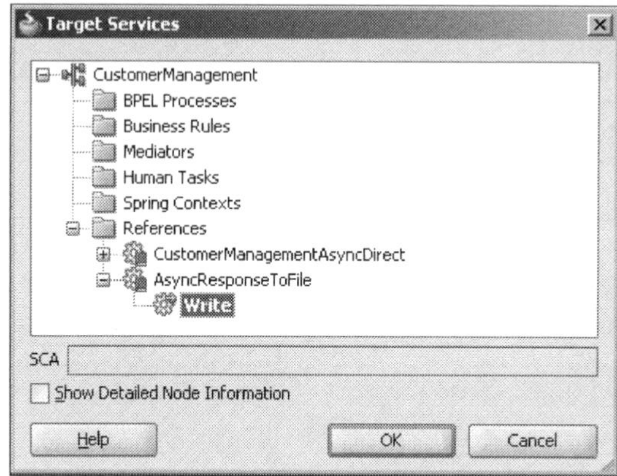

36. Expand the **AsyncResponseToFile** node, select **Write**, and click on **OK**.
37. Click on the icon next to the **Assign Value** of the callback.
38. In the **Assign Value** pop-up window click on the green plus icon.
39. In the **From** section, select **expression** for the **Type** drop-down listbox.
40. Enter `$in.parameters/tns:FindCustomerResponse` into the **Expression** field.
41. In the **To** section, select **expression** for the **Type** drop-down listbox.
42. Enter `$out.body/imp1:FindCustomerResponse` into the **Expression** field.
43. Deploy the project to the SOA server.
44. Retest the **CustomerManagement** composite in Enterprise Manager (repeat Steps 50 to 55).
45. On the **Response** tab, click on **Launch Flow Trace** to see the trace of the test:

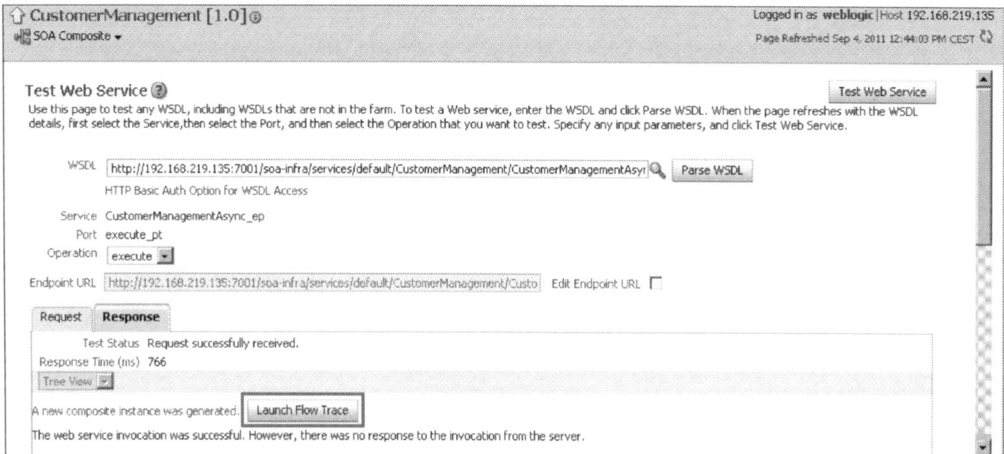

The SOA Suite composite instance flow trace is displayed and we can see that the instance got a response and then invoked the file adapter:

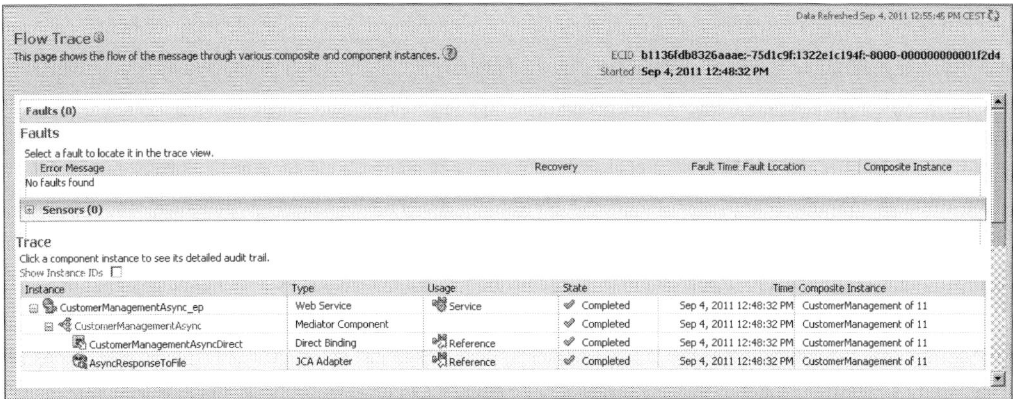

A file called `async_response_1.xml` containing the callback message should be available at `c:\temp`. We have successfully invoked the OSB service and returned the response asynchronously back to the Mediator through an OSB business service. To test it, we have written the callback message to a file.

How it works...

This recipe demonstrated the use case, where an asynchronous SCA service component in a SCA composite invokes an OSB WSLD-based proxy service through the SB transport. To invoke this SB proxy service, the SCA service component needs to use a Direct Binding reference of target type **Oracle Service Bus**. Because of the asynchronous interface, the proxy service is only handling the inbound side (the request message), the callback message, when the processing on the OSB is finished, is sent by a business service through the SOA-DIRECT transport.

In the recipe, the OSB is not doing any real processing except for creating the response message. In a real case, the OSB proxy service would probably call an external service (maybe with an asynchronous interface as well) and then return the response from that external service through the business service back to the SCA component of the SOA Suite.

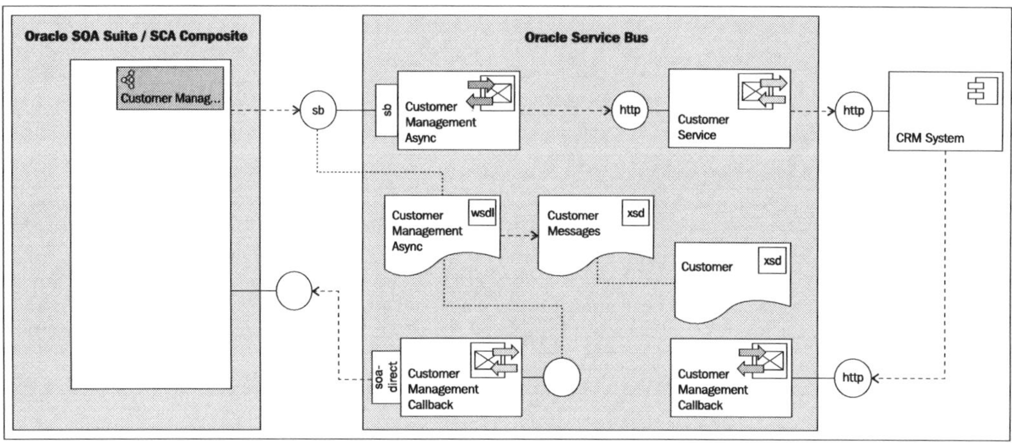

As the callback is sent to a different connection, OSB must be able to remember the original callback location when calling back the SCA component.

When using WS-Addressing, the callback address is sent to the request proxy service in the **ReplyTo** address header. Before invoking the external service, the request proxy service passes this address as a **referenceParameter** property inside the **ReplyTo** header. Following the WS-Addressing specification, the **referenceParameter** property is inserted in the SOAP header block of the callback from the external service.

The callback proxy service can then extract this callback address and set the callback business service URI through a **Transport Options** action as shown in this recipe.

9

Communication, Flow Control, and Message Processing

In this chapter, we will cover:

- Using the **Service Callout** action to invoke a service
- Using the **Publish** action to asynchronously invoke a service
- Using the **Java Callout** action to invoke Java code
- Using the **Java Callout** action with XMLBeans
- Using custom XPath functions
- Using the **For Each** action to process a collection
- Using dynamic Split-Join to perform work in parallel
- Using the **Validate** action to perform message validation
- Enabling/disabling a **Validate** action dynamically
- Creating private proxy service

Introduction

In this chapter, we will show how to use different actions from the **Communication**, **Flow Control**, and **Message Processing** section of the OSB Design Palette.

We will show the various options to invoke other logic, such as **Service Callout**, **Publish**, and the **Java Callout** action as well as the ability to create custom XPath functions. Another topic covered is the processing of collections either through a loop sequentially or by a Split-Join in parallel. The validation of messages and the creation of *private* proxy services are also covered in this chapter.

Using Service Callout action to invoke a service

In this recipe, we will use a **Service Callout** action to call another service from a proxy service message flow.

We will use the sample setup from the first chapter of this book and add an additional service call to another service **Credit Card Info Service**, which returns the credit card information. The service call will be done using the **Service Callout** action. Both the information from the **Credit Card Info Service** and from the **Customer Service** will then be merged by the XQuery transformation into one single response returned by the proxy service.

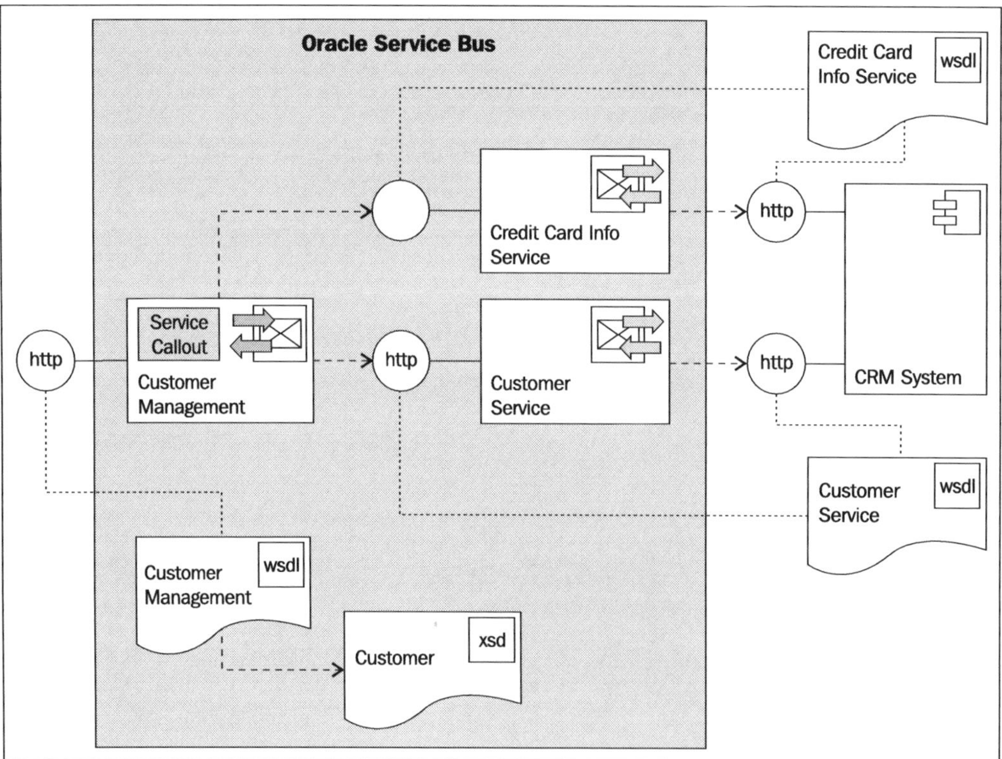

Getting ready

You can import the OSB project containing the base setup for this recipe into Eclipse OEPE from `\chapter-9\getting-ready\using-service-callout`.

Start the soapUI mock services simulating the two external services on the CRM system by double-clicking on `start-CreditCardInfoServiceCRM.cmd` and `start-CustomerServiceCRM.cmd` in the `\chapter-9\getting-ready\misc` folder.

How to do it...

First, we will create a new business service which will wrap the additional **Credit Card Info Service** interface on the CRM system. In Eclipse OEPE, perform the following steps:

1. Create a new business service in the `business` folder and name it `CreditCardInfoService`.
2. On the **General** tab choose **WSDL Web Service** for the **Service Type** option and click **Browse**.
3. Click **Consume** and select **URI** from the **Service Resource** drop-down listbox.
4. Enter the endpoint URI of the soapUI mock service `http://localhost:8090/mockCreditCardInfoServiceSOAP?WSDL` into the **URI** field and click **OK**.
5. Select the **CreditCardInfoServiceSOAP (port)** node and click **OK**.
6. Confirm the pop-up window by clicking **OK**.
7. Rename the imported WSDL from `mockCreditCardInfoServiceSOAP.wsdl` to `CreditCardInfoService.wsdl` and move it into the `wsdl` folder.

By doing that, we have created the new business service. Now, let's add the **Service Callout** action to the proxy service calling the new business service. In Eclipse OEPE, perform the following steps:

8. Open the **Message Flow** tab of the **CustomerManagement** proxy service.
9. In the **FindCustomer** branch, right-click on the **Response Action** flow of the **Routing** action and select **Insert Into | Communication | Service Callout** to add a **Service Callout** action just before the **Replace** action. We want to enrich the message, before the transformation to the canonical format is made.
10. On the **Properties** tab of the **Service Callout** action, click **Browse** and select the **CreditCardInfoService** business service.
11. Select **RetrieveCreditCardById** from the **Invoking** drop-down listbox.
12. Select the **Configure Soap Body** option.

13. Enter `creditCardInfoRequest` into the **Request Body** field and `creditCardInfoResponse` into the **Response Body** field.

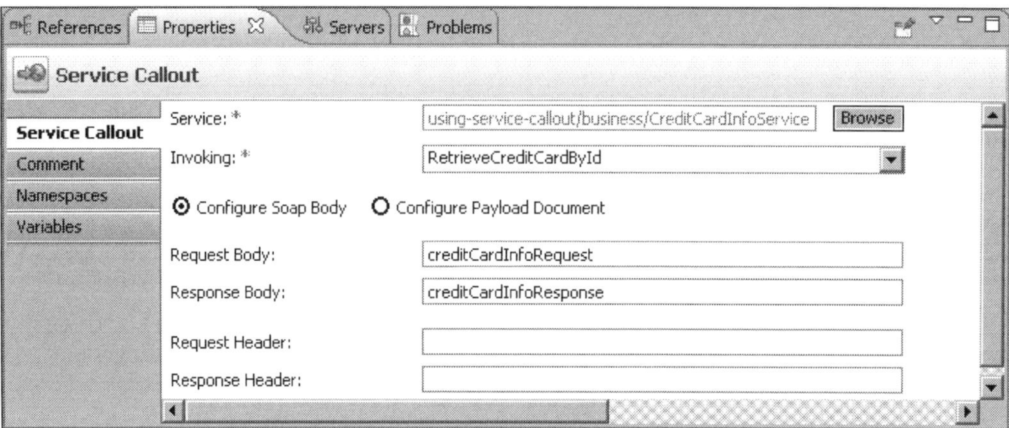

14. Insert an **Assign** action into the **Request Action** flow of the **Service Callout** action.
15. On the **Properties** tab of the **Assign** action, click on **<Expression>** and enter the following XML fragment into the **Expression** field:

```
<soap-env:Body>
    <cred:RetrieveCreditCardById>
        <id>{$body/cus:FindCustomer/ID/text()}</id>
    </cred:RetrieveCreditCardById>
</soap-env:Body>
```

16. Navigate to the **Namespace Definition** tab, add a namespace with `cred` for the **Prefix** and `http://www.crm.org/CreditCardInfoService/` for the **URI** field and click **OK**.
17. Enter `creditCardInfoRequest` into the **Variable** field.

We have added the **Service Callout** action to the proxy service. The message flow should look as shown in the following screenshot:

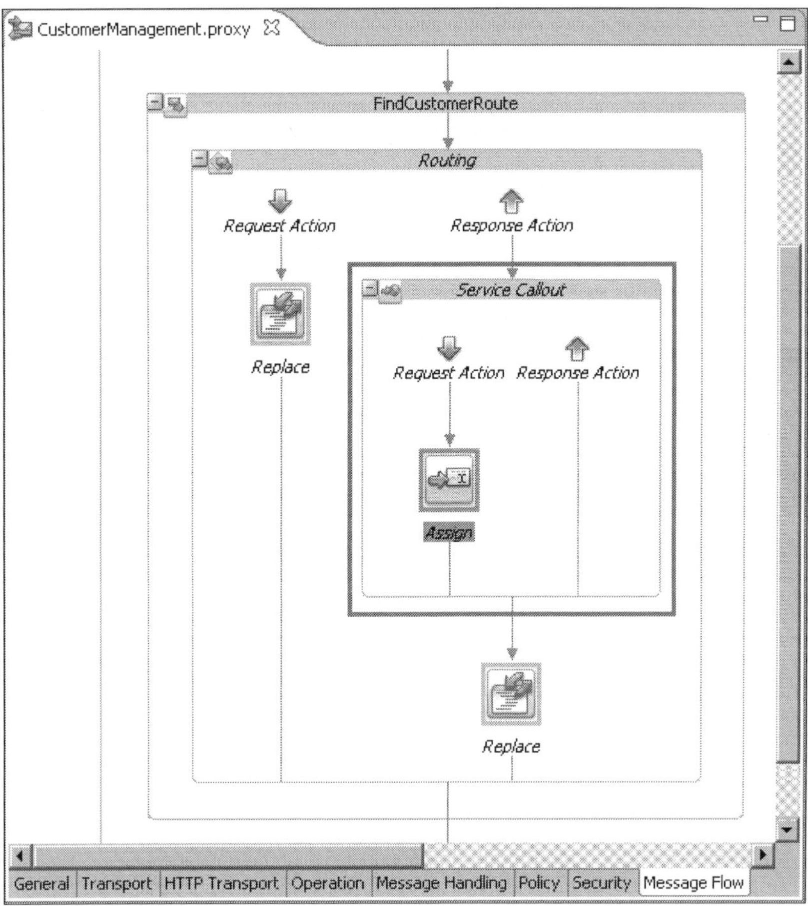

The result of the **Service Callout** action is available in the `creditCardInfoResponse` variable. We now have to adapt the XQuery transformation to merge the message from the **Service Callout** and the **Routing** into one single response message. In Eclipse OEPE, perform the following steps:

18. Open the **TransformFindCustomerResponse.xq** XQuery transformation and navigate to the **Source** tab.
19. Add an additional parameter to the XQuery transformation by adding the following line to the top:

```
(:: pragma bea:global-element-parameter parameter="$retrieveCredi
tCardInfoByIdResponse1" element="ns4:RetrieveCreditCardByIdRespon
se" location="../wsdl/CreditCardInfoService.wsdl" ::)
```

20. Declare an additional namespace:

```
declare namespace ns4 =
    "http://www.crm.org/CreditCardInfoService/";
```

21. Add the parameter to the declaration of the `TransformFindCustomerResponse` function:

```
declare function xf:TransformFindCustomerResponse
    ($retrieveCustomerByCriteriaResponse1 as
        element(ns0:RetrieveCustomerByCriteriaResponse),
    $retrieveCreditCardInfoByIdResponse1 as
        element(ns4:RetrieveCreditCardByIdResponse))
    as element(ns3:FindCustomerResponse) {
        <ns3:FindCustomerResponse>
```

22. Declare an additional variable and add the variable to the invocation call:

```
declare variable $retrieveCreditCardInfoByIdResponse1 as
    element(ns4:RetrieveCreditCardByIdResponse) external;

xf:TransformFindCustomerResponse(
    $retrieveCustomerByCriteriaResponse1,
    $retrieveCreditCardInfoByIdResponse1)
```

23. Navigate back to the **Design** tab and the new parameter with the Credit Card Info data will be shown. Map the credit card information to the **FindCustomerResponse** message. The mapping should look as shown in the following screenshot:

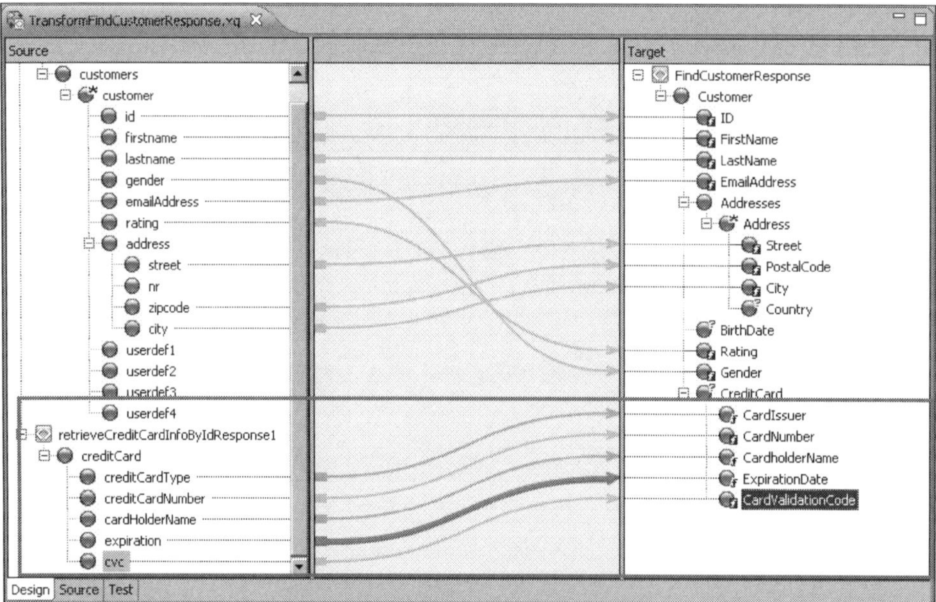

Last but not least we have to change the existing invoke of the XQuery in the **Replace** action so that the additional parameter is passed. In Eclipse OEPE, perform the following steps:

24. Select the **Replace** action following the **Service Callout** action and navigate to the **Properties** tab.
25. Click on the link to the right of **Expression** to reselect the XQuery transformation.
26. Click **Browse**, select the **TransformFindCustomerResponse.xq** XQuery resource and click **OK**.
27. Enter `$body/ext:RetrieveCustomerByCriteriaResponse` into the **retrieveCustomerByCriteriaResponse1** field and `$creditCardInfoResponse/cred: RetrieveCreditCardByIdResponse` into the **retrieveCreditCardInfoByIdResponse1** field.
28. Click **OK**.
29. Deploy the project to the OSB server.

Now let's test the proxy service from soapUI:

30. Import the `CustomerManagement-soapui-project.xml` from the `\chapter-9\getting-ready\misc` folder.
31. Double-click on **Request 1** inside the **FindCustomer** operation.
32. Check that the endpoint of the proxy service is correctly set up in the drop-down listbox on the top.
33. Click on the green arrow to execute the test and make sure that the **CreditCard** information is returned in the response.

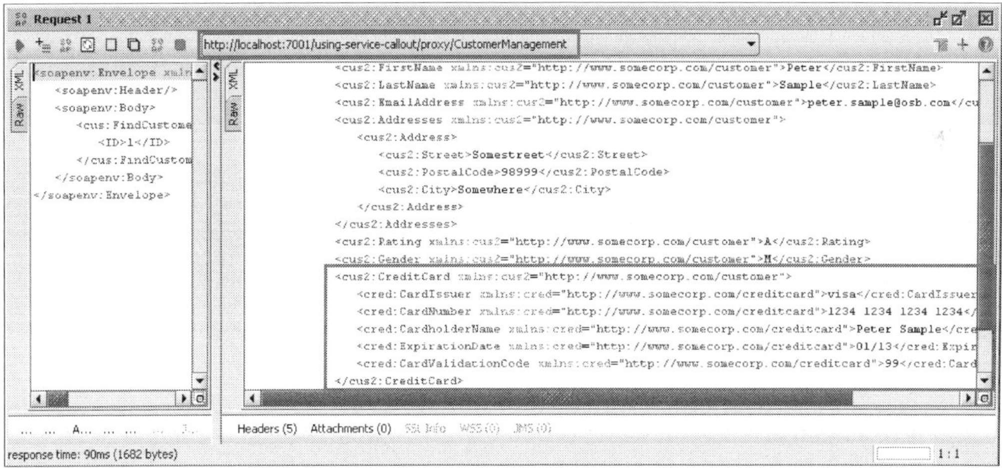

How it works...

We have used the **Service Callout** action in this recipe to invoke an additional service besides the one already called through the **Routing** action. By doing that, we are able to, for example, enrich a message, either before or after doing the routing. In our case, we have added the credit card information to the canonical response message returned to the consumer. By adding the **Service Callout** action into the **Response Action** of the **Routing** action, we decided that the callout is done after the **Routing** has been successfully executed.

A **Service Callout** only works with WSDL operation which implements the request/response message exchange pattern. One-way operations cannot be invoked by the **Service Callout** action, use the **Publish** action instead.

There's more...

In this recipe, we have seen the **Service Callout** in action. But what is the difference between a **Service Callout** and a **Routing** action?

A **Routing** action can only be used inside a **Route** node and will always have to be placed at the end of the proxy service message flow. No other actions can follow a routing node in the message flow. The **Routing** action will define where the request thread stops and where the response thread starts. The request and response pipeline of an OSB proxy service are always executed in two different threads. A **Routing** action supports both request/response as well as one-way message exchange patterns.

The **Service Callout** action can be placed anywhere where an OSB action is valid. There is no limit for the number of **Service Callout** actions which can be used. A **Service Callout** placed in the request pipeline will be performed by the request thread, a **Service Callout** in the response pipeline by the response thread. A **Service Callout** only supports the request/response message exchange pattern and will always be synchronous, that is, it waits for the response message.

Using the Publish action to asynchronously invoke a service

In this recipe, we will use the **Publish** action to asynchronously invoke a service from the proxy service message flow, without having to wait for the calling service to finish its processing.

For this recipe, we have an external **Processing Service**, available as a soapUI mock service which takes quite some time to do its processing. The interface in the **Processing Service** WSDL is defined synchronous. We have a business service **Processing** which allows us to invoke the external service from a proxy service.

Instead of directly invoking the business service from the **Publish** proxy service, an additional proxy service **Processing** is added, which only exposes a one-way interface. By doing that, the **Publish** proxy service can use a **Publish** action to invoke the **Processing** proxy service without having to wait for external service to complete.

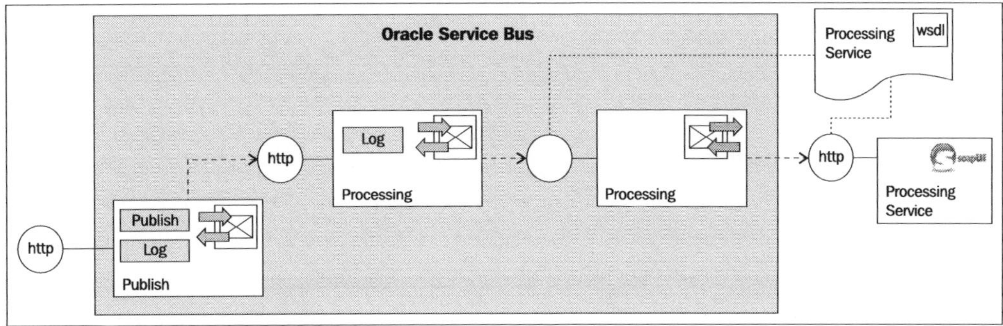

Getting ready

You can import the OSB project containing the base setup for this recipe, with the **Processing Service** business and proxy service already implemented into Eclipse OEPE from `\chapter-9\getting-ready\using-publish`.

Start the soapUI mock service simulating the **Processing Service** by double-clicking on `start-ProcessingService.cmd` in the `\chapter-9\getting-ready\misc` folder.

How to do it...

Let's implement the **Publish** proxy service, which will use the **Publish** action to invoke the **Processing** proxy service. In Eclipse OEPE, perform the following steps:

1. Create a new proxy service in the `proxy` folder and name it `Publish`.
2. On the **General** tab select **Any XML Service** for the **Service Type** option.
3. Navigate to the **Message Flow** tab.
4. Insert a **Pipeline Pair** node and name it `PublishPipelinePair`.
5. Insert a **Stage** node into the **Request Pipeline** and name it `PublishStage`.
6. Insert a **Publish** action into the **Stage**.
7. On the **Properties** tab of the **Publish** action, click **Browse**.
8. Select the **Processing** proxy service inside the `proxy` folder and click **OK**.
9. Insert a **Log** action after the **Publish** action.

10. On the **Properties** tab of the **Log** action, click **<Expression>** and enter `'Publish completed, continue with processing in Publish proxy service'` into the **Expression** field.
11. Click **OK**.
12. Select **Warning** from the **Severity** drop-down listbox.
13. Deploy the project to the OSB server.

Now, let's test OSB project by performing the following steps in the Service Bus console:

14. In the **Project Explorer** navigate to `proxy` folder inside the **using-publish-to-async-invoke-service** project.
15. Click on the **Launch Test Console** icon of the **Publish** proxy service.
16. Leave the **Payload** field empty and directly click **Execute**.
17. The output of the **Log** action from the **Publish** proxy service should be shown first in the Service Bus console window, followed a few seconds later by the output of the **Log** action from the **Processing** proxy service, which is shown after the external service has completed its work.

```
OSB Cookbook 11R2 PS3 (11.1.1.4)
d continue processing>
<20.11.2011 19:20 Uhr MEZ> <Warning> <ALSB Logging> <BEA-000000> < [RouteToLonge
<20.11.2011 21:33 Uhr MEZ> <Warning> <ALSB Logging> <BEA-000000> < [PublishPipel
inePair, PublishPipelinePair_request, PublishStage, REQUEST] Publish completed,
continue with processing in Publish proxy service>
<20.11.2011 21:33 Uhr MEZ> <Warning> <ALSB Logging> <BEA-000000> < [RouteToLonge
rRunningService, null, null, RESPONSE] Answer from Processing Service>
```

How it works...

We have used the **Publish** action in this recipe to asynchronously invoke a service, the **Processing** proxy service, with a one-way service interface. The **Processing** proxy service wraps some processing which takes longer to complete. Actually the external service, mocked by soapUI will use the ID passed (which is hardcoded in the **Replace** action of the **Processing** proxy service to the value of `10`) to the **Processing Service** as the time in seconds to wait until the response is sent back. Therefore, the **Processing** proxy service will only show its **Log** output after a bit more than 10 seconds. However, because the **Publish** proxy service uses the **Publish** action to invoke the **Processing** proxy service, he/she does not have to wait and the **Publish** action finishes immediately. The processing of the **Processing** proxy service is done in a separate thread and is completely independent from the invoking service. The **Log** action in the **Publish** proxy service executes immediately and is therefore shown first in the Service Bus console log window.

See also

- See the *Creating private proxy services* recipe for another usage of the **Publish** action and how to use the local protocol on a proxy service, to hide it from external consumers.
- Check the *Using the Service Callout action to invoke a service* recipe for how to call another service synchronously.

Using the Java Callout action to invoke Java code

In this recipe, we will show how we can use a **Java Callout** action to invoke Java code, which might already exist. This is an easy way to extend the standard functionality of the service bus.

We will use the **Java Callout** action to call a Java method which returns the **Checksum** of the message passed as the parameter. The functionality of calculating a checksum is not available as an XPath/XQuery function and adding it through a **Java Callout** action is of course much simpler and more efficient than using a *real* web service.

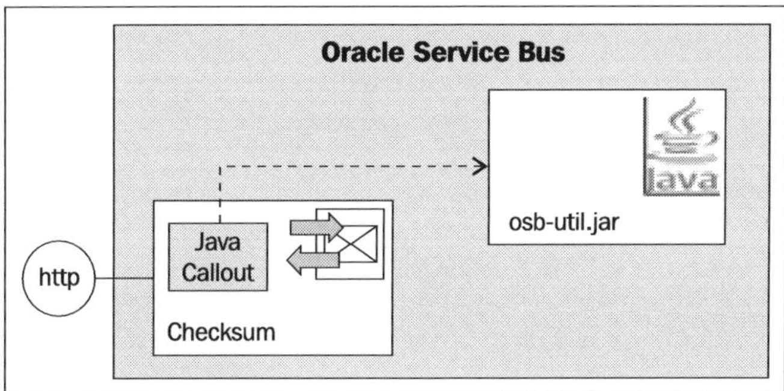

Getting ready

You can import the OSB project containing the base setup for this recipe into Eclipse OEPE from `\chapter-9\getting-ready\using-java-callout-to-invoke-java`.

How to do it...

We will first create the Java project with the Java class holding the checksum calculation functionality. In Eclipse OEPE, perform the following steps:

1. Right-click on the **Project Explorer** and select **New** | **Project**.
2. Enter `java` into the **Wizards** field, select **Java Project** and click **Next**.

3. Enter `osb-checksum-util` into the **Project name** field.
4. Click **Finish** and confirm the pop-up window with **Yes** to switch to the Java perspective.
5. Right-click on the **osb-checksum-util** project and select **New | Class**.
6. Enter `osbcookbook.util.checksum` into the **Package** field.
7. Enter `ChecksumUtil` into the **Name** field and click **Finish**.
8. Implement the following static method inside the **ChecksumUtil** class:

```
public static long calculateChecksum(String data) {
    Checksum checksum = new CRC32();
    checksum.update(data.getBytes(), 0,
        data.getBytes().length);
return checksum.getValue();
}
```

9. Right-click on the source and select **Source | Organize Imports**.

By doing that, the checksum functionality is ready to be used. In order to invoke it through a **Java Callout**, it needs to be packaged into a **Java Archive** (**JAR**) file and copied into the OSB project. In Eclipse OEPE, perform the following steps:

10. Right-click on the **osb-checksum-util** project and select **Export**.
11. Enter `java` into **Select an export destination** and select **JAR** file.
12. Click **Next**.
13. In the **Select the resources to export** tree, select the **osb-checksum-util** project.
14. Click **Browse** right to the **JAR** file drop-down listbox.
15. Navigate to the `jar` folder inside the **using-java-callout-to-invoke-java** OSB project, enter `osb-checksum-util.jar` into the **File name** field and click **Save**.
16. Click **Next** and then **Finish**.

Now, let's switch to the OSB project and implement the proxy service calling our new Java calls through a **Java Callout**. In Eclipse OEPE, perform the following steps:

17. Switch to the **Oracle Service Bus perspective**.
18. Refresh the `jar` folder inside the **using-java-callout-to-invoke-java** project by pressing *F5* and check that the JAR file created previously is located inside the `jar` folder.
19. Create a new proxy service inside the `proxy` folder and name it `Checksum`.
20. On the **General** tab, select **Messaging Service** for the **Service Type** option.
21. Navigate to the **Messaging** tab and select **Text** for both the **Request Message Type** and **Response Message Type** option.

22. Navigate to the **Message Flow** tab.
23. Insert a **Pipeline Pair** node and name it **CalculateChecksumPipelinePair**.
24. Insert a **Stage** into the **Request Pipeline** and name it `CalculateChecksumStage`.
25. Insert a **Java Callout** action into the stage.
26. On the **Properties** tab of the **Java Callout** action, click **Browse** to select the method to call.
27. Navigate to **osb-checksum-util.jar** in the `jar` folder of the project and click **OK**.
28. Select the **public static long calculateChecksum(java.lang.String)** method and click **OK**.
29. Click **<Expression>** and enter `$body/text()` into the **Expression** field and click **OK**.
30. Enter `checksumValue` into the **Result Value** field.

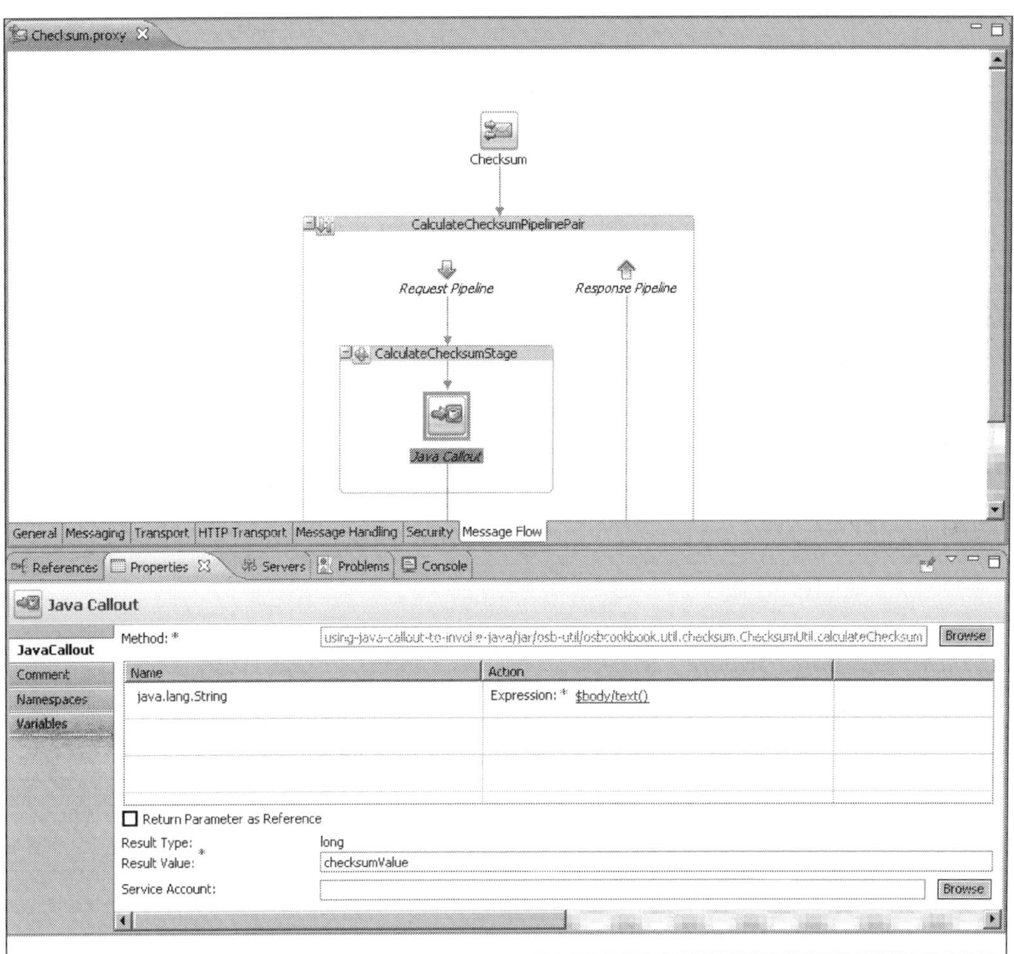

We have added the **Java Callout** action to invoke our Java method and after that the checksum value is available in the `checksumValue` variable. Let's add a **Replace** action to return the checksum in the body variable. In Eclipse OEPE, perform the following steps.

31. Insert a **Replace** action after the **Java Callout** action.
32. Enter `$checksumValue` into the **Expression** field.
33. Enter `body` into the **In Variable** field.
34. Deploy the project to the OSB server.

Now let's test the proxy service by performing the following steps in the Service Bus console:

35. In the **Project Explorer** navigate to `proxy` folder inside the **using-java-callout-to-invoke-java** project.
36. Click on the **Launch Test Console** icon of the **Checksum** proxy service.
37. Enter some text to calculate the checksum on into the **Payload** field and click on **Execute**.
38. The output of the **Java Callout** action and the checksum calculation will be shown in the **Response Document** section.

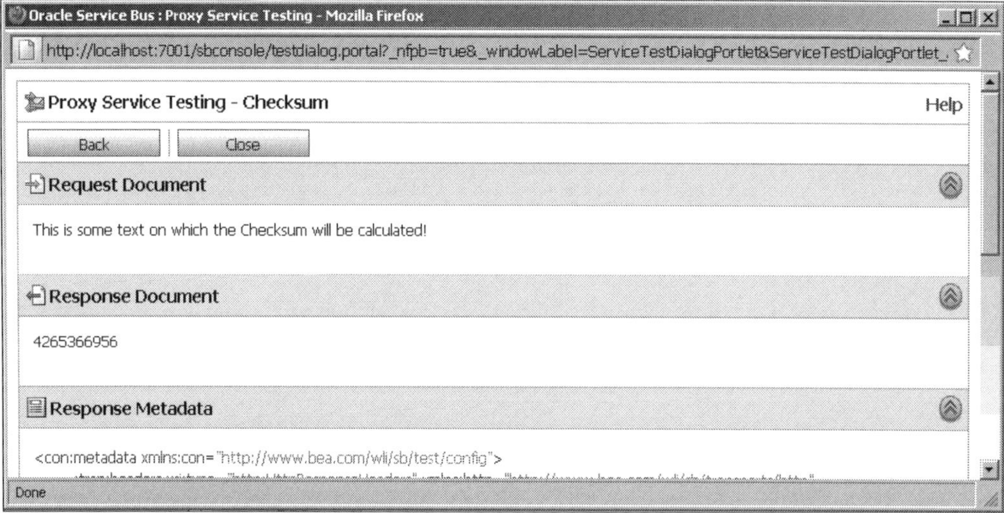

How it works...

We have created a Java class, packaged it as a JAR and invoked it from the OSB proxy service through a **Java Callout** action. Only static methods can be invoked through the **Java Callout** action; other, non-static methods will not be shown when browsing the classes/methods.

The JAR is deployed with the OSB project to the OSB server and it will always run inside the OSB server.

It's recommended that the JARs are kept as simple as possible, any large bodies of code or other large frameworks that the JAR invokes should be placed in the `[OSB-DOMAIN]/lib` folder. Any change to a JAR will cause all service which references it to be redeployed. Therefore, dependencies between JARs and services should be kept on a minimum. To achieve that, only dependent and overlapping classes should be placed in the same JAR.

In our case, the `ChecksumUtil` Java class only uses another class from the Java library, which is directly available on the OSB. If we create dependencies to other Java frameworks, such as Apache Commons, then the corresponding JARs have to be copied manually to the `domain\lib` folder, that is, `[WL_HOME]\user_projects\domains\osb_cookbook_domain\lib`.

There's more...

Spring is a powerful framework which can help to implement Java code which is more loosely coupled. In order to use the Spring framework inside a class used in a **Java Callout**, make sure that Spring 2.5.x is used. This version of Spring is already included with WebLogic server, so no additional JAR has to be placed in the `domain\lib` folder.

A solution of the recipe, which supports different implementations of the **Checksum** interface through a Spring context configuration, is available in the folder `\chapter-9\solution\using-java-callout-to-invoke-java\spring`.

Using the Java Callout action with XMLBeans

In this recipe, we will show how to use a **Java Callout** action to invoke a Java method, which will return XML messages. We have already seen that a Java method can return Java primitives or String values in the *Using the Java Callout action to invoke Java code* recipe. But the **Java Callout** action can also work with Apache XMLBeans, which allows us to directly pass XML message from a Java method to an OSB proxy service and vice versa, without having them serialized from String to XML. The Oracle Service Bus natively works with these XMLBean objects.

We will implement a proxy service which invokes a Java class inside a JAR using the **Java Callout** action, as shown in the following screenshot:

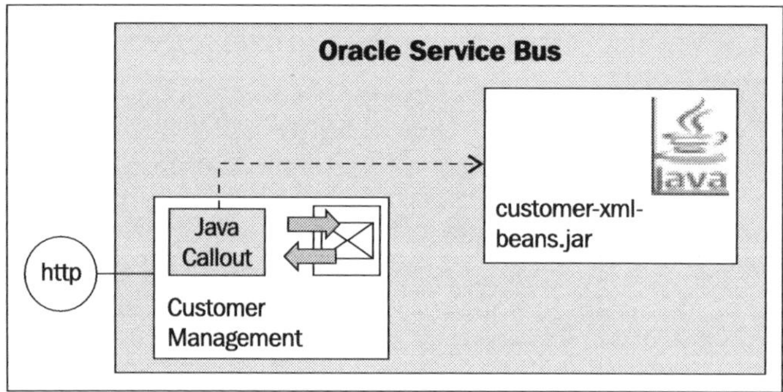

The Java class will format an XML message using Apache XMLBeans and return it to the proxy service. The message is then returned to the caller of the proxy service.

Getting ready

You can import the OSB project containing the base setup for this recipe into Eclipse OEPE from `\chapter-9\getting-ready\using-java-callout-with-xmlbeans\using-java-callout-with-xmlbeans`.

How to do it...

We will first create the Oracle Service Bus project. In Eclipse OEPE, perform the following steps:

1. In the `proxy` folder, create a new proxy service and name it `CustomerService`.
2. On the **General** tab select **Any XML Service** for the **Service Type**.
3. Navigate to the **Message Flow** tab and insert a **Pipeline Pair** node named **HandleMessagePipeline**.
4. Insert a **Stage** node into the **Pipeline Pair** and name it `FindCustomer`.

Now we first have to create the Java class, which will use XMLBeans to create an XML message, which will then be returned to the proxy service through a **Java Callout** action. In Eclipse OEPE, perform the following steps to create a Java project to hold the Java class:

5. Create a new java project in the workspace by selecting **New | Project...** from the **File** menu.
6. Enter `java` into the **Wizards** field, select the **Java Project** node and click **Next**.

7. Name the project `customer-xml-beans` and click **Finish**.
8. Confirm the pop-up window with **Yes** to switch to the **Java EE** perspective.

To be able to work with XMLObjects, we need to add the Apache XMLBeans JAR file to the build path of the new Java project. In Eclipse OEPE, perform the following steps:

9. Right-click on the **customer-xml-beans** project and select **Properties | Java Build Path**.
10. Navigate to the **Libraries** tab and click **Add External JARs**.
11. Navigate to the folder `<ORACLE_HOME>\modules\` and select the following JAR file: `com.bea.core.xml.xmlbeans_2.1.0.0_2-5-1.jar` (actual version of the library while writing the book).
12. Click **Open** and then click **OK**.
13. Right-click on the **customer-xml-beans** project and select **New | Class** to create new Java class.
14. Enter `cookbook.model.services` into the **Package** field.
15. Enter `CustomerManagement` into the **Name** field and click **Finish**.
16. Add the following Java method to the **CustomerManagement** class:

```
public static XmlObject findCustomer(long id) throws XmlException
{
String customer = String
  .format("<?xml version=\"1.0\" encoding=\"UTF-8\"?>\n"
  + "<tns:Customer
    xmlns:credit=\"http://www.somecorp.com/creditcard\"
    xmlns:tns=\"http://www.somecorp.com/customer\"
    xmlns:xsi=\"http://www.w3.org/2001/XMLSchema-instance\">\n"
  + "<tns:ID>%s</tns:ID>\n"
  + "<tns:FirstName>Cookbook</tns:FirstName>\n"
  + "<tns:LastName>XmlObject</tns:LastName>\n"
  + "<tns:EmailAddress>osb.cookbook@packt.com
    </tns:EmailAddress>\n"
  + "<tns:Addresses>\n"
  + "<tns:Address>\n"
  + "<tns:Street>String</tns:Street>\n"
  + "<tns:PostalCode>String</tns:PostalCode>\n"
  + "<tns:City>String</tns:City>\n"
  + "<tns:Country>String</tns:Country>\n"
  + "</tns:Address>\n"
  + "</tns:Addresses>\n"
  + "<tns:BirthDate>1967-08-13</tns:BirthDate>\n"
  + "<tns:Rating>A</tns:Rating>\n"
```

```
        + "<tns:Gender>String</tns:Gender>\n"
        + "<tns:CreditCard>\n"
        + "<credit:CardIssuer>visa</credit:CardIssuer>\n"
        + "<credit:CardNumber>String</credit:CardNumber>\n"
        + "<credit:CardholderName>cookbook user
          </credit:CardholderName>\n"
        + "<credit:ExpirationDate>2012-01-01</credit:ExpirationDate>\n"
        + "<credit:CardValidationCode>2147483647
          </credit:CardValidationCode>\n"
        + "</tns:CreditCard>\n" + "</tns:Customer>\n",
        Long.toString(id));

        XmlObject customerXmlObject = XmlObject.Factory.parse(customer);
        return customerXmlObject;
    }
```

17. Right-click on the source and select **Source** | **Organize Imports**.

This method receives an ID and will return an XML message back. In order to be able to call the Java method from an OSB proxy service, we first have to create a JAR archive. In Eclipse OEPE, perform the following steps:

18. Right-click on the **customer-xml-beans** project and select **Export**.
19. Enter `java` into the **Select an export destination**, select **JAR file** and click **Next**.
20. In the **Select the resources to export** tree, select the **customer-xml-beans** project.
21. Click **Browse** right to the **JAR** file drop-down listbox.
22. Navigate to the `jar` folder inside the **using-java-callout-with-xmlbeans** OSB project, enter `customer-xml-beans.jar` into the **File name** field and click **Save**.
23. Click **Next** and then **Finish**.

Now we can continue with the implementation of our proxy service. In Eclipse OEPE, perform the following steps:

24. Refresh the `jar` folder by pressing *F5* and check that the JAR file created previously is located inside the `jar` folder.
25. Insert a **Java Callout** action into the **FindCustomer** stage.
26. On the **Properties** tab of the **Java Callout** action, click **Browse**.
27. Navigate to the `customer-xml-beans.jar` inside the `jar` folder and click **OK**.
28. Select the **public static org.apache.xmlbean.XmlObject findCustomer(long)** method and click **OK**.
29. Click the **Expression** link in the **Action** column.

30. Enter the value of `10` into the **Expression** field.
31. Enter `findCustomerResult` into the **Result Value** field.

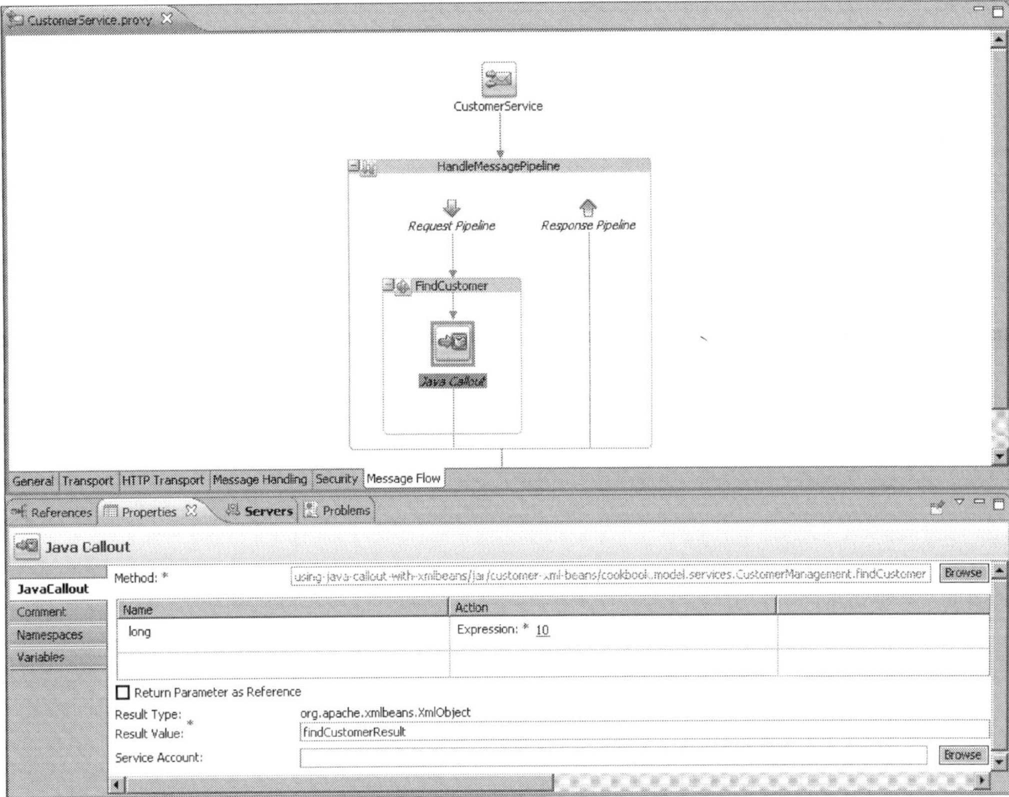

Let's add a **Replace** action to return the result in the `body` variable.

32. Insert a **Replace** action after the **Java Callout** action.
33. Enter `$findCustomerResult` into the **Expression** field.
34. Enter `body` into the **In Variable** field.
35. Deploy the project to the OSB server.

Let's test the proxy service by performing the following steps in the Service Bus console:

36. In the **Project Explorer**, navigate to the `proxy` folder inside the **using-java-callout-with-xml-beans** project.
37. Click on the **Launch Test Console** icon of **CustomerManagement** proxy service.
38. There is no **Request Document** needed, directly click on **Execute**.

39. The output of the **Java Callout** is shown in the **Response Document** section.

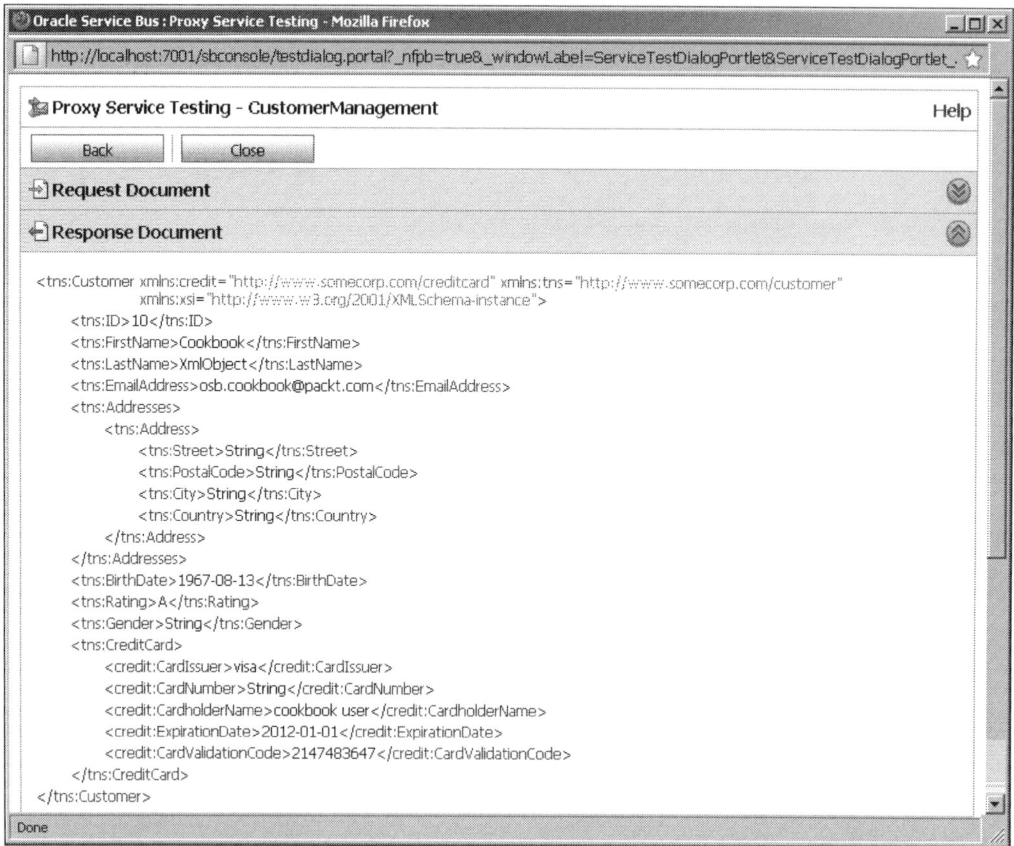

How it works...

This recipe showed how we can use the **Java Callout** action of the OSB to call a Java method which does not return Java primitive or String values, but whole XML messages using Apache XMLBeans. Inside the Java method, we just used normal String concatenation operations to first build the XML fragment as a String object and then we have used the XMLBean Factory to parse the string into an XMLObject.

The Java class is then made available to the proxy service as a Java Archive.

There's more...

We can also use XMLBeans to generate Java classes based on XML schema definitions and then use these generated classes in our Java class to build the XML document to return to the proxy service. This really simplifies the creation of the XML message compared to the approach of using String concatenation shown previously.

We will use an Ant script to first perform the generation of the Java classes. In Eclipse OEPE, perform the following steps:

1. Copy the `build.xml` and `build.properties` files from the `\chapter-9\getting-ready\using-java-callout-with-xmlbeans\misc` folder into the root of the **customer-xml-beans** project.
2. Open the `build.properties` file and configure the paths so they match the environment.
3. Copy the `schemas` folder from `\chapter-9\getting-ready\using-java-callout-with-xmlbeans\misc` folder into the root of the **customer-xml-beans** project.
4. Run Ant by right-clicking on `build.xml` build script and select **Run As | Ant Build**.

The Ant build generated the necessary Java classes representing the XML type definitions of the XML schemas. It also created a JAR file inside the `build/lib` folder. Now let's use the generated Java classes to build the corresponding XML message instead of the String concatenation used previously. In Eclipse OEPE, perform the following steps:

5. Navigate to the **CustomerManagement** class and add the following method:

```
public static CustomerTyp findCustomerObject(long id) {
    CustomerDocument custDoc =
        CustomerDocument.Factory.newInstance();
    CustomerTyp customer = custDoc.addNewCustomer();
    customer.setID(id);
    customer.setFirstName("Cookbook");
    customer.setLastName("XmlObject");
    customer.setEmailAddress("osb.cookbook@packt.com");
    customer.setAddresses(null);

    CreditCardDocument creditDoc =
        CreditCardDocument.Factory.newInstance();
    CreditCardTyp creditCard = creditDoc.addNewCreditCard();
    creditCard.setCardholderName("cookbook user");
    creditCard.setCardIssuer(CardIssuerTyp.VISA);
    customer.setCreditCard(creditCard);
    return customer;
}
```

6. Right-click on the source and select **Source | Organize Imports**.
7. Delete the `customer-xml-beans.jar` from the `build/lib` folder so that it is regenerated with the next run of the Ant build script.
8. Run Ant again, by right-clicking on `build.xml` build script and select **Run As | Ant Build**.

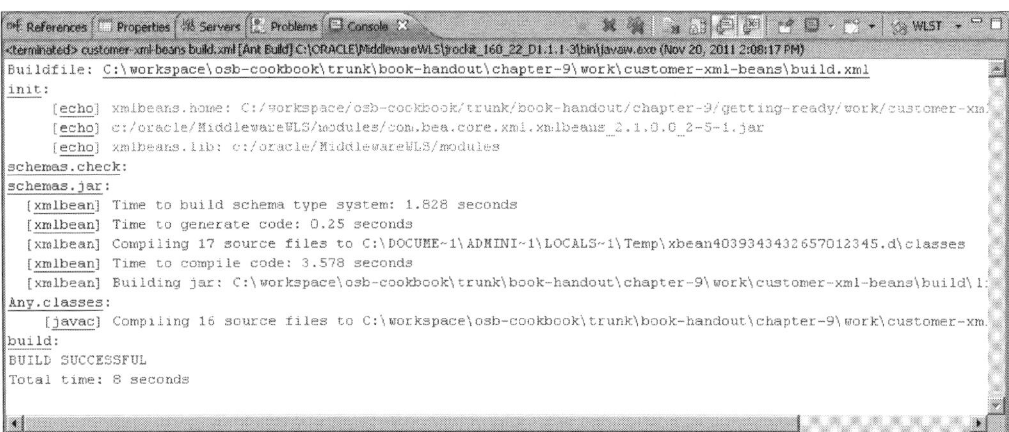

9. Copy the newly generated `customer-xml-beans.jar` into the `jar` folder inside the **using-the-java-callout-with-xmlbeans** Oracle Service Bus project.
10. Click **Yes** on the pop-up window to confirm overwriting the older one.

Now let's clone the proxy service from above and change it so that the new Java method is used in the **Java Callout** action. In Eclipse OEPE, perform the following steps:

11. Navigate back to the **using-the-java-callout-with-xmlbeans** project.
12. Right-click on the **CustomerManagement** proxy service and select **Copy**.
13. Right-click on the `proxy` folder and select **Paste**.
14. On the **Name Conflict** pop-up window, enter `CustomerManagement2.proxy` into the field.
15. Navigate to the **Transport** tab of the new proxy service and change the **Endpoint URI** field to `/using-java-callout-with-xmlbeans/proxy/CustomerManagement2`.
16. Navigate to the **Message Flow** tab.
17. On the **Properties** tab of the **Java Callout** action, click **Browse** to reselect the Java method.
18. Select the `customer-xml-beans.jar` inside the `jar` folder and click **OK**.

19. Select the **public static com.somecorp.customer.CustomerTyp findCustomerObject(long)** method inside the **cookbook.model.services.CustomerManagement** class and click **OK**.
20. Click the **Expression** link in the **Action** column, enter `10` into the **Expression** and click **OK**.
21. Enter `findCustomerResult` into the **Result Value** field.
22. Deploy the project to the OSB server.

Test the **CustomerManagement2** proxy service through the OSB Test console. The output should represent the XML message we have created with the new method.

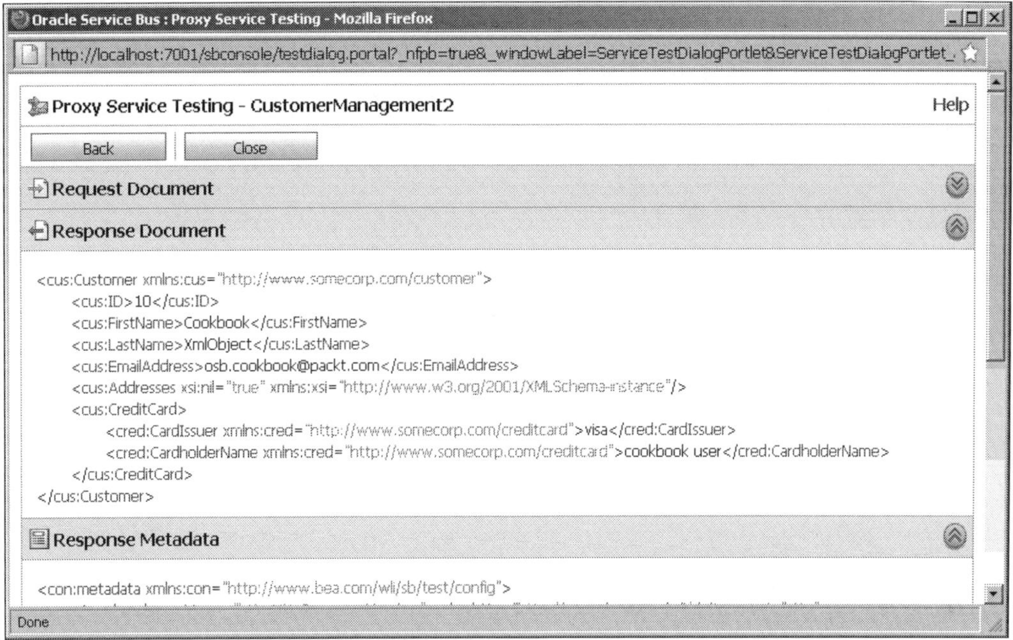

Building the XML message in the Java class is much easier and less-error prone through the Java classes generated by XMLBeans than through the String concatenation. There is an additional effort for creating the Java classes and for keeping them up-to-date if the XML schemas change, but this effort is worth it, comparing the two methods shown here with the usage of the String concatenation and the usage of the generated Java classes representing the XML schema types.

Using custom XPath functions

In this recipe, we will show how to implement custom XPath functions, which extends the collection of XPath functions available with the OSB platform. We will use the same functionality that we used in the *Using the Java Callout action to invoke Java code* recipe, but now make the calculate checksum functionality available as an XPath function.

Getting ready

You can import the OSB project containing the base setup for this recipe into Eclipse OEPE from `\chapter-9\getting-ready\using-custom-xpath-function`.

How to do it...

First we have to create the Java functionality we like to expose as a custom XPath function. We will reuse the same Java class we used in the *Using the Java Callout action to invoke Java code* recipe which is shown here:

```
package osbcookbook.util.checksum;

import java.util.zip.CRC32;
import java.util.zip.Checksum;

public class ChecksumUtil {
  public static long calculateChecksum(String data) {
    Checksum checksum = new CRC32();
    checksum.update(data.getBytes(), 0,
      data.getBytes().length);
    return checksum.getValue();
  }
}
```

A JAR with this class is available in `\chapter-9\getting-ready\misc\osb-checksum-util.jar`.

Next, we need to configure the XPath function on the OSB server and map it to the `calculateChecksum` method of the `ChecksumUtil` class. The configuration for the XPath functions is held in the `[WL_HOME]/Oracle_OSB1/config/xpath-functions`. Perform the following steps in an Explorer window.

1. Navigate to the `[WL_HOME]/Oracle_OSB1/config/xpath-functions` folder.
2. Copy the `osb-built-in.xml` file and paste it as a new file called `osb-cookbook.xml` which will hold the definition of the custom XPath function.

3. Open the `osb-cookbook.xml` file in an Editor.
4. Remove all the existing `<xpf:function>` elements and add our function as shown in the following screenshots:

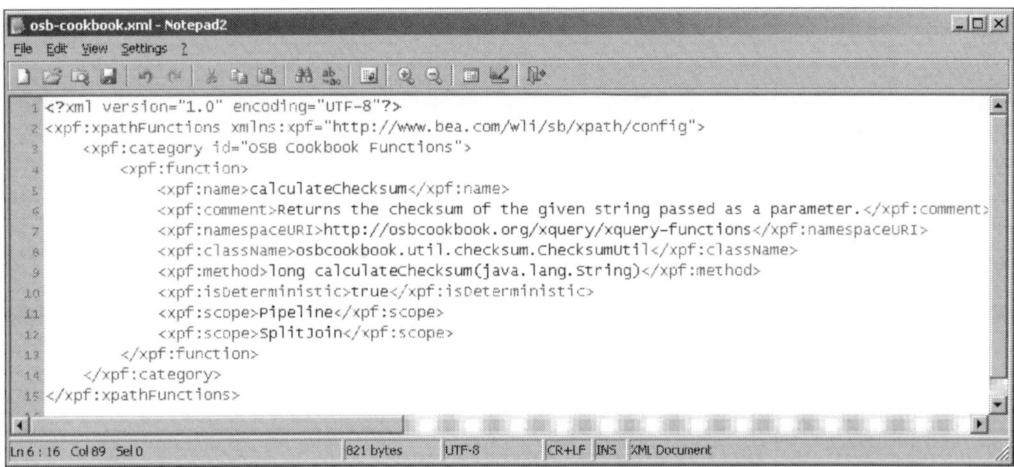

5. Save the file.

Now we have to make the JAR available to the OSB Server:

6. Copy `osb-checksum-util.jar` from the `\chapter-9\getting-ready\misc` to the `[WL_HOME]/Oracle_OSB1/config/xpath-functions` folder.
7. Restart both Eclipse OEPE and the OSB server to reload the configuration.

Now let's use our new XPath function. In Eclipse OEPE, perform the following steps:

8. Open the **Checksum** proxy service and navigate to the **Message Flow** tab.
9. Insert a **Replace** action into **CalculateChecksumStage**.
10. On the **Properties** tab of the **Replace** action, enter `body` into the **In Variable** field.

11. Click **<Expression>** and select the **XQuery Functions** tab.

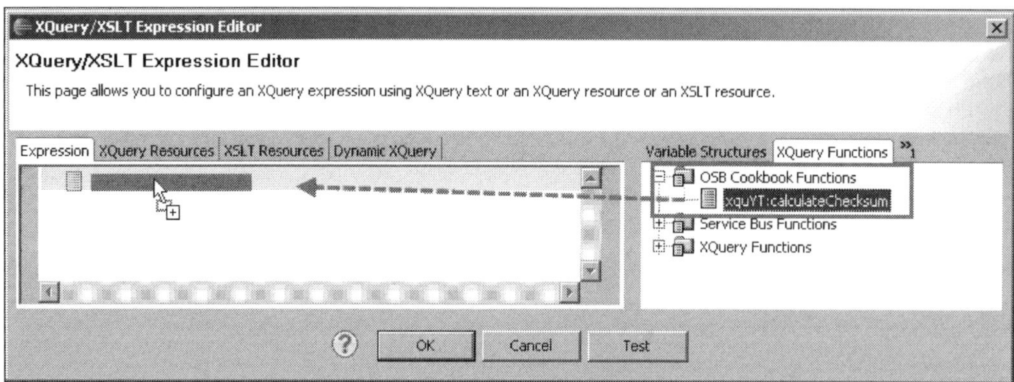

12. Replace the `$arg-string` in the parameter list by `$body/text()` and click **OK**.

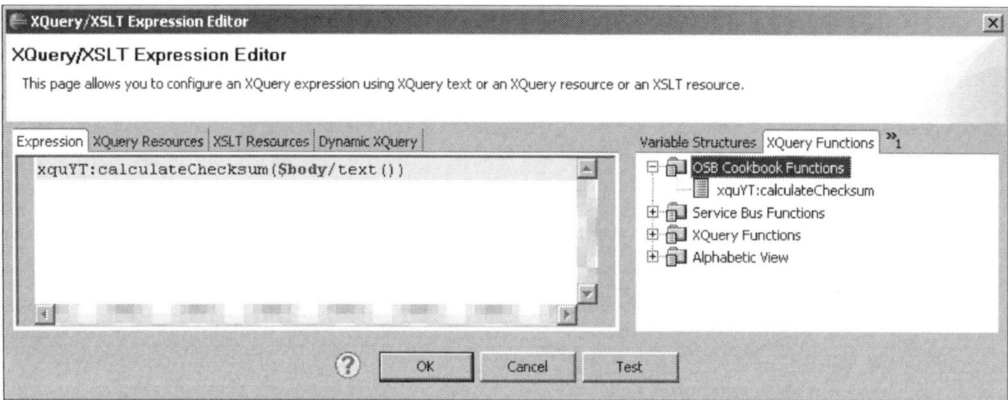

13. Select the **Replace node contents** option.
14. Deploy the project to the OSB server.

Now let's test the proxy service by performing the following steps in the Service Bus console:

15. In the **Project Explorer** navigate to `proxy` folder inside the **using-custom-xpath-function** project.
16. Click on the **Launch Test Console** icon of the **Checksum** proxy service.
17. Enter `This is some text on which the Checksum will be calculated!` into the **Payload** field and click **Execute**.
18. The output in the **Response Document** section should show the same checksum value `4265366956` as in the recipe with the **Java Callout** action.

How it works...

We have seen how we can extend the set of XPath functions available on the OSB platform by custom XPath function. A custom XPath function is implemented by some Java code. In order to map the Java functionality to the custom XPath function, the Java code needs to be exposed as a public static method in a public Java class.

The Java method should not produce side-effects; for example, it should not update any databases or participate in a global transaction. Such code should be invoked by a **Java Callout** action, as shown in the *Using the Java Callout action to invoke Java code* recipe.

A custom function will only appear in Eclipse OEPE if the OSB can find the Java class. Such a custom XPath function can be used both in inline XQuery expression, as shown with the Replace, and in XQuery resources, just as any other functions provided by the Oracle Service Bus.

The `isDeterministic` property in the configuration specifies whether the function is deterministic or non-deterministic. Deterministic functions always provide the same results whereas non-deterministic functions return the unique results. The XQuery standard recommends that functions should be deterministic, so that the XQuery engine is able to perform optimizations.

There's more...

A custom XPath function can also be invoked in an XQuery resource, as shown in the following screenshot:

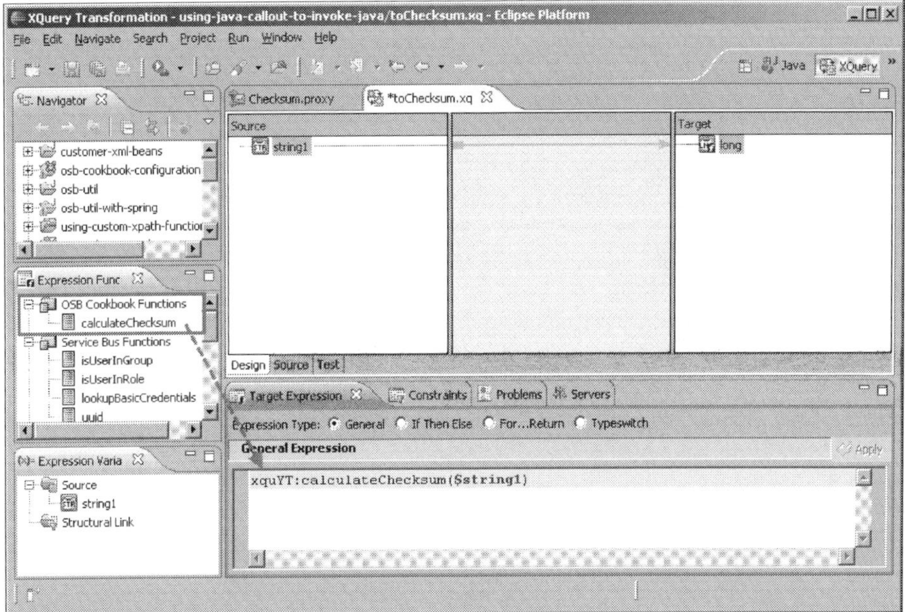

Just drag the XPath function from the **Expression Functions** tree into the **Expression** window, as with any other built-in XPath function.

Using the For Each action to process a collection

This recipe will show we can loop over a collection of information by using the **For Each** action. We will implement a proxy service accepting a **Customer** element through a one-way interface. The proxy service will use the **For Each** action in its message flow to loop over the single addresses inside the addresses collection.

Each address will then be sent to an **Address Checking Service** which would check the address for correctness. In our case, this service is a mock service implemented in soapUI. To better see the sequential nature of the processing, the **Address Checking Service** is written so that it takes four seconds to respond.

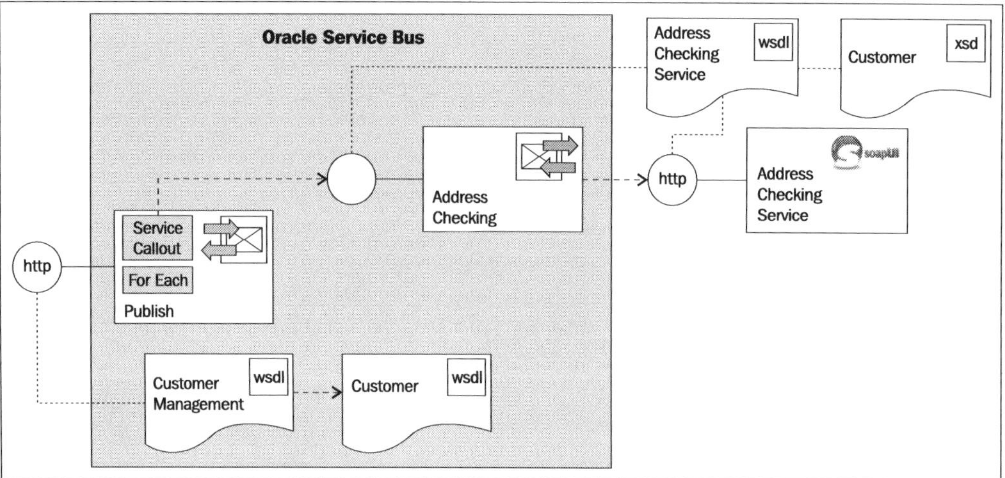

Getting ready

You can import the OSB project containing the base setup for this recipe into Eclipse OEPE from `\chapter-9\getting-ready\using-foreach-to-process-collection`.

Start the soapUI mock service simulating the **Address Checking Service** by double-clicking on `start-AddressCheckingService.cmd` in the `\chapter-9\getting-ready\misc` folder.

How to do it...

Let's create the proxy service with a one-way interface accepting a Customer XML Schema type. In Eclipse OEPE, perform the following steps:

1. In the **using-foreach-to-process-collections** project, open the **ForEach** proxy service and navigate to the **Message Flow** tab.
2. Insert a **Pipeline Pair** node into the **StoreCustomer** branch and name it `ProcessAddressesPipelinePair`.
3. Insert a **Stage** into the **Request Pipeline** and name it `ProcessAddressesStage`.
4. Insert a **For Each** action into the stage.
5. On the **Properties** tab of the **For Each** action, enter `address` into the **For Each Variable** field.
6. Click on the **<XPath>** link and enter `./cus1:StoreCustomer/Customer/cus:Addresses/cus:Address` into the **Expression** field.
7. Enter `body` into the **In Variable** field, `index` into the **Index Variable** field and `count` into the **Count Variable** field.

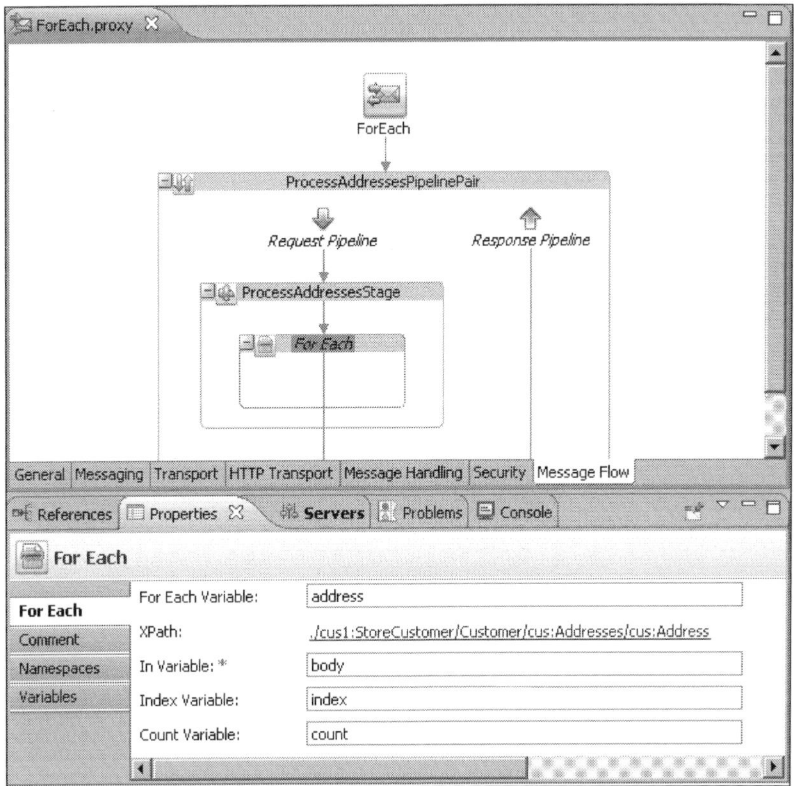

8. By doing that, we have implemented the loop over the addresses collection using a **For Each** action. But we are not yet doing anything inside the loop. So let's add a **Log** action to show a log output for each item (address) of the collection and pass the address to the **AddressChecking** business service. In Eclipse OEPE, perform the following steps:
9. Insert a **Log** action into the **For Each** action.
10. On the **Properties** tab of the **Log** action click **<Expression>**.
11. Enter `concat('Address ', $index, ' of ', $count, ' = ', $address)` into the **Expression** field and click **OK**.
12. Select **Warning** from the **Severity** drop-down listbox.
13. Insert a **Service Callout** action after the **Log** action.
14. On the **Properties** tab of the **Service Callout** action click **Browse** and then select the **AddressChecking** business service from `business` folder.
15. Select **CheckAddress** from the **Invoking** drop-down listbox.
16. Select the **Configure Payload Document** option.
17. Enter `request` into the **Request Variable** and `response` into the **Response Variable** field.
18. Insert an **Assign** action into the **Request Action** of the **Service Callout** action.
19. On the **Properties** tab of the **Assign** action click **<Expression>** and enter the following XML fragment into the **Expression** field:

```
<add:CheckAddress
  xmlns:add="http://www.osbcookbook.org/AddressCheckingService/">
  {$address}
</add:CheckAddress>
```

20. Click **OK**.

21. Enter `request` into the **Variable** field.

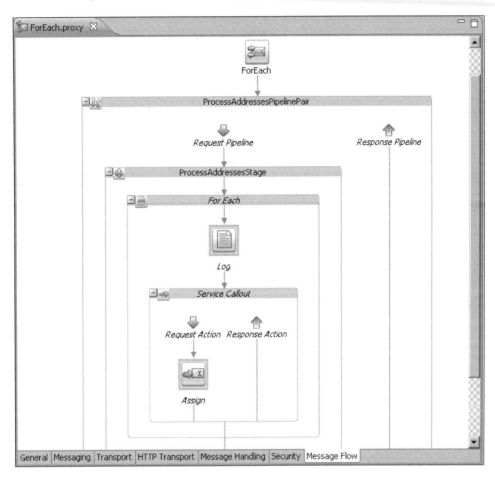

22. Deploy the project to the OSB server.

Now we can test the proxy service. In the Service Bus console, perform the following steps:

23. In the **Project Explorer** navigate to `proxy` folder inside the **using-foreach-to-process-collections** project.
24. Click on the **Launch Test Console** icon of the **ForEach** proxy service.

25. Enter a message with two addresses into the **Payload** field as shown in the following screenshot and click **Execute**.

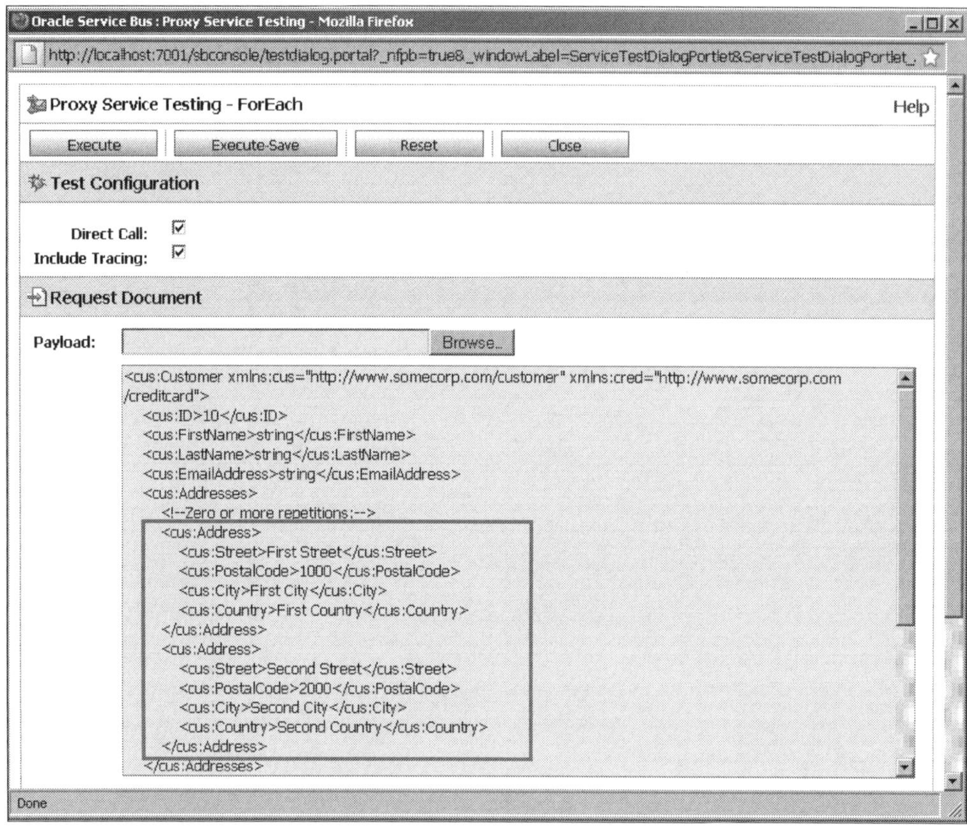

26. Two log statements should be shown in the Service Bus console log window, with a four seconds delay in between the first and the second.

```
OSB Cookbook 11R2 PS3 (11.1.1.4)
<20.11.2011 16:12 Uhr MEZ> <Warning> <ALSB Logging> <BEA-000000> < [ProcessAddre
ssesPipelinePair, ProcessAddressesPipelinePair_request, ProcessAddressesStage, R
EQUEST] Address 1 of 2 =
        First Street
        1000
        First City
        First Country
  >
<20.11.2011 16:12 Uhr MEZ> <Warning> <ALSB Logging> <BEA-000000> < [ProcessAddre
ssesPipelinePair, ProcessAddressesPipelinePair_request, ProcessAddressesStage, R
EQUEST] Address 2 of 2 =
        Second Street
        2000
        Second City
        Second Country
  >
```

27. The service will take around eight seconds to respond with the result window.

How it works...

The **For Each** action allows us to implement a loop to process each single item of a collection. The loop body can include all the different actions the Oracle Service Bus provides. However, it's not possible to include a node such as a **Pipeline Pair** or **Route** inside a loop. Therefore, it's not possible to execute a **Routing** action inside a loop. To call a service for each item of a collection, a **Service Callout** or **Publish** action has to be used in the loop body.

See also

- Check the *Using dynamic Split-Join to perform work in parallel* recipe to see how the processing can also be done in parallel by using a **Split-Join** instead of the **For Each** action.
- Check the *Using the Service Callout action to invoke a service* recipe to see the **Service Callout** action.

Using dynamic Split-Join to perform work in parallel

In this recipe, we will use the Split-Join functionality of the Oracle Service Bus to handle outgoing service callouts in parallel instead of the usually used sequential method.

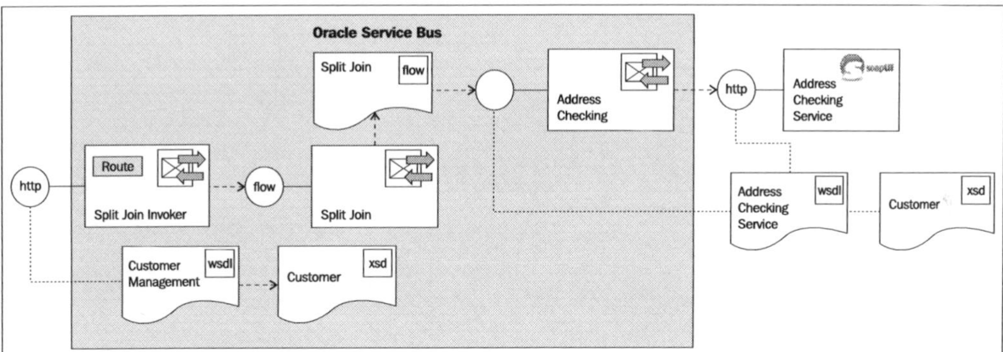

Getting ready

You can import the OSB project containing the base setup for this recipe into Eclipse OEPE from `\chapter-9\getting-ready\using-dynamic-split-join`.

Start the soapUI mock service simulating the **Address Checking Service** by double-clicking on `start-AddressCheckingService.cmd` in the `\chapter-9\getting-ready\misc` folder.

How to do it...

A Split-Join is a separate artifact, which we will create first. In Eclipse OEPE, perform the following steps:

1. Create an additional folder `flow` in the project **using-dynamic-split-join**.
2. Right-click on flow and select **New | Split-Join**.
3. Enter `SplitJoin` into the **File name** field and click **Next**.
4. Navigate to the **operation: StoreCustomer** node of the `CustomerManagement.wsdl` file and click **Finish**.
5. The **SplitJoin** flow artifact will be shown in the detail window.
6. Drag a **For Each** operation from the **Flow Control** section of the **Design Palette** to the flow between **Receive** and **Reply**.

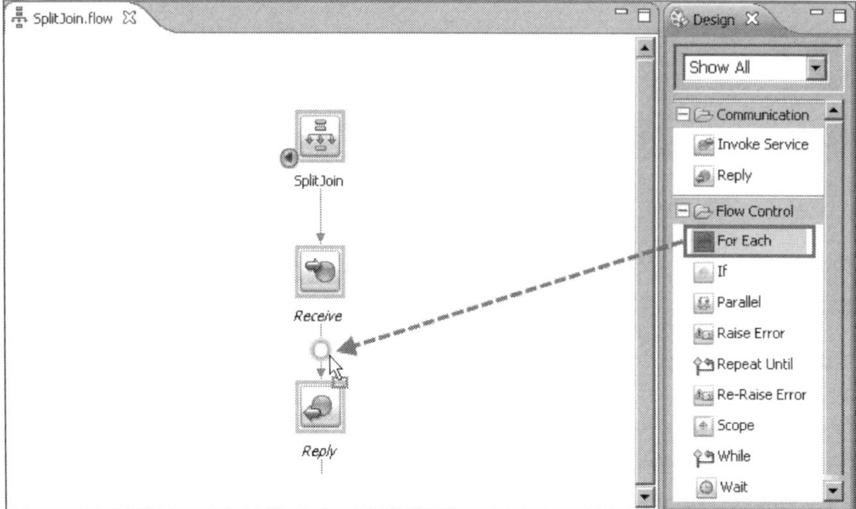

7. On the **Properties** tab of the **For Each** operation, click **<Counter Name>** and enter `counter` into the **Counter Variable Name** field on the pop-up window. Click **OK**.
8. Enter `number(1)` into the **Start Counter Value** field.

9. Enter `count($request.parameters/Customer/cus:Addresses/cus:Address)` into the **Final Counter Value** field.

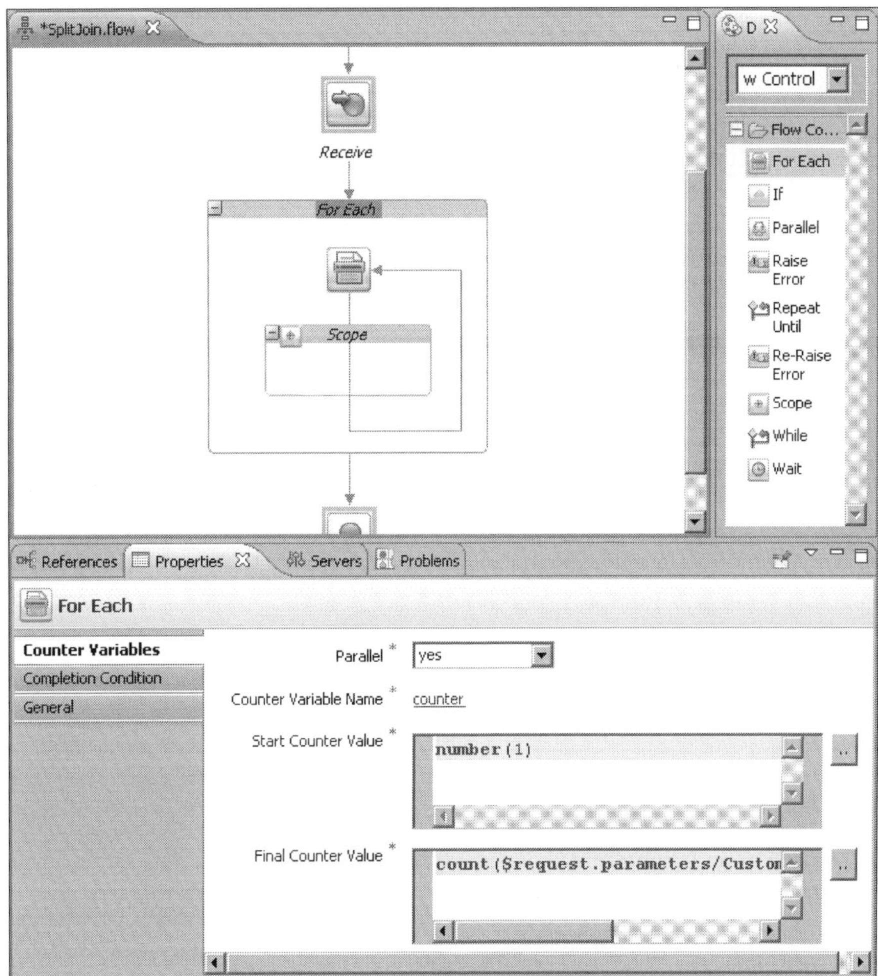

10. Drag an **Invoke Service** operation from the **Communication** section of the **Design Palette** into the **For Each** operation.
11. On the **Properties** tab of the **Invoke Service** operation, click **Browse** and select the **operation: CheckAddress** node from the **AddressChecking** business service in the `business` folder.
12. Click **OK**.

13. Navigate to the **Input Variable** tab and select the **Create Message Variable** item of the **Message Variable** drop-down listbox.
14. Enter `addressCheckRequest` into the **Name** field and click **OK**.
15. Navigate to the **Output Variable** tab and select the **Create Message Variable** item of the **Message Variable** drop-down listbox.
16. Enter `addressCheckResponse` into the **Name** field and click **OK**.
17. Drag an **Assign** operation from the **Assign Operations** section of the **Design Palette** and drop it before the **Invoke Service** operation.
18. On the **Properties** tab of the **Assign**, select **addressCheckRequest.parameters** from the **Variable** drop-down listbox.
19. Click on **<Expression>** and enter the following XML fragment into the **Expression** field:

```
<add:CheckAddress
  xmlns:add="http://www.osbcookbook.org/AddressCheckingService/">
{$request.parameters/Customer/cus:Addresses/cus:Address[$counter]}
</add:CheckAddress>
```

20. Click **OK**.
21. Drag an **Assign** operation from the **Assign Operations** section of the **Design Palette** and drop it after the **Invoke Service** operation.

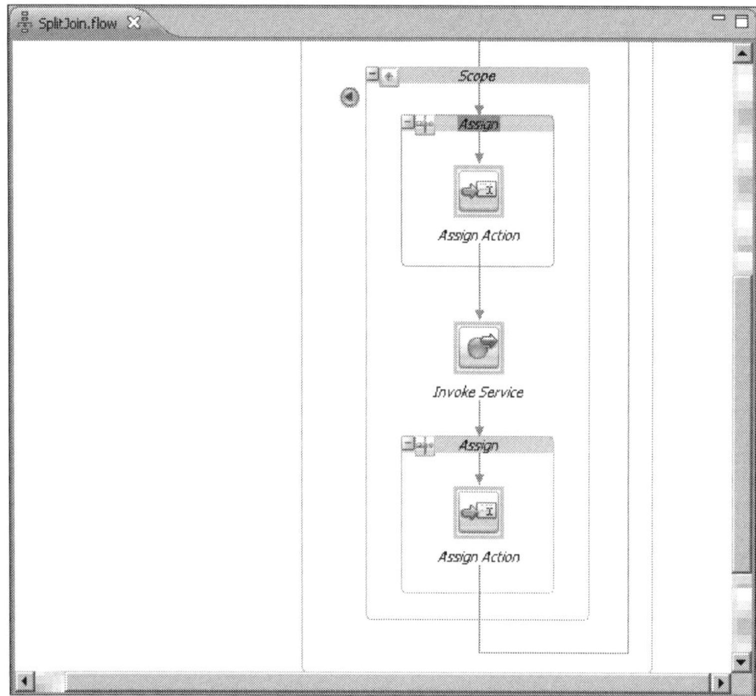

22. On the **Properties** tab of the **Assign**, select **response.parameters** from the **Variable** drop-down listbox.
23. Click on **<Expression>** and enter the following XML fragment into the **Expression** field:

    ```
    <out>COMPLETED</out>
    ```

We have successfully created the Split-Join flow artifact. Now, let's create the business service, which will invoke the Split-Joint through the **flow** transport. The business service can easily be generated by performing the following steps in Eclipse OEPE:

24. Right-click on the **SplitJoin.flow** artifact and select **Oracle Service Bus | Generate Business Service**.
25. Select the `business` folder in the **Service Location** tree and enter `SplitJoin` into the **Service Name** field and click **OK**.

Now, let's add the call of the business service to the already existing **SplitJoinInvoker** proxy service. In Eclipse OEPE, perform the following steps:

26. Open the **SplitJoinInvoker** proxy service and navigate to the **Message Flow** tab.
27. Insert a **Route** node into the **StoreCustomer** branch and name it `InvokeSplitJoinRoute`.
28. Insert a **Routing** action into the **Route** node.
29. On the **Properties** tab of the **Routing** action, click **Browse** and select the **SplitJoin** business service. Click **OK**.
30. Select the **StoreCustomer** operation from the **Invoking** drop-down listbox.
31. Deploy the project to the OSB server.

Now, we can test the proxy service. In the Service Bus console, perform the following steps:

32. In the **Project Explorer** navigate to `proxy` folder inside the **using-dynamic-split-join** project.
33. Click on the **Launch Test Console** icon of the **SplitJoinInvoker** proxy service.
34. Select the **StoreCustomer** operation from the **Available Operations** drop-down listbox.

35. Enter a message with two addresses into the **Payload** field as shown in the following screenshot:

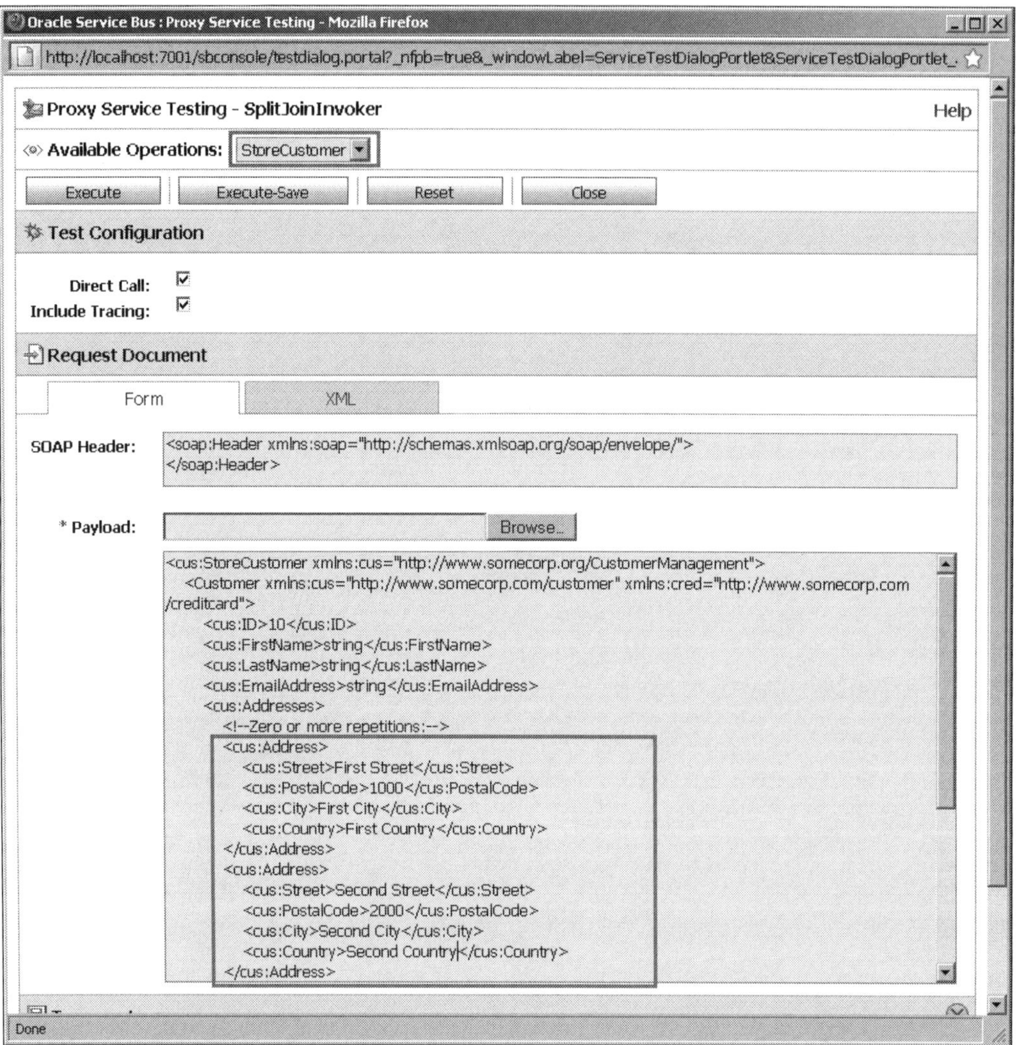

36. Click on **Execute**.
37. It should not take more than four seconds until the Test console response window is shown (each single **Address Checking Service** call is taking four seconds to answer).
38. Click **Back** to retest.
39. Enter a message with four addresses into the **Payload** field and click **Execute**.
40. It should still take about four seconds until the response window is shown. The four calls to the **Address Checking Service** are done in parallel.

How it works...

We have seen how the OSB's advanced mediation feature, called Split-Join, can help to improve the performance of the service by concurrently processing individual parts of a message. The Split-Join first splits the input message payload into submessages (split), processes these submessages concurrently and then aggregates the responses into one return message (join). In our case, the splitting has been done on the collection of addresses in the customer request message and the concurrent processing involves the invocation of the **Address Checking Service** in parallel.

Split-Joins are useful for optimizing the overall response time when parts of the request messages need to be processed by slower services, that is, each individual address has to be handled by a call to the **Address Checking Service**, taking four seconds to respond. Because of the parallel nature, the whole Split-Join finishes in little more than four seconds. This is a huge benefit compared to the solution with the **For Each** action shown in the *Using the For Each action to process a collection* recipe.

The Split-Join of the Oracle Service Bus comes in two flavors:

- **Static Split-Join** – branches from the main execution thread of the OSB message flow by splitting the payload into a fixed number of branches according to the configuration of the Split-Join at design time.
- **Dynamic Split-Join** – branches from the main execution thread of the OSB message flow by dynamically creating new branches according to the contents of the incoming payload. Conditional logic is used to determine the number of branches at runtime.

In this recipe, we have used the dynamic Split-Join.

See also

Check the *Using the For Each action to process a collection* recipe to see how the processing of the addresses can be done sequentially inside the OSB message flow using a **For Each** action.

Using the Validate action to perform message validation

In this recipe, we will show how to use the **Validate** action to perform message validation. We will use the same proxy service setup we have used in the *Using the For Each action to process a collection* recipe, with a proxy service with a **Messaging Service** type interface accepting a customer element. We will use the **Validate** action in the proxy service to make sure that the message passed in is a valid customer.

Getting ready

You can import the OSB project containing the base setup for this recipe into Eclipse OEPE from `\chapter-9\getting-ready\using-validate-to-do-message-validation`.

How to do it...

Let's add the **Validate** action to the proxy service we imported previously in the *Getting ready* section. In Eclipse OEPE, perform the following steps:

1. Open the **MessageValidation** proxy service and navigate to the **Message Flow** tab.
2. Insert a new stage into the **MessageProcessingPipelinePair** and name it `MessageValidationStage`.
3. Insert a **Validate** action into the stage.
4. On the **Properties** tab of the **Validate** action, enter `body` into the **In Variable** field.
5. Click **<XPath>** and enter `./cus:Customer` into the **Expression** field. Click **OK**.
6. Click **Browse** to the right of **Against Resource** and select the **Customer (element)** in the **xsd/Customer.xsd** XML Schema. Click **OK**.
7. Select the **Raise Error** option.
8. Deploy the project to the OSB server.

Now let's test the validation of our proxy service. In the Service Bus console, perform the following steps:

9. In the **Project Explorer** navigate to `proxy` folder inside the **using-validate-to-do-message-validation** project.
10. Click on the **Launch Test Console** icon of the **MessageValidation** proxy service.

11. Enter a message with an invalid **CardIssuer** (only the lowercase values **visa** and **mastercard** are valid) and click **Execute**.

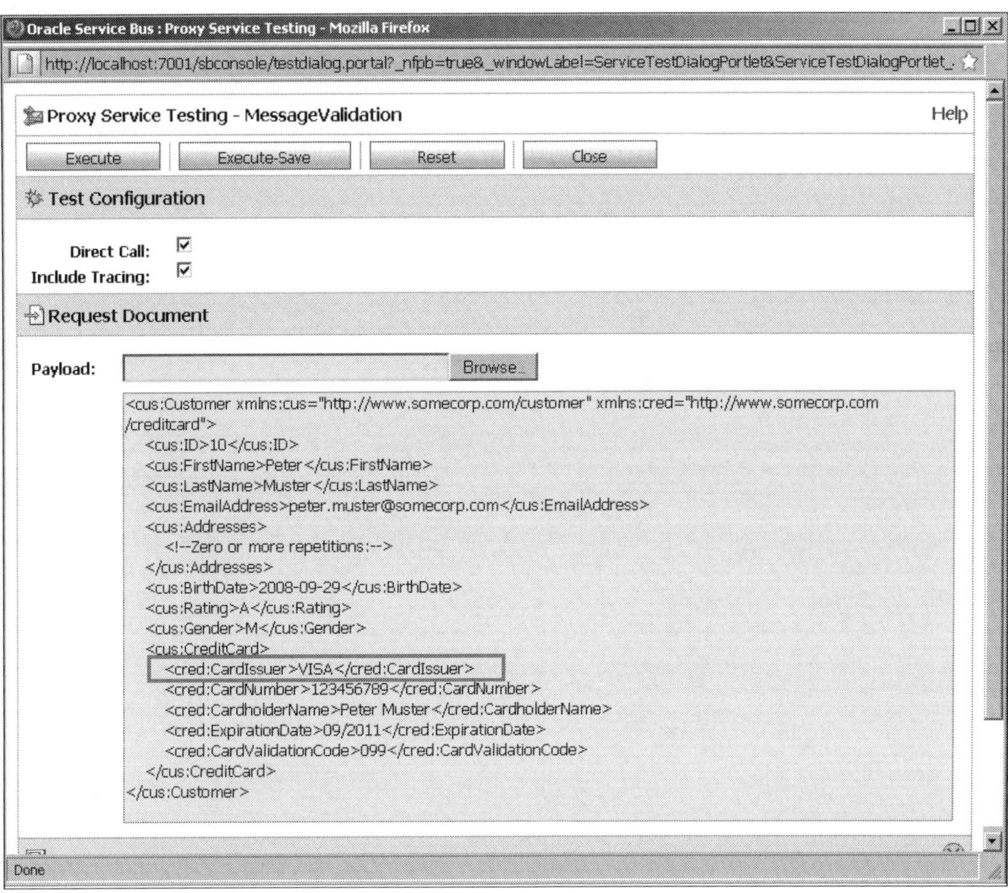

12. The **Validate** action will raise a validation error, which is shown in the following screenshot:

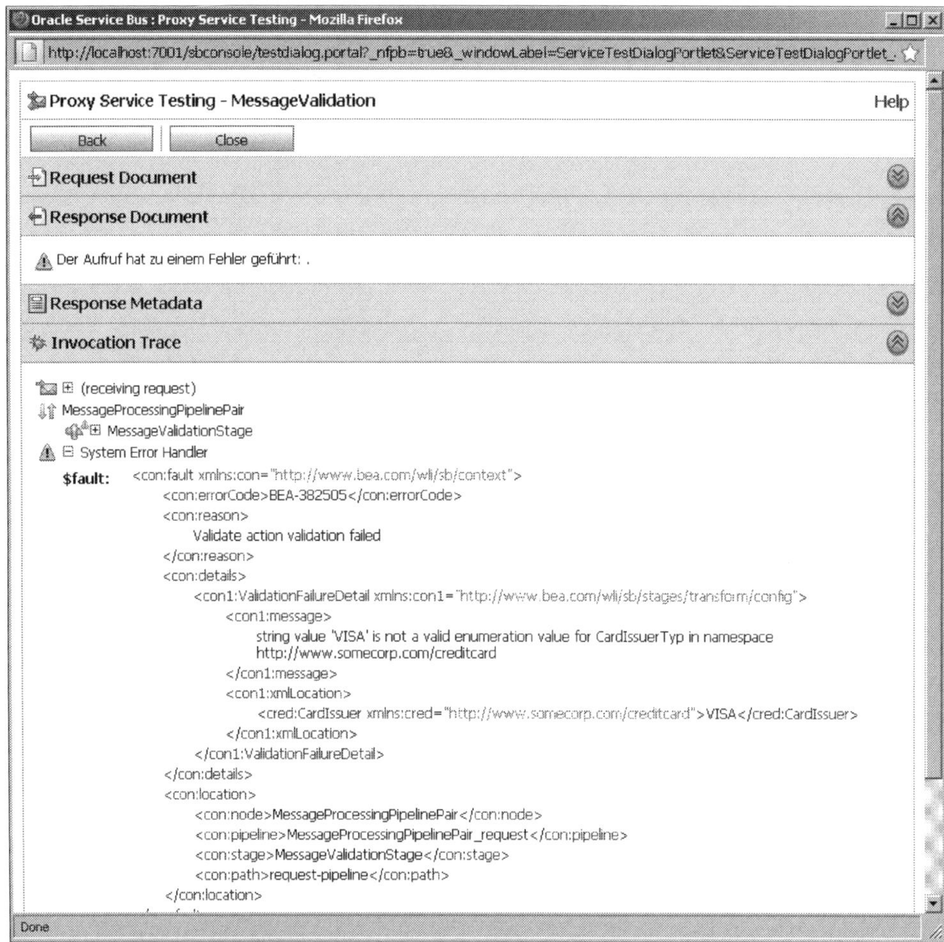

How it works...

The **Validate** action can be used to check the content of any variable against an element or type of an XML schema. The validation can be configured to either save the Boolean result of the validation in a variable or to raise an error if the validation fails. An error will hold the error code `BEA-382505` and the message will hold further details about the failed validation.

By using the XPath expression, it's also possible to only check fragments, inside a larger XML message, for validity.

The **Validate** action cannot be disabled, if it's included in the **Message Flow** tab, then it will always be executed. To programmatically exclude it, it can be wrapped inside an **If Then** action. Refer the *Enabling/Disabling a Validate action dynamically* recipe for how to achieve that.

Enabling/disabling a Validate action dynamically

In the previous recipe, we have seen how to use a **Validate** action for performing message validation. The problem of using message validation is that it can involve quite some overhead and often it's no longer necessary after some period of testing. Instead of removing it from the code, it would be nice to keep it in the code, so that it can be enabled dynamically if needed. This recipe will show how this can be achieved with a **Java Callout** and an **If Else** action.

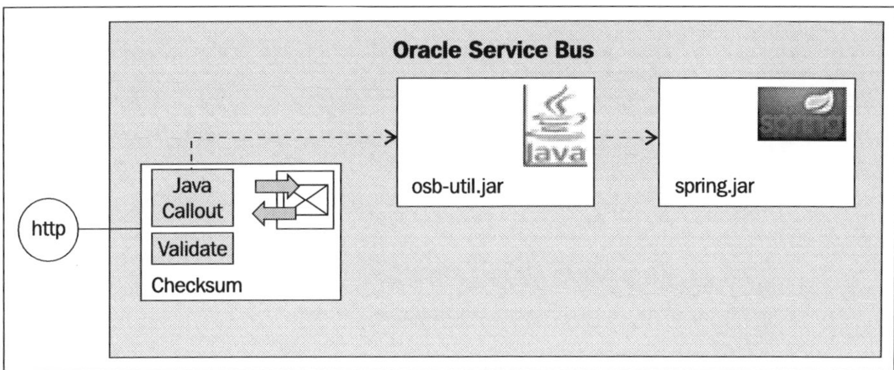

The **Java Callout** action will invoke a Java method which accesses a bean configured by the Spring framework application context. This bean holds the condition of whether the validation should be performed or not. Spring makes it easy to expose a bean through JMX, which we will use to dynamically enable/disable the message validation.

Getting ready

You can import the OSB project containing the solution of the previous recipe into Eclipse OEPE from `\chapter-9\getting-ready\enabling-validate-dynamically`. We will continue from there and add to the solution of the previous recipe.

How to do it...

We will start with the necessary Java logic supporting the enabling/disabling of the validation. The Java Class `ValidationUtil` will be invoked through the **Java Callout** action and holds a static method called `shouldValidate()`.

```
public class ValidationUtil {
    private static ApplicationContext ctx =
        new ClassPathXmlApplicationContext
        ("classpath:applicationContext.xml");

    public static boolean shouldValidate() {
        ValidationConfiguration config = (ValidationConfiguration)
            ctx.getBean("validationConfiguration");
        return config.isValidationEnabled();
    }
}
```

This method retrieves a Spring bean called `validationConfiguration` from the Spring application context. The `ValidationConfiguration` Java class holds a `ValiationEnabled` Boolean property. The value of the property is exposed to JMX through the `@ManagedResource` and `@ManagedAttribute` annotations.

```
@ManagedResource
public class ValidationConfiguration {
    private boolean validationEnabled = true;

    @ManagedAttribute
    public boolean isValidationEnabled() {
        return validationEnabled;
    }

    @ManagedAttribute
    public void setValidationEnabled(boolean validationEnabled) {
        this.validationEnabled = validationEnabled;
    }

}
```

The Spring application context defines the `validationConfiguration` bean and makes sure that the bean annotated by `@ManagedResource` is exposed by JMX.

```
<?xml version="1.0" encoding="UTF-8"?>
<beans xmlns="http://www.springframework.org/schema/beans"
    xmlns:xsi="http://www.w3.org/2001/XMLSchema-instance"
```

```
    xmlns:context="http://www.springframework.org/schema/context"
    xsi:schemaLocation="http://www.springframework.org/schema/beans
    http://www.springframework.org/schema/beans/spring-beans-2.5.xsd
    http://www.springframework.org/schema/context
    http://www.springframework.org/schema/context/
        spring-context-2.5.xsd">

    <context:mbean-export/>

    <bean id="validationConfiguration"
        class="osbcookbook.util.validation.ValidationConfiguration">
    <property name="validationEnabled" value="true"/>
    </bean>

</beans>
```

The complete Java project with this code is available in `\chapter-9\solution\java\osb-validation-util`. The JAR file of that project has already been created and resides inside the `JAR` folder of the imported OSB project.

Let's adapt the proxy service so that the **Validate** action is only executed, if the flag in the `ValdationConfiguration` is set to true. We will use a **Java Callout** action to invoke the `ValdationUtil` and process the return value by an **If Then** action. In Eclipse OEPE, perform the following steps:

1. Open the **MessageValidation** proxy service and navigate to the **Message Flow** tab.
2. Insert a **Java Callout** action right before the **Validate** action.
3. On the **Properties** tab of the **Java Callout** action, click **Browse** and select the `osb-validation-util.jar` file in the `jar` folder of the **enabling-validate-dynamically** project. Click **OK**.
4. Select the **public static Boolean shouldValidate()** Java method and click **OK**.
5. Enter `shouldValidate` into the **Result Value** field.
6. Insert an **If Then** action after the **Java Callout** action.
7. Click on the **If:<Condition>** branch in the message flow and on the **Properties** tab click **<Condition>**.
8. Enter `string($shouldValidate) = 'true'` into the **Expression** field and click **OK**.

9. Drag the **Validate** action into the **If: string** branch.

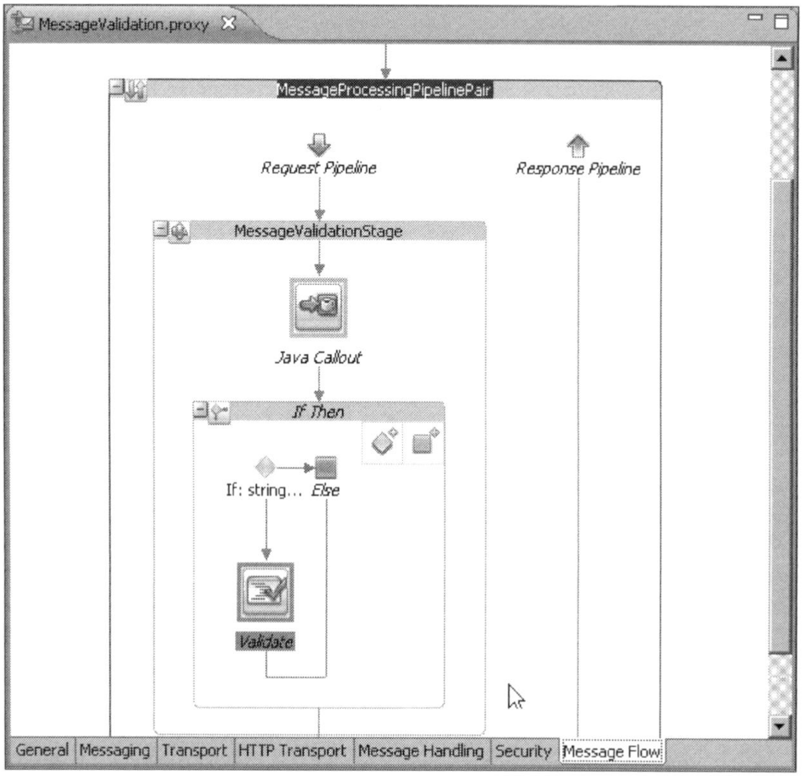

10. Deploy the project to the OSB server.

Now, let's test the validation of our proxy service. In the Service Bus console, perform the following steps:

11. In the **Project Explorer** navigate to `proxy` folder inside the **enabling-validate-dynamically** project.
12. Click on the **Launch Test Console** icon of the **MessageValidation** proxy service.
13. Enter a message with an invalid **CardIssuer** (only the lowercase values **visa** and **mastercard** are valid) and a validation error should be returned.

We can see that the validation is enabled by default. Now, let's disable the validation by changing the `ValidationEnabled` flag to `false` through a JMX, without having to redeploy the proxy service.

14. Launch a command line window and enter `jconsole` to start Java console.
15. In the **New Connection** screen select **weblogic.Server** from the **Local Process** listbox and click **Connect**.

16. Navigate to the **MBeans** tab.
17. From the tree on the left, select the `ValidationEnabled` attribute of the `ValidationConfiguration` class.
18. Enter `false` into the **Value** column and click **Refresh**.

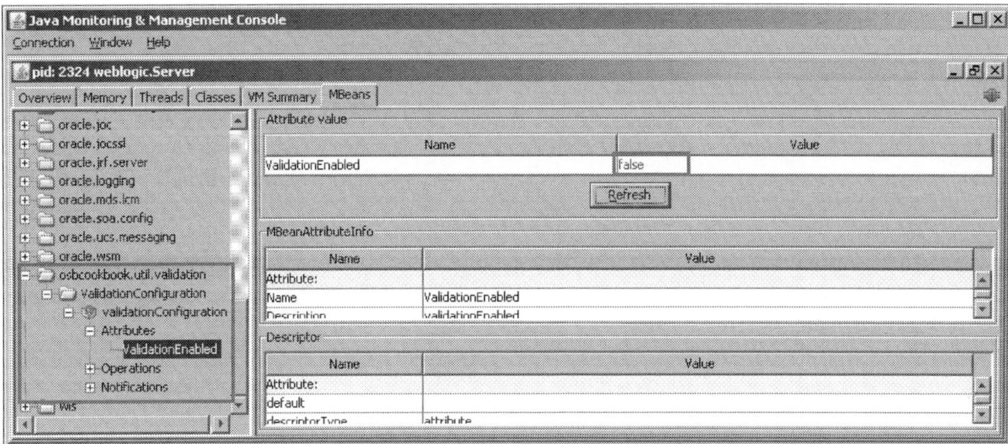

Now, let's retest the validation. In the Service Bus console, perform the following steps:

19. In the **Project Explorer** navigate to `proxy` folder inside the **enabling-validate-dynamically** project.
20. Click on the **Launch Test Console** icon of the **MessageValidation** proxy service.
21. Enter a message with an invalid **CardIssuer** (only the lowercase values **visa** and **mastercard** are valid). Because we have disabled the validation, the validation error will no longer occur.

How it works...

In this recipe, we have added a condition around the **Validate** action, so that the message validation can be enabled/disabled at runtime. The condition is based on a Boolean flag, which we get through a **Java Callout** action. Because we have used Spring with its possibility to easily expose beans as JMX managed beans, we were able to change the value of the flag on the fly, using any program which supports JMX, such as the JConsole.

Creating private proxy service

In this recipe, we will create a proxy service which can be reused and which is only available for other proxy services within the same OSB configuration, therefore we call it *private* proxy service in this recipe. The setup of the recipe is shown in the following screenshot:

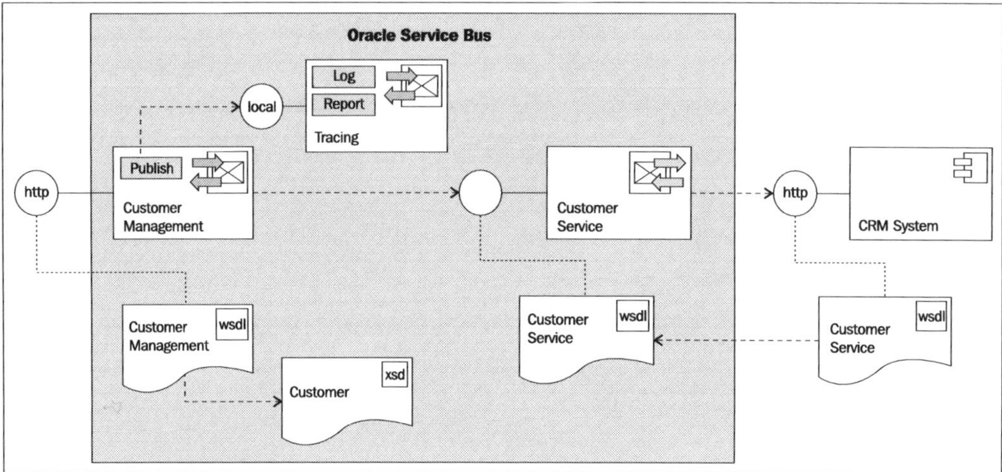

Getting ready

Make sure to have the latest state of the `basic-osb-service` project from the first chapter available in Eclipse OEPE. We will use it for this recipe. If necessary, it can be imported from here: `\chapter-1\solution\with-transformation-proxy-service-created`.

How to do it...

First, we will create a new proxy service which will provide the internal functionality that can be reused by other proxy services. In Eclipse OEPE, perform the following steps:

1. Create a new proxy service in the `proxy` folder and name it `Tracing`.
2. On the **General** tab choose **Any XML Service** for the **Service Type** option.
3. On the **Transport** tab choose **local** from the protocol drop-down listbox.
4. Navigate to the **Message Flow** tab and add a **Pipeline Pair** node and name it `TracingPipeline`.
5. Insert a **Stage** into the **Request Pipeline** and name it `TracingStage`.
6. Insert a **Log** action into the **Stage**.
7. On the **Properties** tab of the **Log** action, click on **<Expression>**.

8. Enter `$body/custom/correlationID/text()` into the **Expression** field.
9. Enter `Message received with ID` into the **Annotation** field.
10. Select **Warning** from the **Severity** drop-down listbox.
11. Insert a **Report** action after the **Log** action just created previously.
12. On the **Properties** tab of the **Report** action, click **<Expression>**.
13. Enter `$body` into the **Expression** field and click **OK**.
14. Click **Add a Key**.
15. Enter `CorrelationId` into the **Name** field.
16. Click on **<XPath>** and enter `./custom/correlationID` into the **Expression** field and click **OK**.
17. Enter `body` into the **In Variable** field.

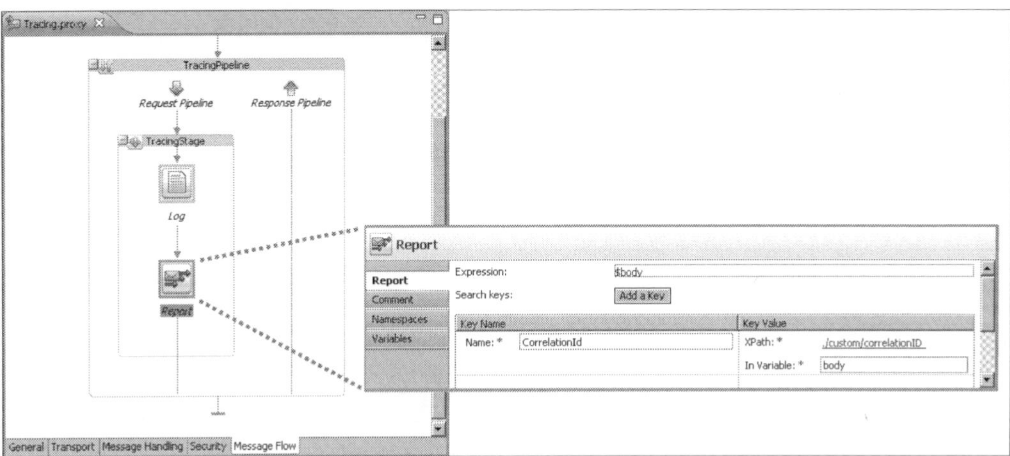

Our reusable tracing functionality is now available. Let's use it from the **CustomerManagement** proxy service.

18. Open **CustomerManagement** proxy service and navigate to **Message Flow** tab.
19. Navigate to the **Design Palette** and drag a **Publish Action** from the **Stage Actions** into the **Request Action** of the **Routing** action in the **StoreCustomerRoute** node.
20. On the **Properties** tab of the **Publish** action click **Browse**.
21. Select the **Tracing** proxy service and click **OK**.
22. Add a **Replace** action into the **Request Action** flow of the **Publish** action.
23. On the **Properties** tab of the **Replace** action, enter `body` into the **In Variable** field
24. Click **<Expression>**, enter `$header/custom` into the **Expression** field and click **OK**.

25. Select the **Replace node contents** option.
26. Copy the created **Publish** action into the **Request Action** of the **Routing** action of the **FindCustomerRoute** node.

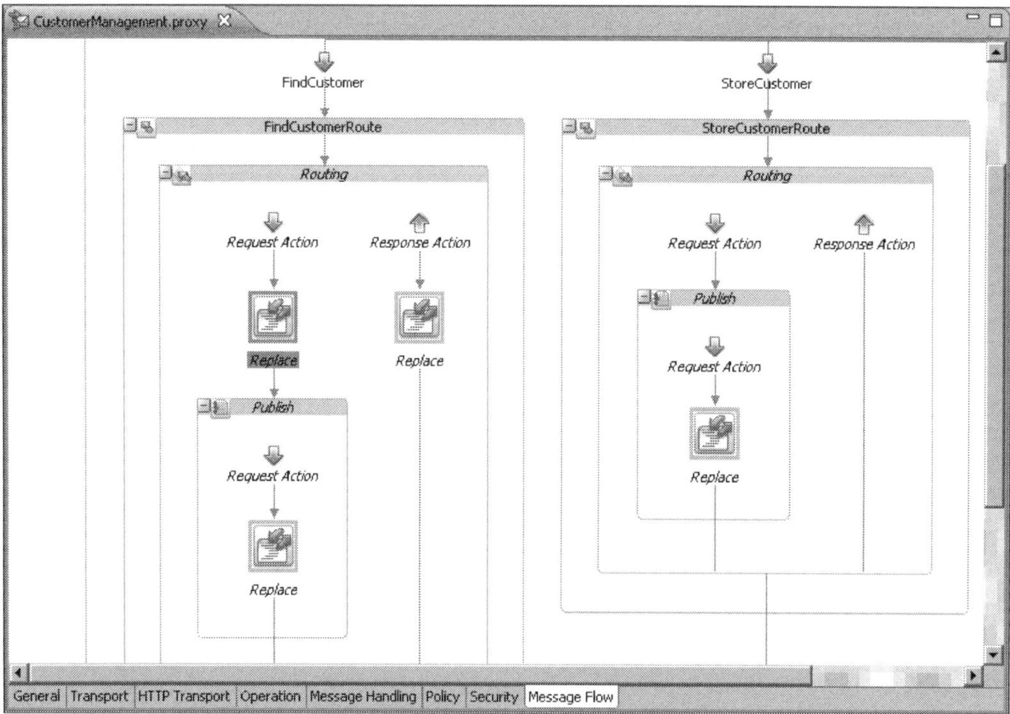

27. Deploy the project to the OSB server.

Now, let's test the added functionality through the Test console. In the Service Bus console, perform the following steps:

28. In the **Project Explorer**, navigate to the **CustomerManagement** proxy service and click on **Launch Test Console** icon.
29. In the **SOAP Header** field insert `<custom><correlationID>abcd1234</correlationID></custom>` in between the **soap:Header** element and click **Execute**.

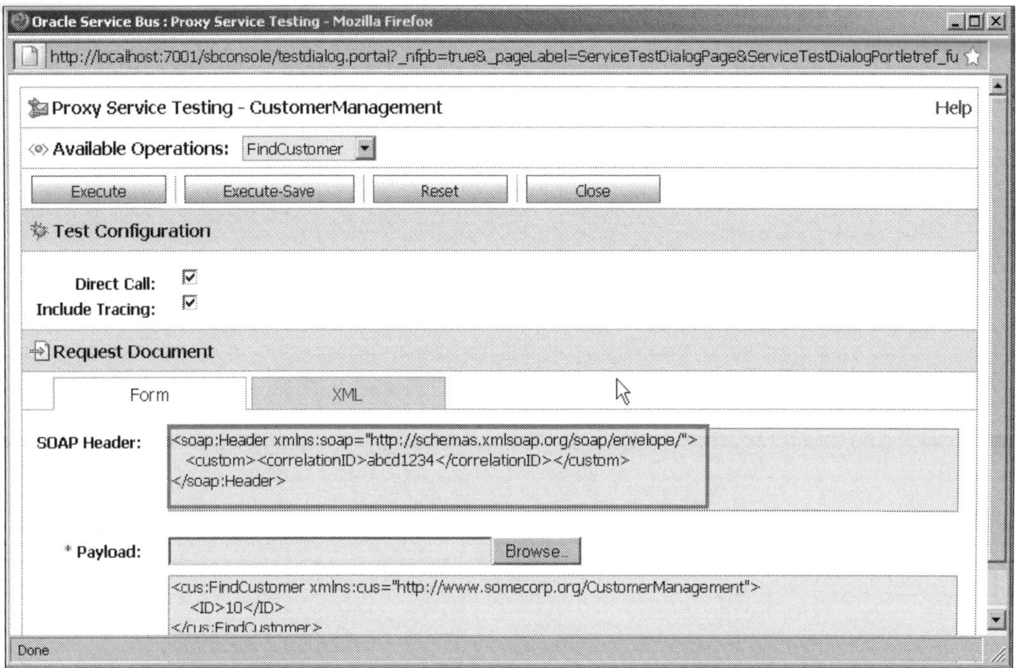

How it works...

The **CustomerManagement** proxy service calls the **Tracing** proxy for all incoming messages. Because we have used a **Publish** action instead of a **Service Callout** action, the **Tracing** proxy gets invoked by the **CustomerManagement** proxy service without waiting for any response. The information written by the **Reporting** action can be viewed through the Oracle Service Bus console by clicking on **Message Reports** in the **Reporting** section.

When using the **Local** transport for a proxy service, as shown in this recipe for the **Tracing** proxy service, no **Endpoint URI** has to be configured. The reason for that is that a local proxy service can never be called from outside the OSB; it's only available for other proxy services within the same OSB.

We used a simple example to centrally use the **Log** and **Report** action of the OSB. However, private proxy services can be used for multiple tasks which have a high repetitive nature. Think of error handling or similar transformation of XML messages in multiple operations.

10
Reliable Communication with the OSB

In this chapter, we will cover the following topics:

- Configuring Retry handling in JMS
- Enabling JMS Message Persistence
- Working with global transactions and Quality of Service
- Using Reliable Messaging (WS-RM) with WS transport
- Sending SOAP over JMS

Introduction

The consequence of not thinking about reliable communication or not implementing it in our OSB services can lead to many problems in case of error. It can lead to the loss of your messages, a destination can receive multiple messages and this means that the sending application can't trust the service bus. The application needs to monitor its own requests.

Reliable communication is all about Distributed Transactions—**XA**, **Quality of Service** (**QoS**), and persistence.

XA is a transaction that can be shared across multiple resources such as a JMS queue, coherence, direct binding, JCA binding, or an EJB session bean. Be aware that the HTTP transport does not support XA and can't take part in the so called global transaction. When an OSB transport or a JCA adapter starts a transaction, this transaction will be handled or controlled by the **Java Transaction API** (**JTA**) of the WebLogic server. XA will use a two-phase commit so all resources either do a commit or a rollback together.

When a destination does not take part in the global transaction, the message can be delivered more than once if there is a rollback and the OSB process is retried.

Besides XA, QoS is also important for reliable communication. With QoS. We can also control if the destination will take part in the global transaction. Choose, for example, *exactly Once* for joining the global transaction or *best effort* for not. *Exactly once* means reliability through message assurance, as the OSB is trying to deliver the messages from inbound to outbound exactly once.

With XA and QoS, it is possible to create a loop when there is a rollback and the messages are retried infinitely. This leads to **Denial of Service** (**DOS**) on the OSB server. When the message is retried and the destination does not take part in the global transaction, then it is possible that the message is delivered to the destination more than once.

The third aspect of reliable communication is persistence. Persistence is important when the WebLogic server goes down unexpectedly. When the messages are stored in memory, they are lost in cases of a server crash or a reboot. To make persistence highly available, the storage subsystem plays an important role as well, that is, the persistent store must be configured on a shared disk.

If either the sending or the receiving application can detect failures or duplicate messages, then reliable communication might not be necessary. However, in most cases we should think about it and implement it in a good way. At least we should know what the behavior of a proxy or business service is in case of an error and test all the possible scenarios.

Off course, reliable communication also has some downsides such as the transaction overhead and the performance will be less with Exactly Once QoS.

In terms of reliable SOAP messaging, you can choose SOAP over JMS or WS-RM. With SOAP over JMS, we need to define a queue and change the endpoint. With WS-RM, we don't need to change anything and the reliable communication will be handled by the client and the service.

Configuring Retry handling in JMS

In this recipe we will configure the redelivery limit and expiration policy on a Queue that will take part in a reliable communication. This option prevents an infinite loop: when the redelivery limit is reached, the message will be moved to the error queue. The redelivery limit on the queue will always override the value set on the message itself.

Getting ready

For this recipe we need the two queues from the standard environment and a proxy service that consumes the messages from the SourceQueue. The proxy service will initially just log the content of the message to the console using a **Log** action.

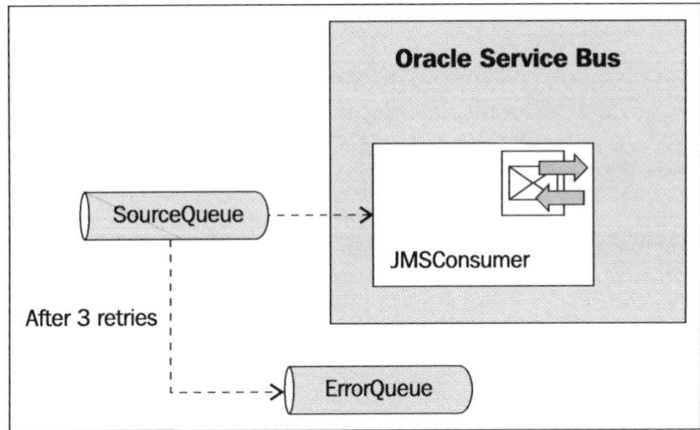

Import the OSB project into Eclipse from `\chapter-10\getting-ready\configuring-retry-handling` and deploy it to the OSB server. In the WebLogic console, perform the following steps to send a message to the queue for testing:

1. Select **Services | Messaging**.
2. Click on **JMS Modules** and in the list of modules click on **OsbCookbookResources**.
3. Click on the **SourceQueue** queue.
4. Navigate to the **Monitoring** tab.
5. Enable the checkbox in front of **OsbCookbookResources!SourceQueue** and click on **Show Messages**.
6. Click on **New** to create a message.
7. Type `<message>OSB Cookbook</message>` into the **Body** field.

8. Click on **OK**:

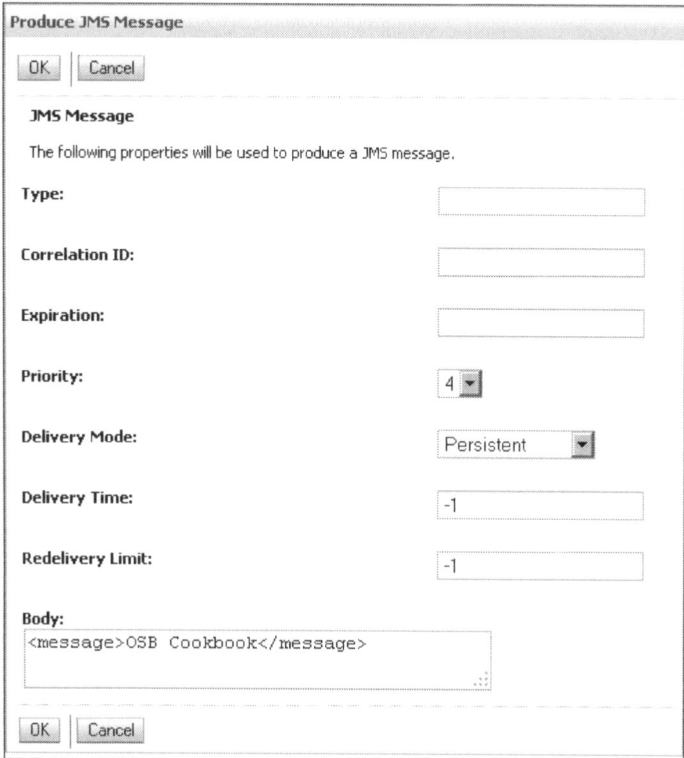

Make sure that the log entry shows up in the OSB console window:

```
OSB Cookbook 11gR1 PS3
56.ear/META-INF/application.xml. A version attribute is required, but this versi
on of the Weblogic Server will assume that the JEE5 is used. Future versions of
the Weblogic Server will reject descriptors that do not specify the JEE version.
>
<06.07.2011 14:33 Uhr MESZ> <Warning> <Munger> <BEA-2156203> <A version attribut
e was not found in element application in the deployment descriptor in C:\ORACLE
\MiddlewareWLS\user_projects\domains\osb_cookbook_domain\servers\AdminServer\tmp
\_WL_user\_ALSB_1309955613156\lmxf9/META-INF/application.xml. A version attribut
e is required, but this version of the Weblogic Server will assume that the JEE5
 is used. Future versions of the Weblogic Server will reject descriptors that do
 not specify the JEE version.>
<06.07.2011 14:33 Uhr MESZ> <Warning> <Munger> <BEA-2156203> <A version attribut
e was not found in element ejb-jar in the deployment descriptor in C:\ORACLE\Mid
dlewareWLS\user_projects\domains\osb_cookbook_domain\servers\AdminServer\tmp\_WL
_user\_ALSB_1309955613156\lmxf9\ejb.jar/META-INF/ejb-jar.xml. A version attribut
e is required, but this version of the Weblogic Server will assume that the JEE5
 is used. Future versions of the Weblogic Server will reject descriptors that do
 not specify the JEE version.>
<06.07.2011 14:40 Uhr MESZ> <Warning> <ALSB Logging> <BEA-000000> < [PipelinePai
rNode1, PipelinePairNode1_request, stage1, REQUEST] After consuming:: <soapenv:B
ody xmlns:soapenv="http://schemas.xmlsoap.org/soap/envelope/">
  <message>OSB Cookbook</message>
</soapenv:Body><jms:JMSXDeliveryCount xmlns:jms="http://www.bea.com/wli/sb/trans
ports/jms">1</jms:JMSXDeliveryCount>>
```

The message has been consumed by the proxy service and the log output shows the successful processing of the message.

How to do it...

To test the retry handling, we first need to make sure that the proxy service fails. We can easily do that by adding a **Raise Error** action to the message flow:

In Eclipse OEPE, perform the following steps:

1. Navigate to the **Message Flow** tab of the proxy service.
2. Add a **Raise Error** action after the **Log** action inside the **ProcessingStage**.
3. Set APP-00001 into the **Code** field and **Error happended when processing JMS message!** into the **Message** field.
4. Deploy the project to the OSB server.

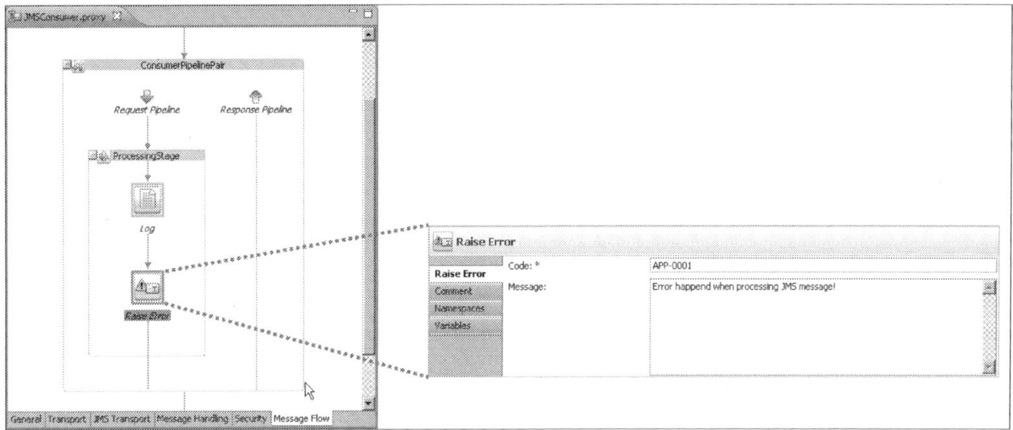

Now let's configure the retry behavior. In WebLogic Console, perform the following steps:

5. Select **Services** | **Messaging**.
6. Click on **JMS Modules** and in the list of modules click on **OsbCookbookResources**.
7. Click on the **SourceQueue** queue.
8. Select the **Delivery Failure** tab located inside the **Configuration** tab.
9. Enter `20000` (to wait for 20 seconds) into the **Redelivery Delay Override** field.
10. Enter `3` into the **Redelivery Limit** field (to redeliver the message three times).
11. Select **Redirect** as **Expiration Policy**.

12. Select **ErrorQueue** as the **Error Destination** value.
13. Click on **Save**:

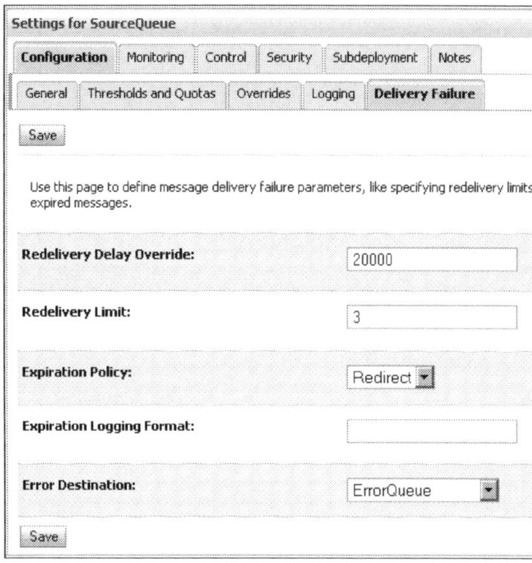

To test it, create a new message in the queue in the same way as shown in the *Getting Ready* section. Just make sure to overwrite the `-1` in the **Redelivery Limit** field to the same value as specified on the queue:

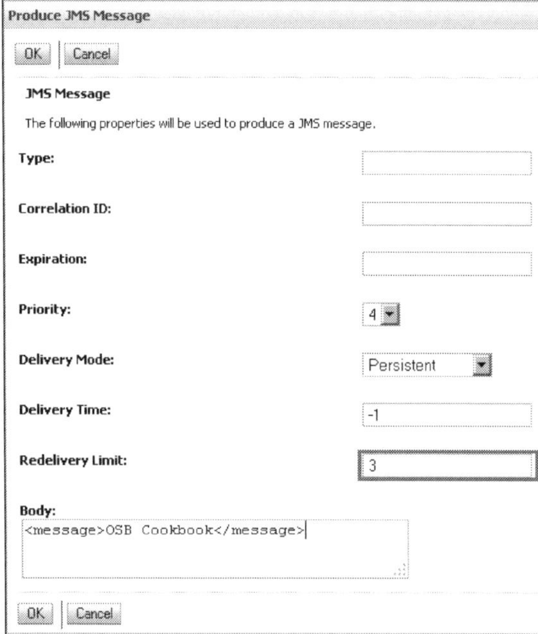

Otherwise the **-1** will overwrite the setting on the queue and it will again retry forever. This seems to be a limitation of the Weblogic console Produce JMS message client. If the message is sent from a real client, such as another OSB business service, then it would not be necessary and the settings on the queue would be taken.

How it works...

When a proxy service reads a message from the SourceQueue and there is an error somewhere in the process, the message will be rolled back and stays on the queue. WebLogic will detect this and wait for 20 seconds before the proxy service can consume it again. If this happens three times then WebLogic will move the message automatically to the error queue. Such an error queue can be monitored for new messages through the WebLogic diagnostic module. An administrator might be able to solve the problem and remove the message or move it back into the original queue.

There's more...

We can also set these properties in the **Advanced Settings** section on the **JMS Transport** tab of the proxy service. In that case, they will overwrite any settings specified directly on the JMS queue:

JMSConsumer.proxy

JMS Transport Configuration

Configuration

Use this page to configure protocol-dependent transport information for this service.

Destination Type	(•) Queue / ( ) Topic
Is Response Required	[ ]
Dispatch Policy	default
Request Encoding	UTF-8
JMS Service Account	[Browse]

⊟ Advanced Settings

Use SSL	[ ]
Message Selector	
Durable Subscription	[ ]
Retry Count	3
Retry Interval	20000
Error Destination	jms.ErrorQueue
Expiration Policy	Redirect
Is XA Required	[ ]

General | Transport | JMS Transport | Message Handling | Security | Message Flow

Enabling JMS message persistence

When we send messages to a JMS queue, the **Message Delivery Mode** option controls if a message is guaranteed to be delivered once, and if it is safely stored in the persistent store of the JMS server. There is also a non persistent option, where the messages are stored in memory and may be lost in case of a WebLogic or JMS server failure, or when the WebLogic server is rebooted.

In this recipe, we will set the delivery mode option on a JMS message with the OSB **Transport Header** action.

Getting ready

For this recipe, we will use a simple OSB project with one proxy and one business service:

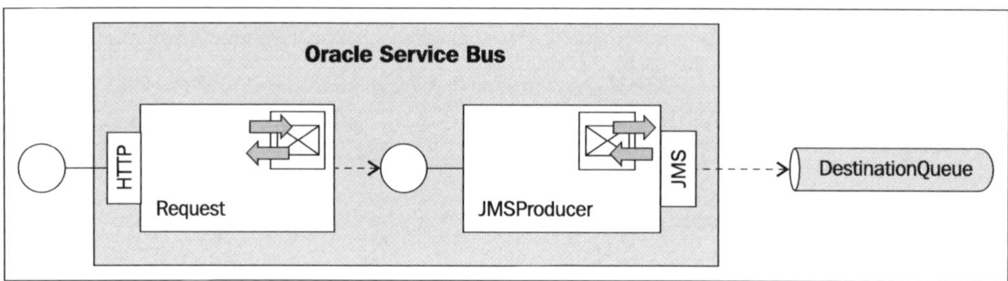

You can import the OSB project into Eclipse from `\chapter-10\getting-ready\enabling-jms-message-persistence`.

How to do it...

In OPEP, perform the following steps:

1. Navigate to the proxy service **Request**.
2. Navigate to the **Message Flow** tab.
3. Drag a **Transport Header** action and drop it on the **Request action** lane of the **Route** action.
4. On the **Properties** tab of the **Transport Header** select **Outbound Request** as the value for the **Direction** field.
5. Click on **Add Header**.
6. Select **jms** and then **JMSDeliveryMode** from the **Defined** drop-down list.

7. Type 2 into the **Set Header to** field (1 = non-persistent and 2 = persistent).

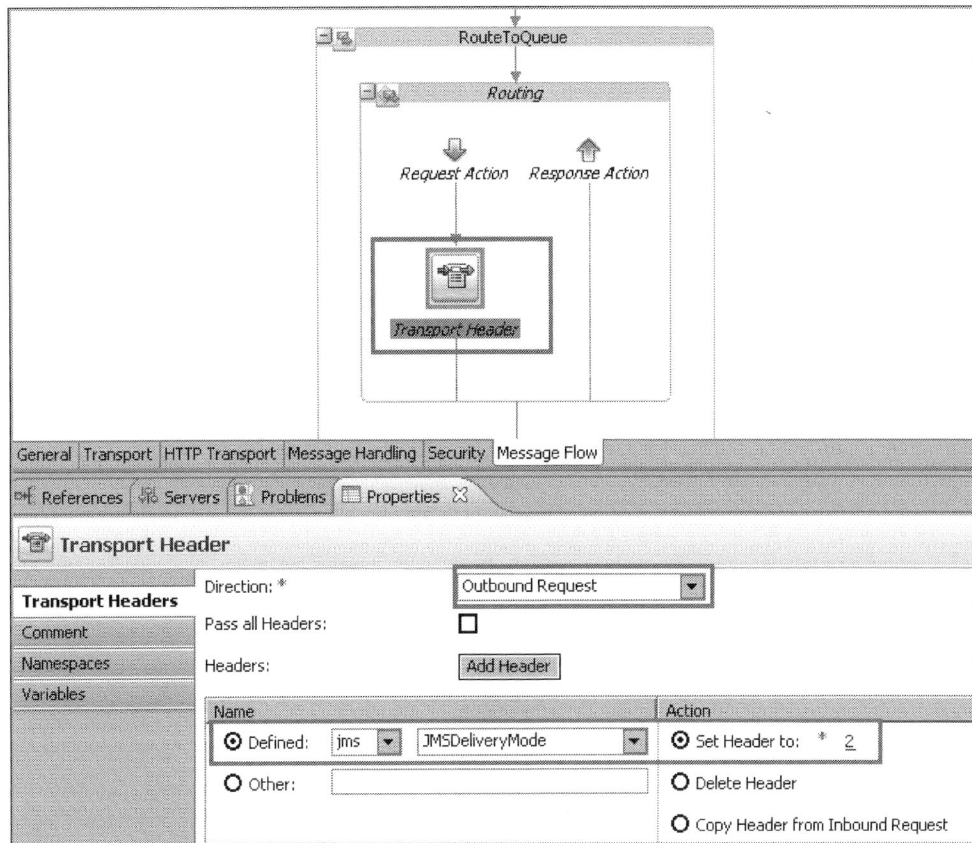

8. Publish the project to the OSB server.

By adding the **Transport Header** action into the message flow we are able to define the delivery mode of the JMS queue. By setting the **JMSDeliveryMode** to 2 we are defining that the messages should be persistent.

We can easily check the result by invoking the proxy service with a test message and then browsing the message through the WebLogic console.

To invoke the proxy service, perform the following steps through the service bus console:

9. In the **Project Explorer** navigate to the proxy folder inside the enabling-jms-message-persistence project.

10. Click on the **Launch Test Console** icon of the **Request** proxy service.
11. Enter `<message>OSB Cookbook</message>` into the **Payload** field and click on **Execute**.

To browse for the message inside the DestinationQueue, perform the following steps through the WebLogic console:

12. Select **Services** | **Messaging**.
13. Click on **JMS Modules** and in the list of modules, click on **OsbCookbookResources**.
14. Click on the **DestinationQueue** queue.
15. Navigate to the **Monitoring** tab.
16. Enable the checkbox in front of **OsbCookbookResources!DestinationQueue** and click on **Show Messages**.
17. Click on the **ID** link of the message and the **JMS Message Detail** window will be shown:

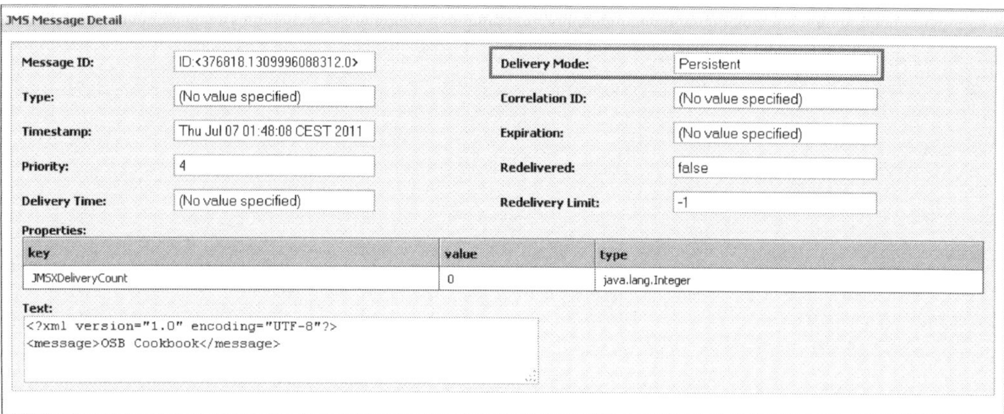

How it works...

With a **Transport Header** action, we can set the transport-specific (header) properties on the business service. In case of a JMS business service, you can use the predefined JMS header properties. These JMS properties will be used when the business service sends a message to the queue.

There's more...

We can also override the delivery mode in WebLogic, which takes precedence over all the settings that the producer of the message specifies in the delivery mode.

In WebLogic Console, perform the following steps to override the delivery mode:

1. Navigate to the **Configuration** tab of your queue.
2. Click on the **Overrides** tab and set the **Delivery Mode Override** to **Persistent**:

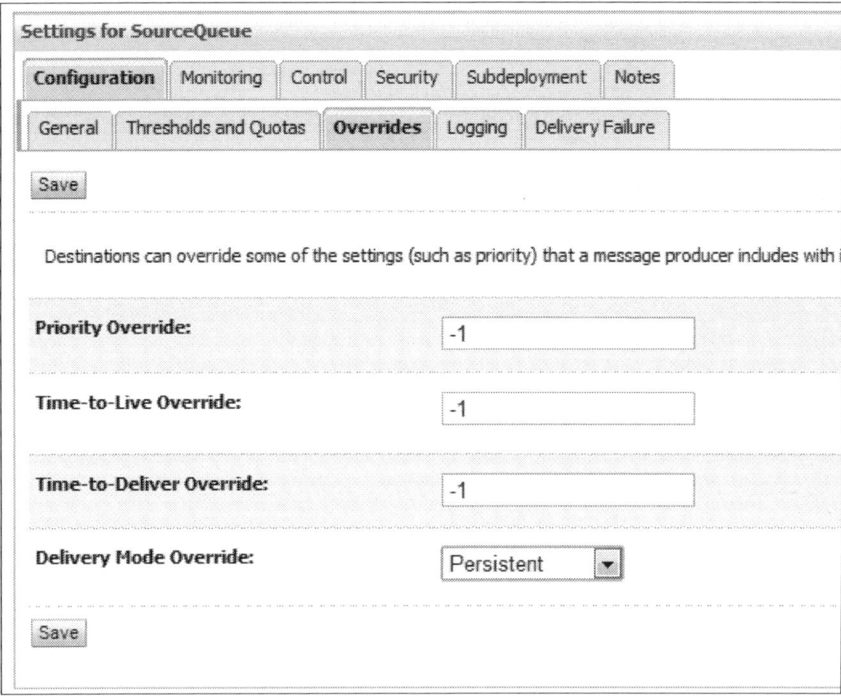

Even if the producer of the message specifies the non-persistent delivery mode, the message will be made persistent due to the override.

If we don't override the delivery mode in WebLogic, we can define it on the **JMS Transport** tab of the business service. Just enable the **Enable Message Persistence** checkbox:

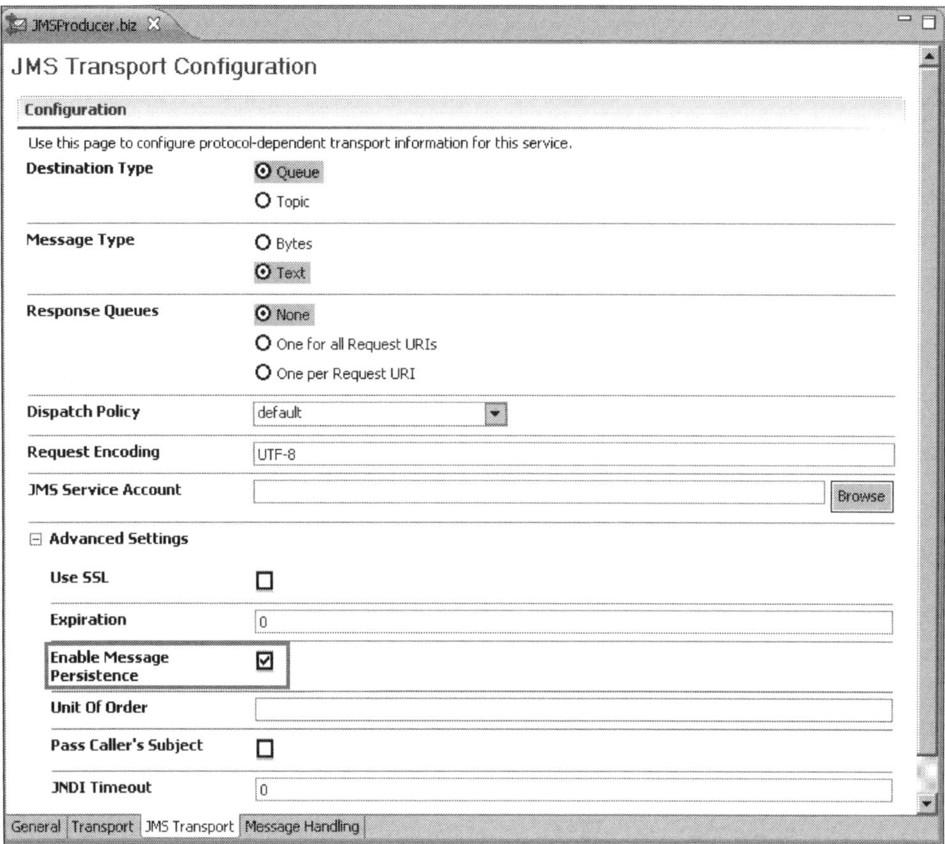

The **Enable Message Persistence** property on the business service will not override what we have set in a **Transport Header** action.

Working with global transactions and quality of service

This recipe will show the different error scenarios, which we can have with XA and non XA enabled resources and how QoS can influence this.

Getting ready

For this recipe, we will use a setup with three queues from the standard environment, a proxy service that consumes messages from a JMS queue, and a business service that sends the messages to another JMS queue:

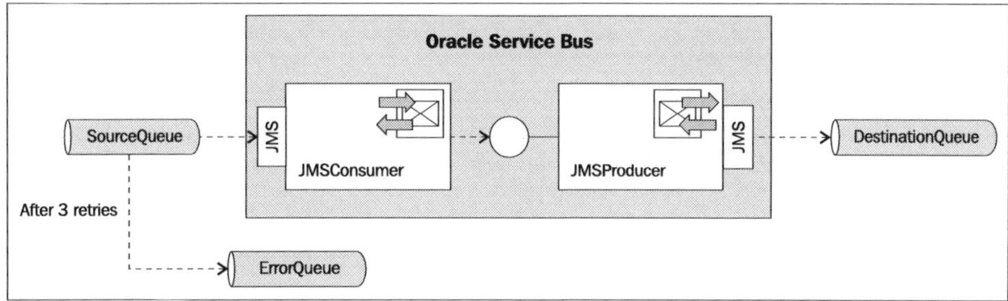

You can import the OSB project into Eclipse from `\chapter-10\getting-ready\working-with-global-transactions-and-qos`.

How to do it...

First, we will show you the behaviour of the service without a global transaction.

In Eclipse OEPE, perform the following steps:

1. Navigate to the proxy service **JMSConsumer**.
2. Navigate to the **Transport** tab.
3. Change the **Endpoint URI** to use the non-XA JMS Connection Factory : `jms://[OSBServer]:[Port]/weblogic.jms.ConnectionFactory/jms.SourceQueue`

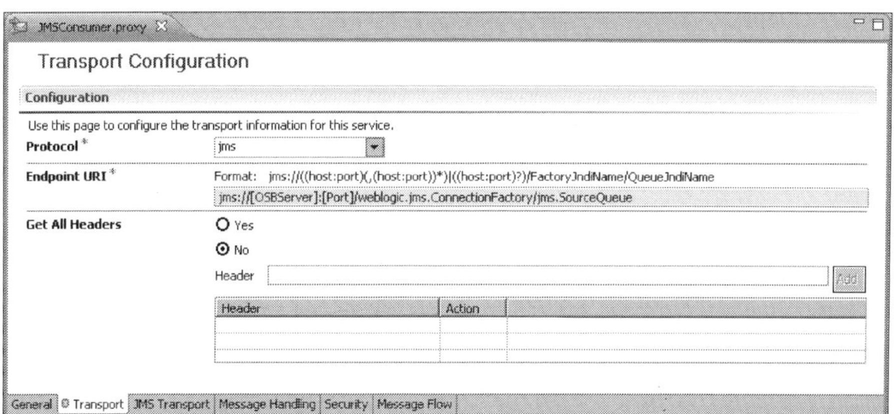

4. Navigate to the **Message Flow** tab.
5. The message flow contains a **Pipeline Pair** node and a **Route** node with a **Routing** action that invokes the JMS business service.
6. Add a **Stage** to the **Request Pipeline** of the **InterceptorPipelinePair** node and name it `ErrorStage`.
7. Add a **Raise Error** action to this Stage.
8. Enter `APP-00001` to the **Code** field and `An error occurred!` into the **Message** field:

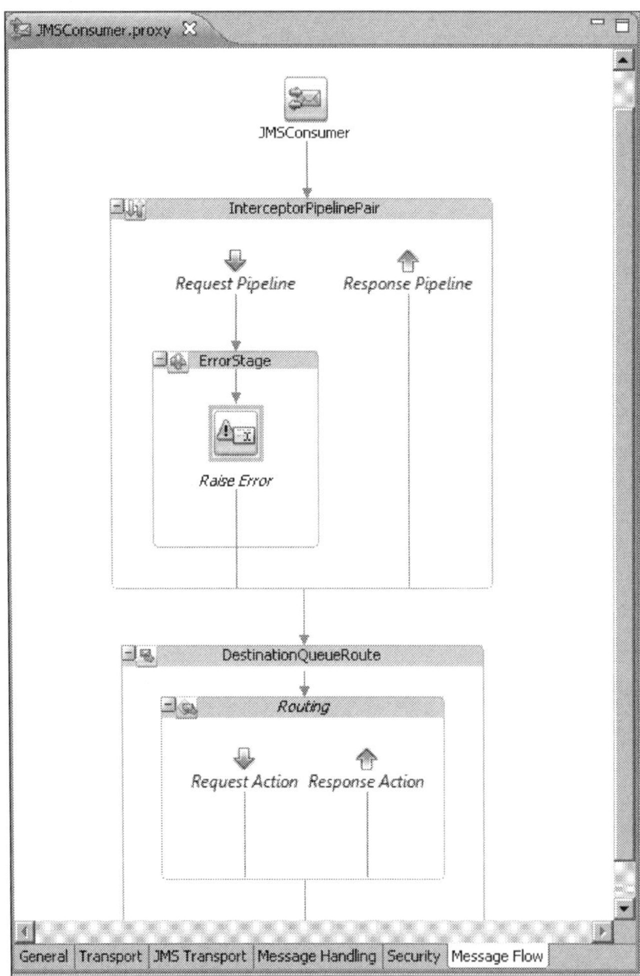

9. Navigate to the business service **JMSProducer**.
10. Navigate to the **Transport** tab.

11. Change the **Endpoint URI** so it uses a Non XA Connection Factory `jms://[OSBServer]:[Port]/weblogic.jms.ConnectionFactory/DestinationQueue`:

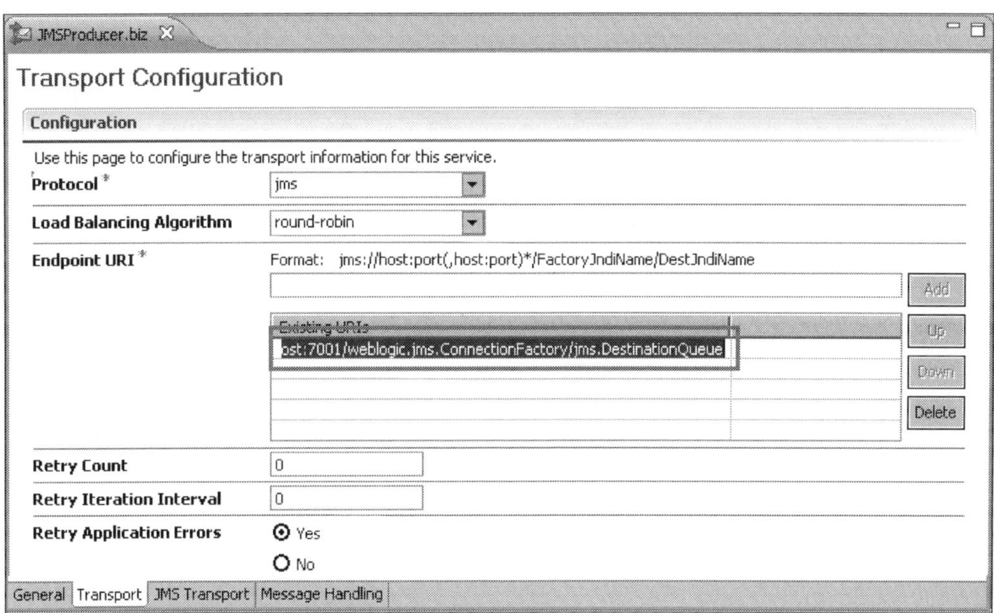

12. Deploy the project to the OSB server.

Now it's time to test the behavior. In WebLogic console, perform the following steps to add a message to the SourceQueue:

13. Go to **Services** | **Messaging** | **JMS Modules**.
14. Open the **OsbCookbookResources** | **SourceQueue**.
15. Navigate to the **Monitoring** tab.
16. Select the **OsbCookbookResources!SourceQueue** and click on **Show Messages**.
17. Click on **New**.
18. Type `3` into the **Redelivery Limit** field.
19. Type `<message>OSB Cookbook</message>` into the **Body** field and click on **OK**.
20. Open the **Monitoring** tab of the three queues—SourceQueue, DestinationQueue, and ErrorQueue and check that the message is gone.

    The message is lost because the processing of the proxy service has been done in a local transaction. Because of the error, the OSB transaction rolls back, but the consumption from the SourceQueue has happened in a different transaction and was already commited, so the message is lost!

Now let's change the setup to use a global transaction. In Eclipse OEPE, perform the following steps:

21. Open the **JMSConsumer** proxy service.
22. Click to the **Transport** tab.
23. Change the **Endpoint URI** so it uses a XA Connection Factory: `jms://[OSBServer]:[Port]/weblogic.jms.XAConnectionFactory/SourceQueue`
24. Navigate to the **Message Handling** tab.
25. Enable **Same Transaction For Response**.
26. Navigate to the **Message Flow** tab.
27. By drag-and-drop, move the **ErrorStage** to the **Response Pipeline** of the pipeline pair.
28. Open the **JMSProducer** business service.
29. Navigate to the **Transport** tab.
30. Change the **Endpoint URI** so it uses a XA Connection Factory: `jms://[OSBServer]:[Port]/weblogic.jms.XAConnectionFactory/DestinationQueue`
31. Deploy the project to the OSB server.

Let's now retest the behavior by adding a message to the SourceQueue. In WebLogic Console perform the following steps:

32. Go to **Services | Messaging | JMS Modules**.
33. Open the **JMS Module**.
34. Open the **SourceQueue**.
35. Navigate to the **Monitoring** tab.
36. Select the **OsbCookbookResources!SourceQueue** and click on **Show Messages**.
37. Click on **New** to create a message.
38. Type `3` into the **Redelivery Limit** field.
39. Type `<message>OSB Cookbook</message>` into the **Body** field and click on **OK**.
40. Open the **Monitoring** tab of the three queues, SourceQueue, DestinationQueue, and ErrorQueue and check that the message arrives in the ErrorQueue.

This time the processing of the proxy service is in the same global transaction as the consummation of the queue. Therefore, the message is rolled back and three times a redelivery is tried. After that the message is sent to the ErrorQueue.

We have moved the ErrorStage into the response processing. Therefore, the routing to the business service has already happened. Because the enqueue of the message to the DestinationQueue happens in the same global transaction, it is also rolled-back, and no message can be found in the DestinationQueue.

Now let's change the setup and enable QoS. In OEPE, perform the following steps:

42. Open the **JMSProducer** business service.
43. Navigate to the **Transport** tab and verify that a XA JMS Connection Factory is used in the **Endpoint URI** field.
44. Open the **JMSConsumer** proxy service.
45. Navigate to the **Transport** tab and verify that a XA Connection Factory is used in the **Endpoint URI** field.
46. Navigate to the **Message Handling** tab.
47. Enable the **Same Transaction For Response** property.
48. Navigate to the **Message Flow** tab.
49. Leave the stage with the **Raise Error** action on the **Response Pipeline** of the **InterceptorPipelinePair** node.
50. Add a **Routing Options** action on the **Request Action** of the **Routing** Node.

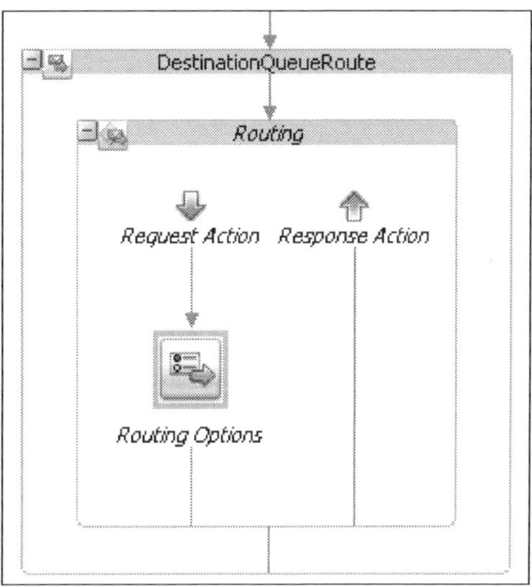

51. On the **Properties** of the **Routing Options** action, enable the **QoS** checkbox and choose **Best Effort** as the value of the drop-down listbox:

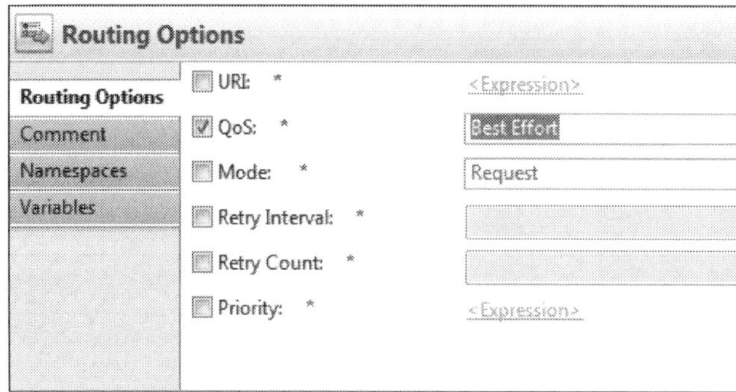

52. Deploy the project to the OSB Server.

Let's test the behavior of the new settings again. Add a message to the SourceQueue by performing the following steps in the WebLogic Console:

53. Click on **Services | Messaging | JMS Modules**.
54. Open the **JMS Module**.
55. Click on the **SourceQueue**.
56. Navigate to the **Monitoring** tab.
57. Select the **OsbCookbookResources!SourceQueue** and click on **Show Messages**.
58. Click on **New** to create a message.
59. Type `3` into the **Redelivery Limit** field.
60. Type `<message>OSB Cookbook</message>` into the **Body** field and click on **OK**.
61. Open the **Monitoring** tab of the three queues, SourceQueue, DestinationQueue, and ErrorQueue and check that the message is four times in the DestinationQueue and once in the ErrorQueue.

By setting the QoS setting in the **Routing Options** to **Best Effort,** we force the business service not to use the global transaction. This means that the enqueue of the message into the `DestinationQueue` happens in its own local transaction and is therefore, commited independently of the global transaction. Because the global transaction retries three times, we get four messages in the `DestinationQueue`, one for the original request and three for the retries. This is probably not the behavior we want and therefore, we have to be careful when using the **Best Effort** QoS setting.

How it works...

When we use XA-enabled resources, enable **Same Transaction For Response**, and use **Exactly Once QoS** on the outbound transport, every resource will be rolled-back in case of an error in the **Request** or **Response** lane. To make this work, we should check if we are using a XA or non-XA resource and what the value of the QoS is, otherwise the resource won't take part in the global transaction.

In this recipe, we don't need to set QoS to *Exactly Once* because this is the default value when we use JMS with a XA Connection Factory as inbound transport.

To know the QoS values of your proxy service, we can read the following transport variables:

- `$inbound/ctx:transport/ctx:qualityOfService`
- `$outbound/ctx:transport/ctx:qualityOfService`

The inbound variable value can't be changed and OSB uses the inbound value as a default value for the outbound transport. We can change the outbound QoS value with a **Routing Options** action.

Only use the **Exactly Once** of QoS when there is a transaction involved. The following inbound transports such as e-mail, FTP, File, JMS/XA, SFTP, and Transactional Tuxedo can start a transaction and have **Exactly Once** as the default value of QoS. This is because the E-mail, FTP, and File transport internally use a JMS queue with a XA Connection Factory.

In case of a **Publish** or a **Service Callout** action, the default value of QoS is always **Best Effort**. This means in case of a JCA resource such as a DB or an AQ adapter we need to set the **dataSourceName** property of the resource adapter and not using the **xADataSourcename** property, otherwise we will get a runtime error. If the **Publish** or **Service Callout** action should be part of the global transaction, then use the **Routing Options** action and set the QoS to **Exactly Once**. In the case of a JCA adapter, we need to use the **xADataSourceName** property of the resource adapter.

If our business service **Publish** action or **Service Callout** does not support XA, then with each retry of the proxy service, the service will be invoked. This can lead to many duplicate messages or invokes.

We can also force this behavior in a XA-enabled business service by adding a **Routing Option** in the **Request Action** of the **Route** Node. In the **Routing Options**, you need to enable QoS and set it to **Best Effort**. With **Best Effort**, the resource won't take part in the global transaction even when XA is enabled.

Don't use the OSB console for testing XA. The test of the proxy or business service in the OSB console is not the same as when putting a message on a queue. The OSB console can't start a transaction.

Using WS-Reliable Messaging (WS-RM) with WS transport

In this recipe, we will create a one-way (fire and forget) proxy service that contains a long running **WS-RM** (**Reliable Messaging**) policy and test this WS-RM policy in a JDeveloper web service proxy client.

We will use the WS transport, which implements both inbound and outbound requests for SOAP-based services with a WS-RM policy.

Getting ready

For this recipe, we will use a setup with a very simple proxy service based on a WSDL containing only a one-way operation. For the WS-RM client we will use JDeveloper.

You can import the OSB project into Eclipse from `\chapter-10\getting-ready\using-reliable-msg-with-ws-transport`.

How to do it...

First, let's change the proxy service to use the WS transport and add the reliable messaging policy. In Eclipse OEPE, perform the following steps:

1. Open the **Provider** proxy service and navigate to the **Transport** tab.
2. Select **ws** in the **Protocol** field to specify the WS transport.
3. Navigate to the **Policy** tab.
4. Select the **From Pre-defined Policy or WS-Policy Resource** option.
5. Select **Service Level Policies** in the following tree.
6. Click on **Add**.
7. Click on **Browse** on the left of the **Name** field (you might have to scroll down in order to see it):

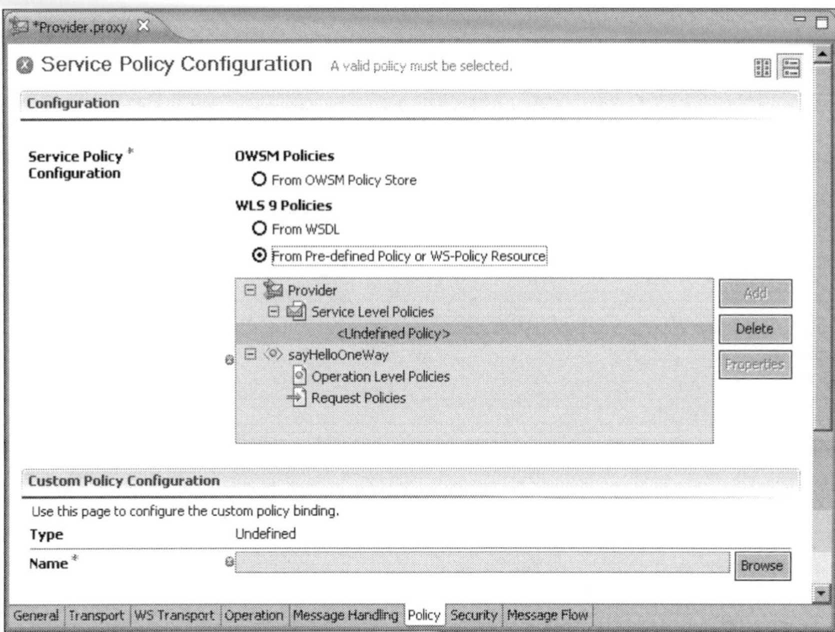

8. Select the **Predefined Policy** option in the **Select a Policy Resource** dialog.
9. Select the **LongRunningReliability.xml** policy resource.
10. Click on **OK**.
11. The **Service Level Policies** now contains the `LongRunningReliability.xml` policy:

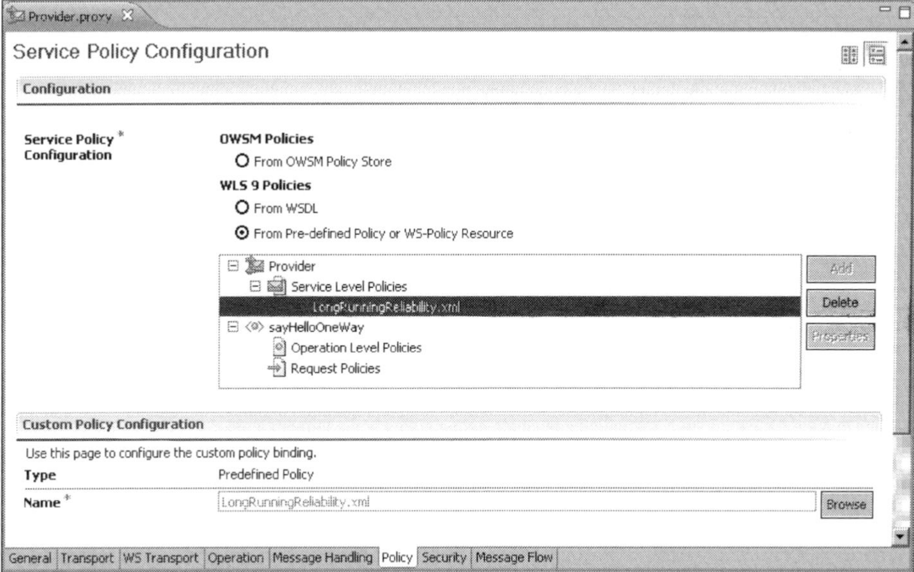

12. Navigate to the **Message Flow** tab.
13. Check the **Log** action, which will log the content of `$body`.
14. Deploy the project to the OSB Server.

In a browser, perform the following steps:

15. Open the `WSDL` of the WS-RM proxy service by entering the following URL: `http://[OSBServer]:[Port]/using-reliable-msg-with-ws-transport/Provider?wsdl`.
16. Make sure that the `WSDL` contains the RM assertion, as shown in the following screenshot:

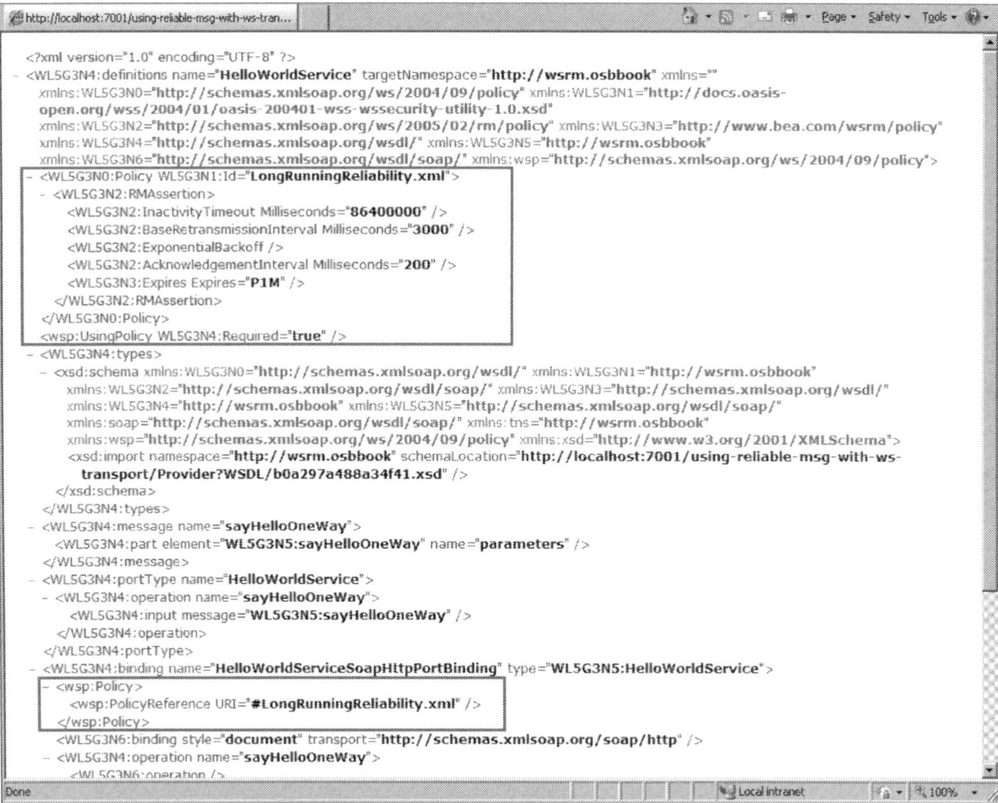

Now with the service implemented, let's create a client to test the behaviour. In JDeveloper, perform the following steps:

17. Create a new application by selecting **File | New**.
18. Enter `Generic` into the **search** field, select **Generic Application** and click on **OK**.

19. Enter `ReliableMessaging` into the **Application Name** field and click on **Next**.
20. Enter `WsClient` into the **Project Name** field and click on **Finish**.
21. Right-click on the **WsClient** project in the project navigator and select **New**.
22. In the **search** field enter `Web Service Proxy`.
23. Select **Web Service Proxy** from the list of items on the right and click on **OK**.
24. The **Create Web Service Proxy** window will open and click on **Next**.
25. Choose the **JAX-WS Style** option as the **Client Style** and click on **Next**.
26. Provide WSDL URL of the OSB proxy service: `http://[OSBServer]:[Port]/using-reliable-msg-with-ws-transport/Provider?wsdl`.
27. Click on **Next**.
28. Enter `wsrm.client` into the **Package Name** field.
29. Enter `wsrm.types` into the **Root Package for Generated Types** field.
30. Click on **Next**.
31. Click on **Next** two more times.
32. Select **oracle/wsrm10_policy** from the **Reliability** drop-down list.
33. Click on **Finish**:

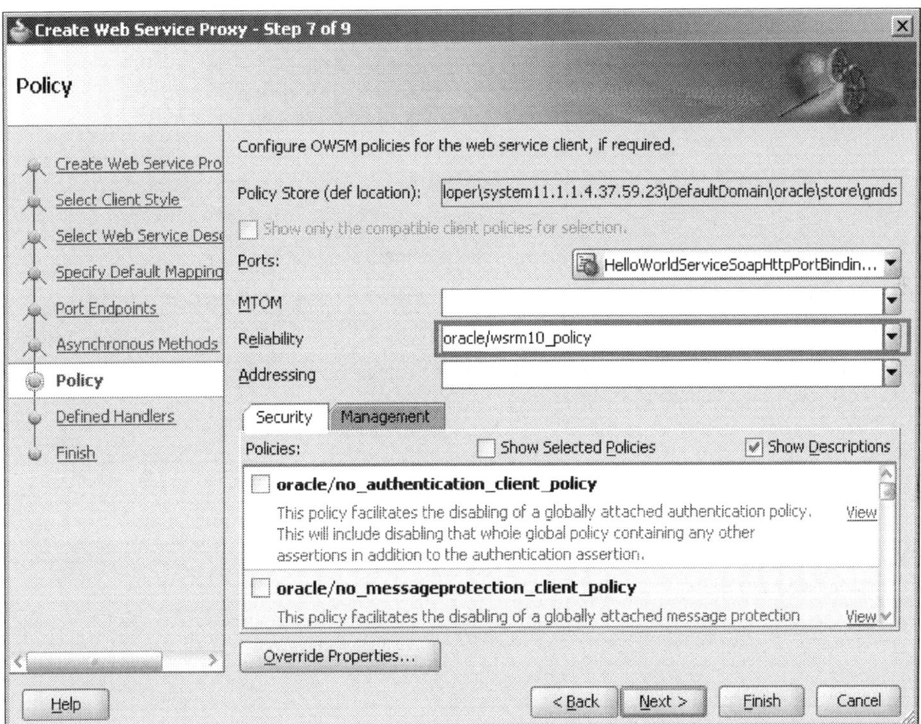

34. JDeveloper will open the generated `HelloWorldServiceSoapHttpPortBindingQSPortClient` class.
35. Remove all the methods after the static main method.
36. Change the code of the `main()` method to invoke the `sayHelloOneWay` operation as shown in the following screenshot:

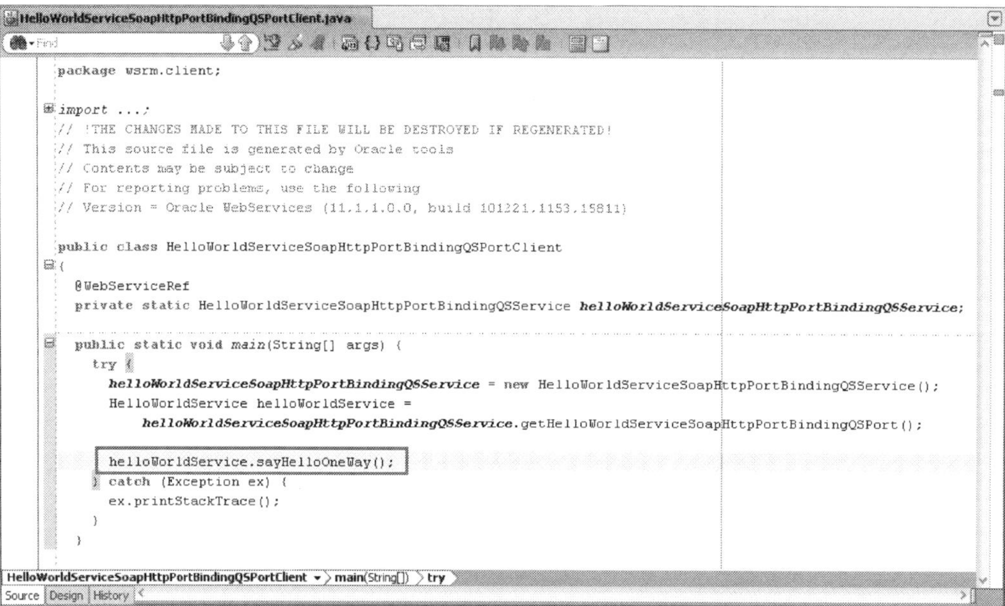

37. From the **Tools** menu select **HTTP Analyzer**.
38. Start the analyzer by clicking on the green arrow icon. All the communication between JDeveloper and the OSB server wil be intercepted.
39. Right-click on **HelloWorldServiceSoapHttpPortBindingQSPortClient** and select **Run** to execute the class.
40. The JDeveloper **log window** will show operations on a persistent file store, which is created in the generic project folder:

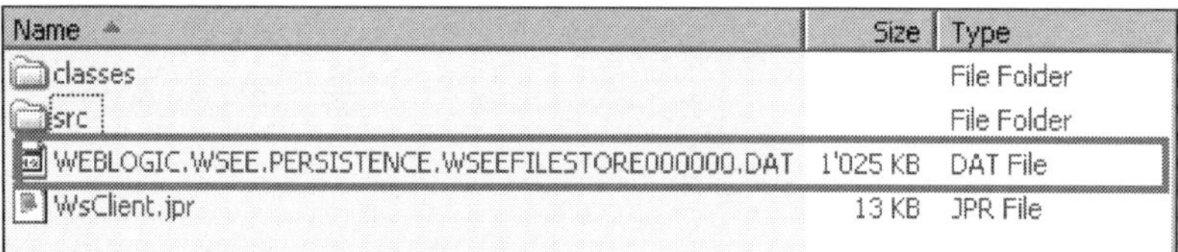

41. Check the **OSB Console log** window to see the log output of the request just made.
42. In JDeveloper, navigate to the **HTTP Analyzer** tab where we can see two instances:

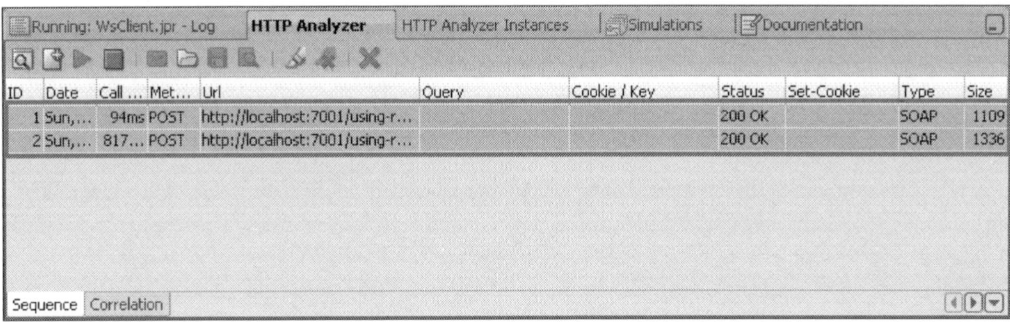

43. Click on the first instance and the message detail window with the request/response is shown, containing the create sequence interaction:

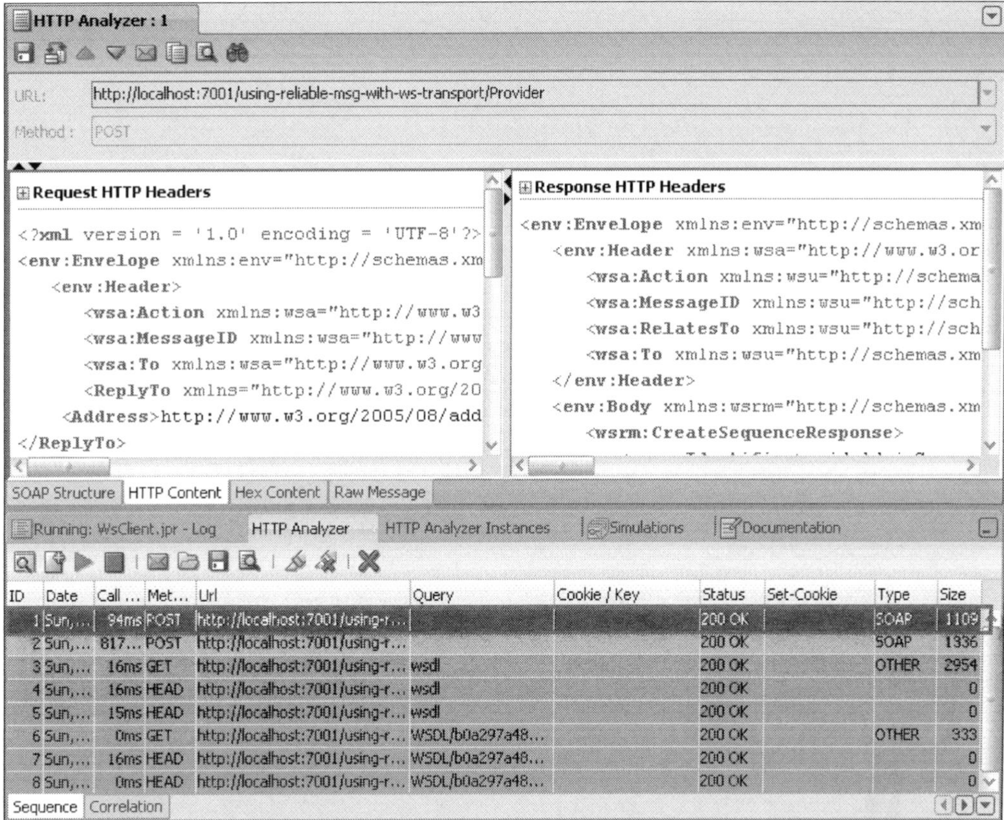

The request sent to the OSB with the `CreateSequence` is shown in the following screenshot:

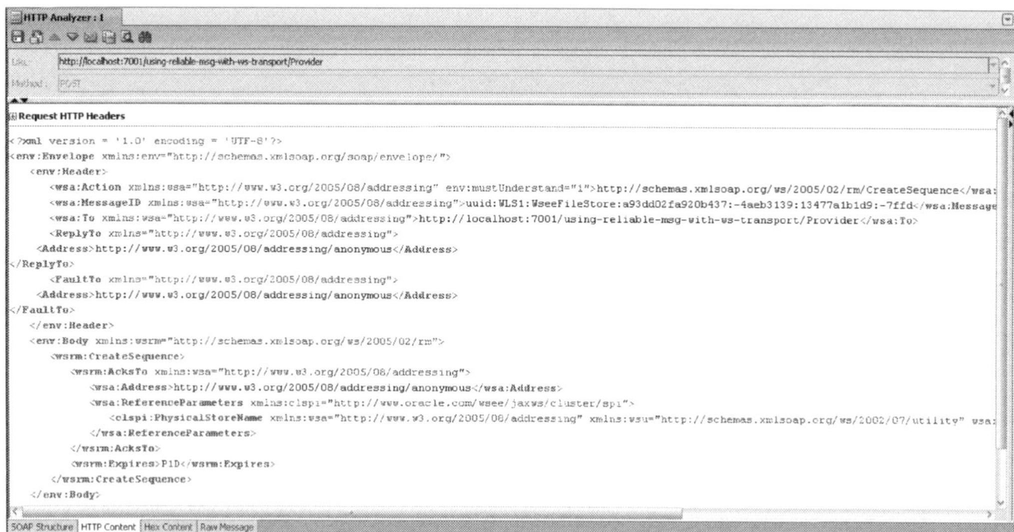

The response to the `CreateSequence` returned by the OSB is shown in the following screenshot:

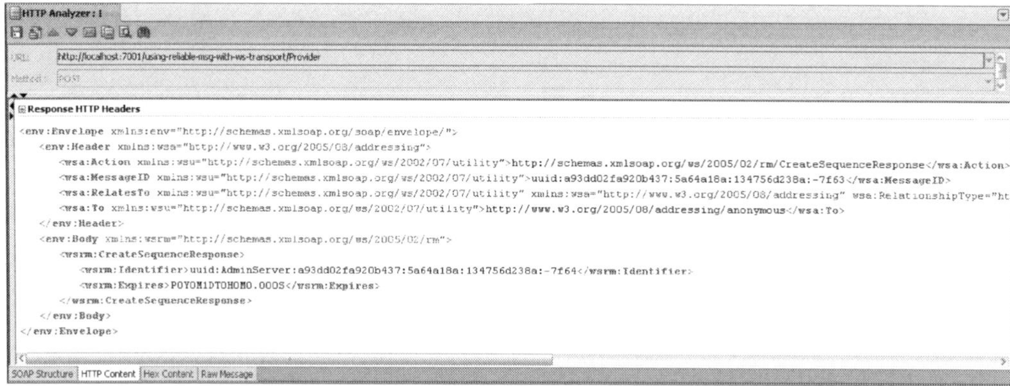

44. Click on the second instance and again the message detail window is shown.

    The request with the real payload sent to the OSB is shown in the following screenshot:

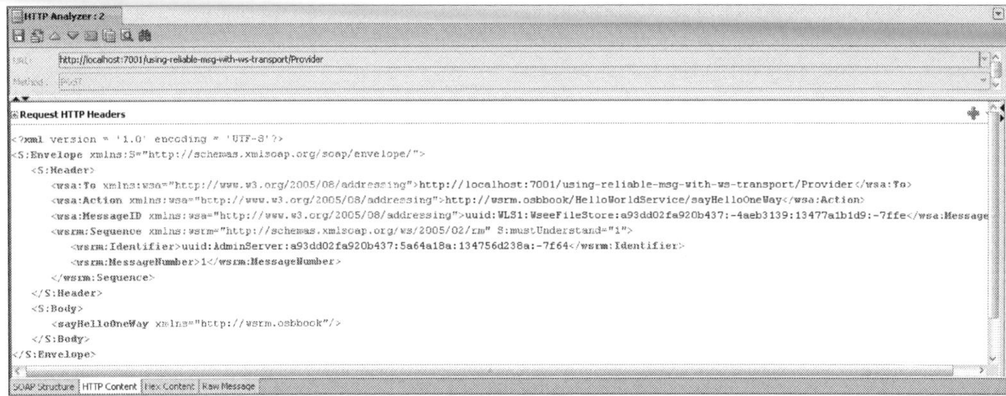

The response of the OSB is shown in the following screenshot:

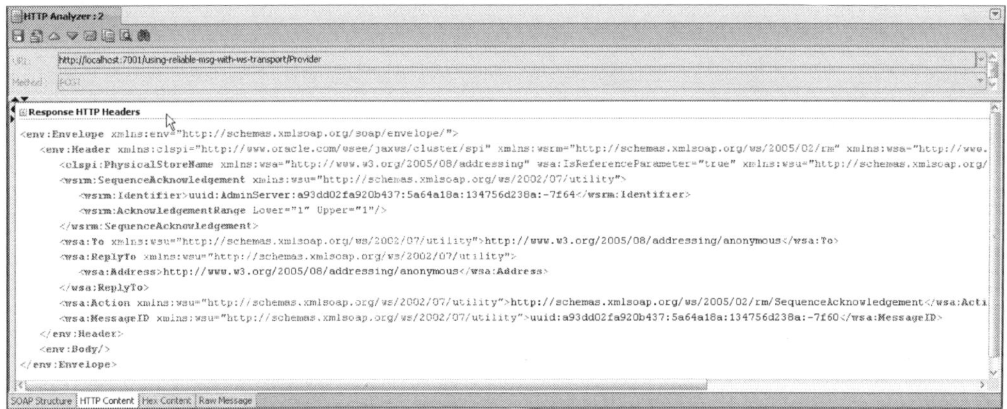

How it works...

In WS-RM, the JDeveloper Web Service proxy and the OSB proxy server both have or start agents that handle, intercept the message communication, and are responsible for the retries of these messages. In this case, JDeveloper is the RM Source and the OSB is the RM Destination.

To make sure these messages are not lost, we will see that JDeveloper creates a file persistence that stores the request and the status of these requests.

In this recipe, we used WS-RM in a one-way messaging pattern. Beside one way, WS-RM can also support asynchronous communication. It's important to know that the WS transport of OSB, only supports WS-RM 1.0 and that the response in the asynchronous communication does not take part in reliable communication.

The following steps explain how WS-RM works in a one-way messaging pattern.

1. JDeveloper sends the request and this will be intercepted by the **RM Source agent**. This agent starts the process by sending a `CreateSequence` request. The OSB **RM Destination agent** intercepts the message and responds with a `CreateSequence` response, which contains a sequence identifier ID. The identifier ID should be used in every communication between the RM Source and Destination.
2. The RM Source sends the original request, containing the sequence identifier ID together with a unique message number in the SOAP header. The message number starts with 1, so the RM agents can keep track of the messages.
3. The RM Destination delivers the request to the OSB proxy service. The RM Destination also responds with a `Sequence Acknowledgement` in the SOAP header and an empty SOAP body (because of the one-way communication). The `Sequence Acknowledgement` says that every message is received and handled.

   If something goes wrong, the JDeveloper RM Source will resend those requests until it gets the `Sequence Acknowledgement`.

There's more...

In this recipe, we used the pre-defined `LongRunningReliability.xml` as our WS-RM policy. Beside this `LongRunningReliability.xml` policy, we can also use the `DefaultReliability.xml` policy or even create our own. The difference between these two policies is that the activity timeout of `LongRunningReliability.xml` is 24 hours and in `DefaultReliability.xml`, it is 10 minutes.

When we start the JDeveloper WEB Service proxy client, we can get a persistence store error. To solve this, it is necessary to remove the persistence store in the generic project folder.

SOAP over JMS

In this recipe, we will implement reliable SOAP communication over JMS and not over HTTP. The only difference is that your request and response will be published on a queue. This way the request can't be lost (when it has JMS persistence with XA/QoS). The response will also be published on the queue and the client can consume this response.

Getting ready

For this recipe, we will use an OSB project with a proxy service that is based on a WSDL with a synchronous request/response operation. The SOAP message will be sent over JMS instead of HTTP. JDeveloper will be used to generate a test client:

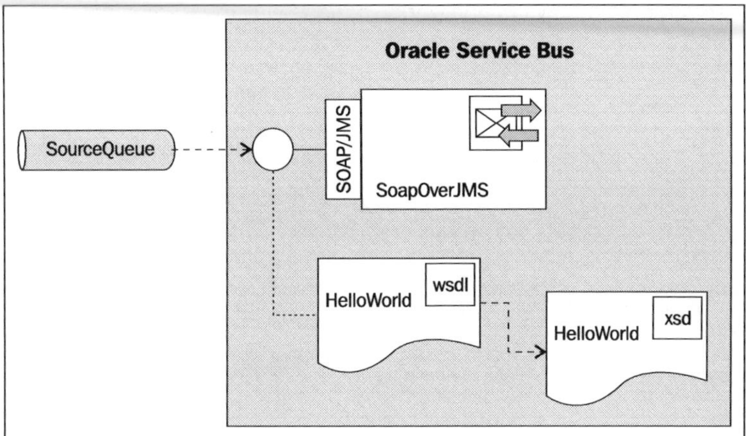

You can import the OSB project into Eclipse OEPE from `\chapter-10\getting-ready\sending-soap-over-jms`.

How to do it...

First we will need to change the proxy service to use the JMS instead of the HTTP transport. In Eclipse OEPE, perform the following steps:

1. Open the **SoapOverJMS** proxy service.
2. Click on the **Transport** tab.
3. Choose **jms** in the **Protocol** field.
4. The **Endpoint URI** must use a **XA Connection Factory**. The URI must look like this `jms://[OSBServer]:[Port]/weblogic.jms.XAConnectionFactory/SourceQueue`
5. Navigate to the **JMS Transport** tab.
6. Enable **Is Response Required**.
7. Select **JMSMessageID** in the **Response Pattern** field.
8. Select **Text** in the **Response Message Type** field.
9. Click on the **Message Flow** tab.

10. Add a **Transport Header** action after the **Replace** action:

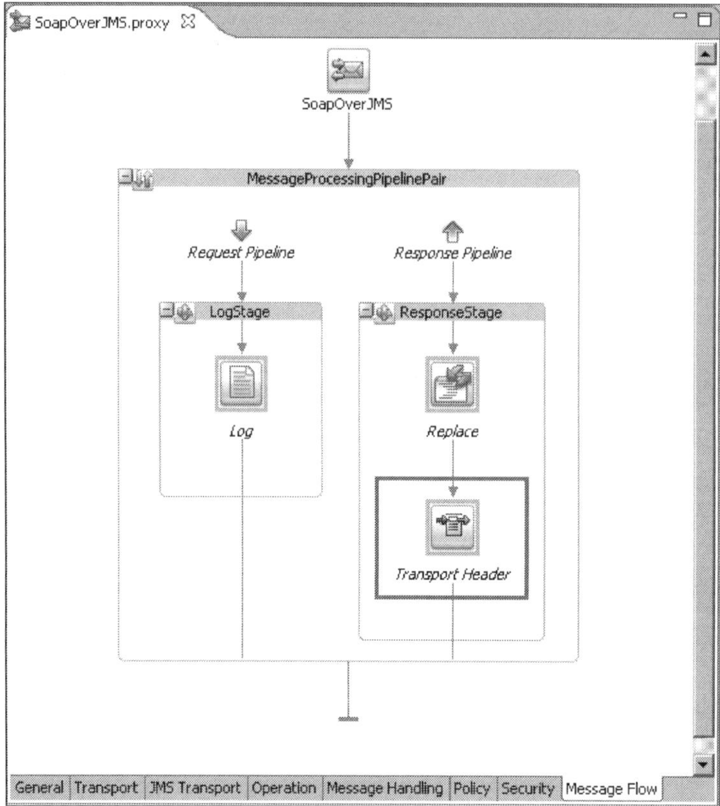

11. On the **Properties** of the **Transport Header**, choose **Inbound Response** from the **Direction** drop-down listbox.
12. Click on **Add Header**.
13. Select the **Other** option and enter `_wls_mimehdrContent_Type` into the field.
14. Select the **Set Header** option to and click on **Expression**.
15. Enter `text/xml; charset=utf-8` into the **Expression** field and click on **OK**.
16. Deploy the project to the OSB Server.

Now let's test the service by implementing a simple Java client in JDeveloper. First we need to retrieve the WSDL of the OSB proxy service from the OSB server. In the Service Bus console, perform the following steps for saving the WSDL into a file:

17. In the **Project Explorer**, select the `sending-soap-over-jms` project.
18. Click on the `proxy` folder on the right.

19. Navigate to the **SoapOverJMS** proxy service and click on the **Export WSDL** icon (the third icon in the **Actions** cell).
20. Click on **Save**.
21. Save the `SoapOverJMS_wsdl.jar` to a temporary folder.

In JDeveloper, perform the following steps:

22. Create a new application by selecting **File** | **New**.
23. Enter `Generic` into the **search** field, select **Generic Application**, and click on **OK**.
24. Enter `SoapOverJms` into the **Application Name** field and click on **Next**.
25. Enter `SoapOverJMSClient` into the **Project Name** field and click on **Finish**.
26. Right-click on the **SoapOverJMSClient** in the project navigator and select **New**.
27. Enter `ant` in the **search** field, select **Empty Buildfile (Ant)**, and click on **OK**.
28. Leave **build.xml** as the file name and click on **OK**.
29. Open the **build.xml** and enter the following Ant script:

```
<project default="clientOSB">

  <path id="weblogic">
    <pathelement path="C:/oracle/MiddlewareJdev11gR1PS4/
wlserver_10.3/server/lib/weblogic.jar" />
  </path>

 <taskdef name="clientgen" classname="weblogic.wsee.tools.
anttasks.ClientGenTask"
          classpathref="weblogic"/>

 <target name="clientOSB">
  <clientgen wsdl="file:Helloworld.wsdl"
             destdir="src"
             packagename="osb.book.soap.jms"
             type="JAXRPC"/>
  <javac srcdir="src"
         destdir="classes"
         includes="osb.book.soap.jms/**/*.java"/>
 </target>
</project>
```

30. Change the path to the `weblogic.jar` so it matches with your environment.
31. Open the `SoapOverJMS_wsdl.jar` file that we just created and extract the `Helloworld.wsdl` and `Helloworld.xsd` into the `project` folder.

32. Right-click on the **build.xml** and select **Run Ant Target | clientOSB**.
33. JDeveloper creates the Web Service proxy client code. Confirm that this was successful by checking the **Ant Log** tab for the **BUILD SUCCESSFUL** message.
34. Right-click on the **SoapOverJMSClient** project and select **Project Properties**.
35. In the tree on the left, navigate to **Libraries and Classpath** and click on **Add Library**.
36. In the pop-up window select the **WebLogic 10.3 Remote-Client** library and click on **OK**.
37. Close the **Project Properties** window by clicking on **OK**.
38. Right-click on the **SoapOverJMSClient** project and select **New**.
39. Enter `java class` into the **search** field, select **Java Class**, and click on **OK**.
40. Enter `TestService` into the **Name** field, enable the **Main Method** checkbox, and click on **OK**.
41. Add the following import statements to the `TestService` Java class:

```
import java.net.URISyntaxException;
import java.rmi.RemoteException;

import javax.xml.rpc.ServiceException;
import javax.xml.rpc.Stub;

import osb.book.soap.jms.HelloWorldService;
import osb.book.soap.jms.
HelloWorldServiceSoapHttpPortBindingQSService;
import osb.book.soap.jms.
HelloWorldServiceSoapHttpPortBindingQSService_Impl;

import weblogic.wsee.connection.transport.jms.JmsTransportInfo;
```

Replace the main method by the following code:

```
public static void main(String[] args) throws ServiceException,
                                              URISyntaxException,
                                              RemoteException {

    HelloWorldServiceSoapHttpPortBindingQSService service =
        new HelloWorldServiceSoapHttpPortBindingQSService_Impl();
    HelloWorldService port =
        service.getHelloWorldServiceSoapHttpPortBindingQSPort();

    Stub stub = (Stub)port;
    String uri = "jms://[OSBServer]:[Port]?URI=SourceQueue";
    JmsTransportInfo ti =  new JmsTransportInfo(uri);
```

```
        stub._setProperty("weblogic.wsee.connection.transportinfo"
                                , ti);

        try {
            String result = null;
            System.out.println("start");
            result = port.sayHello();
            System.out.println("Got JMS result: " + result);
        } catch (RemoteException e) {
            e.printStackTrace();
        }
    }
```

42. Replace `[OSBServer]` and `[Port]` with the settings of the OSB server installation.

Now let's test the Java class.

43. Right-click on the `TestService.java` class and select **Run**:

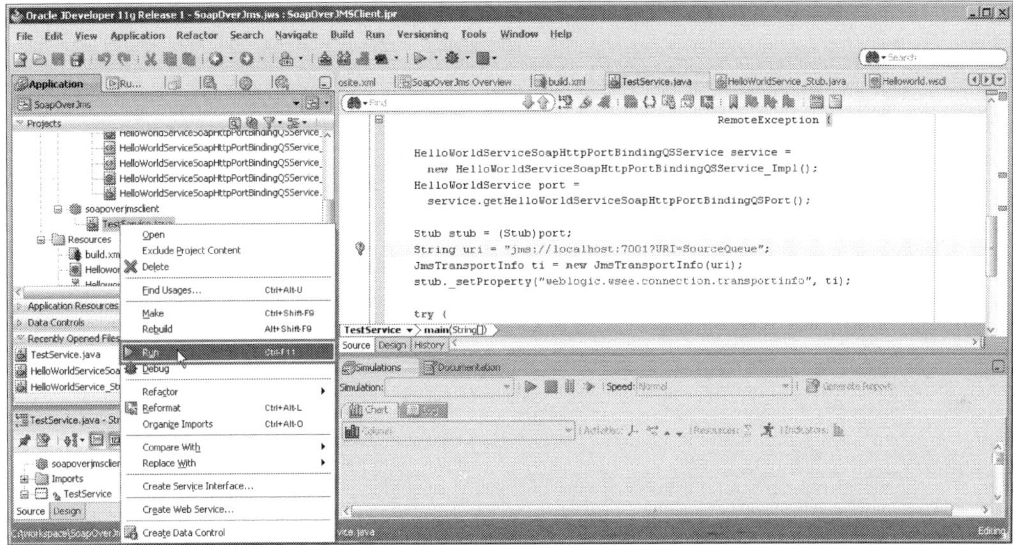

44. The **log** window will show the result of the call as shown in the following screenshot:

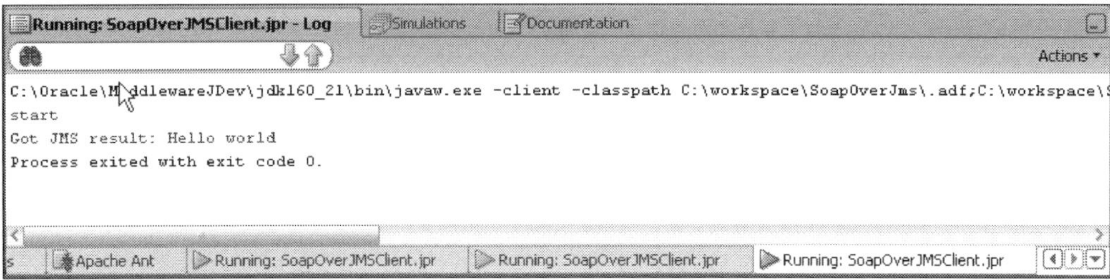

How it works...

SOAP over JMS works in the same manner as HTTP, but JMS will be more reliable. The JAX-RPC client in JDeveloper generates a request and puts it in a WebLogic queue. The proxy service consumes the request from the queue and executes the normal message flow. The proxy service publishes the response that is also on the queue and uses the value of the **JMSMessagId** property of the request as the `JMSCorrelationId`. The client listens on the queue for the response message with this `JMSCorrelationId`.

SOAP over JMS has the following disadvantages:

- The WSDL is only accessible in the Oracle Service Bus console
- On the client, you need to change the endpoint
- Only the JAX-RPC framework supports JMS. JAX-WS only supports HTTP
- On the server, we need to change the transport of the proxy service to JMS and enable correlation

11 Handling Message-level Security Requirements

In this chapter, we will cover:

- Preparing OSB server to work with OWSM
- Configuring OSB server for OWSM
- Securing a proxy service by Username Token authentication
- Securing a proxy service by protecting the message
- Securing a proxy service by using Username Token authentication and protecting the message
- Securing a proxy service by using certificate authentication and protecting the message
- Securing a proxy service with authorization through Message Access Control
- Using JDeveloper to test a secured service
- Calling a secured service from OSB

Introduction

Security has always played and still plays an important role in today's information-driven business processes. Consumers of information must know who sent the information and whether it has not been changed or read by others. Only then can they trust the message and do the transaction.

When thinking about security it's important to distinguish between Transport and Message-level security.

Transport-level security represents a technique where the underlying operating system or application servers are handling security features. Recipes for transport-level security are covered in the next chapter.

Message-level security represents a technique where all information related to security is encapsulated in the message. This is what WS-Security specifies for web services. Securing messages using message-level security instead of using transport-level security has several advantages that include:

- Flexibility – parts of the message can be signed or encrypted. This means that intermediary nodes can see parts of the message that are indented for them. This might be necessary in a routing scenario, so that the intermediary can determine where to send the message to.
- Supports multiple protocols – secured messages can be sent over different protocols such as FTP, HTTP, or e-mail without having to use the protocol level security.

Oracle Service Bus (OSB) supports both Transport and Message-level security. The level of security available on the OSB is dependent on the transport protocol used.

In this chapter, we will only cover Message-level security related recipes. The recipes for Transport-level security are covered in the next chapter.

Security in the OSB is handled by the **Oracle Web Service Manager** (**OWSM**). OWSM was introduced in the 11gR1 version of the OSB. Before 11gR1, we could only use the WLS 9.2 policies. Oracle recommends using the OWSM policies because in the next major releases of OSB, the old WLS 9.2 policies will no longer be supported.

Preparing OSB server to work with OWSM

Before OWSM can be used, we need to create a Metadata Service (MDS) database repository. The OWSM policies will be stored in the MDS and these policies can be used at design time by Eclipse OEPE or the Service Bus console, and at runtime by the OSB server. The second step is to extend our OSB domain with the OWSM and the Enterprise Manager options.

This recipe will show how to create an OWSM-enabled OSB domain.

Getting ready

1. For this recipe, you will need the following in place. A WebLogic domain which has the OSB version 11gR1 option will need to be enabled.
2. An Oracle Database in version 10*g* R2, 11*g* R1, or 11*g* R2. The database should be on the latest patch set.

3. A database schema user which has the `sysdba` privilege that can be used by the **Repository Creation Utility** (**RCU**).
4. Download the Repository Creation Utility. It can be downloaded from `http://www.oracle.com/technetwork/middleware/soasuite/downloads/index.html`, here we should accept license agreement and open the **Prerequisites & Recommended Install Process** of the SOA Suite. The version of SOA Suite should match with the OSB version we are using in this cookbook.

How to do it...

First we need to start the Repository Creation Utility which we will use to create the Metadata Service schema in the Oracle Database.

1. Extract the `ofm_rcu_win_11.1.1.4.0_disk1_1of1.zip` file to the following folder `c:\temp\ofm_rcu_win_11.1.1.4.0_disk1_1of1`.
2. **Open Windows Explorer** and browse to `c:\temp\ofm_rcu_win_11.1.1.4.0_disk1_1of1\rcuHome\BIN`.
3. Double-click on the `rcu.bat` command file to start the **Repository Creation Utility** and click **Next**.
4. Choose **Create** at the **Create Repository** step.
5. Choose **Oracle Database** as the value of the **Database Type** drop-down listbox.
6. Enter the name of the server where the database is running into the **Host Name** field.
7. Enter the port on which the database listener is listening (often `1521`) into the **Port** field.
8. Enter the service name for the database into the **Service Name** field.
9. Enter the username for the database into the **Username** field. The user must have the SYSDBA privilege.
10. Enter the password of the database user into the **Password** field and click **Next**.
11. This will open the **Checking Prerequisites** window and some checks are started. A pop-up window will indicate if the wrong database version has been specified.
12. Click **OK**.
13. Select **Create a new Prefix** in the **Select Components** step.
14. Type **COOKBOOK** as the value in the **Create a new Prefix** field.

15. Expand the **AS Common Schemas** item in the component tree and enable the **Metadata Services** option and click **Next**.

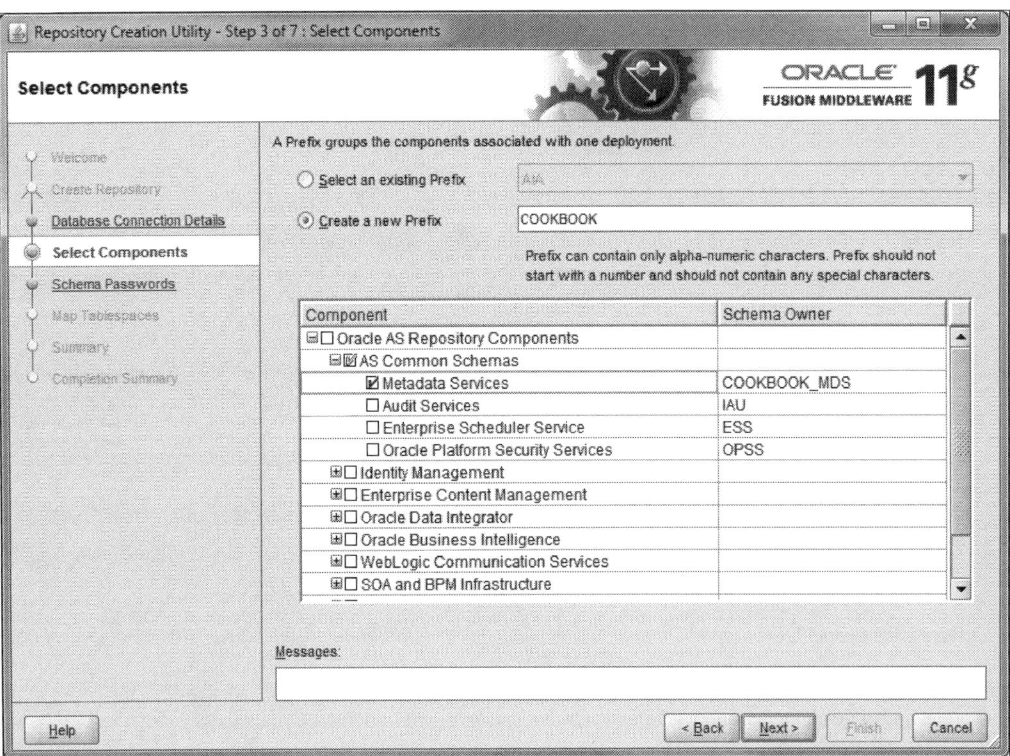

16. This will again open the **Checking Prerequisites** window and some checks are started. All checks should be ok this time.

17. Click **OK**.

18. In the **Schema Passwords** step, select **Use same passwords for all schemas** and type `welcome` as the value for the **Password** and **Confirm Password** field.

19. Click **Next** twice.

20. Click **OK** to confirm the creation of the tablespaces for the Metadata Services repository.

21. A check will run to see if the RCU can create the tablespaces.

22. Click **OK**.

23. On the **Summary** step, click **Create**.

24. After the creation of the Metadata Services schema and tablespaces, the RCU will show a completion summary. The status column should have the value **Success**.

25. Finish the RCU by clicking **Close**.

Next we will add the OWSM product to an existing WebLogic domain. Start the configuration wizard `config.cmd` located in the `[OSB-HOME]\wlserver_10.3\common\bin` folder and perform the following steps:

26. Choose **Extend an existing WebLogic domain** and click **Next**.
27. In the **Select a WebLogic Domain Directory** window, navigate to `user_projects\domains\`, choose `osb_cookbook_domain` and click **Next**.
28. In the **Select Extension Source** window, choose the following products, if not already selected and click **Next**:

    Oracle WSM Policy Manager

    Oracle Service Bus OWSM Extension

    Oracle Enterprise Manager

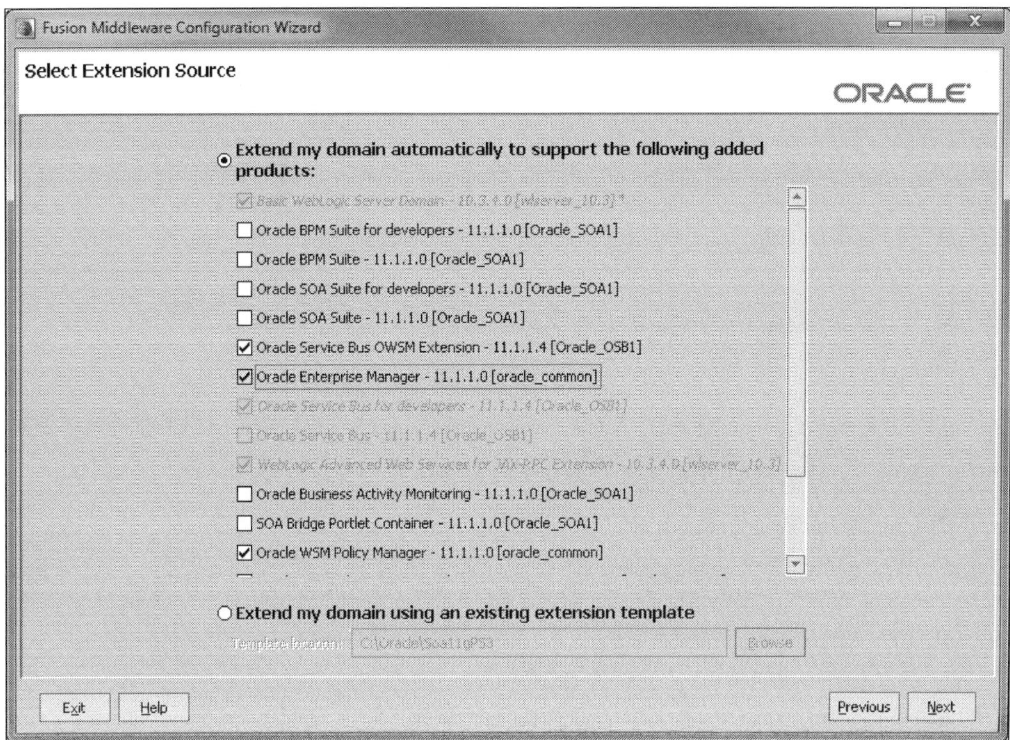

29. In the **Configure JDBC Component Schema** window, select the **OWSM MDS Schema** checkbox. Enter **COOKBOOK_MDS** for the **Schema Owner** field.
30. Enter `welcome` into the **Schema Password** field.
31. Provide the database details in the **DBMS/Service**, **Host Name** and the **Port** fields.

32. Click **Next** to test the JDBC connection.

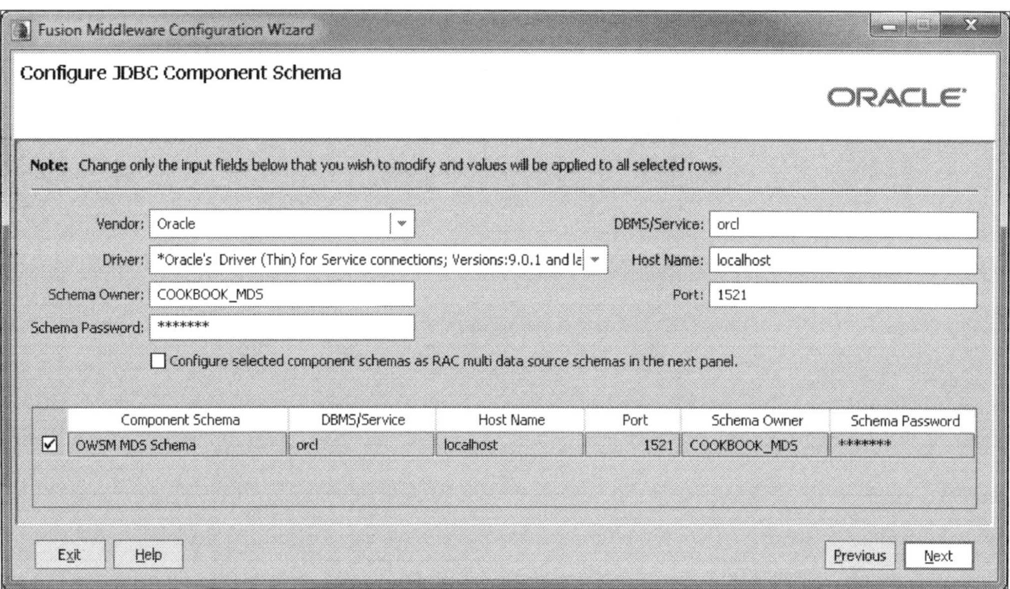

33. The test should return the **Test Successful!** message.
34 Click **Next** twice.
35. In the **Configuration Summary** window, click **Extend**.
36. After reaching 100 percent in the progress bar, click **Done**.

We have successfully added the OWSM schema to the database repository and extended the existing OSB domain by OWSM.

How it works...

The WebLogic domain configuration wizard configures the Metadata Services with the OWSM policies by adding the OWSM product to the WebLogic domain. The Metadata Services is a database repository and is created by the RCU. The WebLogic domain now contains a reference to these OWSM policies and at design time, the Eclipse OEPE or the Service Bus console can retrieve these policies from our WebLogic domain.

Configuring OSB server for OWSM

After installing the OWSM component to our WebLogic domain, we will be configuring the OSB server for OWSM. For this, we need to generate a custom Java keystore which contains the server certificates and configure it in **Enterprise Manager** (**EM**).

How to do it...

First, let's create a Java keystore which will be used by OWSM. On the command line, perform the following steps:

1. Navigate to the `bin` folder of the JDK used by the OSB:

   ```
   cd c:\[FMWHome]\jrockit-jdk1.6.0_20-R28.1\bin
   ```

2. Generate a new Java keystore with a self-signed server key:

   ```
   keytool -genkey -alias serverKey -keyalg "RSA" -sigalg
     "SHA1withRSA" -dname "CN=server, C=US"
     -keypass welcome -keystore c:\server.jks -storepass welcome
   ```

3. Copy the Java keystore `server.jks` located at `c:\` to the `config\fmwconfig` folder of the OSB domain:

   ```
   cd ..\..
   ```

   ```
   cd user_projects\domains\osb_cookbook_domain\config\fmwconfig
   ```

   ```
   copy c:\server.jks .
   ```

Next, we have to import the Java keystore into **Enterprise Manager**. Open **Enterprise Manager** in a browser window (`http://localhost:7001/em`) and perform the following steps:

4. Login with the **weblogic** user account.
5. In the tree to the left, expand the **WebLogic Domain** tree node.
6. Click on **osb_cookbook_domain**.
7. In the right window, click on the **WebLogic Domain** to open the drop-down menu.

8. Select **Security | Security Provider Configuration.**

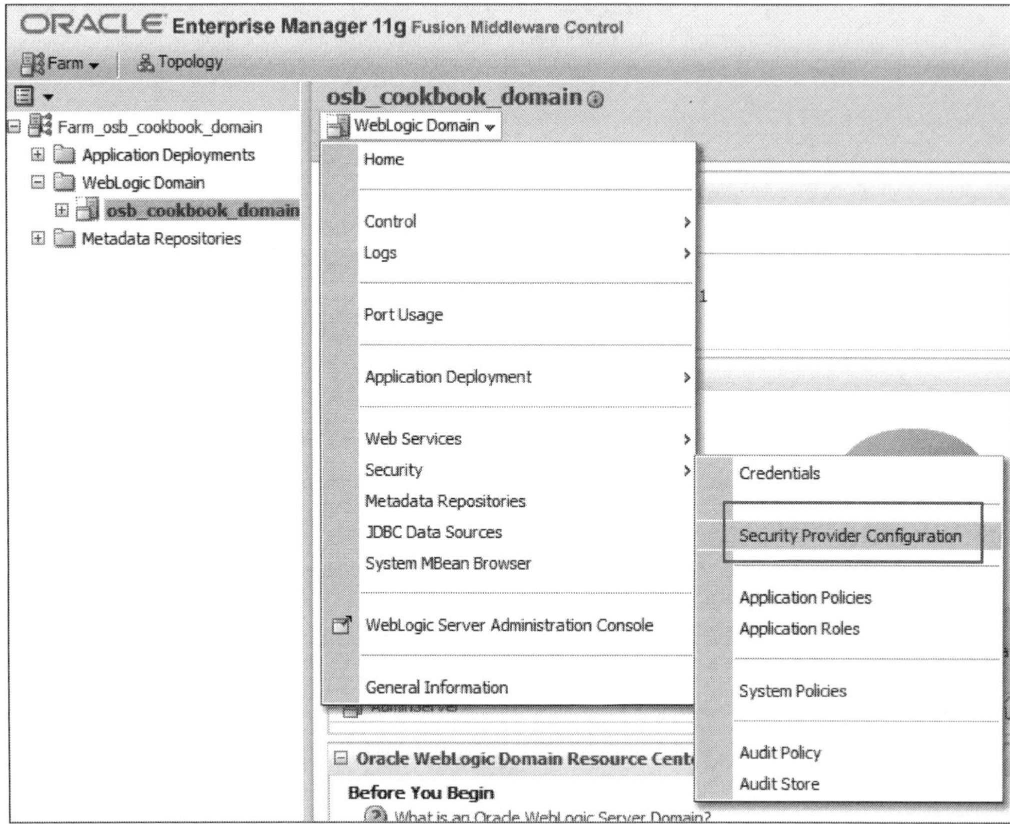

9. In the **Security Provider Configuration** page, expand the **Keystore** option.

10. Click **Configure...**.

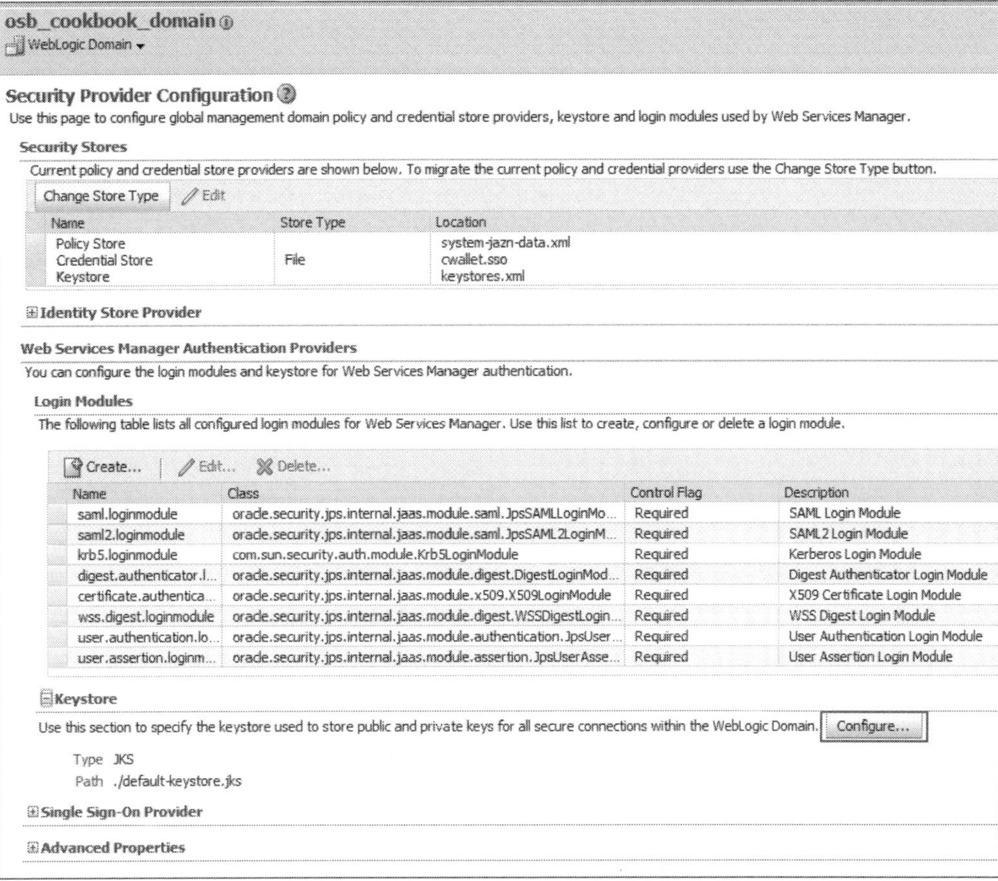

11. Enter `./server.jks` into the **Keystore Path** field.
12. Enter `welcome` into the **Password** and **Confirm Password** field.
13. Enter `serverKey` into the **Key Alias** field in the **Signature Key** section.
14. Enter `welcome` into the **Signature Password** and **Confirm Password** field.
15. Enter `serverKey` into the **Crypt Alias** field in the **Encryption Key** section.
16. Enter `welcome` into the **Crypt Password** and **Confirm Password** field.

17. Click **OK**.

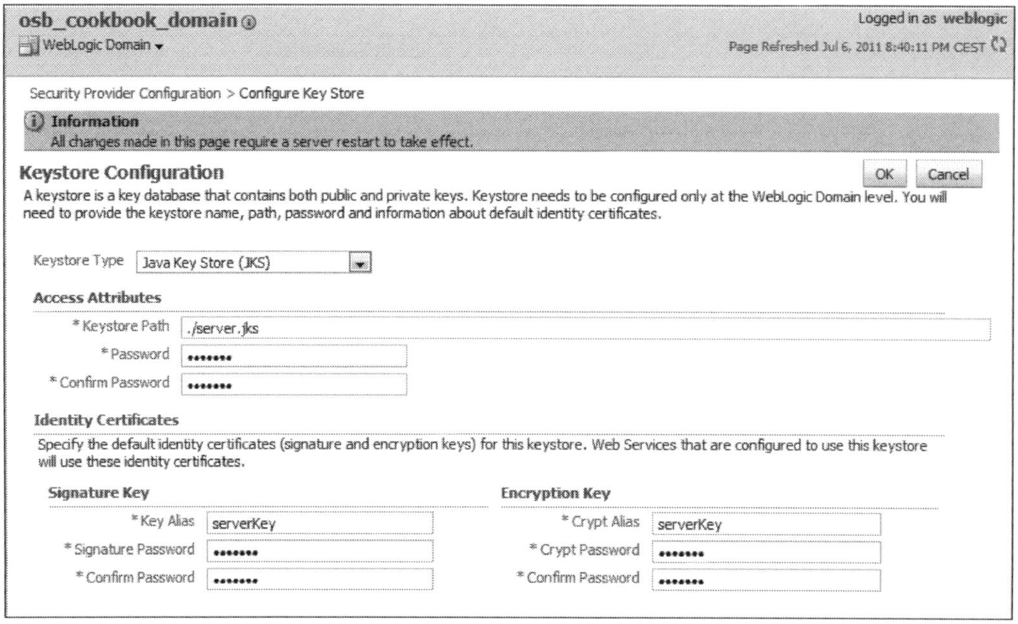

18. Restart the server.

We have successfully created a Java keystore and configured it for our OSB domain.

Now, let's create a user we will use for the authentication later. In the Service Bus console, perform the following steps:

19. Navigate to the **Security Configuration** using the menu on the left side.
20. Select the **Users** menu item and click **Add New**.
21. Enter `osbbook` into the **User Name** field and `welcome1` into the **New Password** and **Confirm Password** fields.
22. Leave **DefaultAuthenticator** for the **Authentication Provider** and click **Save**.

Adding a new user through the Service Bus console can be done outside a change session.

Next we need to add the `osbbook` user to the domain credential store. A credential store is a repository of security data. The credential is used later by the Service Bus test console in order to look up the username and password. In **Enterprise Manager**, perform the following steps to add a credential to the credential store:

23. In the tree to the left, expand the **WebLogic Domain** entry and select the domain.

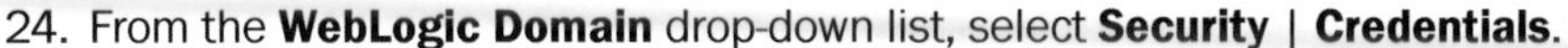

24. From the **WebLogic Domain** drop-down list, select **Security | Credentials**.

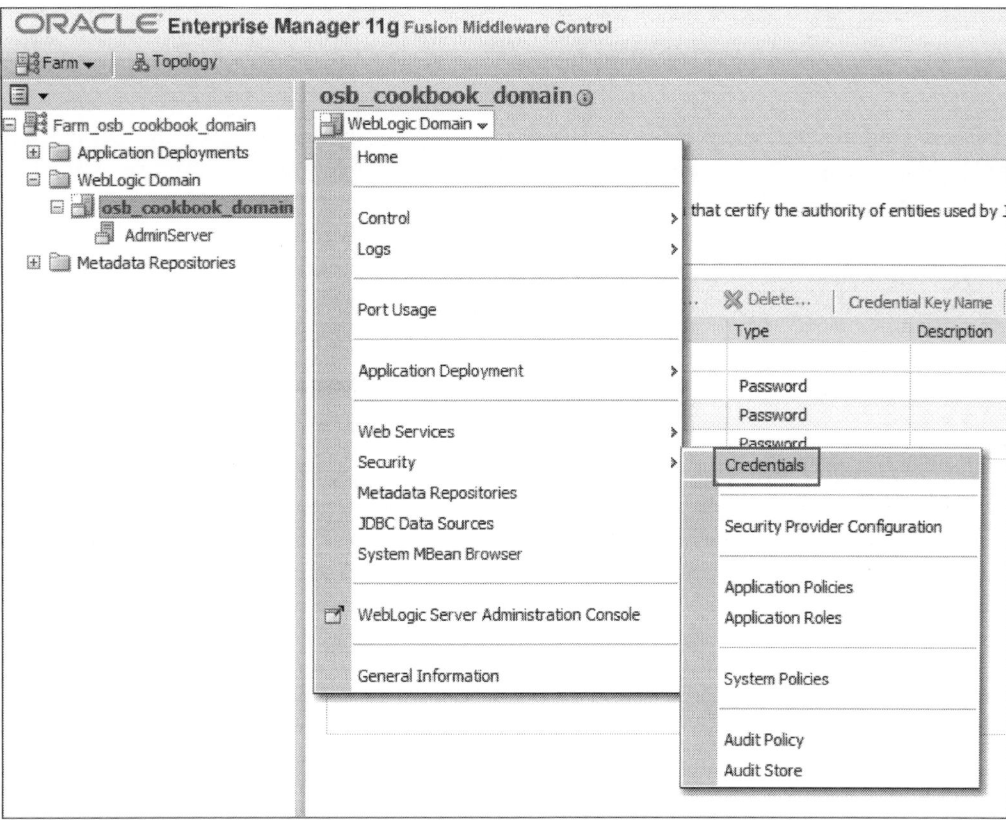

25. In the **Credentials** page, expand the **oracle.wsm.security** node.
26. Click **Create Key** and the **Create Key** pop-up window will be shown.

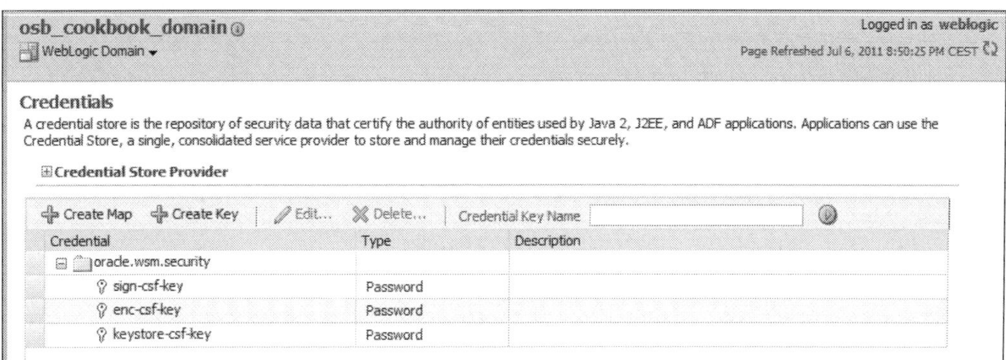

27. Enter `osbbook-key` into the **Key** field
28. Enter `osbbook` into the **User Name** field and `welcome1` into the **Password** and **Confirm Password** field.
29. Click **OK**.

We have now set up the OSB server to work with OWSM and also created and configured the `osbbook` user which we will use later.

How it works...

In this recipe, we created a Java keystore and this keystore contains a self-signed Server Key which will be used by OWSM. For production it is better to use a certificate which is signed by a known **Certificate Authority** (**CA**). The Server Key consists of two parts: the private key part will be used by the receiver to decrypt the incoming messages and to sign the messages and the public key part is used by the sender to encrypt the message and to check the signature.

Enterprise Manager uses the **Credential Store Framework** (**CSF**) to store the credentials, such as username/password combinations, tickets, and public key certificates. The configuration of the CSF is maintained in the `jps-config.xml` file in the domain folder.

There's more...

A credential can also be created from the command line using **Web Logic Scripting Toolkit (WLST)**. In a command window, perform the following steps:

1. Run `wlst.cmd` located in the `[FMWHome]\oracle_common\common\bin` folder.
2. Connect to the domain:

```
connect('weblogic','welcome1','t3://localhost:7001')
```

3. Create the **osbbook-key** credential:

```
createCred(map="oracle.wsm.security", key="osbbook-key",
  user="osbbook", password="welcome1",desc="osbbook-key")
```

4. Disconnect from WLST:

```
disconnect()
exit()
```

Securing a proxy service by Username Token authentication

In this recipe, we will secure a proxy service with an OWSM server policy using Eclipse OEPE.

Getting ready

For this recipe, we will use a simple OSB project with one proxy. Import the `getting-ready` project into Eclipse OEPE from `\chapter-11\getting-ready\\securing-a-proxy-service-with-username-token`.

The OSB Server must be up and running and configured using the first two recipes of this chapter. This server needs to be defined in the Eclipse OEPE for this recipe to work.

How to do it...

In Eclipse OEPE, perform the following steps to add an OWSM policy to a proxy service:

1. Open the **CustomerManagement.proxy** in the `proxy` folder of the **securing-a-proxy-service-with-username-token** project.
2. Navigate to the **Policy** tab.
3. Enable **From OWSM Policy Store**.
4. Click **Service Level Policies**, which will enable the **Add** button.
5. Click **Add** and the **OWSM Policy Configuration** window will open.

6. Click **Browse**.

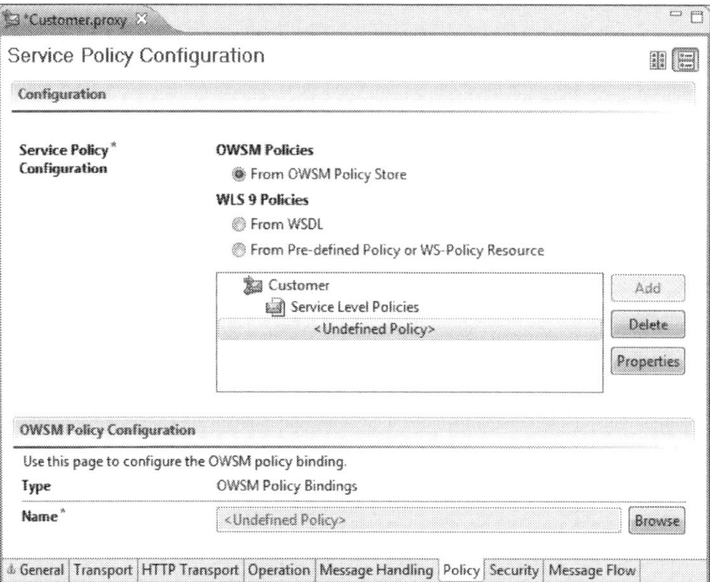

7. In the **Select OWSM Policy** window we need to choose a security or management policy.
8. Enter `*username*` into the **Name** field and click **Search**.

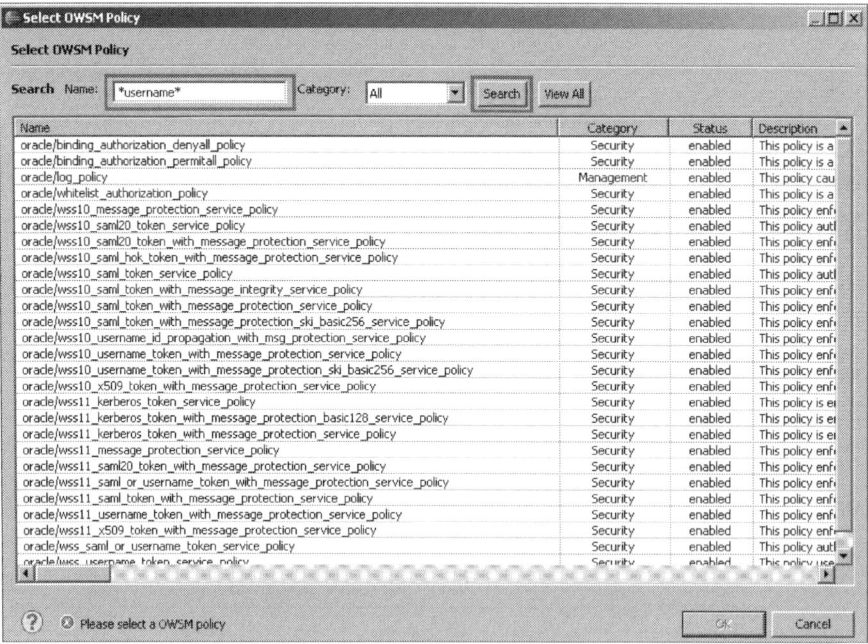

9. Select the **oracle/wss_username_token_service_policy** from the list of policies and click **OK**.
10. The Username Token policy will be displayed in the **Policy** tab of the proxy service.

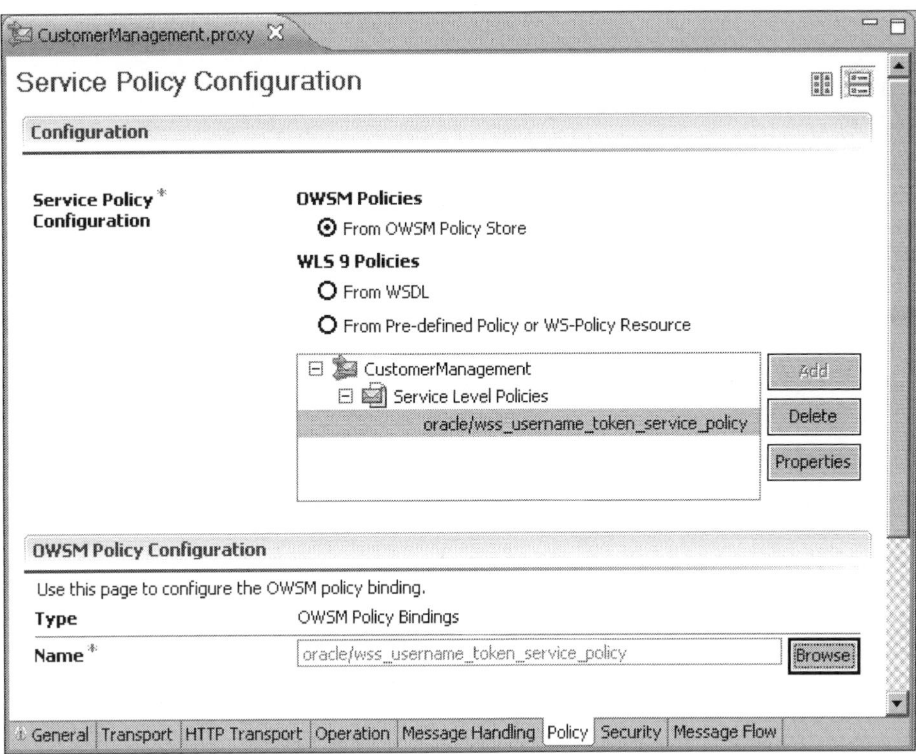

11. Save the project and deploy it to the OSB server.

We have successfully secured our proxy service using `UsernameToken` WS-Security SOAP headers to authenticate users.

Now let's test it first using the Service Bus test console. In the Service Bus console, perform the following steps:

12. Navigate to the **CustomerManagement** proxy service (in **Project Explorer**, click on the project and then on the `proxy` folder) and click on the **Launch Test Console** icon (with the bug).
13. Click **Execute** (the value passed in the **ID** does not have an effect; the answer of the proxy service is hardcoded).

14. We get an error because we have not passed a username and password.

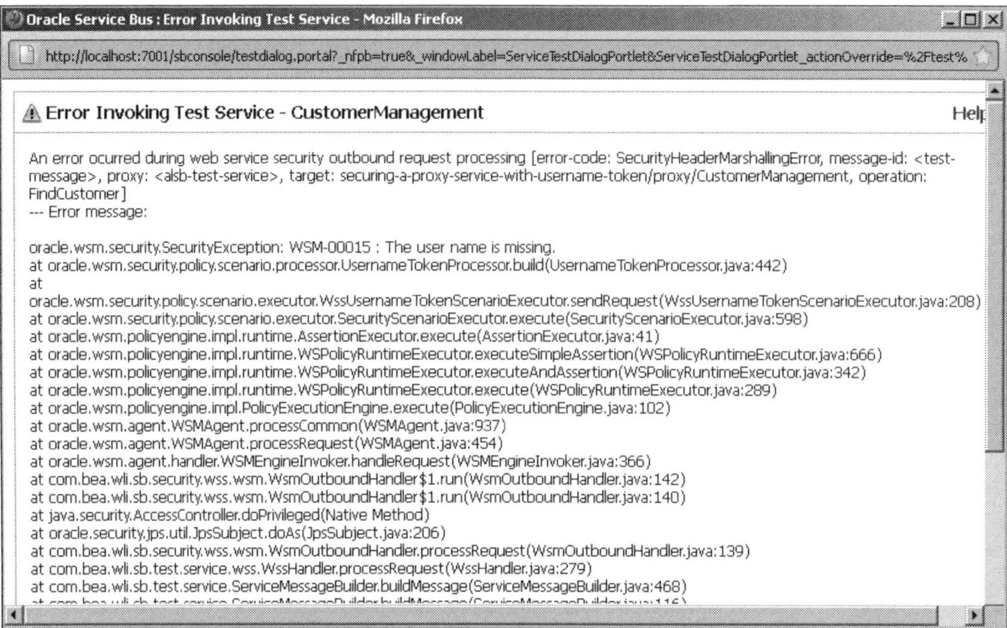

15. Click **Back** to specify the username and password.
16. In the test console, scroll down until the **Security** area is visible.
17. Enter `osbbook-key` into the **Override Value** field and click **Execute**.

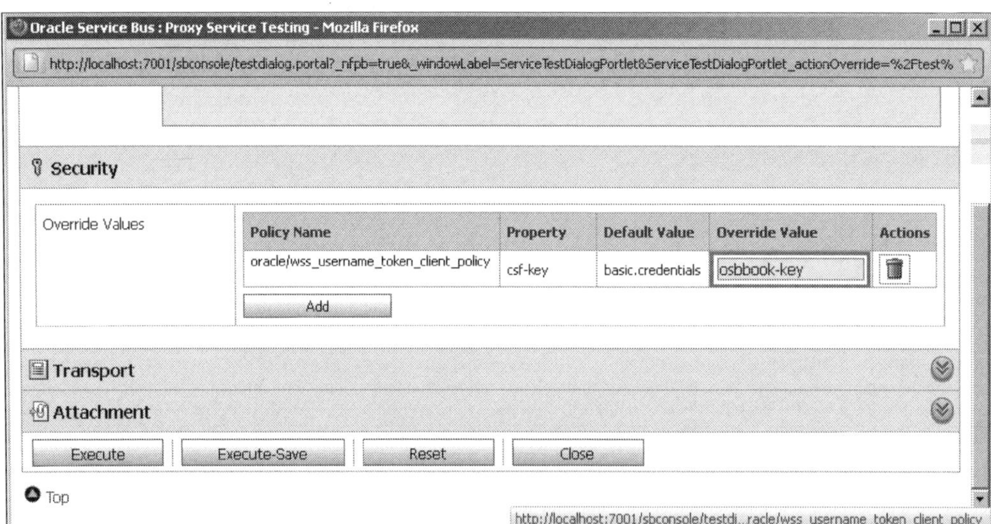

18. The test should now work and a valid response should be returned by the proxy service. The test console also shows the SOAP header with the Username Token necessary for the authentication.

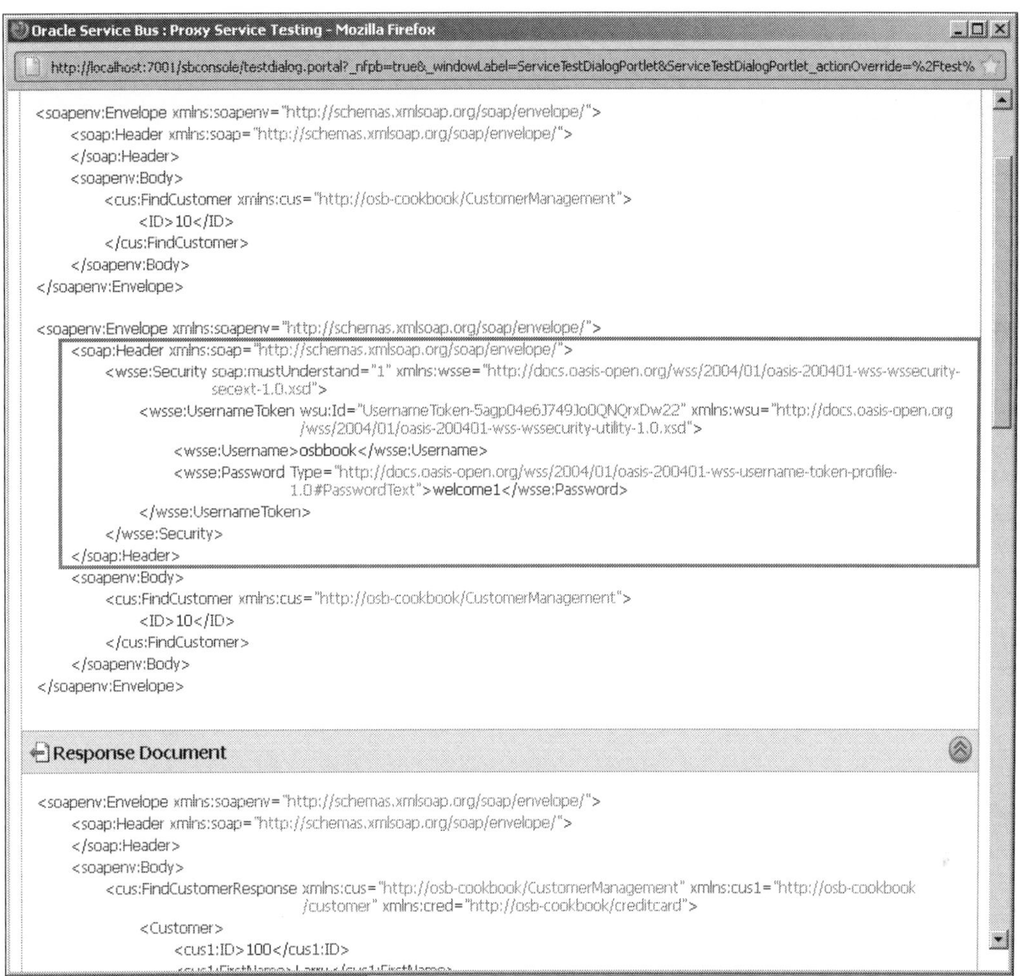

How it works...

The Username Token authentication policy uses the credentials in the `UsernameToken` WS-Security header to authenticate users. Only the plain text mechanism is supported. The credentials are authenticated against the configured identity store on WebLogic server.

The usernames used in the user authentication policies will be validated against the users of the WebLogic security realm and the SOAP body will not be encrypted.

To add the OWSM policy to the proxy service, Eclipse OEPE needs to contact the OSB WebLogic server to retrieve the available OWSM server policies. We can add one or more OWSM policy references to a proxy service. These policies can only be added or verified when the OSB WebLogic server is running.

When the proxy service is deployed to the OSB Server, we can retrieve the WSDL of the proxy service. This WSDL will contain the WS security policies which can be used by the clients of this proxy service.

There's more...

SoapUI can also be used to test secured web services. To test the proxy service just created previously, perform the following steps in soapUI:

1. Create a new soapUI project by consuming the WSDL from the proxy service, which is available under: `http://[OSBServer]:[port]/securing-a-proxy-service-with-username-token/proxy/CustomerManagement?wsdl`.
2. Double-click on the new project in the project tree.
3. Navigate to the **WS-Security Configurations** tab.
4. Within the **WS-Security Configurations**, navigate to the **Outgoing WS-Security Configurations** tab.
5. Click on the **+** button to create a new outgoing configuration.
6. Enter `UsernameToken` into the **Name** cell and click **OK**.
7. Click on the **+** button below the new configuration to add a WSS entry.
8. From the drop-down list, select **Username**.
9. Click **OK**.
10. Enter `osbbook` into the **Username** filed and `welcome1` into the **Password** field.

11. Select **PasswordText** for the **Password Type**.

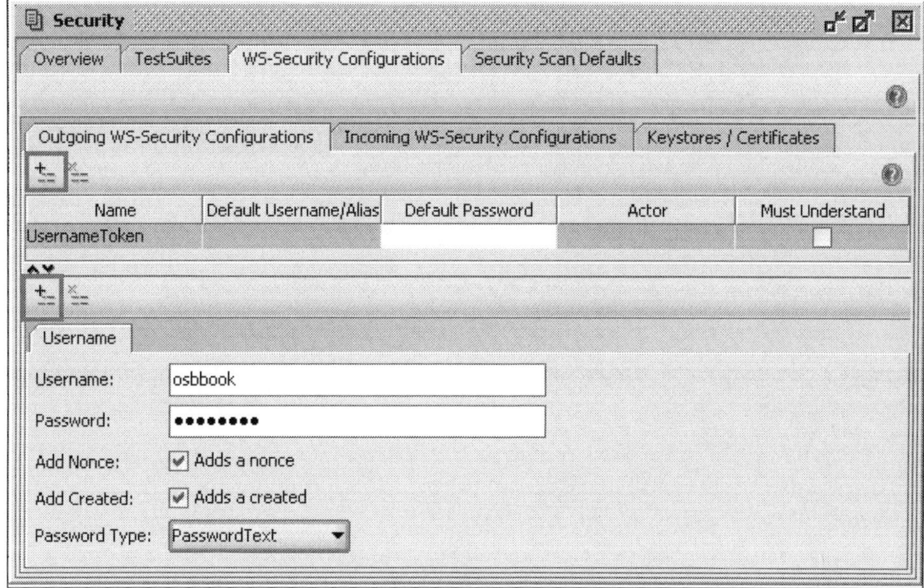

12. Close the window.
13. Open **Request 1** for the **FindCustomer** operation.
14. Replace the **?** with **1** in the **ID** element.
15. Run the test by clicking on the green arrow icon. A security error will be returned, because the WSS configuration is not yet used.
16. Click the **Aut** button in the lower-left corner (marked red in the following screenshot):

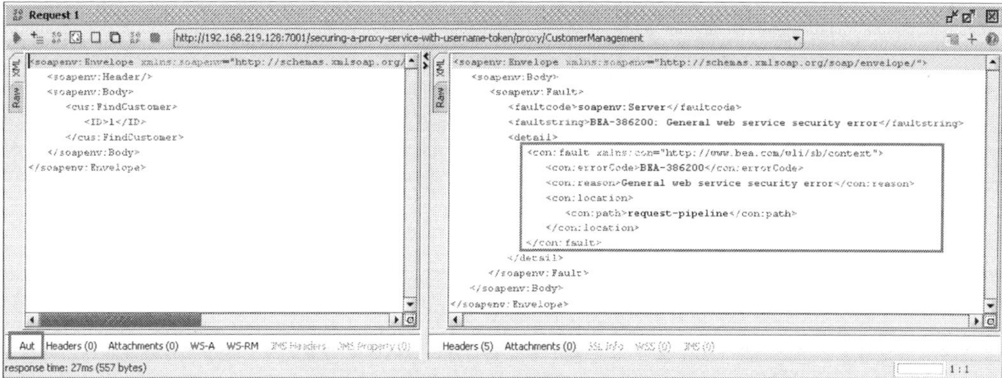

17. Select **UsernameToken** in the **Outgoing WSS** drop-down list.
18. Rerun the test and a valid response should be returned.

Securing a proxy service by protecting the message

Apart from requiring the user to authenticate themselves to the proxy service, we can also enforce that a message be encrypted and signed using the message protection policies. In this recipe, we will enable the message protection to guarantee message integrity through digital signature and message confidentiality through XML encryption.

For this to work, we need to have the public key of the server certificate.

Getting ready

For this we will use the same simple OSB project as in the previous *Securing a proxy service using Username Token authentication* recipe.

Import the `getting-ready` project into Eclipse from `\chapter-11\getting-ready\securing-a-proxy-service-with-message-protection`.

How to do it...

The steps to execute in this recipe are the same as in the previous *Securing a proxy service using Username Token Authentication* recipe, only another policy needs to be selected. In the Eclipse OEPE, perform the following steps:

1. Open the **CustomerManagement.proxy** in the `proxy` folder of the **securing-a-proxy-service-with-message-protection** project.
2. Navigate to the **Policy** tab.
3. Enable **From OWSM Policy Store**.
4. Click **Service Level Policies**, which will enable the **Add** button.
5. Click **Add** and the **OWSM Policy Configuration** window will open.
6. Click **Browse**.
7. In the **Select OWSM Policy** window, we need to choose a security or management policy.
8. Enter `*message_protection_service*` in the **Name** field and click **Search**.
9. Select the **oracle/wss11_message_protection_service_policy** from the list of policies.

10. Click **OK**.
11. The message protection policy will be displayed in the **Policy** tab of the proxy service.

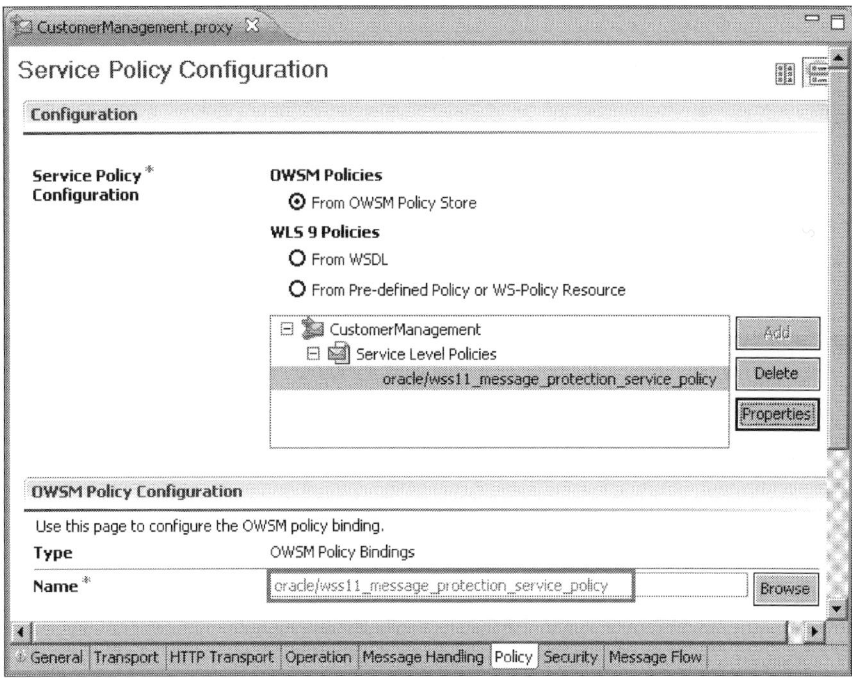

12. Save the project and deploy it to the OSB server.

Instead of `oracle/wss11_message_protection_service_policy`, we could also use `oracle/wss10_message_protection_service_policy` on this proxy service.

In the Service Bus console, perform the following steps for testing the service:

13. Navigate to the **CustomerManagement** proxy service (in **Project Explorer**, click on the **securing-a-proxy-service-with-message-protection** project and then on the `proxy` folder) and click on the **Launch Test Console** icon (the bug).
14. Click on **Execute** (the value passed in the **ID** does not have an effect; the answer of the proxy service is hardcoded).
15. We may get an error because we have not defined a certificate.
16. Click **Back** to specify the username and password.
17. In the test console, scroll down until the **Security** area is visible.

18. Enter `serverkey` into the **Override Value** field for the property **keystore.recipient.alias**.
19. Enter `enc-csf-key` into the **Override Value** field for the property **keystore.enc.csf.key**.
20. Click **Execute**.

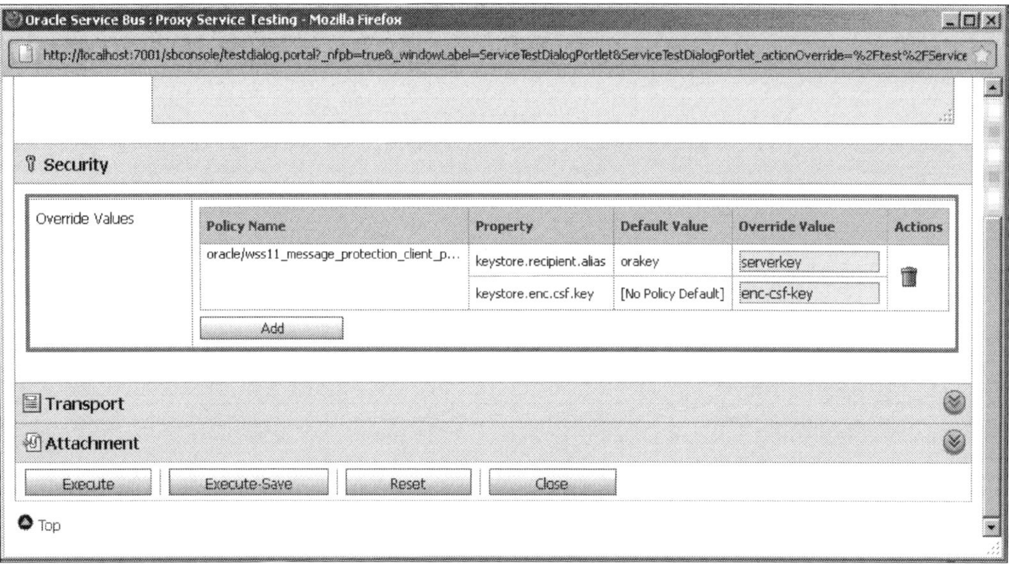

21. The test should now work and a valid response should be returned by the proxy service. The test console also shows the SOAP headers passed in the request message with the encrypted key.

How it works...

With the message protection policy, the public key of the server is used to encrypt the SOAP body. OWSM will use the private key of the server to decrypt the SOAP body.

The CSF keys used in the Service Bus test console match the entries we have seen when setting up the credential store (**WebLogic Domain** | **Security** | **Credentials**)

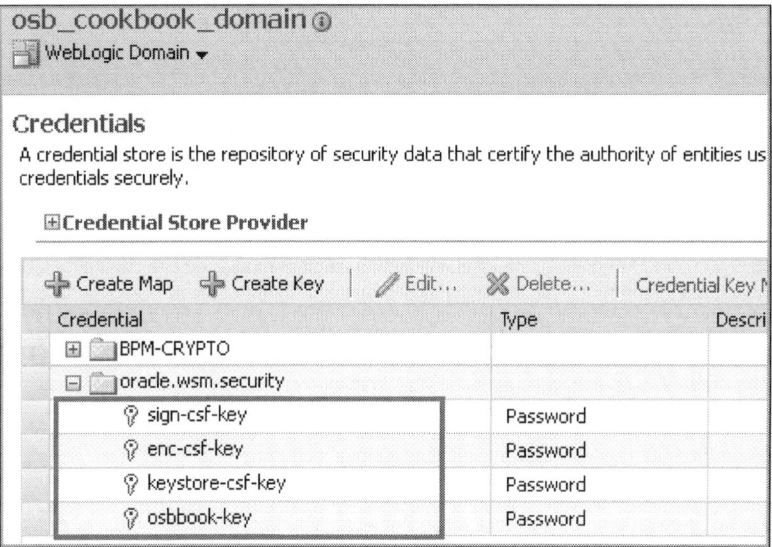

There's more...

Policies can also be directly manipulated on the OSB server through the OSB console.

To remove the old policy and add the new one for the message protection used in this recipe, perform the following steps in the Service Bus console:

1. Click on the **Project Explorer**.
2. Click on the **securing-a-proxy-service-with-username-token** project.
3. Click on the `proxy` folder.
4. Click on **Create** in the **Change Center** in the upper-left corner, to start a new change session.

5. Click on the **CustomerManagement** proxy service.

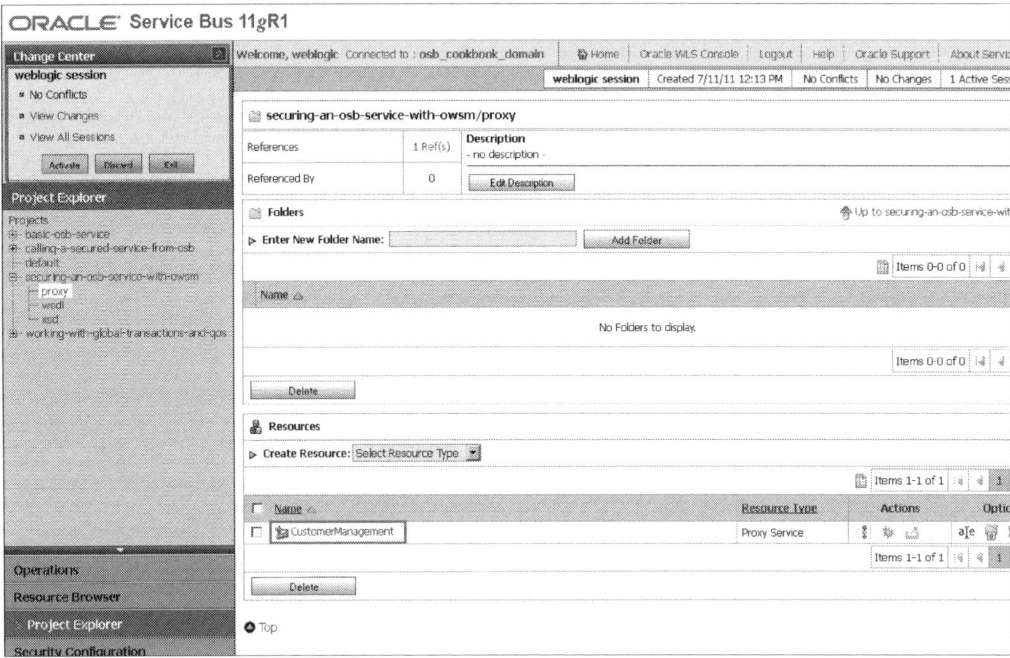

6. Navigate to the **Policies** tab.
7. Click on the garbage bin icon to delete the `oracle/wss_username_token_policy` service-level policies.
8. Click **Add**.
9. The **Select OWSM Policy** window is shown.
10. Enter `*message_protection_service*` into the **Name** field of the **Search** section and click **Search**.
11. Select **oracle/wss11_message_protection_service_policy** and click **Submit**.
12. Click **Update**.
13. Click **Activate** in the **Change Center** section to apply the changes.
14. Enter `Replaced wss_username_token_policy by message_protection_service_policy` into the **Description** field to document the change and click **Submit**.

Securing a proxy service by using Username Token authentication and protecting the message

In this recipe, we will combine message protection with user authentication. For this we can reuse the client Java keystore and the `osbbook` user from the preceding recipes.

Getting ready

For this we will use the same simple OSB project as in the previous *Securing a proxy service using username and password authentication through OWSM* recipe.

Import the `getting-ready` project into Eclipse OEPE from `\chapter-11\getting-ready\securing-a-proxy-service-with-auth-and-message-protection`.

How to do it...

The steps to execute in this recipe are the same as in the previous *Securing a proxy service using username and password authentication through OWSM* recipe, only another policy needs to be selected. In the Eclipse OEPE, perform the following steps:

1. Open the **CustomerManagement.proxy** in the `proxy` folder of the **securing-a-proxy-service-with-auth-and-message-protection** project.
2. Navigate to the **Policy** tab.
3. Enable **From OWSM Policy Store**.
4. Click **Service Level Policies**, which will enable the **Add** button.
5. Click **Add** and the **OWSM Policy Configuration** window will open.
6. Click **Browse**.
7. In the **Select OWSM Policy** window, we need to choose a security or management policy.
8. Enter `*username_token_with*` into the **Name** field and click **Search**.

9. Select the **oracle/wss11_username_token_with_message_protection_service_policy** from the list of policies and click **OK**.

   The Username Token policy will be displayed in the **Policy** tab of the proxy service.

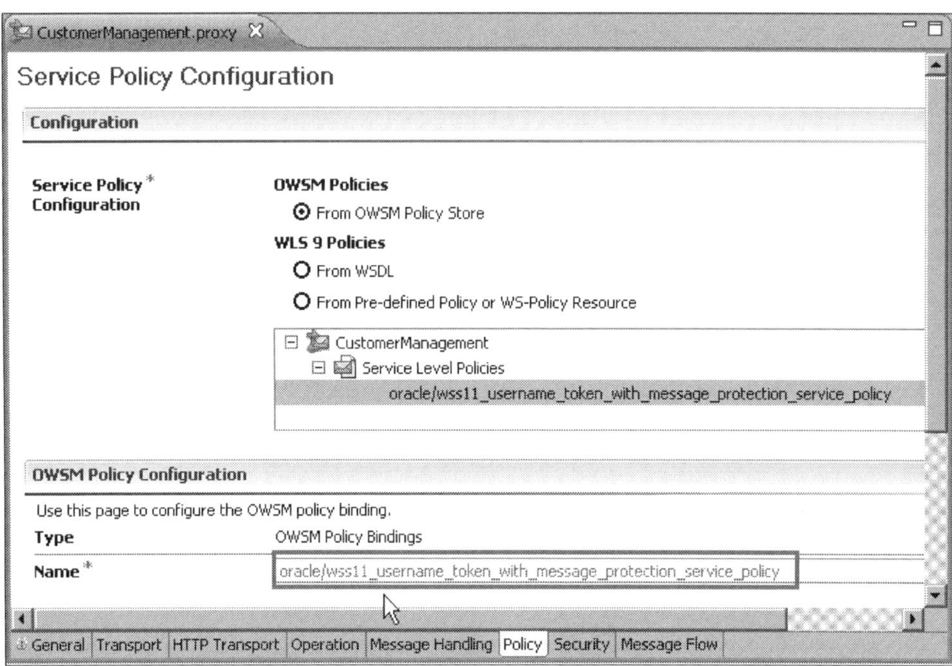

10. Save the project and deploy it to the OSB server.

Instead of the `oracle/wss11_username_token_with_message_protection_service_policy` we could also use `oracle/wss10_username_token_with_message_protection_service_policy` for this proxy service.

In the Service Bus console, perform the following steps for testing the service:

11. Navigate to the **CustomerManagement** proxy service (in the **Project Explorer**, click on the **securing-a-proxy-service-with-auth-and-message-protection** project and then on the `proxy` folder) and click on the **Launch Test Console** icon (with the bug).
12. Click **Execute** (the value passed in the **ID** does not have an effect; the answer of the proxy service is hardcoded).
13. We will get an error saying that the username is missing.
14. Click **Back** to specify the username and password.
15. In the test console, scroll down until the **Security** area is visible.

16. Enter `serverkey` into the **Override Value** field for the property **keystore.recipient.alias**.
17. Enter `enc-csf-key` into the **Override Value** field for the property **keystore.enc.csf.key**.
18. Enter `osbbook-key` into the **Override Value** field for the property **csf.key**.
19. Click **Execute**.

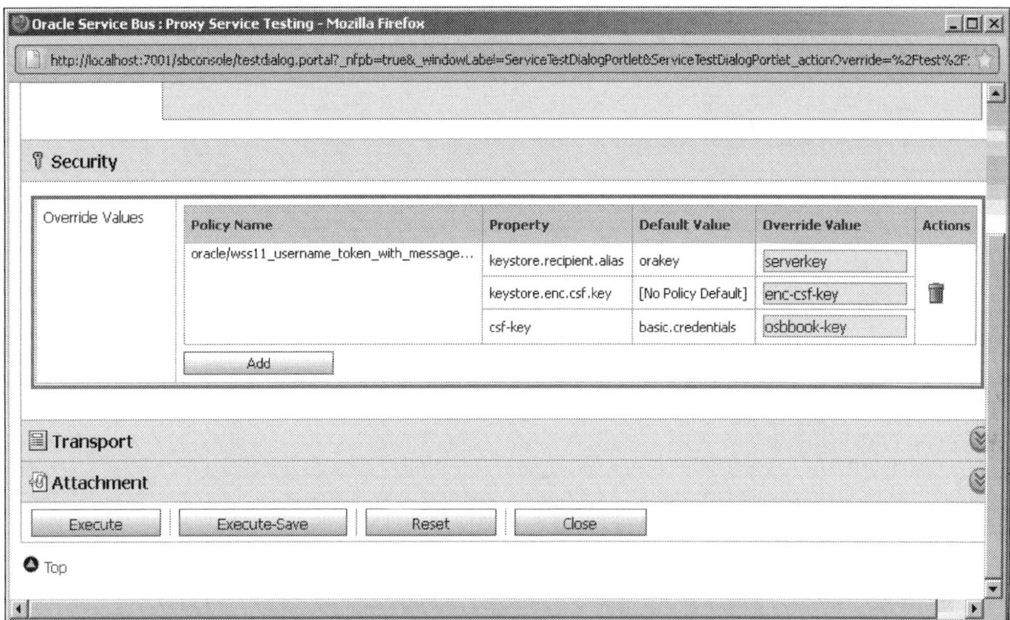

20. The test should now work and a valid response should be returned by the proxy service. The test console also shows the various SOAP headers passed in the request message holding the security information.

How it works...

The Username Token authentication, together with message protection policy, authenticates the service consumer using the Username Token and also encrypts the SOAP body.

The public key of the server is used to encrypt the SOAP body.

Securing a proxy service by using certificate authentication and protecting the message

In this recipe, we will also use the message protection similar to the previous recipes but replace the username/password authentication with a client certificate authentication. For this, we need to generate a client certificate and add the public key of the client certificate to the server Java keystore. This way, OWSM can verify the client signature which is added to the SOAP message.

Getting ready

For this recipe, we will use the same simple OSB project as in the previous *Securing a proxy service using username and password authentication through OWSM* recipe.

Import the `getting-ready` project into Eclipse OEPE from `\chapter-11\getting-ready\securing-a-proxy-service-with-cert-auth-and-msg-protect`.

How to do it...

The steps to execute in this recipe are the same as in the previous *Securing a proxy service using username and password authentication through OWSM* recipe, only another policy needs to be selected. In the Eclipse OEPE, perform the following steps:

1. Open the **CustomerManagement.proxy** in the `proxy` folder of the **securing-a-proxy-service-with-cert-auth-and-msg-protect** project.
2. Navigate to the **Policy** tab.
3. Enable **From OWSM Policy Store**.
4. Click **Service Level Policies**, which will enable the **Add** button.
5. Click **Add** and the **OWSM Policy Configuration** window will open.
6. Click **Browse**.
7. In the **Select OWSM Policy** window, we need to choose a security or management policy.
8. Enter `*x509*` into the **Name** field and click **Search**.
9. Select the **/wss11_x509_token_with_message_protection_service_policy** from the list of policies.
10. Click **OK**.

11. The Username Token policy will be displayed in the **Policy** tab of the proxy service.

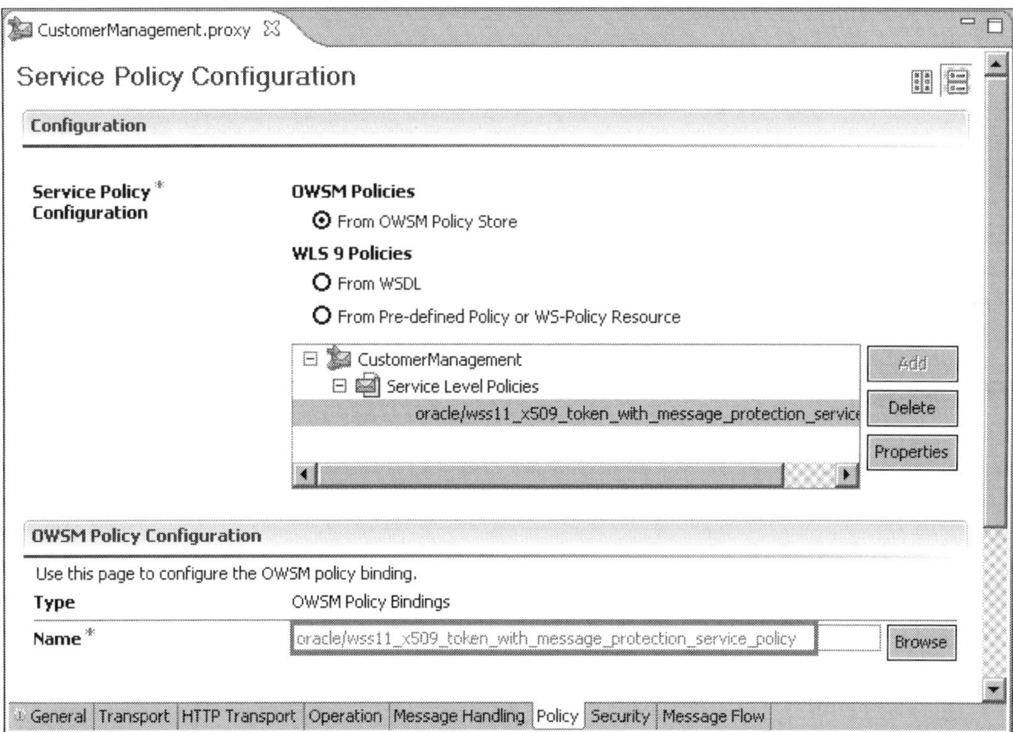

12. Save the project and deploy it to the OSB server.

Instead of the `oracle/wss11_x509_token_with_message_protection_service_policy` we could also use `oracle/wss10_x509_token_with_message_protection_service_policy` on this proxy service.

Now, we have to generate a client certificate and exchange the public certificates of the client and the server. Open a command line window and perform the following steps:

13. Navigate to the `bin` folder of the JDK used by the OSB:

    ```
    cd  c:\[FMWHome]\jrockit-jdk1.6.0_20-R28.1\bin
    ```

14. Generate a new client certificate with `client` as common name (CN) attribute and store it in the `client_2.jks` keystore:

    ```
    keytool -genkey -alias clientKey -keyalg "RSA" -sigalg
      "SHA1withRSA" -dname "CN=client, C=US" -keypass welcome
      -keystore c:\client_2.jks -storepass welcome
    ```

15. Export the public key of the server certificate:

```
keytool -exportcert -alias serverKey -storepass welcome -keystore
  c:\server.jks -file c:\server.cer
```

16. Import the public key:

```
keytool -import -file c:\server.cer -alias serverKey  -keystore
  c:\client_2.jks -storepass welcome -keypass welcome
```

17. Choose **yes** for the question about whether you trust the certificate:
18. Export the public key of the client certificate:

```
keytool -exportcert -alias clientKey -storepass welcome -keystore
  c:\client_2.jks -file c:\client_2.cer
```

19. Import the key in the server Java keystore:

```
keytool -import -file c:\client_2.cer -alias clientKey -keystore
  c:\server.jks -storepass welcome -keypass welcome
```

20. Copy the updated Java keystore `server.jks` located at `c:\` to the `config\fmwconfig` folder of the OSB domain:

```
cd ..\..
cd user_projects\domains\osb_cookbook_domain\config\fmwconfig
copy c:\server.jks .
```

21. Confirm the overwrite warning by entering **yes**.
22. Restart the WebLogic servers so that the updated server Java keystore is loaded.

Next we have to add the user called `client` to the `myrealm` security realm of the WebLogic server. The name of the user must match with the common name (CN=client) of the client certificate.

In the Service Bus console, perform the following steps:

23. Navigate to the **Security Configuration** using the menu on the left side.
24. Select the **Users** menu item and click **Add New**.
25. Enter `client` into the **User Name** field and `welcome1` into the **New Password** and **Confirm Password** fields.
26. Leave **DefaultAuthenticator** for the **Authentication Provider**.
27. Click **Save**.

The password of the client user is not important because we will use the public key of the client certificate to verify the SOAP signature.

We can use the next recipe, *Using JDeveloper to test a secured service* to test the implementation.

How it works...

The X509 Token authentication together with message protection policy authenticates the service consumer using a client certificate.

The public key of the server is used to encrypt the SOAP body and the private key of the client is used to sign the SOAP body. The signature of the SOAP message can be verified by OWSM because it has the public key of the client and OWSM will use the private key of the server to decrypt the SOAP body.

The common name of the client certificate is also checked against the users of the WebLogic security realm.

See also

Check the *Using JDeveloper to test a secured service* recipe for how to test the service with JDeveloper.

Securing a proxy service with authorization through Message Access Control

In the *Securing a proxy service by Username Token authentication* recipe we have made sure that only authenticated users have access to services through the use of OWSM. With this recipe, we will extend this security configuration with authorization to make sure that only selected users, roles, or groups have access to the proxy service.

Getting ready

For this we will need the OSB project from the previous *Securing a proxy service by Username Token authentication* recipe.

The finished solution can be imported into Eclipse OEPE from `\chapter-11\solution\securing-a-proxy-service-with-username-token`.

How to do it...

In the Service Bus console, perform the following steps to configure **Message Access Control**:

1. In the menu to the left, click **Project Explorer**.
2. Navigate to the **CustomerManagement** proxy service.
3. Navigate to the **Security** tab.
4. Click **Create** in the **Change Center** on the upper-left corner to create a new change session.
5. Make sure that the option **Process WS-Security Header** is set to **Yes**.
6. Click on the **CustomerManagement** link in the **Message Access Control** row.

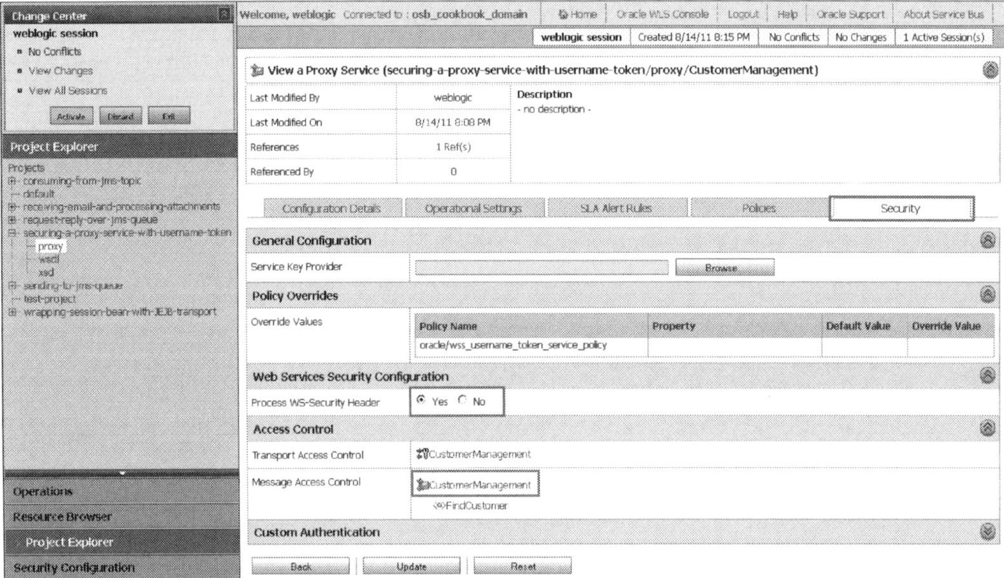

7. Click **Add Conditions**.
8. Select **User** from **Predicate List** drop-down list and click **Next**.
9. Enter `osbbook` into the **User Argument Name** field to allow access only for the osbbook user and click **Add**.
10. Click **Finish**.

11. Click **Save**.

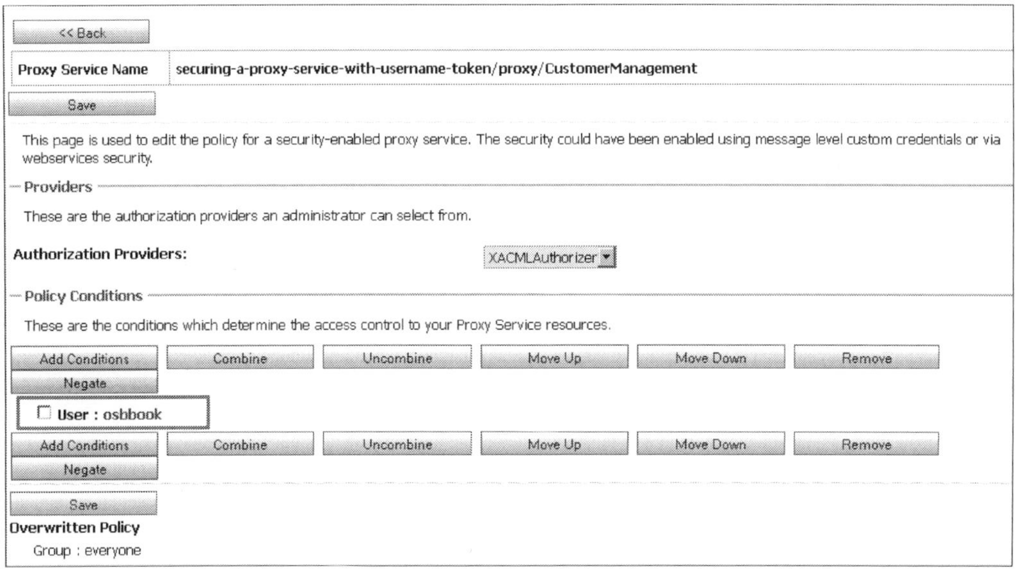

<< Back

Proxy Service Name securing-a-proxy-service-with-username-token/proxy/CustomerManagement

Save

This page is used to edit the policy for a security-enabled proxy service. The security could have been enabled using message level custom credentials or via webservices security.

Providers

These are the authorization providers an administrator can select from.

Authorization Providers: XACMLAuthorizer

Policy Conditions

These are the conditions which determine the access control to your Proxy Service resources.

Add Conditions Combine Uncombine Move Up Move Down Remove
Negate

User : osbbook

Add Conditions Combine Uncombine Move Up Move Down Remove
Negate

Save

Overwritten Policy
Group : everyone

12. Click **Activate** in the **Change Center** to activate the changes.

Use soapUI to test the service as shown in the *Securing a proxy service by Username Token authentication* recipe. Make sure that the `osbbook` user is used for authentication.

How it works...

Due to the OWSM policy, the incoming message will contain a WS-Security `UsernameToken`. The username will be extracted and first used for authenticating against the list of known users and then used to authorize against the Message Access Control list before access to the proxy service is granted.

If we test the OSB service with a different user such as `weblogic`, the authentication would still be successful. But because the `weblogic` user is not configured in the Message Access Control list, a **Message-level authorization denied** error is shown.

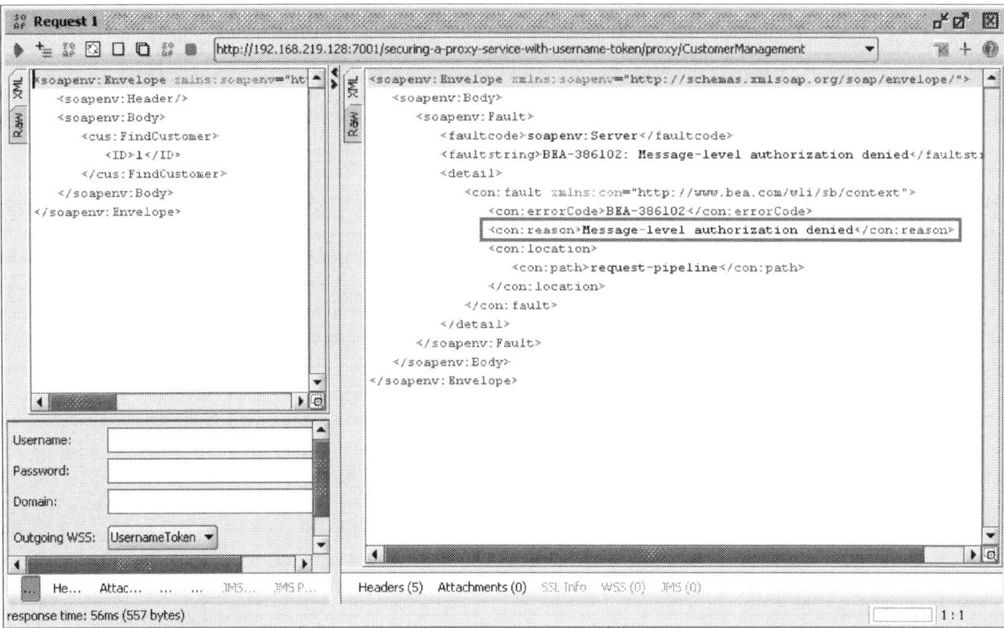

There's more...

Besides authorizing based on the user, other predicates are available to make up security policy conditions, such as predicates for groups, roles, time/date, and context elements. The next screenshot shows the possible values of the **Predicate List** drop-down listbox.

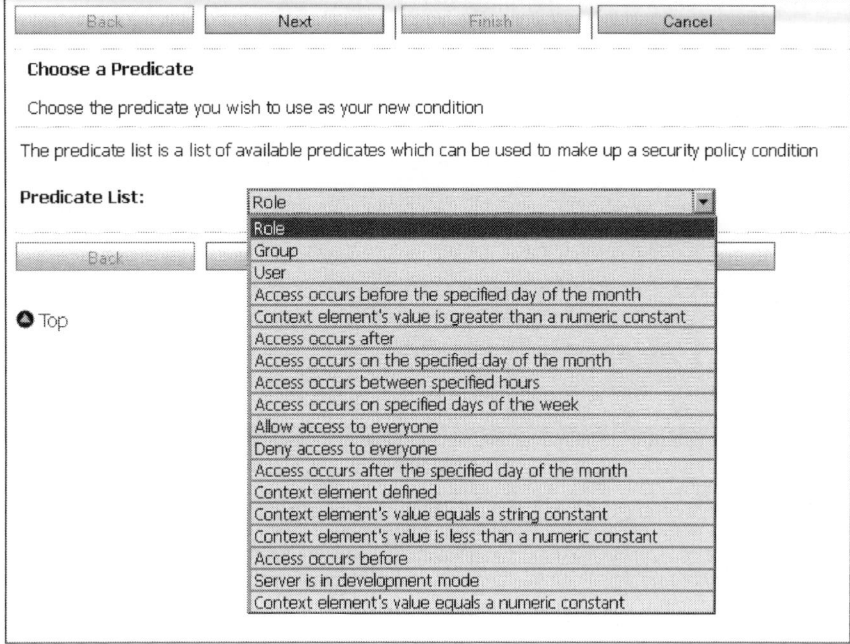

Using users, groups, and roles instead of individual users

Instead of adding individual users to allow access, you can use **Role** or **Group** to work with roles and groups to simplify maintenance.

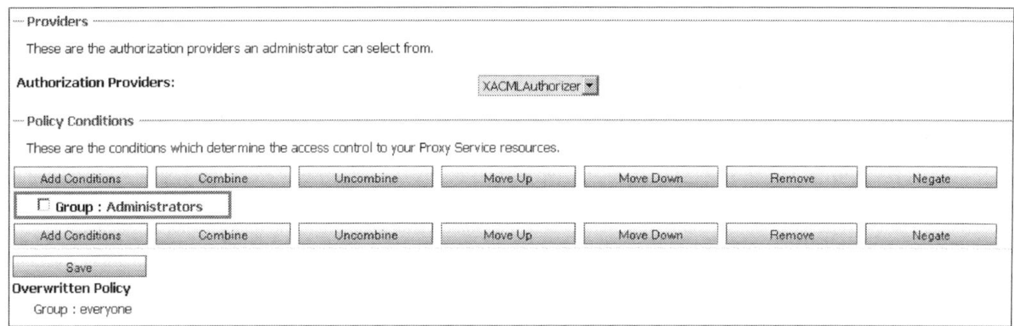

Making a resource available only during working hours

We can also make sure that a resource, that is, a proxy service is only available during certain hours of a day. For that we have to select the **Access occurs between specified hours** from the **Predicate List** drop-down listbox.

We can use the same predicate twice to make sure the proxy service can only be accessed in the morning from 9:00 to 11:45 and then in the afternoon from 1:30 to 6:30.

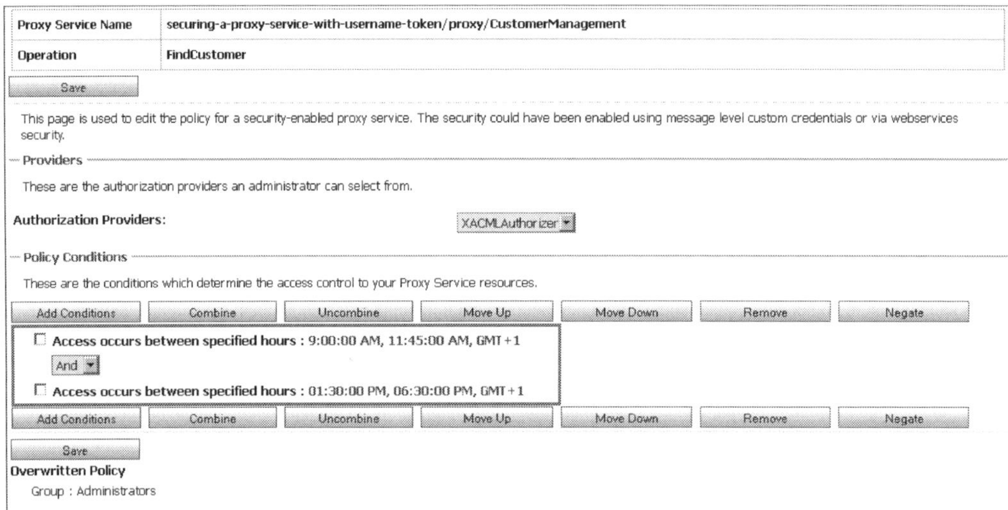

Using JDeveloper to test a secured service

In this recipe, we will create a JDeveloper client for testing the secured OSB service created in the previous recipe. We will use the client certificate store created in the previous recipe.

Getting ready

For this we will need the OSB project from the previous *Securing a proxy service using certificate authentication and protecting the message* recipe.

The finished solution can be imported into Eclipse OEPE from `\chapter-11\solution\securing-a-proxy-service-with-cert-auth-and-msg-protect`.

How to do it...

In JDeveloper, we will create a new application workspace with a generic project. The generic project will be used to generate a web service proxy based on the WSDL of the customer proxy service.

In JDeveloper, perform the following steps:

1. Click **File** | **New...**.
2. Choose **Generic Application** in the **General** category.
3. Enter `OWSM` into the **Application Name** field.
4. Click **Browse**, right to the **Directory** field and select the `workspace` folder.
5. Enter `osb.cookbook.owsm` into the **Application Package Prefix** field and click **Next**.
6. Enter **CustomerManagementClient** into the **Project Name** field.
7. In the **Project Technologies** tab, select the **Web Service** technology from the **Available** section and move it to the **Selected** technologies section.
8. Click **Next**.
9. Click **Finish**.

A new JDeveloper application with an empty project has been generated. Now let's create a consumer of the web service as a Java class. Still in JDeveloper, perform the following steps:

10. Click **File** | **New...**.
11. Click on the **Business Tier** | **Web Services** category.
12. Select the **Web Service Proxy** from the list of items to the right and click **OK**.

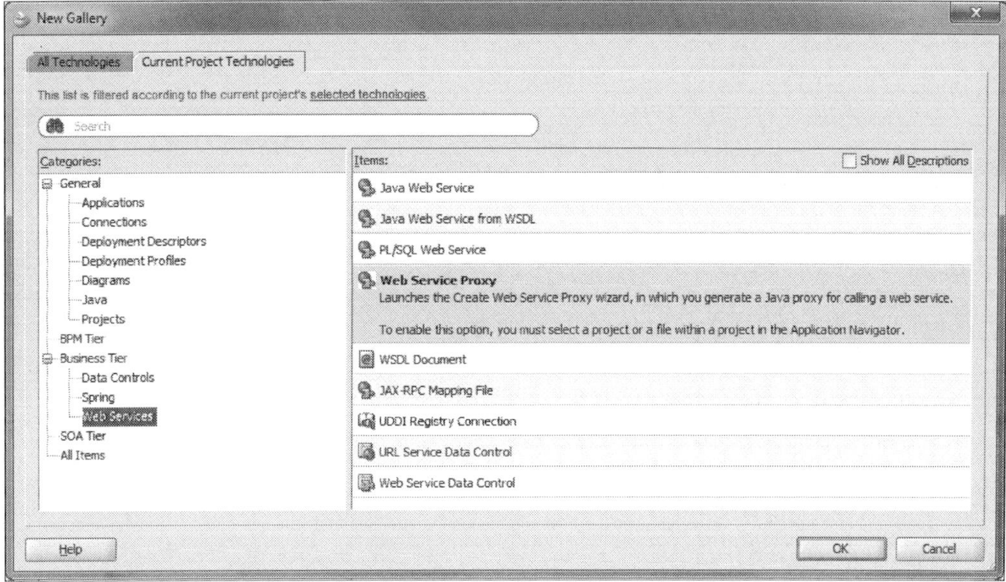

13. The **Create Web Service Proxy** wizard will open.
14. Click **Next**.
15. Choose **Client Style** for the **JAX-WS Style** option and click **Next**.
16. Enter the URL of the WSDL for the **CustomerManagement** proxy service into the **WSDL Document URL** field: `http://localhost:7001/securing-a-proxy-service-with-cert-auth-and-msg-protect/proxy/CustomerManagement?wsdl`
17. Click **Next**.
18. Enter `osb.cookbook.owsm.client` into the **Package Name** field and `osb.cookbook.owsm.types` into the **Root Package for Generated Types** field.
19. Click **Next** three times.
20. The **Policy** step of the wizard will be shown and JDeveloper detects the matching OWSM client policy.
21. Select the **oracle/wss11_x509_token_with_message_protection_client_policy** OWSM policy in the **Policies** list and click **Finish**.

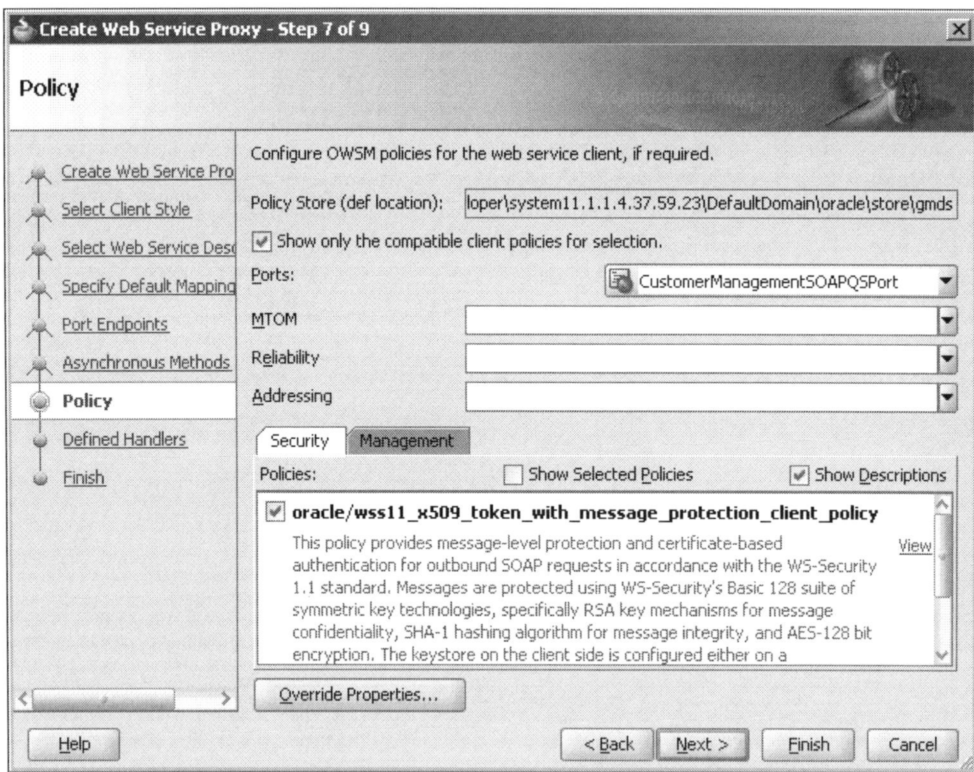

22. JDeveloper will generate the necessary Web service proxy code to invoke the service provider.

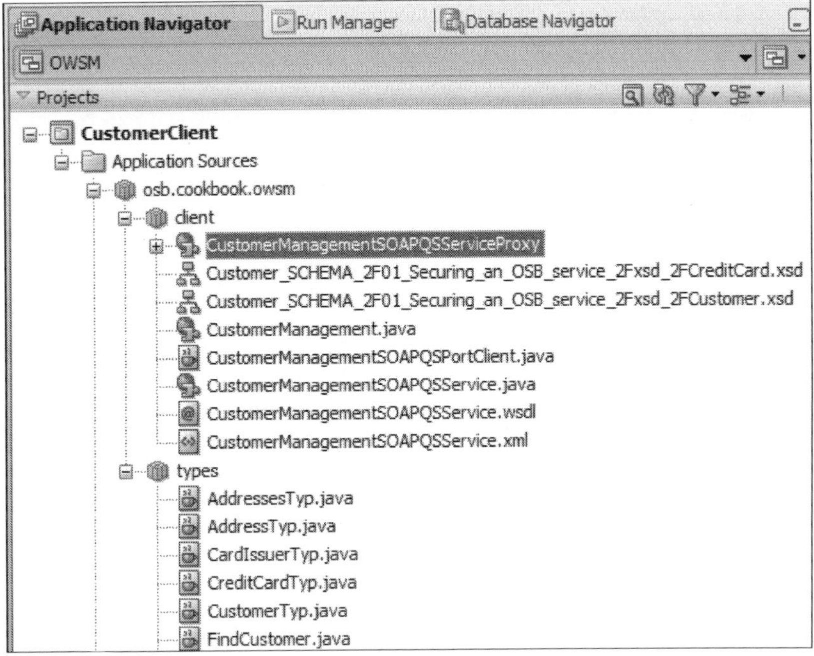

23. The test client Java class called **CustomerManagementSOAPQSPortClient.java** will be opened.

```
package osb.cookbook.owsm.client;

import ...;
// !THE CHANGES MADE TO THIS FILE WILL BE DESTROYED IF REGENERATED!
// This source file is generated by Oracle tools
// Contents may be subject to change
// For reporting problems, use the following
// Version = Oracle WebServices (11.1.1.0.0, build 101221.1153.15811)

public class CustomerManagementSOAPQSPortClient
{
  @WebServiceRef
  private static CustomerManagementSOAPQSService customerManagementSOAPQSService;

  public static void main(String [] args)
  {
    customerManagementSOAPQSService = new CustomerManagementSOAPQSService();
    SecurityPoliciesFeature securityFeatures =
      new SecurityPoliciesFeature(new String[] { "oracle/wss11_x509_token_with_message_protection_client_policy" });
    CustomerManagement customerManagement = customerManagementSOAPQSService.getCustomerManagementSOAPQSPort(securityFeatures);
    // Add your code to call the desired methods.
  }
}
```

24. Replace the line **// Add your code to call the desired methods.** with the following code block:

```
Map<String, Object> reqContext = ((BindingProvider)
  customerManagement).getRequestContext();

reqContext.put(ClientConstants.WSSEC_KEYSTORE_TYPE, "JKS");
reqContext.put(ClientConstants.WSSEC_KEYSTORE_LOCATION,
  "c:/client_2.jks");
reqContext.put(ClientConstants.WSSEC_KEYSTORE_PASSWORD,
  "welcome");

reqContext.put(ClientConstants.WSSEC_ENC_KEY_ALIAS, "serverKey");
reqContext.put(ClientConstants.WSSEC_ENC_KEY_PASSWORD, "welcome");
reqContext.put(ClientConstants.WSSEC_RECIPIENT_KEY_ALIAS,
  "serverKey");

reqContext.put(ClientConstants.WSSEC_SIG_KEY_ALIAS, "clientKey");
reqContext.put(ClientConstants.WSSEC_SIG_KEY_PASSWORD, "welcome");

// call the operation.
CustomerTyp customer = customerManagement.findCustomer(10L);
System.out.println( "Firstname: "+customer.getFirstName()
  +" Lastname: "+customer.getLastName());
```

25. There will be some red lines because of missing imports. Hit *Alt* + *Enter* on the marked classes and let JDeveloper add the import statements.
26. Right-click on the code window and select **Run** to run the Java class.

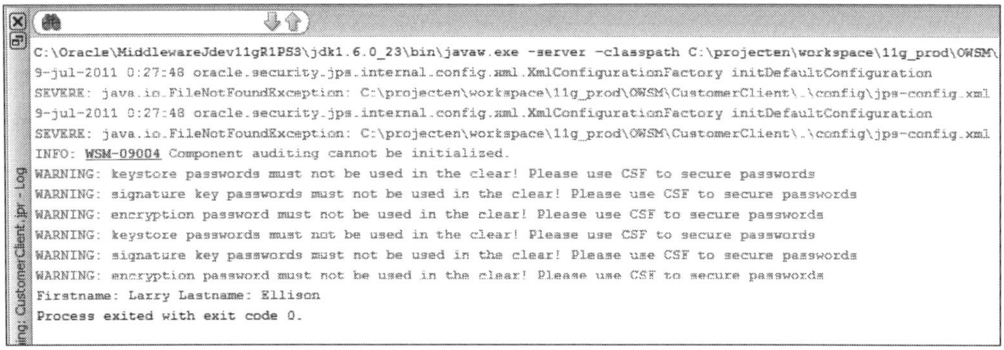

```
C:\Oracle\MiddlewareJdev11gR1PS3\jdk1.6.0_23\bin\javaw.exe -server -classpath C:\projecten\workspace\11g_prod\OWSM\
9-jul-2011 0:27:48 oracle.security.jps.internal.config.xml.XmlConfigurationFactory initDefaultConfiguration
SEVERE: java.io.FileNotFoundException: C:\projecten\workspace\11g_prod\OWSM\CustomerClient\.\config\jps-config.xml
9-jul-2011 0:27:48 oracle.security.jps.internal.config.xml.XmlConfigurationFactory initDefaultConfiguration
SEVERE: java.io.FileNotFoundException: C:\projecten\workspace\11g_prod\OWSM\CustomerClient\.\config\jps-config.xml
INFO: WSM-09004 Component auditing cannot be initialized.
WARNING: keystore passwords must not be used in the clear! Please use CSF to secure passwords
WARNING: signature key passwords must not be used in the clear! Please use CSF to secure passwords
WARNING: encryption password must not be used in the clear! Please use CSF to secure passwords
WARNING: keystore passwords must not be used in the clear! Please use CSF to secure passwords
WARNING: signature key passwords must not be used in the clear! Please use CSF to secure passwords
WARNING: encryption password must not be used in the clear! Please use CSF to secure passwords
Firstname: Larry Lastname: Ellison
Process exited with exit code 0.
```

We will get some *file not found exceptions* but we can ignore this because we are testing this from a Java client and not from a WebLogic server.

The last blue line is the result of the `findCustomer` operation of the **CustomerManagement** proxy service. We can see that the authentication worked!

How it works...

The **Web Service Proxy** wizard generates a set of Java classes necessary to invoke the secured OSB service. The classes are created based on the WSDL retrieved from the proxy service. Because of the server policy definition, JDeveloper knows what client policy to use. As a developer, all we need to do is set up the request context map with the corresponding credential information.

There's more...

The following two sections show the necessary changes in the code to test the proxy service with the Username Token authentication and with the message protection.

Implementing a JDeveloper test client for service with Username Token authentication

To generate a JDeveloper test client for testing the Username Token authentication, the same steps 1 – 17 from this recipe have to be executed. Just replace the URL of the WSDL in step 9 with the one from the Username Token authentication recipe: `http://localhost:7001/securing-a-proxy-service-with-username-token/proxy/CustomerManagement/proxy/CustomerManagement?wsdl`

This WSDL will automatically show the right corresponding client-side policy in step 13 and in step 18, the following code block has to be used instead.

```
// Add the user
Map<String, Object> reqContext = ((BindingProvider)
  customerManagement).getRequestContext();
reqContext.put(BindingProvider.USERNAME_PROPERTY, "osbbook" );
reqContext.put(BindingProvider.PASSWORD_PROPERTY, "welcome1" );

// call the operation.
CustomerTyp customer = customerManagement.findCustomer(10L);
System.out.println( "Firstname: "+customer.getFirstName()
  +" Lastname: "+customer.getLastName());
```

Implementing a JDeveloper test client for service with message protection

To generate a JDeveloper test client for testing the Username Token authentication, the same steps 1 – 17 from this recipe have to be executed. Just replace the URL of the WSDL in step 9 with the one from the Username Token authentication recipe: `http://localhost:7001/securing-a-proxy-service-with-message-protection/proxy/CustomerManagement/proxy/CustomerManagement?wsdl`

This WSDL will automatically show the right corresponding client-side policy in step 13 and in step 18, the following code block has to be used instead.

```
// Add the user
Map<String, Object> reqContext = ((BindingProvider)
  customerManagement).getRequestContext();

// message protection
reqContext.put(ClientConstants.WSSEC_KEYSTORE_TYPE, "JKS");
reqContext.put(ClientConstants.WSSEC_KEYSTORE_LOCATION,
  "c:/client_1.jks");
reqContext.put(ClientConstants.WSSEC_KEYSTORE_PASSWORD, "welcome");
reqContext.put(ClientConstants.WSSEC_ENC_KEY_ALIAS, "serverKey");
reqContext.put(ClientConstants.WSSEC_ENC_KEY_PASSWORD, "welcome");
reqContext.put(ClientConstants.WSSEC_RECIPIENT_KEY_ALIAS,
  "serverKey");

// call the operation.
CustomerTyp customer = customerManagement.findCustomer(10L);
System.out.println( "Firstname: "+customer.getFirstName()
  +" Lastname: "+customer.getLastName());
```

Calling a secured service from OSB

In this recipe, we will call a secured web service by adding an OWSM client policy to a business service. For this we create a new business service that uses the WSDL of our previous recipe. This WSDL contains the OWSM server policy.

Getting ready

For this we will use a simple OSB project with one proxy. Import the `getting-ready` project into Eclipse OEPE from `\chapter-11\getting-ready\calling-a-secured-service-form-OSB`. Make sure that the solution from the *Securing a proxy service using username and password authentication through OWSM* recipe is deployed to the OSB server.

How to do it...

Open the WSDL of the secured proxy service and check whether the WSDL contains some WS-Security policies. In Eclipse OEPE, perform the following steps:

1. Expand the `wsdl` folder of the **calling-a-secured-service-from-osb** project.
2. Double-click on the **CustomerManagement.wsdl**. This is the WSDL consumed from the service provider.

3. Check that the WSDL has a **wsp:Policy** element.

```
<wsdl:definitions name="CustomerManagement"
    targetNamespace="http://osb-cookbook/CustomerManagement" xmlns:wsdl="http://schemas.xmlsoap.org/wsdl/"
    xmlns:WL5G3N2="http://schemas.xmlsoap.org/wsdl/soap/" xmlns:WL5G3N0="http://schemas.xmlsoap.org/wsdl/"
    xmlns:WL5G3N1="http://osb-cookbook/CustomerManagement">
    <wsp:Policy
        orawsp:provides="{http://docs.oasis-open.org/ns/opencsa/sca/200903}authentication, {http://docs.oasis-open.org/ns/o
        wsu:Id="wss_username_token_service_policy" xmlns:wsp="http://schemas.xmlsoap.org/ws/2004/09/policy"
        xmlns="http://schemas.xmlsoap.org/ws/2004/09/policy" xmlns:orawsp="http://schemas.oracle.com/ws/2006/01/policy"
        xmlns:wsu="http://docs.oasis-open.org/wss/2004/01/oasis-200401-wss-wssecurity-utility-1.0.xsd"
        xmlns:xsi="http://www.w3.org/2001/XMLSchema-instance">
        <sp:SupportingTokens
            xmlns:sp="http://schemas.xmlsoap.org/ws/2005/07/securitypolicy">
            <wsp:Policy>
                <sp:UsernameToken
                    sp:IncludeToken="http://schemas.xmlsoap.org/ws/2005/07/securitypolicy/IncludeToken/AlwaysToRecipient">
                    <wsp:Policy>
                        <sp:WssUsernameToken10 />
                    </wsp:Policy>
                </sp:UsernameToken>
            </wsp:Policy>
        </sp:SupportingTokens>
    </wsp:Policy>
    <wsdl:types>
        <xsd:schema targetNamespace="http://osb-cookbook/CustomerManagement"
            xmlns:WL5G3N3="http://schemas.xmlsoap.org/wsdl/soap/" xmlns:WL5G3N4="http://schemas.xmlsoap.org/wsdl/soap/"
```

4. Also check that the service binding section holds the correct endpoint location matching the OSB server configuration.

```
<WL5G3N2:address
  location="http://localhost:7001/securing-a-proxy-service-with-
  username-token/proxy/CustomerManagement" />
```

Next we will create a business service and add the necessary OWSM client policy to this service so that it will properly authenticate itself against the service provider.

In Eclipse OEPE, perform the following steps:

5. Click on the `business` folder, right-click and select **New | Business Service**.
6. Enter **CustomerManagement** into the **File name** field.
7. In the **General** tab, click on the **WSDL Web Service** option for the **Service Type**.
8. Click **Browse**.
9. In the **Select a WSDL** dialog, open the **CustomerManagement.wsdl** and then click on the **CustomerManagementSOAPQSPort(port)**.
10. Click **OK.**
11. Confirm the **Transport Configuration Change** message by clicking **Yes**.
12. Navigate to the **Transport** tab.
13. The **Endpoint URI** from the `CustomerManagement.wsdl` is used.
14. Navigate to the **Policy** tab.

15. Enable the **From OWSM Policy Store** option.
16. Select the **Service Level Policies** and click **Add Compatible** and the matching OWSM client policy will be added.

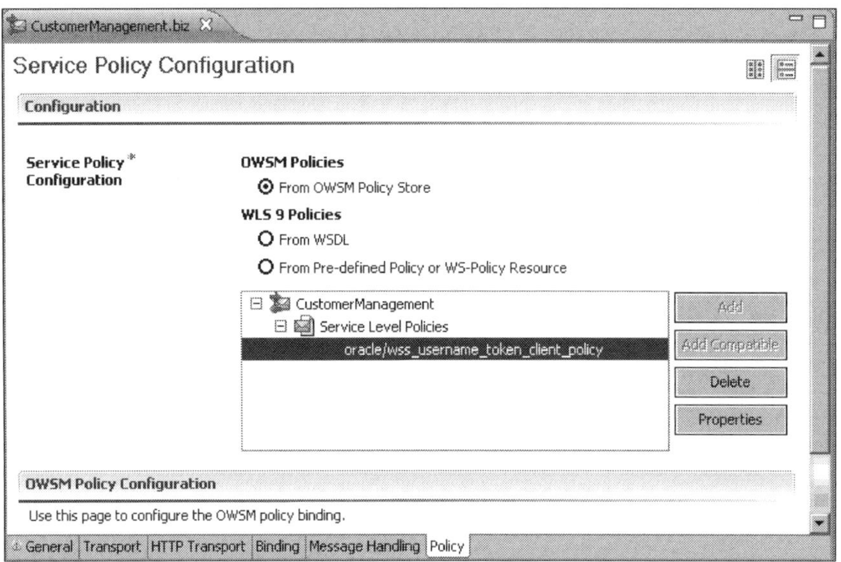

17. Save the project and deploy it to the OSB server.

To test it, perform the following steps in the Service Bus console:

18. In **Project Explorer**, click the project **calling-a-secured-service-from-osb** and click the **business** link.
19. Click the **Launch Test Console** icon of the **CustomerManagement** business service and click **Execute**.
20. An error will be returned: **The username is missing**.

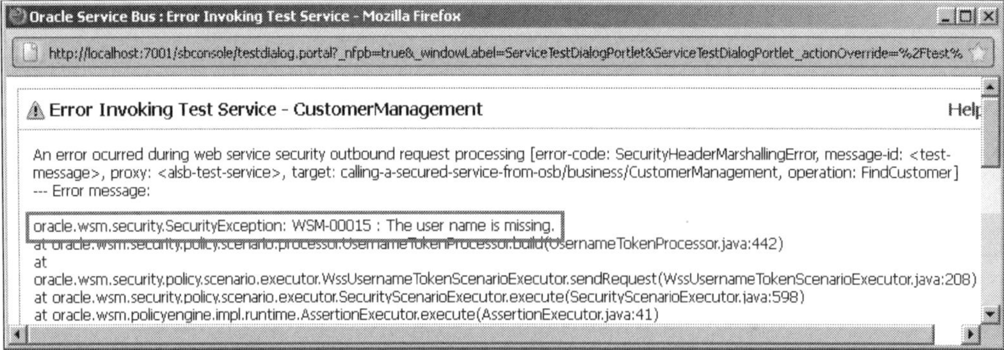

This is due to the fact that the business service is by default using the credential with the name **basic.credentials** from the credential store. Since we have not yet configured it, we get the error. We can either configure the basic credential or overwrite the default on the policy configuration on the business service.

Here we will show and use the second approach and overwrite the default value on the policy. In Eclipse OEPE, perform the following steps:

21. Open the **CustomerManagement** business service.
22. Navigate to the **Policy** tab.
23. Select the **oracle/wss_username_token_client_policy** policy entry under **Service Level Policies**.
24. Click **Properties** tab.
25. Enter `osbbook-key` into the **Override Value** column of the **csf-key** row.

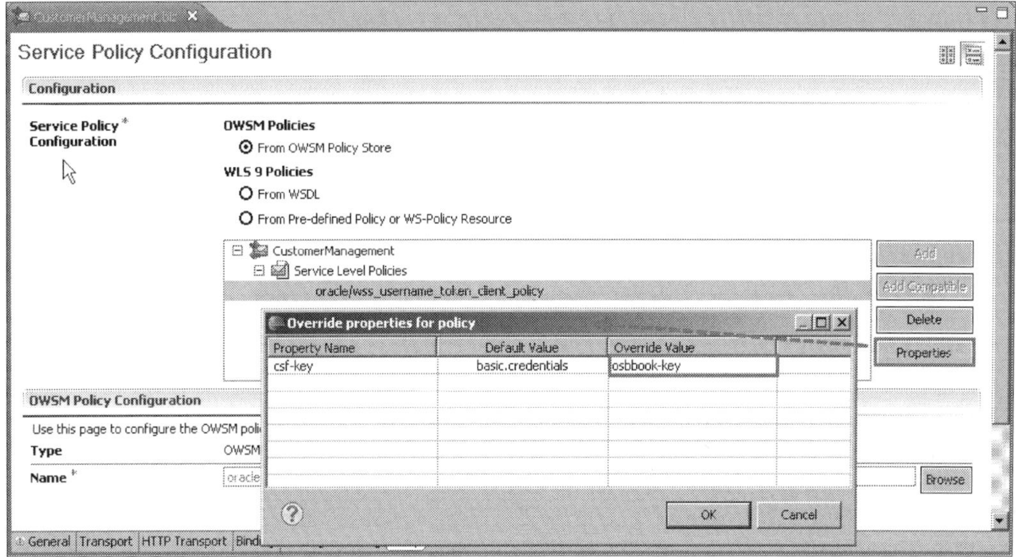

26. Save and deploy to the OSB server.

Retest the business service as shown previously from the Service Bus console. The test should now be successful.

How it works...

The business service can detect the WS-Security policies from the WSDL and Eclipse OEPE tries to find the matching OWSM client policies.

It's not required to use the **Add Compatible** button; we can also use the **Add** button and choose the matching OWSM client policy manually.

There's more...

In this section, we will cover how to configure the business service to work with the default credential and how to specify the key used for encryption and signing if message protection is enabled on a business service.

Making the business service work with the default credential

In order to not have to overwrite the default value on the policy of the business service, we need to create a **basic.credentials** credential in the **oracle.wsm.security** security map of the credential store.

We have seen how to create the **osbbook-key** credential both from the Enterprise Manager as well as on the command line through WLST in the *Configuring OSB server for OWSM* recipe

After configuring the **basic.credentials**, it should be shown in the list of credentials of the **oracle.wsm.security** map.

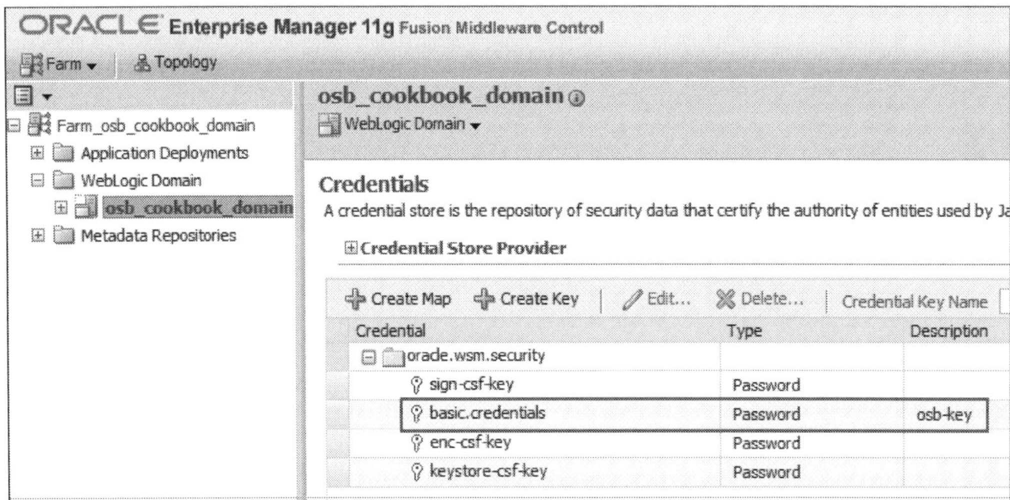

Keys used for signing and encrypting if a message protection client policy is configured on the business service

A business service with message protection and signing policies uses the **Signature Key** to sign the SOAP message and the **Encryption Key** to encrypt the SOAP body, which are both configured in OWSM.

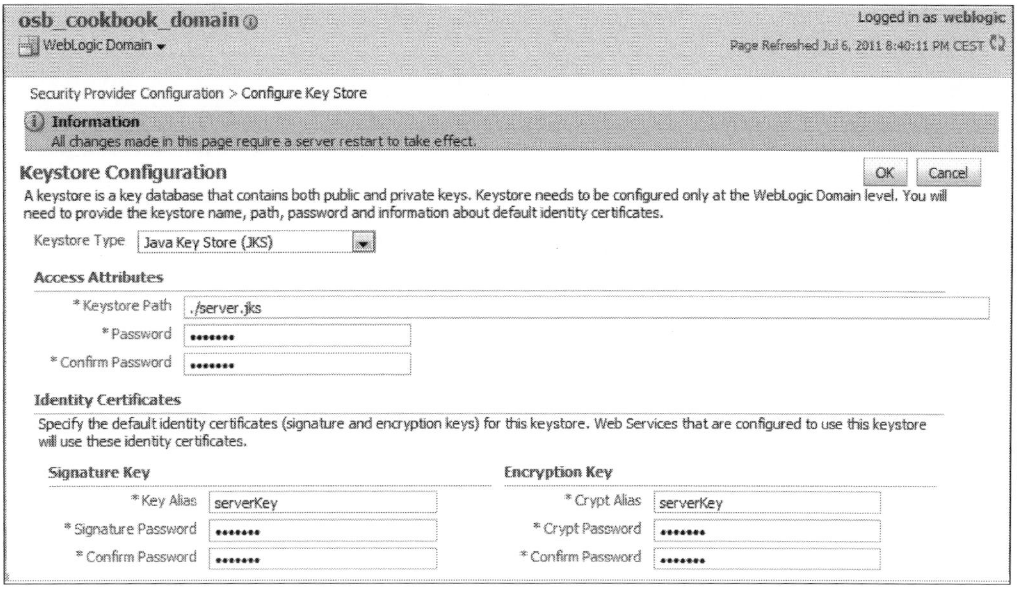

12
Handling Transport-level Security Requirements

In this chapter, we will cover:

- Using service accounts with OSB for basic authentication
- Configuring WebLogic network connection filters
- Preparing OSB server to work with SSL
- Configuring a proxy service to use HTTPS security

Introduction

In this chapter, we cover recipes related to transport-level security, which represents the technique where the underlying operating system or application servers are handling security features. For data confidentiality, the **Secure Sockets Layer** (**SSL**) is often used to provide encryption. If a message needs to go through multiple points to reach a destination, each intermediate node (that is, an OSB) must forward the message over a new SSL connection. The original message from the service consumer is not cryptographically protected on the intermediary nodes and additional computationally expensive cryptographic operations are performed for each new SSL connection that is established.

Message-level security has been covered in *Chapter 11, Handling Message-level Security Requirements*.

Using service accounts with OSB

In this recipe, we will discuss an OSB feature called service accounts. A **service account** (**SA**) is mainly used by proxy and business services for setting up an outbound connection to external resources such as a JMS, FTP, or E-mail server, where authentication is necessary. Apart from that it can be used for simple transport-level authentication to remote web services where HTTP basic authentication is necessary.

The setup for that recipe is shown in the following figure. We can see that both the **Customer Management** proxy service on the left and the **Mock CustomerService** proxy service on the right (the mock implementation) require **Basic authentication**. In between, we have the **Customer Service** business service which we will configure in this recipe so that the credentials are passed-through.

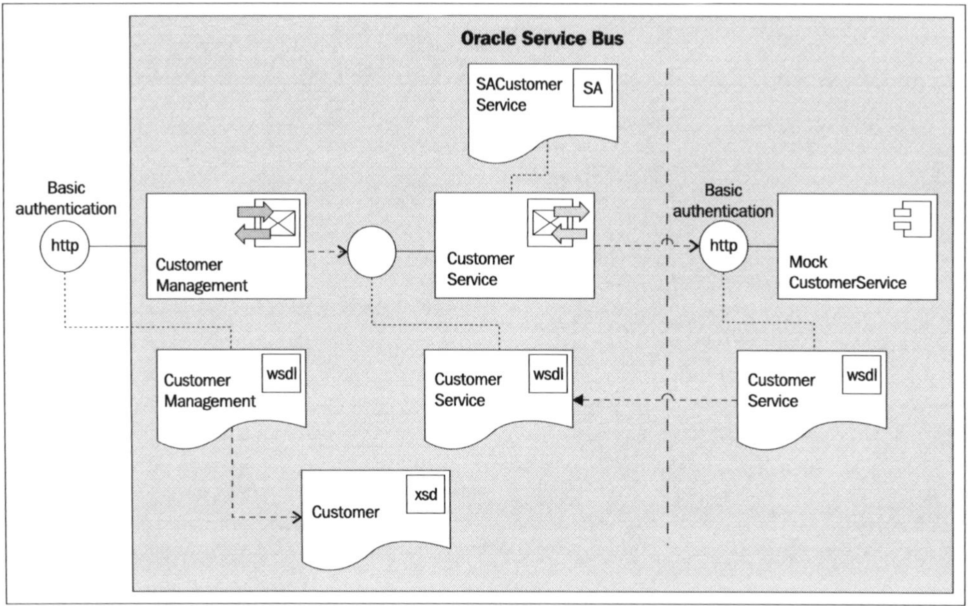

Getting ready

Make sure to have access to a working Eclipse OEPE. We will continue with a project from *Chapter 1, Creating a Basic OSB Service*, which we made available as a new import in the folder `\chapter-12\getting-ready\using-service-accounts-with-osb`. Import both projects into Eclipse OEPE. The `using-service-accounts-with-osb` project holds the solution from *Chapter 1, Creating a Basic OSB Service*, and the `using-service-accounts-with-osb-mockservice` contains the implementation of a mock service required for testing the basic authentication. This is not possible with a soapUI mock service; therefore we have implemented another proxy service on the OSB that acts as a mock service.

Click on the proxy service **MockCustomerService.proxy** in the **proxy** folder of the **using-service-accounts-with-osb** project and navigate to the **HTTP Transport** tab.

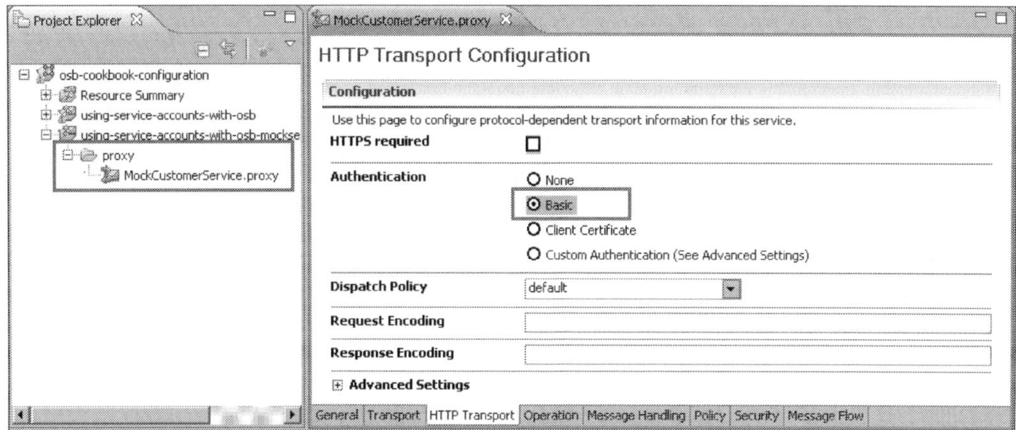

The proxy service specifies that basic authentication is required, but without using HTTPS. If we check the **Message Flow** tab, we see that the mock service returns a hardcoded response and uses the **Log** action to write the value of the `$inbound` variable (holding the authenticated user) to the **Service Bus Console Output** window.

Deploy the two OSB projects to the OSB server.

How to do it...

Before we change anything, let's test the behavior of the current setup. We will use soapUI to invoke the `CustomerManagement` proxy service as we have seen in *Chapter 1, Creating a Basic OSB Service*. In soapUI, perform the following steps:

1. Click on the **File** menu and select **Import Project** to import an existing project.
2. Navigate to the `\chapter-12\getting-ready\using-service-accoutns-with-osb\soapui\CustomerManagement-soapui-project.xml` file and click **Open**.
3. Navigate to **Request 1** of the **FindCustomer** operation in the project tree and click on it.

4. Execute the request by clicking on the green arrow on the upper-left corner. A **BEA-380000: Unauthorized** error occurs as shown in the following screenshot:

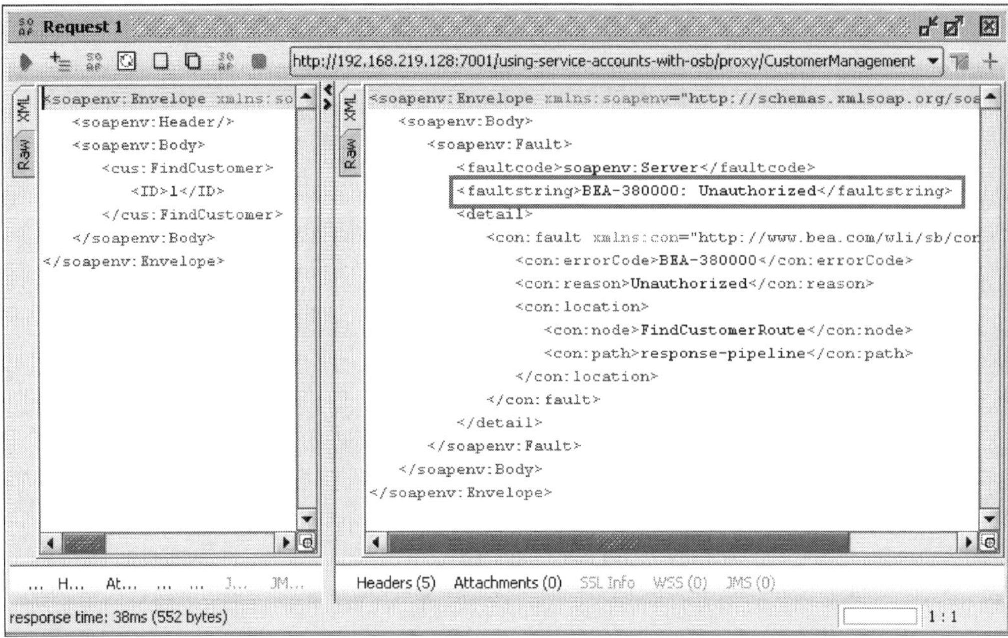

This is because the mock service requires proxy authentication but we don't send any credentials.

We will now show you how to configure a proxy and business service so that the credentials are passed through the OSB to the mock service using basic authentication on both ends.

In Eclipse OEPE, we will extend the project with a service account and change configuration of the business service and soapUI to activate HTTP basic authentication.

First we will configure a service account object, which will then be used by the business service to configure the basic authentication. In Eclipse OEPE, perform the following steps:

5. Create a new folder and name it `security`.
6. Right-click on the `security` folder and select **New | Service Account**.
7. Enter `SACustomerService` into the **File name** field.
8. Leave the **Resource Type** option on **Pass Through**.

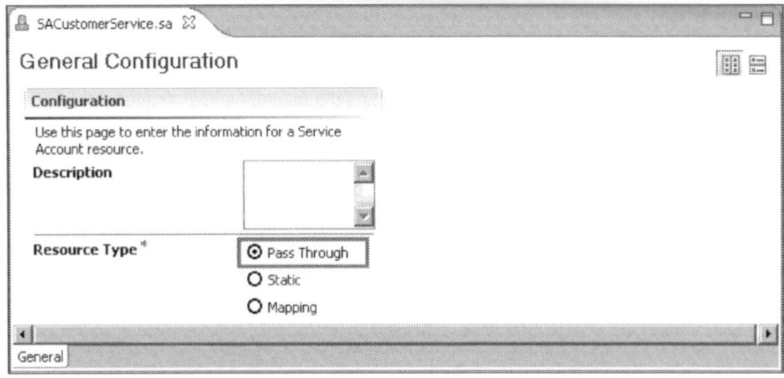

9. Close the **Service Account** artifact.

Now with the service account in place, let's configure the business service to use it together with basic authentication.

10. Click on the business service `CustomerService.biz` in the `business` folder.
11. Navigate to the **HTTP Transport** tab.
12. Change the **Authentication** option to **Basic**.
13. Click **Browse** and a pop-up window will appear.
14. Expand the `security` folder from the tree and select the **SACustomerService Service Account**.
15. Click **OK**.

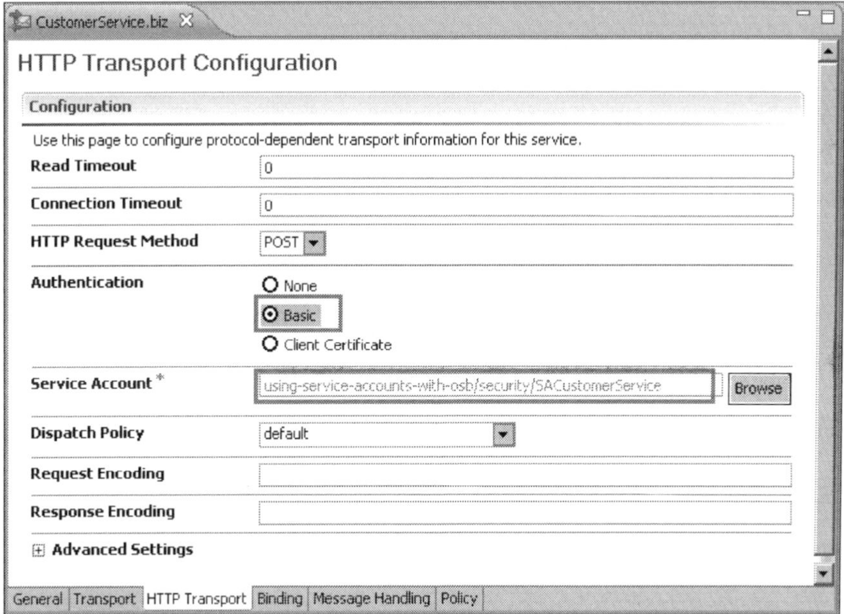

Last but not least, we also have to tell the proxy service to use basic authentication:

16. Click on the proxy service `CustomerManagement.proxy` in the `proxy` folder.
17. Navigate to the **HTTP Transport** tab.
18. Select the **Basic** option for the **Authentication**.

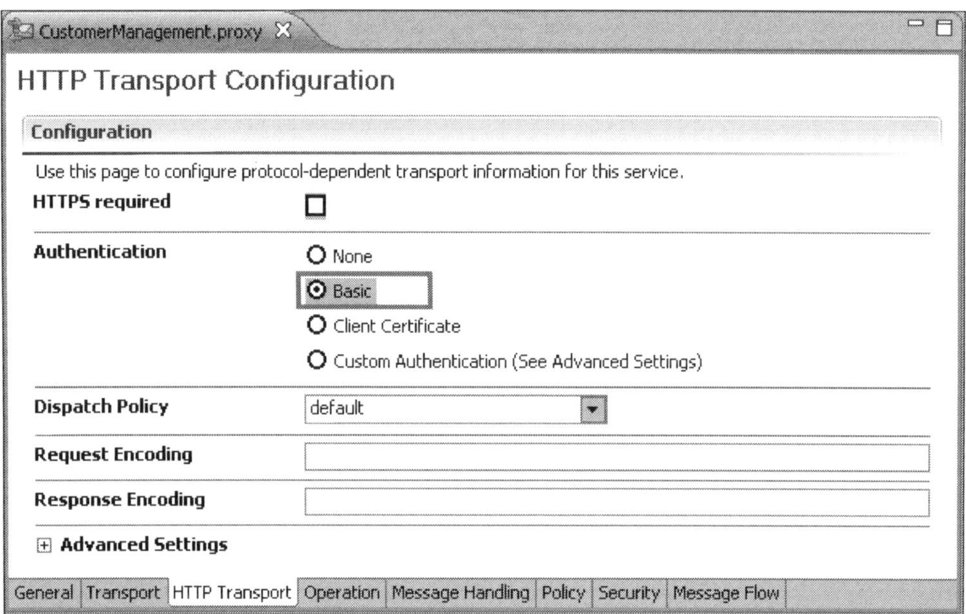

19. Save the project and deploy it to the OSB server.

This finishes the end-to-end configuration of the basic authentication with the OSB just passing it through to the CRM system (that is, the mock service).

Before we can test that the basic authentication to the CRM system works, we need a user to test with. Since OSB uses the WebLogic security framework, we will need to add the username/password to the WebLogic security realm.

In WebLogic console, perform the following steps:

20. Navigate to the **Security Realms** in the **Domain Structure** tree on the left.
21. Click on **myrealm**.
22. Navigate to the **Users and Groups** tab.
23. Click **New**.

24. Enter `crmuser` in the **Name** field, `welcome1` into the **Password** and **Confirm Password** field.
25. Click **OK**.

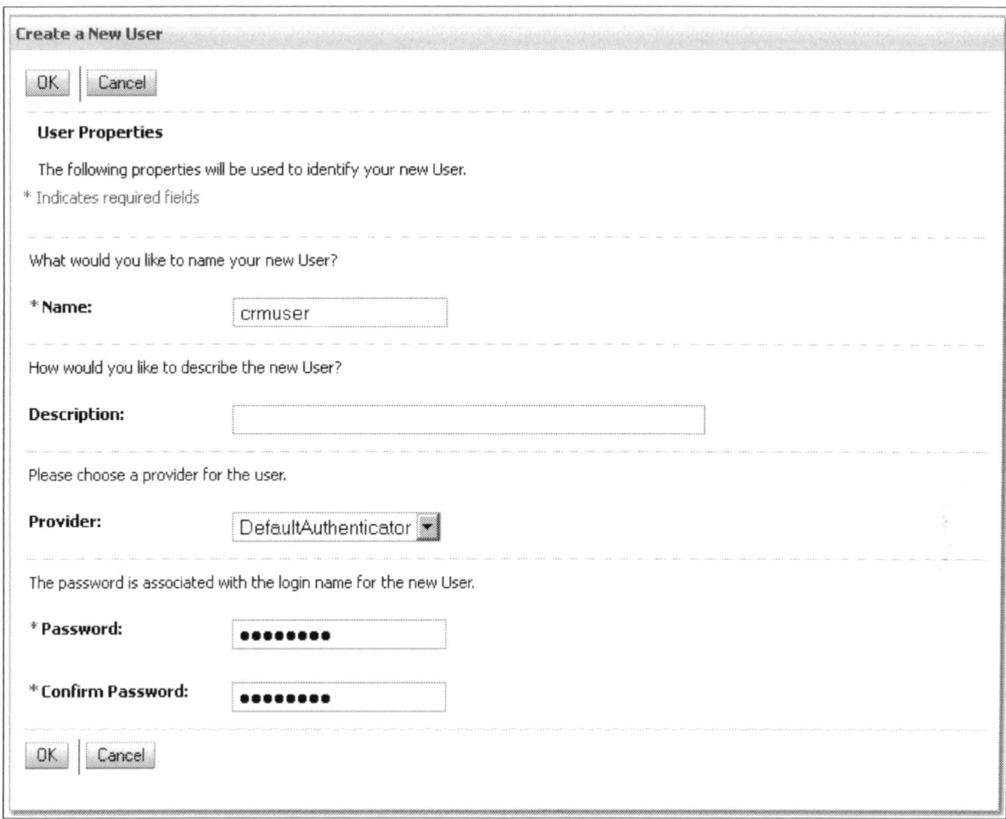

Next, we will setup the soapUI mock service from *Chapter 1, Creating a Basic OSB Service*, to require basic authentication.

Let's go back to soapUI and perform the following steps to test the new behavior:

26. Navigate again to **Request 1** of the **FindCustomer** operation.
27. Click on the green arrow to send the request.

28. An **HTTP/1.1 401 Unauthorized** error will occur as shown in the following screenshot. This is because we have not yet passed the credentials, so now the OSB server complains with that error.

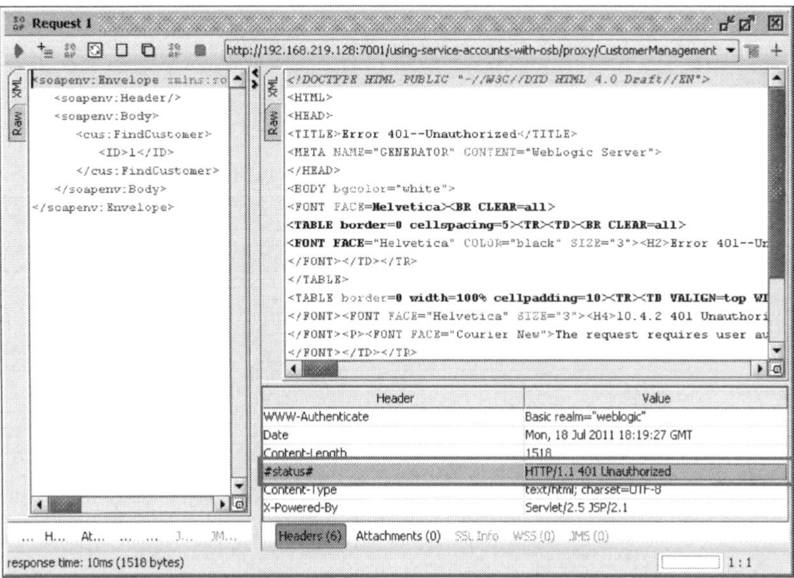

29. Click on the left tab labeled **...** or **Aut** at the bottom of the request window.
30. Enter `crmuser` into the **Username** field and `welcome1` into the **Password** field.
31. Re-execute the test by clicking on the green arrow.

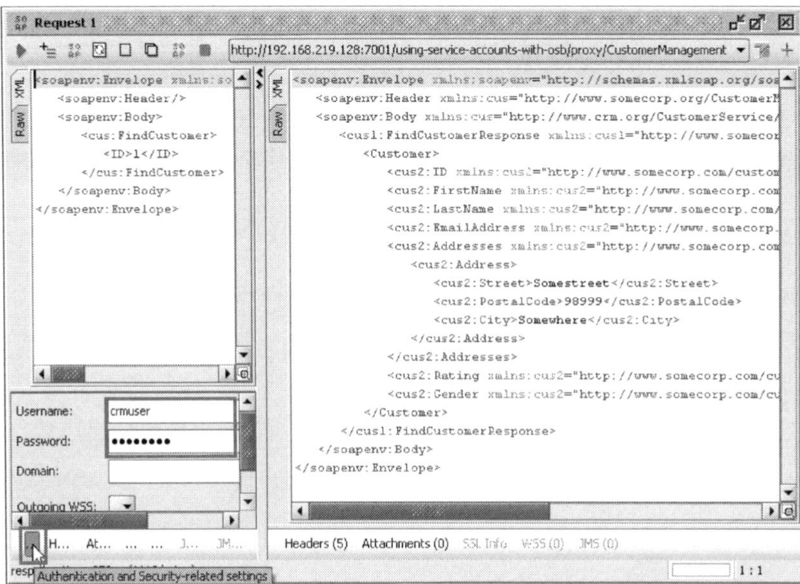

32. A valid response should be returned.

33. If we click on the **Raw** tab on the left, we can see the additional HTTP header **Authorization** over which the username and password is passed as an encoded string.

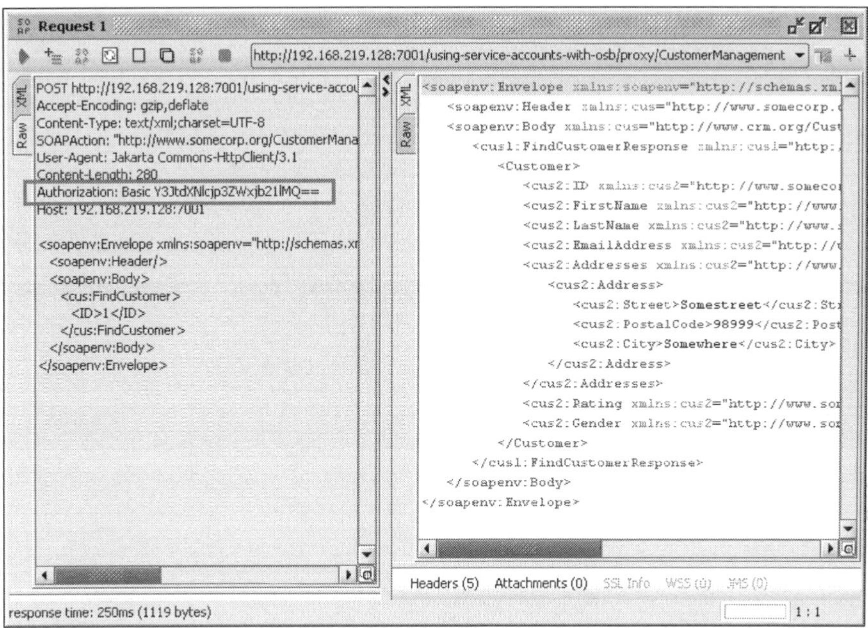

34. On the Service Bus Console output, we should see the value of the `$inbound` variable which the mock service logs. `$inbound` contains transport related header information as well as some security information including where the authenticated user can be found (that is, **crmuser** in our case).

```
OSB Cookbook 11gR1 PS3
      </tran:headers>
      <tran:encoding xmlns:tran="http://www.bea.com/wli/sb/transports">utf-8</tr
an:encoding>
      <http:client-host>127.0.0.1</http:client-host>
      <http:client-address>127.0.0.1</http:client-address>
      <http:http-method>POST</http:http-method>
    </con:request>
    <con:response xsi:type="http:HttpResponseMetaData" xmlns:http="http://www.be
a.com/wli/sb/transports/http" xmlns:xsi="http://www.w3.org/2001/XMLSchema-instan
ce">
      <tran:headers xsi:type="http:HttpResponseHeaders" xmlns:tran="http://www.b
ea.com/wli/sb/transports">
        <http:Content-Type>text/xml</http:Content-Type>
      </tran:headers>
      <tran:response-code xmlns:tran="http://www.bea.com/wli/sb/transports">0</t
ran:response-code>
    </con:response>
  </con:transport>
  <con:security>
    <con:transportClient>
      <con:username>crmuser</con:username>
    </con:transportClient>
  </con:security>
</con:endpoint>
```

This shows that the end-to-end security is working. The consumer of the proxy service (soapUI) sends a request using basic authentication and the same user is passed through the OSB and used on the other end to invoke the mock service (representing the CRM system).

How it works...

The account used in the custom HTTP header will be validated against available authenticators of the WebLogic security realm and then passed through by the OSB business service to the CRM system. The pass-through behavior comes from the setup of the service account object, which is then being linked to the business service.

The authorization value **Y3JtdXNlcjp3ZWxjb21lMQ==** is actually a base64 encoded string. This is not a safe way to authenticate because the encoded string, although unreadable for a human, can be easily decoded. Basic authentication is therefore only advised in combination with transport security as SSL and is shown later in the recipe *Configuring a proxy service to use HTTPS security*.

There's more...

In this section, we show some other ways of using the service account artefact in the OSB.

Static service accounts

In this recipe, we demonstrated how to pass a username and password from a service client through the OSB. However, it is also possible to simply configure the service account to static. With static, we can provide the **User Name** and **Password** directly in the OSB without having to go to the WebLogic security realm.

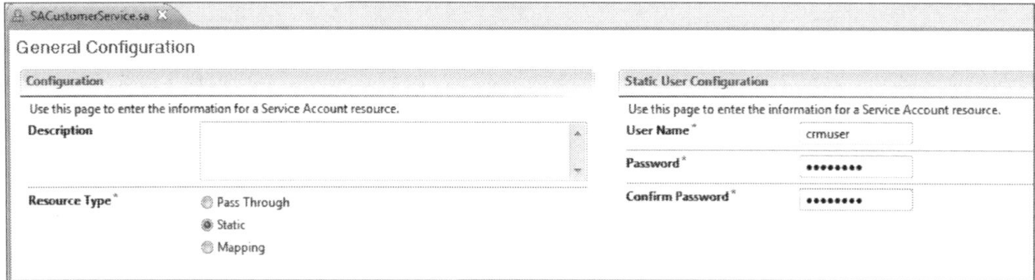

Mapping service accounts

The last **Resource Type** option in the service account configuration is **Mapping**. With mapping, we can map an authenticated user on a proxy service to a user that will be used in the business service.

The **Local User Mappings** table will contain users authenticated by the proxy service for an incoming request. This table must contain users available in the WebLogic security realm. The **Remote Users** table contains users and passwords used by the business service for their remote callout. These users do not have to be part of the WebLogic security realm.

In the following example, we configure the **crmuser** to be the remote user and the **osbbook** user, which we have added in the recipe *Configuring OSB server for OWSM* of *Chapter 11, Handling Message-Level Security Requirements*, as the local user.

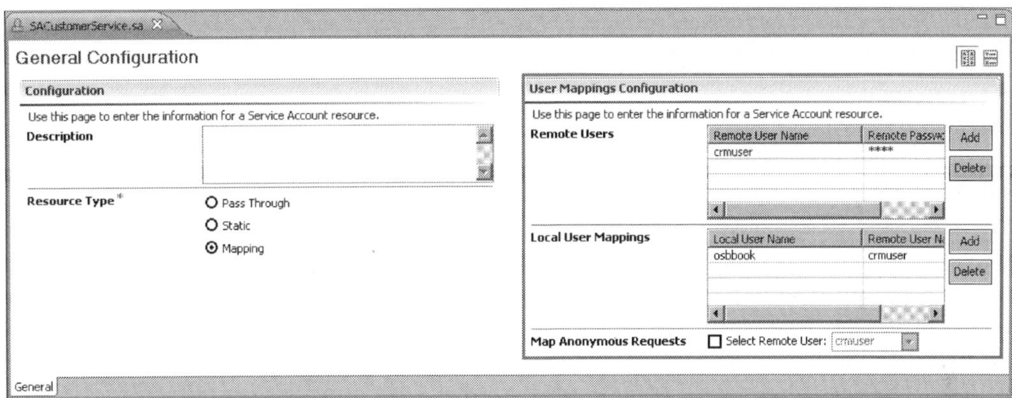

So now we can use the **osbbook** user in soapUI and everything should still work as before. If we check on the Service Bus Console output we can also see that the business service is using the **crmuser** to authenticate against the CRM service (the mock service).

Service accounts from XQuery

In a XQuery transformation on the OSB, it's possible to read a service account configuration using the function `fn-bea:lookupBasicCredentials`. This is useful when we need to map a username and password into the content of a SOAP header or body structure. This function can only be used with a service account that is configured with the **Static Resource** type. The correct syntax for using the function in our current project is:

```
fn-bea:lookupBasicCredentials('using-service-accounts-with-osb/
security/SACustomerService')
```

This will return the following XML fragment:

```
<UsernamePasswordCredential xmlns="http://www.bea.com/wli/sb/services/
security/config">
   <username>crmuser</username>
   <password>welcome1</password>
</UsernamePasswordCredential>
```

Configuring WebLogic network connection filters

In this recipe, we will actually discuss a WebLogic feature that is called network connection filters. These filters are a sort of firewall feature that can be used to allow or deny access to the server for certain protocols and addresses. A typical use is to restrict access to the Administrator port to prevent unauthorized access.

Getting ready

Make sure you have access to the WebLogic console.

How to do it...

We will configure WebLogic to use a network connection filter. In this filter, we will only allow certain addresses and protocols to have access to the Administrator console and the services.

In WebLogic console, perform the following steps:

1. Click on the domain name in the **Domain Structure** tree.
2. Navigate to the **Security** tab.
3. Navigate to the **Filter** sub tab with the **Security** tab.
4. Enter `weblogic.security.net.ConnectionFilterImpl` into the **Connection Filter** field.
5. Enter the following values into the **Connection Filter Rules** field:

   127.0.0.1 * 7001 allow #local ipv4

   server01 * 7001 allow #local hostname

   0:0:0:0:0:0:0:1 * 7001 allow #local ipv6

   0.0.0.0/0 * 7001 deny #all other traffic

6. Click **Save**.

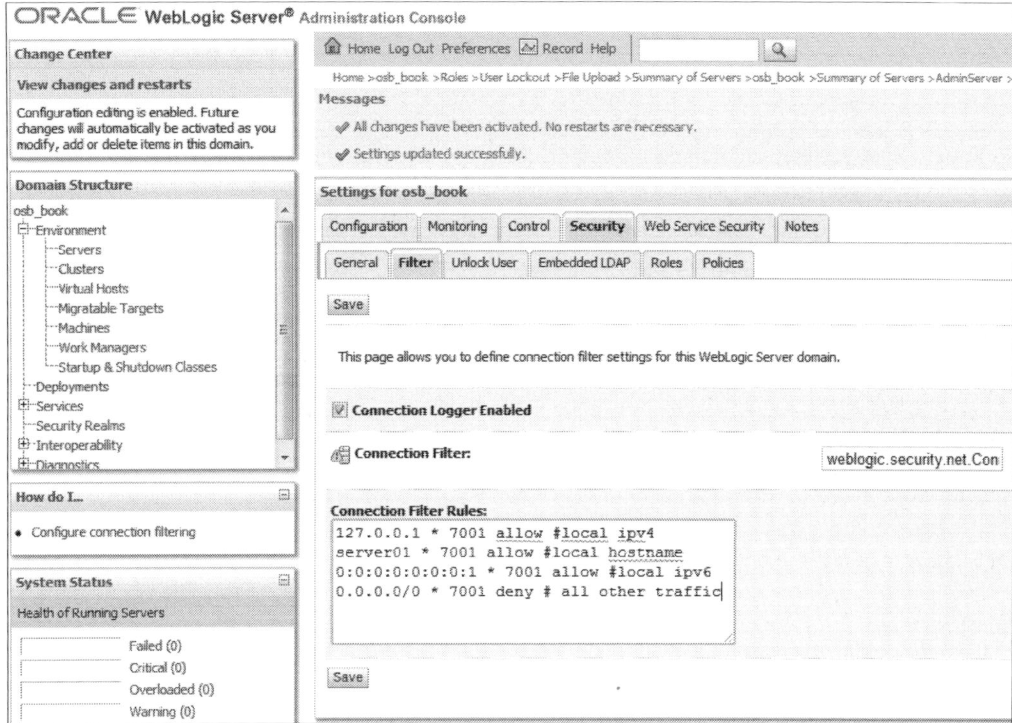

7. Restart the servers in your domain by clicking on **Environment** | **Servers**.
8. Navigate to the **Control** tab.
9. Select all servers.
10. Click on **Shutdown** and select the **Force Shutdown Now** item.
11. Restart the domain as normal.

How it works...

We implemented the WebLogic filter implementation class that is provided as part of the WebLogic Server product. By default, it accepts all incoming connections. Therefore we configured the filter rules to allow or deny certain traffic to the Admin Server. Filter rules are evaluated in the order they are written. The first rule to match determines how the connection is treated. If no rules match, the connection is permitted.

In our case, the last rule is a deny rule which locks down all traffic to the 7001 Administrator port except for connections allowed by one of the preceding rules. As a result of the connection filter rules, the Admin Server is now only available from the server itself.

Filter rules have a syntax of:

```
targetAddress localAddress localPort action protocols
```

where:

- `targetAddress`: specifies the address to filter.
- `localAddress`: defines the host address of the WebLogic server (* matches all local addresses).
- `localPort`: defines the port of the WebLogic server (* matches all ports).
- `action`: specifies the type of rule and may contain allow or deny.
- `protocols`: contains a list of protocols to match (http, https, t3, t3s, giop, giops, dcom, ftp, ldap). When no protocol is defined, all protocols will match the rule.

By implementing the filter implementation class, we needed to restart the WebLogic servers. However, changing the filter rules does not require a restart but will be instantly active.

Filters apply to all servers in your WebLogic domain, so not just the Admin Server but also all Managed Servers.

There's more...

In this recipe, we locked down port 7001 and only allowed access to the Admin Server from local addresses. If we want to filter on a subnet to only allow access to the OSB Managed Server for given subnet, the following configuration can be used:

```
10.20.30.0/24 10.20.30.2 8011 allow http #osb services
0.0.0.0/0 * 8011 deny                     #osb services
```

The OSB server runs on `10.20.30.2:8011` and the allowed subnet is from `10.20.30.1` to `10.20.30.254`.

When unauthorized access occurs on the server, the following line will appear in the log file of the specific server:

```
<datetime> <Notice> <Socket> <BEA-000445> <Connection rejected, filter blocked Socket[addr=10.50.30.203,port=54144,localport=7001], weblogic.security.net.FilterException: [Security:090220]rule 4>
```

In this example, the external address `10.50.30.203` did not match any of the first three filter rules and therefore is denied access by the fourth filter rule.

Preparing OSB server to work with SSL

In this recipe, we will configure the OSB to use SSL. The WebLogic server standard installation already comes with a default certificate and keystore, but in this recipe we will use the custom keystore that we created in *Chapter 11, Handling Message-level Security Requirements*.

Getting ready

We will need access to Eclipse OEPE, soapUI client, and the `server.jks` and `client.jks` files.

How to do it...

First, we will configure the OSB server to use the `server.jks` keystore we created earlier.

In WebLogic console, perform the following steps:

1. Click on **Environment** in the tree on the left and select **Servers | AdminServer(admin)** on the detail view.
2. Navigate to the **Configuration | Keystores** tab.
3. Click **Change** and change the value to **Custom Identity and Custom Trust for the Keystores** field.
4. Enter `./config/fmwconfig/server.jks` into the **Custom Identity Keystore** field.
5. Enter `JKS` into the **Custom Identity Keystore Type** field.
6. Enter `welcome` into the **Custom Identity Keystore Passphrase** field.
7. Enter `welcome` into the **Confirm Custom Identity Keystore Passphrase** field.
8. Enter `./config/fmwconfig/server.jks` into the **Custom Trust Keystore** field.
9. Enter `JKS` into the **Custom Trust Keystore Type** field.
10. Enter `welcome` into the **Custom Trust Keystore Passphrase** field.
11. Enter `welcome` into the **Confirm Custom Trust Keystore Passphrase** field.

12. Click **Save**.

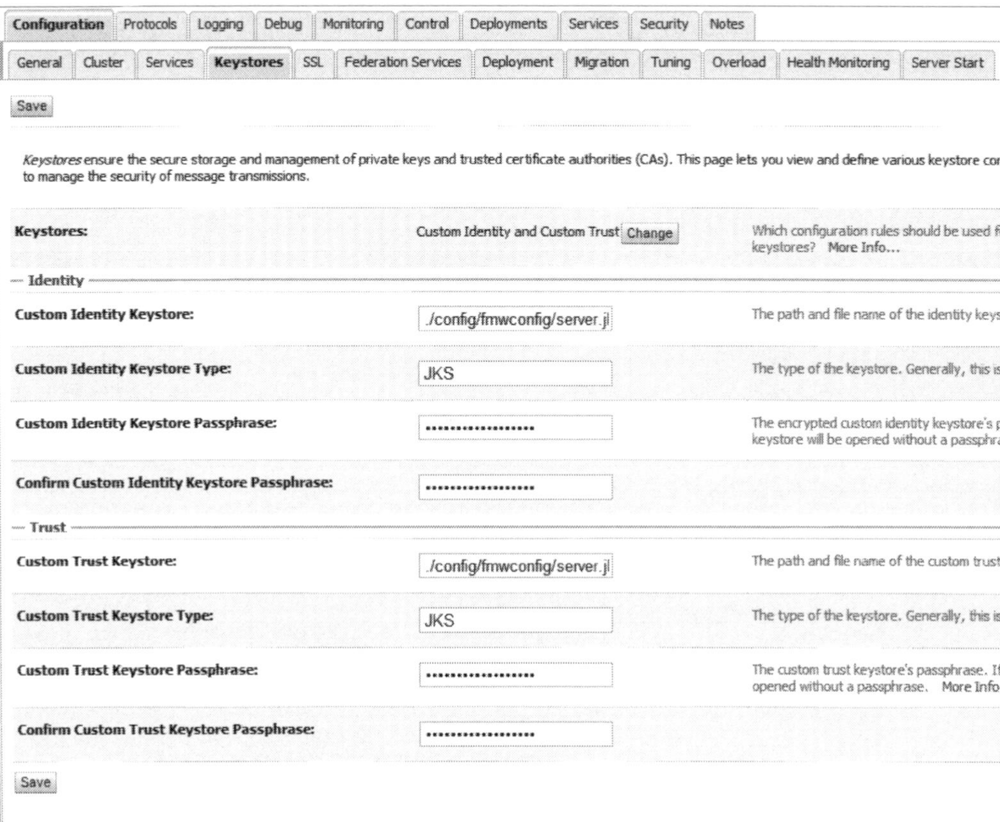

Next, we have to configure the SSL identity of the server.

13. Click on **Environment** in the tree on the left and select **Servers | AdminServer(admin)**.
14. Navigate to the **Configuration | SSL** tab.
15. Enter `serverKey` into the **Private Key Alias** field.
16. Enter `welcome` into the **Private Key Passphrase** field.
17. Enter `welcome` into the **Confirm Private Key Passphrase** field and click **Save**.
18. Click on the **Advanced** link.
19. Select **None** for **Hostname Verification**.

20. Click **Save**.

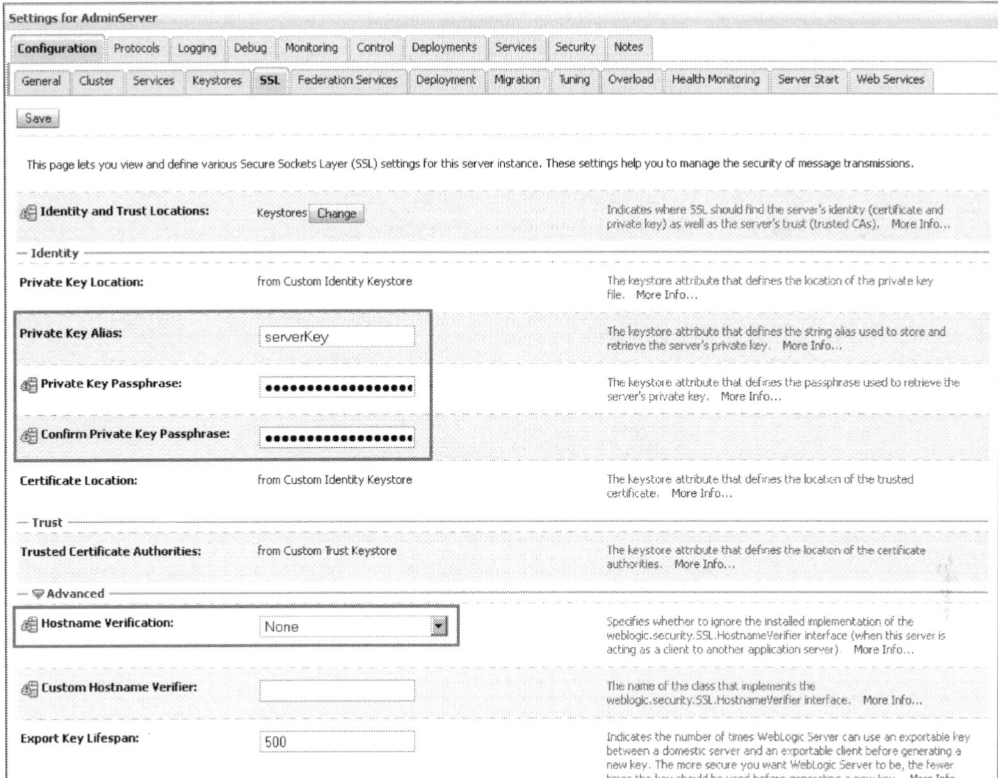

Next, we will configure the Admin Server in order to enable HTTPS traffic.

21. Click on **Environment** in the tree on the left and select **Servers | AdminServer(admin)**.
22. Navigate to the **Configuration | General** tab.
23. Check the option **SSL Listen Port Enabled**.
24. Leave the **SSL Listen Port** on the default of **7002**.

25. Click **Save**.

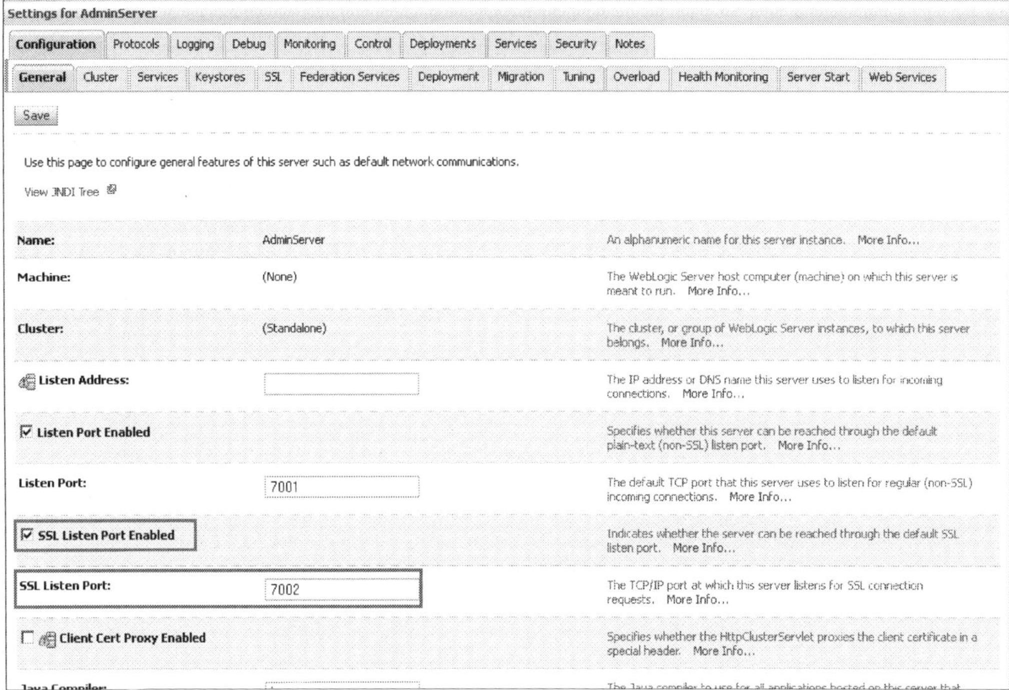

Next we need to create a **PKICredentialProvider** in the WebLogic security realm.

26. Click **Security Realm** in the tree on the left and select **myRealm**.
27. Navigate to the **Providers | Credential Mapping** tab.
28. Click **New**.
29. Enter `PKICredentialMapper` into the **Name** field.
30. Select **PKICredentialMapper** from the **Type** drop-down listbox.
31. Click **OK**.
32. Click on the new **PKICredentialMapper**.
33. Navigate to the **Configuration | Provider Specific** tab.
34. Enter `JKS` into the **Keystore Type** field.
35. Enter `./config/fmwconfig/server.jks` into the **Keystore File Name** field.
36. Enter `welcome` into the **Keystore Pass Phrase** field.
37. Enter `welcome` into the **Confirm Keystore Pass Phrase** field.

38. Click **Save**.

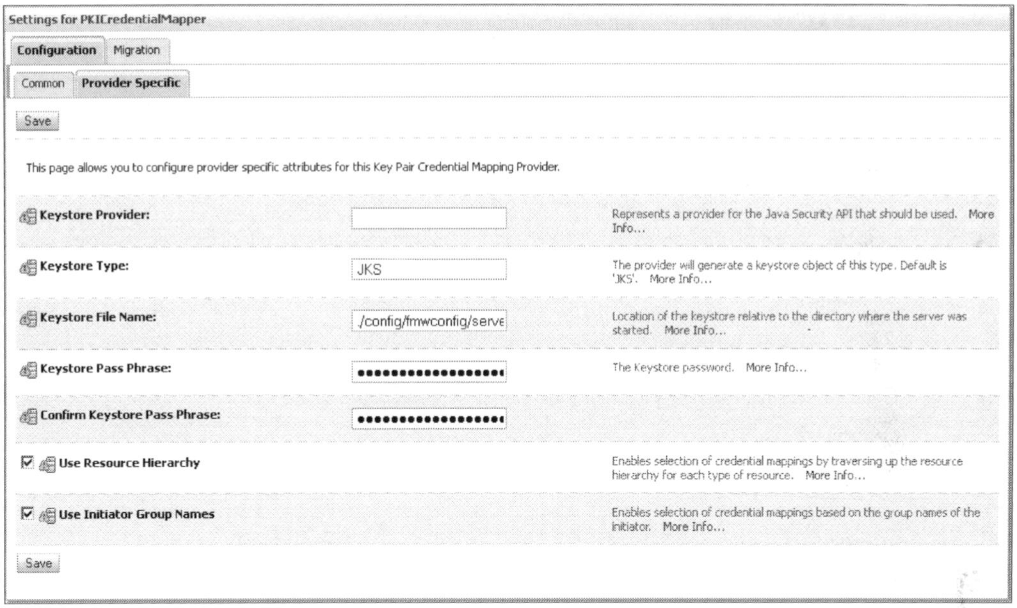

Settings for PKICredentialMapper

Configuration | Migration

Common | Provider Specific

Save

This page allows you to configure provider specific attributes for this Key Pair Credential Mapping Provider.

Keystore Provider:		Represents a provider for the Java Security API that should be used. More Info...
Keystore Type:	JKS	The provider will generate a keystore object of this type. Default is 'JKS'. More Info...
Keystore File Name:	./config/fmwconfig/serve	Location of the keystore relative to the directory where the server was started. More Info...
Keystore Pass Phrase:	••••••••••••••••••	The Keystore password. More Info...
Confirm Keystore Pass Phrase:	••••••••••••••••••	
☑ Use Resource Hierarchy		Enables selection of credential mappings by traversing up the resource hierarchy for each type of resource. More Info...
☑ Use Initiator Group Names		Enables selection of credential mappings based on the group names of the initiator. More Info...

Save

39. Restart the server.

How it works...

Due to the fact that OSB uses the WebLogic security framework for SSL transport security, the whole configuration takes place in the WebLogic console. First, we need to configure the server to activate the SSL traffic. For the OSB cookbook, we use a development installation with the OSB installed on the Admin Server. If the OSB Server is installed on its own Managed Server, which will be the case in a production environment, then SSL needs to be enabled on all Managed Servers, where it is required. After that we configure the **PKICredentialMapper** on WebLogic for using key pair or certificate credential mappings.

Configuring a proxy service to use HTTPS security

In this recipe, we will configure a proxy service to use transport-level security based on HTTPS. By that we can ensure that the communication between the consumer and the OSB service is encrypted, but the proxy service gets the message in plain text.

If message-level security is necessary, where the message itself is encrypted, a recipe such as *Securing a proxy service by protecting the message* covered in *Chapter 11, Handling Message-level Security Requirements*, should be considered.

Getting ready

Make sure the OSB server is configured to work with SSL by applying the previous recipe *Preparing the OSB server to work with SSL*.

Make sure the solution from the recipe *Using service accounts with OSB* for basic authentication is available in Eclipse OEPE. If not, import it from here: `\chapter-12\solution\using-service-accounts-with-osb`. Make sure you import both the `using-service-accounts-with-osb` and the `using-service-accounts-with-osb-mockservice` projects. Deploy the two projects to the OSB server.

Import the soapUI project from `\chapter-12\solution\using-service-accounts-with-osb\soapui` into soapUI and execute **Request 1** of the **FindCustomer** operation.

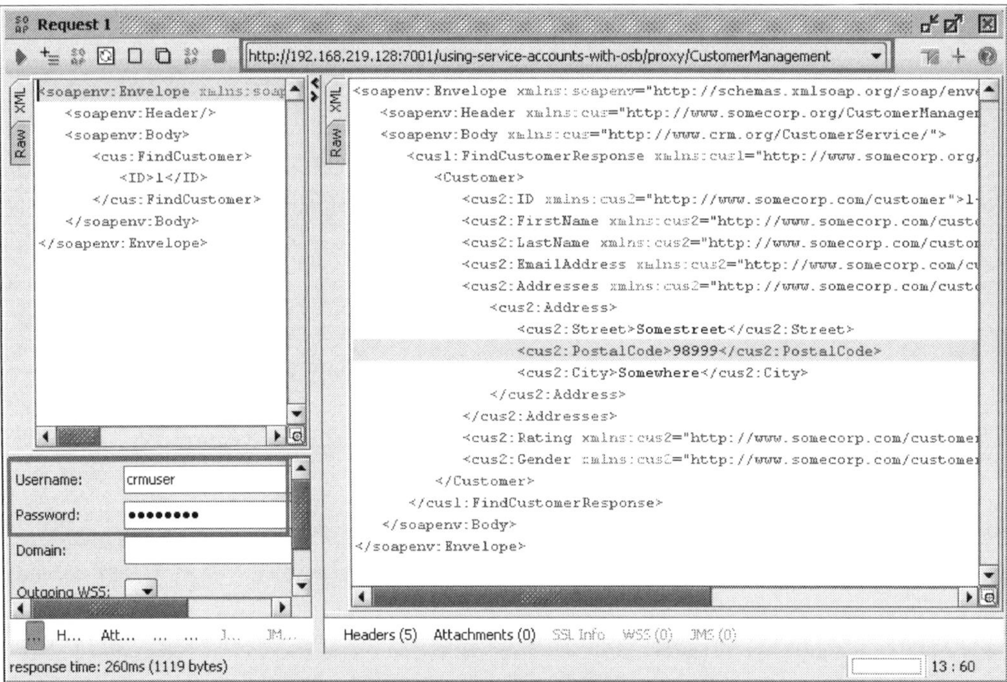

You can see that we are using HTTP by checking the endpoint on the top and that we pass the **crmuser** for basic authentication.

Let's now configure the proxy service so that the request is sent securely over SSL using HTTPS.

How to do it...

In Eclipse OEPE, perform the following steps:

1. Open the proxy service **CustomerManagement.proxy** in the `proxy` folder.
2. Navigate to the **HTTP Transport** tab.
3. Enable the **HTTPS required** checkbox and confirm that the option **Basic** is still set for **Authentication**.

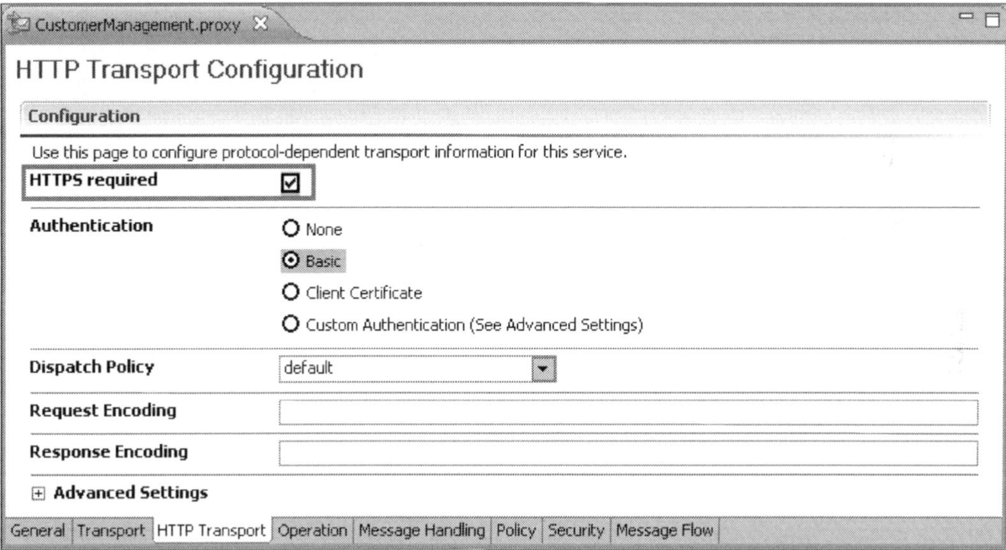

4. Deploy the project to the OSB server.

Now, let's test the behavior of our proxy service. In soapUI, perform the following steps:

5. Re-execute the **Request 1** test case like in the *Getting Ready* section.
6. An **HTTP/1.1 401 Unauthorized** error will occur. This is because the server now only accepts SSL.

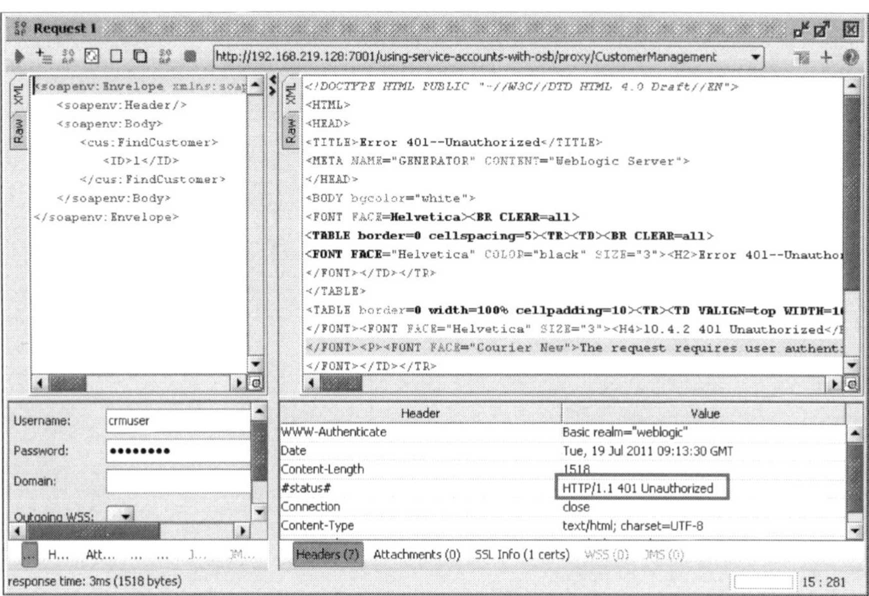

7. Click on the endpoint drop-down listbox on the top and select **[add new endpoint..]** and a pop-up window will appear.

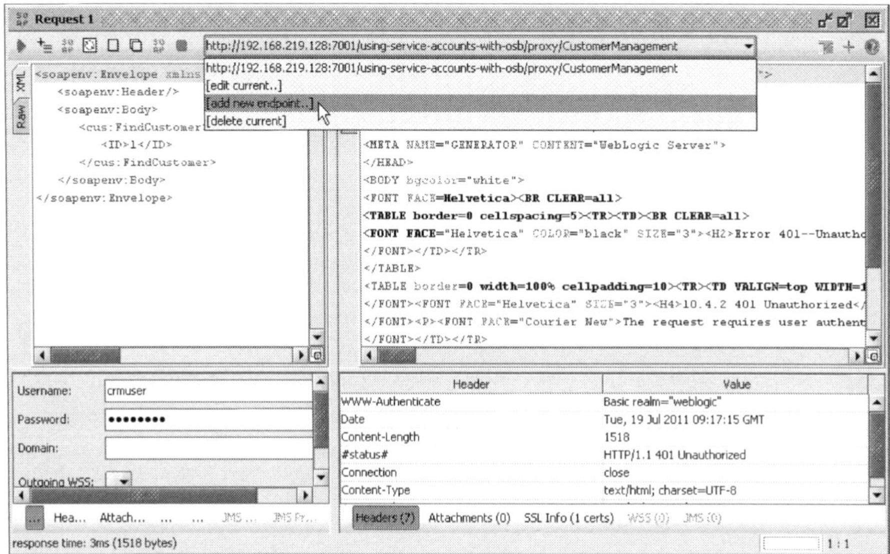

8. Enter `https://192.168.219.128:7002/using-service-accounts-with-osb/proxy/CustomerManagement` into the **Add new endpoint for interface** field. We will need to change to **https** and replace the port with **7002**.
9. Click **OK**.
10. Rerun the **Request 1** test case by using the new endpoint. It should run successfully using HTTPS.

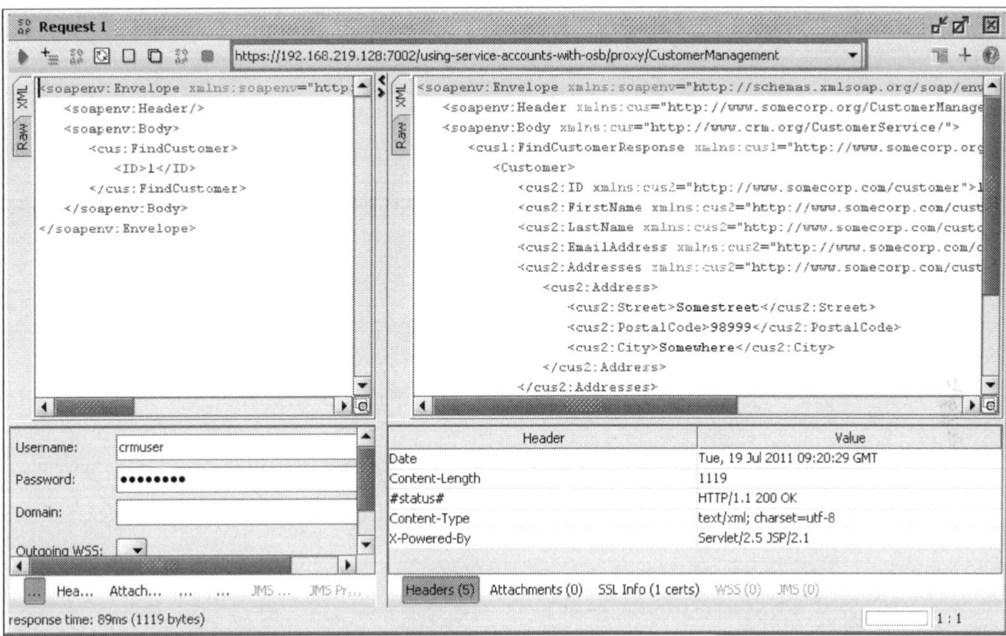

We have now successfully added transport-level security by changing the protocol from HTTP to HTTPS on the proxy service.

How it works...

By simply enabling the HTTPS option required on the proxy services we can enforce that a consumer uses HTTPS to communicate with the OSB service. This only works if SSL is enabled on the WebLogic server beforehand.

By doing this, basic authentication is more secure, because the username/password is no longer sent as plain text over the communication channel. But on the OSB server in the proxy service, the message is still readable. We can check that by just adding a log action into the message flow of the proxy service and log the value of the `$body` variable. If the message should also be protected inside the OSB, then we have to use message-level security covered in *Chapter 11, Handling Message-level Security Requirements*, and apply a recipe such as the *Securing a proxy service by protecting the message*.

Index

Symbols

A

B

C

D

E

F

P

Q

T

U

V

W

Thank you for buying
Oracle Service Bus 11*g* Development Cookbook

About Packt Publishing

Packt, pronounced 'packed', published its first book "*Mastering phpMyAdmin for Effective MySQL Management*" in April 2004 and subsequently continued to specialize in publishing highly focused books on specific technologies and solutions.

Our books and publications share the experiences of your fellow IT professionals in adapting and customizing today's systems, applications, and frameworks. Our solution-based books give you the knowledge and power to customize the software and technologies you're using to get the job done. Packt books are more specific and less general than the IT books you have seen in the past. Our unique business model allows us to bring you more focused information, giving you more of what you need to know, and less of what you don't.

Packt is a modern, yet unique publishing company, which focuses on producing quality, cutting-edge books for communities of developers, administrators, and newbies alike. For more information, please visit our website: `www.PacktPub.com`.

About Packt Enterprise

In 2010, Packt launched two new brands, Packt Enterprise and Packt Open Source, in order to continue its focus on specialization. This book is part of the Packt Enterprise brand, home to books published on enterprise software – software created by major vendors, including (but not limited to) IBM, Microsoft and Oracle, often for use in other corporations. Its titles will offer information relevant to a range of users of this software, including administrators, developers, architects, and end users.

Writing for Packt

We welcome all inquiries from people who are interested in authoring. Book proposals should be sent to `author@packtpub.com`. If your book idea is still at an early stage and you would like to discuss it first before writing a formal book proposal, contact us; one of our commissioning editors will get in touch with you.

We're not just looking for published authors; if you have strong technical skills but no writing experience, our experienced editors can help you develop a writing career, or simply get some additional reward for your expertise.

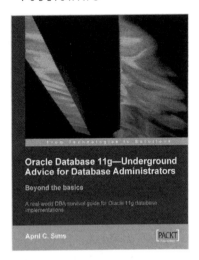

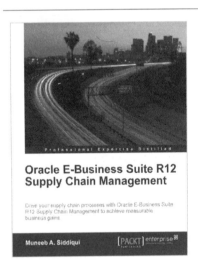

[PACKT] enterprise
professional expertise distilled
PUBLISHING

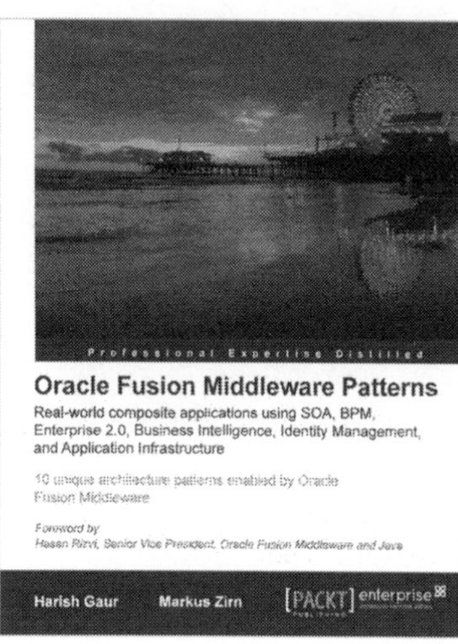

Oracle Fusion Middleware Patterns

ISBN: 978-1-847198-32-7 Paperback: 224 pages

10 unique architecture patterns enabled by Oracle Fusion Middleware

1. First-hand technical solutions utilizing the complete and integrated Oracle Fusion Middleware Suite in hardcopy and ebook formats
2. From-the-trenches experience of leading IT Professionals
3. Learn about application integration and how to combine the integrated tools of the Oracle Fusion Middleware Suite - and do away with thousands of lines of code

---

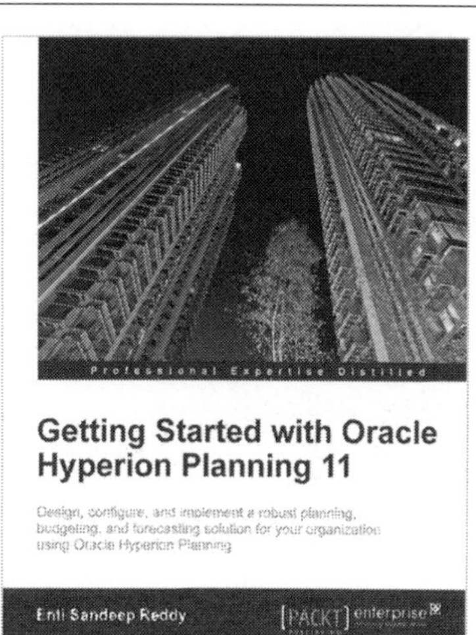

Getting Started with Oracle Hyperion Planning 11

ISBN: 978-1-84968-138-4 Paperback: 620 pages

Design, configure, and implement a robust planning, budgeting, and forecasting solution in your organization using Oracle Hyperion Planning

1. Successfully implement Hyperion Planning—one of the leading planning and budgeting solutions—to manage and coordinate all your business needs with this book and eBook
2. Step-by-step instructions taking you from the very basics of installing Hyperion Planning to implementing it in an enterprise environment
3. Test and optimize Hyperion Planning to perfection with essential tips and tricks

Please check **www.PacktPub.com** for information on our titles

Made in the USA
Lexington, KY
20 April 2012